Entrepreneurship
A Contemporary Approach

Fourth Edition

Donald F. Kuratko

Ball State University

Richard M. Hodgetts

Florida International University

THE DRYDEN PRESS
Harcourt Brace College Publishers

Fort Worth   Philadelphia   San Diego   New York   Orlando   Austin   San Antonio
Toronto   Montreal   London   Sydney   Tokyo

Publisher	George Provol
Acquisitions Editor	John Weimeister
Product Manager	Lisé Johnson
Developmental Editor	Dona Hightower
Project Editor	D. W. Salisbury
Production Manager	Darryl King
Art Director	Bill Brammer
Picture and Rights Editor	Adele Krause
Cover Art	Phil Henslee

Address for Orders
Harcourt Brace College Publishers
6277 Sea Harbor Drive
Orlando, FL 32887-6777
1-800-782-4479

Address for Editorial Correspondence
The Dryden Press
301 Commerce Street, Suite 3700
Fort Worth, TX 76102

Library of Congress Catalog Card Number: 97-66401

ISBN: 0-03-024594-X

Printed in the United States of America

9 0 1 2 3 4 5 6 039 9 8 7

The Dryden Press
Harcourt Brace College Publishers

To our children and their entrepreneurial perspectives:
Christina and Kellie Kuratko
Steven and Jennifer Hodgetts

The Dryden Press Series in Entrepreneurship

Advisory Editor for Entrepreneurship—Donald F. Kuratko, The Stoops Distinguished Professor in Business & Director of the Entrepreneurship Program at Ball State University

Foegen
Business Plan Guidebook with Financial Spreadsheets
Revised Edition

Hodgetts and Kuratko
Effective Small Business Management

Kuratko and Hodgetts
Entrepreneurship: A Contemporary Approach
Fourth Edition

Kuratko and Welsch
Entrepreneurial Strategy: Text and Cases

Ryan, Eckert, and Ray
Small Business: An Entrepreneur's Plan
Fourth Edition

Preface

The United States has developed into an entrepreneurial economy, and the creation of new ventures is at the center of the activity. New enterprises are being developed at a record pace. Celebrity entrepreneurs such as Steven Jobs of Apple and NeXT Computer, Debbie Fields of Mrs. Fields Cookies, Sam Walton of Wal-Mart, Inc., and Fred Smith of Federal Express all emerged to create business dynasties for the 1980s and 1990s by applying entrepreneurship, creativity, and risk taking. Entrepreneurs have become the heroes of economic development and contemporary enterprises.

Business students today need courses and programs that set forth a basic framework for understanding the process of entrepreneurship. Successful entrepreneurship requires more than merely luck and money. It is a cohesive process of creativity, risk taking, and planning. We wrote this textbook to structure and illustrate the discipline of entrepreneurship in a manner that is as unique and creative as enterpreneurship itself. Text, cases, and exercises appear in *Entrepreneurship,* fourth edition, to bring together in one place the most significant resources for exploring the development of new and emerging ventures and are presented in an exciting, organized, and challenging manner.

Organization

The chapter sequence in *Entrepreneurship: A Contemporary Approach,* fourth edition, is systematically organized around the creation, assessment, growth development, and operation of new and emerging ventures. Each major part of the text contains chapters that specifically address these pertinent concepts of entrepreneurship.

Part 1 (Chapters 1–3) introduces the contemporary world of entrepreneurship. The emerging trends of women and minority entrepreneurs are examined as the fastest growing segment of business ownership today. Examining the entrepreneurial revolution throughout the world, this part reveals the evolving nature of entrepreneurship and its importance to the entire world economy. Finally, the concept of intrapreneurship is introduced as an emerging corporate strategy to foster entrepreneurial creativity *within* the larger domain.

Part 2 (Chapters 4–6) addresses the entrepreneurial perspective that resides within individuals. We explore creativity for individuals and the concept of innovation. We also focus on the ethical perspective that entrepreneurs need to take in developing a more socially conscious approach to business.

Part 3 (Chapters 7–10) focuses on the development of an entrepreneurial plan. We discuss the assessment of industrial, competitive, and local environments and their impact on new and emerging ventures.

We also address the issues of marketing that affect the preparation, planning, and operating of entrepreneurial start-ups as well as the financial tools that entrepreneurs need.

Finally, the development of a clear and comprehensive business plan is examined. A complete sample business plan appears in the Entrepreneurial Case Analysis following Chapter 10.

Part 4 (Chapters 11–14) examines the initiation of entrepreneurial ventures. The methods of assessing new ventures and business opportunities are presented. We examine the legal structures of organizations; sole proprietorships, partnerships, and corporations; as well as certain critical legal issues such as proprietary protection (patents, copyrights, and trademarks) and bankruptcy laws. This part concludes with a thorough examination of the sources of capital formation available to entrepreneurs.

Part 5 (Chapters 15–17) focuses on the growth and development of entrepreneurial ventures, which are diverse yet interrelated areas. The need for strategic planning, the challenge of managing entrepreneurial growth, and the global opportunities available to entrepreneurs are all discussed within this part.

Part 6 (Chapters 18–20) is devoted to some contemporary issues in the world of entrepreneurship. We discuss, from a family business perspective, final challenges facing growing entrepreneurial ventures. First, the valuation process needed to acquire a business venture (or sell an existing firm). Second, the critical considerations of management succession and continuity are explored. Finally, the challenge of total quality and the human factor is explored with emphasis on quality tools and techniques for growing firms.

Distinguishing Features

Entrepreneurship: A Contemporary Approach is an organized, systematic study of entrepreneurship. We believe that certain distinguishing features enhance its usefulness for both students and professors. Each chapter contains these specific learning items.

Opening Quotations for Each Chapter   Thought-provoking quotes capture the students' interest about the basic idea for the chapter.

Chapter Objectives   A clear set of learning objectives provides a preview of the chapter material and can be used by students to check whether or not they have understood and retained important points.

Figures and Tables   Numerous charts and tables illustrate specific text material, expand chapter ideas, or refer to outside source material.

Chapter Summary and Discussion Questions   Each chapter closes with a summary of key points to be retained. The discussion questions are a complementary learning tool that will enable students to check their understanding of key issues, to think beyond basic concepts, and to determine areas that require further study. The summary and discussion questions help students discriminate between main and supporting points and provide mechanisms for self-teaching.

Key Terms   The most important terms appearing in each chapter are shown in boldface where they first appear. A list of the key terms appears at the end of each chapter and a complete glossary appears at the end of the book.

Cases   Short cases provide current material for student analysis and classroom discussion. These cases serve as an opportunity for students to sharpen their diagnostic skills, apply important chapter concepts, and determine the areas that require further research and study.

Video Cases   A continued innovation in this edition is the inclusion of eight video cases. A written case is provided at the end of selected chapters and is accompanied by a video for the instructor to show to students in class. The videos greatly enhance class discussion because students can see the company and more directly apply management concepts. The cases examine small entrepreneurial ventures as well as intrapreneurial successes.

Experiential Exercises   A short exercise at the end of each chapter applies principles presented in the chapter, giving students practice on such topics as developing a business plan, analyzing funding sources, and self-tests to determine whether they are high achievers.

Challenging and Innovative Learning Tools

Contemporary Entrepreneurship   Boxed items throughout the text illustrate one or more contemporary ideas related to entrepreneurship. The topics range from finding an entrepreneurial niche to revealing the secrets of the entrepreneurial spirit. Each one is unique in its application to entrepreneurial activity in the 1990s.

The Entrepreneurial Edge   Short vignettes about entrepreneurs are included throughout the text to show how practicing entrepreneurs handle specific challenges and opportunities that are considered the leading edge today.

Entrepreneurial Case Analyses   Comprehensive case studies that illustrate venture creations or managerial ideas confronted by actual firms culminate the six major parts of the text. The companies are real so students can appreciate the value of analyzing the situations and data presented and compare their conclusions with the actual outcomes of the cases provided in the *Instructor's Resource Manual*.

Comprehensive Exercises   A comprehensive exercise that encourages students to go beyond the text material to apply the concepts and experience activities related to the entrepreneur is provided at the end of most parts.

Supplementary Materials

Materials to supplement the text have become increasingly important in teaching most business subjects. Many instructors face large classes with limited resources, and supplementary materials provide a way to expand and improve the students' learning experience. The learning package provided with *Entrepreneurship: A Contemporary Approach* was specifically designed to meet the needs of instructors facing a variety of teaching conditions.

Instructor's Resource Manual, Test Bank, and Transparency Masters   The *Instructor's Resource Manual* contains chapter outlines, lecture outlines, suggested additional experiential exercises, and a test bank of 25 true/false questions and 50 multiple-choice questions for each chapter. The questions are related to specific subject headings in each chapter. The *Instructor's Resource Manual* also provides suggested answers to the discussion and case questions in each chapter. Finally, 40 transparency masters (enlargements of text tables and figures) are included.

Computerized Test Bank   A *Computerized Test Bank* for IBM computers is available free to adopters. The *Computerized Test Bank* allows instructors to select and edit test items from the printed *Test Bank* as well as add an unlimited number of their own questions. Up to 99 versions of each test can be custom printed.

Computerized Instructor's Resource Manual   A disk will be available to instructors that contains most elements of the *Instructor's Resource Manual.* Teachers can electronically cut and paste together the parts of the manual they desire for customized lecture outlines.

Videos   Adopters receive a set of eight video programs that coordinate with the video cases throughout the textbook.

Acknowledgments

Many individuals played an important role in helping us write, develop, and refine our text, and they deserve special recognition. Our families, from whom we took so much time, deserve our deepest love and appreciation. We would also like to express our apprecaition to the staff at The Dryden Press who worked closely with us on this project, in particular, John Weimeister, Yvette Rubio, Adele Krause, Bill Brammer, and Darryl King.

The professionals who reviewed the manuscript and offered copious suggestions for improvement played a decisive role in the final result. We would like to thank the reviewers for the earlier editions. They include David H. Gobeli, *Oregon State University;* Charles C. Green, *University of Texas at Dallas;* E. L. Murphree, Jr., *George Washington University;* Roger Hutt, *Arizona State University;* Lorie L. Mazzaroppi, *Fairleigh Dickinson University;* James Powell, *North Texas State University;* Sherman Timmins, *University of Toledo;* and Warren Weber, *California State Polytechnic University, Pomona;* Michael Czinkota, *Georgetown University;* Richard Lorentz, *University of Wisconsin–Eau Claire;* Thomas Monroy, *Baldwin Wallace College;* and Kim Stewart, *University of Denver.* We would like to especially thank the reviewers for this edition: Frank Hoy, *University of Texas at El Paso;* Amit Shah, *Frostburg State University;* Arthur Shriberg, *Xavier University;* Jack L. Sterrett, *Southeast Missouri State University;* Charles N. Toftoy, *George Washington University;* and Anatoly V. Zhuplev, *Loyola Marymount University.*

We also thank the author of the "Roaring '20s" business plan that appears as an Entrepreneurial Case Analysis following Chapter 10. Michael Y. Graham has prepared an excellent, comprehensive example from which students are sure to benefit.

Special recognition is given to Melissa A. Ewen, Associate Director of the Midwest Entrepreneurial Education Center, for her preparation of the Entrepreneurial Edge vignettes that appear in every chapter. Thanks to her diligent efforts, these sections add special interest to each chapter.

In addition, a special acknowledgment to Kelli M. Hurley, Executive Director of the Midwest Entrepreneurial Education Center, for her constant dedication, support, and passion throughout this entire project.

We would also like to express our appreciation to our colleagues at both Florida International University and Ball State University for their continued support of our efforts. In particular, we thank Harold Wyman, dean of the College of Business, Florida International University; Gary Dessler, chairman of the Management and International Business Department, Florida International University; Ray V. Mantagno, chairman of the Management Department, Ball State University. Additional recognition is given to Frank J. Sabatine, Ball State University, for his development of the creativity section in Chapter 5, and

Professor William Shannon, St. Mary's College, for his expert assistance on the women entrepreneurs section. Finally, thanks to Neil A. Palomba, dean of the College of Business, Ball State University, for his enthusiastic support.

Donald F. Kuratko
Ball State University

Richard M. Hodgetts
Florida International University

Donald F. Kuratko, D.B.A., is The Stoops Distinguished Professor in Business and Director of the Entrepreneurship Program, College of Business, at Ball State University. He is the first professor to be named a Distinguished Professor for the College of Business at Ball State University. He has published more than 100 articles on aspects of entrepreneurship, new venture development, and corporate intrapreneurship. Dr. Kuratko is the Advisory Editor on Entrepreneurship for The Dryden Press/Harcourt Brace & Company and has been a Consulting Editor for *Entrepreneurship Theory & Practice Journal.* He has also been a consultant on corporate intrapreneurship to major corporations such as Blue Cross/ Blue Shield, AT&T, Union Carbide Corp., Ameritech, and United Technologies. Professor Kuratko's work has been published in such journals as *Strategic Management Journal, Journal of Small Business Management, Entrepreneurship Theory & Practice, Training & Development Journal, Entrepreneurship Development Review, Advanced Management Journal,* and *The Small Business Forum.* Professor Kuratko has written seven books, including *Effective Small Business Management* (Dryden Press/Harcourt Brace, 1998); *Entrepreneurial Strategy* (Dryden Press/Harcourt Brace, 1994); and *Management* (Dryden Press/Harcourt Brace, 1991).

The academic program in entrepreneurship that Dr. Kuratko developed at Ball State University has received national acclaim with such honors as the George Washington Medal of Honor (1987); the Leavey Foundation Award for Excellence in Private Enterprise (1988); the National Model Entrepreneurship Program Award (1990); and The NFIB Excellence Award (1993). In addition, the program has been continuously ranked by *Success* and *Business Week* magazines as one of the Top 25 Entrepreneurship Programs in the country.

Dr. Kuratko was named Professor of the Year for five consecutive years at the College of Business, Ball State University; Outstanding Young Faculty for Ball State University in 1987; recipient of Ball State University's Outstanding Teaching Award in 1990; and named the university's Outstanding Faculty Member in 1996. Dr. Kuratko was also honored as the 1990 Entrepreneur of the Year for the State of Indiana (sponsored by Ernst & Young, *Inc.* magazine, and Merrill Lynch), inducted into the Institute of American Entrepreneurs Hall of Fame in 1990, named National Outstanding Entrepreneurship Educator in 1993; and was selected one of the Top Three Entrepreneurship Professors in the country in 1994 by Kauffman Foundation, Ernst & Young, and Merrill Lynch.

Richard M. Hodgetts is a professor of business at Florida International University, with a Ph.D from the University of Oklahoma and an MBA from Indiana University. He has been named Outstanding Teacher of the Year twice, at both the University of Nebraska and Florida International University. He has lectured in Mexico, Venezuela, Peru, Chile, Jamaica, Trinidad, Denmark, Kuwait, and many U.S. colleges and universities. He has consulted for a number of Fortune 500 firms and in recent years has provided training for a wide variety of companies, including AT&T Technologies, Delco Electronics, Eastman Kodak, General Electric, IBM, Motorola, Texas Instruments, and Wal-Mart. His articles have appeared in a host of journals including the *Academy of Management Journal, Personnel, Personnel Journal, Organizational Dynamics, Management International Review; Compensation and Benefits Review, International Human Resource Management Review, Management Advisor,* and *Strategy and Executive Action.* Dr. Hodgetts is also the author or co-author of 40 books, including *Modern Human Relations at Work, International Management, International Business,* and *Effective Small Business Management,* which he co-authored with Dr. Kuratko. Professor Hodgett is a fellow of the Academy of Management and is a past member of the Academy's Board of Governors. He also serves on three academic review boards and writes a weekly column on small business and entrepreneurship in the *Ft. Lauderdale Sun Sentinel.*

Contents in Brief

Contents

THE CONTEMPORARY WORLD OF ENTREPRENEURSHIP

Chapter 1

$\mathscr{T}$HE ENTREPRENEURIAL REVOLUTION

CHAPTER OBJECTIVES

1. To explain the importance of entrepreneurs for economic growth

2. To introduce the concept of an entrepreneurial perspective within individuals

3. To examine the entrepreneurial revolution taking place today

4. To illustrate the entrepreneurial environment

5. To examine some of the most influential trends in entrepreneurship—women and minorities

6. To highlight some of the latest trends in entrepreneurial research

It's not the critic who counts, nor the observer who watches from a safe distance. Wealth is created only by doers in the arena who are marred with dirt, dust, blood, and sweat. These are producers who strike out on their own, who know high highs and low lows, great devotions, and who overextend themselves for worthwhile causes. Without exception, they fail more than they succeed and appreciate this reality even before venturing out on their own. But when these producers of wealth fail, they at least fail with style and grace, and their gut soon recognizes that failure is only a resting place, not a place in which to spend a lifetime. Their places will never be with those nameless souls who know neither victory nor defeat, who receive weekly paychecks regardless of their week's performance, who are hired hands in the labor in someone else's garden. These doers are producers and no matter what their lot is at any given moment, they'll never take a place beside the takers, for theirs is a unique place, alone, under the sun. They are entrepreneurs!

Joseph R. Mancuso
Center for Entrepreneurial Management

ENTREPRENEURS—CHALLENGING THE UNKNOWN

Entrepreneurs are individuals who recognize opportunities where others see chaos, or confusion. They are aggressive catalysts for change within the marketplace. They have been compared to Olympic athletes challenging themselves to break new barriers, to long-distance runners dealing with the agony of the miles, to symphony orchestra conductors who balance the different skills and sounds into a cohesive whole, or to top-gun pilots who continually push the envelope of speed and daring. Whatever the passion, because they all fit in some way, entrepreneurs are the heroes of today's marketplace. They start companies and create jobs at a breathtaking pace. The U.S. economy has been revitalized because of the efforts of entrepreneurs, and the world has turned now to free enterprise as a model for economic development. The passion and drive of entrepreneurs move the world of business forward. They challenge the unknown and continuously create the future.

One anonymous quote found by Jeffry A. Timmons sums up the realities for entrepreneurs. "Anyone [can be an entrepreneur] who wants to experience the deep, dark canyons of uncertainty and ambiguity; and who wants to walk the breathtaking highlands of success. But I caution, do not plan to walk the latter, until you have experienced the former."[1]

---

[1] Jeffry A. Timmons, *New Venture Creation* (Burr Ridge, IL: Irwin, 1994), 3.

5

ENTREPRENEURSHIP: A PERSPECTIVE

Entrepreneurship is more than the mere creation of business. Although that is certainly an important facet, it's not the complete picture. The characteristics of seeking opportunities, taking risks beyond security, and having the tenacity to push an idea through to reality combine into a special perspective that permeates entrepreneurs. As we will illustrate in Chapter 4, an entrepreneurial perspective can be developed in individuals. This perspective can be exhibited inside or outside an organization, in profit or not-for-profit enterprises, and in business or nonbusiness activities for the purpose of bringing forth creative ideas. Thus, entrepreneurship is an integrated concept that permeates an individual's business in an innovative manner. It is this perspective that has revolutionized the way business is conducted at every level and in every country. *Inc.* magazine reported on the cover of one issue some time ago that "America is once again becoming a nation of risk takers and the way we do business will never be the same." So it is. The revolution has begun in an economic sense, and the entrepreneurial perspective is the dominant force.

OUR ENTREPRENEURIAL ECONOMY—THE ENVIRONMENT FOR ENTREPRENEURSHIP

Entrepreneurship is the symbol of business tenacity and achievement. Entrepreneurs were the pioneers of today's business successes. Their sense of opportunity, their drive to innovate, and their capacity for accomplishment have become the standard by which free enterprise is now measured. This standard has taken hold throughout the entire world.

We are experiencing an "Entrepreneurial Revolution" in the United States. This revolution will be as powerful to the twenty-first century as the Industrial Revolution was to the twentieth century (if not more!).

Entrepreneurs will continue to be critical contributors to economic growth through their leadership, management, innovation, research and development effectiveness, job creation, competitiveness, productivity, and formation of new industry.

To understand the nature of entrepreneurship, it is important to consider from two perspectives the environment in which entrepreneurial firms operate. The first perspective is statistical, providing actual aggregate numbers to emphasize the importance of small firms in our economy. The second perspective examines some of the trends in entrepreneurial research and education in order to reflect the emerging importance of entrepreneurship in academic developments.

Predominance of New Ventures in the Economy

The past decade has demonstrated the powerful emergence of entrepreneurial activity in the United States. Many statistics illustrate this fact. For example, during the past ten years, new business incorporations averaged 600,000 *per year.* Although many of these incorporations may have been sole proprietorships or partnerships previously, it still demonstrates venture activity, whether it was through start-ups, expansion, or development. More specifically, 807,000 new small firms were established in 1995, an all-time record. Let's examine some of the latest tabulated numbers.[2]

---

[2] *The State of Small Business: A Report of the President* (Washington, DC: Government Printing Office, 1995), 13.

FIGURE 1.1   **WHAT CONSTITUTES SMALL FIRMS IN AMERICA**

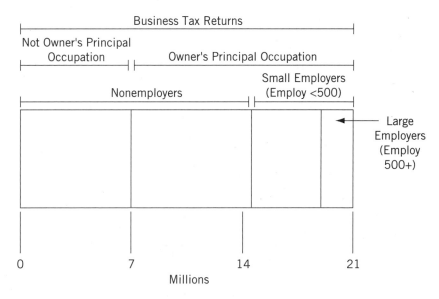

SOURCE: William J. Dennis Jr., *A Small Business Primer* (Washington, DC: The NFIB Foundation, 1993), 3.

Small firms constitute more than 90 percent of the entire business population. Granted, this figure depends on the definition of the term "small"; however, the Internal Revenue Service (IRS) reports that 21 million businesses exist based on business tax returns. Figure 1.1 was developed by the **National Federation of Independent Business (NFIB)** in order to demonstrate the breakdown. Approximately 12 million businesses have owners whose *principal* occupation is owning and operating them. Approximately 7 million (out of 12 million) have owners who work for themselves without employing anyone else. Of the 5 million remaining firms, only 15,000 employ 500 or more people.

Keep in mind that when a business consists of a single establishment, the enterprise and establishment concepts are identical. Sometimes, however, small establishments may be owned by larger enterprises; in that case, they may not be considered small firms.

Three types of establishments have been identified by the Small Business Administration: (1) "small" establishments owned by small enterprises, (2) "apparent small" establishments owned by large enterprises, and (3) "large" establishments owned by large enterprises. Small enterprises are defined as having 100 or fewer employees; large enterprises have more than 100 employees.

Small enterprises are the most common form of enterprise-established relationships regardless of industry, and most small businesses consist of a single establishment. Figure 1.2 demonstrates the employment size of U.S. firms. More than half of all businesses employ fewer than 5 people. More significantly, almost 90 percent of firms employ fewer than 20 people.

This employment number is important, since the small entrepreneurial firms have created the most *net* new jobs in the U.S. economy from 1977 to 1990 (see Figure 1.3). In addition, the smallest of our enterprises have created a *steady supply* of net new jobs over the business cycle from 1977 to 1990. It is important to recognize that historically, employment growth in the United States is correlated directly with new-business growth. This fact

FIGURE 1.2 **THE EMPLOYEE SIZE OF U.S. BUSINESSES**

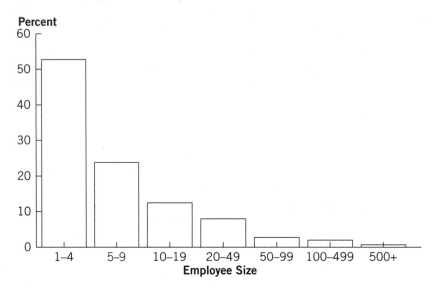

SOURCE: William J. Dennis Jr., *A Small Business Primer* (Washington, DC: The NFIB Foundation, 1993), 11.

FIGURE 1.3 **THE SMALLEST BUSINESSES CREATE THE MOST NET NEW JOBS**

(EMPLOYMENT SHARE AND AVERAGE NET NEW EMPLOYMENT SHARE
BY BUSINESS EMPLOYEE SIZE, 1977–1990)

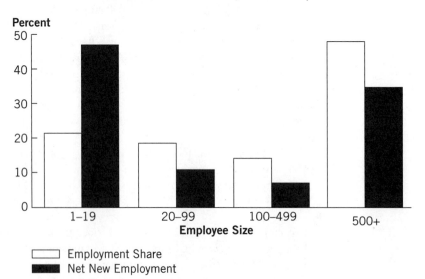

SOURCE: William J. Dennis Jr., *A Small Business Primer* (Washington, DC: The NFIB Foundation, 1993), 17.

TABLE 1.1	SMALL BUSINESS DOMINATION OF EXPANDING INDUSTRIES

INDUSTRIES PROJECTED TO GROW MOST RAPIDLY
(1990–2005) BY DOMINANT FIRM GROUP

Fastest Growing in Output (percentage basis)[a]

√ Manufacturers of computer equipment—*large dominated*

√ Manufacturers of semiconductors, related devices—*large dominated*

√ Residential care—*small dominated*

√ Health services, necessary—*small dominated*

√ Manufacturers of medical instruments and supplies—*indeterminant*

√ Computer/data processing services—*small dominated*

√ Business services—*small dominated*

√ Manufacturers of miscellaneous plastic products—*small dominated*

Fastest Growing in Employment (percentage basis)[b]

√ Residential care—*small dominated*

√ Computer/data processing services—*small dominated*

√ Health services—*small dominated*

√ Offices of health practitioners—*small dominated*

√ Individual and miscellaneous social services—*small dominated*

√ Legal services—*small dominated*

√ Nursing and personal care facilities—*small dominated*

√ Elementary and secondary schools—*small dominated*

[a] Includes only industries projected to employ 200,000 or more.
[b] Includes only industries projected to employ 500,000 or more.

SOURCE: William J. Dennis Jr., *A Small Business Primer* (Washington, DC: The NFIB Foundation, 1993), 15.

has been traced back to 1960, demonstrating that new-business formations are the critical foundations for any net increase in U.S. employment. As a final note to the importance of small enterprises and employment, we present Table 1.1 to outline the projected growth industries through the year 2005 and how small firms dominate these groups. Thus, our employment growth and industry expansions are closely tied to new-venture development. All of this detailed information provides insight into the U.S. economy, and our economic future may well lie in the development of our entrepreneurial abilities.

Research and Education

As we continue our study of entrepreneurship, it is important to note the research and educational developments that have occurred over the past few years. The major new themes that characterize recent research about entrepreneurs and new-venture creation can be summarized as follows:

1. The entrepreneurial and managerial domains are not mutually exclusive but overlap to a certain extent. The former is more opportunity driven, and the latter is more resource and "conservation" driven.

2. Venture financing, including both the new wave of venture capital financing and other innovative financing techniques, emerged again in the 1990s with unprecedented strength, fueling another decade of entrepreneurialism. Both the techniques of venture financing and the amount of money available are important information for entrepreneurs.

3. Intrapreneurship, or entrepreneurship within large organizations, and entrepreneurial cultures and management techniques have gained much attention during the past few years.[3]

4. Entrepreneurial entry strategies and career patterns have been identified that show some important common denominators, issues, and trade-offs.

5. The great variety among types of entrepreneurs and the methods they have used to achieve success defy notions of any single psychological profile that can predict future success.

6. The risks and trade-offs of an entrepreneurial career, particularly its demanding and stressful nature, have been a subject of keen research interest relevant to would-be and practicing entrepreneurs alike.

7. Women and minority entrepreneurs have emerged in unprecedented numbers. They appear to face obstacles and difficulties different from those other entrepreneurs face, although they share many aspects in common with them.

8. The entrepreneurial spirit is universal, judging by the enormous growth of interest in entrepreneurship around the world in the past few years.

9. The economic and social contributions of entrepreneurs, venture capitalists, and new companies have been shown to make immensely disproportionate contributions to job creation, innovation, and economic renewal, compared with the contributions the 1,000 or so largest companies make.

10. Entrepreneurial education has become one of the hottest topics at American business and engineering schools. The number of schools teaching a new-ventures or similar course has grown from as few as two dozen 20 years ago to more than 500 at this time.[4]

Additionally, a number of major academic institutions have developed programs in entrepreneurial research, and every year a symposium titled "Frontiers in Entrepreneurship

---

[3] See Donald F. Kuratko and Ray V. Montagno, "The Intrapreneurial Spirit," *Training and Development Journal* (October 1989): 83–87; and Austin K. Pryor and E. Michael Shays, "Growing the Business with Intrapreneurs," *Business Quarterly* (spring 1993): 43–50.

[4] Robert D. Hisrich, "Entrepreneurship: Past, Present and Future," *Journal of Small Business Management* (October 1988): 1–4; Gerhard R. Plaschka and Harold P. Welsch, "Emerging Structures in Entrepreneurship Education: Curricular Designs and Strategies," *Entrepreneurship Theory and Practice* (spring 1990): 55–71; and Karl H. Vesper, *Entrepreneurship Education,* 1993, The Anderson School, University of California, Los Angeles, 1993.

Research"[5] is conducted on one of the campuses. Since 1981 the conference has provided an outlet for the latest developments in entrepreneurship. Most of the university centers for entrepreneurship have focused on three major areas: (1) entrepreneurial education, (2) outreach activities with entrepreneurs, and (3) entrepreneurial research. These centers have been and will most likely continue to be the leaders in developing entrepreneurial research. Also, many universities are expanding programs and designing curricula specifically for entrepreneurship, with national recognition now given to the top entrepreneurial schools (see the Contemporary Entrepreneurship box). For a complete listing of university programs, see Karl H. Vesper, *Entrepreneurship Education* (Los Angeles: Entrepreneurial Studies Center, University of California, Los Angeles, 1993).

It is interesting to note that during the 1970s entrepreneurial courses were offered at only a handful of schools. Today that number has increased to more than 500, and schools are reporting a record number of students enrolling in such courses.

THE AGE OF THE GAZELLES

New and smaller firms create the most jobs in the U.S. economy. The facts speak for themselves. The vast majority of these job-creating companies are fast-growing businesses. David Birch of Cognetics, Inc., has named these firms "gazelles."[6] A **gazelle,** by Birch's definition, is a business establishment with at least 20 percent sales growth every year from 1990 to 1994 (the last year for which Cognetics has complete numbers), starting with a base of at least $100,000.

Despite the continual downsizing in major corporations, the gazelles produced 5 million jobs and brought the net employment growth to 4.2 million jobs (see Table 1.2).

Innovation

Gazelles are leaders in innovation, as shown by the following:

- New and smaller firms have been responsible for 55 percent of the innovations in 362 different industries and 95 percent of all radical innovations.
- Gazelles produce twice as many product innovations per employee as do larger firms.
- New and smaller firms obtain more patients per sales dollar than do larger firms.

TABLE 1.2	GROWTH BY GAZELLES, 1990–1994	
Jobs created by gazelles	**5.0 million**	
Jobs lost by other companies	**−0.8**	
Net employment growth	**4.2 million**	

[5] See, for example, *Frontiers of Entrepreneurship Research* (Wellesley, MA: Babson College, series of volumes, 1981–1997).

[6] David Birch's research firm, Cognetics, Inc., traces the employment and sales records of some 9 million companies with a Dun & Bradstreet file.

CONTEMPORARY ENTREPRENEURSHIP

The 25 Best Business Schools for Entrepreneurs, 1996

Institution	Description
University of Arizona Karl Eller Graduate School of Management Tucson, AZ	A concentration in entrepreneurship. The Karl Eller Center recruits fellows who are local entrepreneurs.
Babson College F.W. Olin Graduate School of Business Wellesley, MA	Entrepreneurship is the distinctive competence of Babson's curriculum.
Ball State University College of Business Muncie, IN	M.B.A. in entrepreneurship is broadcast on television to more than 60 locations interactively. Offers master's degree in entrepreneurship.
Baylor University Hankamer School of Business Waco, TX	Six chairs in entrepreneurship provide students with regional and international experiences.
Brigham Young University Marriott School of Management Provo, UT	Recruits area entrepreneurs for case development, lectures, and conferences with students. Offers a concentration in entrepreneurship.
University of California at Los Angeles (UCLA) The Anderson School Los Angeles, CA	The Anderson School offers a concentration in entrepreneurship.
Carnegie Mellon University Graduate School of Industrial Administration Pittsburgh, PA	Offers a concentration in entrepreneurship. Program works with students to develop business plans for real businesses.
University of Colorado Graduate School of Business Administration Boulder, CO	The Center for Entrepreneurship is a joint venture between the business and engineering schools.
Cornell University Johnson Graduate School of Management Ithaca, NY	Offers a variety of courses in entrepreneurship. Strengths: unique multidisciplinary nature of the program.
DePaul University Charles H. Kellstadt Graduate School of Business Chicago, IL	Offers master's degree in entrepreneurship.
University of Georgia Terry College of Business Athens, GA	Offers a concentration in entrepreneurship that can create an equivalent to an M.B.A. in entrepreneurship.
Harvard University Harvard Business School Boston, MA	Focus on practical research and case development.

Growth

Note how these growth data indicate the current "Age of the Gazelles":

- During the past ten years, business incorporations have averaged more than 600,000 per year, with 1995 experiencing an all-time high of 807,000.

Institution	Description
University of Illinois—Chicago *College of Business Administration* Chicago, IL	Offers a concentration in entrepreneurship. Entrepreneurship Hall of Fame.
University of Maryland at College Park *The Maryland Business School* College Park, MD	Nine courses and a field project are taught, with emphasis on finance, franchising, and technology-based entrepreneurship.
University of Nebraska—Lincoln *College of Business Administration* Lincoln, NE	Offers a concentration in entrepreneurship. Specializes in international entrepreneurship.
New York University (NYU) *Leonard N. Stern School of Business* New York, NY	Offers Executive M.B.A. with entrepreneurship course. Includes mentor program.
Northwestern University *J.L. Kellogg Graduate School of Management* Evanston, IL	Offers a concentration in entrepreneurship. Kellogg has an advisory board of business leaders.
University of Pennsylvania *The Wharton School* Philadelphia, PA	Courses in entrepreneurship at all levels, including undergraduate, M.B.A., and Ph.D. Master's degree in entrepreneurship available.
Rensselaer Polytechnic Institute *Lally School of Management and Technology* Troy, NY	Infuses entrepreneurship into the schools of management, engineering, and science. Strengths in technology and research.
St. Louis University *School of Business and Administration* St. Louis, MO	Has a doctoral program in management with a concentration in entrepreneurship. Hosts the Gateways Entrepreneurship Research Conference.
University of St. Thomas *Graduate School of Business* Minneapolis, MN	Master's degree in entrepreneurship, M.B.A. concentration in franchise management, venture management.
San Diego State University *College of Business Administration* San Diego, CA	Offers a concentration in entrepreneurship. Sponsors the NASDAQ-SDSU business plan competition.
University of Southern California *School of Business Administration* Los Angeles, CA	Offers a master's degree in entrepreneurship with specialized courses in technology transfer and growth management.
University of South Carolina *College of Business and Administration* Columbia, SC	Offers a concentration or cluster in entrepreneurship.
The University of Texas at Austin *Graduate School of Business* Austin, TX	Master's degree in entrepreneurship. MOOT CORP, "The Super Bowl of World Business Plan Competition."

- Of approximately 21.5 million businesses in the United States (based on IRS tax returns), only 14,000 qualify as "large" businesses.
- The compound growth rate in the number of businesses over a 12-year span is 3.9 percent.

- Each year about 14 percent of firms with employees drop from the unemployment insurance rolls while about 16 percent new and successor firms—firms with management changes—are added each year. This represents the disappearance or reorganization of half of all listed firms every five years!
- By the year 2010, demographers estimate, 30 million firms will exist in the United States, up significantly from the 21.5 million firms existing in the mid-1990s.

THE EMERGING TRENDS IN ENTREPRENEURSHIP

Women-Owned Businesses

The 1990s have been designated the decade of women in leadership.[7] This new leadership position for women has been most notable in their entrepreneurial pursuits. Rather than just climbing the corporate ladder of success, women are creating their own corporations.

On October 25, 1988, President Ronald Reagan signed into law the **Women's Business Ownership Act** to establish programs and initiate efforts to assist the development of women-owned businesses.[8] This law has brought greater recognition to women as entrepreneurs through their remarkable growth in entrepreneurship as evidenced by the aggregate statistics.

Women-owned businesses are the fastest-growing segment of small business in the nation, with an increase from 2.6 million businesses in 1982 to 6.4 million in 1997. Before 1970, women owned 5 percent of all U.S. businesses. Today women own nearly 34 percent of all businesses, 50 percent of all retail businesses, and 29 percent of all service companies.

> At a time when America is suffering from huge budget and trade deficits, and from a chronic failure to significantly increase productivity, it is vital for public policy makers to seek means to catalyze the tremendous pool of talent and energy these women represent. These women are part of the most educated generation of women that has ever existed. They are a gold mine of human capital . . . it is vitally important for our future competitiveness that public policy, in partnership with the private sector, affirm and assist this economic revolution. As part of this effort, it is essential that remaining barriers to women entrepreneurship be eliminated.[9]

Women in the labor force have been steadily increasing in numbers. Today, more than 53 million U.S. women over the age of 16 are in the workforce.

What role will women play in the labor force of the twenty-first century? Of the 26 million net increase in the civilian labor force between 1990 and 2005, women will account for 15 million or 62 percent of the net growth. In 1990 women were 45 percent of the civilian labor force and will become 47 percent of it in 2005. Employment by women-owned firms rose by more than 100 percent from 1987 to 1992, compared to a 38 percent increase in employment by all firms. For women-owned companies with 100 or more

---

[7] John Naisbitt and Patricia Aburdene, *Megatrends 2000* (New York: William Morrow, 1990), 216–40.

[8] Public Law 100-533: Women's Business Ownership Act, October 25, 1988.

[9] U.S. Small Business Administration, *Second Annual Report to the President and Congress by the National Women's Business Council* and *A Statistical Report to Congress: Statistical Information on Women in Business* (Washington, DC: Government Printing Office, 1990), 9; and *The State of Small Business: A Report of the President* (Washington, DC: Government Printing Office, 1992), 50.

workers, employment increased by 158 percent—more than double the rate for all U.S. firms of similar size. Employment growth in women-owned businesses exceeds the national average in nearly every region of the country and in nearly every major industry. Women-owned businesses employ one out of every five U.S. workers—a total of 18.5 million employees.

Female labor-force participation from all racial groups will rise during the period between 1990 and 2005. The net labor force for all women between 1990 and 2005 is projected to increase 26 percent. Hispanic and Asian American women will exhibit the fastest growth, both at 80 percent. Black women's labor-force growth of 34 percent also will exceed the growth average for all women. White women will remain the dominant female participants, but their labor-force growth of 23 percent will be the least among all female groups.

Labor-force participation rates, the percentage of employed women, for both white and black women are expected to exceed 60 percent, but for the first time, during the decade of the turn of the century, white women's participation rate (63.5 percent) is projected to exceed that of black women (61.7 percent). The projected rate for Hispanic women will be 58 percent in 2005, up from 53 percent in 1990. During the same period, the enormous rise in labor-force participation for Asian American women will result in a projected participation rate of 58.9 percent, just slightly above that of Hispanic women.[10]

Receipts from businesses owned by women increased 183 percent from $98.3 billion to $278.1 billion from 1982 to 1987. Such skillful delivery of real goods and services into a global and complex regional marketplace is the basic activity required of all American businesses to continue to feed our national economy.

FUTURE CHALLENGES FOR WOMEN ENTREPRENEURS

What does the future hold for women entrepreneurs? The number of women starting businesses will continue to increase, and their presence will be seen in virtually every industry. It is likely, however, that women entrepreneurs will continue to be prominent in the service industry. This is because (1) the service industry is less capital intensive than most others; hence, financial barriers to entry are lower; and (2) the service industry tends to offer more opportunities to develop selected niches that are critical during the start-up and growth phases of operations. Some challenges that still exist for women entrepreneurs that we will discuss are the work/home role conflict, the closing funding gap, the growth of the service sector, and the changing preparation for a business career. Research on women entrepreneurs continues, addressing questions for the future.

Work/Home Role Conflict

The growth of women-owned businesses is a reflection of the changes in U.S. society. The concepts of dual-income families and professional women in the workplace are ever-expanding notions. However, this societal change also poses a critical problem for women

---

[10] The National Women's Business Council, *Second Annual Report to the President and Congress* (Washington, DC: Government Printing Office, 1990), 7; "Women Workers: Outlook to 2005," *Facts on Working Women* (Washington, DC: Department of Labor Women's Bureau, 1992), 1.2; and *1996 Statistical Update,* The National Foundation for Women Business Owners.

entrepreneurs. A tension exists in the form of **interrole conflict,** in which the pressures from the entrepreneurial role and the homemaker role become incompatible.[11]

A number of variables have been identified that affect the role conflict. For example, the time pressures of an entrepreneurial venture bear heavily on the level of conflict. In addition, family size can affect the tension due to the demands of younger children. The degree of family support for a woman in her venture also may affect the tension level and thus the role conflict. Another variable that has been suggested is a woman's satisfaction level with a job, her marriage, and her life.

In a study of 300 women entrepreneurs, four major findings concerning work/home role conflict were revealed. First, women owners are likely to experience work/home conflict regardless of their family structure or the absolute amount of time spent at work. Second, work/home role conflict for women entrepreneurs is associated with the level of business satisfaction and perceived business success. Third, if the business should meet or exceed the owner's expectations, she is likely to receive business and personal satisfaction, which may, in turn, reduce the level of conflict. Fourth, role conflict is more prevalent in owners who have lower self-esteem or self-worth, and these areas, in turn, are strongly affected by business satisfaction and the financial health of the business.[12]

In a larger study of 1,500 professional women, researchers found that women who were entrepreneurs experienced less role conflict due to significantly higher levels of family-life satisfaction and the recognized autonomy that self-employment provides.[13] In a more recent study, it was pointed out that women entrepreneurs' personal value systems affected the business strategy they pursued. This study called for more research in the area of women's values and their business strategy choice.[14]

Overall, these findings suggest that women business owners need to be prepared to cope with work/home role conflicts, particularly in the early years in the life of the firm. However, entrepreneurship may be the most successful professional outlet for reducing that conflict if autonomy and satisfaction are present.

Closing the Funding Gap

One barrier many women entrepreneurs face is that of securing initial financing. As noted earlier, most men entrepreneurs rely, at least partially, on outside financing to help seed their venture. Women, on the other hand, depend most heavily on personal funds and personal loans. This trend is beginning to change as more venture capitalists begin providing financing to women entrepreneurs. The **funding gap** is the difference between the desired level of available capital for all women-owned businesses and the actual level available.[15] This gap will continue to close as financiers begin to realize they have been neglecting a major source of profitable investments. The gap also will diminish as women begin gaining more experience in the financial arena and become more proficient at making financial forecasts, structuring financial packages, and negotiating financial terms.

---

[11] Charles R. Stoner, Richard J. Hartman, and Raj Arora, "Work-Home Role Conflict in Female Owners of Small Business: An Exploratory Study," *Journal of Small Business Management* (January 1990): 30–38.

[12] Ibid.

[13] Charles R. Stoner, Richard I. Hartman, and Raj Arora, "Differences between Female Entrepreneurs and Female Professional Managers," *Proceedings: Midwest Business Administration Association,* 1990, 41–48.

[14] Shirley R. Olson and Helen M. Currie, "Female Entrepreneurs: Personal Value Systems and Business Strategies in a Male-Dominated Industry," *Journal of Small Business Management* (January 1989): 32–37.

[15] Jill Andresky Fraser, "Desperately Seeking Capital," *Working Women,* July 1993, 59–79.

Service Sector

As the economy continues to grow, the service sector will provide increased opportunities for new ventures. Many of these enterprises will be labor intensive (restaurants, boutiques, florists) and will be small to medium sized. The service industry thus will be a major target for would-be entrepreneurs. The fact that many of these entrepreneurs have low barriers to entry and exit also will make them attractive. Entrepreneurs will need only a limited investment to set up operations and can withdraw without paying an exorbitant exit cost. Currently, approximately 58 percent of all women entrepreneurs are in the service industry. By the turn of the century, this percentage of the owner-managers in the industry will have declined, but women entrepreneurs will still represent a large percentage of the owner-managers in the industry.

Changing Preparation

Most women entrepreneurs of the 1980s had little formal preparation for a business career. Many worked at a job, felt they were underpaid and could do the work better than their employer, and broke away to start their own enterprise. Others pondered a business of their own, saved their money, and finally decided to take the plunge. For most, the new venture was a learning experience. Dealing with bankers, drawing up business plans, hiring and firing personnel, and making expansion decisions were all matters learned through first-hand experience.

Today major changes in the way women entrepreneurs prepare to start their own venture are occurring. More formal training, greater economic opportunities, and changing social mores are influencing the entrepreneurial environment.[16] The woman entrepreneur of the 1990s is quite different from her counterpart of one or two decades earlier. Women are becoming a formidable force in the world of entrepreneurship. Where the 1980s was a decade of gaining lost ground, the 1990s is becoming a decade of full equality in terms of financial funding, representation, and market presence. Many women have long believed their place is at the head of a company. During the 1990s this belief has become a reality for thousands of them.

Future Research

Are women entrepreneurs very different from their male counterparts? Research shows they are not.[17] For example, both are motivated by the desire to achieve and to attain personal independence.[18] In many cases both have been influenced by frustration or dissatisfaction with their former occupation and by a desire to change their personal circumstances. Both rely heavily on personal assets and savings to start their firm. Both are goal oriented, are enthusiastic and energetic, and find strong support for their efforts from their spouse and close friends. The values of both groups are also similar, with the desires for power and economic payoff tending to head the list.

The future will reveal greater attention to research on women entrepreneurs. In particular, a new focus will be emphasized as researchers recognize a more "integrated

---

[16] Lois A. Stevenson, "Against All Odds: The Entrepreneurship of Women," *Journal of Small Business Management* (October 1986): 30–36.

[17] Sue Birley, "Female Entrepreneurs: Are They Really Any Different?" *Journal of Small Business Management* (January 1989): 32–37.

[18] Carole E. Scott, "Why More Women Are Becoming Entrepreneurs," *Journal of Small Business Management* (October 1986): 37–44.

perspective." This perspective is that women business owners conceive of their business ventures as cooperative networks of relationships rather than merely profit-making entities. Researcher Candida G. Brush believes women business owners are at the center of these various mutual relational interactions and their role is to bring these connections together. This **integrated perspective** suggests different interpretations of the variables across the four main dimensions involved in venture creation or acquisition and begs different questions for future research.[19]

Under the four dimensions—individual, organizational, process, and environmental—Brush suggests the following research questions for the future:[20]

INDIVIDUAL DIMENSION

1. How do women business owners view their business? Does a variation in business perspective among types of women business owners exist based on dimensions such as age, location, work experience, life-cycle stage, or cultural background?

2. Is the perspective that female business owners have of their business similar or different from that of male business owners? What are the implications for the difference in perspectives (if any) between men and women on the business strategy, goals, and performance of their enterprises?

3. How do women business owners view their primary role in business operations? How is this role related to other roles women business owners assume?

4. What factors lead to the decision by women to become business owners? What is the effect of these factors on the start-up process? Do differences exist between male and female business owners on this aspect?

5. Do women business owners differ from men in their motivations for business creation/ownership across age, family life cycle, or background?

6. How do women business owners make critical decisions? How do they frame decisions and make choices?

7. How do women business owners measure personal success? Does a variation in the view of success exist among different types of women business owners based on location, education, experience, or life-cycle stage?

ORGANIZATIONAL DIMENSION

1. What are the primary business goals of women-owned businesses? To what degree are these economic or noneconomic goals? How do these goals arise, and do these goals vary over the business cycle or by business type?

2. How do women business owners organize their businesses and allocate responsibilities among employees?

3. What are the implications of any differences in structural and design dimensions for the business operations of male- and female-owned businesses?

[19] Candida G. Brush, "Research on Women Business Owners: Past Trends, a New Perspective and Future Directions," *Entrepreneurship Theory and Practice* (summer 1992): 5–30.

[20] Brush, "Research on Women Business Owners," 19–23.

4. How is business performance measured by female business owners? How is this similar or different from male business owners?

5. What are the perceptions of the business performance of women-owned businesses from the viewpoint of employees? Customers? The community?

6. How do women business owners conceive of planning? What are the content and process of their planning activities?

PROCESS DIMENSION

1. How do women business owners create or acquire their own businesses? What are the roles of family and business relationships in this process?

2. What are the effects of various background factors, such as family life-cycle state, cultural background, or educational and occupational experience, on the process of venture creation or acquisition?

3. What are the management approaches of women business owners? What is the relationship of management style to employee perceptions of job satisfaction? To overall business performance?

4. How do work/family conflicts arise, and how do women business owners manage these?

5. What is the role of the expectations of employees, family, and other stakeholders in the operations and performance of women-owned businesses?

ENVIRONMENTAL DIMENSION

1. To what degree do women business owners view the environment as connected to their business, work, and family? What is the effect of different work, family, social, and cultural experiences on the environmental perspective of women business owners?

2. What is the role of women's associations and groups in establishing relationships and networks for women business owners? Do these associations perform the same functions as organizations that are not gender based?

3. What are the political, governmental, technological, and economic factors that encourage or discourage women's business ownership?

Overall, the future of entrepreneurship will be guided by public understanding of the emerging impact of women entrepreneurs. As *The State of Small Business* reported, "Women-owned businesses have attained an important place alongside businesses owned by men. Moreover, women can be expected to continue their progress into the labor force and business ownership. Their determination and increasing industrial diversification represent important steps toward economic and personal fulfillment as well as economic growth and strength for the nation."[21]

---

[21] *The State of Small Business: A Report of the President* (Washington, DC: Government Printing Office, 1992), 331.

FIGURE 1.4   **MINORITY-OWNED BUSINESSES**

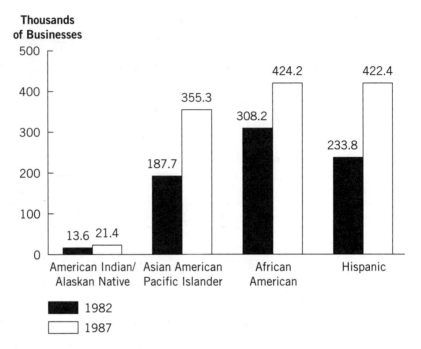

Thousands of Businesses

Category	1982	1987
American Indian/Alaskan Native	13.6	21.4
Asian American Pacific Islander	187.7	355.3
African American	308.2	424.2
Hispanic	233.8	422.4

■ 1982
□ 1987

SOURCE: U.S. Department of Commerce, Bureau of the Census, *1987 Survey of Minority-Owned Business Enterprises* (Washington, DC: Government Printing Office, 1991).

MINORITY-OWNED BUSINESSES

In recent years the number of minority-owned firms have increased dramatically. Asian American–owned firms increased 394 percent; Native American–owned firms, 40 percent; Hispanic-owned firms, 93 percent; and African American–owned firms, 87 percent. Cumulatively, these firms generated more than $78 billion in gross receipts. These statistics correspond to more than 1,213,570 minority-owned businesses that, in addition to providing salaries for more than 300,000 proprietorships, provided paid employment for 836,000 people.[22]

These figures represent 8.9 percent of all businesses within the scope of the Bureau of Census and 3.9 percent of the receipts of those businesses. African American–owned businesses accounted for the largest share of minority-owned business receipts (42.6 percent). Businesses owned by Asian Americans and Pacific Islanders had the largest share of minority-owned businesses in terms of average annual receipts, with receipts per firm of $93,221, compared to an average of $64,131 for minority-owned businesses overall.[23]

The number of minority-owned businesses increased in every category from 1982 to 1987 (see Figure 1.4). The number of businesses owned by **North American Indians,** including Alaskan Native Americans, rose from 13,573 to 21,380, an increase of 57.5

[22] John R. Winston, "Minority-Owned Business: A Look Ahead," *The National Public Accountant* (July 1992): 36–39; and Dayton J. Watkins, "Minority Entrepreneurs and the Future of the American Economy," *Journal of Small Business Strategy* (spring 1993): 71–72.

[23] *The State of Small Business,* 331.

percent. The total receipts of these businesses rose 84 percent from $495 million to $911 million. The receipts of businesses owned by North American Indians and Alaskan Native Americans accounted for 0.2 percent of all U.S. businesses and about 0.05 percent of total U.S. business receipts.

The number of businesses owned by Asian Americans and Pacific Islanders rose from 187,691 to 355,311, an increase of 89.3 percent. The total receipts of these businesses rose from $12.7 billion in 1982 to $33.1 billion in 1987, an increase of 161.8 percent. Asian Americans and Pacific Islanders accounted for 2.6 percent of all U.S. businesses and 1.7 percent of total U.S. business receipts.

African American–owned businesses rose from 308,000 to 424,000, an increase of 38.0 percent. The receipts of these businesses rose by 105.4 percent from $9.6 billion in 1982 to $19.8 billion in 1987. African American–owned businesses accounted for roughly 3 percent of all U.S. businesses and about 1 percent of total U.S. business receipts.

Hispanic-owned businesses rose from 233,800 to 422,373, an increase of 80.5 percent. The total receipts of Hispanic-owned businesses more than doubled over this same period, rising from $11.76 billion in 1982 to $24.73 billion in 1987.

Future Challenges for Minority Entrepreneurs

Minority-owned enterprises are not only emerging at a record pace, but, more important, they also are succeeding. One study of the largest African American–owned firms found impressive ten-year growth rates, including some reaching 300–400 percent.[24] In a more recent study, researchers studied the long-term patterns of black and white female-owned businesses and found the **staying power** (longevity) of the black female-owned firms were equal to that of white female-owned firms.[25] This study, which pointed out the smaller number of black persons entering into entrepreneurship, reinforces the need for increasing entrepreneurial opportunities and education for potential minority entrepreneurs.

EDUCATION AND CAPITAL   The two most frequently cited areas that need improvement for minority entrepreneurs are education in business skills and access to start-up capital, although problems in these areas do not differ much from those women or nonminority entrepreneurs experience.

Minority entrepreneurs do recognize their lack of abilities in some business skills. A continued effort is needed to encourage these entrepreneurs to seek out the programs they need. The frustration with start-up capital is shared by all entrepreneurs. As will be pointed out in the "Sources of Capital" chapter, "angel" financing may need to be disseminated in the minority communities. Also, the emerging minority-owned banks, community development groups, and Minority Enterprise Small Business Investment Companies (MESBICs) may provide better initial capital opportunities for minority entrepreneurs in the years to come.[26]

Finally, it should be pointed out that successful minority entrepreneurs do exist and their numbers are growing. Each year *Black Enterprise* magazine reports on some of the finest

[24] Matthew C. Sonfield, "An Exploratory Analysis of the Largest Black-Owned U.S. Companies," *Journal of Small Business Management* (January 1994): 18–26.

[25] Arthur L. Dolinsky, Richard K. Caputo, and Kishore Rasumarty, "Long Term Entrepreneurship Patterns: A National Study of Black and White Female Entry and Stayer Status Differences," *Journal of Small Business Management* (January 1994): 18–26.

[26] Bradford McKee and Sharon Nelton, "Building Bridges to Minority Firms," *Nation's Business,* December 1992, 29–31.

ENTREPRENEURIAL

EDGE

Business Opportunities—Unlimited

In order to illustrate just how many potential opportunities exist for entrepreneurs, *Entrepreneur* magazine identifies 500 business opportunities *every year.* These opportunities are grouped into five major classifications: dealers/distributors, licensees, coin operated, multilevel marketing/direct sales, and cooperative buying groups. Although the magazine only provides a list and these opportunities *must* be carefully researched before pursuing them, the publication of these opportunities may help potential entrepreneurs realize the huge world of possibility. The list includes the following types of business opportunities:

Dealer/Distributors

Advertising Services
    Direct mail/publishing services
    Miscellaneous advertising products/
        services
Apparel
    Jewelry
    Miscellaneous apparel and accessories

Automotive
Building Services
    Hot tubs
    Prefabricated homes
    Roofing systems
    Miscellaneous building products/
        services
Business Systems
Children's Businesses
Financial Systems
Food
Home-Improvement Products/
    Services
Maintenance
    Porcelain repair
    Miscellaneous maintenance products/
        services
Photo Products
Retail Sales
    Computer products
    Cosmetics
    Gifts and novelties
    Personal-care products/services
    Recreational products
    Stationery/paper goods
    Miscellaneous products
Security Systems
Telecommunications
Travel
Water

African American–owned enterprises in the United States.[27] The need to showcase these successes and expose potential minority entrepreneurs to them is critical. One study stresses the importance of having successful minority entrepreneurs as role models for guidance and encouragement.[28] It is through these role models that future minority entrepreneurs will find opportunity, set goals, and succeed in greater numbers than ever imagined. With the numbers of minority-owned businesses increasing, the U.S. economy's revitalization may need the success of these enterprises.

[27] See Kevin D. Thompson, "The Freshman Class of '93," *Black Enterprise,* June 1993, 131–40.

[28] Kofi Q. Dadzie and Youngil Cho, "Determinants of Minority Business Formation and Survival: An Empirical Assessment," *Journal of Small Business Management* (July 1989): 56–61.

Photo
  Aerial photography
  Image transfer systems
  Miscellaneous photo/video
    businesses
Service
  Balloon wrapping/gift canning
  Computer-based businesses
  Dating services
  Engraving/monogramming systems
  Home inspection services
  Packaging and postal centers
  Referral businesses
  Yard signs

Coin-Operated

Candy/Snack Vending
Public Phone/Faxes
Ultrasonic Golf Club Cleaning Machines
Miscellaneous Coin-Operated Businesses

Licensees

Apparel
  Screen-printing businesses
  Miscellaneous apparel businesses
Automotive
  Antifreeze recycling services
  Auto appearance services
  Auto marketing systems
  Windshield repair
  Miscellaneous auto services
Beauty/Personal-Care
Business Service
  Advertising services
  Auditing services
  Medical claims processing
  Miscellaneous business services

Children's Businesses
  Personalized children's products
  Miscellaneous children's businesses
Computer
  Internet businesses
  Toner cartridge recharging
  Computer maintenance businesses
Educational/Financial Aid Services
Financial Services
Food
Home
  Carpeting businesses
  Wall printing
  Miscellaneous home-improvement
    businesses
Maintenance
  Blind cleaning
  Carpet and upholstery cleaning
  Vinyl repair
  Miscellaneous maintenance services
Recreation Business
  Miniature golf
  Travel agencies
  Miscellaneous recreation businesses
Telecommunications Systems
Miscellaneous Products and Services

Multilevel Marketing/Direct Sales

Cosmetics/Health-Care Products
Home-Decorating Products
Long-Distance Services
Miscellaneous Products and Services

Cooperative Buying Groups

SOURCE: Adapted from Stephani Osowski, "Business Opportunities 500," *Entrepreneur,* July 1996, 168–69. Reprinted with permission from *Entrepreneur Magazine* (Special Issue BIZ OPP 500) July 1996.

ENTREPRENEURIAL OPPORTUNITIES

Free enterprise is the economic basis for all entrepreneurial activity. This means any individual is free to transform an idea into a business. The opportunities for potential entrepreneurs are unlimited. The constantly changing economic environment provides a continuous flow of potential opportunities *if* an individual can recognize a profitable idea amid the chaos and cynicism that also permeates such an environment. Thousands of alternatives exist since every individual creates and develops ideas with a unique frame of reference.

Whether the motivation is profit or independence, or the challenge of developing one's own business, entrepreneurs are actively pursuing ideas and opportunities at a record pace. The Bureau of Labor Statistics reported that self-employment grew from 7,575,000 to 8,944,000, an increase of 18.1 percent between 1992 and 1994. In addition, as noted earlier the U.S. Small Business Administration reported that more than 600,000 *new firms* are being developed each year.[29]

Entrepreneurial opportunities will continue to exist for individuals willing to take the risk. As we will see throughout the following chapters, the discipline of entrepreneurship can be learned in order to better prepare oneself for an entrepreneurial opportunity. Thus, your ability to act entrepreneurially may be enhanced. The decision to act is and always will be yours!

✳ SUMMARY

This chapter attempted to provide a broad perspective of the entrepreneurial revolution occurring throughout the United States and the world. Beginning with the concept of entrepreneurship and then exploring a perspective of it, the chapter discussed important statistics supporting our entrepreneurial economy. The major forces in contemporary entrepreneurial research as well as the new educational programs were described. The emerging trends in entrepreneurship were then discussed. The number of women entrepreneurs continues to increase dramatically. Approximately 5 million women own their business, and they represent 32 percent of all businesses. Reasons for this growth include economic conditions, the availability of opportunities, dissatisfaction with wage and salary jobs, and a desire for supplementary income.

The future will reveal an increased number and acceptance of women entrepreneurs. The funding gap will continue to decrease, women will continue to better prepare themselves for a business career, and opportunities for women in all business sectors will increase. Future research in the area of women entrepreneurs will provide greater insights into an integrated perspective based on the individual, the organization, the process, and the environment.

Minority-owned enterprises are another emerging trend. African American–owned firms have increased 87 percent; Hispanic-owned firms, 93 percent; Asian American–owned firms, 394 percent; and Native American–owned firms, 40 percent. Along with improving business education and access to start-up capital, the importance of recognizing and showcasing successful minority entrepreneurs as role models is critical to developing future entrepreneurs in U.S. minority groups.

Key Terms and Concepts

African American–owned businesses	National Federation of Independent
Asian Americans	Businesses (NFIB)
Entrepreneurship	North American Indians
Funding gap	Pacific Islanders
Gazelle	Staying power
Hispanic-owned businesses	Women entrepreneurs
Integrated perspective	Women-owned businesses
Interrole conflict	Women's Business Ownership Act
Minority entrepreneurs	

[29] *The State of Small Business.*

Review and Discussion Questions

1. Briefly describe what is meant by the term *entrepreneurship.*
2. Describe the predominance of new ventures in the economy.
3. What is the record number of new small firms being established?
4. Describe the three types of small business establishments identified by the Small Business Administration.
5. How have most *net* new jobs been created in the economy?
6. Identify some of the projected growth industries through the year 2005.
7. Define a "gazelle" and discuss its importance.
8. Describe the increase in business ownership among women and use actual statistics.
9. What are three reasons for the rapid growth of business ownership among women?
10. Why is the "funding gap" likely to diminish during the 1990s?
11. Describe the emerging trend in minority entrepreneurship. Present some statistical data.
12. Describe the future challenges for minority entrepreneurship.

Experiential Exercise   *Separating Fact from Fiction*

Many myths, or fictons, exist about women and minority entrepreneurs. The following statements can be divided into two groups: fiction and facts. Place an *FI* before the fictions and an *FA* before the facts. Answers are provided at the end of the exercise.

_____ 1. More and more women entrepreneurs are failing in their business ventures and are going back to their jobs in large corporations.

_____ 2. Women entrepreneurs today represent approximately 30 percent of all business ownerships in the United States.

_____ 3. About 100,000 women-owned businesses exist in the United States today.

_____ 4. Women entrepreneurs now have gross receipts of about $278 billion annually.

_____ 5. Research shows that in most ethnic groups in the U.S. economy the percentage of minority-owned businesses is increasing.

_____ 6. If the present growth trend continues, by the year 2000 women will own 50 percent of the nation's small businesses.

_____ 7. Almost 50 percent of all retail trade businesses are owned by women.

_____ 8. Hispanic and Asian American women are predicted to show the fastest growth in the labor force by the year 2005.

_____ 9. The African American women's labor force will grow 34 percent by 2005.

_____ 10. In recent years, the percentage of Hispanic-owned firms has increased more than any other minority group.

_____ 11. Women entrepreneurs are not very different from their male counterparts in terms of ability and desire to succeed.

_____ 12. Women and minority entrepreneurs are very high risk takers.

_____ 13. Women entrepreneurs draw the greatest support from their spouse, friends, and family.

———— 14. Women entrepreneurs often rely heavily on personal assets and savings to start their firm.

———— 15. Minority-owned enterprises are emerging at a record pace, and they are succeeding.

———— 16. Role models are ineffective tools for minority entrepreneurs to use for guidance.

Answers

1. FI	5. FA	9. FA	13. FA
2. FA	6. FI	10. FI	14. FA
3. FI	7. FA	11. FA	15. FA
4. FA	8. FA	12. FI	16. FI

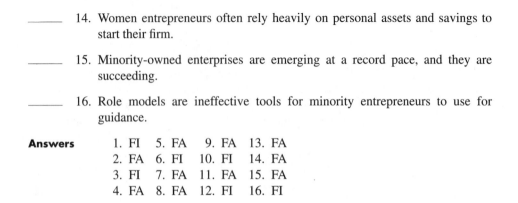

VIDEO CASE 1.1

Two Women Boxing: The Art of Entrepreneurship

Linda Finnell and Julie Cohn are two artists who accidentally became successful entrepreneurs. In 1983, a photographer commissioned Finnell to make portfolio boxes. She asked her best friend, Julie Cohn, to help. "There was no idea at the time there would ever be a business because we were art students. We were purists; we were going to do the art thing," Finnell says with a laugh. The day the photographer arrived to pick up his boxes, he discovered Finnell and Cohn working amid piles of boxes. "As we were stacked up to our heads with boxes on either side, I said, 'You know, if we ever have a business we should call it Two Women Boxing,'" Cohn recalls.

Thirteen years later, Finnell and Cohn are the creative heart and soul of a growing design business with a tony account list that includes Neiman Marcus, Barneys, Bergdorf Goodman, and other upscale retailers. "Julie and I have sculpted out of our art not only the nature of ourselves as artists but a way to make a living doing our art, and that's really gratifying," Finnell says. Inside the company's Dallas studio and bindery, they craft a visually rich collection of boxes, picture frames, photo albums, and journals. "We take a lot of risks by putting different types of patterns together in odd juxtapositions," Finnell reveals. "There's a sense of color that people have come to associate with us."

In the beginning, Finnell and Cohn had to do everything themselves: make their products, market them, nurture supplier relations, and oversee the business details. "As time has gone on, we've been able to actually hire people who have the skills to do those jobs and allow us to do what we do best and love doing the most, which is designing," Finnell says. Today, a lean manufacturing staff—just 12 women—shape, glue, and sew every unique, handmade item.

Although their one-of-a-kind creations have been the core of Two Women Boxing's success, manufacturing everything by hand has presented some real limitations for the company's growth. "Now we have a real global awareness that is essential to the business," Finnell admits. "It's no longer the luxury of Linda and Julie just making a few things that they think are pretty and they'd like to get out on the market. It's having to be aware of everything else that's going on, from the flow of retail sales to the price of products that we import to how we get things in from the Orient during monsoon season to being sometimes frightfully aware of where we are in our own cash flow and our profit and loss."

Finnell and Cohn hope to expand their business by focusing their attention on their greatest strength: their unique design talents. In addition to the 'Two Women Boxing by Hand' product line, Finnell and Cohn are now licensing their designs to other companies. Recently, they created a china pattern for Fitz and Floyd and a collection of journals for Chronicle Books. "The work with Chronicle Books has been wonderful because it has really expanded our audience," Finnell says. "Someone who can't afford a $70 handmade Two Women Boxing baby book can get something that is very different but equally wonderful in a bookstore in cities all over the country for $29.95."

Although potentially lucrative, licensing has presented some new challenges. "There's been some frustration with the outcome of the product," Cohn explains. "With Fitz and Floyd there were more compromises to be made because of pricing. That is something we've actually confronted in all of our licensing situations. We've overdesigned for the market. We've overdesigned for the price point." Still, Finnell and Cohn are enthusiastic about designing products for other companies. They've recently created a line of tabletop items for Silvestry and a distinctive canister set that Neiman Marcus will sell exclusively—all gratifying accomplishments for artists who sometimes worried that they abandoned their art. "We no longer feel like 'Oh, we sold out; we aren't artists; we're only business-women,' but that we have realized a way to spend our lives doing what we really love doing the most," Finnell concludes.

Questions

1. Describe how Linda Finnell and Julie Cohn fit the emerging trend of women entrepreneurs.
2. What potential problems do you think they will face?
3. What typical challenges to women entrepreneurs have Finnell and Cohn already overcome?

 **CASE** **1.2**

Breaking Away

For the past five years Joan Kimball has worked for a small interior-decorating company. The firm does both home and business decorating, although most of its work is in private residences. When Joan started with the firm, she was responsible for talking to clients and getting a preliminary idea of what type of decorating they wanted. She then would take this information back to the company, where initial pricing would be done and preliminary sketches worked up. If the customer accepted the plan, then others in the interior decorating company would take over.

After six months, Joan's responsibilities were expanded, and she was assigned to help with job pricing. This required her to visit dealers and manufacturers' representatives who sell textiles, furniture, bathroom fixtures, wallpaper, and a wide range of other materials used in interior decorating. This experience helped Joan get a firsthand look at prices and profit margins in the industry.

Over the past two years Joan has been performing a wide range of functions—calling on potential clients, pricing jobs, lining up subcontractors, buying the necessary materials, overseeing jobs, and arranging for final payment. Other than the two women who founded the firm, only Joan has this wide a range of responsibilities.

Joan likes her job very much. She has, however, been thinking about breaking away and starting her own operation. "I know basically all there is to know about this business," she told her husband. "The biggest problem will be initial capital and hiring the right people. Also, I'll have to learn how to run an office and do some financial planning. But I think I can do it if I can get the initial financing."

Questions

1. What traits or characteristics would Joan need in order to succeed in this business?
2. How could Joan go about financing her proposed venture? Which avenue would be most available to her?
3. What does Joan need to learn in order to run her new venture most effectively? Be complete in your answer.

 **CASE   1.3**

A Research Orientation

Henry Schalley received his Ph.D. last year and joined a major university shortly thereafter. Henry teaches business strategy and is looking for an area in which he can do research and publish. "You've got to find a niche where there has not been much work done," his department chairperson told him, "and start investigating the area. Minority entrepreneurship would be a good choice. A great deal is known about entrepreneurs, but not very much has been learned specifically about minority entrepreneurs. There are many areas you could investigate."

Henry believes that his department chairperson is right. However, he is unsure of how to proceed. What types of research questions should he ask? What specific areas of inquiry would be most profitable? Henry believes his first step should be to review the current literature and find out what types of articles have been written and what data have been uncovered about minority entrepreneurs. This, he hopes, will help him decide on a course of action. He also intends to look over the journals in the field and determine the types of research they are most likely to accept for publication.

Henry knows he has a total of three more years to generate three or four research articles. It will take him approximately one year to collect data, write a couple of articles, and get them submitted to journals. It will take at least ten weeks to get back a review and, if it is favorable, another two to three weeks to make changes based on reviewer comments. Because of this long time lag from the start of a research project to its fruition in the form of an article, Henry knows he has little time to waste. He must formulate a course of action and begin work immediately.

Questions

1. What are three research questions Henry could pursue?
2. Discuss any important findings that have emerged in research conducted on minority entrepreneurs.
3. Discuss an area of research you think would be most fruitful for Henry.

Chapter 2

ENTREPRENEURSHIP: AN EVOLVING CONCEPT

CHAPTER OBJECTIVES

1. To examine the historical development of entrepreneurship

2. To explore and debunk the myths of entrepreneurship

3. To define and explore the major schools of entrepreneurial thought

4. To explain the process approaches to the study of entrepreneurship

5. To set forth a comprehensive definition of entrepreneurship

Most of what you hear about entrepreneurship, says America's leading management thinker, is all wrong. It's not magic; it's not mysterious; and it has nothing to do with genes. It's a discipline and, like any discipline, it can be learned.

Peter F. Drucker
Innovation and Entrepreneurship,
(New York: Harper & Row, 1985)

THE EVOLUTION OF ENTREPRENEURSHIP

The word *entrepreneur* is derived from the French *entreprendre,* meaning "to undertake." The **entrepreneur** is one who undertakes to organize, manage, and assume the risks of a business. In recent years entrepreneurs have been doing so many things that it is necessary to broaden this definition. Today, an entrepreneur is an innovator or developer who recognizes and seizes opportunities; converts those opportunities into workable/marketable ideas; adds value through time, effort, money, or skills; assumes the risks of the competitive marketplace to implement these ideas; and realizes the rewards from these efforts.[1]

The entrepreneur is the aggressive catalyst for change in the world of business. He or she is an independent thinker who dares to be different in a background of common events. The literature of entrepreneurial research reveals some similarities, as well as a great many differences, in the characteristics of entrepreneurs. Chief among these characteristics are personal initiative, the ability to consolidate resources, management skills, a desire for autonomy, and risk taking. Other characteristics include aggressiveness, competitiveness, goal-oriented behavior, confidence, opportunistic behavior, intuitiveness, reality-based actions, the ability to learn from mistakes, and the ability to employ human relations skills.[2]

Although no single definition of *entrepreneur* exists and no one profile can represent today's entrepreneur, research is providing an increasingly sharper focus on the subject. A brief review of the history of entrepreneurship illustrates this.

America currently is in the midst of a new wave of business and economic development, and entrepreneurship is its catalyst. Yet the social and economic forces of entrepreneurial

---

[1] For a compilation of definitions, see Robert C. Ronstadt, *Entrepreneurship* (Dover, MA: Lord Publishing, 1984), 28; Howard H. Stevenson and David E. Gumpert, "The Heart of Entrepreneurship," *Harvard Business Review* (March/April 1985): 85–94; and J. Barton Cunningham and Joe Lischeron, "Defining Entrepreneurship," *Journal of Small Business Management* (January 1991): 45–61.

[2] See Calvin A. Kent, Donald L. Sexton, and Karl H. Vesper, *Encyclopedia of Entrepreneurship* (Englewood Cliffs: Prentice-Hall, 1982); Ray V. Montagno and Donald F. Kuratko, "Perception of Entrepreneurial Success Characteristics," *American Journal of Small Business* (winter 1986): 25–32; and Thomas M. Begley and David P. Boyd, "Psychological Characteristics Associated with Performance in Entrepreneurial Firms and Smaller Businesses," *Journal of Business Venturing* (winter 1987): 79–91.

30

activity existed long before the 1990s. In fact, as noted in Chapter 1, the entrepreneurial spirit has driven many of humanity's achievements.

> Humanity's progress from caves to campuses has been explained in numerous ways. But central to virtually all of these theories has been the role of the "agent of change," the force that initiates and implements material progress. Today we recognize that the agent of change in human history has been and most likely will continue to be the entrepreneur.[3]

The recognition of entrepreneurs dates back to eighteenth-century France when economist Richard Cantillon associated the "risk-bearing" activity in the economy with the entrepreneur. In England during the same period, the Industrial Revolution was evolving, with the entrepreneur playing a visible role in risk taking and the transformation of resources.[4]

The association of entrepreneurship and economics has long been the accepted norm. In fact, until the 1950s the majority of definitions and references to entrepreneurship had come from economists. For example, Cantillon (1725), just mentioned; Jean Baptiste Say (1803), the renowned French economist; and Joseph Schumpeter (1934), a twentieth-century economic genius, all wrote about entrepreneurship and its impact on economic development.[5] Over the decades writers have continued to try to describe or define what entrepreneurship is all about. Here are some examples:

> Entrepreneurship . . . consists in doing things that are not generally done in the ordinary course of business routine; it is essentially a phenomenon that comes under the wider aspect of leadership.[6]

> Entrepreneurship, at least in all nonauthoritarian societies, constitutes a bridge between society as a whole, especially the noneconomic aspects of that society, and the profit-oriented institutions established to take advantage of its economic endowments and to satisfy, as best they can, its economic desires.[7]

> In . . . entrepreneurship, there is agreement that we are talking about a kind of behavior that includes: (1) initiative taking, (2) the organizing or reorganizing of social economic mechanisms to turn resources and situations to practical account, and (3) the acceptance of risk of failure.[8]

After reviewing the evolution of entrepreneurship and examining its varying definitions, Robert C. Ronstadt put together a summary description:

> Entrepreneurship is the dynamic process of creating incremental wealth. This wealth is created by individuals who assume the major risks in terms of equity, time, and/or career commitment of providing value for some product or service. The product or service

---

[3] Kent, Sexton, and Vesper, *Encyclopedia of Entrepreneurship,* xxix.

[4] Israel M. Kirzner, *Perception, Opportunity, and Profit: Studies in the Theory of Entrepreneurship* (Chicago: University of Chicago Press, 1979), 38–39.

[5] See Ronstadt, *Entrepreneurship,* 9–12.

[6] Joseph Schumpeter, "Change and the Entrepreneur," in *Essays of J. A. Schumpeter,* ed. Richard V. Clemence (Reading, MA: Addison-Wesley, 1951), 255.

[7] Arthur Cole, *Business Enterprise in Its Social Setting* (Cambridge, MA: Harvard University Press, 1959), 27–28.

[8] Albert Shapero, *Entrepreneurship and Economic Development,* Project ISEED, Ltd. (Milwaukee, WI: Center for Venture Management, summer 1975), 187.

itself may or may not be new or unique but value must somehow be infused by the entrepreneur by securing and allocating the necessary skills and resources.[9]

Entrepreneurship as a topic for discussion and analysis was introduced by the economists of the eighteenth century, and it continued to attract the interest of economists in the nineteenth century. In the present century, the word has become synonymous or at least closely linked with free enterprise and capitalism. Also, it is generally recognized that entrepreneurs serve as agents of change; provide creative, innovative ideas for business enterprises; and help businesses grow and become profitable.

Whatever the specific activity they engage in, entrepreneurs today are considered the heroes of free enterprise. Many of them have used innovation and creativity to build multimillion-dollar enterprises from fledgling businesses—some in less than a decade! These individuals have created new products and services and have assumed the risks associated with these ventures. Many people now regard entrepreneurship as "pioneership" on the frontier of business.

> Entrepreneurship is the ability to create and build a vision from practically nothing: fundamentally it is a human, creative act. It is the application of energy to initiating and building an enterprise or organization, rather than just watching or analyzing. This vision requires a willingness to take calculated risks—both personal and financial—and then to do everything possible to reduce the chances of failure. Entrepreneurship also includes the ability to build an entrepreneurial or venture team to complement your own skills and talents. It is the knack for sensing an opportunity where others see chaos, contradiction, and confusion. It is possessing the know-how to find, marshal, and control resources (often owned by others).[10]

THE MYTHS OF ENTREPRENEURSHIP

Throughout the years many myths have arisen about entrepreneurship. These myths are the result of a lack of research on entrepreneurship. As many researchers in the field have noted, the study of entrepreneurship is still emerging, and thus "folklore" will tend to prevail until it is dispelled with contemporary research findings. Ten of the most notable myths with an explanation to dispel each myth appear next.

Myth 1: Entrepreneurs Are Doers, Not Thinkers

Although it is true entrepreneurs tend toward action, they are also thinkers. Indeed, they are often very methodical people who plan their moves carefully. The emphasis today on the creation of clear and complete business plans (see Part 2) is an indication that "thinking" entrepreneurs are as important as "doing" entrepreneurs.

Myth 2: Entrepreneurs Are Born, Not Made

The idea that the characteristics of entrepreneurs cannot be taught or learned, that they are innate traits one must be born with, has long been prevalent. These traits include aggressiveness, initiative, drive, a willingness to take risks, analytical ability, and skill in human relations. Today, however, the recognition of entrepreneurship as a discipline is helping to

---

[9] Ronstadt, *Entrepreneurship*, 28.

[10] Jeffry A. Timmons, *New Venture Creation*, 4th ed. (Homewood, IL: Irwin, 1994), 7–8.

CONTEMPORARY ENTREPRENEURSHIP

The E-Myth

Michael E. Gerber has written a book titled *The E-Myth: Why Most Businesses Don't Work and What to Do about It*. He clearly delineates the differences among the types of persons involved with contemporary small businesses. These persons are the following:

- The *entrepreneur* invents a business that works without him or her. This is a visionary who makes a business unique by imbuing it with a special and exciting sense of purpose and direction. The entrepreneur's far-reaching perspective enables him or her to anticipate changes and needs in the marketplace and to initiate activities to capitalize on them.

- The *manager* produces results through employees by developing and implementing effective systems and, by interacting with employees, enhances their self-esteem and ability to produce good results. The manager can actualize the entrepreneur's vision through planning, implementation, and analysis.

- The *technician* performs specific tasks according to systems and standards management developed. The technician, in the best of businesses, not only gets the work done but also provides input to supervisors for improvement of those systems and standards.

Understanding these definitions is important, because Gerber contends that most small businesses *don't work;* their *owners* do. In other words, he believes that today's small-business owner works too hard at a *job* that he or she has created for himself or herself rather than working to create a *business*. Thus, most small businesses fail because the owner is more of a "technician" than an "entrepreneur." Working only as a technician, the small-business owner realizes too little reward for so much effort, and eventually, according to Gerber, the business fails.

The E-Myth is that today's business owners are *not* true entrepreneurs who create businesses but merely technicians who now have created a job for themselves. The solution to this myth lies in the owner's willingness to begin thinking and acting like a true entrepreneur: to imagine how the business would work without him or her. In other words, the owner must begin working *on* the business, in addition to working *in* it. He or she must leverage the company's capacity through systems development and implementation. The whole key is a person developing an "Entrepreneurial Perspective."

SOURCE: Adapted from Michael E. Gerber, *The E-Myth: Why Most Businesses Don't Work and What to Do about It* (New York: Harper Business, 1986); and personal interview, 1993.

dispel this myth. Like all disciplines, entrepreneurship has models, processes, and case studies that allow the topic to be studied and the knowledge to be acquired.

Myth 3: Entrepreneurs Are Always Inventors

The idea that entrepreneurs are inventors is a result of misunderstanding and tunnel vision. Although many inventors are also entrepreneurs, numerous entrepreneurs encompass all sorts of innovative activity.[11] For example, Ray Kroc did not invent the fast-food franchise, but his innovative ideas made McDonald's the largest fast-food enterprise in the world. A contemporary understanding of entrepreneurship covers more than just invention. It requires a complete understanding of innovative behavior in all forms.

Myth 4: Entrepreneurs Are Academic and Social Misfits

The belief that entrepreneurs are academically and socially ineffective is a result of some business owners having started successful enterprises after dropping out of school or quitting a job. In many cases such an event has been blown out of proportion in an attempt to "profile" the typical entrepreneur. Historically, in fact, educational and social organizations did not recognize the entrepreneur. They abandoned him or her as a misfit in a world of corporate giants. Business education, for example, was aimed primarily at the study of corporate activity. Today the entrepreneur is considered a hero—socially, economically, and academically. No longer a misfit, the entrepreneur is now viewed as a professional.

Myth 5: Entrepreneurs Must Fit the "Profile"

Many books and articles have presented checklists of characteristics of the successful entrepreneur. These lists were neither validated nor complete; they were based on case studies and on research findings among achievement-oriented people. Today we realize that a standard entrepreneurial profile is hard to compile. The environment, the venture itself, and the entrepreneur have interactive effects, which result in many different types of profiles. Contemporary studies conducted at universities across the United States will, in the future, provide more accurate insights into the various profiles of successful entrepreneurs. As we will show in Chapter 4, an "Entrepreneurial Perspective" within individuals is more understandable than a particular profile.

Myth 6: All Entrepreneurs Need Is Money

It is true a venture needs capital to survive; it is also true a large number of business failures occur because of a lack of adequate financing. Yet having money is not the only bulwark against failure. Failure due to a lack of proper financing often is an indicator of other problems: managerial incompetence, lack of financial understanding, poor investments, poor planning, and the like. Many successful entrepreneurs have overcome the lack of money while establishing their ventures. To those entrepreneurs, money is a resource but never an end in itself.

Myth 7: All Entrepreneurs Need Is Luck

Being at "the right place at the right time" is always an advantage. But "luck happens when preparation meets opportunity" is an equally appropriate adage. Prepared entrepreneurs who seize the opportunity when it arises often seem "lucky." They are, in fact, simply better prepared to deal with situations and turn them into successes. What appears to be luck really is preparation, determination, desire, knowledge, and innovativeness.

---

[11] John B. Miner, Norman R. Smith, and Jeffrey S. Bracker, "Defining the Inventor-Entrepreneur in the Context of Established Typologies," *Journal of Business Venturing* (March 1992): 103–13.

Myth 8: Ignorance Is Bliss for Entrepreneurs

The myth that too much planning and evaluation lead to constant problems, that over-analysis leads to paralysis, does not hold up in today's competitive markets, which demand detailed planning and preparation. Identifying a venture's strengths and weaknesses, setting up clear timetables with contingencies for handling problems, and minimizing these problems through careful strategy formulation are all key factors for successful entrepreneurship. Thus careful planning—not ignorance of it—is the mark of an accomplished entrepreneur.

Myth 9: Entrepreneurs Seek Success but Experience High Failure Rates

It is true many entrepreneurs suffer a number of failures before they are successful. They follow the adage "If at first you don't succeed, try, try, again." In fact, failure can teach many lessons to those willing to learn and often leads to future successes. This is clearly shown by the **corridor principle,** which states that with every venture launched, new and unintended opportunities often arise. The 3M Corporation invented Post-it notes using a glue that had not been strong enough for its intended use. Rather than throw away the glue, the company focused on finding another use for it and, in the process, developed a multimillion-dollar product. Yet, the statistics of entrepreneurial failure rates have been misleading over the years. In fact, one researcher, Bruce A. Kirchoff, has reported that the "high failure rate" most commonly accepted may be misleading. Tracing 814,000 businesses started in 1977, Kirchoff found that more than 50 percent were still surviving under their original owners or new owners. Additionally, 28 percent voluntarily closed down, and only 18 percent actually "failed" in the sense of leaving behind outstanding liabilities.[12]

Myth 10: Entrepreneurs Are Extreme Risk Takers (Gamblers)

As we will show in Chapter 4, the concept of risk is a major element in the entrepreneurial process. However, the public's perception of the risk most entrepreneurs assume is distorted. Although it may appear that an entrepreneur is "gambling" on a wild chance, the fact is the entrepreneur is usually working on a moderate or "calculated" risk. Most successful entrepreneurs work hard through planning and preparation to minimize the risk involved in order to better control the destiny of their vision.

These ten myths have been presented to provide a background for today's current thinking on entrepreneurship. By sidestepping the "folklore," we can build a foundation for critically researching the contemporary theories and processes of entrepreneurship.

APPROACHES TO ENTREPRENEURSHIP

In the study of contemporary entrepreneurship, one concept recurs: Entrepreneurship is interdisciplinary. As such it contains various approaches that can increase one's understanding of the field.[13] Thus we need to recognize the diversity of theories as an emergence of entrepreneurial understanding. One way to examine these theories is with a "schools of

---

[12] "A Surprising Finding on New-Business Mortality Rates," *Business Week,* 14 June 1993, 22.

[13] William B. Gartner, "What Are We Talking about When We Talk about Entrepreneurship?" *Journal of Business Venturing* (January 1990): 15–28; see also Lanny Herron, Harry J. Sapienza, and Deborah Smith Cook, "Entrepreneurship Theory from an Interdisciplinary Perspective," *Entrepreneurship Theory and Practice* (spring 1992): 5–12.

FIGURE 2.1 **ENTREPRENEURIAL SCHOOLS-OF-THOUGHT APPROACH**

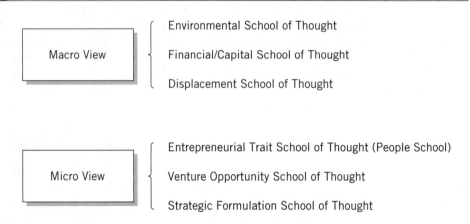

Macro View
- Environmental School of Thought
- Financial/Capital School of Thought
- Displacement School of Thought

Micro View
- Entrepreneurial Trait School of Thought (People School)
- Venture Opportunity School of Thought
- Strategic Formulation School of Thought

thought'' approach that divides entrepreneurship into specific activities. These activities may be within a ''macro'' view or a ''micro'' view, yet all address the conceptual nature of entrepreneurship.

The Schools of Entrepreneurial Thought

In this section we shall highlight the ideas emanating from the macro and micro views of entrepreneurial thought, and we will further break down these two major views into six distinct schools of thought, three within each entrepreneurial view (see Figure 2.1). Although this presentation does not purport to be all inclusive, neither does it claim to limit the schools to these six, for a movement may develop for unification or expansion. Whatever the future holds, however, it is important to become familiar with these conceptual ideas on entrepreneurship in order to avoid the semantic warfare that has plagued general management thought for so many years.[14]

THE MACRO VIEW The **macro view of entrepreneurship** presents a broad array of factors that relate to success or failure in contemporary entrepreneurial ventures. This array includes external processes that are sometimes beyond the control of the individual entrepreneur, for they exhibit a strong **external locus of control** point of view.

Three schools of entrepreneurial thought represent a breakdown of the macro view: (1) the environmental school of thought, (2) the financial/capital school of thought, and (3) the displacement school of thought. The first of these is the broadest and the most pervasive school.

The Environmental School of Thought This school of thought deals with the external factors that affect a potential entrepreneur's lifestyle. These can be either a positive or a negative force in the molding of entrepreneurial desires. The focus is on institutions,

[14] See Harold Koontz, ''The Management Theory Jungle Revisited,'' *Academy of Management Review* (April 1980): 175–87; Richard M. Hodgetts and Donald F. Kuratko, ''The Management Theory Jungle—Quo Vadis?'' *Southern Management Association Proceedings* (November 1983): 280–83; J. Barton Cunningham and Joe Lischeron, ''Defining Entrepreneurship,'' *Journal of Small Business Management* (January 1991): 45–61; and Ian C. MacMillan and Jerome A. Katz, ''Idiosyncratic Milieus of Entrepreneurship Research: The Need for Comprehensive Theories,'' *Journal of Business Venturing* (January 1992): 1–8.

TABLE 2.1	FINANCIAL ANALYSIS EMPHASIS	
Venture Stage	**Financial Consideration**	**Decision**
Start-up or acquisition	Seed capital Venture capital sources	Proceed or abandon
Ongoing	Cash management Investments Financial analysis and evaluation	Maintain, increase, or reduce size
Decline or succession	Profit question Corporate buyout Succession question	Sell, retire, or dissolve operations

values, and mores that, grouped together, form a sociopolitical environmental framework that strongly influences the development of entrepreneurs.[15] For example, if a middle manager experiences the freedom and support to develop ideas, initiate contracts, or create and institute new methods, the work environment will serve to promote that person's desire to pursue an entrepreneurial career. Another environmental factor that often affects the potential development of entrepreneurs is their social group. The atmosphere of friends and relatives can influence the desire to become an entrepreneur.

The Financial/Capital School of Thought This school of thought is based on the capital-seeking process. The search for seed and growth capital is the entire focus of this entrepreneurial emphasis. Certain literature is devoted specifically to this process, whereas other sources tend to treat it as but one segment of the entrepreneurial process.[16] In any case, the venture capital process is vital to an entrepreneur's development. Business-planning guides and texts for entrepreneurs emphasize this phase, and development seminars focusing on the funds application process are offered throughout the country on a continuous basis. This school of thought views the entire entrepreneurial venture from a financial management standpoint. As is apparent from Table 2.1, decisions involving finances occur at every major point in the venture process.

The Displacement School of Thought This school of thought focuses on group phenomena. It holds that the group affects or eliminates certain factors that project the individual into an entrepreneurial venture. As Ronstadt has noted, individuals will *not* pursue a venture unless they are prevented or displaced from doing other activities.[17] Three major types of displacement illustrate this school of thought:

1. *Political displacement.* This is caused by factors ranging from an entire political regime that rejects free enterprise (international environment) to governmental regulations and policies that limit or redirect certain industries.

---

[15] See Andrew H. Van de Ven, "The Development of an Infrastructure for Entrepreneurship," *Journal of Business Venturing* (May 1993): 211–30.

[16] See Ian C. MacMillan, David M. Kullow, and Roubina Khoylian, "Venture Capitalists' Involvement in Their Investments: Extent and Performance," *Journal of Business Venturing* (January 1989): 27–48; and David J. Brophy and Joel M. Shulman, "A Finance Perspective on Entrepreneurship Research," *Entrepreneurship Theory and Practice* (spring 1992): 61–71.

[17] Ronstadt, *Entrepreneurship.*

ENTREPRENEURIAL

EDGE

A New Breed of Entrepreneurs

A new breed of entrepreneurs is trying to learn the ropes of small business ownership. And for some it hasn't been easy. This emerging group of entrepreneurs comprises large-corporation executives who have been laid off, downsized, or bought out. Many of these displaced workers have a great deal of management experience, years of industry knowledge, and a variety of contacts, which are ideal characteristics for individuals considering venturing out on their own, whether by choice or by force. Regardless of these advantages, these former executives are finding that small business ownership is hard work. The transition from manager to entrepreneur and loneliness have been their biggest obstacles. But even so, many agree that the vast rewards of entrepreneurship are well worth the effort.

The volatile business climate that started in the 1980s has intensified in the 1990s due to fierce global competition. As a result, the layoffs that began in the past decade in the automotive, steel, and rubber industries have spread to all industries. This era of widespread employee displacement has been a result of the corporate emphasis on achieving and maintaining a competitive edge in the intense global market. In many cases, businesses are finding that outsourcing certain business functions is more cost effective than handling them internally. In addition, they are replacing workers with new technology, including machines and robots. And, finally, the escalation of mergers in recent times has added to the numbers of displaced managers and executives. In 1995 alone, mergers worth $866 billion took place in the United States, according to Challenger, Gray & Christmas, a Chicago-based corporate outplacement company. The result was 72,000 layoffs, and nothing indicates future relief. "The competition big business faces today isn't going to get any better in the next five or ten years. If anything, it'll get even more intense," Ken Goldstein of The Conference Board, a New York City economic research firm, says.

With a wealth of knowledge and experience under their belt, displaced executives are exploring the world of small

2. *Cultural displacement.* This deals with social groups precluded from professional fields. Ethnic background, religion, race, and sex are all examples of factors that figure in the minority experience. Increasingly, this experience will turn various individuals from standard business professions toward entrepreneurial ventures. According to the U.S. government, the number of minority businesses grew by nearly half a million during the last ten years and represents one-tenth of all the nation's businesses.[18]

[18] Small Business Administration, *The State of Small Business: 1995: A Report of the President* (Washington, DC: Government Printing Office, 1995).

business by starting their own. The number of layoff victims who have turned to entrepreneurship has nearly doubled in only two years, rising from 6 percent in 1993 to 15 percent in 1995, according to Challenger, Gray & Christmas. These entrepreneurs are finding that although the working conditions are very different from those in a corporation, the rewards are very satisfying. The earning potential is unlimited, and they can maintain a position of authority, in addition to working without the daily fear of getting a pink slip.

Their biggest challenge? Former executives are having difficulty adjusting from a narrowly defined job into an all-encompassing entrepreneurial role. Most people who are accustomed to working in corporations have to get used to "wearing all the hats" and taking responsibility for everything themselves. David Keillor had this experience. After working for International Business Machines (IBM) in Rochester, Minnesota, for 30 years, he accepted a buyout and opened Technology Concepts, Inc., a software company. Keillor, like many start-up entrepreneurs, assumed most of the burden of the daily operations. Rather than calling someone to fix problems or purchase merchandise, Keillor realized he had to handle it all himself,

and those many little jobs added up to one big job.

In addition, loneliness is a common grievance for executives who are used to the social interplay in the corporate environment. As a small-business owner, they are finding it requires a certain amount of effort to maintain human contact on a daily basis. Wanda Schiele, who accepted a buyout package from US West and started her own business, tries to maintain social contact by meeting people for lunch, attending networking events, and rekindling old business friendships. She has learned to search out people for social interactions in a way she didn't have to before, Schiele says.

Although many laid-off corporate workers continue to feel a lot of economic and emotional pain, others are turning these unfortunate situations into opportunities by pursuing their lifelong dream of owning their own business. In addition, many former executives who start a business out of necessity are finding they were cut out for entrepreneurship all along. Whether they leave the corporate life by force or by choice, this new rank of entrepreneurs is taking control and making it big on their own.

SOURCE: Heather Page, "Executive Decision," *Entrepreneur,* July 1996, 149–53.

3. *Economic displacement.* This is concerned with the economic variations of recession and depression. Job loss, capital shrinkage, or simply "bad times" can create the foundation for entrepreneurial pursuits, just as it can affect venture development and reduction.

These examples of displacement illustrate the external forces that can influence the development of entrepreneurship. Cultural awareness, knowledge of political and public policy, and economic indoctrination will aid and improve entrepreneurial understanding

TABLE 2.2   **DEFINITIONS AND CRITERIA OF ONE APPROACH TO THE MICRO VIEW**

Entrepreneurial Model	Definition	Measures	Questions
"Great Person"	"Extraordinary Achievers"	Personal principles Personal histories Experiences	What principles do you have? What are your achievements?
Psychological Characteristics	Founder Control over the means of production	Locus of control Tolerance of ambiguity Need for achievement	What are your values?
Classical	People who make innovations bearing risk and uncertainty "Creative destruction"	Decision making Abilities to see opportunities Creativity	What are the opportunities? What is your vision? How do you respond?
Management	Creating value through the recognition of business opportunity, the management of risk taking . . . through the communicative and management skills to mobilize . . .	Expertise Technical knowledge Technical plans	What are your plans? What are your capabilities? What are your credentials?
Leadership	"Social architect" Promotion and protection of values	Attitudes, style Management of people	How do you manage people?
Intrapreneurship	Those who pull together to promote innovation	Decision making	How do you change and adapt?

SOURCE: Adapted from J. Barton Cunningham and Joe Lischeron, "Defining Entrepreneurship," *Journal of Small Business Management* (January 1991): 56.

under the displacement school of thought. The broader the educational base in economics and political science, the stronger the entrepreneurial understanding.

THE MICRO VIEW   The **micro view of entrepreneurship** examines the factors that are specific to entrepreneurship and are part of the **internal locus of control.** The potential entrepreneur has the ability, or control, to direct or adjust the outcome of each major influence in this view. Although some researchers have developed this approach into various definitions and segments, as shown in Table 2.2, our approach presents the entrepreneurial trait theory (sometimes referred to as the "people school of thought"), the venture opportunity theory, and the strategic formulation theory. Unlike the macro approach, which focuses on events from the outside looking in, the micro approach concentrates on specifics from the inside looking out. The first of these schools of thought is the most widely recognized.

The Entrepreneurial Trait School of Thought   Many researchers and writers have been interested in identifying traits common to successful entrepreneurs.[19] The approach is grounded in the study of successful people who tend to exhibit similar characteristics that

[19] Kelly G. Shaver and Linda R. Scott, "Person, Process, Choice: The Psychology of New Venture Creation," *Entrepreneurship Theory and Practice* (winter 1991): 23–45.

if copied would increase success opportunities for the emulators. For example, achievement, creativity, determination, and technical knowledge are four factors that *usually* are exhibited by successful entrepreneurs. Family development and educational incubation are also examined. Certain researchers have argued against educational development of entrepreneurs because they believe it inhibits the creative and challenging nature of entrepreneurship.[20] Other authors, however, contend that new programs and new educational developments are on the increase because they have been found to aid in entrepreneurial development.[21] The family development idea focuses on the nurturing and support that exist within the home atmosphere of an entrepreneurial family. This reasoning promotes the belief that certain traits established and supported early in life will lead eventually to entrepreneurial success.

The Venture Opportunity School of Thought   This school of thought focuses on the opportunity aspect of venture development. The search for idea sources, the development of concepts, and the implementation of venture opportunities are the important interest areas for this school. Creativity and market awareness are viewed as essential. Additionally, according to this school of thought, developing the right idea at the right time for the right market niche is the key to entrepreneurial success.

Another development from this school of thought is the previously described *corridor principle*. New pathways or opportunities will arise that lead entrepreneurs in different directions. The ability to recognize these opportunities when they arise and to implement the necessary steps for action are key factors. The maxim that preparation meeting opportunity equals ''luck'' underlies this corridor principle. Proponents of this school of thought believe that proper preparation in the interdisciplinary business segments will enhance the ability to recognize venture opportunities.

The Strategic Formulation School of Thought   George Steiner has stated that ''Strategic planning is inextricably interwoven into the entire fabric of management; it is not something separate and distinct from the process of management.''[22] The strategic formulation approach to entrepreneurial theory emphasizes the planning process in successful venture development.[23]

Ronstadt views strategic formulation as a leveraging of unique elements.[24] Unique markets, unique people, unique products, or unique resources are identified, used, or constructed into effective venture formations. The interdisciplinary aspects of strategic adaptation become apparent in the characteristic elements listed here with their corresponding strategies:

- *Unique markets:* Mountain versus **mountain gap strategies,** which refers to identifying major market segments as well as interstice (in-between) markets that arise from larger markets.

---

[20] See Albert Shapero, ''The Displaced, Uncomfortable Entrepreneur,'' *Psychology Today* (November 1975): 8–13.

[21] See Donald F. Kuratko and William R. LaFollette, ''A Small Business Management/Entrepreneurship Curriculum: A Dual Progression Experience,'' *Journal of Business Education* (March 1986): 267–71; Donald F. Kuratko, ''New Venture Creation: A Laboratory Course for Entrepreneurship Education,'' *Journal of Business Education* (March 1989): 248–50; and Zenas Block and Stephen A. Stumpf, ''Entrepreneurship Education Research: Experience and Challenge'' in *The State of the Art of Entrepreneurship,* ed. Donald L. Sexton and John D. Kasarda (Boston, MA: PWS-Kent, 1992), 17–42.

[22] George A. Steiner, *Strategic Planning* (New York: Free Press, 1979), 3.

[23] See Jeffrey G. Covin and Dennis P. Slevin, ''New Venture Strategic Posture, Structure, and Performance: An Industry Life Cycle Analysis,'' *Journal of Business Venturing* (March 1990): 123–35; and Marjorie A. Lyles, Inga S. Baird, J. Burdeane Orris, and Donald F. Kuratko, ''Formalized Planning in Small Business: Increasing Strategic Choices,'' *Journal of Small Business Management* (April 1993): 38–50.

[24] Ronstadt, *Entrepreneurship,* 112–15.

- *Unique people:* **Great chef strategies,** which refers to the skills or special talents of one or more individuals around whom the venture is built.
- *Unique products:* **Better widget strategies,** which refers to innovations that encompass new or existing markets.
- *Unique resources:* **Water well strategies,** which refers to the ability to gather or harness special resources (land, labor, capital, raw materials) over the long term.

Without question, the strategic formulation school encompasses a breadth of managerial capability that requires an interdisciplinary approach.

SCHOOLS OF ENTREPRENEURIAL THOUGHT: A SUMMARY   Although the knowledge and research available in entrepreneurship is in an emerging stage, it is still possible to piece together and describe current schools of thought in the field. From this point we can begin to develop an appreciation for the schools and view them as a foundation for entrepreneurial theory. However, just as the field of management has used a "jungle" of theories as a basis for understanding the field and its capabilities, so too must the field of entrepreneurship use a number of theories in its growth and development.

PROCESS APPROACHES

Another way to examine the activities involved in entrepreneurship is through a process approach. Although numerous methods and models attempt to structure the entrepreneurial process and its various factors, we shall examine three of the more traditional process approaches here.[25] First, we will discuss the "entrepreneurial events" approach, as described by William D. Bygrave.[26] Bygrave's model incorporates theoretical and practical concepts as they affect entrepreneurship activity. The second approach is an assessment process based on an entrepreneurial perspective developed by Robert C. Ronstadt. The third process approach, developed by William B. Gartner, is multidimensional and interrelates the concepts of individual, environment, organization, and process. All of these methods attempt to describe the entrepreneurial process as a consolidation of diverse factors, which is the thrust of this book.

Entrepreneurial Events Approach

Entrepreneurship is not a series of isolated activities or undertakings. It is a process by which individuals plan, implement, and control their entrepreneurial activities. In addition, a number of elements affect each event in the entrepreneurial process. The entrepreneurial events approach focuses on the process of entrepreneurial activity and includes the following factors:

- *Initiative:* An individual or group takes the initiative.
- *Organization:* Resources are brought together in organizational form to accomplish some objective (or the resources in an existing organization are reorganized).
- *Administration:* Those who took the initiative take over management of the organization.

---

[25] See the special issue dealing with models, of *Entrepreneurship: Theory and Practice* 17, no. 2 (1993).

[26] William D. Bygrave, "The Entrepreneurship Paradigm: A Philosophical Look at Its Research Methodologies," *Entrepreneurship: Theory and Practice* (fall 1989): 7–26.

FIGURE 2.2 ENTREPRENEURIAL EVENTS FORMATION PROCESS

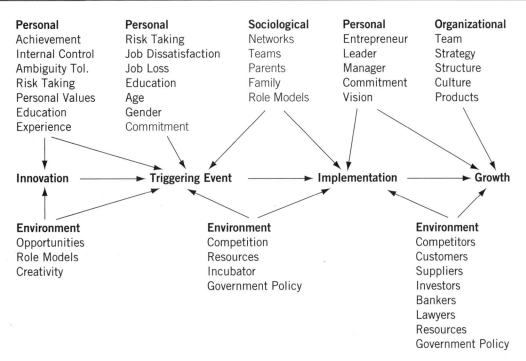

SOURCE: William D. Bygrave, "The Entrepreneurship Paradigm: A Philosophical Look at Its Research Methodologies," *Entrepreneurship: Theory and Practice* (fall 1989): 9.

- *Relative autonomy:* The initiators assume relative freedom to dispose of and distribute resources.
- *Risk taking:* The organization's success or failure is shared by the initiator's supervisors and employees.
- *Environment:* This includes the opportunities, resources, competitors, and so forth that affect the entrepreneurial events at different stages.

Bygrave has outlined a model that mixes theoretical concepts from basic social sciences with practical concepts from applied sciences. Figure 2.2 illustrates the four distinct events: innovation → triggering event → implementation → growth. The diagram depicts some of the numerous elements that affect each event in the process.

Entrepreneurial Assessment Approach

Another model, developed by Robert C. Ronstadt, stresses making assessments qualitatively, quantitatively, strategically, and ethically in regard to the entrepreneur, the venture, and the environment.[27] (Figure 2.3 depicts this model.) To examine entrepreneurship, the results of these assessments must be compared to the stage of the entrepreneurial career— early, midcareer, or late. Ronstadt termed this process "the entrepreneurial perspective."

[27] Ronstadt, *Entrepreneurship,* 39.

FIGURE 2.3   **ENTREPRENEURIAL ASSESSMENT APPROACH**

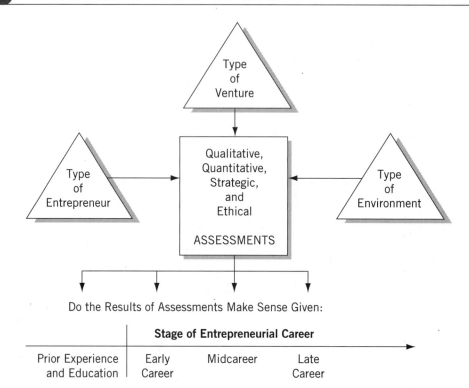

SOURCE: Robert C. Ronstadt, *Entrepreneurship* (Dover, MA: Lord Publishing Co., 1984), 39.

We focus on this term in Chapter 4 when we examine the individual characteristics of entrepreneurship.

Multidimensional Approach

A more detailed process approach to entrepreneurship is the **multidimensional approach.**[28] In this view entrepreneurship is a complex, multidimensional framework that emphasizes the individual, the environment, the organization, and the venture process. Specific factors that relate to each of these dimensions follow.

THE INDIVIDUAL

1. Need for achievement

2. Locus of control

3. Risk-taking propensity

4. Job satisfaction

[28] Bradley R. Johnson, "Toward a Multidimensional Model of Entrepreneurship: The Case of Achievement Motivation and the Entrepreneur," *Entrepreneurship: Theory and Practice* (spring 1990): 39–54.

5. Previous work experience

6. Entrepreneurial parents

7. Age

8. Education

THE ENVIRONMENT

1. Venture capital availability

2. Presence of experienced entrepreneurs

3. Technically skilled labor force

4. Accessibility of suppliers

5. Accessibility of customers or new markets

6. Governmental influences

7. Proximity of universities

8. Availability of land or facilities

9. Accessibility of transportation

10. Attitude of the area population

11. Availability of supporting services

12. Living conditions

THE ORGANIZATION

1. Type of firm

2. Entrepreneurial environment

3. Partners

4. Strategic variables
   a) Cost   *b)* Differentiation   *c)* Focus

5. Competitive entry wedges

THE PROCESS

1. Locating a business opportunity

2. Accumulating resources

3. Marketing products and services

4. Producing the product

5. Building an organization

6. Responding to government and society[29]

Figure 2.4 depicts the interaction of the four major dimensions of this entrepreneurial, or new-venture, process and lists more variables. This type of process moves entrepreneurship from a segmented school of thought to a dynamic, interactive process approach.

INTRAPRENEURSHIP

Recently the term **intrapreneurship** has become popular in the business community, but very few executives thoroughly understand the concept. Gifford Pinchot has defined an intrapreneur as "any of the dreamers who do. . . ." However, he goes on to say, ". . . take hands-on responsibility for creating innovation of any kind within an organization. The intrapreneur may be the creator or the inventor but is always the dreamer who figures out how to turn an idea into a profitable reality."[30] This definition has definite similarities to entrepreneurship except intrapreneurship takes place *within* an organization. The major thrust of intrapreneuring, then, is to create or develop the entrepreneurial spirit within

[29] William B. Gartner, "A Conceptual Framework for Describing the Phenomenon of New Venture Creation," *Academy of Management Review* (October 1985): 702.

[30] Gifford Pinchot III, *Intrapreneuring* (New York: Harper & Row, 1985), ix.

FIGURE 2.4   **VARIABLES IN NEW-VENTURE CREATION**

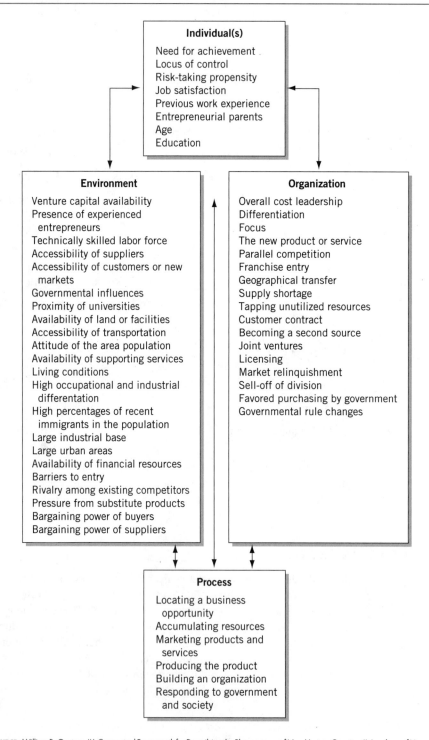

Individual(s)

Need for achievement
Locus of control
Risk-taking propensity
Job satisfaction
Previous work experience
Entrepreneurial parents
Age
Education

Environment

Venture capital availability
Presence of experienced
  entrepreneurs
Technically skilled labor force
Accessibility of suppliers
Accessibility of customers or new
  markets
Governmental influences
Proximity of universities
Availability of land or facilities
Accessibility of transportation
Attitude of the area population
Availability of supporting services
Living conditions
High occupational and industrial
  differentation
High percentages of recent
  immigrants in the population
Large industrial base
Large urban areas
Availability of financial resources
Barriers to entry
Rivalry among existing competitors
Pressure from substitute products
Bargaining power of buyers
Bargaining power of suppliers

Organization

Overall cost leadership
Differentiation
Focus
The new product or service
Parallel competition
Franchise entry
Geographical transfer
Supply shortage
Tapping unutilized resources
Customer contract
Becoming a second source
Joint ventures
Licensing
Market relinquishment
Sell-off of division
Favored purchasing by government
Governmental rule changes

Process

Locating a business
  opportunity
Accumulating resources
Marketing products and
  services
Producing the product
Building an organization
Responding to government
  and society

SOURCE: William B. Gartner, "A Conceptual Framework for Describing the Phenomenon of New Venture Creation," *Academy of Management Review* (October 1985): 702. Reprinted with permission.

corporate boundaries, thereby allowing an atmosphere of innovation to prosper.[31] More about this specific application of entrepreneurship is presented in Chapter 3.

KEY CONCEPTS

Before concluding our discussion of the nature of entrepreneurship, we need to put into perspective three key concepts: entrepreneurship, entrepreneur, and entrepreneurial management.

Entrepreneurship

Entrepreneurship is a process of innovation and new-venture creation through four major dimensions—individual, organizational, environmental, process—that is aided by collaborative networks in government, education, and institutions. All of the macro and micro positions of entrepreneurial thought must be considered while recognizing and seizing opportunities that can be converted into marketable ideas capable of competing for implementation in today's economy.

Entrepreneur

The *entrepreneur* is a catalyst for economic change who uses purposeful searching, careful planning, and sound judgment when carrying out the entrepreneurial process. Uniquely optimistic and committed, the entrepreneur works creatively to establish new resources or endow old ones with a new capacity, all for the purpose of creating wealth.

Entrepreneurial Management

The underlying theme of this book is the discipline of *entrepreneurial management,* a concept that has been delineated as follows:

> Entrepreneurship is based upon the same principles, whether the entrepreneur is an existing large institution or an individual starting his or her new venture single-handed. It makes little or no difference whether the entrepreneur is a business or a nonbusiness public-service organization, nor even whether the entrepreneur is a governmental or nongovernmental institution. The rules are pretty much the same, the things that work and those that don't are pretty much the same, and so are the kinds of innovation and where to look for them. In every case there is a discipline we might call Entrepreneurial Management.[32]

The techniques and principles of this emerging discipline will drive the entrepreneurial economy of our time.

---

[31] See Donald F. Kuratko and Ray V. Montagno, "The Intrapreneurial Spirit," *Training and Development Journal* (October 1989): 83–86.

[32] Peter F. Drucker, *Innovation and Entrepreneurship* (New York: Harper & Row, 1985), 143. See also Howard H. Stevenson and J. Carlos Jarillo, "A Paradigm of Entrepreneurship: Entrepreneurial Management," *Strategic Management Journal* (summer 1990): 17–27.

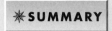

This chapter examined the evolution of entrepreneurship, providing a foundation for further study of this dynamic and developing discipline. Exploring the early economic definitions as well as selected contemporary ones, the chapter presented a historical picture of how entrepreneurship has been viewed. In addition, the ten major myths of entrepreneurship were discussed to permit a better understanding of the folklore surrounding this newly developing field of study. Contemporary research is broadening the horizon for studying entrepreneurship and is providing a better focus on the what, how, and why behind this discipline.

The approaches to entrepreneurship were examined from two different perspectives: schools of thought and process. Six selected schools of thought were presented, and three approaches for understanding contemporary entrepreneurship as a process were discussed. The chapter concluded with definitions of entrepreneurship, entrepreneur, and entrepreneurial management.

Key Terms and Concepts

Better widget strategies	Financial/capital school of thought
Corridor principle	Great chef strategies
Displacement school of thought	Internal locus of control
Entrepreneur	Intrapreneurship
Entrepreneurial assessment approach	Macro view of entrepreneurship
Entrepreneurial events approach	Micro view of entrepreneurship
Entrepreneurial management	Mountain gap strategies
Entrepreneurial trait school of thought	Multidimensional approach
Entrepreneurship	Strategic formulation school of thought
Environmental school of thought	Venture opportunity school of thought
External locus of control	Water well strategies

Review and Discussion Questions

1. Briefly describe the evolution of the term *entrepreneurship*.
2. What are the ten myths associated with entrepreneurship? Debunk each.
3. What is the macro view of entrepreneurship?
4. What are the schools of thought that use the macro view of entrepreneurship?
5. What is the micro view of entrepreneurship?
6. What are the schools of thought that use the micro view of entrepreneurship?
7. What are the three specific types of displacement?
8. In the strategic formulation school of thought, what are the four types of strategies involved with unique elements? Give an illustration of each.
9. What is the process approach to entrepreneurship? In your answer describe the entrepreneurial assessment approach.
10. What are the major elements in the framework for entrepreneurship presented in Figure 2.4? Give an example of each.

Experiential Exercise   *Understanding Your Beliefs about Successful Entrepreneurs*

Read each of the following ten statements, and to the left of each indicate your agreement or disagreement. If you fully agree with the statement, put a *10* on the line at the left. If you totally disagree, put a *1*. If you tend to agree more than you disagree, give a response between *6* and *9*, depending on how much you agree. If you tend to disagree, give a response between *2* and *5*.

_____ 1. Successful entrepreneurs are often methodical and analytical individuals who carefully plan out what they are going to do and then do it.

_____ 2. The most successful entrepreneurs are born with special characteristics such as high achievement drive and a winning personality, and these serve them well in their entrepreneurial endeavors.

_____ 3. Many of the characteristics needed for successful entrepreneurship can be learned through study and experience.

_____ 4. The most successful entrepreneurs are those who invent a unique product or service.

_____ 5. Highly successful entrepreneurs tend to have very little formal schooling.

_____ 6. Most successful entrepreneurs admit that dropping out of school was the best thing they ever did.

_____ 7. Because they are unique and individualistic in their approach to business, most successful entrepreneurs find it hard to socialize with others; they just do not fit in.

_____ 8. Research shows that although it is important to have adequate financing before beginning an entrepreneurial venture, it is often more important to have managerial competence and proper planning.

_____ 9. Successful entrepreneurship is more a matter of preparation and desire than it is of luck.

_____ 10. Most successful entrepreneurs do well in their first venture, and this encourages them to continue; failures tend to come later on as the enterprise grows.

Put your answers on the following list in this way: *(a)* Enter answers to numbers 1, 3, 8, and 9 just as they appear, and then *(b)* subtract the answers to 2, 4, 5, 6, 7, and 10 from 11 before entering them here. Thus, if you gave an answer of *8* to number 1, put an *8* before number 1 here. However, if you gave an answer of *7* to number 2 here, place a *4* before number 2 here. Then add both columns of answers and enter your total on the appropriate line.

_____ 1   _____ 6*

_____ 2*   _____ 7*

_____ 3   _____ 8

_____ 4*   _____ 9

_____ 5*   _____ 10*   _____ Total

Interpretation: This exercise measures how much you believe the myths of entrepreneurship. The lower your total, the stronger your beliefs; the higher your total, the less strong your beliefs. Numbers 1, 3, 8, and 9 are accurate statements; numbers 2, 4, 5, 6, 7, and 10 are inaccurate statements. Here is the scoring key:

80–100	Excellent. You know the facts about entrepreneurs.
61–79	Good, but you still believe in a couple of myths.
41–60	Fair. You need to review the chapter material on the myths of entrepreneurship.
0–40	Poor. You need to reread the chapter material on the myths of entrepreneurship and study these findings.

VIDEO CASE   **2.1**

Drew Pearson Companies: Super Bowl Champ Puts a Cap on Success

When Drew Pearson, a wide receiver for the Dallas Cowboys, played in his third Super Bowl, he had no idea he'd become the CEO of one of the nation's top designers and manufacturers of sports caps. "When I left professional football, it was hard to imagine that my earning power off the field would ever eclipse my earning power on the field," Pearson reveals. But in the megabuck business of logo-licensed headwear, Drew Pearson Companies (DPC) has racked up some impressive statistics since it was formed in 1985. Sales have skyrocketed from $3 million in 1985 to $10 million in 1989 to $77.5 million in 1993. DPC is one of only six companies to have scored licenses with the National Football League (NFL), National Basketball Association, Major League Baseball, and the National Hockey League. Equally impressive is the fact that DPC is the only company to have exclusive worldwide rights with the Walt Disney Company.

Nicknamed "The Clutch" during his Cowboy days, Pearson was accustomed to making spectacular plays. But DPC's superstar rise in the headwear industry hasn't been without a few fumbles along the way. "Of course, being a former NFL player, I thought the natural thing would be to approach the NFL first," Pearson says. "Roger Staubach, who was an initial investor, and I went to New York to meet with NFL Properties. The meeting lasted maybe 35 minutes. They just told us no."

In time, Pearson proved that DPC had the financial resources and capabilities to produce quality products, and it became the first minority-owned business to secure a licensing agreement with the NFL. But more important, DPC discovered its competitive edge. "What's really set us apart from our competitors is our innovative designs," Pearson admits. Colorful, intricately stitched hats with names like "The Jagged Edge" are DPC's trademark. Early on, DPC embraced technology to create its fashion-forward caps. "We were able to bring together in our creative services area the first computer that generated art that could show three-dimensional variations in designs—forward looks, backward looks—things that our competition had no clue as to how we were generating. While they were trying to figure out the technology, we were gaining market share," DPC president Ken Shead explains.

In 1995, DPC shipped 30 million trendsetting caps to 7,500 retailers throughout the United States, making it the industry's fastest growing headwear company. The company's aggressive growth has been the payoff for Pearson's winning vision. "We knew that the sports licensing industry, especially in the headwear category, is very competitive. We had to do something to set ourselves apart." DPC began courting the entertainment industry and was rewarded with lucrative licensing rights to feature Mickey Mouse, Looney Tunes characters, the Flintstones, Barney, Garfield, and other pop-culture icons on DPC headwear. "Our number-one-selling hat is Mickey Mouse," Pearson says. "It outsells the NFL; it outsells Major League Baseball; it even outsold the Chicago Bulls with Michael Jordan."

Impressive sales in the domestic market have served as a catalyst for DPC's expansion worldwide. "DPC is a global company. We made that decision to focus on the international market worldwide approximately three years ago," Mike Russell, executive vice president of marketing, says. "From the standpoint of developing products to sell internationally, we're somewhat unique in our industry since Mickey Mouse doesn't change whether he's sold in the Far East or Central America. We have a definitive line of products that transcend international markets, and the demand for American logo products is continually growing internationally."

With new products and new markets on the horizon, Drew Pearson Companies is poised to extend its winning streak well into the next century. But the former NFL star turned CEO knows his team can't rest on its laurels. "When you win a Super Bowl, you're not necessarily satisfied with winning one Super Bowl. You want to go back and win it again. You like the adulation and the accolades that come along with success. We try to implement that same feeling, that same strategy at the Drew Pearson Companies. No matter what level of success we reach, we know there's more to attain. There's more to garner. We're not the number one headwear company in the world, and that's a goal of ours."

Questions

1. What myths in entrepreneurship does DPC and Drew Pearson seem to debunk?
2. Describe the schools of entrepreneurial thought that may apply to Drew Pearson and his venture.
3. Using Figure 2.3, explain how Pearson's venture fits into the entrepreneurial assessment approach?

 **CASE 2.2**

Paul's Four Shortcomings

Paul Enden has always been very reliable and a hard worker. For the past eight years Paul has been working in a large auto service garage. During this time he has made a number of recommendations to the owner regarding new services that could be provided to customers. One of these is called the "fast lube." With this service people who want to have their oil changed and their car lubricated do not have to leave the auto and come back later in the day. Three service racks handle this job. It generally takes less than 10 minutes to take care of a car, and most people can have the job completed within 25 minutes of the time they arrive. The service, which has become extremely popular with customers, resulted in an increase in overall profits of 5 percent last year.

Paul's wife believes he has a large number of ideas that could prove profitable. "You ought to break away and open your own shop," she has told him. Paul would like to do so, but he believes four things help account for entrepreneurial success and he has none of them. Here is how he explained it to his wife:

"To be a successful entrepreneur, you have to be a thinker, not a doer. I'm a doer. Thinking bores me. I wouldn't like being an entrepreneur. Second, those guys who do best as entrepreneurs tend to be inventors. I'm not an inventor. If anything, I think of new approaches to old ways of doing business. I'm more of a tinkerer than an inventor. Third, you've got to be lucky to be a successful entrepreneur. I'm hard working; I'm not lucky. Fourth, you have to have a lot of money to do well as an entrepreneur. I don't have much money. I doubt whether $50,000 would get me started as an entrepreneur."

Questions

1. Does Paul need to be an inventor in order to be an effective entrepreneur? Explain your answer.
2. How important is it that Paul have a lot of money if he hopes to be an entrepreneur? Explain your answer.
3. What is wrong with Paul's overall thinking? Be sure to include a discussion of the myths of entrepreneurship in your answer.

Chapter 3

*I*NTRAPRENEURSHIP: DEVELOPING ENTREPRENEURSHIP IN THE CORPORATION

CHAPTER OBJECTIVES

1. To define the term *intrapreneurship*

2. To illustrate the need for corporate entrepreneuring

3. To describe the corporate obstacles preventing innovation from existing in corporations

4. To discuss the intrapreneurship considerations involved in reengineering corporate thinking

5. To describe the specific elements of an intrapreneurial strategy

6. To profile intrapreneurial characteristics and myths

7. To illustrate the interactive process of intrapreneurship

There is nothing more difficult to take in hand, more perilous to conduct, than to take a lead in the introduction of a new order of things, because the innovation has for enemies all those who have done well under the old conditions and lukewarm defenders in those who may do well under the new.

Machiavelli,
The Prince

The current decade is seeing corporate strategies focused heavily on innovation. This new emphasis on entrepreneurial thinking developed during the *entrepreneurial economy* of the 1980s.[1] Peter Drucker, the renowned management expert, described four major developments that explain the emergence of this economy. First, the rapid evolution of knowledge and technology promoted the use of high-tech entrepreneurial start-ups. Second, demographic trends such as two-wage-earner families, continuing education of adults, and the aging population added fuel to the proliferation of newly developing ventures. Third, the venture-capital market became an effective funding mechanism for entrepreneurial ventures. Fourth, American industry began to learn how to manage entrepreneurship.[2]

The contemporary thrust of entrepreneurship as the major force in American business has led to a desire for this type of activity *inside* enterprises. Although some researchers have concluded that entrepreneurship and bureaucracies are mutually exclusive and cannot coexist,[3] others have described entrepreneurial ventures within the enterprise framework.[4] Successful corporate ventures have been used in many different companies, including 3M, Bell Atlantic, AT&T, Acordia, and Polaroid.[5] Today, a wealth of popular business literature describes a new "corporate revolution" taking place thanks to the infusion of entrepreneurial thinking into large bureaucratic structures.[6] This infusion is referred to as **corporate**

[1] Peter F. Drucker, "Our Entrepreneurial Economy," *Harvard Business Review* (January/February 1984): 59–64.

[2] Ibid., 60–61.

[3] See, for example, C. Wesley Morse, "The Delusion of Intrapreneurship," *Long Range Planning* 19 (1986): 92–95; and W. Jack Duncan et al., "Intrapreneurship and the Reinvention of the Corporation," *Business Horizons* (May/June, 1988): 16–21.

[4] Robert A. Burgelman, "Designs for Corporate Entrepreneuring," *California Management Review* 26 (1984): 154–66; Rosabeth M. Kanter, "Supporting Innovation and Venture Developments in Established Companies," *Journal of Business Venturing* (January 1985): 47–60; Donald F. Kuratko and Ray V. Montagno, "The Intrapreneurial Spirit," *Training and Development Journal* (October 1989): 83–86; and Donald F. Kuratko and Jeffrey S. Hornsby, "Developing Entrepreneurial Leadership in Contemporary Organizations," *Journal of Management Systems* 8, no. 1 (1997): 17–24.

[5] For example, see Michael H. Morris and J. Don Trotter, "Institutionalizing Entrepreneurship in a Large Company: A Case Study at AT&T," *Industrial Marketing Management* 19 (1990): 131–34; and Brian McWilliams, "Strength from Within—How Today's Companies Nurture Entrepreneurs," *Enterprise,* April 1993, 43–44.

[6] See, for example, Joseph H. Boyett and Henry P. Conn, *Workplace 2000* (New York: Dutton Books, 1991); Kenneth C. Green and Daniel T. Seymour, *Who's Going to Run General Motors?* (Princeton, NJ: Peterson's Guides, 1991); Robert L. Kuhn, *Generating Creativity and Innovation in Large Bureaucracies* (Westport, CT: Quorum Books, 1993); and Zenas Block and Ian C. Macmillan, *Corporate Venturing* (Boston: Harvard Business School Press, 1993).

entrepreneurship[7] or **intrapreneurship.**[8] Why has this concept become so popular? One reason is that it allows corporations to tap the innovative talents of their own workers and managers. Steven Brandt puts it this way:

> The challenge is relatively straightforward. The United States must upgrade its innovative prowess. To do so, U.S. companies must tap into the creative power of their members. Ideas come from people. Innovation is a capability of the many. That capability is utilized when people give commitment to the mission and life of the enterprise and have the power to do something with their capabilities. Noncommitment is the price of obsolete managing practices, not the lack of talent or desire.
>
> Commitment is most freely given when the members of an enterprise play a part in defining the purposes and plans of the entity. Commitment carries with it a de facto approval of and support for the management. Managing by consent is a useful managing philosophy if more entrepreneurial behavior is desired.[9]

THE NATURE OF INTRAPRENEURSHIP

In recent years the subject of intrapreneurship has been popularized, but very few people thoroughly understand the concept. Most researchers agree that the term refers to entrepreneurial activities that receive organizational sanction and resource commitments for the purpose of innovative results.[10] The major thrust of intrapreneuring is to develop the entrepreneurial spirit within organizational boundaries, thus allowing an atmosphere of innovation to prosper.

The Need for Corporate Entrepreneuring

Many companies today are realizing the need for corporate entrepreneuring. Articles in popular business magazines (*Business Week, Fortune, Success, Forbes*) are reporting the infusion of entrepreneurial thinking into large bureaucratic structures. In fact, in many of his books, Tom Peters has devoted entire sections to innovation in the corporation.[11] Quite obviously, business firms and consultants/authors are recognizing the need for in-house entrepreneurship.

This need has arisen in response to a number of pressing problems, including a rapidly growing number of new and sophisticated competitors, a sense of distrust in the traditional methods of corporate management, an exodus of some of the best and brightest people who are leaving corporations to become small-business entrepreneurs, international

---

[7] Donald F. Kuratko, Jeffrey S. Hornsby, Douglas W. Naffziger, and Ray V. Montagno, "Implementing Entrepreneurial Thinking in Established Organizations," *Advanced Management Journal* (winter 1993): 28–34.

[8] Gifford Pinchot III, *Intrapreneuring* (New York: Harper & Row, 1985).

[9] Steven C. Brandt, *Entrepreneuring in Established Companies* (Homewood, IL: Dow-Jones-Irwin, 1986), 54.

[10] See Robert A. Burgelman, "Designs for Corporate Entrepreneurship," *California Management Review* (winter 1984): 154–66; Rosabeth M. Kanter, "Supporting Innovation and Venture Development in Established Companies," *Journal of Business Venturing* (winter 1985): 47–60; and Donald F. Kuratko, "Intrapreneurship: Developing Innovation in the Corporation," *Advances in Global High Technology Management* 3 (1993): 3–14.

[11] Tom Peters, *Liberation Management* (New York: Alfred A. Knopf, 1992); and Tom Peters, *The Pursuit of Wow* (New York: Vintage Books, 1994).

competition, downsizing of major corporations, and an overall desire to improve efficiency and productivity.[12]

The first of these, the problem of competition, is one that has always plagued businesses. However, today's high-tech economy is finding a far greater number of competitors than ever before. In contrast to previous decades, changes, innovations, and improvements are now very common in the marketplace. Thus corporations must either innovate or become obsolete.

Another of these problems, losing the brightest people to entrepreneurship, is escalating as a result of two major developments. First, entrepreneurship is on the rise in terms of status, publicity, and economic development. This enhancement of entrepreneurship has made the choice more appealing to both young and seasoned employees. Second, in recent years venture capital has grown into a large industry capable of financing more new ventures than ever before. Thus a capital market enables new entrepreneurs to launch their projects. This development is encouraging people with innovative ideas to leave large corporations and strike out on their own.

The modern corporation, then, is forced into seeking avenues for developing in-house entrepreneuring. To do otherwise is to wait for stagnation, loss of personnel, and decline. This new "corporate revolution" represents an appreciation for and a desire to develop intrapreneurs within the corporate structure.

Corporate Venturing Obstacles

The obstacles to corporate entrepreneuring are usually based on the ineffectiveness of traditional management techniques applied to new-venture development. Although it is unintentional, the adverse impact of a particular traditional management technique can be so destructive the individuals within an enterprise will tend to avoid corporate entrepreneurial behavior. Table 3.1 provides a list of traditional management techniques, their adverse effects (when the technique is rigidly enforced), and the recommended actions to change or adjust the practice.

Understanding these obstacles is critical to fostering corporate entrepreneuring because they are the foundation points for all other motivational efforts. In order to gain support and foster excitement for new-venture development, managers must remove the perceived obstacles and seek alternative management actions.[13]

After recognizing the obstacles, managers need to adapt to the principles of successful innovative companies. James Brian Quinn, an expert in the innovation field, found the following factors in large corporations that are successful innovators.

- *Atmosphere and vision:* Innovative companies have a clear-cut vision of and the recognized support for an innovative atmosphere.
- *Orientation to the market:* Innovative companies tie their visions to the realities of the marketplace.
- *Small, flat organizations:* Most innovative companies keep the total organization flat and project teams small.

---

[12] Robert H. Hayes and William J. Abernathy, "Managing Our Way to Economic Decline," *Harvard Business Review* (July/ August 1980): 67–77; see also Amanda Bennett, *The Death of the Organization Man* (New York: Simon and Schuster, 1990); and Donald F. Kuratko, "Developing Entrepreneurship within Organizations Is Today's Challenge," *Entrepreneurship, Innovation, and Change* 4, no. 2 (June 1995): 99–104.

[13] Hollister B. Sykes and Zenas Block, "Corporate Venturing Obstacles: Sources and Solutions," *Journal of Business Venturing* (winter 1989): 159–67; and Ian C. MacMillan, Zenas Block, and P. M. Subba Narasimha, "Corporate Venturing: Alternatives, Obstacles Encountered, and Experience Effects," *Journal of Business Venturing* (spring 1986): 177–91.

| TABLE 3.1 | SOURCES OF AND SOLUTIONS TO OBSTACLES IN CORPORATE VENTURING |

Traditional Management Practices	Adverse Effects	Recommended Actions
Enforce standard procedures to avoid mistakes	Innovative solutions blocked, funds misspent	Make ground rules specific to each situation
Manage resources for efficiency and ROI	Competitive lead lost, low market penetration	Focus effort on critical issues, e.g., market share
Control against plan	Facts ignored that should replace assumptions	Change plan to reflect new learning
Plan long term	Nonviable goals locked in, high failure costs	Envision a goal, then set interim milestones, reassess after each
Manage functionally	Entrepreneur failure and/or venture failure	Support entrepreneur with managerial and multidiscipline skills
Avoid moves that risk the base business	Missed opportunities	Take small steps, build out from strengths
Protect the base business at all costs	Venturing dumped when base business threatened	Make venturing mainstream, take affordable risks
Judge new steps from prior experience	Wrong decisions about competition and markets	Use learning strategies, test assumptions
Compensate uniformly	Low motivation and inefficient operations	Balance risk and reward, employ special compensation
Promote compatible individuals	Loss of innovators	Accommodate "boat rockers" and "doers"

SOURCE: Reprinted by permission of the publisher from "Corporate Venturing Obstacles: Sources and Solutions," by Hollister B. Sykes and Zenas Block, *Journal of Business Venturing* (winter 1989): 161. Copyright 1989 by Elsevier Science Publishing Co., Inc.

- *Multiple approaches:* Innovative managers encourage several projects to proceed in parallel development.
- *Interactive learning:* Within an innovative environment, learning and investigation of ideas cut across traditional functional lines in the organization.
- *Skunkworks:* Every highly innovative enterprise uses groups that function outside traditional lines of authority. This eliminates bureaucracy, permits rapid turnaround, and instills a high level of group identity and loyalty.[14]

Reengineering Corporate Thinking

To establish corporate entrepreneuring, companies need to provide the freedom and encouragement intrapreneurs require to develop their ideas.[15] This is often a problem in enterprises because many top managers do not believe entrepreneurial ideas can be nurtured and developed in their environment. They also find it hard to implement policies that encourage freedom and unstructured activity. But managers need to develop policies that

[14] James Brian Quinn, "Managing Innovation: Controlled Chaos," *Harvard Business Review* (May/June 1985): 73–84.

[15] Dennis P. Slevin and Jeffrey G. Covin, "Juggling Entrepreneurial Style and Organizational Structure: How to Get Your Act Together," *Sloan Management Review* (winter 1990): 43–53.

ENTREPRENEURIAL

EDGE

Open-Book Success

With the new global market and fierce competition on the rise, the old top-down, chain-of-command way of running a business is nearly extinct. During the past decade, managers have been scrambling for *the* management cure that would lead them into the next century and beyond. The search for such a cure brought about many new concepts in management: Total quality management (TQM); Teams; Empowerment; Reengineering. While all these efforts may have been effective for some, most have not proved to be cures. Quality efforts only improve quality. Reengineering only cuts costs. Teamwork and empowerment have faded. Rosabeth Moss Kanter, one of the nation's best-known business thinkers, states "Each of the 'management buzzwords and fads of the last decade is like a way station' on the road to a comprehensive rethinking of the business organization."

Finally, there does seem to be a new paradigm or a comprehensive rethinking of management that really works. It's being called *open-book management*. This new way of thinking is helping companies compete in today's brutal marketplace by getting everybody on the payroll to think and act like a businessperson, an owner, rather than like a traditional hired hand. Open-book management is being tried by all types of businesses in all types of industries, and many of them are seeing startling results. Springfield Manufacturing Corp. (SRC), in Springfield, MO, transformed itself from a small money-losing division of International Harvester into a profitable miniconglomerate with revenues near $100 million. Profits for Mid-States Technical, a staffing company headquartered in Davenport, IA, nearly tripled within two years after adopting the new approach. Some companies claim that open-book management is the key to their competitive advantage while others claim that it has changed employee attitudes, builds trust, and even reduces stress.

Open-book management works by getting everyone to focus on helping the business make money by taking the latest management ideas—TQM, empowerment, and teams—and giving them a business logic. Employees are taught to understand why they are being called upon to solve problems, cut costs, and give the customers better service. They are taught to stop thinking of themselves as hired hands and to start realizing that they are businesspeople. Their job secu-

will help innovative people reach their full potential. Four important steps for establishing this new thinking follow:

1. Set *explicit goals.* These need to be mutually agreed on by worker and management so specific steps are achieved.

rity, their chances for advancement, their hopes for the future all depend on the company's success and the contributions of each individual.

So, how does open-book management teach employees to think like businesspeople? There are three distinct differences between conventional business practices and open-book management.

1. Every employee in the company learns to understand the company's financials and other important numbers in tracking the business's performance. And they see them on a regular basis, hence the name "open-book." Employees know when they're making money, how much they're making, and why they are making money.
2. Employees learn that part of their job is to move those numbers toward profitability. Every employee from salespeople to telephone operators are accountable to one another for their unit's performance.
3. Employees have a direct stake in the company's success so that when the company is making profits, the employees get their share and vice versa.

The management fads of the past decade have only taught employees the "how-to" of their jobs—how to cut costs, how to improve quality, how to provide better service. The key to open-book management's success is that it teaches the employees the "want-to." Rather than telling employees how to cut defects, it asks them to improve profits and lets them figure out how. In turn, the employees experience the challenge, the fun, and the excitement of providing solutions and sharing the proceeds, which is a great motivator.

There are four steps in implementing an open-book management system. The first step is to show employees the financial statements and other key numbers. They should see the cash flow statements, the balance sheets, and the income statements. The second step is teaching employees the basics of business so they are able to understand the financials and how they relate to the overall operation of the business. The third step is to empower people to make decisions based on what they know. And finally, the fourth step is to make sure that everyone shares directly in the company's success—and in the risk of failure.

In summary, the goal of open-book management is to create "a business of businesspeople." Employees aren't just doing as they are told, they're figuring out what needs to be done and doing it, bearing full responsibility for their actions. They are expected to understand the big picture. These companies are providing employees with the tools they need to become businesspeople and everyone, businesses and employees alike, are profiting.

SOURCE: *Inc.*, "The Open-Book Revolution: Open-Book Management: Special Report," by John Case, June 1995, 26–29.

2. Create a system of *feedback* and *positive reinforcement.* This is necessary in order for potential inventors, creators, or intrapreneurs to realize acceptance and reward exist.

3. Emphasize *individual responsibility.* Confidence, trust, and accountability are key features in the success of any innovative program.

4. Give *rewards* based on results. Reward systems should enhance and encourage others to risk and to achieve.[16]

Although each enterprise must develop a philosophy most appropriate for its own entrepreneurial process, a number of key questions can assist in establishing the type of process an organization has. Organizations can use the following questions to assess their enterprise. Applying these questions helps them feed back to the planning process for a proper approach.

• *Does your company encourage self-appointed intrapreneurs?* Intrapreneurs appoint themselves to their role and receive the corporation's blessing for their self-appointed task. Despite this, some corporations foolishly try to appoint people to carry out an innovation.

• *Does your company provide ways for intrapreneurs to stay with their enterprises?* When the innovation process involves switching the people working on an idea—that is, handing off a developing business or product from a committed intrapreneur to whoever is next in line—that person is often not as committed as the originator of a project.

• *Are people in your company permitted to do the job in their own way, or are they constantly stopping to explain their actions and ask for permission?* Some organizations push decisions up through a multilevel approval process so the doers and the deciders never even meet.

• *Has your company evolved quick and informal ways to access the resources to try new ideas?* Intrapreneurs need discretionary recources to explore and develop new ideas. Some companies give employees the freedom to use a percentage of their time on projects of their own choosing and set aside funds to explore new ideas when they occur. Others control resources so tightly that nothing is available for the new and unexpected. The result is nothing new.

• *Has your company developed ways to manage many small and experimental products and businesses?* Today's corporate cultures favor a few well-studied, well-planned attempts to hit a home run. In fact, nobody bats 1,000, and it is better to try more times with less careful and expensive preparation for each.

• *Is your system set up to encourage risk taking and to tolerate mistakes?* Innovation cannot be achieved without risk and mistakes. Even successful innovation generally begins with blunders and false starts.

• *Can your company decide to try something and stick with the experiment long enough to see if it will work, even when that may take years and several false starts?* Innovation takes time, even decades, but the rhythm of corporations is annual planning.

• *Are people in your company more concerned with new ideas or with defending their turf?* Because new ideas almost always cross the boundaries of existing patterns of organization, a jealous tendency to "turfiness" blocks innovation.

• *How easy is it to form functionally complete, autonomous teams in your corporate environment?* Small teams with full responsibility for developing an intraprise solve many of the basic innovation problems. But some companies resist their formation.

• *Do intrapreneurs in your company face monopolies, or are they free to use the resources of other divisions and outside vendors if they choose?* Entrepreneurs live in a multioption

---

[16] See Susan R. Quinn, "Supporting Innovation in the Workplace," *Supervision* (February 1990): 3–5; and Rick Brown and Joseph L. Meresman, "Balancing Stability and Innovation to Stay Competitive," *Personnel* (September 1990): 49–52.

universe. If one venture capitalist or supplier can't or won't meet their needs, they have many more to choose from. Intrapreneurs, however, often face single-option situations that may be called internal monopolies. They must have their product made by a certain factory or sold by a specific sales force. Too often these groups lack motivation or are simply wrong for the job, and a good idea dies an unnecessary death.[17]

Another way to create an innovative corporate atmosphere is to apply rules for innovation. The following rules can provide a hands-on guideline for developing the necessary innovative philosophy:

1. Encourage action.

2. Use informal meetings whenever possible.

3. Tolerate failure and use it as a learning experience.

4. Persist in getting an idea to market.

5. Reward innovation for innovation's sake.

6. Plan the physical layout of the enterprise to encourage informal communication.

7. Expect clever **bootlegging** of ideas—secretly working on new ideas on company time as well as on personal time.

8. Put people on small teams for future-oriented projects.

9. Encourage personnel to circumvent rigid procedures and bureaucratic red tape.

10. Reward and promote innovative personnel.

When these rules are followed, they create an environment conducive to and supportive of potential entrepreneurs. The result is a corporate philosophy that supports intrapreneurial behavior.

What can a corporation do to reengineer its thinking to foster the intrapreneurial process? First, the organization needs to examine and revise its management philosophy. Many enterprises have obsolete ideas about cooperative cultures, management techniques, and the values of managers and employees. Unfortunately, doing old tasks more efficiently is not the answer to new challenges; a new culture with new values has to be developed. Bureaucrats and controllers must learn to coexist with or give way to the designer and intrapreneur. Unfortunately, this is easier said than done. However, organizations can take some steps to help restructure corporate thinking and encourage an intrapreneurial environment: (1) early identification of potential intrapreneurs, (2) top management sponsorship of intrapreneurial projects, (3) creation of both diversity and order in strategic activities, (4) promotion of intrapreneurship through experimentation, and (5) development of collaboration between intrapreneurial participants and the organization at large.[18]

A number of advantages to developing an intrapreneurial philosophy exist. One is that this type of atmosphere often leads to the development of new products and services and

---

[17] Pinchot III, *Intrapreneuring*, 198–99.

[18] William E. Souder, "Encouraging Entrepreneurship in the Large Corporation," *Research Management* (May 1981): 18–22; see also Robert D. Russel, "An Investigation of Some Organizational Correlates of Entrepreneurship: Toward a Systems Model of Organizational Innovation," *Entrepreneurship, Innovation, and Change* 4, no. 4 (December 1995): 295–314; and Deborah Dougherty, "Managing Your Core Incompetencies for Corporate Venturing," *Entrepreneurship Theory and Practice* (spring 1995): 113–35.

CONTEMPORARY ENTREPRENEURSHIP

The Champion Program at Bell Atlantic

An effective intrapreneurship program creates a management environment in which innovation can flourish, and it transforms ordinary people into successful introcorporate entrepreneurs. These intrapreneurs create new possibilities within the company in a way that neither they nor the company has dreamed possible. They may even do it first while handling their existing jobs. Experience has shown that intrapreneurial efforts develop a greater sense of ownership within the company.

One example of a successful intrapreneurial experience is the Bell Atlantic Champion Program. The program was structured into three phases: early business opportunity exploration; full business planning, and trials; and commercial rollout.

These were the six major operating guidelines for the program:

1. Only five hours of company time per week were allowed on the project during the early phases. The rest of the time required had to be moonlighted out of the person's own time.

2. An expense-only budget of $1,000 per project was placed under the full discretionary control of the intrapreneur.

3. When ready, the project was presented to a cross-functional middle management review committee and either passed on to the next phase or terminated.

4. Regardless of whether the project was passed or terminated, the intrapreneur was eligible for up to $1,000 as an award for due diligence in evaluating the opportunity.

5. Candidates had a choice of either bringing their own ideas to the meeting or adopting one from the company's backlog.

6. The program was generally limited to lower and middle levels of management.

helps the organization expand and grow. A second is it creates a workforce that can help the enterprise maintain its competitive posture. A third is it promotes a climate conducive to high achievers and helps the enterprise motivate and keep its best people.

SPECIFIC ELEMENTS OF A CORPORATE INTRAPRENEURIAL STRATEGY

When attempting to create an intrapreneurial strategy, organizations should be aware of the following considerations for reinventing the corporation:

Thirty-five intrapreneurial candidates were put through an intensive four days of initial training and two sessions of follow-up training and coaching, each lasting two days. Between formal sessions the intrapreneurs were supported by the New Business Development Department as needed.

If, after three to four months of effort, candidates recommended more intensive effort to the screening committee—and were accepted—then they went through another three days of intensive training and coaching, followed by additional follow-up training days about six weeks apart. At this point, some were lent full time to the New Business Group to work on their projects. Others negotiated roles within their home departments that permitted them to devote up to half of their time to their intrapreneurial projects.

If the project was then accepted for commercialization, Bell provided a compensation choice. Intrapreneurs were allowed to invest 10 percent of their salary, taken as a salary reduction, plus their individual performance award for a period of three years. In return, they received 5 percent of the pretax profits from their project up to a cap of ten times their investment. Alternatively, the intrapreneur could retain regular compensation and progress with the project.

Eight projects made it into the second phase of development, which was initiated by another three days of training and intensive coaching, ending with a presentation of a 90-day action plan for the project. Intrapreneurs whose projects did not make it through to the second phase could at their discretion either return to the drawing board for more investigation or terminate the project. Regardless, a celebration was held, and awards were given to the intrapreneurs.

The program expanded throughout the company, with more than 130 intrapreneurs championing more than 100 projects. At least 15 products are on or near the market, and 15 patents have been awarded. Potential revenues estimated for these projects total at least $100 million within five years.

SOURCE: Adapted from Austin K. Pryor and E. Michael Shays, "Growing the Business with Intrapreneurs," *Business Quarterly* (spring 1993): 43–50.

1. The corporations that promote personal growth will attract the best people.

2. The challenge of the 1990s is to retrain the manager as coach, teacher, and mentor.

3. The best people seek ownership, and the best companies will provide it with bonus plans, stock incentive plans, employee stock-option plans, profit sharing, and even employee ownership per se.

4. Authoritarian management is being replaced by a networking, people style of management, characterized by horizontal coordination and support.

5. Intrapreneurship within the corporation allows employees the satisfaction of developing their ideas without the risk of leaving the company.

FIGURE 3.1   **SHARED VISION**

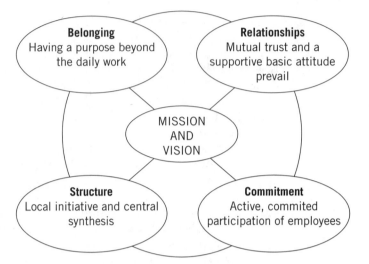

SOURCE: Jon-Arild Johannessen, "A Systemic Approach to the Problem of Rooting a Vision in the Basic Components of an Organization," *Entrepreneurship, Innovation, and Change* 3, no. 1 (March 1994): 47. Reprinted with permission from Plenum Publishing Corporation.

6. Large companies are taking lessons from small businesses and learning how to be flexible, to promote innovation, and to create spirit.[19]

Corporations that create an intrapreneurial strategy find that the ethos of the original enterprise often changes dramatically. Traditions are set aside in favor of new processes and procedures. Some people, unaccustomed to operating in this environment, will leave; the others will discover a new motivational system that encourages creativity, ingenuity, risk taking, teamwork, and informal networking, all designed to increase productivity and make the organization more viable. Some people thrive in an intrapreneurial environment; others dislike it intensely.

The four critical steps of an intrapreneurial strategy are (1) developing the vision, (2) encouraging innovation, (3) structuring for an intrapreneurial climate, and (4) developing venture teams. Each of these are now discussed in greater detail.

Developing the Vision

The first step in planning an intrapreneurial strategy for the enterprise is sharing the vision of innovation the corporate leaders wish to achieve. Since it is suggested that corporate entrepreneuring results from the creative talents of people within the organization, employees need to know about and understand this vision. Shared vision is a critical element for a strategy that seeks high achievement (see Figure 3.1). This shared vision requires identification of specific objectives for corporate entrepreneuring strategies and of the programs needed to achieve those objectives. Author and researcher Rosabeth Moss Kanter has described three major objectives and their respective programs designed for venture development within companies. These are outlined next.

[19] John Naisbitt and Patricia Aburdene, *Re-inventing the Corporation* (New York: Warner Books, 1985), 45–46. Copyright © 1985 by Megatrends, Inc.

OBJECTIVES AND PROGRAMS FOR VENTURE DEVELOPMENT

Objectives	Programs
Make sure current systems, structures, and practices do not present insurmountable road-blocks to the flexibility and fast action needed for innovation.	Reduce unnecessary bureaucracy, and encourage communication across departments and functions.
Provide the incentives and tools for intrapreneurial projects.	Use internal "venture capital" and special project budgets. (This has been termed **intracapital** to signify a special fund for intrapreneurial projects.) Allow discretionary time for projects (sometimes referred to as "bootlegging" time).
Seek synergies across business areas so new opportunities are discovered in new combinations.	Encourage joint projects and ventures among divisions, departments, and companies. Allow and encourage employees to discuss and brainstorm new ideas.

SOURCE: Adapted by permission of the publisher from "Supporting Innovation and Venture Development in Established Companies," by Rosabeth Moss Kanter, *Journal of Business Venturing* (winter 1985): 56–59. Copyright © 1985 by Elsevier Science Publishing Co., Inc.

Encouraging Innovation

As will be discussed in Chapter 5, innovation is the specific tool of the entrepreneur. Therefore, corporations must understand and develop innovation as the key element in their strategy. Numerous researchers have examined the importance of innovation within the corporate environment.[20]

Innovation is described as chaotic and unplanned by some authors,[21] while other researchers insist it is a systematic discipline.[22] Both of these positions can be true depending on the nature of the innovation. One way to understand this concept is to focus on two different types of innovation: radical and incremental.[23]

Radical innovation is the launching of inaugural breakthroughs such as personal computers, Post-it Notes, disposable diapers, and overnight mail delivery. These innovations take experimentation and determined vision, which are not necessarily managed but *must* be recognized and nurtured.

Incremental innovation refers to the systematic evolution of a product or service into newer or larger markets. Examples include microwave popcorn, popcorn used for packaging (to replace Styrofoam), frozen yogurt, and so forth. Many times the incremental innovation will take over after a radical innovation introduces a breakthrough (see Figure 3.2). The structure, marketing, financing, and formal systems of a corporation can help implement incremental innovation. Jan Carlzon, CEO of SAS Airlines, has explained that his organization did not do one thing *1,000 percent* better. Rather, his organization (referring to his people) did 1,000 things *1 percent* better.

[20] See, for example, Dean M. Schroeder, "A Dynamic Perspective on the Impact of Process Innovation upon Competitive Strategies," *Strategic Management Journal* 2 (1990): 25–41; and C. Marlene Fiol, "Thought Worlds Colliding: The Role of Contradiction in Corporate Innovation Processes," *Entrepreneurship Theory and Practice* (spring 1995): 71–90.

[21] Thomas J. Peters, *Thriving on Chaos* (New York: Harper & Row, 1987).

[22] Peter F. Drucker, "The Discipline of Innovation," *Harvard Business Review* (May/June 1985): 67–72.

[23] Harry S. Dent Jr., "Reinventing Corporate Innovation," *Small Business Reports* (June 1990): 31–42.

FIGURE 3.2   **RADICAL VERSUS INCREMENTAL INNOVATION**

SOURCE: Harry S. Dent Jr., "Reinventing Corporate Innovation," *Small Business Reports* (June 1990): 33.

Both types of innovation require vision and support. This support takes different steps for effective development (see Table 3.2). In addition, they both need a **champion**—the person with a vision and the ability to share it.[24] And finally, both types of innovation require an effort by the top management of the corporation to develop and educate employees concerning innovation and intrapreneurship, a concept known as **top management support.**

Encouraging innovation requires a willingness to not only tolerate failure but also to learn from it. For example, one of the founders of 3M, Francis G. Oakie, had an idea to replace razor blades with sandpaper. He believed men could rub sandpaper on their face rather than use a sharp razor. He was wrong and the idea failed, but his ideas evolved until he developed a waterproof sandpaper for the auto industry, a blockbuster success!

Thus, 3M's philosophy was born. Innovation is a numbers game; the more ideas, the better the chances for a successful innovation. In other words, to master innovation companies must have a tolerance for failure. This philosophy has paid off for 3M. Antistatic videotape, translucent dental braces, synthetic ligaments for knee surgery, heavy-duty reflective sheeting for construction signs, and, of course, Post-it Notes are just some of the great innovations developed at 3M. From 1994 to 1995, 3M's net sales increased 10.8 percent from $12.15 to $13.46 million. Overall, the company has a catalog of 60,000 products.[25]

Today 3M follows a set of innovative rules that encourage employees to foster ideas. The key rules include the following:

---

[24] Jane M. Howell and Christopher A. Higgins, "Champions of Change: Identifying, Understanding, and Supporting Champions of Technology Innovations," *Organizational Dynamics* (summer 1990): 40–55.

[25] See Russell Mitchell, "Masters of Innovation," *Business Week,* 10 April 1989, 58–63; and *3M Annual Report,* 1995.

TABLE 3.2	DEVELOPING AND SUPPORTING RADICAL AND INCREMENTAL INNOVATION

Radical	**Incremental**
Stimulate through challenges and puzzles	Set systematic goals and deadlines
Remove budgetary and deadline constraints when possible	Stimulate through competitive pressures
Encourage technical education and exposure to customers	Encourage technical education and exposure to customers
Allow technical sharing and brainstorming sessions	Hold weekly meetings that include key management and marketing staff
Give personal attention—develop relationships of trust	Delegate more responsibility
Encourage praise from outside parties	Set clear financial rewards for meeting goals and deadlines
Have flexible funds for opportunities that arise	
Reward with freedom and capital for new projects and interests	

SOURCE: Adapted from Harry S. Dent Jr., "Growth through New Product Development," *Small Business Reports* (November 1990): 36.

- *Don't kill a project.* If an idea can't find a home in one of 3M's divisions, a staffer can devote 15 percent of his or her time to prove it is workable. For those who need seed money, as many as 90 Genesis grants of $50,000 are awarded each year.
- *Tolerate failure.* Encouraging plenty of experimentation and risk taking allows more chances for a new product hit. The goal: Divisions must derive 25 percent of sales from products introduced in the past five years. The target may be boosted to 30 percent.
- *Keep divisions small.* Division managers must know each staffer's first name. When a division gets too big, perhaps reaching $250 million to $300 million in sales, it is split up.
- *Motivate the champions.* When a 3M employee has a product idea, he or she recruits an action team to develop it. Salaries and promotions are tied to the product's progress. The champion has a chance to someday run his or her own product group or division.
- *Stay close to the customer.* Researchers, marketers, and managers visit with customers and routinely invite them to help brainstorm product ideas.
- *Share the wealth.* Technology, wherever it is developed, belongs to everyone.

Structuring for an Intrapreneurial Climate

When reestablishing the drive to innovate in today's corporations, the final and possibly most critical step is to invest heavily in *entrepreneurial activities* that allow new ideas to flourish in an innovative environment. This concept, when coupled with the other elements of an innovation strategy, can enhance the potential for employees to become venture developers. To develop employees as a source of innovations for corporations, companies

FIGURE 3.3   **INTRAPRENEURIAL DEVELOPMENT: JOINT FUNCTION OF INDIVIDUAL AND ORGANIZATIONAL FACTORS**

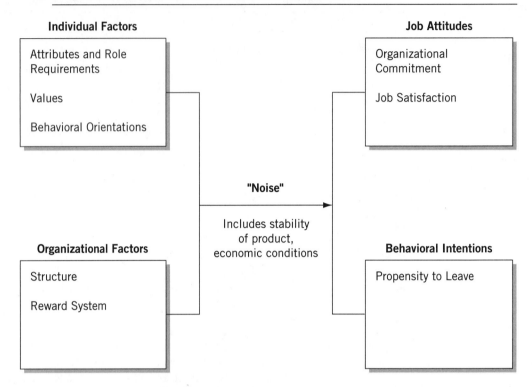

SOURCE: Deborah V. Brazeal, "Organizing for Internally Developed Corporate Ventures," *Journal of Business Venturing* 8, no. 1 (1993): 80.

need to provide more nurturing and information-sharing activities.[26] In addition to establishing entrepreneurial ways and nurturing intrapreneurs, they need to develop a climate that will help innovative-minded people reach their full potential. Employee perception of an innovative climate is critical for stressing the importance of management's commitment to not only the organization's people but also to the innovative projects.

The importance of an organizational climate for intrapreneurship is further emphasized by researcher Deborah V. Brazeal's model for internally developed ventures.[27] Figure 3.3 illustrates the model's focus of a joint function between innovative individuals and organizational factors. Brazeal defines corporate venturing as "an internal process that embraces the ultimate goal of growth through the development of innovative products, processes, and technologies" that should be institutionalized with an emphasis on long-term prosperity. Thus, in order for organizations to promote innovation among their employees, they must give careful attention to the melding of an individual's attitudes, values, and behavioral orientations with the organizational factors of structure and reward. Ulti-

---

[26] David Krackhardt, "Entrepreneurial Opportunities in an Entrepreneurial Firm: A Structural Approach" *Entrepreneurship Theory and Practice* (spring 1995): 53–70.

[27] Deborah V. Brazeal, "Organizing for Internally Developed Corporate Ventures," *Journal of Business Venturing* 8, no. 1 (1993): 75–90.

mately, the key objective is to enhance a firm's innovative abilities through an organizational environment supportive of individuals.

As a way for organizations to develop key environmental factors for intrapreneurial activity, an intrapreneurship training program (ITP) often induces the change needed in the work atmosphere. It is not our intent to elaborate completely on the content of a training program here, but a brief summary of an actual program is presented to provide a general understanding of how such a program is designed to introduce an intrapreneurial environment in a company. This award-winning training program was intended to create an awareness of intrapreneurial opportunities in an organization. The ITP consisted of six four-hour modules, each designed to train participants to support intrapreneurship in their own work area.[28] The modules and a brief summary of their contents follow:

1. *Introduction.* This consisted of a review of managerial and organizational behavior concepts, definitions of intrapreneurship and related concepts, and a review of several intrapreneurial cases.

2. *Personal creativity.* This module attempted to define and stimulate personal creativity. It involved a number of creativity exercises and had participants develop a personal creative enrichment program.

3. *Intrapreneuring.* A review of the current literature on the topic was presented here, as well as in-depth analyses of several intrapreneuring organizations.

4. *Assessment of current culture.* A climate survey (not the research instrument) was administered to the training group for the purpose of generating discussion about the current facilitators and barriers to change in the organization.

5. *Business planning.* The intrapreneurial business planning process was outlined and explained. The specific elements of a business plan were identified and illustrated, and an example of an entire business plan was presented.

6. *Action planning.* In this module participants worked in teams and created action plans designed to bring about change to foster intrapreneurship in their own workplaces.

To validate the training program's effectiveness, a questionnaire titled the **"Intrapreneurship Assessment Instrument"** (IAI) was developed by researchers Donald F. Kuratko, Jeffrey S. Hornsby, and Ray V. Montagno to provide for a psychometrically sound instrument that measured key entrepreneurial climate factors from the existing intrapreneurship literature. The responses to the IAI were statistically analyzed and resulted in five identified factors. Each of these factors identified next are aspects of the organization over which management has some control. Each is briefly defined with illustrations of specific elements of a firm's environment relative to each dimension.

> *Management support.* This is the extent the management structure itself encourages employees to believe innovation is, in fact, part of the role set for all organization members. Some of the specific conditions reflecting management support would be quick adoption of employee ideas, recognition of people who bring ideas forward, support for small experimental projects, and seed money to get projects off the ground.

---

[28] Kuratko and Montagno, "The Intrapreneurial Spirit," 83–87; see also Kuratko and Hornsby, "Developing Entrepreneurial Leadership in Contemporary Organizations," 17–24.

Autonomy/work discretion. Workers have discretion to the extent they are able to make decisions about performing their own work in the way they believe is most effective. Organizations should allow employees to make decisions about their work process and should avoid criticizing them for making mistakes when innovating.

Rewards/reinforcement. Rewards and reinforcement enhance the motivation of individuals to engage in innovative behavior. Organizations must be characterized by providing rewards contingent on performance, providing challenge, increasing responsibility, and making the ideas of innovative people known to others in the organizational hierarchy.

Time availability. The fostering of new and innovative ideas requires that individuals have time to incubate these ideas. Organizations must moderate the workload of people, avoid putting time constraints on all aspects of a person's job, and allow people to work with others on long-term problem solving.

Organizational boundary. These are the boundaries, real and imagined, that prevent people from looking at problems outside their own jobs. People must be encouraged to look at the organization from a broad perspective. Organizations should avoid having standard operating procedures for all major parts of jobs and should reduce dependence on narrow job descriptions and rigid performance standards.[29]

The statistical results from the IAI demonstrated support for this underlying set of internal environmental factors that organizations need to focus on when seeking to introduce an intrapreneurial strategy. These factors, as well as the previous research mentioned, are the foundation for the critical steps involved in introducing an intrapreneurial climate.

Another researcher, Vijay Sathe, has suggested a number of areas corporations must focus on if they are going to facilitate intrapreneurial behavior. The first is to encourage, not mandate, intrapreneurial activity. Managers should use financial rewards and strong company recognition rather than rules or strict procedures to encourage corporate entrepreneurship. This is actually a stronger internal control and direction method than traditional parameters.

Another area is the proper control of human resource policies. Managers need to remain in positions for a period long enough to allow them to learn an industry and a particular division. Rather than move managers around in positions, as is the case in many companies, Sathe suggests "selected rotation," in which managers are exposed to different but related territories. This helps managers gain sufficient knowledge for new-venture development.

A third factor is for management to sustain a commitment to intrapreneurial projects long enough for momentum to occur. Failures will inevitably occur, and learning must be the key aftermath of those failures. Thus, sustained commitment is an important element in managing corporate entrepreneurship.

A final element Sathe mentioned is to bet on people, *not* on analysis. Although analysis is always important to judge a project's progression, it should be done in a supportive rather than an imposed style. The supportive challenge can help intrapreneurs realize errors, test their convictions, and accomplish a self-analysis.[30] It should be mentioned that the exact rewards for corporate entrepreneuring are not yet agreed on by most researchers.[31] Some believe allowing the inventor to take charge of the new venture is the best reward. Others say it is allowing the corporate entrepreneur more discretionary time to work on

[29] Donald F. Kuratko, Ray V. Montagno, and Jeffrey S. Hornsby, "Developing an Intrapreneurial Assessment Instrument for an Effective Corporate Entrepreneurial Environment," *Strategic Management Journal* 11 (1990): 49–58.

[30] Vijay Sathe, "From Surface to Deep Corporate Entrepreneurship," *Human Resource Management* (winter 1988): 389–411.

[31] See John J. Kao, *The Entrepreneur* (Englewood Cliffs: Prentice Hall, 1991), 197–98.

future projects. Still others insist that special capital, called *intracapital,* should be set aside for the corporate entrepreneur to use whenever investment money is needed for further research ideas.

In light of these climate elements, it is clear that change in the corporate structure is inevitable if intrapreneurial activity is going to exist and prosper. The change process consists of a series of emerging constructions of people, corporate goals, and existing needs. In short, the organization can encourage innovation by relinquishing controls and changing the traditional bureaucratic structure.[32]

Developing Venture Teams

Venture teams and the potential they hold for producing innovative results are recognized as the productivity breakthrough of the 1990s. Certainly, no one doubts their popularity is on the rise. Companies that have committed to a venture team approach often label the change they have undergone a "transformation" or a "revolution." This new breed of work team is a new strategy for many firms. It is referred to as self-directing, self-managing, or high performing, but a venture team includes all of those descriptions.[33]

In examining the entrepreneurial development for corporations, Robert Reich found that intrapreneurship is not the sole province of the company's founder or its top managers. Rather, it is diffused throughout the company, where experimentation and development occur all the time as the company searches for new ways to build on the knowledge already accumulated by its workers. Reich's definition of **collective entrepreneurship** follows.

> In collective entrepreneurship, individual skills are integrated into a group; this collective capacity to innovate becomes something greater than the sum of its parts. Over time, as group members work through various problems and approaches, they learn about each other's abilities. They learn how they can help one another perform better, what each can contribute to a particular project, how they can best take advantage of one another's experience. Each participant is constantly on the lookout for small adjustments that will speed and smooth the evolution of the whole. The net result of many such small-scale adaptations, effected throughout the organization, is to propel the enterprise forward.[34]

In keeping with Reich's focus on collective entrepreneurship, venture teams offer corporations the opportunity to use the talents of individuals but with a sense of teamwork.

A **venture team** is comprised of two or more people who formally created and share the ownership of a new organization.[35] The unit is semiautonomous in the sense it has a budget plus a leader who has the freedom to make decisions within broad guidelines. Sometimes the leader is called a "product champion" or an "intrapreneur." The unit is often separated from other parts of the firm, in particular from parts involved with daily activities. This prevents the unit from procedures that can stifle innovative activities. If the venture proves successful, however, it eventually is treated the same as other outputs the organization produces. It is integrated into the larger organization.[36]

[32] See Kuratko, Hornsby, Naffziger, and Montagno, "Implementing Entrepreneurial Thinking," 28–33.

[33] Chris Lee, "Beyond Teamwork," *Training* (June 1990): 25–32; and Michael F. Wolff, "Building Teams—What Works," *Research Technology Management* (November/December 1989): 9–10.

[34] Robert B. Reich, "The Team as Hero," *Harvard Business Review* (May/June 1987): 81.

[35] Judith B. Kamm and Aaron J. Nurick, "The Stages of Team Venture Formulation: A Decision-Making Model," *Entrepreneurship, Theory, and Practice* 17, no. 2 (winter, 1993): 17–27.

[36] Philip D. Olson, "Choices for Innovation-Minded Corporations," *Journal of Business Strategy* (January/February 1990): 42–46.

CONTEMPORARY ENTREPRENEURSHIP

Signode's V-Teams

Robert F. Hettinger, a venture manager with Signode Industries, Inc., in Glenview, Illinois, smiles as he recounts the strategy initiated by Jack Campbell, director of corporate development. "He strongly believed," Hettinger says, "that you have to kiss a lot of frogs in order to find a prince. Most ideas in raw form aren't winners—you really have to work them out before success sets in."

Signode, a $750 million-a-year manufacturer of plastic and steel strapping for packaging and materials handling, wanted to chart new directions to become a $1 billion–plus firm by 1990. In pursuit of this goal, Signode set out in 1983 to devise an aggressive strategy for growth: developing "new legs" for the company to stand on. It formed a corporate development group to pursue markets outside the company's core businesses but within the framework of its corporate strengths.

Before launching the first of its venture

teams, Signode's top management identified the firm's global business strengths and broad areas with potential for new product lines: warehousing/shipping; packaging; plastics for nonpackaging, fastening, and joining systems; and product identification and control systems. Each new business opportunity a venture team suggested was to have the potential to generate $50 million in business within five years. In addition, each opportunity had to build on one of Signode's strengths: industrial customer base and marketing expertise, systems sales and service capabilities, containment and reinforcement technology, steel and plastic process technology, machine and design capabilities, and productivity and distribution know-how.

The criteria was based on business-to-business selling only; Signode did not want to market directly to retailers or consumers. The basic technology to be employed in the new business had to al-

In many ways, a venture team is a small business operating within a large business, and its strength is its focus on design (i.e., structure and process) issues for innovative activities. One organization that operated successfully with the venture team concept was the Signode Corporation (see the Contemporary Entrepreneurship box).

Specific intrapreneurship strategies vary from firm to firm. However, they all have similar patterns, seeking a proactive changing of the status quo and a new, flexible approach to operations management.

THE INTERACTIVE PROCESS OF INTRAPRENEURSHIP

Who Are Intrapreneurs?

Intrapreneurs are not necessarily the inventors of new products or services but are the persons who can turn ideas or prototypes into profitable realities. They are the people behind a product or service. They are team builders with a commitment and a strong drive

ready exist and had to have a strong likelihood of attaining a major market share within a niche. Finally, the initial investment in the new opportunity had to be $30 million or less.

Based on these criteria, Signode began to build its "V-Team" (venture team) approach to intrapreneurship. It took three months to select the first team members. The six initial teams had three common traits: high risk-taking ability, creativity, and the ability to deal with ambiguity. All were multidisciplinary volunteers who would work full-time on developing new consumer-product packaging businesses. The team members came from such backgrounds as design engineering, marketing, sales, and product development. They set up shop in rented office space five miles from the firm's headquarters. "We put them off-campus in order to create an entrepreneurial environment," Hettinger recalls.

The first venture team recommendation, complete with a business plan, was to produce plastic trays for frozen entrees that could be used in either regular or microwave ovens. The business potential for this product was estimated to be in excess of $50 million a year within five years.

Signode launched a total of six teams between October 1983 and April 1986. Two teams have already finished their strategic tasks and the other four are scheduled to make presentations to top management. All team volunteers passed a rigorous selection process. Typically, the employees are borrowed from operating divisions; after their team's work is finished, they either return to their old positions or take on positions with the newly formed business unit and further champion the new ideas.

According to Hettinger, the V-Team experience rekindled enthusiasm and affected morale overall. In every case a V-Team member became a better contributor to Signode. Most important, the V-Team approach became a strategy for members to invent their future rather than waiting for things to happen.

SOURCE: Mark Frohman and Perry Pascarella, "Achieving Purpose-Driven Innovation," *Industry Week*, 19 March 1990, 20–26; and personal interview.

to see their ideas become a reality. Perhaps most surprising, they are typically of average or slightly above-average intelligence—they are not geniuses.

Most intrapreneurs begin their "intraprise" with an idea. This idea typically starts as a vision, often referred to as the "daydreaming phase." Here the intrapreneur mentally goes through the process of taking the idea to fruition. Different pathways are thought through, and potential obstacles and barriers are mentally examined. The intrapreneur of the Pontiac Fiero, Hulki Aldikacti, provides an example of this process. When Aldikacti first came up with the idea for the Fiero, he was unsure of what the car would look like. So he built a wooden mock-up of the passenger compartment. He then sat in the model and imagined what it would feel like to drive the finished car. This helped him develop and perfect the final product.

Initially, the intrapreneur is the general manager of a new business that does not yet exist. In the beginning the individual may specialize in one area, such as marketing or research and development, but once the intraprise is started, he or she quickly begins to learn all the project's facets. The intrapreneur soon becomes a generalist with many skills.

TABLE 3.3   **THE TEN COMMANDMENTS OF AN INTRAPRENEUR**

1. Come to work each day willing to be fired.

2. Circumvent any orders aimed at stopping your dream.

3. Do any job needed to make your project work, regardless of your job description.

4. Network with good people to assist you.

5. Build a spirited team: Choose and work with only the best.

6. Work underground as long as you can—publicity triggers the corporate immune mechanism.

7. Be loyal and truthful to your sponsors.

8. Remember it is easier to ask forgiveness than for permission.

9. Be true to your goals, but be realistic about the ways to achieve them.

10. Keep the vision strong.

SOURCE: Adapted from *Intrapreneuring* by Gifford Pinchot III, 1985, 22. Copyright © 1985 by Gifford Pinchot III. Adapted by permission of HarperCollins Publishers.

Intrapreneurs are sometimes captured by the description as "a dreamer who does." They tend to be action oriented. They can move quickly to get things done. They are goal oriented, willing to do whatever it takes to achieve their objectives. They are also a combination of thinker, doer, planner, and worker. They combine vision and action. Dedication to the new idea is paramount. As a result, intrapreneurs often expect the impossible from themselves and consider no setback too great to make their venture successful. They are self-determined goal setters who go beyond the call of duty in achieving their goals.[37] (See Table 3.3 for the intrapreneur's ten commandments.)

When faced with failure or setback, intrapreneurs employ an optimistic approach. First, they do not admit they are beaten; they view failure as a temporary setback to be learned from and dealt with. It is not seen as a reason to quit. Second, they view themselves as responsible for their own destiny. They do not blame their failure on others but instead focus on learning how they might have done better. By objectively dealing with their own mistakes and failures, intrapreneurs learn to avoid making the same mistakes again, and this, in turn, is part of what helps make them successful.

Intrapreneurial Myths Dispelled

A great similarity exists between entrepreneurs and intrapreneurs. Consequently, some of the myths about entrepreneurs have carried over as myths about intrapreneurs. These myths sometimes affect the impressions peers and supervisors have of intrapreneurs. They follow, along with a discussion of each:

1. *Myth:* The primary motivation of intrapreneurs is a desire for wealth; hence, money is the prime objective.

[37] See Kao, *The Entrepreneur,* 18–20.

Fact: The primary motivation of intrapreneurs is the process of innovation: The freedom and ability to innovate is *the* prime motivator. Money is only a tool and a symbol of success.

2. *Myth:* Intrapreneurs are high risk takers—they are gamblers who play for high stakes.
Fact: Moderate risk taking is a more realistic description of intrapreneurs' actions. Because of their insatiable desire to achieve, small, calculated, and analyzed risks are the favorite stepping-stones of these individuals.

3. *Myth:* Because intrapreneurs lack analytical skills, they "shoot from the hip." This has led to a philosophy of "luck is all you need."
Fact: Intrapreneurs are extremely analytical. Although it may appear they are lucky and shoot from the hip, in truth, they are well prepared, understand innovation, and perceive market needs very well.

4. *Myth:* Intrapreneurs lack morals or ethics due to their strong desire to succeed. They do not care how they succeed, just as long as they do succeed.
Fact: In today's demanding, educated, and critical society, intrapreneurs must be highly ethical and have moral convictions consistent with society's expectations. If they do not have these convictions, they do *not* survive.

5. *Myth:* Intrapreneurs have a power-hungry attitude and are most interested in building an empire. They want the venture to grow as big and as fast as it can.
Fact: Most intrapreneurial enterprises are small and conservative. They are more interested in profit and growth than in empire building. The focus is on doing things right rather than doing them big.

Table 3.4 compares the characteristics and skills of the intrapreneur with those of the traditional manager and entrepreneur.

The Interactive Process of Individual and Organizational Characteristics

As we emphasized in Chapter 2, the entire new-venture creation process is an interaction of many factors.[38]

This is clear from the specific organizational strategies for intrapreneurship and the individual traits and characteristics of intrapreneurs. One research model was developed to illustrate the critical interaction of several activities rather than events that occur in isolation. Figure 3.4 on page 78 illustrates the key elements of this process. Researchers Jeffrey S. Hornsby, Douglas W. Naffziger, Donald F. Kuratko, and Ray V. Montagno believe the decision to act intrapreneurially occurs as a result of interactions among organizational characteristics, individual characteristics, and some kind of precipitating event. The precipitating event provides the impetus to behave intrapreneurially when other conditions are conducive to such behavior.[39]

Researcher Shaker Zahra identified a number of influencing factors in corporate entrepreneurship that could be viewed as types of precipitating events. These include environmental factors such as hostility (threats to a firm's mission through rivalry), dynamism

---

[38] David B. Greenberger and Donald L. Sexton, "An Interactive Model of New Venture Creation," *Journal of Small Business Management* 26 (1988): 1–7.

[39] Jeffrey S. Hornsby, Douglas W. Naffziger, Donald F. Kuratko, and Ray V. Montagno, "An Interactive Model of the Corporate Entrepreneurship Process," *Entrepreneurship Theory and Practice* (spring 1993): 29–37.

TABLE 3.4		WHO IS THE INTRAPRENEUR?	
Characteristic	**Traditional Manager**	**Entrepreneur**	**Intrapreneur**
Primary motives	Wants promotion and other traditional corporate rewards; power motivated	Wants freedom; goal oriented, self-reliant, and self-motivated	Wants freedom and access to corporate resources; goal-oriented and self-motivated, but also responds to corporate rewards and recognition
Time orientation	Responds to quotas and budgets; to weekly, monthly, quarterly, and annual planning horizons; and to the next promotion or transfer	Uses end goals of 5- to 10-year growth of the business as guides; takes action now to move to next step along the way	End goals of 3 to 15 years, depending on the type of venture; urgency to meet self-imposed and corporate timetables
Tendency to action	Delegates action; supervising and reporting take most energy	Gets hands dirty; may upset employees by suddenly doing their work	Gets hands dirty; may know how to delegate but, when necessary, does what needs to be done
Skills	Professional management; often business-school trained; uses abstract analytical tools, people-management and political skills	Knows business intimately; more business acumen than managerial or political skill; often technically trained if in technical business; may have had formal profit-and-loss responsibility in the company	Very much like the entrepreneur, but the situation demands greater ability to prosper within the organization; needs help with this
Attitude toward courage and destiny	Sees others being in charge of his or her destiny; can be forceful and ambitious but may be fearful of others' ability to do him or her in	Self-confident, optimistic, and courageous	Self-confident and courageous; many are cynical about the system but optimistic about their ability to outwit it
Focus of attention	Primarily on events inside corporation	Primarily on technology and marketplace	Both inside and outside; sells insiders on needs of venture and marketplace but also focuses on customers
Attitude toward risk	Cautious	Likes moderate risk; invests heavily but expects to succeed	Likes moderate risk; generally not afraid of being fired, so sees little personal risk
Use of market research	Has market studies done to discover needs and guide product conceptualization	Creates needs; creates products that often cannot be tested with market research; potential customers do not yet understand them; talks to customers and forms own opinions	Does own market research and intuitive market evaluation, like the entrepreneur
Attitude toward status	Cares about status symbols (corner office, etc.)	Happy sitting on an orange crate if job is getting done	Considers traditional status symbols a joke; treasures symbols of freedom

(instability of a firm's market because of changes), and heterogeneity (developments in the market that create new demands for a firm's products).[40]

These influencing factors seem to include some type of environmental or organizational change that precipitates or ignites the interaction of organizational and individual charac-

[40] Shaker Zahra, "Predictors and Financial Outcomes of Corporate Entrepreneurship: An Exploratory Study," *Journal of Business Venturing* 6 (1991): 259–85.

TABLE 3.4	WHO IS THE INTRAPRENEUR? *(continued)*		
Characteristic	**Traditional Manager**	**Entrepreneur**	**Intrapreneur**
Attitude toward failure and mistakes	Strives to avoid mistakes and surprises; postpones recognizing failure	Deals with mistakes and failures as learning experiences	Sensitive to need to appear orderly; attempts to hide risky projects from view in order to learn from mistakes without political cost of public failure
Decision-making style	Agrees with those in power; delays making decisions until a feel of what bosses want is obtained	Follows private vision; decisive, action oriented	Adept at getting others to agree with private vision; somewhat more patient and willing to compromise than the entrepreneur but still a doer
Who serves	Pleases others	Pleases self and customer	Pleases self, customers, and sponsors
Attitude toward the system	Sees system as nurturing and protective; seeks position within it	May rapidly advance in a system; then, when frustrated, may reject the system and form his or her own company	Dislikes the system but learns to manipulate it
Problem-solving style	Works out problems within the system	Escapes problems in large and formal structures by leaving and starting over alone	Works out problems within the system or bypasses them without leaving
Family history	Family members worked for large organizations	Entrepreneurial small-business, professional, or farm background	Entrepreneurial small-business, professional, or farm background
Relationship with parents	Independent of mother; good relations with father but slightly dependent	Absent father or poor relations with father	Better relations with father but still stormy
Socioeconomic background	Middle class	Lower class in some early studies; middle class in more recent ones	Middle class
Educational level	Highly educated	Less well educated in earlier studies; some graduate work but not Ph.D. in later ones	Often highly educated, particularly in technical fields, but sometimes not
Relationships with others	Perceives hierarchy as basic relationship	Perceives transactions and deal making as basic relationship	Perceives transactions within hierarchy as basic relationship

SOURCE: Table adapted from *Intrapreneuring* by Gifford Pinchot III, 1985, 54–56. Copyright © 1985 by Gifford Pinchot III. Adapted by permission of HarperCollins Publishers.

teristics to cause intrapreneurial events. Some specific examples of precipitating events in the corporate entrepreneurship process could include the development of new procedures, a change in company management, a merger or acquisition, a competitor's move to increase market share, the development of new technologies, cost reduction, a change in consumer demand, and economic changes.

The next major element after the decision to act intrapreneurially is to develop an effective business plan. The entire plan will encompass all phases of the start-up research

FIGURE 3.4   **AN INTERACTIVE MODEL OF CORPORATE ENTREPRENEURING**

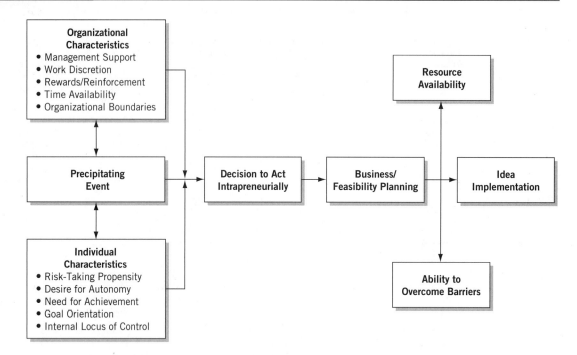

SOURCE: Jeffrey S. Hornsby, Douglas W. Naffziger, Donald F. Kuratko, and Ray V. Montagno, "An Interactive Model of the Corporate Entrepreneurship Process," *Entrepreneurship Theory and Practice* (spring 1993): 31.

needed to clarify the operations of a new internal venture. (A complete analysis of business plan development is covered later in Chapter 10).

Although an accurate business plan is essential, its implementation and the ultimate success of the intrapreneurial idea depend on two factors. First, is the organization able to provide the needed resources, and, second, can the intrapreneur overcome the organizational and individual barriers that may prohibit the new project?

The implementation of an intrapreneurial idea is the result of the interaction of the factors described in this chapter. After developing the feasibility analysis, acquiring the resources necessary for the new venture, and overcoming any existing organizational barriers, the intrapreneur is in a position to implement the idea and initiate the innovation.

As in Chapter 2, we emphasized that understanding the process of entrepreneuring is more important than understanding the entrepreneur; understanding the intrapreneur is only one part of understanding the intrapreneurial process. The interactive nature of the process cannot be overstated. Intrapreneurship is multidimensional and relies on the successful interaction of several organizational and individual activities.

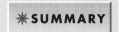

✳SUMMARY

Intrapreneurship is the process of profitably creating innovation within an organizational setting. Most companies are realizing the need for corporate entrepreneuring. This need has arisen as a response to (1) the rapidly growing number of new, sophisticated competitors, (2) a sense of distrust in the traditional methods of corporate management, and (3) an exodus of some of the best and brightest people who are leaving corporations to become small-business entrepreneurs.

When creating the climate for in-house entrepreneurial ways, companies must develop four climate characteristics: (1) explicit goals, (2) a system of feedback and positive reinforcement, (3) an emphasis on individual responsibility, and (4) rewards based on results. Organizations create corporate intrapreneuring in a number of ways. The first step is to understand the obstacles to corporate venturing. These are usually based on the adverse impact of traditional management techniques. The next step is to adapt to innovative principles that include atmosphere and vision, multiple approaches, interactive learning, and skunkworks.

Specific strategies for corporate entrepreneurship entail the development of a vision as well as the development of innovation. Two types of innovation exist: radical and incremental. In order to facilitate the development of innovation, corporations need to focus on the key factors of top management support, time, resources, and rewards. Thus, commitment to and support of intrapreneurial activity are critical.

Venture teams are the semiautonomous units that have the collective capacity to develop new ideas. Sometimes referred to as self-managing or high-performance teams, venture teams are emerging as the new breed of work teams formed to strengthen innovative developments.

Intrapreneurs have a number of similar characteristics and traits. Among these traits are a generalist point of view, an action orientation, an optimistic approach, self-determination, ambitious goal setting, dedication to new ideas, and a willingness to accept their mistakes and learn from them.

At the end of this chapter we discussed the interactive process of intrapreneurship. We identified and attempted to dispel some of the myths about intrapreneurs. In addition, we examined the role of individual and organizational characteristics that impact intrapreneurship.

Key Terms and Concepts

Bootlegging	Intracapital
Champion	Intrapreneurship
Collective entrepreneurship	Intrapreneurship Assessment Instrument (IAI)
Corporate entrepreneurship	Radical innovation
Entrepreneurial economy	Skunkworks
Incremental innovation	Top management support
Interactive learning	Venture teams

Review and Discussion Questions

1. In your own words, what is an intrapreneur?
2. What are two reasons such a strong desire in recent years to develop intrapreneurs has arisen?
3. What are some of the corporate obstacles that must be overcome in order to establish an intrapreneurial environment?
4. What are some of the innovative principles identified by James Brian Quinn that companies need to establish?

5. A number of corporations today are working to reengineer corporate thinking and encourage an intrapreneurial environment. What types of steps would you recommend? Offer at least three and explain each.
6. What are five useful rules for innovation?
7. What are three advantages of developing an intrapreneurial philosophy?
8. Identify the four key elements managers should concentrate on to develop an intrapreneurial strategy.
9. Explain the differences between radical and incremental innovation.
10. Identify the five specific entrepreneurial climate factors that organizations need to address in structuring their environment.
11. Why are venture teams emerging as part of a new strategy for many corporations?
12. Of the key intrapreneurial considerations set forth in Table 3.4, which three are of most value to practicing managers? Why?
13. How does an entrepreneur differ from an intrapreneur? Compare and contrast the two.
14. Why is it useful to understand some of the myths that have sprung up about intrapreneurs? Explain, using two of these myths as examples.
15. What exactly is the "interactive process" of intrapreneurship? Be specific.

Experiential Exercise   *Developing Intrapreneurship*

Many ways of developing intrapreneurship exist. Some of these are presented in the following list. Write *yes* next to those that would help develop intrapreneurship and *no* next to those that would not help develop intrapreneurship.

_____   1. Create an innovative climate.

_____   2. Set implicit goals.

_____   3. Provide feedback on performance.

_____   4. Provide positive reinforcement.

_____   5. Encourage structured activity.

_____   6. Develop a well-defined hierarchical structure and stick to it.

_____   7. Tolerate failure.

_____   8. Encourage a bias for action.

_____   9. Make extensive use of formal meetings.

_____   10. Allow bootlegging of ideas.

_____   11. Reward successful personnel.

_____   12. Fire those who make mistakes as a way of creating a good example for others.

_____   13. Make extensive use of informal meetings.

_____   14. Encourage communication throughout the organization.

_____   15. Discourage joint projects and ventures among different departments.

_____   16. Encourage brainstorming.

_____   17. Encourage moderate risks.

_____ 18. Encourage networking with others in the enterprise.

_____ 19. Encourage personnel not to fear failing.

_____ 20. Encourage personnel to be willing to succeed even if it means doing unethical things.

Answers

1. Y	6. N	11. Y	16. Y
2. N	7. Y	12. N	17. N
3. Y	8. Y	13. Y	18. Y
4. Y	9. N	14. Y	19. Y
5. N	10. Y	15. N	20. N

VIDEO CASE **3.1**

Southwest Airlines: Positively Outrageous Leadership

When Southwest Airlines first taxied onto the runway of Dallas's Love Field in 1971, industry gurus predicted it would be a short trip to bankruptcy for the Texas-based airline. But the first short-haul, low-fare, high-frequency, point-to-point carrier took a unique idea and made it fly. Today, Southwest Airlines is the most profitable commercial airline in the world.

But it took more than a wing and a prayer for Southwest to soar to such lofty altitudes. It took a maverick spirit. From the beginning, Southwest has flown against convention. Southwest's fleet of 737s—the newest and safest in the industry—still only makes short hauls to 45 cities. The average flight distance is 394 miles. The airline does not offer baggage transfers or give seat assignments, and the only food it serves passengers is a bag of peanuts. But what Southwest may lack in amenities, it seems to more than make up for in what could be called positively outrageous service. "FUN" is the company's mandate! Leading the way is founder and CEO Herb Kelleher. "Herb Kelleher is definitely the zaniest CEO in the world," Libby Sartain, vice president of Southwest Airlines' People Department, admits. "Where else would you find a CEO who dresses up as Elvis Presley, who's on a first-name basis with 20,000 employees, and who has a heart as big as the state of Texas? His style has fostered an atmosphere where people feel comfortable being themselves—where they can have a good time when they work."

Legendary for his love of laughter, Kelleher calls his unique leadership style *management by fooling around.* "An important part of leadership, I think, is enjoying what you're doing and letting it show to the people that you work with," Kelleher reveals. "And I would much rather have a company that is bound by love, rather than bound by fear." Kelleher's philosophy has been enthusiastically embraced by a workforce that is 85 percent unionized. "Southwest's culture is designed to promote high spirit and avoid complacency. We have little hierarchy here. Our employees are encouraged to be creative and innovative, to break rules when they need to in order to provide good service to our customers," Sartain explains. "If you create the type of environment that a person really feels valued and they feel they make a difference, then they're going to be motivated. That's the type of environment we create here for our employees," Rita Bailey, Southwest's director of training, adds.

Beginning with its new employee orientation, the airline nurtures intrapreneurship by grooming a workforce of leaders. "You can do whatever it takes to keep this airline on top,'' an orientation instructor tells his class of newly hired staffers. At Southwest Airlines's University for People, future managers and supervisors attend a course titled "Leading with Integrity." Through a series of role-playing exercises, employees learn that trust, cooperation, mutual respect, and good communication are the components of success. "An organization that has an esprit, that does things cooperatively and voluntarily rather than through coercion, is the most competitive organization you can have," Kelleher asserts. These guiding principles have earned Southwest Airlines the distinction of being named one of the ten best companies to work for in America.

Employees are valued and recognized in many ways for their achievements. Perhaps the most prestigious is Southwest's "Heroes of the Heart" award. Each year, one outstanding department has its name tattooed on a Southwest Jet. Southwest was the first airline to offer stock options to its employees. Today, employees own approximately 10 percent of the company.

In the lobby of Southwest Airlines's corporate headquarters is a prominent tribute to the men and women of Southwest. It reads: "The people of Southwest Airlines are the creators of what we have become—and what we will be. Our people transformed an idea into a legend. That legend will continue to grow only so long as it is nourished by our people's indomitable spirit, boundless energy, immense goodwill, and burning desire to excel. Our thanks and our love to the people of Southwest Airlines for creating a marvelous family and wondrous airline."

Questions

1. Describe some of the factors needed to reengineer corporate thinking that Southwest Airlines already exhibits.
2. What specific elements of a corporate entrepreneurial strategy are apparent within Southwest Airlines?
3. How has Herb Kelleher structured a climate conducive to entrepreneurial activity?

PART 1

ENTREPRENEURIAL CASE ANALYSIS

Odysseum: An Intrapreneur's Vision at Polaroid

Development of the Vision

In a report on the experience industry for Stanford Research Institute in 1985, James Ogilvy wrote:

> It is no longer enough merely to travel. It's not the mileage that counts but the quality and intensity of the experience. And to guarantee an intense quality experience it is not enough merely to transport a passenger to a distant place, not even to a place that is off the beaten track or visually extravagant. After you've seen Niagara Falls or Yosemite, innocent awe gives way to a thirst for more complex experiences. A childlike gawking at the natural sublime gives way to a more mature hunger for psychological involvement. It is not enough to stand at a distance and witness the wonders of nature: one wants to become involved in the mysteries of culture. One wishes to leave the audience and join the drama of human participation.

Joline Godfrey continually thought about these very words as she searched for *the* idea that could be developed into a new venture for the Polaroid Corporation.

While on vacation in Mexico, Joline stood on the balcony of her hotel room and gazed on the beauty of the sunrise on the landscape of the Acapulco terrain. What a breathtaking experience! She had, in effect, experienced seeing a beautiful happening. Joline thought about this experience and wondered how many people travel to wonderful places on their vacations and "see" various sights but do not "experience" them. The problem, she felt, was due to the fact vacationers quickly snap photographs of many sights and attractions but never stop long enough to gaze, observe, and appreciate what they are seeing. In other words, they never allow themselves the "experience" of what they see.

"What if . . ." she thought, "what if an actual business concept could be developed around this idea of experiences. A business that would provide a variety of creative, interactive games and programs designed for visual fun, enjoyment, and experiences."

This was the beginning of an intrapreneur's vision at Polaroid.

Joline Godfrey

Joline Godfrey was 35 years old, single, and employed at Polaroid for ten years. She had worked during those years in human resources, marketing, and strategic planning. Educated as a social psychologist, Joline had always looked at the "inner side" of projects proposed at Polaroid. Naturally, in a products-oriented company this was not the traditional line of analysis.

More recently her involvement with a new-product task force at Polaroid allowed her to learn the dynamics of creating a new idea and transforming it into a business. She had been on the developmental team that launched the Polaroid Spectra camera. For more than 18 months Joline was involved in designing, producing, and marketing this new product. She found the experience challenging and exhilarating. When this assignment was over, Joline was truly "spoiled" in that she yearned to develop another

---

SOURCE: This case was prepared by Dr. Donald F. Kuratko of the College of Business at Ball State University as a basis for class discussion rather than to illustrate either effective or ineffective handling of an administrative situation. Presented to the Midwest Society for Case Research Workshop, 1989. All rights reserved to the author and to the Midwest Society for Case Research. Copyright © 1989 by Donald F. Kuratko.

concept. The question was what concept and how could she convince Polaroid to give her the autonomy to work on it. Joline realized, however, that Polaroid's research and development teams *always* operated under the limitations that new developments were to be camera or film related. In other words, new ventures were product-related ideas.

Joline decided to introduce this "experience" idea to Polaroid and request a product development team that would attempt to develop a viable business opportunity. Polaroid had just issued its latest mission statement that, in effect, focused on the high-technology market. However, Joline proposed the notion of a products company thinking like a service company. And the best way to accomplish that was to actually establish something in the service industry. To Joline's amazement, Polaroid's executive board agreed to allow her a venture team for six months to develop, test, and establish her concept.

Background on Polaroid

Polaroid began in Boston, Massachusetts, in 1948 with the first retail sales of the now famous "picture in a minute" Polaroid Land Camera. Edwin Land's initial research, in 1926, was on means of polarizing light. In 1932 he and an associate created the Land-Wheelwright Laboratories, Inc., to develop, manufacture, and sell light-polarizing filters. The company's first product was the Polaroid filter; the name *Polaroid* was derived from the fact that the filter was composed of celluloid material that polarized light.

The first two customers of any great size for Land-Wheelwright were Eastman Kodak Company, which signed a contract in 1934 for the purchase of Polascreens, and American Optical Company, which signed a contract in 1935 for the purchase of filter material to be used in Polaroid Day Glasses (sunglasses). The money from these contracts provided the young company with funds to continue its development of Polaroid filter products. An additional $750,000 supplied by two investment banking firms in 1937 (in the form of a private placement) enabled the company to continue its search for profitable applications for the filter.

Polaroid's sales grew from $142,000 in 1937 to $1,481,000 in 1948, most of the increase represented by sales of Polaroid filter material for use in sunglasses. In 1949, the first full year of sales for the Polaroid camera, the firm's sales more than quadrupled (to $6.7 million) over those of the previous year. Twenty-seven years later the company's sales broke the $800 million mark, proving to all the skeptics that what they had considered a mere "fad" was, in fact, one of the most dramatic achievements in the history of photography. In the 28-year period, from 1947 to 1975, Polaroid's sales grew at an average annual compounded rate of more than 25 percent, while profits and the common stock price advanced by more than 17 percent per year. In an accomplishment matched by only a handful of companies, Polaroid's average price/earnings ratio during this entire period was 44. By 1969 each dollar invested in Polaroid common stock in 1948 had grown to more than $500.

Today, the Polaroid Corporation designs, manufactures, and markets a variety of products primarily in the instant-image-recording fields. These include instant cameras and films, magnetic media, light-polarizing filters and lenses, and diversified chemical, optical, and commercial products. The principal company products are used in amateur and professional photography, industry, science, medicine, and education. Selected financial data for 1985 include the following (in millions):

Current assets	$1,035.7	Sales	$1,295.2
Inventory	335.0	EBIT	62.5
Total assets	1,384.7	EAT	36.9
Current liabilities	337.9		

Some of Polaroid's major products are cameras that focus and control exposure automatically. These cameras use advanced computer-like circuitry to make more than 30 complex focusing and exposure decisions within fifty-thousandths of a second. The cameras, film, accessories, and services involved are collectively called the Spectra System. This system was Polaroid's major product innovation for 1986.*

Through the years Polaroid's strategy was committed to the proprietary aspects of manufacturing. Polaroid has never appeared to be interested in diver-

---

*Background information adapted from Michael E. Porter, *Cases in Competitive Strategy* (New York: The Free Press, 1983), 76–78; and Samuel C. Certo and J. Paul Peter, *Strategic Management* (New York: Random House, 1988), 273–74.

sification. Every new product introduced since 1948 has related completely to the instant photographic process.

One interesting aspect of Polaroid strategy was the total involvement of Edward W. Land. His entrepreneurial spirit was apparent through the years as he conveyed a management style that has been described as more of a philosophy than a direction. According to researcher Michael E. Porter, "Annual meetings at Polaroid were always a unique experience for stockholders; sales and earnings figures were hardly ever mentioned. At typical meetings Land would demonstrate one or more new products or processes he and his large research team had developed. Most often these demonstrations, which in many cases were much like seminars or lectures, were totally unrelated to the products the company intended to introduce in the future." From time to time Land would remind his stockholders why Polaroid existed: "Our function is to sense a deep human need . . . then satisfy it. . . . Our company has been dedicated throughout its life to making only those things which others cannot make. . . . We proceed from basic science to highly desirable products."*

The Early Concept

Using their Polaroid knowledge and experience, Joline Godfrey's venture team developed a photo game titled Odysseum with programs that emphasize *SEE*. The name is actually a combination of Odysseus, the great explorer in ancient Greek mythology, and Lyceum, which represented a place of entertainment. Thus, it is a place to explore for entertainment. The game would be played by vacationers using 35mm cameras to take pictures that would fit a riddle provided for them. The players would use the surrounding environment (terrain, landscape, buildings, artifacts, etc.), fellow players, or even passersby to take photographs to illustrate various captions in the riddle. Thus, the game could develop into a treasure hunt for visual clues that would solve the riddle. Participants would gather together at the end of the specified period in order to compare their photos (in slide format for all to share) and discuss their discoveries, observations, and perspectives.

With this concept, vacationers would analyze sights far more carefully, and, through the fun of a visual game, they would begin to experience many of the beautiful, though sometimes ignored, parts of the location. What a wonderful way to help people appreciate the sights of their vacation much more than ever before!

As wonderful as this idea seemed, however, the venture team needed to develop it into a *profitable new business* for Polaroid. A profitable new business is defined by Polaroid as a $200 million business. Although that seemed inappropriate for the Odysseum concept, the team proposed to develop five distinct $20 million businesses. However, this could be accomplished only if the first attempt at the venture proved successful.

Polaroid agreed to allow Joline and her small team (three people) to test their concept in the marketplace if a sponsor could be found to volunteer its site. The Sonesta Beach Hotel in Bermuda was approached, and it agreed to be the test site.

Joline launched a three-month trial effort with vacationers at the Sonesta Beach Hotel. The games were offered at no charge in order to attract more people during the trial run. Although the attendance never reached the numbers Joline had hoped for, those that did attend and participate truly enjoyed the experience. Thus, once in the door, participants were convinced the "seeing experience" was worth their time. The problem was getting vacationers convinced to try it. Only large numbers of participants could make this concept a profitable reality at Polaroid.

Polaroid's Reaction

Polaroid reacted to Joline's trial effort by analyzing other possible outlets or uses for her idea. Jerry Sudbey, vice president of marketing, saw a number of possibilities in using Joline's idea to sell Polaroid products. In other words, Polaroid could sponsor these "games" if participants purchased cameras and equipment from Polaroid. Thus, it could be a unique marketing tool. A number of other similar alternatives were suggested, all revolving around the use of Joline's work to sell products. Richard Clapp, assistant to the president at Polaroid, believed it was time

---

*Porter, *Competitive Strategy*, 78.

to pull Joline's team in and put members under the marketing division to work these product/promotion ideas into Polaroid's traditional emphasis.

Joline Godfrey was called to an executive board meeting where the fate of Odysseum would be decided. With a few days to go before this scheduled meeting, Joline and her team prepared their strategy for keeping the project a separate entity with potential for venture success.

The Strategy

Joline and her team established a menu of programs that would provide entertainment from a visual perspective. This menu is described here.

Photo Odyssey

Teams of players are given automatic 35mm cameras for interpreting a series of captions such as "Off The Wall" or "Human Exposure." The teams use their surrounding environment, fellow players, and passers-by to take photographs to illustrate the assigned captions. The challenge is for each team to express its creativity and illustrate the captions in the most unique way possible. A rousing finale slide show presents each team's creative results.

Private Eye

Teams of "detective agencies," outfitted with authentic investigator's paraphernalia, "snoop" out a series of clues that require them to draw on their skills of persuasion, observation, negotiation, and "interagency" cooperation to solve a puzzling mystery.

Power Vision

A learning workshop to stimulate creativity and innovation by developing essential but often neglected visual skills, the one-hour Power Vision program leads participants through a five-part training program in the skill of seeing: Discovery, Observation, Analysis, Perspective, Imagination, Focus, and Appreciation.

Advanced Power Vision

A two-day applied training session includes a diagnostic workshop covering baseline visual skills as well as lectures and small-group discussions on the application of visual skills to product development, communications, product design, and corporate cul-

ture. Participants play a special session of Photo Odysee, which allows them to experience their new skills, and they also produce their own dazzling audiovisual show as a finale.

Mask

Participants create a lightweight, fast-drying mask of their partner that then can be decorated to wear at a *bal masque* or displayed as a "place mask" at dinner or as a work of art. "Mask" provides a relaxing yet exciting experience for smaller groups.

Scrutiny for the Bounty

An exciting contemporary treasure hunt challenges teams to use strategic and deductive skills in locating the hidden prize in a series of clues. The level of difficulty can be adjusted; each program is specially designed for the location and group.

READJUSTMENT OF THE MARKET

The expanded menu of games was not the only change in strategy for Joline. She also decided to readjust the market niche at which Odysseum was aiming. Rather than limiting her market to the vacationers at specific resorts around the world, Godfrey also would position Odysseum into the corporate meeting industry. The reason for this came from "listening to the market," as she put it. During the three-month trial period, Joline was contacted by a number of large corporations that were sending their managers on corporate retreats or to off-site meetings in Bermuda. They inquired about her unique games, and, in many cases, their people became participants. This led Joline to the realization of a stronger market niche. She would aim the visual games at the "adult play" portion of corporate off-site meetings. Joline and her team gathered research that showed major corporations hold an estimated 900,000 off-site meetings annually. In addition, of the $35 billion companies spend on these meetings, $5.2 billion is earmarked for specialty programs that educate, entertain, or amuse participants.

For expanding into the corporate meeting market, the team developed Odysseum's strategy to relate specifically to the importance of corporations understanding adult experiences. Joline explained:

> Adult play is more sophisticated and challenging because it does more than simply fill time.

Ashley Montagu has said that "adults are nothing more than deteriorated children." To the extent that the experiences you provide fill time with absorbing opportunities for discovery and mastery, these "deteriorated children" will return home refreshed—renewed with the energy and enthusiasm of the playful child. With this in mind, there are a few rules to consider when designing and selecting the kinds of experiences you want to offer on your next incentive trip:

1. Make it participatory. The more involved your "participants" are in creating the fun, the more pride and achievement they'll feel. Active, absorbing experiences produce strong memories.
2. Make it fun, enriching, entertaining. Your attendees will tell you they "want to have a good time." When they receive added value with their fun (a tidbit learned, a new skill mastered), they go home truly enriched.
3. Eliminate all possibility of participant feelings of anxiety, rejection, or incompetence. Those are experiences of childhood play that don't need to be re-created.
4. Make sure your programs are facilitated by professionals who can provide an environment that is conducive to positive group interaction.
5. Give opportunities for camaraderie. Design groups and group identity to enhance feelings of shared spirit, pleasure, and fun. The Miller Beer commercials work because many people yearn to feel like "one of the gang."
6. Make sure there's a "take-home" item that will trigger memories of the experience. It's better to spend less money on a funny or memorable artifact than more money on a souvenir that has no inherent meaning and will simply be stored in a closet.

If Odysseum could capture a major portion of this market in addition to its current market of vacationers, then the team could establish a more lucrative business for Polaroid. In other words, this new market allowed Joline to at least talk to Polaroid's executive board about the opportunity to establish a $200 million business.

The Meeting

The meeting day came, and Joline felt extremely well prepared with her new strategy to keep Odysseum alive. However, as the meeting progressed, she realized the company was seeking to put the concept into marketing as a tool for selling cameras. Joline realized this was now the day she would quit or be fired because she was not going to give up her idea as just another marketing ploy for camera sales.

Joline pressed hard during her presentation to the board and emphasized her dedication to this concept as a viable business opportunity. During a question-and-answer period, she refused to relent on this idea becoming anything but what she envisioned—a full-blown business concept.

The president and CEO of Polaroid, I. MacAllister Booth, stood up at the close of the meeting and thanked Joline for her hard work and courage to stick with this concept. He assured her Polaroid would decide the fate of Odysseum based on what was best for Polaroid. They promised her a decision by 8:00 A.M. the next day.

Questions

1. As a member of Polaroid's executive board, what decision would you make concerning Odysseum? Why?
2. If you were Joline Godfrey, what would you do if Polaroid did not accept your idea?
3. What major problems do you see for this venture to succeed at Polaroid?
4. What benefits can be realized by Polaroid in accepting the idea?
5. Has Joline developed a feasible venture idea? Why or why not? Be specific.

EXERCISES

Determine Your EQ (Entrepreneurial Quotient)

- *Definition:* An "EN-TRE-PRE-NEUR" is an individual who creates, develops, and manages a business venture, with personal risk, for a potential profit.
- *Description:* The EQ, more commonly known as the Entrepreneur Quotient, is a self-directed learning tool. It is not a test, but rather a method by which an individual can compare his or her own personal characteristics with those of successful entrepreneurs.
- *Instructions:* Answer each question to the best of your ability. There is no time limit. Correct answers are given to each question to further stimulate your interest.
- *Interpretation:* Remember, this is not a test. If you cannot answer any of the questions, do not be alarmed. You can learn to be an entrepreneur. For those individuals who prefer a scoring format, the procedure below provides rough guidelines.
- *Correct Number:*
  100 If you're not already an entrepreneur, you should be.
  85 You're compatible. Get started.
  70 You have potential. Study the rules.
  55 You're behind, but you can still make it.
  40 You don't seem to be interested, but that doesn't mean you can't make it.
  25 You still have a chance. Go for it.
  0 You're probably dead.

1. As a child, did you have a paper route, sell candy or magazine subscriptions, or shine shoes for money?

   Yes _____   No _____

2. Did you come from a family that owned a business?

   Yes _____   No _____

3. Do you have a relative who is in business?

   Yes _____   No _____

4. Have you ever worked for a small firm where you had close contact with the owner?

   Yes _____   No _____

5. Are you between the ages of 16 and 44?

   Yes _____   No _____

6. Have you ever worked for a large company where you worked closely with a top manager?

   Yes _____   No _____

7. Have you ever been fired from a job?

   Yes _____   No _____

8. Do you have experience in organization, planning, budgeting, personnel, marketing, advertising, administration, evaluation?

   Yes _____   No _____

9. If you are married, is your spouse supportive of the personal and financial risks involved in starting a business?

   Yes _____   No _____

10. Do you have a library of "self-help" success books?

   Yes _____   No _____

SOURCE: The EQ was created by James W. Kuntz for use by the Institute for the Development of Entrepreneur Abilities, Copyright 1984, App. H. From *Entrepreneurship Education,* ed. Kathryn Greenwood, Garry Bice, Raymond LaForge, and Dianne Wimberley (School of Occupational and Adult Education, College of Education, Oklahoma State University, Stillwater, OK 74078). Reprinted with permission.

11. Are you respected by your peers at work and by your friends in other areas of your life?

    Yes _____   No _____

12. Are you inquisitive, inventive, creative, innovative, and aggressive?

    Yes _____   No _____

13. Do you enjoy solving problems?

    Yes _____   No _____

14. Would you rather be your own boss?

    Yes _____   No _____

15. Do you like to make things happen?

    Yes _____   No _____

16. Do you enjoy taking personal and financial risks?

    Yes _____   No _____

17. Were you a first-born child in your family?

    Yes _____   No _____

18. Are you male or female?

    Male _____   Female _____

19. Are you married or single?

    Married _____   Single _____

20. Do you consider yourself a free and independent spirit?

    Yes _____   No _____

21. Do you have a high need for achievement?

    Yes _____   No _____

22. Did you have a good relationship with your father?

    Yes _____   No _____

23. Small businesses employ over 50 percent of the workforce, generate 50 percent of all new jobs, and account for 44 percent of the gross national product.

    True _____   False _____

24. Do you take rejection personally?

    Yes _____   No _____

25. Do you like to move around a lot?

    Yes _____   No _____

26. Is it true that entrepreneurs make good managers?

    Yes _____   No _____

27. To be a successful entrepreneur, an individual needs a lot of good luck.

    True _____   False _____

28. Successful entrepreneurs often use the advice of expert outside consultants.

    True _____   False _____

29. Do you believe that you can control your own destiny?

    Yes _____   No _____

30. Are you a consistent goal setter and a results-oriented individual?

    Yes _____   No _____

31. Have you ever been forced to move, gone through a divorce, or suffered a death of a spouse or parent?

    Yes _____   No _____

32. Do you have specific experience in the area of business you plan to go into?

    Yes _____   No _____

33. Personal savings is the most important source of start-up funds for entrepreneurs.

    True _____   False _____

34. Do you have managerial skills?

    Yes _____   No _____

35. Are you willing to work longer hours for the same salary you now make?

    Yes _____   No _____

36. Do you have a college degree or special skills and knowledge from a vocational or technical school?

    Yes _____   No _____

37. Do you know how to raise money for starting a business?

    Yes _____   No _____

38. Do you like people?

    Yes _____   No _____

39. Can you make quick decisions?

    Yes _____   No _____

40. Do you have a high energy level?

    Yes _____   No _____

41. Do your friends and acquaintances place a great deal of faith and trust in you?

    Yes _____   No _____

42. Do you follow through with implementation when a decision has been made?

    Yes _____   No _____

43. Do you believe in your own power to accomplish goals?

    Yes _____   No _____

44. Are you willing to change your negative habit patterns?

    Yes _____   No _____

45. Do you have high moral and ethical standards?

    Yes _____   No _____

46. Do you have a good idea or product and/or know how to get one?

    Yes _____   No _____

47. Do you know how to tap the power of your subconscious mind?

    Yes _____   No _____

48. Are you dedicated and committed to being in business for yourself?

    Yes _____   No _____

49. Do you know how to develop a business plan for presentation to a group of investors?

    Yes _____   No _____

50. Can you inspire and motivate other individuals?

    Yes _____   No _____

51. Do you know how to use radio, TV, direct mail, and space advertising?

    Yes _____   No _____

52. Do you know what the four Ps of marketing are?

    Yes _____   No _____

53. Are you familiar with the OPM principle?

    Yes _____   No _____

54. Do you know how to multiply your talents?

    Yes _____   No _____

55. Do you know how the 20/80 rule affects success?

    Yes _____   No _____

56. Have you ever made an assessment of your personality characteristics?

    Yes _____   No _____

57. Have you ever determined your net worth?

    Yes _____   No _____

58. Do you know what the 12 laws of universal success are?

    Yes _____   No _____

59. Have you ever explored your career potential?

    Yes _____   No _____

60. Do you believe in the power and success of self-directed learning?

    Yes _____   No _____

61. Do you wake up happy 99 percent of the time?

    Yes _____   No _____

62. Do you provide a period during each day for thinking, studying, planning, or relaxation?

    Yes _____   No _____

63. Do you consider yourself ambitious?

    Yes _____   No _____

64. Do you enjoy power, control, and authority?

    Yes _____   No _____

65. Would you be willing to quit your job today and start at the bottom?

    Yes _____   No _____

66. Do you know how to determine the "break-even" point?

    Yes _____   No _____

67. Do you know what motivates customer behavior and buying habits?

    Yes _____   No _____

68. Student organizations such as ATA, VICA, DECA, FFA, and others help students learn about entrepreneurship.

    True _____   False _____

69. Do you know where to get information on franchising?

    Yes _____   No _____

70. Do you know the rules of buying an existing business?

    Yes _____   No _____

71. Are you willing to follow a proven success system even if it differs from yours?

    Yes _____   No _____

72. The National Federation of Business is the largest small business organization in the United States.

    True _____   False _____

73. Can you accept failure without admitting defeat?

    Yes _____   No _____

74. Do you know how to project cash flow?

    Yes _____   No _____

75. Do you know how to read a balance sheet and profit and loss statement?

    Yes _____   No _____

76. Are you familiar with the current business and tax laws?

    Yes _____   No _____

77. Are you familiar with the laws affecting recruitment and selection of personnel?

    Yes _____   No _____

78. Do you know, or are you willing to learn, how to sell?

    Yes _____   No _____

79. Do you consider yourself enthusiastic, imaginative, and tenacious?

    Yes _____   No _____

80. Are you willing to participate in both the profits and losses of a business?

    Yes _____   No _____

81. Do you know how to protect your ideas from thieves?

    Yes _____   No _____

82. Do you have a savings account?

    Yes _____   No _____

83. Are you familiar with the principles of bartering?

    Yes _____   No _____

84. Are you familiar with the rules and laws pertaining to investments?

    Yes _____   No _____

85. Are you familiar with the 30,000 occupational titles in the United States?

    Yes _____   No _____

86. Do you know how to get free publicity for your product or service?

    Yes _____   No _____

87. Are you dissatisfied with your present employment or school work?

    Yes _____   No _____

88. Women entrepreneurs represent about 7 percent of all self-employed.

    True _____   False _____

89. Minority entrepreneurs represent about 5.5 percent of all self-employed.

    True _____   False _____

90. On the average, incorporated self-employed persons make more than self-employed proprietors.

    True _____   False _____

91. On the average, women entrepreneurs make less than men.

    True _____   False _____

92. Do you know where to find business and operating ratios for specific industries?

    Yes _____   No _____

93. Are you familiar with the differences between a general corporation, partnership, subchapter S, and proprietorship?

    Yes _____   No _____

94. Do you know how to find adult training programs in entrepreneurship?

    Yes _____   No _____

95. Are you familiar with the services offered by the SBA?

    Yes _____   No _____

96. Are you familiar with the services offered by the Minority Business Development Agency and the Minority Business Development Centers?

    Yes _____   No _____

97. Are you familiar with federal government contracting and R&D monies available to small business?

    Yes _____   No _____

98. If you are a parent or teenager, are you familiar with entrepreneur programs available in high schools and colleges?

    Yes _____   No _____

99. Are you familiar with business control systems such as accounting, record keeping, financial analysis, bookkeeping, profit center, collections, forecasting, etc.?

    Yes _____   No _____

100. Do you know the secrets of working with bankers, accountants, and attorneys?

    Yes _____   No _____

101. The failure rate of most small-business start-ups is about 80 percent within the first three years.

    True _____   False _____

102. Immigrants have a high rate of entrepreneurship in the United States.

    True _____   False _____

103. Over 90 percent of all businesses in the United States are small, employ fewer than 20 persons, and are organized as sole proprietorships.

    True _____   False _____

Correct Answers

1. Yes	15. Yes	29. Yes	43. Yes
2. Yes	16. Yes	30. Yes	44. Yes
3. Yes	17. Yes	31. Yes	45. Yes
4. Yes	18. Either	32. Yes	46. Yes
5. Yes	19. Either	33. True	47. Yes
6. Yes	20. Yes	34. Yes	48. Yes
7. Yes	21. Yes	35. Yes	49. Yes
8. Yes	22. Yes	36. Yes	50. Yes
9. Yes	23. True	37. Yes	51. Yes
10. Yes	24. No	38. Yes	52. Yes
11. Yes	25. Yes	39. Yes	53. Yes
12. Yes	26. No	40. Yes	54. Yes
13. Yes	27. True	41. Yes	55. Yes
14. Yes	28. True	42. Yes	56. Yes

57. Yes	69. Yes	81. Yes	93. Yes
58. Yes	70. Yes	82. Yes	94. Yes
59. Yes	71. Yes	83. Yes	95. Yes
60. Yes	72. True	84. Yes	96. Yes
61. Yes	73. Yes	85. Yes	97. Yes
62. Yes	74. Yes	86. Yes	98. Yes
63. Yes	75. Yes	87. Yes	99. Yes
64. Yes	76. Yes	88. True	100. Yes
65. Yes	77. Yes	89. True	101. True
66. Yes	78. Yes	90. True	102. True
67. Yes	79. Yes	91. True	103. True
68. True	80. Yes	92. Yes	

THE ENTREPRENEURIAL PERSPECTIVE

Chapter 4

Understanding the Entrepreneurial Perspective in Individuals

CHAPTER OBJECTIVES

1. To describe the three major sources of information useful in profiling the entrepreneurial perspective

2. To identify and discuss the most commonly cited characteristics found in successful entreprcncurs

3. To discuss the "dark side" of entrepreneurship

4. To identify and describe the different types of risk entrepreneurs face as well as the major causes of stress for these individuals and the ways they can handle stress

5. To examine entrepreneurial motivation

The study of new venture creation began with some reasonable assumptions about the psychological characteristics of "entrepreneurs." Through the years, more and more of these personological characteristics have been discarded, debunked, or at the very least, found to have been measured ineffectively. The result has been a tendency to concentrate on almost anything except the individual. Economic circumstances are important; marketing is important; finance is important; even public agency assistance is important. But none of these will, alone, create a new venture. For that we need a person, in whose mind all of the possibilities come together, who believes that innovation is possible, and who has the motivation to persist until the job is done. Person, process, and choice: for these we need a truly psychological perspective on new venture creation.

Kelly G. Shaver and Linda R. Scott,
Entrepreneurship Theory and Practice

THE ENTREPRENEURIAL PERSPECTIVE

Every person has the potential and free choice to pursue a career as an entrepreneur. Exactly what motivates individuals to make a choice for entrepreneurship has not been identified, at least not as one single event, characteristic, or trait. As we demonstrated in Chapter 2, researchers are continually striving to learn more about the entire entrepreneurial process in order to better understand the driving forces within entrepreneurs.[1] Throughout this book, the chapters are designed to concentrate on learning the discipline of entrepreneurship. However, this chapter is devoted to a more psychological look at entrepreneurs.

This chapter describes the most common characteristics associated with successful entrepreneurs as well as the elements associated with the "dark side" of entrepreneurship. In this manner we can become more acquainted with the complete perspective involved with entrepreneurial behavior. We call this the **entrepreneurial perspective** an individual exhibits. Although certainly not an exact science, this perspective provides an interesting look at the entrepreneurial potential within every individual.

---

[1] See, for example, William D. Bygrave and Charles W. Hofer, "Theorizing about Entrepreneurship," *Entrepreneurship Theory and Practice* (winter 1991): 12–22; and Ivan Bull and Gary E. Willard, "Towards a Theory of Entrepreneurship," *Journal of Business Venturing* 8 (May 1993): 183–96.

Who Are Entrepreneurs?

Frank Carney, the founder of Pizza Hut, Inc., once described entrepreneurs as the cornerstone of the American enterprise system, the self-renewing agents for our economic environment. Normally defined as risk takers in new-venture creations, entrepreneurs are uniquely optimistic, hard-driving, committed individuals who derive great satisfaction from being independent. Starting a new business requires more than just an idea; it requires a special person, an entrepreneur, who uses sound judgment and planning along with risk taking to ensure the success of his or her own business.

Entrepreneurs, driven by an intense commitment and determined perseverance, work very hard. They are optimists who see the cup half full rather than half empty. They strive for integrity. They burn with the competitive desire to excel. They use failure as a tool for learning. They have enough confidence in themselves to believe they personally can make a major difference in the final outcome of their ventures.

The substantial failure rate of new ventures attests to the difficulty of entrepreneurship. Inexperience and incompetent management are the main reasons for failure. But what are the factors for success? Do they apply to all components of entrepreneurship? These are some of the issues we shall explore in this chapter.

Sources of Research on Entrepreneurs

Three major sources of information supply data related to the entrepreneurial perspective. The first source is publications, research-based as well as popular.[2] The following are among the more important of these publications:

1. *Technical and professional journals.* These are refereed journals that contain articles dealing with research—methodology, results, and application of results—that are well designed and tightly structured. Examples include the *Journal of Small Business Management, Entrepreneurship Theory and Practice, Journal of Business and Entrepreneurship, Journal of Business Venturing, Strategic Management Journal, Journal of Small Business Strategy,* and the *Small Business Forum.*

2. *Textbooks on entrepreneurship.* These texts typically address the operation of small firms and nonprofit organizations. Sections or chapters are frequently devoted to research on entrepreneurs. Examples include *New Venture Creation, Effective Small Business Management,* and *Entrepreneurial Strategy.*[3]

3. *Books about entrepreneurship.* Most of these books are written as practitioners' "how-to" guides. Some deal with the problems facing the individual who starts a business; others deal with a specific aspect of the subject. Examples include *Startup, In the Owner's Chair, Small Business: An Entrepreneur's Plan,* and *The Business Planning Guide.*[4]

---

[2] For more on publications, see John A. Hornaday, "Research about Living Entrepreneurs," *Encyclopedia of Entrepreneurship,* ed. Calvin Kent, Donald Sexton, and Karl Vesper (Englewood Cliffs: Prentice-Hall, 1982), 21–22.

[3] Jeffry A. Timmons, *New Venture Creation* (Homewood, IL: Irwin, 1990); Richard M. Hodgetts and Donald F. Kuratko, *Effective Small Business Management* (Fort Worth: The Dryden Press, 1995); and Donald F. Kuratko and Harold P. Welsch, *Entrepreneurial Strategy* (Fort Worth: The Dryden Press, 1994).

[4] William J. Stolze, *Startup: An Entrepreneur's Guide to Launching and Managing a New Venture* (Hawthorne, NJ: Career Press, 1992); Ronald W. Torrence, *In the Owner's Chair* (Englewood Cliffs: Prentice-Hall, 1992); Lee A. Eckert, J. D. Ryan, and Robert J. Ray, *Small Business: An Entrepreneur's Plan* (Fort Worth: The Dryden Press, 1993); and David N. Bangs, *The Business Planning Guide,* 7th ed. (Chicago: Upstart Publishing, 1995).

4. *Biographies or autobiographies of entrepreneurs.* Examples include *Going for It* and *Boone.*[5]

5. *Compendiums about entrepreneurs.* These are collections that deal with several selected individuals or that present statistical information or overviews of perceived general trends. Examples include *The Entrepreneurs,*[6] which is a compendium of information about selected living entrepreneurs, and *The Enterprising Americans,*[7] which provides a summary of trends.

6. *News periodicals.* Many newspapers and news periodicals run stories on entrepreneurs either regularly or periodically. Examples include *Business Week, Forbes, Fortune,* and *The Wall Street Journal.*

7. *Venture periodicals.* A growing number of new magazines are concerned specifically with new business ventures. Most, if not all, of each issue's contents are related to entrepreneurship. Examples include *Black Enterprise, Entrepreneur, In Business, Inc.,* and *Family Business.*

8. *Newsletters.* A number of newsletters are devoted exclusively to entrepreneurship. The *Liaison* of the U.S. Association for Small Business and Entrepreneurship is an example.

9. *Proceedings of conferences.* Publications relating to annual or periodic conferences deal at least in part with entrepreneurship. Examples include *Proceedings of the Academy of Management, Proceedings of the International Council for Small Business, Proceedings of the U.S. Association for Small Business and Entrepreneurship,* and *Frontiers in Entrepreneurship Research* (proceedings of the Babson College Annual Entrepreneurship Conference).

10. *Government publications.* The U.S. government publishes a wealth of information on entrepreneurship, small-business operations, and specific small businesses. Examples include myriad Small Business Administration (SBA) pamphlets.

The second major source of information about the entrepreneurial perspective is direct observation of practicing entrepreneurs. Through the use of interviews, surveys, and case studies, the experiences of individual entrepreneurs can be related. Analysis of these experiences can provide insights into the traits, characteristics, and personalities of individual entrepreneurs and leads to the discovery of commonalities that help explain the perspective.

The final source of entrepreneurial information is speeches and presentations (including seminars) by practicing entrepreneurs. This source may not be as thorough as the other two, but it does provide an opportunity to learn about the entrepreneurial perspective. Entrepreneur-in-residence programs at various universities illustrate the added value oral presentations may have in educating people about entrepreneurship.

Common Characteristics Associated with Entrepreneurs

A review of the literature related to entrepreneurial characteristics reveals the existence of a large number of factors that can be consolidated into a much smaller set of profile

---

[5] Victor Kiam, *Going for It* (New York: Morrow, 1986); and T. Boone Pickens, *Boone* (Boston: Houghton-Mifflin, 1987).

[6] Robert L. Shook, *The Entrepreneurs* (New York: Harper & Row, 1980). See also Robert Sobel, *The Entrepreneurs: Explorations within the American Business Tradition* (New York: Weybright and Talley, 1974).

[7] John Chamberlin, *The Enterprising Americans: A Business History of the United States* (New York: Harper & Row, 1963).

dimensions. For example, if the work of John Kao is considered, 11 common characteristics can be identified:[8]

- Total commitment, determination, and perseverance
- Drive to achieve and grow
- Opportunity and goal orientation
- Taking initiative and personal responsibility
- Persistent problem solving
- Realism and a sense of humor
- Seeking and using feedback
- Internal locus of control
- Calculated risk taking and risk seeking
- Low need for status and power
- Integrity and reliability

Stevenson and Gumpert present an outline of the entrepreneurial organization that reveals such characteristics as imagination, flexibility, and willingness to accept risks.[9] Gartner examined the literature and found a diversity of reported characteristics.[10] Hornaday examined various research sources and formulated a list of 42 characteristics often attributed to entrepreneurs (see Table 4.1).

In the simplest of theoretical forms for studying entrepreneurship, entrepreneurs cause entrepreneurship. That is, $E + f(e)$ states that entrepreneurship is a function of the entrepreneur. Thus, the continuous examination of entrepreneurial characteristics does help in the evolving understanding of entrepreneurship.[11] One author provides the following description:

> Would-be entrepreneurs live in a sea of dreams. Their destinations are private islands—places to build, create, and transform their particular dreams into reality. Being an entrepreneur entails envisioning your island, and even more important, it means getting in the boat and rowing to your island. Some leave the shore and drift aimlessly in the shallow waters close to shore, while others paddle furiously and get nowhere, because they don't know how to paddle or steer. Worst of all are those who remain on the shore of the mainland, afraid to get in the boat. Yet, all those dreamers may one day be entrepreneurs if they can marshal the resources—external and internal—needed to transform their dreams into reality.
>
> Everyone has dreams. We all dream while asleep, even if we don't remember dreaming. Entrepreneurs' dreams are different. Their dreams are not limited to dreams about fantasy islands or fast cars. Theirs are about business.[12]

Entrepreneurship also has been characterized as the interaction of the following skills: inner control, planning and goal setting, risk taking, innovation, reality perception, use of feedback, decision making, human relations, and independence. In addition, many people believe successful entrepreneurs are individuals who are not afraid to fail.

---

[8] John J. Kao, *The Entrepreneur* (Englewood Cliffs: Prentice-Hall, 1991).

[9] Howard H. Stevenson and David E. Gumpert, "The Heart of Entrepreneurship," *Harvard Business Review* (March/April 1985): 85–94.

[10] See William B. Gartner, "Some Suggestions for Research on Entrepreneurial Traits and Characteristics," *Entrepreneurship Theory and Practice* (fall 1989): 27–38.

[11] Ibid.

[12] Lloyd E. Shefsky, *Entrepreneurs Are Made Not Born* (New York: McGraw-Hill, Inc., 1994).

TABLE 4.1	CHARACTERISTICS OFTEN ATTRIBUTED TO ENTREPRENEURS

1. Confidence	22. Responsibility
2. Perseverance, determination	23. Foresight
3. Energy, diligence	24. Accuracy, thoroughness
4. Resourcefulness	25. Cooperativeness
5. Ability to take calculated risks	26. Profit orientation
6. Dynamism, leadership	27. Ability to learn from mistakes
7. Optimism	28. Sense of power
8. Need to achieve	29. Pleasant personality
9. Versatility; knowledge of product, market, machinery, technology	30. Egotism
10. Creativity	31. Courage
11. Ability to influence others	32. Imagination
12. Ability to get along well with people	33. Perceptiveness
13. Initiative	34. Toleration for ambiguity
14. Flexibility	35. Aggressiveness
15. Intelligence	36. Capacity for enjoyment
16. Orientation to clear goals	37. Efficacy
17. Positive response to challenges	38. Commitment
18. Independence	39. Ability to trust workers
19. Responsiveness to suggestions and criticism	40. Sensitivity to others
20. Time competence, efficiency	41. Honesty, integrity
21. Ability to make decisions quickly	42. Maturity, balance

SOURCE: John A. Hornaday, "Research about Living Entrepreneurs," in *Encyclopedia of Entrepreneurship*, ed. Kent/Sexton/Vesper, © 1982, 26–27. Adapted by permission of Prentice-Hall, Englewood Cliffs, NJ.

New characteristics are continually being added to this ever-growing list. At this point, however, let us examine some of the most often cited entrepreneurial characteristics. Although this list admittedly is incomplete, it does provide important insights into the entrepreneurial perspective.

COMMITMENT, DETERMINATION, AND PERSEVERANCE   More than any other factor, total dedication to success as an entrepreneur can overcome obstacles and setbacks. Sheer determination and an unwavering commitment to succeed often win out against odds many people would consider insurmountable. They also can compensate for personal shortcomings. Often, entrepreneurs with a high-potential venture and a plan that includes venture capital financing can expect investors to measure their commitment in several ways. Examples include a willingness to mortgage their house, take a cut in pay, sacrifice family time, and reduce their standard of living.

DRIVE TO ACHIEVE   Entrepreneurs are self-starters who appear to others to be internally driven by a strong desire to compete, to excel against self-imposed standards, and to pursue and attain challenging goals. This need to achieve has been well documented in the entrepreneurial literature, beginning with David McClelland's pioneering work on motivation in the 1950s and 1960s.[13] High achievers tend to be moderate risk takers. They examine a situation, determine how to increase the odds of winning, and then push ahead. As a result, high-risk decisions for the average businessperson often are moderate risks for the well-prepared high achiever.

OPPORTUNITY ORIENTATION   One clear pattern among successful, growth-minded entrepreneurs is their focus on opportunity rather than on resources, structure, or strategy. They start with the opportunity and let their understanding of it guide other important issues. They are goal oriented in their pursuit of opportunities. Setting high but attainable goals enables them to focus their energies, to selectively sort out opportunities, and to know when to say no. Their goal orientation also helps them to define priorities and provides them with measures of how well they are performing.

INITIATIVE AND RESPONSIBILITY   Historically, the entrepreneur has been viewed as an independent and highly self-reliant innovator. Most researchers agree that effective entrepreneurs actively seek and take the initiative. They willingly put themselves in situations where they are personally responsible for the success or failure of the operation. They like to take the initiative in solving a problem or in filling a vacuum where no leadership exists. They also like situations where their personal impact on problems can be measured. This is the action-oriented nature of the entrepreneur expressing itself.

PERSISTENT PROBLEM SOLVING   Entrepreneurs are not intimidated by difficult situations. In fact, their self-confidence and general optimism seem to translate into a view that the impossible just takes a little longer. Yet they are neither aimless nor foolhardy in their relentless attack on a problem or an obstacle that is impeding business operations. If the task is extremely easy or perceived to be unsolvable, entrepreneurs often will give up sooner than others. Simple problems bore them; unsolvable ones do not warrant their time. Moreover, although entrepreneurs are extremely persistent, they are realistic in recognizing what they can and cannot do and where they can get help in solving difficult but unavoidable tasks.

SEEKING FEEDBACK   Effective entrepreneurs often are described as quick learners. Unlike many people, however, they also have a strong desire to know how well they are doing and how they might improve their performance. In attempting to make these determinations, they actively seek out and use feedback. Feedback is also central to their learning from their mistakes and setbacks.

INTERNAL LOCUS OF CONTROL   Successful entrepreneurs believe in themselves. They do not believe the success or failure of their venture will be governed by fate, luck, or similar forces. They believe their accomplishments and setbacks are within their own

[13] David C. McClelland, *The Achieving Society* (New York: Van Nostrand, 1961); and "Business Drive and National Achievement," *Harvard Business Review* (July/August 1962): 99–112.

control and influence and they can affect the outcome of their actions. This attribute is consistent with a high-achievement motivational drive, the desire to take personal responsibility, and self-confidence.

TOLERANCE FOR AMBIGUITY   Start-up entrepreneurs face uncertainty compounded by constant changes that introduce ambiguity and stress into every aspect of the enterprise. Setbacks and surprises are inevitable; lack of organization, structure, and order is a way of life. Yet successful entrepreneurs thrive on the fluidity and excitement of such an ambiguous existence. Job security and retirement generally are of no concern to them.

CALCULATED RISK TAKING   Successful entrepreneurs are not gamblers. When they decide to participate in a venture, they do so in a very calculated, carefully thought-out manner. They do everything possible to get the odds in their favor, and they often avoid taking unnecessary risks. These strategies include getting others to share inherent financial and business risks with them—for example, by persuading partners and investors to put up money, creditors to offer special terms, and suppliers to advance merchandise.

INTEGRITY AND RELIABILITY   Integrity and reliability are the glue and fiber that bind successful personal and business relationships and make them endure. Investors, partners, customers, and creditors alike highly value these attributes. Integrity and reliability help build and sustain trust and confidence. Small-business entrepreneurs, in particular, find these two characteristics crucial to success.

TOLERANCE FOR FAILURE   Entrepreneurs use failure as a learning experience. The iterative, trial-and-error nature of becoming a successful entrepreneur makes serious setbacks and disappointments an integral part of the learning process. The most effective entrepreneurs are realistic enough to expect such difficulties. Furthermore, they do not become disappointed, discouraged, or depressed by a setback or failure. In adverse and difficult times, they look for opportunity. Many of them believe they learn more from their early failures than from their early successes.

HIGH ENERGY LEVEL   The extraordinary workloads and the stressful demands entrepreneurs face place a premium on energy. Many entrepreneurs fine-tune their energy levels by carefully monitoring what they eat and drink, establishing exercise routines, and knowing when to get away for relaxation.

CREATIVITY AND INNOVATIVENESS   Creativity was once regarded as an exclusively inherited trait. Judging by the level of creativity and innovation in the United States compared with that of equally sophisticated but less creative and innovative cultures, it appears unlikely this trait is solely genetic. An expanding school of thought believes creativity can be learned. Chapter 5 provides a comprehensive examination of this critical characteristic. New ventures often have a collective creativity that emerges from the joint efforts of the founders and personnel and produces unique goods and services.

VISION   Entrepreneurs know where they want to go. They have a vision or concept of what their firm can be. For example, Steve Jobs of Apple Computer fame wanted his firm to provide microcomputers that could be used by everyone from schoolchildren to

CONTEMPORARY ENTREPRENEURSHIP

The E-Generation: Young Successes

An entrepreneur's success may be limited by the economy, demographics, finances, or governmental regulations, but it's certainly not limited by age. A new generation of young, street-smart, and business-savvy entrepreneurs is making waves. Today's entrepreneurs are starting younger and younger, and for many reasons.

One reason is the insecure job market with its massive downsizing and widespread layoffs. Due to these changing economic circumstances, traditional job options for students fresh out of college are not what they used to be. But according to Jennifer Kushell, the president of her own company, The Young Entrepreneurs Network, "The opportunities for younger people are now more plentiful than ever before. These people can start their own businesses and graduate as president of a company."

Administrators at universities also are seeing a change in the attitudes and mind-sets of students. Young people are taking charge of their own destiny, and for many that means starting their own business. In addition, young people have more entrepreneurial role models than

ever before. Traditionally, success was associated with professionals such as doctors, lawyers, and judges. America's idea of success now turns to individuals such as Bill Gates and other entrepreneurs. And, finally, the universities can take some credit for turning these traditional students into unconventional business owners. Many of the most noted universities are offering entrepreneurial programs to prepare students for the rigors of the lifestyle. The practical classes offered in these programs offer students a head start in the race for success in owning a business. The following are some shining examples of young people who are making it big on their own.

Suzanne Lowe, 30
Company: Mizanne, Inc.
Year started: 1993
Start-up costs: $50,000
1996 projections: $1 million plus
Suzanne Lowe was fed up with shopping for golf clothing for herself. "As far as sportswear markets go, women's golf clothing is one of the most undeveloped," Lowe says. Lowe obtained the financing

businesspeople. The computer would be more than a machine. It would be an integral part of the person's life in terms of learning and communicating. This vision helped make Apple a major competitor in the microcomputer industry. Not all entrepreneurs have predetermined visions for their firm. In many cases this vision develops over time as the individual begins to realize what the firm is and what it can become.

SELF-CONFIDENCE AND OPTIMISM   Although entrepreneurs often face major obstacles, their belief in their ability seldom wavers. During these down periods they maintain their confidence and let those around them know it. This helps the others sustain their own optimism and creates the level of self-confidence necessary for efficient group effort.

to launch her business while still attending graduate school. Mizanne, Inc., markets a line of tailored, European-styled clothing designed by Lowe's sister Alison Smith. The line can be purchased at Nordstrom department store, country clubs, and resorts across the country. The clothing has become so popular that women who don't even play golf are sporting the stylish attire.

Tracy Melton, 28
Company: Melton International Tackle
Year started: 1993
Start-up costs: $300,000
1996 projections: $1.5 million plus

Tracy Melton loved to fish. So much that he spent the night of his college graduation traveling to a fishing tournament in Hawaii. So much that he takes three to five fishing vacations each year. So much that he left his father's machine shop to launch a mail-order company that sells big-game fishing tackle and accessories. Melton's catalog is almost 90 pages and features more than 3,000 of the finest fishing products available. Melton made the move because he wanted to do something he really enjoyed. And if you were to ask him what makes his business so successful, he would say it is definitely his passion for the sport of fishing.

Andrew and Thomas Parkinson, 38 and 36
Company: Peapod LP
Year started: 1989
Start-up costs: $50,000
1996 projections: $30 million

Many customers are claiming Peapod has changed their lives. Peapod is a computer grocery-shopping and delivery service the Parkinson brothers started. They developed a software program that would enable them to route, bill, and process orders in an economical way. The service not only saves consumers time, but it also allows them to shop smarter by skimming nutritional labels and sorting by fat content, unit price, sales price, and much more. Although in the beginning the brothers did all of the shopping and delivery themselves, they now have more than 600 shoppers and drivers. Peapod now delivers to customers in Chicago, San Francisco, Boston, and Columbus, Ohio, with plans to enter 20 other major cities by the year 2000.

SOURCE: Lynn Beresford, "Young Guns," *Entrepreneur,* October 1996, 158–63; and Janean Chun, Debra Phillips, Heather Page, Lynn Beresford, Holly Celeste Fink, and Charlotte Mulhern, "Young Millionaires," *Entrepreneur,* November 1996, 118–34.

INDEPENDENCE   The desire for independence is a driving force behind contemporary entrepreneurs. Their frustration with rigid bureaucratic systems coupled with a sincere commitment to "make a difference" adds up to an independent personality trying to accomplish tasks his or her own way. This is not to say entrepreneurs must make *all* the decisions; however, they do want the authority to make the important ones.

TEAM BUILDING   The desire for independence and autonomy does not preclude the entrepreneur's desire to build a strong entrepreneurial team. Most successful entrepreneurs have highly qualified, well-motivated teams that help handle the venture's growth and development. In fact, although the entrepreneur may have the clearest vision of where the firm is (or should be) headed, the personnel are often more qualified to handle the day-to-day implementation challenges.[14]

THE DARK SIDE OF ENTREPRENEURSHIP

A great deal of literature is devoted to extolling the rewards, successes, and achievements of entrepreneurs. However, a **dark side of entrepreneurship** also exists. This aspect of the entrepreneurial perspective has a destructive source that exists within the energetic drive of successful entrepreneurs. In examining this dual-edged approach to the entrepreneurial personality, researcher Manfred Kets de Vries has acknowledged the existence of certain negative factors that may envelop entrepreneurs and dominate their behavior.[15] Although each of these factors possesses a positive aspect, it is important for entrepreneurs to understand the potential destructive vein of these factors.

The Entrepreneur's Confrontation with Risk

Starting or buying a new business involves **risk,** and the higher the rewards, the greater the risk entrepreneurs usually face. This is why entrepreneurs tend to evaluate risk very carefully.

In an attempt to describe the risk-taking activity of entrepreneurs, researchers Thomas Monroy and Robert Folger developed a typology of entrepreneurial styles.[16] Figure 4.1 illustrates the classifications in terms of the financial risk endured when undertaking a new venture. In this model, the financial risk is measured against the level of profit motive (defined as the desire for monetary gain or return from the venture), with the characteristic or risk coupled with the type of activity. Profit-seeking activity is associated with the strong desire to maximize profit, and activity seeking refers to other activities associated with entrepreneurship, such as independence or the work of the venture itself. The thrust of this theory argues that entrepreneurs vary in the relation between risk and financial return. This typology highlights the need to explore in economic theory the styles or entrepreneurial motivations that deviate from the styles most characterizing the rational person.

"If different entrepreneurial styles exist, then not every person who founds a new business enterprise does so by seeking to minimize financial risk and maximize financial return. Models of organization formation would thus have to be adjusted for differences among those who form organizations."[17] Thus, not all entrepreneurs are driven solely by monetary gain, and the level of financial risk cannot be completely explained by profit opportunity. Entrepreneurial risk is a far more complex issue than a simple economic risk-versus-return explanation.

---

[14] For some recent articles on entrepreneurial characteristics, see John B. Miner, Norman R. Smith, and Jeffrey S. Bracker, "Defining the Inventor-Entrepreneur in the Context of Established Typologies," *Journal of Business Venturing* (March 1992): 103–13; Rita Gunther McGrath, Ian C. MacMillan, and Sari Scheinberg, "Elitists, Risk Takers, and Rugged Individualists? An Exploratory Analysis of Cultural Differences between Entrepreneurs and Non-Entrepreneurs," *Journal of Business Venturing* (March 1992): 115–36; and Ellen A. Fagenson, "Personal Value Systems of Men and Women Entrepreneurs versus Managers," *Journal of Business Venturing* (September 1993): 409–30.

[15] Manfred F. R. Kets de Vries, "The Dark Side of Entrepreneurship," *Harvard Business Review* (November/December 1985): 160–67.

[16] Thomas Monroy and Robert Folger, "A Typology of Entrepreneurial Styles: Beyond Economic Rationality," *Journal of Private Enterprise* IX, no. 2 (1993): 64–79.

[17] Ibid., 75–76.

FIGURE 4.1 TYPOLOGY OF ENTREPRENEURIAL STYLES

Level of Personal Financial Risk

		Low	**High**
Level of Profit Motive	**Low**	Risk avoiding Activity seeking	Risk accepting Activity seeking
	High	Risk avoiding Profit seeking	Risk accepting Profit seeking

SOURCE: Thomas Monroy and Robert Folger, "A Typology of Entrepreneurial Styles: Beyond Economic Rationality," *Journal of Private Enterprise* IX, no. 2 (1993): 71.

It should be noted that "People who successfully innovate and start businesses come in all shapes and sizes. But they do have a few things others do not. In the deepest sense, they are willing to accept risk for what they believe in. They have the ability to cope with a professional life riddled by ambiguity, a consistent lack of clarity. Most have a drive to put their imprint on whatever they are creating. And while unbridled ego can be a destructive thing, try to find an entrepreneur whose ego isn't wrapped up in the enterprise."[18]

Entrepreneurs face a number of different types of risk. These can be grouped into four basic areas.[19]

FINANCIAL RISK   In most new ventures the individual puts a significant portion of his or her savings or other resources at stake. This money or these resources will, in all likelihood, be lost if the venture fails. The entrepreneur also may be required to sign personally on company obligations that far exceed his or her personal net worth. The entrepreneur is thus exposed to personal bankruptcy. Many people are unwilling to risk their savings, house, property, and salary to start a new business.

CAREER RISK   A question frequently raised by would-be entrepreneurs is whether they will be able to find a job or go back to their old job if their venture should fail. This is a major concern to managers who have a secure organizational job with a high salary and a good benefit package.

[18] Michael O'Neal, "Just What Is an Entrepreneur?" *Business Week,* Special Enterprise Issue 1993, 104–12.

[19] Patrick R. Liles, *New Business Ventures and the Entrepreneur* (Homewood, IL: Irwin, 1974), 14–15.

FAMILY AND SOCIAL RISK   Starting a new venture uses much of the entrepreneur's energy and time. Consequently, his or her other commitments may suffer. Entrepreneurs who are married, and especially those with children, expose their families to the risks of an incomplete family experience and the possibility of permanent emotional scars. In addition, old friends may vanish slowly because of missed get-togethers.

PSYCHIC RISK   The greatest risk may be to the well-being of the entrepreneur. Money can be replaced; a new house can be built; spouse, children, and friends can usually adapt. But some entrepreneurs who have suffered financial catastrophes have been unable to bounce back, at least not immediately. The psychological impact has proven to be too severe for them.

STRESS AND THE ENTREPRENEUR

Some of the most common entrepreneurial goals are independence, wealth, and work satisfaction. Research studies of entrepreneurs show that those who achieve these goals often pay a high price.[20] A majority of entrepreneurs surveyed had back problems, indigestion, insomnia, or headaches. In order to achieve their goals, however, these entrepreneurs were willing to tolerate these effects of stress. The rewards justified the costs.

What Is Entrepreneurial Stress?

In general, **stress** can be viewed as a function of discrepancies between a person's expectations and ability to meet demands, as well as discrepancies between the individual's expectations and personality. If a person is unable to fulfill role demands, then stress occurs. To the extent entrepreneurs' work demands and expectations exceed their abilities to perform as venture initiators, they are likely to experience stress. One researcher has pointed out how entrepreneurial roles and operating environments can lead to stress. Initiating and managing a business requires taking significant risk. As previously mentioned, these risks may be described as financial, career, family, social, or psychic. Also, entrepreneurs must engage in constant communication activities, interacting with relevant external constituencies including customers, suppliers, regulators, lawyers, and accountants, which is stressful.

Lacking the depth of resources, entrepreneurs must bear the cost of their mistakes while playing a multitude of roles, such as salesperson, recruiter, spokesperson, and negotiator. These simultaneous demands can lead to role overload. Owning and operating a business require a large commitment of time and energy, often at the expense of family and social activities. Finally, entrepreneurs are often working alone or with a small number of employees and therefore lack the support from colleagues that may be available to managers in a large corporation.[21]

In addition to the roles and environment entrepreneurs experience, stress can result from a basic personality structure. Referred to as "Type A" behavior, this personality structure describes people who are impatient, demanding, and overstrung. These individuals gravitate toward heavy workloads and find themselves completely immersed in their business

---

[20] Adebowale Akande, "Coping with Entrepreneurial Stress," *Leadership & Organization Development Journal* 13, no. 2 (1992): 27–32; and E. Holly Buttner, "Entrepreneurial Stress: Is It Hazardous to Your Health?" *Journal of Managerial Issues* (summer 1992): 223–40.

[21] Buttner, "Entrepreneurial Stress." See also: M. Afzalur Rabin, "Stress, Strain, and Their Moderators: An Empirical Comparison of Entrepreneurs and Managers," *Journal of Small Business Management* (January 1996): 46–58.

demands. Some of the distinguishing characteristics associated with Type A personalities follow:

- Chronic and severe sense of time urgency. For instance, Type A people become particularly frustrated in traffic jams.
- Constant involvement in multiple projects subject to deadlines. Somehow Type A people take delight in the feeling of being swamped with work.
- Neglect of all aspects of life except work. Workaholics live to work rather than work to live.
- A tendency to take on excessive responsibility, combined with the feeling that "Only I am capable of taking care of this matter."
- Explosiveness of speech and a tendency to speak faster than most people. Type A people are thus prone to ranting and swearing when upset. A widespread belief in the stress literature is that Type A behavior is related to coronary heart disease and that stress is a contributor to heart disease.[22]

Thus, in order to better understand stress, entrepreneurs need to be aware of their particular personality as well as the roles and operating environments that differentiate their business pursuits.[23]

Sources of Stress

Boyd and Gumpert have identified four causes of entrepreneurial stress: (1) loneliness, (2) immersion in business, (3) people problems, and (4) the need to achieve.[24]

LONELINESS   Although entrepreneurs are usually surrounded by others—employees, customers, accountants, and lawyers—they are isolated from persons in whom they can confide. Long hours at work prevent them from seeking the comfort and counsel of friends and family members. Moreover, they tend not to participate in social activities unless they provide a business benefit.

IMMERSION IN BUSINESS   One of the ironies of entrepreneurship is that successful entrepreneurs make enough money to partake of a variety of leisure activities, but they cannot take that exotic cruise, fishing trip, or skiing vacation because their business will not allow their absence. Most entrepreneurs are married to their business. They work long hours, leaving little time for civic organizations, recreation, or further education.

PEOPLE PROBLEMS   Entrepreneurs must depend on and work with partners, employees, customers, bankers, and professionals. Most experience frustration, disappointment, and aggravation in their experiences with these people. Successful entrepreneurs are to some extent perfectionists and know how they want things done; often they spend a lot of time trying to get lackadaisical employees to meet their performance standards. And, frequently, because of irreconcilable conflict, many partnerships are dissolved.

---

[22] See K. A. Mathews and S. C. Haynes, "Type A Behavior Pattern and Coronary Disease Risk," *American Journal of Epistemiology* 123 (1986): 923–60.

[23] Akande, "Coping with Entrepreneurial Stress."

[24] David P. Boyd and David E. Gumpert, "Coping with Entrepreneurial Stress," *Harvard Business Review* (March/April 1983): 46–56.

ENTREPRENEURIAL
EDGE

Entrepreneurial Terror

The terror an entrepreneur experiences has its own taste, its own smell, and its own gut-wrenching pain. And it does not go away as long as the person remains an entrepreneur. It becomes an organization entrepreneurs join—the Club of Terror. Although the club is very exclusive, admission is automatic; permission is neither needed nor sought, and tenure is indefinite. The terror entrepreneurs experience cannot be expected, cannot be escaped, and cannot be prepared against. Because most entrepreneurs do not admit they have experienced this entrepreneurial terror, it remains a deep, dark secret. And because it is not talked about, most entrepreneurs feel they are the the only ones who have ever experienced it.

According to Wilson Harrell, an entrepreneur from Jacksonville, Florida, this entrepreneurial terror is much different from simple fear. Fear is usually acciden-

tal, unexpected, and short lived, such as the sudden rush of adrenaline experienced when you almost get hit by a bus, he explains. On the other hand, entrepreneurial terror is self-inflicted. It is a private world where no sleep occurs, and wide-awakening nightmares filled with monsters constantly try to destroy every morsel of the entrepreneur's being.

What causes this terror? Well, it is not the money, for any entrepreneur will explain that money is just a bonus of the accomplishment, and losing money is one of the risks taken. "Fear of failure" has a lot to do with it. Entrepreneurs do not want to become just another businessperson and pass into oblivion without leaving their mark. What induces this complex fear or terror has yet to be determined.

For Harrell, the fear came while starting his own food brokerage business to sell products on military bases in Europe. Harrell was appointed a representative

NEED TO ACHIEVE   Achievement brings satisfaction. During the Boyd and Gumpert study, however, it became clear that a fine line exists between attempting to achieve too much and failing to achieve enough. More often than not, the entrepreneur was trying to accomplish too much. Many are never satisfied with their work no matter how well it was done. They seem to recognize the dangers (e.g., to their health) of unbridled ambition, but they have a difficult time tempering their achievement need. They seem to believe that if they stop or slow down, some competitor is going to come from behind, and everything they have built will fall apart.

Dealing with Stress

It is important to point out that not all stress is bad. Certainly, if stress becomes overbearing and unrelenting in a person's life, it wears down the body's physical abilities. However, if

of Kraft Food Company and did so well increasing its sales that he sold himself out of a job. Because he had made his job look so easy, it was suggested to Kraft's management team that its own salespeople could do the work better and cheaper. So what did Harrell do? Because losing the Kraft account would put him out of business, he put everything on the line and proposed that if Kraft kept brokering through his company and took over the brokering in Germany, then Harrell would help it take over the food industry everywhere. After Harrell experienced 30 days of immeasurable terror, Kraft made the decision to trust Harrell and continue brokering through his company. Although he later sold his business, 30 years later the company still represents Kraft Inc., not only in Europe but also in the Far East and many other countries. The company has grown into the largest military-representative organization in the field and was sold in 1985 for more than $4 million.

What is the secret to entrepreneurship, given such terror? Its reward. No matter what pain is experienced through the terror, the elation felt from success subsides it. That high, along with terror, is an emotion reserved for entrepreneurs and becomes food for the spirit. Addicting? It is more like a roller-coaster ride. In the beginning, imagine pulling yourself up the incline very slowly, making any tough decisions with a growing sense of excitement and foreboding. Then when you hit the top, for a brief moment it is frightening, and the anticipation accelerates before you feel no more feelings of control. As you go screaming into the unknown, terror takes over. At first, all you feel is fear; then, suddenly, the ride is over, and the terror is gone, but the exhilaration remains. What is next for the entrepreneur? He or she buys another ticket.

So what is the key ingredient for entrepreneurial success? According to Wilson Harrell, it is the ability to handle terror. For he believes it is the lonely entrepreneur living with his or her personal terror who breathes life and excitement into an otherwise dull and mundane world.

SOURCE: Wilson Harrell, "Entrepreneurial Terror," *Inc.*, February 1987, 74–76.

---

stress can be kept within constructive bounds, then it could increase a person's efficiency and improve performance.[25]

Boyd and Gumpert made a significant contribution to defining the causes of entrepreneurial stress, but what makes their study particularly noteworthy is the presentation of stress reduction techniques—ways entrepreneurs can improve the quality of their business and personal lives.[26] Although classical stress reduction techniques such as transcendental meditation, biofeedback, muscle relaxation, and regular exercise help reduce stress, Boyd and Gumpert suggest that another important step entrepreneurs can take is to clarify the causes of their stress. Having identified these causes, entrepreneurs then can combat

---

[25] J. M. Ivancevich and M. T. Matteson, *Stress and Work: A Managerial Perspective* (Glenview, IL: Scott, Foresman & Co., 1980).

[26] Boyd and Gumpert, "Coping with Entrepreneurial Stress."

excessive stress by (1) acknowledging its existence, (2) developing coping mechanisms, and (3) probing unacknowledged personal needs.

Presented here are five specific ways entrepreneurs can cope with stress.

NETWORKING   One way to relieve the loneliness of running a business is to share experiences by networking with other business owners. The objectivity gained from hearing about the triumphs and errors of others is itself therapeutic.

GETTING AWAY FROM IT ALL   The best antidote to immersion in business, report many entrepreneurs, is a holiday. If vacation days or weeks are limited by valid business constraints, short breaks still may be possible. Such interludes allow a measure of self-renewal.

COMMUNICATING WITH EMPLOYEES   Entrepreneurs are in close contact with employees and can readily assess the concerns of their staffs. The personal touches often unavailable in large corporations, such as company-wide outings, flexible hours, and small loans to tide workers over until payday, are possible. In such settings employees often are more productive than their counterparts in large organizations.

FINDING SATISFACTION OUTSIDE THE COMPANY   Countering the obsessive need to achieve can be difficult because the entrepreneur's personality is inextricably bound in the company fabric. Entrepreneurs need to get away from the business occasionally and become more passionate about life itself; they need to gain some new perspectives.

DELEGATING   Implementation of coping mechanisms requires implementation time. To gain this time, the entrepreneur has to delegate tasks. Entrepreneurs find delegation difficult, because they think they have to be at the business all of the time and be involved in every aspect of the operation. But if time is to be gained for alleviation of stress, then appropriate delegatees must be found and trained.

THE ENTREPRENEURIAL EGO

In addition to the challenges of risk and stress, the entrepreneur also may experience the negative effects of an inflated ego. In other words, certain characteristics that usually propel entrepreneurs into success also can be exhibited to their extreme. We examine four of these characteristics that may hold destructive implications for entrepreneurs.[27]

An Overbearing Need for Control

Entrepreneurs are driven by a strong desire to control both their venture and their destiny. This internal focus of control spills over into a preoccupation with controlling everything. An obsession for autonomy and control may cause entrepreneurs to work in structured situations *only* when they have created the structure on *their* terms. This, of course, has serious implications for networking in an entrepreneurial team, since entrepreneurs can visualize the external control by others as a threat of subjection or infringement on their

[27] Manfred F. R. Kets de Vries, "The Dark Side of Entrepreneurship," *Harvard Business Review* (November/December 1985): 160–67.

will. Thus, the same characteristic that entrepreneurs need for successful venture creation also contains within it a destructive side.

Sense of Distrust

In order to remain alert to competition, customers, and government regulations, entrepreneurs are continually scanning the environment. They try to anticipate and act on developments that others might recognize too late. This distrustful state can result in their focusing on trivial things, causing them to lose sight of reality, to distort reasoning and logic, and to take destructive actions. Again, distrust is a dual-edged characteristic.

Overriding Desire for Success

The entrepreneur's ego is involved in the desire for success. Although many of today's entrepreneurs believe they are living on the edge of existence, constantly stirring within them is a strong desire to succeed in spite of the odds. Thus the entrepreneur rises up as a defiant person who creatively acts to deny any feelings of insignificance. The individual is driven to succeed and takes pride in demonstrating that success. Therein lie the seeds of possible destructiveness. If the entrepreneur seeks to demonstrate achievement through the erection of a monument—such as a huge office building, an imposing factory, or a plush office—then the danger exists that the individual will become more important than the venture itself. Losing perspective like this can, of course, be the destructive side of the desire to succeed.

Unrealistic Optimism

The ceaseless optimism that emanates from entrepreneurs (even through the bleak times) is a key factor in the drive toward success. Entrepreneurs maintain a high enthusiasm level that becomes an external optimism that allows others to believe in them during rough periods. However, when taken to its extreme, this optimistic attitude can lead to a fantasy approach to the business. A self-deceptive state may arise in which entrepreneurs ignore trends, facts, and reports and delude themselves into thinking everything will turn out fine. This type of behavior can lead to an inability to handle the reality of the business world.

These examples do not imply that *all* entrepreneurs fall prey to these scenarios nor that each of the characteristics presented always gives way to the "destructive" side. Nevertheless, all potential entrepreneurs need to know that the dark side of entrepreneurship exists.

ENTREPRENEURIAL MOTIVATION

Examining why people start businesses and how they differ from those who do not (or those who start unsuccessful businesses) may help explain how the motivation entrepreneurs exhibit during start-up is linked to the sustaining behavior exhibited later. Lanny Herron and Harry J. Sapienza have stated, "Because motivation plays an important part in the creation of new organizations, theories of organization creation that fail to address this notion are incomplete."[28]

[28] Lanny Herron and Harry J. Sapienza, "The Entrepreneur and the Initiation of New Venture Launch Activities," *Entrepreneurship Theory and Practice* (fall 1992): 49–55.

Researcher Bradley R. Johnson in his review of achievement motivation and the entrepreneur stated, "It remains worthwhile to carefully study the role of the individual, including his or her psychological profile. Individuals are, after all, the energizers of the entrepreneurial process."[29]

Thus, although research on the psychological characteristics of entrepreneurs has not provided an agreed on "profile" of an entrepreneur, it is still important to recognize the contribution of psychological factors to the entrepreneurial process.[30] In fact, the quest for new-venture creation as well as the willingness to *sustain* that venture is directly related to an **entrepreneur's motivation.** One research study examined the importance of satisfaction to an entrepreneur's willingness to remain with the venture. Particular goals, attitudes, and backgrounds were all important determinants of an entrepreneur's eventual satisfaction.[31] In that vein, one research approach is the motivational process an entrepreneur experiences.[32] Figure 4.2 illustrates the key elements of this approach.

The decision to behave entrepreneurially is the result of the interaction of several factors. One set of factors includes the individual's personal characteristics, the individual's personal environment, the relevant business environment, the individual's personal goal set, and the existence of a viable business idea. In addition, the individual compares his or her perception of the probable outcomes with the personal expectations he or she has in mind. Next, an individual looks at the relationship between the entrepreneurial behavior he or she would implement and the expected outcomes.

According to the model, the entrepreneur's expectations are finally compared with the actual or perceived firm outcomes. Future entrepreneurial behavior is based on the results of all of these comparisons. When outcomes meet or exceed expectations, the **entrepreneurial behavior** is positively reinforced, and the individual is motivated to continue to behave entrepreneurially, either within the current venture or possibly through the initiation of additional ventures, depending on the existing entrepreneurial goal. When outcomes fail to meet expectations, the entrepreneur's motivation will be lower and will have a corresponding impact on the decision to continue to act entrepreneurially. These perceptions also affect succeeding strategies, strategy implementation, and management of the firm.[33]

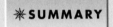

✳SUMMARY

In attempting to explain the "entrepreneurial perspective" within individuals, this chapter presented the most common characteristics exhibited by successful entrepreneurs. Then a review of the "dark side" of entrepreneurship reveals certain factors that possess a de-

[29] Bradley R. Johnson, "Toward a Multidimensional Model of Entrepreneurship: The Case of Achievement Motivation and the Entrepreneur," *Entrepreneurship Theory and Practice* (spring 1990): 39–54.

[30] See Kelly G. Shaver and Linda R. Scott, "Person, Process, Choice: The Psychology of New Venture Creation," *Entrepreneurship Theory and Practice* (winter 1991): 23–45.

[31] Arnold C. Cooper and Kendall W. Artz, "Determinants of Satisfaction for Entrepreneurs," *Journal of Business Venturing* (November 1995): 439–58.

[32] Douglas W. Naffziger, Jeffrey S. Hornsby, and Donald F. Kuratko, "A Proposed Research Model of Entrepreneurial Motivation," *Entrepreneurship Theory and Practice* (spring 1994): 29–42.

[33] Donald F. Kuratko, Jeffrey S. Hornsby, and Douglas W. Naffziger, "An Examination of Owner's Goals in Sustaining Entrepreneurship," *Journal of Small Business Management* (January 1997): 24–33.

FIGURE 4.2   **A MODEL OF ENTREPRENEURIAL MOTIVATION**

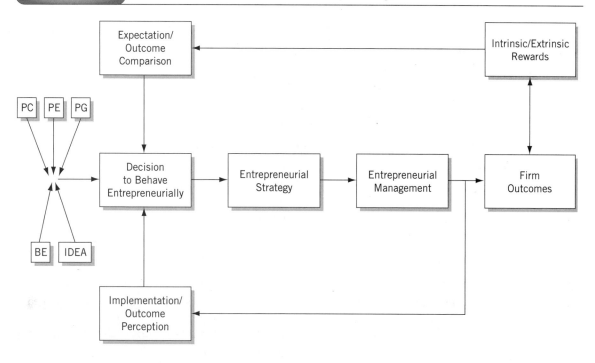

PC = **Personal Characteristics**
PE = **Personal Environment**
PG = **Personal Goals**
BE = **Business Environment**

SOURCE: Douglas W. Naffziger, Jeffrey S. Hornsby, and Donald F. Kuratko, "A Proposed Research Model of Entrepreneurial Motivation," *Entrepreneurship Theory and Practice* (spring 1994): 33.

structive vein for entrepreneurs. Finally, a motivational model of entrepreneurship was discussed.

First it is important to recognize that a number of sources of information relating to the entrepreneurial perspective exist. Three major ones are publications, direct observation, and presentations by or case studies of practicing entrepreneurs.

Several studies have been conducted to determine the personal qualities and traits of successful entrepreneurs. Some of these were examined in the chapter: commitment, determination, and perseverance; drive to achieve; opportunity orientation; initiative and responsibility; persistent problem solving; seeking feedback; internal locus of control; tolerance for ambiguity; calculated risk taking; integrity and reliability; tolerance for failure; high energy level; creativity and innovativeness; vision; self-confidence and optimism; independence; and team building.

The next part of the chapter focused on the dark side of entrepreneurship, including the confrontation with risk, the problems of stress, and the particular traits that may permeate the entrepreneurial ego.

Finally, the chapter introduced a model of entrepreneurial motivation. Recognizing the contribution of psychological factors to the process of entrepreneurship, this model demonstrated the importance of entrepreneurs' perceived expectations and actual outcomes in their motivation to start and sustain a venture.

Key Terms and Concepts

Calculated risk taking	Immersion in business
Career risk	Loneliness
Dark side of entrepreneurship	Need for control
Delegating	Networking
Drive to achieve	Opportunity orientation
Entrepreneurial behavior	Psychic risk
Entrepreneurial motivation	Stress
Entrepreneurial perspective	Tolerance for ambiguity
External optimism	Tolerance for failure
Family and social risk	Vision
Financial risk	

Review and Discussion Questions

1. Identify and describe the three major sources of information that supply data related to the entrepreneurial perspective.
2. How do the following traits relate to entrepreneurs: desire to achieve, opportunity orientation, initiative, and responsibility?
3. Some of the characteristics attributed to entrepreneurs include persistent problem solving, continuous seeking of feedback, and internal locus of control. What does this statement mean? Be complete in your answer.
4. Entrepreneurs have a tolerance for ambiguity, are calculated risk takers, and have a high regard for integrity and reliability. What does this statement mean? Be complete in your answer.
5. Is it true most successful entrepreneurs have failed at some point in their business careers? Explain.
6. In what way is "vision" important to an entrepreneur? Self-confidence? Independence?
7. Entrepreneurship has a "dark side." What is meant by this statement? Be complete in your answer.
8. What are the four specific areas of risk entrepreneurs face? Describe each.
9. What are four causes of stress among entrepreneurs? How can an entrepreneur deal with each of them?
10. Describe the factors associated with the entrepreneurial ego.
11. What is the concept of entrepreneurial motivation?
12. How does the model depicted in the chapter illustrate an entrepreneur's motivation? Be specific.

Experiential Exercise   *Are You a High Achiever?*

One of the most important characteristics of a successful entrepreneur is the desire to be a high achiever. The following ten questions are designed to help identify your achievement drive. Write the letter preceding your answer in the blank to the left of each. Scoring information is provided at the end of the exercise.

_____ 1. An instructor in one of your college classes has asked you to vote on three grading options: *(a)* Study the course material, take the exams, and receive the grade you earn; *(b)* roll a die and get an A if you roll an odd number and a D if you roll an even number; *(c)* show up for all class lectures, turn in a short term paper, and get a C. Which of these options would you choose?

_____ 2. How would you describe yourself as a risk taker? *(a)* high, *(b)* moderate, *(c)* low.

_____ 3. You have just been asked by your boss to take on a new project in addition to the many tasks you are already doing. What would you tell your boss? *(a)* Since I'm already snowed under, I can't handle any more. *(b)* Sure, I'm happy to help out; give it to me. *(c)* Let me look over my current workload and get back to you tomorrow about whether or not I can take on any more work.

_____ 4. Which one of these people would you most like to be? *(a)* Steve Jobs, founder of Apple Computers, *(b)* Lee Iacocca of Chrysler fame, *(c)* Jack Welch, CEO of General Electric.

_____ 5. Which one of these games would you most like to play? *(a)* monopoly, *(b)* bingo, *(c)* roulette.

_____ 6. You have decided to become more physically active. Which one of these approaches has the greatest attraction for you? *(a)* join a neighborhood team, *(b)* work out on your own, *(c)* join a local health club.

_____ 7. With which one of these groups would you most enjoy playing poker? *(a)* friends, *(b)* high-stake players, *(c)* individuals who can challenge you.

_____ 8. Which one of these persons would you most like to be? *(a)* a detective solving a crime, *(b)* a politician giving a victory statement, *(c)* a millionaire sailing on his or her yacht.

_____ 9. Which one of these activities would you prefer to do on an evening off? *(a)* visit a friend, *(b)* work on a hobby, *(c)* watch television.

_____ 10. Which one of these occupations has the greatest career appeal for you? *(a)* computer salesperson, *(b)* corporate accountant, *(c)* criminal lawyer.

Scoring: Transfer each of your answers to the scoring key below by circling the appropriate number (e.g., if your answer to question 1 is *c,* you will circle the number 2 in row 1). Then total all three columns to arrive at your final score.

	a	**b**	**c**
1.	10	0	2
2.	2	10	2
3.	6	2	10
4.	7	10	5
5.	10	0	0

6.	2	10	6
7.	4	2	10
8.	10	7	4
9.	4	10	4
10.	10	5	10

_____ + _____ + _____ = _____

High achievers	76–100
Moderate achievers	50–75
Low achievers	Less than 50

Interpretation:

1. High achievers take personal responsibility for their actions. They do not like to rely on luck. The third option *(c)* assumes the class time saved by not having to study for exams will be used to study for other classes; otherwise the answer would be a zero.
2. High achievers are moderate risk takers in important situations.
3. High achievers like to study a situation before committing themselves to a course of action.
4. Jobs is a high-achieving individual but is more interested in design and engineering than in goal accomplishment; Iacocca is an extremely high-achieving salesperson/ executive; Jack Welch is more driven by the need for power than the need to achieve.
5. Monopoly allows the high achiever to use his or her skills; bingo and roulette depend on luck.
6. The high achiever would work out on his or her own. The second-best choice is to join a health club, which allows less individual freedom but gives the chance to get feedback and guidance from individuals who understand how to work out effectively.
7. High achievers like challenges but not high risks. If you are a very good poker player and you chose *b,* you then can raise your score on this question from *2* to *10.*
8. Because high achievers like to accomplish goals, the detective would have the greatest appeal for them. The politician is more interested in power, and the millionaire is simply enjoying himself or herself.
9. High achievers like to do constructive things that help them improve themselves, so working on a hobby would be their first choice.
10. The computer salesperson and the criminal lawyer have a much higher need to achieve than does the corporate accountant.

 **CASE** **4.1**

Jane's Evaluation

Paul Medwick is a commercial banker. In the past month he has received loan applications from three entrepreneurs. All three have fledgling businesses with strong potential. However, Paul believes it is important to look at more than just the business itself; the individual also needs close scrutinization.

The three entrepreneurs are (1) Robin Wood, owner of a small delicatessen located in the heart of a thriving business district; (2) Richard Trumpe, owner of a ten-minute oil-change-and-lube operation; and (3) Phil Hartack, owner of a bookstore that specializes in best-sellers and cookbooks. Paul has had the bank's outside consultant, Professor Jane Jackson, interview each of the three entrepreneurs. Jane has done a lot of work with entrepreneurs and after a couple of hours of discussion is usually able to evaluate a person's entrepreneurial qualities. In the past Jane has recommended 87 people for loans, and only two of these ventures have failed. This success rate is much higher than that for commercial loans in general. Here is Jane's evaluation of the three people whom she interviewed.

Characteristic	Robin Wood	Richard Trumpe	Phil Hartack
Perseverance	H	M	M
Drive to achieve	M	H	M
Initiative	M	H	M
Persistent problem solving	M	M	H
Tolerance for ambiguity	L	M	H
Integrity and reliability	H	M	H
Tolerance for failure	H	H	H
Creativity and innovativeness	M	H	M
Self-confidence	H	H	H
Independence	H	H	H

H = High

M = Medium

L = Low

Questions

1. Which of the three applicants do you think comes closest to having the perspective of an ideal entrepreneur? Why?
2. To which applicant would you recommend that the bank lend money? (Assume each has asked for a loan of $50,000.) Defend your answer.
3. Can these three entrepreneurs do anything to improve their entrepreneurial profile and their chances for success? Be specific in your answer.

 **CASE 4.2**

To Stay or to Go?

Mary Gunther has been a sales representative for a large computer firm for seven years. She took this job after graduation from a large university, where she had majored in computer science. Recently Mary has been thinking about leaving the company and starting her own business. Her knowledge of the computer field would put her in an ideal position to be a computer consultant.

Mary understands computer hardware and software, is knowledgeable about the strong and weak points of all the latest market offerings, and has a solid understanding of how to implement a computer system throughout an organization. Mary believes many medium-sized firms around the country would like to introduce computer technology but do not know how to do so. The large manufacturers, such as the one for which she works, are more interested in selling hardware than in helping their clients develop a fully integrated, company-wide computer system. Small consulting firms have to be brought in to do this. Mary feels that as a consultant she not only would be able to evaluate a computer's effectiveness, but she also would know how to set up these machines so they will provide maximum benefit to the company.

Mary estimates that if she were to leave the computer firm tomorrow, she could line up ten clients immediately. This would provide her with sufficient income for six months. She is sure that during this period she would have little difficulty getting more clients. Six of these ten firms are located on the East Coast, two of them are in the Midwest, and the remaining two are in California. Mary estimates that it would take about two weeks to install a system and have it working, and it would probably take another 2 days to correct any problems that occur later on. These problems would be handled on a follow-up visit, usually 10 to 14 days later.

The idea of starting her own venture appeals to Mary. However, she is not sure she wants to leave her job and assume all the responsibilities associated with running her own operation. Before going any further, she has decided to evaluate her own abilities and desires and make certain this is the right career move for her.

Questions
1. Identify three major characteristics Mary should have if she hopes to succeed in this new venture. Defend your choices.
2. How can Figure 4.1 help Mary decide if she is sufficiently entrepreneurial to succeed in this new venture? Which quadrant would she have to be in to succeed in the new venture?

Chapter 5

DEVELOPING CREATIVITY AND UNDERSTANDING INNOVATION

CHAPTER OBJECTIVES

1. To examine the role of creativity and to review the major components of the creative process: knowledge accumulation, incubation process, idea experience, evaluation, and implementation

2. To present ways of developing personal creativity: recognize relationships, develop a functional perspective, use your "brains," and eliminate muddling mind-sets

3. To introduce the four major types of innovation: invention, extension, duplication, and synthesis

4. To define and illustrate the sources of innovation for entrepreneurs

5. To review some of the major myths associated with innovation and to define the ten principles of innovation

6. To illustrate the financial support for innovation

The era of the intelligent man/woman is almost over and a new one is emerging—the era of the creative man/woman.

Pinchas Noy

INNOVATION AND THE ENTREPRENEUR

Innovation is a key function in the entrepreneurial process. Most researchers and authors in the field of entrepreneurship are, for the most part, in agreement with Drucker about the concept of innovation:

> Innovation is the specific function of entrepreneurship. . . . It is the means by which the entrepreneur either creates new wealth-producing resources or endows existing resources with enhanced potential for creating wealth.[1]

Innovation is the process by which entrepreneurs convert opportunities into marketable ideas. It is the means by which they become catalysts for change.[2]

More than Just a Good Idea

The innovation process is more than just a good idea. The origin of an idea is important, and the role of creative thinking may be vital to that development.[3] However, a major difference exists between an idea arising from mere speculation and one that is the product of extended thinking, research, experience, and work. More important, a prospective entrepreneur must have the desire to bring a good idea through the development stages. Thus innovation is a combination of the vision to create a good idea and the perseverance and dedication to remain with the concept through implementation.

Entrepreneurs blend imaginative and creative thinking with a systematic, logical process ability. This combination is a key to success. In addition, potential entrepreneurs are always looking for unique opportunities to fill needs or wants. They sense economic potential in business problems by continually asking "What if . . . ?" or "Why not . . . ?" They develop an ability to see, recognize, and create opportunity where others find only problems. It has been said that the first rule for developing entrepreneurial vision is to recognize that

---

[1] Peter F. Drucker, *Innovation and Entrepreneurship* (New York: Harper & Row, 1985), 20.

[2] Jane M. Howell and Christopher A. Higgins, "Champions of Change: Identifying, Understanding, and Supporting Champions of Technological Innovations," *Organizational Dynamics* (summer 1990): 40–55; see also Dean M. Schroeder, "A Dynamic Perspective on the Impact of Process Innovation upon Competitive Strategies," *Strategic Management Journal* 11 (1990): 25–41.

[3] Peter F. Drucker, "The Discipline of Innovation," *Harvard Business Review* (May/June 1985): 67–72.

TABLE 5.1	TWO APPROACHES TO CREATIVE PROBLEM SOLVING	

Adaptor	**Innovator**
Employs a disciplined, precise, methodical approach	Approaches tasks from unusual angles
Is concerned with solving, rather than finding, problems	Discovers problems and avenues of solutions
Attempts to refine current practices	Questions basic assumptions related to current practices
Tends to be means oriented	Has little regard for means; is more interested in ends
Is capable of extended detail work	Has little tolerance for routine work
Is sensitive to group cohesion and cooperation	Has little or no need for consensus; often is insensitive to others

SOURCE: Michael Kirton, "Adaptors and Innovators: A Description and Measure," *Journal of Applied Psychology* (October 1976): 623. Copyright 1976 by The American Psychological Association.

problems are to solutions what demand is to supply. Applying this rule means an entrepreneur will analyze a problem from every possible angle: What is the problem? Whom does it affect? How does it affect them? What costs are involved? Can it be solved? Would the marketplace pay for a solution? This is the type of analysis that blends creative thinking with systematic analysis.[4]

In order to give a better perspective of this entrepreneurial vision, this chapter is devoted to examining the role of creativity and the innovation process. These two major topics are keys to understanding opportunity and its development for entrepreneurs.

THE ROLE OF CREATIVITY

It is important to recognize the role of creativity in the innovative process. **Creativity** is the generation of ideas that result in the improved efficiency or effectiveness of a system.[5]

Two important aspects of creativity exist: process and people. The process is goal oriented; it is designed to attain a solution to a problem. The people are the resources that determine the solution. The process remains the same, but the approach the people use will vary. For example, sometimes they will adapt a solution, and at other times they will formulate a highly innovative solution.[6] Table 5.1 compares these two approaches.

One study examined the validity of these two approaches for distinguishing innovative entrepreneurs from adaptive entrepreneurs and found their application very effective.[7]

[4] Lloyd W. Fernald Jr., "The Underlying Relationship between Creativity, Innovation, and Entrepreneurship," *Journal of Creative Behavior* 22, no. 3 (1988): 196–202.

[5] Timothy A. Matherly and Ronald E. Goldsmith, "The Two Faces of Creativity," *Business Horizons* (September/October 1985): 8; see also Bruce G. Whiting, "Creativity and Entrepreneurship: How Do They Relate?" *Journal of Creative Behavior* 22, no. 3 (1988): 178–83.

[6] Michael Kirton, "Adaptors and Innovators: A Description and Measure," *Journal of Applied Psychology* (October 1976): 622–29.

[7] E. Holly Buttner and Nur Gryskiewicz, "Entrepreneurs' Problem-Solving Styles: An Empirical Study Using the Kirton Adaption/Innovation Theory," *Journal of Small Business Management* (January 1993): 22–31.

TABLE 5.2	THE MOST COMMON IDEA STOPPERS

1. "Naah."
2. "Can't" (said with a shake of the head and an air of finality).
3. "That's the dumbest thing I've ever heard."
4. "Yeah, but if you did that . . ." (poses an extreme or unlikely disaster case).
5. "We already tried that—years ago."
6. "We've done all right so far; why do we need that?"
7. "I don't see anything wrong with the way we're doing it now."
8. "That doesn't sound too practical."
9. "We've never done anything like that before."
10. "Let's get back to reality."
11. "We've got deadlines to meet—we don't have time to consider that."
12. "It's not in the budget."
13. "Are you kidding?"
14. "Let's not go off on a tangent."
15. "Where do you get these weird ideas?"

SOURCE: Adapted from *The Creative Process*, ed. Angela M. Biondi, The Creative Education Foundation, 1986.

Thus, understanding the problem-solving orientation of individuals helps develop their creative abilities.

The Nature of the Creative Process

Creativity is a process that can be developed and improved.[8] Everyone is creative to some degree. However, as is the case with many abilities and talents (e.g., athletic, artistic), some individuals have a greater aptitude for creativity than others. Also, some people have been raised and educated in an environment that encouraged them to develop their creativity. They have been taught to think and act creatively. For others the process is more difficult because they have not been positively reinforced, and, if they are to be creative, they must learn how to implement the creative process.[9]

Many people incorrectly believe only a genius can be creative.[10] Most people also assume some people are born creative and others are not, or only the gifted or highly intelligent person is capable of generating creative ideas and insights. Yet, the real barriers to creative thinking are sometimes the inadvertent "killer phrases" we use in our communications. Table 5.2 lists the 15 key "idea stoppers" we use. People may not intentionally

[8] See Edward deBono, *Serious Creativity: Using the Power of Creativity to Create New Ideas* (New York: Harper Business, 1992).

[9] Eleni Mellow, "The Two Conditions View of Creativity," *Journal of Creative Behavior* 30, no. 2 (1996): 126–43.

[10] H. J. Eysenck, *Genius: The Nature of Creativity* (New York: Cambridge University Press, 1995); and B. Taylor, *Into the Open: Reflections on Genius and Modernity* (New York: New York University Press, 1995).

stop a creative idea, but these simple negative phrases prohibit people from thinking any further.

Creativity is not some mysterious and rare talent reserved for a select few. It is a distinct way of looking at the world that is oftentimes illogical. The creative process involves seeing relationships among things others have not seen (e.g., modems—using telephones to transfer data among computers).[11]

The creative process has four commonly agreed on phases or steps. Most experts agree on the general nature and relationships among these phases, although they refer to them by a variety of names.[12] Experts also agree that these phases do not always occur in the same order for every creative activity. For creativity to occur, chaos is necessary but a structured and focused chaos. We shall examine this four-step process using the most typical structural development.

PHASE 1: BACKGROUND OR KNOWLEDGE ACCUMULATION   Successful creations are generally preceded by investigation and information gathering. This usually involves extensive reading, conversations with others working in the field, attendance at professional meetings and workshops, and a general absorption of information relative to the problem or issue under study. Additional investigation in both related and unrelated fields is sometimes involved. This exploration provides the individual with a variety of perspectives on the problem, and it is particularly important to the entrepreneur, who needs a basic understanding of all aspects of the development of a new product, service, or business venture.

People practice the creative search for background knowledge in a number of ways. Some of the most helpful follow: (1) read in a variety of fields; (2) join professional groups and associations; (3) attend professional meetings and seminars; (4) travel to new places; (5) talk to anyone and everyone about your subject; (6) scan magazines, newspapers, and journals for articles related to the subject; (7) develop a subject library for future reference; (8) carry a small notebook and recording useful information; and (9) devote time to pursue natural curiosities.[13]

PHASE 2: THE INCUBATION PROCESS   Creative individuals allow their subconscious to mull over the tremendous amounts of information they gather during the preparation phase. This incubation process often occurs while they are engaged in activities totally unrelated to the subject or problem. It happens even when they are sleeping. This accounts for the advice frequently given to a person who is frustrated by what appears to be an unsolvable problem: "Why don't you sleep on it?"[14] Getting away from a problem and letting the subconscious mind work on it allows creativity to spring forth. Some of the most helpful steps to induce incubation follow: (1) engage in routine, "mindless" activities (cutting the grass, painting the house); (2) exercise regularly; (3) play (sports, board games,

---

[11] See Dale Dauten, *Taking Chances: Lessons in Putting Passion and Creativity in Your Work Life* (New York: New Market Press, 1986).

[12] Edward deBono, *Six Thinking Hats* (Boston: Little, Brown, 1985); and Edward deBono, "Serious Creativity," *The Journal for Quality and Participation* 18, no. 5 (1995): 12.

[13] For a discussion of the development of creativity, see Eugene Raudsepp, *How Creative Are You?* (New York: Perigee Books, 1981); Arthur B. Van Gundy, *108 Ways to Get a Bright Idea and Increase Your Creative Potential* (Englewood Cliffs: Prentice-Hall, 1983); and Roger L. Firestien, *Why Didn't I Think of That?* (Buffalo: United Education Services Inc., 1989).

[14] T. A. Nosanchuk, J. A. Ogrodnik, and Tom Henigan, "A Preliminary Investigation of Incubation in Short Story Writing," *Journal of Creative Behavior* 22, no. 4 (1988): 279–80. (This study reported that an eight-day incubation period was associated with significantly elevated story-writing creativity.)

puzzles); (4) think about the project or problem before falling asleep; (5) meditate or practice self-hypnosis; and (6) sit back and relax on a regular basis.[15]

PHASE 3: THE IDEA EXPERIENCE This phase of the creative process is often the most exciting. It is when the idea or solution the individual is seeking is discovered. Sometimes referred to as the "eureka factor," this phase is also the one the average person incorrectly perceives as the only component of creativity.[16]

As with the incubation process, new and innovative ideas often emerge while the person is busy doing something unrelated to the enterprise, venture, or investigation (e.g., taking a shower, driving on an interstate highway, leafing through a newspaper).[17] Sometimes the idea appears as a bolt out of the blue. In most cases, however, the answer comes to the individual incrementally. Slowly but surely, the person begins to formulate the solution. Because it is often difficult to determine when the incubation process ends and the idea experience phase begins, many people are unaware of moving from Phase 2 to Phase 3.

In any event, here are ways to speed up the idea experience: (1) daydream and fantasize about your project, (2) practice your hobbies, (3) work in a leisurely environment (e.g., at home instead of the office), (4) put the problem on the back burner, (5) keep a notebook at bedside to record late-night or early-morning ideas, and (6) take breaks while working.[18]

PHASE 4: EVALUATION AND IMPLEMENTATION This is the most difficult step of a creative endeavor and requires a great deal of courage, self-discipline, and perseverance. Successful entrepreneurs can identify ideas that are workable and that they have the skills to implement. More important, they do not give up when they run into temporary obstacles.[19] Often they will fail several times before they successfully develop their best ideas. In some cases entrepreneurs will take the idea in an entirely different direction or will discover a new and more workable idea while struggling to implement the original idea. Another important part of this phase is the reworking of ideas to put them into final form. Because frequently an idea emerges from Phase 3 in rough form, it needs to be modified or tested in order to put it in final shape. Some of the most useful suggestions for carrying out this phase follow: (1) increase your energy level with proper exercise, diet, and rest; (2) educate yourself in the business planning process and all facets of business; (3) test your ideas with knowledgeable people; (4) take notice of your intuitive hunches and feelings; (5) educate yourself in the selling process; (6) learn about organizational policies and practices; (7) seek advice from others (e.g., friends, experts); and (8) view the problems you encounter while implementing your ideas as challenges.[20]

---

[15] W. W. Harman and H. Rheingold, *Higher Creativity: Liberating the Unconscious for Breakthrough Insights* (Los Angeles: Tarcher, 1984); and Daniel Goleman, Paul Kaufman, and Michael Ray, *The Creative Spirit* (New York: Penguin Books USA Inc., 1993).

[16] See J. Conrath, "Developing More Powerful Ideas," *Supervisory Management* (March 1985): 2–9; Denise Shekerjian, *Uncommon Genius: How Great Ideas Are Born* (New York: Viking Press, 1990); and Keng L. Siau, "Group Creativity and Technology," *Journal of Creative Behavior* 29, no. 3 (1996). Siau argues that electronic brainstorming instead of in-person brainstorming eliminates "evaluation apprehension" among group participants.

[17] Deborah Funk, "I Was Showering When . . . ," *Baltimore Business Journal* 12, no. 46 (March 1995): 13–14.

[18] For more on idea development, see A. F. Osborn, *Applied Imagination,* 3d ed. (New York: Scribners, 1963); William J. Gordon, *Synectics* (New York: Harper & Row, 1961); and Ted Pollock, "A Personal File of Stimulating Ideas, Little-Known Facts and Daily Problem-Solvers," *Supervision* 56, no. 4 (1 April 1995): 24.

[19] Martin F. Rosenman, "Serendipity and Scientific Discovery," *Journal of Creative Behavior* 22, no. 2 (1988): 132–38.

[20] For more on implementation, see John M. Keil, *The Creative Mystique: How to Manage It, Nurture It, and Make It Pay* (New York: Wiley, 1985); and James F. Brandowski, *Corporate Imagination Plus: Five Steps to Translating Innovative Strategies into Action* (New York: The Free Press, 1990).

FIGURE 5.1   **THE CREATIVE THINKING PROCESS**

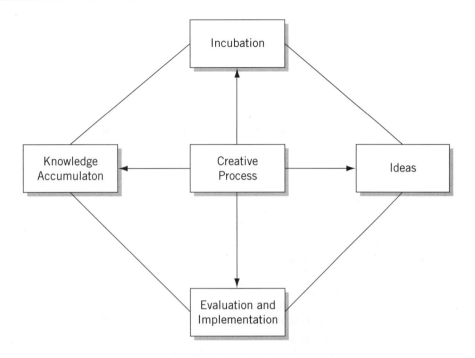

Figure 5.1 illustrates the four phases of the creative thinking process. If a person encounters a major problem while moving through the process, it is sometimes helpful to go back to a previous phase and try again. For example, if an individual is unable to formulate an idea or solution (Phase 3), a return to Phase 1 often helps. By immersing in the data, the individual allows the unconscious mind to begin anew processing the data, establishing cause/effect relationships, and formulating potential solutions.

Developing Your Creativity

You can do a number of things to improve your own creative talents. Becoming aware of some of the habits and mental blocks that stifle creativity is one of the most helpful.[21] Of course, as with most processes, your development will be more effective if you regularly do practice exercises designed to increase your creative abilities. The following section is designed to improve your awareness of some of the thought habits that limit your creativity and to assist you in developing a personalized creativity improvement program.

RECOGNIZING RELATIONSHIPS   Many inventions and innovations are a result of the inventor's seeing new and different relationships among objects, processes, materials, technologies, and people.[22] Examples range widely and include (1) adding fruit juice to soft

---

[21] J. Wajec, *Five Star Minds: Recipes to Stimulate Your Creativity and Imagination* (New York: Doubleday, 1995); and Frank Barron, *No Rootless Flower: An Ecology of Creativity* (New Jersey: Hampton Press, Inc., 1995).

[22] See Dale Dauten, *Taking Chances: Lessons in Putting Passion and Creativity into Your Work Life* (New York: Newmarket Press, 1986); and Gary A. Davis, *Creativity Is Forever* (Dubuque, IA: Kendall/Hunt, 1986).

CONTEMPORARY ENTREPRENEURSHIP

Creativity Is the Key

What would you think if you were in a business meeting with your coworkers and suddenly got hit in the head with a rubber dart? Well, at the Forum Conference & Education Center in Cleveland, it just might happen. Evelyn and Francis Girard started Forum, a facility that provides meeting rooms, six years ago. Many businesses had some doubts about a facility that only provided meeting rooms, not sleeping rooms (as hotels do). But, today, Forum has 20 employees, and its meeting rooms are consistently booked by both *Fortune* 500 companies and smaller companies.

The secret of its success is creativity. The two entrepreneurs are committed to thinking creatively about meeting their client needs. One way they do this is by providing a basket of toys, including dart guns, footballs, and Frisbees. The toys are used to facilitate in-house strategy sessions. "Some of our best ideas happen when darts are flying," Francis Girard claims. The clients believe the toys help people open up and create a flow of ideas. By the end of the day, toys are strung out all over the meeting rooms. The creativity in the Girards' business encompasses the business concept as well as the creation of powerful business magic.

Roger von Oech, author of *A Whack*

on the Side of the Head, says potential for creativity exists in every business and in every job. Businesses need to be creative in everything they do. The product should be creative, the delivery should be creative, the marketing should be creative, and the customer interaction should be creative. The fact creativity lies in small ideas, not just big, bold ideas, is also important. But regardless of idea size, von Oech says "creativity is a business survival skill," and without it you are standing still.

Many people find that being creative is very difficult. Von Oech believes everyone is born creative. Mike Vance, former dean of Disney University (The Walt Disney Company's training program) and now chair of the Creative Thinking Association of America, seems to know why the creativity process is so difficult. He has worked with companies such as Apple and GE to develop creative spirits within their organizations and has found that the techniques found in most books won't increase creativity. So Vance offers his own suggestions on how to heighten creativity.

Vance offers five recommendations for increasing creativity in the workplace. First, think realistically. The question of how things really are should be answered honestly. Don't overestimate anything—

drinks to create Slice, (2) combining combustion engine technology with the wheel to create the automobile, and (3) using a 330-pound defensive football player as a running back and pass receiver.

If you wish to improve your creativity, it helps to look for different or unorthodox relationships among the elements and people around you. This activity involves *perceiving* the product, the competitors, or the consumer demand. This would lead not to creativity but to delusions, Vance says. Second, create an environment where people can speak their minds, even if it causes conflict. Too much harmony can threaten the creativity process. The third suggestion is to use humor to generate ideas. Often what makes us laugh is seeing how things are messed up and then seeing how we can fix them. Fourth, every business needs to have space with supplies designed to nurture creativity, he says. The supplies can be anything that stimulates creativity, such as toys, music, or a chalkboard. And, finally, challenge the status quo. The process of creativity cannot begin until what is known to be true is emptied from the mind, Vance says. Conformity inhibits creativity.

Kathleen R. Allen, a University of Southern California professor, offers some more concrete ways to foster creativity. Applying the following tips can result in great ideas.

- Carry a notebook. Ideas can occur anytime. If you write them down, you will remember them.
- Think opportunistically. Pay attention to everything. Start questioning what you see and why.
- Network. Meet new people and talk to them.
- Think in opposites. Every idea has an opposite. Sometimes opportunities or ideas can be found in it.

- Reinvent the wheel. Think of ways to spice up old products or services. Take a product and make a list of 50 unexpected uses for it. This process may create ideas for something completely new.
- Challenge your ruts. Change the way you do things. Experience something new. Change the radio station, or eat at a different restaurant.

Allen indicates that creativity may not arise from any of these suggestions alone, but great ideas can be created when they are combined. So once the ideas are in place, the next step is to turn them into viable business opportunities. Allen suggests two tactics for making the most of a good idea.

1. Reality test. Test every good idea for its marketability. Gather feedback from friends and potential customers.
2. Keep refining. Criticize ideas and find ways to make them better.

Considering all of these suggestions, the key to creativity is practice. The myth that people are either born creative or they're not is just that, a myth. Creativity can be developed within us all with the help of these suggestions and a little practice. And creativity can be the key to open doors to new ideas and opportunities.

SOURCE: Robert McGarvey, "Turn It On," *Entrepreneur* (November 1996): 154–61.

in a relational mode. You can develop this talent by viewing things and people as existing in a complementary or **appositional relationship** with other things and people. Simply stated, things and people exist in the world in relation to other things and people. Creative people seem to be intuitively aware of this phenomenon and have developed a talent for recognizing new and different relationships. These relationships often lead to visions that result in new ideas, products, and services.[23] In order to develop the ability to recognize new relationships, you must practice perceiving in a relational mode. The following exercise helps with this development.

A Creative Exercise   Analyze and elaborate on how the following pairs relate to each other in a complementary way: nut and bolt, husband and wife, chocolate cake and vanilla ice cream, grass clippings and tomato plants, peanut butter and jelly, athlete and coach, humanity and water, winning and losing, television and overhead projectors, and managers and production workers.

DEVELOPING A FUNCTIONAL PERSPECTIVE   If expanded, the principle of perceiving in a relational mode helps develop a **functional perspective** toward things and people. A creative person tends to view things and people in terms of how they can satisfy his or her needs and help complete a project. For example, the homemaker who cannot find a screwdriver often will use a butter knife to tighten a loose screw. Or the cereal manufacturer will add fruit to its product to create a new product line that appeals to a health-conscious market.

If you wish to become more innovative and creative, you need to visualize yourself in complementary relationships to the things and people of the world. You must learn to look at them in terms of how they complement you in your attempts to satisfy your own needs and to complete your projects. You must begin to look at things and people in nonconventional ways and from a different perspective.[24] The following exercise is designed to help you develop a functional perspective.

A Creative Exercise   Think of and write down all the functions you can imagine for the following items (spend five minutes on each item):

- An egotistical staff member
- A large pebble
- A fallen tree branch
- A chair
- A computer "whiz kid"
- An obsessively organized employee
- The office "gossip"
- An old hubcap
- A new secretary
- An empty roll of masking tape
- A yardstick
- Your sister, a college theater major
- An old coat hanger
- The office tightwad
- This exercise

---

[23] Sidney J. Parnes, *Visionizing: State-of-the-Art Processes for Encouraging Innovative Excellence* (East Aurora, NY: D.O.K., 1988).

[24] See E. Paul Torrance, *The Search for Sartori and Creativity* (Buffalo: Creative Education Foundations, 1979); and Erik K. Winslow and George T. Solomon, "Further Development of a Descriptive Profile of Entrepreneurs," *Journal of Creative Behavior* 23, no. 3 (1989): 149–61.

ENTREPRENEURIAL

EDGE

Challenges for the Creative Entrepreneur

Group Kill   Killer phrases, inaction, group jealousy and sabotage, overwhelming negative reactions, and so forth

Theft or Protecting the Idea   Others stealing the idea and getting to market first

Financing the Idea   Having a great idea but having no luck with financers (e.g., banker) who lack imagination and creativity themselves

Inflexible Perspective   Unwilling to adapt an idea to make it more practical and more easily implemented

Lack of Credit for Idea   Supervisor or someone else taking credit for a successful idea

Pie in the Sky Idea   Having a great idea in theory but unable to make it practical

Researching the Idea   Making sure an idea isn't copyrighted or patented

Real Testing of the Idea   Through focus groups, surveys, pilot programs, and so forth

Lack of Persistence   Tending to move on to new ideas, giving up on an idea because of obstacles

No Time to Incubate Ideas   Too busy putting out fires, getting financing, and so forth

Fixation on an Idea   Falling in love with the idea and failing to objectively evaluate it

Not Brainstorming with Others   Fearing someone will steal the idea and wanting to control everything

USING YOUR BRAINS   Ever since split-brain studies were conducted in the 1950s and 1960s, experts on creativity, innovation, and self-development have emphasized the importance of developing the skills associated with both hemispheres of the brain.[25]

The **right brain** hemisphere helps an individual understand analogies, imagine things, and synthesize information. The **left brain** hemisphere helps the person analyze, verbalize, and use rational approaches to problem solving. Although the two brain hemispheres (right and left) process information differently and are responsible for different brain activities and skills (see Table 5.3), they are integrated through a group of connecting nerve fibers called the corpus callosum. Because of this connection and the nature of the relationship between the activities of each hemisphere, each hemisphere should be viewed as existing and functioning in a complementary relationship with the other hemisphere.[26]

[25] Tony Buzan, *Make the Most of Your Mind* (New York: Simon and Schuster, 1984).

[26] Weston H. Agor, *Intuitive Management: Integrating Left and Right Brain Management Skills* (Englewood Cliffs: Prentice-Hall, 1984); and Tony Buzan, *Using Both Sides of Your Brain* (New York: Dutton, 1976).

| TABLE 5.3 | PROCESSES ASSOCIATED WITH THE TWO BRAIN HEMISPHERES |

Left Hemisphere	Right Hemisphere
Verbal	Nonverbal
Analytical	Synthesizing
Abstract	Seeing analogies
Rational	Nonrational
Logical	Spatial
Linear	Intuitive
	Imaginitive

SOURCE: Betty Edwards, *Drawing on the Right Side of the Brain* (Los Angeles: Tarchor, 1979).

The creative process involves logical and analytical thinking in the knowledge accumulation, evaluation, and implementation stages; and it calls for imagination, intuition, analogy conceptualization, and synthesizing in the incubation and idea creation stages. So in order to become more creative, it is necessary to practice and develop both right- and left-hemisphere skills. The following problem-solving exercise is designed to demonstrate the effectiveness of combining the skills of both hemispheres when solving problems.

A Creative Exercise   Assume you have an idea that will save your organization time and money on processing customer complaints. Your supervisor has been extremely busy and has been unwilling to stop and listen to your idea.

1. Write down all the left-hemisphere-type solutions to this problem you can think of in five minutes.

2. Write down all the right-hemisphere-type solutions to this problem you can think of in five minutes.

3. Compare these lists and combine two or more solutions from each list that will result in a unique and innovative way to solve this problem.

4. Repeat numbers 1, 2, and 3 using a current problem you are facing at work or at home.

Our society and its educational institutions reward individuals who have been successful at developing their logical, analytical, and rational left-brain skills. Little emphasis, however, has been placed on practicing and using right-brain skills. Table 5.4 represents some ways you can practice developing both left- and right-hemisphere skills.[27]

[27] For more on this topic, see Jacquelyn Wonder and Priscilla Donovan, *Whole-Brain Thinking* (New York: Morrow, 1984), 60–61.

TABLE 5.4	WAYS TO DEVELOP LEFT- AND RIGHT-HEMISPHERE SKILLS	
Left-Hemisphere Skills	**Right-Hemisphere Skills**	
1. Step-by-step planning of your work and life activities	1. Using metaphors and analogies to describe things and people in your conversations and writing	
2. Reading ancient, medieval, and scholastic philosophy, legal cases, and books on logic	2. Taking off your watch when you are not working	
3. Establishing timetables for all of your activities	3. Suspending your initial judgment of ideas, new acquaintances, movies, TV programs, etc.	
4. Using and working with a computer program	4. Recording your hunches, feelings, and intuitions and calculating their accuracy	
	5. Detailed fantasizing and visualizing things and situations in the future	
	6. Drawing faces, caricatures, and landscapes	

ELIMINATING MUDDLING MIND-SETS   A number of mental habits block or impede creative thinking. It has been estimated that adults use only 2 to 10 percent of their creative potential.[28] For example, many individuals tend to make quick judgments about new things, people, and ideas. Another inclination is to point out the negative components of a new or different idea because of the psychological discomfort associated with change. Some common mental habits that inhibit creativity and innovation are "either/or" thinking, security hunting, stereotyping, and probability thinking. These habits tend to muddle creative thought processes, and different thought processes must be used to enhance creative thinking.[29]

Either/or Thinking   Because of the speed of change in the modern world, personal lives are filled with a great deal of uncertainty and ambiguity. People often get bogged down with striving for an unreasonable amount of certainty in their lives. But the creative person learns to accept a reasonable amount of ambiguity in his or her work and life. In fact, many exceptionally creative people thrive in an uncertain environment and find it exhilarating.[30]

Security Hunting   Many people try to make the right decision or take the correct action every time. In doing so, they rely on averages, stereotypes, and probability theory to minimize their risks. Although this strategy often is appropriate, at times a creator or innovator must take some calculated risks.[31] Sometimes these risks result in the innovator's being wrong and making mistakes. Yet by recognizing this as part of the innovative game, the creative person learns from his or her mistakes and moves on to create bigger and better

[28] Doris Shallcross and Anthony M. Gawienowski, "Top Experts Address Issues on Creativity Gap in Higher Education," *Journal of Creative Behavior* 23, no. 2 (1989): 75.

[29] Vincent Ryan Ruggiero, *The Art of Thinking: A Guide to Critical and Creative Thought* (New York: Harper Collins, 1995).

[30] David Campbell, *Take the Road to Creativity and Get Off Your Dead End* (Greensboro, NC: Center for Creative Leadership, 1985).

[31] James O'Toole, *Vanguard Management: Redesigning the Corporate Future* (New York: Berkley Books, 1987).

things. We all know Thomas Edison failed numerous times when searching for the correct materials to use inside the incandescent lightbulb.

Stereotyping   It is ironic that although averages and stereotypes are abstractions people fabricate, people act and make decisions based on them as if these were data entities existing in the real world. For example, one could hypothesize that the average homemaker is female, 38 years old, and 5'4" tall; weighs 120 pounds; and has 2 children, a part-time job, and 14.5 years of formal education. If one tried to find a person who fits this description, however, the chances of success would be small. In short, the more descriptive the abstraction or stereotype, the less real it becomes. Predicating actions from stereotypes and averages can cause an individual to act on the basis of a distorted picture of reality. More important, relying on these abstractions can limit a person's perception of the real entities and possibilities in the world. Edward deBono argues that people must alter their thinking to enhance their creativity. Only new patterns of thinking will lead to new ideas and innovations.[32]

Probability Thinking   In their struggle to achieve security, many people also tend to rely on probability theory to make decisions. An overreliance on this decision-making method, however, can distort reality and prohibit one from taking calculated risks that may lead to creative endeavors.

Probability experts report that the predictive power of probability theory increases in proportion to the number of times an event is repeated. If a person wishes to predict the probability of tossing the number *3* when rolling dice a certain number of times, probability theory is extremely useful. However, if the person wishes to know the likelihood of rolling a *4* with one roll of the dice, the predictive ability of probability theory is much less valuable.

In the creative game, often an individual is looking at an opportunity or situation that may occur only once in a lifetime. In a single-event situation, intuition and educated guesses are just as useful, if not more useful, than logic and probability.[33] One way of increasing your creative capacities is to practice looking at some of the situations in your life as a 50/50 game, and then begin to take some risks. Additionally, the following problem-solving exercises are designed to help eliminate muddling mind-sets.

- Practice taking small risks in your personal life and at work, relying on your intuition and hunches. Keep a log of these risks and chart their accuracy and consequences. For example, try to draw to an inside straight in your next family poker game.
- Go out of your way to talk to people who you think conform to a commonly accepted stereotype.
- Take on a number of complex projects at work and at home that do not lend themselves to guaranteed and predictable results. Allow yourself to live with a manageable amount of ambiguity. Notice how you react to this ambiguity.
- When an idea is presented to you, first think of all the positive aspects of the idea, then of all the negative aspects, and finally of all the interesting aspects of the idea.
- When listening to people, suspend initial judgment of them, their ideas, and their information, and simply listen.

---

[32] Edward deBono, *Lateral Thinking: Creativity Step by Step* (New York: Harper and Row, 1970).

[33] Zoa Rockenstein, "Intuitive Processes in Executive Decision Making," *Journal of Creative Behavior* 22, no. 2 (1988): 77–84.

- Try making some decisions in the present. That is, do not let your personal history or your estimates about the future dominate your decision-making process.[34]

The Creative Climate

Creativity is most likely to occur when the business climate is right. No enterprise will have creative owners and managers long if the right climate is not established and nurtured. Some of the important characteristics of this climate follow:

- A trustful management that does not overcontrol the personnel
- Open channels of communication among all business members
- Considerable contact and communication with outsiders
- A large variety of personality types
- A willingness to accept change
- An enjoyment in experimenting with new ideas
- Little fear of negative consequences for making a mistake
- The selection and promotion of employees on the basis of merit
- The use of techniques that encourage ideas, including suggestion systems and brainstorming
- Sufficient financial, managerial, human, and time resources for accomplishing goals[35]

THE INNOVATION PROCESS

Most innovations result from a conscious, purposeful search for new opportunities.[36] This process begins with the analysis of the sources of new opportunities. Drucker has noted that because innovation is both conceptual and perceptual, would-be innovators must go out and look, ask, and listen. Successful innovators use both the right and left sides of their brains. They look at figures. They look at people. They analytically work out what the innovation has to be in order to satisfy the opportunity. Then they go out and look at potential product users to study their expectations, values, and needs.[37]

Most successful innovations are simple and focused. They are directed toward a specific, clear, and carefully designed application. In the process they create new customers and new markets. The Spectra camera from Polaroid is an example. Although the camera is highly sophisticated, it is easy to use and appeals to a specific market niche: people who want instant photography.

Above all, innovation often involves more work than genius. As Thomas Edison once said, "Genius is 1 percent inspiration and 99 percent perspiration." Moreover, innovators rarely work in more than one area. For all his systematic innovative accomplishments, Edison worked only in the electricity field.

---

[34] Adapted from deBono, *Lateral Thinking;* and Eugene Raudsepp, *How to Create New Ideas: For Corporate Profit and Personal Success* (Englewood Cliffs: Prentice-Hall, 1982).

[35] Karl Albrecht, *The Creative Corporation* (Homewood, IL: Dow Jones-Irwin, 1987); also see William C. Miller, *The Creative Edge: Fostering Innovation Where You Work* (New York: Addison-Wesley Publishing, 1987); K. Mark Weaver, "Developing and Implementing Entrepreneurial Cultures," *Journal of Creative Behavior* 22, no. 3 (1988): 184–95; American Management Association, *Creative Edge: How Corporations Support Creativity and Innovation,* New York, 1995; and Michael A. Verespej, "Managing for Creativity: At Broderbund, It's O.K. for Employees and Ideas to Fail," *Industry Week* 244, no. 8 (17 April 1995): 24.

[36] See Peter L. Josty, "A Tentative Model of the Innovation Process," *R & D Management* (January 1990): 35–44.

[37] Drucker, "The Discipline of Innovation," 67.

TABLE 5.5		INNOVATION IN ACTION
Type	**Description**	**Examples**
Invention	Totally new product, service, or process	Wright brothers—airplane Thomas Edison—lightbulb Alexander Graham Bell—telephone
Extension	New use or different application of an already existing product, service, or process	Ray Kroc—McDonald's Nolan Bushnell—Atari Kemmons Wilson—Holiday Inn
Duplication	Creative replication of an existing concept	Wal-Mart—department stores Gateway—personal computers Pizza Hut—pizza parlor
Synthesis	Combination of existing concepts and factors into a new formulation or use	Fred Smith—Federal Express Merrill Lynch—home equity financing

Types of Innovation

Four basic types of innovation exist. These extend from the totally new to modifications of existing products or services. In order of originality, these are the four types:

- **Invention:** the creation of a new product, service, or process, often one that is novel or untried. Such concepts tend to be "revolutionary" (see Table 5.5).
- **Extension:** the expansion of a product, service, or process already in existence. Such concepts make a different application of a current idea.
- **Duplication:** the replication of an already existing product, service, or process. The duplication effort, however, is not simply copying but adding the entrepreneur's own creative touch to enhance or improve the concept to beat the competition.
- **Synthesis:** the combination of existing concepts and factors into a new formulation. This involves taking a number of ideas or items already invented and finding a way so together they form a new application.[38]

Sources of Innovation

Innovation is a tool by which entrepreneurs typically exploit change rather than create change.[39] Although some inventions have created change, these are rare. It is more common to find innovations that take advantage of change. The internal and external areas that serve as innovation sources are presented next.

UNEXPECTED OCCURRENCES   These are successes or failures that, because they were unanticipated or unplanned, often end up proving to be a major innovative surprise to the firm.

---

[38] Adapted from Richard M. Hodgetts and Donald F. Kuratko, *Effective Small Business Management*, 5th ed. (Fort Worth, TX: Dryden, 1995), 21–23.

[39] See Jane M. Howell and Chris A. Higgins, "Champions of Change," *Business Quarterly* (spring 1990): 31–36.

INCONGRUITIES   These occur whenever a gap or difference exists between expectations and reality. For example, when Fred Smith proposed overnight mail delivery, he was told, "If it were that profitable, the U.S. Post Office would be doing it." It turned out Smith was right. An incongruity existed between what Smith felt was needed and the way business was currently conducted.

PROCESS NEEDS   These exist whenever a demand arises for the entrepreneur to innovate and answer a particular need. The creation of health foods and timesaving devices are examples.

INDUSTRY AND MARKET CHANGES   Continual shifts in the marketplace occur, caused by developments such as consumer attitudes, advancements in technology, industry growth, and the like. Industries and markets are always undergoing changes in structure, design, or definition. An example is found in the health care industry, where hospital care has undergone radical change and where home health care and preventive medicine have replaced hospitalization and surgery as primary focus areas. The entrepreneur needs to be aware of and seize these emerging opportunities.

DEMOGRAPHIC CHANGES   These arise from trend changes in population, age, education, occupations, geographic locations, and similar factors. Demographic shifts are important and often provide new entrepreneurial opportunities. For example, as the average population age in Florida has increased (due heavily to the influx of retirees), land development, recreational, and health care industries all have profited.

PERCEPTUAL CHANGES   These changes occur in people's interpretation of facts and concepts. They are intangible yet meaningful. Perception can *cause* major shifts in ideas to take place. The current fitness craze, caused by the perceived need to be healthy and physically fit, has created a demand for both health foods and health facilities throughout the country.

KNOWLEDGE-BASED CONCEPTS   These are the basis for the creation or development of something brand new, tying into our earlier discussion of invention as a type of innovation. Inventions are knowledge based; they are the product of new thinking, new methods, and new knowledge. Such innovations often require the longest time period between initiation and market implementation because of the need for testing and modification. For example, the Spectra camera from Polaroid, which helped revolutionize instant photography, took almost five years to create, perfect, and bring to market.

Some examples of these innovation sources are presented in Table 5.6.

Major Innovation Myths

Presented next is a list of the commonly accepted innovation myths, along with reasons why these are myths and not facts.[40]

MYTH 1: INNOVATION IS PLANNED AND PREDICTABLE   This myth is based on the old concept that innovation should be left to the research and development (R&D)

[40] Adapted from Drucker, *Innovation and Entrepreneurship;* and Thomas J. Peters and Nancy J. Austin, *Passion for Excellence* (New York: Random House, 1985).

CONTEMPORARY ENTREPRENEURSHIP

Five Types of Innovators

Gatekeepers

These people collect and channel information about changes in the technical environment. They stay current with events and ideas through personal contacts, professional meetings, and the news media. When gatekeepers find relevant information, they send it to the appropriate person or unit for follow-up.

Idea Generators

This role involves analysis of information about new technologies, products, or procedures in order to yield a new idea for the company. The fresh idea may be an innovative solution to an existing problem in product or business development or the identification of a new marketplace opportunity.

Champions

Champions advocate and push for the new idea. This role involves obtaining and applying the resources and staff to demonstrate the idea's feasibility. Champions are concerned about results, not risk, and do not spend time studying the consequences of failure. Their mission is to remove obstacles.

Project Managers

Someone has to draw up schedules and budgets; arrange periodic information sessions and status reports; coordinate labor, equipment, and other resources; and monitor progress against the plan. Project managers integrate and administer the tasks, people, and physical resources necessary to move an idea into practice.

Coaches

This function addresses the technical and interpersonal aspects of the work in the innovation process. Coaches provide technical training related to new developments and help people work together to turn an idea into a tangible result.

SOURCE: Mark Frohman and Perry Pascarella, "Achieving Purpose-Driven Innovation," *Industry Week,* 19 March 1990, 20–26.

department under a planned format. In truth, innovation is unpredictable and may be introduced by anyone.

MYTH 2: TECHNICAL SPECIFICATIONS SHOULD BE THOROUGHLY PREPARED
Thorough preparation often takes too long. Quite often it is more important to use a try/test/revise approach.

MYTH 3: CREATIVITY RELIES ON DREAMS AND BLUE-SKY IDEAS   Accomplished innovators are very practical people and create from the opportunities left by reality—not daydreams.

MYTH 4: BIG PROJECTS WILL DEVELOP BETTER INNOVATIONS THAN SMALLER ONES   This myth has been proven false time and time again. Larger firms are now en-

TABLE 5.6	SOURCES OF INNOVATION

Source	Examples
Unexpected occurrences	Unexpected success: Apple Computer (microcomputers) Unexpected failure: Ford's Edsel
Incongruities	Overnight package delivery
Process needs	Sugar-free products Caffeine-free coffee Microwave ovens
Industry and market changes	Health care industry: changing to home health care
Demographic changes	Rest homes or retirement centers for older people
Perceptual changes	Exercise (aerobics) and the growing concern for fitness
Knowledge-based concepts	Video industry; robotics

couraging their people to work in smaller groups, where it often is easier to generate creative ideas.

MYTH 5: TECHNOLOGY IS THE DRIVING FORCE OF INNOVATION AND SUCCESS
Technology is certainly one source for innovation, but it is not the only one. Moreover, the customer or market is the driving force behind any innovation. Market-driven or customer-based innovations have the highest probability of success. A good example is found in Polaroid's Polarvision, a television camera that allowed for instant playback of the film. Polaroid hit the market with this technological advance at the same time videocassette recorders arrived. The result: Polaroid's product was rejected, and the company lost millions of dollars.

Principles of Innovation

Potential entrepreneurs need to realize innovation principles exist. These principles can be learned and, when combined with opportunity, can enable individuals to innovate. The major motivation principles follow:

- *Be action oriented.* Innovators always must be active and searching for new ideas, opportunities, or sources of innovation.
- *Make the product, process, or service simple and understandable.* People must readily understand how the innovation works.
- *Make the product, process, or service customer based.* Innovators always must keep the customer in mind. The more an innovator has the end user in mind, the greater the chance the concept will be accepted and used.
- *Start small.* Innovators should not attempt a project or development on a grandiose scale. They should begin small and then build and develop, allowing for planned growth and proper expansion in the right manner and at the right time.
- *Aim high.* Innovators should aim high for success by seeking a niche in the marketplace.

- *Try/test/revise.* Innovators always should follow the rule of try, test, and revise. This helps work out any flaws in the product, process, or service.
- *Learn from failures.* Innovation does not guarantee success. More important, failures often give rise to innovations.[41]
- *Follow a milestone schedule.* Every innovator should follow a schedule that indicates milestone accomplishments. Although the project may run ahead or behind schedule, it still is important to have the schedule in order to plan and evaluate the project.
- *Reward heroic activity.* This principle applies more to those involved in seeking and motivating others to innovate. Innovative activity should be rewarded and given the proper amount of respect. This also means tolerating and, to a limited degree, accepting failures as a means of accomplishing innovation. Innovative work must be seen as heroic activity that will reveal new horizons for the enterprise.
- *Work, work, work.* This is a simple but accurate exhortation with which to conclude the innovation principles. It takes work, not genius or mystery, to innovate successfully.[42]

FINANCIAL SUPPORT FOR INNOVATION

A financial environment that supports innovation is crucial to the continued nurturing of creative activity. Two major sources of financial backing are venture capital and government support.

Venture-Capital Environment

The activity in venture capital funds has changed dramatically in the past 20 years. Consider the following facts. In 1987, 587 U.S. venture-capital firms existed (a 148 percent increase since 1977), which represented independent private funds, corporate funds, and venture-capital-related small-business investment companies.

Independent private funds, in contrast to venture-capital companies and corporate funds (affiliated with financial and industrial concerns), showed the greatest increase. In 1987, 55 percent of the total venture capital was handled by 64 firms with $100 million in venture capital.[43]

Between 1978 and 1987, the industry gained nearly 800 percent in total capital under management, from $3.5 billion to $31.1 billion. In addition, a 700 percent increase in annual capital commitments, from $600 million to $4.9 billion, occurred. Also, nearly a 600 percent increase in annual disbursements, from $550 million to $3.8 billion, transpired.

In 1989 a slowdown in the venture-capital markets occurred. After the stock market crash of October 1987, the number of individual investors—the backbone of initial public offerings (IPOs)—dropped. Venture capitalists depend on a strong IPO market for their investments.

However, 1990 demonstrated a resurgence in the IPO market with a 29 percent increase over 1989. Dollar volume increased 33 percent, and the number of offerings increased from 69 (1989) to 98 (1990), with the dollar amount increasing from $3.6 billion in 1989 to $5.4

---

[41] For a good example, see Ronald A. Mitsch, "Three Roads to Innovation," *Journal of Business Strategy* (September/October 1990): 18–21.

[42] William Taylor, "The Business of Innovation," *Harvard Business Review* (March/April 1990): 97–106.

[43] For more on venture capital, see Stanley E. Pratt and Jane K. Morris, *Pratt's Guide to Venture Capital Sources,* 10th ed. (Phoenix: Onyx Press, 1986); and Jeffry A. Timmons and William D. Bygrave, "Venture Capital's Role in Financing Innovation for Economic Growth," *Journal of Business Venturing* (winter 1986): 161–76.

billion in 1990.[44] Although the 1990s dropped somewhat to approximately $3.8 billion, a record $7.4 billion in venture capital was invested in 1995.[45] This unprecedented total represents nearly 50 percent growth over the funding level for 1994 and a 125 percent increase since 1991. Venture capitalists deployed this unparalleled amount of capital in a record 1,100 deals. The total number of financings completed in 1995 increased just 15 percent over the total for 1994 and has grown 39 percent since 1991.[46]

Though disbursements have declined since 1987, total capital under management has continued to increase. This phenomenal growth has netted the following changes in the structure and investment philosophy of the industry:

- Increasing size and number of venture capital funds
- Increasing competition among venture capitalists and declining rates of return
- Fewer experienced investment personnel
- Increasing size of average investment
- Increasing amount of coinvestment
- Increasing specialization[47]

Seed capital (initial research funding) accounts for only 2 percent of all dollars invested by venture-capital firms. This is two-and-a-half times more money available than 17 years ago, but, nevertheless, entrepreneurs must be aware of the environment for venture capital.[48]

In the most current research conducted on seed capital funds (1993), the following facts were noted. A total of 67 seed capital funds were examined with an average age of 8.7 years. They reported that their aggregate amount of current funds under management was $4.146 billion, having increased from their initial capitalization of $1.015 billion. They have collectively invested $2.164 billion in 1,914 company investments, and they have experienced 433 company failures (22.6 percent), with a total dollar loss of $231.6 million (10.7 percent). On the positive side, their successful enterprises produced $30.9 billion in revenues in 1992 and supported 218,488 jobs. In addition, the overall average return on investment (ROI) was 17.8 percent for all their investments and 15.5 percent for their seed/start-up-stage investments.

Combination funds exhibited the best ROI at 23 percent and a better-than-average cost per job created of $8,845. Public funds showed the lowest ROI at 6 percent, but their cost per job created was the best at $6,766; public funds also were the smallest in current capitalization at an average of $3.1 million, compared to private funds at $100.8 million. The typical investment by a private fund was $1.5 million versus $188,000 by a public fund. Ninety percent of the funds targeted their investments at technology-based enterprises.[49]

The 1990s have found a continual willingness on the part of investors, yet the trend is toward specialization by venture capitalists. The venture-capital firms are becoming more restrictive on the industry in which they invest, including the company's development stage.

[44] Rosalyn Retkwa, "Venture Capital Industry Now in Transition Period," *Pension World,* July 1990, 24–25.

[45] *The State of Small Business: A Report to the President* (Washington: Government Printing Office, 1995), 287.

[46] Steven P. Galante and David T. Gleba, "An Overview of the Venture Capital Industry and Emerging Changes," *The Private Equity Analyst,* Wellesley, Massachusetts, 1996, 10.

[47] S. Michael Camp and Donald L. Sexton, "Trends in Venture Capital Investment: Implications for High Technology Firms," *Journal of Small Business Management* (July 1992): 11–19.

[48] Marie-Jeanne Juilland, "The Frustrating Search for Seed," *Venture,* June/July 1990, 34.

[49] Richard T. Meyer, Timothy Falvey, and Min Lee, *The 1993 National Census of Seed Capital Funds* (Atlanta: Orion Technical Associates, 1993).

If the quality of innovation is there, then the money will be found. Valuations for start-ups have decreased approximately 30 percent since the mid-1980s, and, thus, entrepreneurs are seeking joint ventures, marketing agreements with larger firms, and foreign investors.

Government Support of Innovation

Government programs to support innovation have been on the rise over the past decade. For example, the Small Business Innovation Development Act of 1982 provides millions of dollars for smaller companies and entrepreneurs involved in research and development.

The Small Business Innovation Development Act directs that small firms get at least a minimum fixed percentage of research and development awards from federal agencies with sizable R&D budgets. The act, signed into law by President Ronald Reagan on July 22, 1982, means that small high-technology firms receive more federal R&D awards than before. In fiscal 1983 $45 million was awarded under this program, and that amount was increased to $483 million by fiscal 1993. By 1995, 11 federal agencies participating in the program had provided more than $4 billion to small high-tech companies throughout the United States that competed for 21,722 awards. Under the act each participating agency in the program publishes solicitations that describe that agency's research and development needs, funds for which are to be awarded by competitive contract, grant, or cooperative agreement through the Small Business Innovation Research (SBIR) programs. The SBA then publishes a master schedule of all SBIR solicitations from the participating agencies.

Small high-technology firms can submit proposals for research projects directly to the appropriate agency through a simplified standard solicitation procedure. Each agency then awards the firms on a competitive basis. Selection criteria are included in each solicitation, and projects with potential for commercialization are encouraged. Thus small high-technology firms have opportunities to (1) compete with other small firms for more federal R&D awards, (2) find out easily about federal R&D projects available through the SBIR programs in participating agencies, and (3) be included in a source file of small firms capable of doing R&D for the federal government. R&D awards in the SBIR programs have three phases. In Phase 1 awards are made for research projects intended to evaluate the scientific and technical merit and feasibility of an idea. These awards generally are $100,000 or less, and the phase lasts about six months. Funding for projects with the most potential are continued. In Phase 2 awards of $750,000 or less are made for further development of the innovation. This phase usually lasts about two years. Phase 3 is characterized by private-sector investment and support that will bring the innovation to the marketplace. When appropriate, this phase also may include follow-up production contracts with a federal agency for the federal government's future use.[50]

✳ SUMMARY

This chapter examined the importance of creativity and innovation to the entrepreneur. The creativity process was described, and ways of developing creativity were presented. Exercises and suggestions were included to help the reader increase the development of his or her creativity. The nature of the creative climate also was described.

[50] Small Business Innovation Research, U.S. Small Business Administration, 1441 L Street NW, Washington, DC 20416.

The four basic types of innovation—invention, extension, duplication, and synthesis—were explained, and the sources of innovation were outlined and examined. The last part of the chapter reviewed the myths commonly associated with innovation, presented the major innovation principles, and discussed financial support for innovation.

Key Terms and Concepts

Appositional relationship	Invention
Creative process	Left brain
Creativity	Muddling mind-sets
Duplication	Probability thinking
Extension	Right brain
Functional perspective	Stereotyping
Incongruities	Synthesis
Innovation	

Review and Discussion Questions

1. In your own words, state what is meant by the term *innovation.*
2. What is the difference between an adaptor and an innovator?
3. What are four major components in the creative process?
4. What are the four steps involved in developing personal creativity?
5. What are four major types of innovation?
6. What are the major sources of innovation? Explain and give an example of each.
7. Briefly describe each of the five major myths commonly associated with innovation.
8. Identify and describe five of the innovation principles.

Experiential Exercise   *Developing Your Personal Creativity*

This exercise is designed to help you develop your personal creativity. To enhance your creativity, you should make improvements in the following areas:

1. *Personal development* (self-discipline, self-awareness, self-confidence, improvement in energy level, etc.)
2. *Problem-solving skills* (problem recognition, etc.)
3. *Mental fluency* (quantity of thoughts/ideas, etc.)
4. *Mental flexibility* (switching gears/approaches, etc.)
5. *Originality* (unusual thoughts and ideas, etc.)

It is best to start small and work on a few things at a time. Follow the step-by-step approach listed next. Use the accompanying worksheet to help you design a personal creativity program.

1. Choose one of the five areas for improvement listed (e.g., mental fluency).
2. Establish a specific objective for this area (e.g., to increase your ability to generate logical and intuitive solutions to problems at work).
3. Decide how much time you will give to this program (e.g., three hours a week).
4. Decide how long you will work in this area (e.g., one month, two months).

5. Decide what actions you will take and what exercises you will perform to improve in this area (e.g., sentence-creation exercises, usage ideas, meditation, suspension of initial judgments).
6. Set up an outline of your program (i.e., day of week, time of day, place, and what you will do during this time).
7. Review your program after completion, and write a similar program for another one of the five areas for improvement.

PERSONAL CREATIVITY PROGRAM WORKSHEET

Area of improvement _____

Specific objective _____

_____

_____

Number of hours per week _____

Duration of program _____

Actions/exercises _____

_____

_____

_____

Outline of Program

Day of the week _____ _____ _____ _____

Time of day _____ _____ _____ _____

Place _____ _____ _____ _____

Actions that day _____ _____ _____ _____

_____ _____ _____ _____

_____ _____ _____ _____

VIDEO CASE   **5.1**

Paradigm Simulation: Reality Bytes in the Virtual World

In 1990, three young, unemployed software engineers—Mike Engledinger, Wes Hoffman, and Ron Toupal—followed their vision and formed Paradigm Simulation. "Originally, we all worked at the same company," Engledinger, Paradigm cofounder and vice president of engineering, says. "That company did simulation and training applications, but they didn't see the computer graphics side as being all that important. They didn't think there was much of a future in it. As it turns out, there is, and we knew there was."

Since it was founded, Paradigm has been blazing a trail in the simulation and virtual-reality industries. Originally, the company began doing high-end, multimillion-dollar simulation for the defense industry. But the company has found an innovative way to make state-of-the-art technology more affordable and user-friendly to a broader consumer base. "Before Paradigm came along, 3-D simulation wasn't accessible to anybody," Hoffman, cofounder and creative director, explains. "It was too expensive. Software products were selling for $70,000 to $80,000 and the hardware was $300,000. We came in and said, 'Well, I think if we drop the price down to $5,000 we can sell thousands more.'"

At the core of their success has been a product called Vega, a software tool that enables programmers and nonprogrammers alike to build interactive 3-D visual simulation and virtual-reality applications.

"Our Vega product was revolutionary because it provided not only an application interface to engineers, but it also provided a graphical user interface—a point-and-click environment—that users could leverage off of," David Gatchel, executive vice president of entertainment, explains. "People in the past haven't been able to use this technology because they weren't a software engineer or an engineer of any sort. With our implementation, they can visualize data, visualize scenarios without ever having to write any software code."

Paradigm's innovative software tools have attracted an impressive client list that includes Chrysler, the National Aeronautics and Space Administration, Silicon Graphics, BMW, and, most recently, the gaming giant—Nintendo. "Nintendo was looking for a company that could help them bring 3-D games to the home market," Gatchel says. Nintendo chose Paradigm to create one of its most challenging games: Pilot Wings 64. Unveiled to glowing reviews, Pilot Wings 64 has proven to be one of Nintendo's best-selling games, giving Paradigm an impressive entrée into a lucrative new market. "We've actually developed a capability in-house which says, 'Hey, we can develop good games! There's a business there. Maybe we should consider building more games,'" Toupal, cofounder and president of Paradigm, says. Soon, another Paradigm creation, a spike-haired, animated ski demon named Egghead, will be an interactive star at Disney's Epcot Center.

Deals with Disney and Nintendo have sent Paradigm soaring. "Every year, the company has doubled in size. And every year my biggest challenge is how I'm going to double it again. The business has to change dramatically," Toupal reveals. While Paradigm's leaders look forward to the rewards of change and growth, they have concerns about the impact the future will have on the relaxed corporate culture that has nurtured the company's creativity. "I think that's really been a challenge to maintain the small-company atmosphere as the company grows," Hoffman admits. "A lot of the reason that we decided to start a company in the first place was because we all worked at large companies and were sick of the bureaucratic nonsense. But maintaining that kind of creative thinking in a large company where people start becoming kind of political and then develop some bureaucracy tends to start inhibiting really creative thinking." "That's the number one challenge that we've had going from 10 to 70 people to 150 people: communicating the vision. Communicating and maintaining the culture. Attracting and retaining the great individuals that we've got," chief financial officer Ron Paige adds.

Despite its rapid-paced growth, Paradigm's leaders are determined to preserve the relaxed, casual atmosphere they believe nurtures professional camaraderie, sparks creativity, and values the contributions of people above technology. "Technology is fleeting," Toupal says. "In the software business, the success of the business is directly attributed to the people. And we don't ever want to lose sight of that."

Questions

1. Explain how the phases of the creative process apply to the founding of Paradigm Simulation?
2. What type of innovation would Paradigm be considered? Why?

3. Identify the source of innovation that best describes the start of Paradigm Simulation.
4. How would the principles of innovation be applied to Paradigm's new growth?

 **CASE   5.2**

Post-it Notes

One way new products are developed is to take a current product and modify it in some way. Another way is to determine how a previously developed product can be marketed or used by a particular group of customers.

The 3M Company is famous for many products, among them adhesives and abrasives. A few years ago one of the 3M managers, a member of a church choir, wanted to mark the pages of his hymnal so he could quickly find them. A bookmark would not do because the piece of paper could easily fall out. The manager needed something that would adhere to the page but not tear it. Back at work, the manager asked one of the members of the research and development department if an adhesive existed that would do this. One did, but it never had been marketed because the company found that the adhesive was not strong enough for industrial use. At the manager's request, a batch of the glue was prepared and applied to small pieces of paper that could be used as bookmarks.

As the manager who had requested the product began to think about the new product, he concluded it had uses other than as a bookmark. Secretaries could use it to attach messages to files, and managers could use it to send notes along with letters and memos. In an effort to spur interest in the product, the manager had a large batch of these "attachable" notes, now called Post-it Notes, made and began distributing them to secretaries throughout the company. Before long more and more people began to ask for them. The manager then ordered the supply cut off and told everyone who wanted them that they would have to contact the marketing department. When that department became inundated with calls for Post-it Notes, it concluded that a strong demand existed throughout industry for these notes, and full production began. Today Post-its is one of the largest and most successful product lines at the 3M Company.

Questions

1. In the development of this product, how did the creative thinking process work? Describe what took place in each of the four steps.
2. Why did the manager have the Post-its sent to secretaries throughout the company? What was his objective in doing this?
3. What type of innovation was this—invention, extension, duplication, or synthesis? Defend your answer.
4. Which of the innovation sources discussed in the chapter help account for this product's success? Explain in detail.

ETHICAL AND SOCIAL RESPONSIBILITY CHALLENGES FOR ENTREPRENEURS

CHAPTER OBJECTIVES

1. To discuss the importance of ethics for entrepreneurs

2. To define the term *ethics*

3. To study ethics in a conceptual framework for a dynamic environment

4. To review the constant dilemma of law versus ethics

5. To examine the role of ethics in the free enterprise system

6. To present strategies for establishing ethical responsibility

7. To introduce the challenge of social responsibility

8. To emphasize the importance of entrepreneurs taking a position of ethical leadership

Managers who fail to provide proper leadership and to institute systems that facilitate ethical conduct share responsibility with those who conceive, execute, and knowingly benefit from corporate misdeeds.

Lynn Sharp Paine,
"Managing for Organizational Integrity"
Harvard Business Review, 1994

The most important contributions of the members of the socially responsible business movement have little to do with recycling, nuts from the rain forest, or employing the homeless. Their gift to us is that they are leading by trying to do something, to risk, to take a chance, to make a change, any change. They're not waiting for "the solution" but acting creatively without guarantees of success. That is what all of us must do. Being visionary has always been given a bad rap by commerce. But without a positive vision for humankind, we can have no meaning, no work, and no purpose.

Paul Hawken and William McDonough,
"Seven Steps to Doing Good Business"
Inc., 1993

Ethical issues in business are of great importance today. And why not? The prevalence of scandals, fraud, and various forms of executive misconduct in corporations has spurred the watchful eye of the public.[1]

Ethics is not a new topic, however. It has figured prominently in philosophical thought since the time of Socrates, Plato, and Aristotle. Derived from the Greek word *ethos,* meaning custom or mode of conduct, ethics has challenged philosophers for centuries to determine what exactly represents right or wrong conduct. For example, Loucks notes that "It was about 560 B.C. . . . when the Greek thinker Chilon registered the opinion that a merchant does better to take a loss than to make a dishonest profit. His reasoning was that a loss may be painful for a while, but dishonesty hurts forever—and it's still timely."[2]

---

[1] See Frank K. Sonnenberg and Beverly Goldberg, "Business Integrity: An Oxymoron?" *Industry Week,* 6 April 1992, 53–56; and Kenneth Labich, "The New Crisis in Business Ethics," *Fortune,* 20 April 1992, 167–76.

[2] Vernon R. Loucks Jr., "A CEO Look at Ethics," *Business Horizons* (March/April 1987): 2.

Today's entrepreneurs are faced with many ethical decisions, especially during the early stages of their new ventures. And, as Sir Adrian Cadbury observes, "There is no simple universal formula for solving ethical problems. We have to choose from our own codes of conduct whichever rules are appropriate to the case in hand; the outcome of these choices makes us who we are."[3]

The purpose of this chapter is to examine some of the issues surrounding ethics and entrepreneurship. It is our hope that aspiring entrepreneurs will realize the powerful impact integrity and ethical conduct have on creating a successful venture.

DEFINING ETHICS

In the broadest sense, **ethics** provide the basic rules or parameters for conducting any activity in an "acceptable" manner. More specifically, ethics represent a set of principles prescribing a behavioral code that explains what is good and right or bad and wrong; ethics may, in addition, outline moral duty and obligations.[4] The problem with most definitions of the term is not in the description but rather in the implications for implementation. The definition is a static description that implies society agrees on certain universal principles. With society operating in a dynamic and ever-changing environment, however, such a consensus does not exist.[5] In fact, continual conflict over the ethical nature of decisions is still quite prevalent.

This conflict arises for a number of reasons. First, business enterprises are confronted by many interests both inside and outside the organization—for example, stockholders, customers, managers, the community, the government, employees, private interest groups, unions, peers, and so on. Second, society is undergoing dramatic change. Values, mores, and societal norms have gone through a drastic evolution in the past few decades. A definition of ethics in such a rapidly changing environment must be based more on a process than on a static code. Figure 6.1 illustrates a conceptual framework for viewing this process. As one ethicist states, "Deciding what is good or right or bad and wrong in such a dynamic environment is necessarily 'situational.' Therefore, instead of relying on a set of fixed ethical principles, we must now develop an ethical process."[6]

The quadrants depicted in Figure 6.1 demonstrate the age-old dilemma between law and ethics. Moving from the ideal ethical and legal position (Quadrant I) to an unethical and illegal position (Quadrant IV), one can see the continuum of activities within an ethical process. Yet legality provides societal standards but not definitive answers to ethical questions.

ETHICS AND LAWS

For the entrepreneur the dilemma of legal versus ethical is a vital one. Just how far can an entrepreneur go in order to establish his or her venture? Survival of the venture is a strong motivation for entrepreneurs, and although the law provides the boundaries for what is

---

[3] Sir Adrian Cadbury, "Ethical Managers Make Their Own Rules," *Harvard Business Review* (September/October 1987): 69.

[4] Verne E. Henderson, "The Ethical Side of Enterprise," *Sloan Management Review* (spring 1982): 38.

[5] Richard Evans, "Business Ethics and Changes in Society," *Journal of Business Ethics* 10 (1991): 871–76.

[6] Henderson, "The Ethical Side," 40.

FIGURE 6.1   **CLASSIFYING DECISIONS USING A CONCEPTUAL FRAMEWORK**

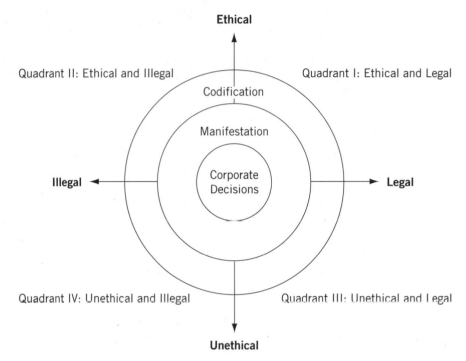

SOURCE: Verne E. Henderson, "The Ethical Side of Enterprise," *Sloan Management Review* (spring 1982): 42.

illegal (even though the laws are subject to constant interpretation), it does not supply answers for ethical considerations.

Managerial Rationalizations

One researcher believes legal behavior represents one of four rationalizations managers use for justifying questionable conduct. The four **rationalizations** are believing that the activity is not "really" illegal or immoral; that it is in the individual's or the corporation's best interest; that it will never be found out; and that because it helps the company, the company will condone it.[7]

These rationalizations appear realistic, given the behavior of many business enterprises today. However, the legal aspect can be the most dubious. This is because the business world (and society) relies heavily on the law to qualify the actions of various situations. The law interprets the situations within the prescribed framework. Unfortunately, this framework does not always include ethical or moral behavior. This is left up to the individual, which is the precise reason for the dilemma.

In any examination of the realm of managerial rationalizations, the idea of morally questionable acts becomes a major concern for understanding ethical conduct. One research study developed a typology of morally questionable acts.[8] Table 6.1 summarizes the dis-

[7] Saul W. Gellerman, "Why Good Managers Make Bad Ethical Choices," *Harvard Business Review* (July/August 1986): 85.

[8] James A. Waters and Frederick Bird, "Attending to Ethics in Management," *Journal of Business Ethics* 5 (1989): 493–97.

CONTEMPORARY ENTREPRENEURSHIP

An Enterpreneur's Success Turns into Disaster

Stew Leonard, an enterpreneur and retail legend from Norwalk, Connecticut, featured by Tom Peter's *In Search of Excellence* as the wizard who transformed a small dairy farm into a $200 million-a-year supermarket Disneyland, shocked the business world when he pleaded guilty to tax fraud in 1993.

Federal agents say he conspired to defraud the government of taxes on $17.5 million. How? He developed a computer software program that allowed him to reduce sales data on an item-by-item basis and skim $17 million in cash over a period from 1981 to 1991. Computer tapes that contained the real financial figures were destroyed, and the company's auditors were given the understated books. In order to divert even more money, Leonard had customers buy gift certificates with cash.

Each day the cash was emptied from the registers into a "money room" where it was counted, placed in bags, and dropped down a chute into the "vault room." Most of the unreported money was taken to the Caribbean, where Leonard owns a second home. Another executive, Leonard's brother-in-law, kept $484,000 hidden behind a false panel in his basement. The computer program itself was also hidden.

The government apparently began investigating Leonard after he was stopped in June 1991 by customs agents as he boarded a flight to the Caribbean with $80,000 in cash. He had not filed the required government forms for taking that amount of money out of the country.

IRS agents identified Leonard's actions as the largest criminal tax evasion in Connecticut's history and as the largest case in the country's history involving a computer program as part of the conspiracy.

Leonard had achieved the pinnacle of success in his industry. Two hundred thousand customers visit his two stores every week. His Norwalk store has the highest sales per square foot, $3,470 compared to the industry average of $300–$500, and it sells 10 million quarts of milk and 8 million ears of corn annually. A former recipient of the Presidential Award for Entrepreneurial Achievement, Leonard now stands disgraced and faces a sentence that includes community service and repayment of $15 million in restitution.

SOURCE: Richard Behar, "Skimming the Cream," *Time*, 2 August 1993, 49; and Clifford J. Levy, "Founder of Renowned Store Pleads Guilty in Fraud Case," *New York Times*, 23 July 1993, A11.

tinctions made in this typology. Morally questionable acts are either "against the firm" or "on behalf of the firm." In addition, the managerial role differs for various acts. **Nonrole** acts are those the person takes outside of his or her role as manager, yet they go against the firm. Examples would include expense account cheating and embezzlement. **Role failure** acts are also against the firm, but they involve a person failing to perform his or her managerial role, including superficial performance appraisals (not totally honest) and not

TABLE 6.1 **TYPES OF MORALLY QUESTIONABLE ACTS**

Type	Direct Effect	Examples
Nonrole	Against the firm	Expense account cheating Embezzlement Stealing supplies
Role failure	Against the firm	Superficial performance appraisal Not confronting expense account cheating Palming off a poor performer with inflated praise
Role distortion	For the firm	Bribery Price fixing Manipulating suppliers
Role assertion	For the firm	Investing in South Africa Using nuclear technology for energy generation Not withdrawing product line in face of initial allegations of inadequate safety

SOURCE: James A. Waters and Frederick Bird, "Attending to Ethics in Management," *Journal of Business Ethics* 5 (1989): 494.

FIGURE 6.2 **OVERLAP BETWEEN MORAL STANDARDS AND LEGAL REQUIREMENTS**

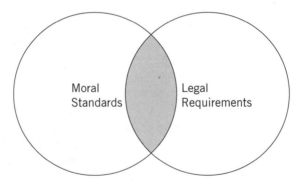

confronting someone who is cheating on expense accounts. **Role distortion** acts and **role assertion** acts are committed on the basis they are "for the firm." These acts involve managers/entrepreneurs who rationalize that the long-run interests of the firm are foremost. Examples include bribery, price fixing, manipulating suppliers, and failing to withdraw a potentially dangerous product from the market.

All four of these roles involved in the morally questionable acts, whether "for" or "against" the firm, illustrate the types of rationalizations that can occur. In addition, this typology presents an interesting insight into the distinctions involved with managerial rationalization.

The Matter of Morality

Ethical conduct may reach beyond the limits of the law. As one group of noted legal writers has pointed out, morals and law are not synonymous but may be viewed as two circles partially superimposed on each other (see Figure 6.2). The area covered by both the moral standards circle and the legal requirements circle represents the body of ideas that are both moral and legal. Yet the largest expanse of area is outside this overlapping portion, indicating the vast difference that sometimes exists between morality (ethics) and law.[9]

LaRue Hosmer has pointed out three conclusions regarding the relationship between legal requirements and moral judgment. First, as noted earlier, the requirements of law may overlap at times but do not duplicate the moral standards of society. Some laws have no moral content whatsoever (e.g., driving on the right side of the road), some laws are morally unjust (e.g., racial segregation laws before the 1960s), and some moral standards have no legal basis (e.g., telling a lie). Second, legal requirements tend to be negative (forbidding acts), whereas morality tends to be positive (encouraging acts). Third, legal requirements usually lag behind the acceptable moral standards of society.[10]

In addition, even if the argument were made that laws are supposed to be the collective moral judgment of society, inherent problems arise when people believe laws represent morality. Whether it is lack of information on issues, misrepresentation of the values or laws, or an imprecise judicial system, the legal environment has difficulty encompassing all ethical and moral expectations. Thus the issue of law and ethics will continue to be a dilemma for entrepreneurs (see Table 6.2).

Economic Trade-Offs

Innovation, risk taking, and venture creation are the backbone of the free enterprise system. From this system emerge the qualities of individualism and competition. These qualities have produced an economic system that creates jobs (approximately 20 million jobs in the past decade) and enormous growth in ventures (more than 600,000 incorporations each year). However, these same qualities also have produced complex trade-offs between economic profits and social welfare, as revealed by the following situations:

- Advertisements for Marlboro and Vantage cigarettes show young, athletic, outdoorsy men and women, yet cigarettes place hundreds of thousands of people in hospital intensive care units and cause about 350,000 deaths per year.
- Among the 50,000 toxic-waste dump sites in the United States, more than 1,000 are very dangerous. Every day, more steel drums rust through, their toxic contents running into streams and lakes and contaminating drinking water.
- During an economic downturn, a manager at Bank of America was faced with laying off, by seniority, most of the more recently hired black and women employees.
- Young financial wizard Dennis Levine made millions of dollars in personal profits using information obtained from those who were a party to proposed mergers. He purchased stock before the news became public, and the stock increased in price.[11]

[9] Al H. Ringlab, Roger E. Meiners, and Frances L. Edwards, *Managing in the Legal Environment, 3d ed.* (St. Paul, MN: West, 1996), 12–14; see also Roger LeRoy Miller and Frank B. Cross, *The Legal Environment Today* (St. Paul, MN: West, 1996), 33–37.

[10] LaRue T. Hosmer, *The Ethics of Management,* 2d ed. (Homewood, IL: Irwin, 1991), 81–83.

[11] Gerald F. Cavanaugh and Philip J. Chmielewski, "Ethics and the Free Market," *America,* 31 Jan. 1987, 79.

TABLE 6.2   **MAJOR PROBLEMS REGARDING LAWS REFLECTING ETHICAL STANDARDS**

1. *The moral standards of members of society may be based on a lack of information relative to issues of corporate conduct.* Most people were apparently unaware of the payments of large foreign bribes until the revelations of the Lockheed case and the subsequent Securities and Exchange Commission study. Many people now may be unaware of the magnitude of the toxic-waste disposal problem, with 231 million metric tons of waste produced annually. It is difficult for personal moral standards to influence the law if relevant information is missing.

2. *The moral standards of members of society may be diluted by the formation of small groups.* People with similar norms, beliefs, and values tend to become associated in small groups, but these standards generally are not precisely similar among all members, and compromises have to be made. Further, many small groups act from motives other than morality; economic benefits and professional prestige often seem to be stressed. It is difficult for personal moral standards to influence the law if they are not conveyed accurately.

3. *The moral standards of members of society may be misrepresented in the consensus of large organizations.* Many organizations do share norms, beliefs, and values, but no evidence indicates each individual and each group within the organization has equal influence, or even equal weighted influence, in determining that consensus. This can be seen in the norms, beliefs, and values of many non-profit organizations, such as hospitals and universities; the standards of the professional personnel—the physicians and the faculty—often seem to predominate.

4. *The moral standards of members of society may be misrepresented in the formulation of the laws.* This is the same point made about shaping the consensus of an organization, though on a larger scale. No guarantees exist that all organizations have equal influence, or even equal influence weighted by size, in determining the law. This can be seen in the provisions of much tax legislation; certain organizations always seem to be favored.

5. *The legal requirements formed through the political process are often incomplete or imprecise and have to be supplemented by judicial court decisions or administrative agency actions.* This can be seen in both product liability cases and equal employment reviews; the meaning and the application of the law have to be clarified outside of the legislative process. It is difficult for personal moral standards to influence the law if they are considered only indirectly—if at all—in two of the means of formulating that law.

SOURCE: Reproduced with permission from LaRue T. Hosmer, *The Ethics of Management,* 2nd ed. (Homewood, IL: Richard D. Irwin, 1991): 91–92. Reproduced with permission of The McGraw-Hill Companies.

These vignettes demonstrate the conflicting needs inherent in the free enterprise system. On the one hand is the generation of profits, jobs, and efficiency. On the other hand is the quest for personal and social respect, honesty, and integrity. A utilitarian ethical norm would calculate what the greatest good for the greatest number would be. This calculation also would take into account future generations.[12] Unfortunately, although the calculation sounds easy, in practice it borders on the impossible. To illustrate, one study reported that 65 percent of the public said executives would do everything they could to make a profit, even if it meant ignoring society's needs.[13] Another study reported that a Darwinistic ethic was now prevailing in business that spreads a "profit-at-any-price" attitude among business owners and managers.[14]

Yet the public's perception may be based more on a misunderstanding of the free enterprise system than a condemnation of it. One ethicist, Margaret Maxey, reminds us that in a complex world of changing technology and valuable innovations, we cannot blame

[12] Ibid., 81.

[13] Edward L. Hennessy, "Business Ethics—Is It a Priority for Corporate America?" *Financial Executive* (October 1986): 14–15.

[14] Myron Magnet, "The Decline and Fall of Business Ethics," *Fortune,* 8 December 1986, 65–72.

single individuals for the ethical problems of free enterprise. Rather, we must understand the total, systematic impact free enterprise has on the common good.[15]

In spite of these misconceptions, the fact remains that unethical behavior does take place. Why? A few possible explanations include (1) greed, (2) distinctions between activities at work and activities at home, (3) a lack of a foundation in ethics, (4) survival (bottom-line thinking), and (5) a reliance on other social institutions to convey and reinforce ethics. Whatever the reasons, ethical decision making is a challenge that confronts every businessperson involved in large or small enterprises.[16]

ESTABLISHING A STRATEGY FOR ETHICAL RESPONSIBILITY

Because the free enterprise system in which the entrepreneur flourishes is fraught with myriad conflicts, entrepreneurs need to commit to an established strategy for ethical responsibility.

Ethical Practices and Codes of Conduct

A **code of conduct** is a statement of ethical practices or guidelines to which an enterprise adheres. Many such codes exist, some related to industry at large and others related directly to corporate conduct. These codes cover a multitude of subjects, ranging from misuse of corporate assets, conflict of interest, and use of inside information to equal employment practices, falsification of books or records, and antitrust violations.

How prevalent are codes of conduct today? One survey of executives by *Personnel Journal* revealed that 72 percent of the organizations had published codes of ethics.[17] The Conference Board found that 227 out of 300 firms surveyed had codes of conduct.[18]

Based on the results of such research, two important conclusions can be reached. First, codes of conduct are becoming more prevalent in industry. Management is not just giving lip service to ethics and moral behavior; it is putting its ideas into writing and distributing these guidelines for everyone in the organization to read and follow. Second, in contrast to earlier codes, the more recent ones are proving to be more meaningful in terms of external legal and social development, more comprehensive in terms of their coverage, and easier to implement in terms of the administrative procedures used to enforce them.[19]

Of course, the most important question still remains to be answered: Will management really adhere to a high moral code? Many managers would respond to this question by answering yes. Why? The main reason is that it is good business. One top executive put the idea this way: Singly or in combination, unethical practices have a corrosive effect on free markets and free trade, which are fundamental to the survival of the free enterprise

[15] Margaret N. Maxey, "Bioethical Reflections on the Case for Private/Free Enterprise," in *The Future of Private Enterprise,* ed. Craig E. Aronoff, Randall B. Goodwin, and John L. Ward (Atlanta: Georgia State University Publications, 1986), 145–64.

[16] Charles R. Stoner, "The Foundation of Business Ethics: Exploring the Relationship between Organization Culture, Moral Values, and Actions," *SAM Advanced Management Journal* (summer 1989): 38–43; and Robert A. Cooke, *Business Ethics: A Perspective* (Chicago: Arthur Anderson & Co., monograph, 1988).

[17] James Court, "A Question of Corporate Ethics," *Personal Journal* (September 1988): 37–38.

[18] Susan J. Harrington, "What Corporate America Is Teaching about Ethics," *Academy of Management Executive* 5, no. 1 (1991): 21–30.

[19] For more on this topic, see Donald R. Cressey and Charles A. Moore, "Managerial Values and Corporate Codes of Conduct," *California Management Review* (summer 1983): 121–27; Steven Weller, "The Effectiveness of Corporate Codes of Ethics," *Journal of Business Ethics* (July 1988): 389–95; and Diane E. Kirrane, "Managing Values: A Systematic Approach to Business Ethics," *Training & Development Journal* (November 1990): 53–60.

system. They subvert the laws of supply and demand, and they short-circuit competition based on classical ideas of product quality, service, and price. Free markets become replaced by contrived markets. The need for constant improvement in products or services is thus removed.[20]

A second, related reason is that by improving the moral climate of the enterprise, the corporation can eventually win back the public's confidence. This would mark a turnaround in that many people today question the moral and ethical integrity of companies and believe businesspeople try to get away with everything they can. Only time will tell whether codes of conduct will serve to improve business practices. Current trends indicate, however, that the business community is working hard toward this objective.[21]

Approaches to Managerial Ethics

When focusing on an ethical position, entrepreneurs should analyze various organizational characteristics. One study examined ethical norms, motives, goals, orientation toward law, and strategy for three distinct types of management: **immoral management, amoral management,** and **moral management.**[22] Table 6.3 provides a summary of each characteristic within each of the ethical types. These characteristics are important for gaining insight into the continuum of behaviors that can be exhibited. Before entrepreneurs set forth any strategy, it is imperative they analyze their own reactions to these characteristics and thus their own ethical styles.

Moving from an immoral or amoral position to a moral position requires a great deal of personal effort. Whether it is a commitment to sending employees to training seminars on business ethics, establishing codes of conduct, or exhibiting tighter operational controls, the entrepreneur needs to develop particular areas around which a strategy can be formulated.

A HOLISTIC APPROACH   One author has suggested a holistic management approach that encompasses ethics in its perspective. It is a dual-focused approach that includes "knowing how" and "knowing that." Admittedly, it is an aesthetic, philosophical perspective, but the understanding of it "reminds the administrator that there exist complementary forms of acquiring managerial knowledge."[23] In other words, managerial practices as well as the ethical implications of those practices need to be acquired.

To apply a holistic approach, entrepreneurs can develop specific principles that will assist them in taking the right external steps as their venture develops. Presented here are one executive's four principles for ethical management:

• Principle 1: *Hire the right people.* Employees who are inclined to be ethical are the best insurance you can have. They may be the only insurance. Look for people with

---

[20] Reported in Darrell J. Fashing, "A Case of Corporate and Management Ethics," *California Management Review* (spring 1981): 84.

[21] Amitai Etzioni, "Do Good Ethics Ensure Good Profits?" *Business and Society Review* (summer 1989): 4–10; L. J. Brooks, "Corporate Ethical Performance: Trends, Forecasts, and Outlooks," *Journal of Business Ethics* 8 (1989): 31–38; Susan J. Harrington, "What Corporate America Is Teaching about Ethics," *Academy of Management Executive* (February 1991): 21–30; and Simcha B. Werner, "The Movement for Reforming American Business Ethics: A Twenty Year Perspective," *Journal of Business Ethics* 11 (1992).

[22] Archie B. Carroll, "In Search of the Moral Manager," *Business Horizons* (March/April 1987): 7–15.

[23] F. Neil Brady, "Aesthetic Components of Management Ethics," *Academy of Management Review* (April 1986): 344.

TABLE 6.3   **APPROACHES TO MANAGERIAL ETHICS**

Organizational Characteristics	Immoral Management	Amoral Management	Moral Management
Ethical norms	Managerial decisions, actions, and behavior imply a positive and active opposition to what is moral (ethical). Decisions are discordant with accepted ethical principles. An active negation of what is moral is implied.	Management is neither moral nor immoral, but decisions lie outside the sphere to which moral judgments apply. Managerial activity is outside or beyond the moral order of a particular code. A lack of ethical perception and moral awareness may be implied.	Managerial activity conforms to a standard of ethical, or right, behavior. Managers conform to accepted professional standards of conduct. Ethical leadership is commonplace on the part of management.
Motives	Selfish: Management cares only about its or the company's gains.	Well-intentioned but selfish: The impact on others is not considered.	Good: Management wants to succeed but only within the confines of sound ethical precepts (fairness, justice, due process).
Goals	Profitability and organizational success at any price	Profitability; other goals not considered	Profitability within the confines of legal obedience and ethical standards
Orientation toward law	Legal standards are barriers management must overcome to accomplish what it wants.	Law is the ethical guide, preferably the letter of the law. The central question is what managers can do legally.	Obedience is toward the letter and spirit of the law. Law is a minimal ethical behavior. Managers prefer to operate well above what the law mandates.
Strategy	Exploit opportunities for corporate gain. Cut corners when it appears useful.	Give managers free rein. Personal ethics may apply but only if managers choose. Respond to legal mandates if caught and required to do so.	Live by sound ethical standards. Assume leadership position when ethical dilemmas arise. Enlightened self-interest prevails.

SOURCE: Archie B. Carroll, "In Search of the Moral Manager," *Business Horizons* (March/April 1987): 12. Copyright © 1987 by the Foundation for the School of Business at Indiana University. Reprinted by permission.

principles. Let them know that those principles are an important part of their qualifications for the job.

- Principle 2: *Set standards more than rules.* You can't write a code of conduct airtight enough to cover every eventuality. A person inclined to fraud or misconduct isn't going to blink at signing your code anyway. So don't waste your time on heavy regulations. Instead, be clear about standards. Let people know the level of performance you expect—and that ethics are not negotiable.

CONTEMPORARY ENTREPRENEURSHIP

Shaping an Ethical Strategy

The development of an organizational climate for responsible and ethically sound behavior requires continuing effort and investment of time and resources. A code of conduct, ethics officers, training programs, and annual ethics audits do not necessarily add up to a responsible, ethical organization. A formal ethics program can serve as a catalyst and a support system, but organizational integrity depends on the integration of the company's values into its driving systems.

Here are a few key elements entrepreneurs should keep in mind when developing an ethical strategy.

- *The entrepreneur's guiding values and commitments must make sense and be clearly communicated.* They should reflect important organizational obligations and widely shared aspirations that appeal to the organization's members. Employees at all levels must take them seriously, feel comfortable discussing them, and have a concrete understanding of their practical importance.

- *Entrepreneurs must be personally committed, credible, and willing to take action on the values they espouse.* They are not mere mouthpieces. They

must be willing to scrutinize their own decisions. Consistency on the part of leadership is key. Entrepreneurs must assume responsibility for making tough calls when ethical obligations conflict.

- *The espoused values must be integrated into the normal channels of the organization's critical activities:* planning innovation, resource allocation, information communication, and personnel promotion and advancement.

- *The venture's systems and structures must support and reinforce its values.* Information systems, for example, must be designed to provide timely and accurate information. Reporting relationships must be structured to build in checks and balances to promote objective judgment.

- *Employees throughout the company must have the decision-making skills, knowledge, and competencies needed to make ethically sound decisions every day.* Ethical thinking and awareness must be part of every employee's skills.

SOURCE: Adapted from Lynn Sharp Paine, "Managing for Organizational Integrity," *Harvard Business Review* (March/April 1994): 106–17.

- Principle 3: *Don't let yourself get isolated.* You know managers can lose track of markets and competitors by moving into the ivory tower. But they also can lose sight of what's going on in their own operations. The only problem is you are responsible for whatever happens in your office or department or corporation, whether you know about it or not.

- Principle 4: *The most important principle is to let your ethical example at all times be absolutely impeccable.* This isn't just a matter of how you act in matters of accounting, competition, or interpersonal relationships. Be aware also of the signals you send to those around you. Steady harping on the importance of quarterly gains in earnings, for example, rather easily leads people to believe you don't care much about how the results are achieved.

- *Note:* Mark Twain once said, "Always do the right thing. This will surprise some people and astonish the rest." It will also motivate them to do the right thing. Indeed, without a good example from the top, ethical problems (and all the costs that go with them) are probably inevitable within your organization.[24]

ETHICAL RESPONSIBILITY It must be kept in mind that establishing a strategy for ethical responsibility is not an easy task for entrepreneurs. No single ideal approach to organizational ethics exists. Entrepreneurs need to analyze the ethical consciousness of their organization, the process and structure devised to enhance ethical activity, and, finally, their own commitment to institutionalize ethical objectives in the company.[25] Keeping these points in mind, entrepreneurs eventually can begin to establish a strategy for ethical responsibility. This strategy should encompass three major elements: ethical consciousness, ethical process and structure, and institutionalization.[26]

Ethical Consciousness The development of ethical consciousness is the responsibility of the entrepreneur since his or her vision created the venture. The key figure to set the tone for ethical decision making and behavior is the entrepreneur. An open exchange of issues and processes within the venture, established codes of ethics for the company, and the setting of examples by the entrepreneur are all illustrations of how this is done. One interesting example from a large corporation is Motorola. When the company's CEO discovered bookkeeping discrepancies in one of the departments, he directed the 20 implicated employees to make retribution by donating $8,500 to charity.[27] This action commanded positive ethical action and set the tone for ethical expectations.

Ethical Process and Structure Ethical process and structure refer to the procedures, position statements (codes), and announced ethical goals designed to avoid ambiguity. Having all key personnel read the venture's specific ethical goals and sign affidavits affirming their willingness to follow those policies is a good practice for ventures.

Institutionalization Institutionalization is a deliberate step to incorporate the entrepreneur's ethical objectives with the economic objectives of the venture. At times an entrepreneur may have to modify policies or operations that become too intense and infringe on the ethics of the situation. This is where the entrepreneur's commitment to ethics and values is tested. Constant review of procedures and feedback in operations are vital to institutionalizing ethical responsibility.

[24] Adapted from Vernon R. Loucks Jr., "A CEO Looks at Ethics," *Business Horizons* (March/April 1987): 6. Copyright © 1987 by the Foundation for the School of Business at Indiana University. Reprinted by permission.

[25] Patrick E. Murphy, "Creating Ethical Corporate Structures," *Sloan Management Review* (winter 1989): 81–87.

[26] Joseph A. Raelin, "The Professional as the Executive's Ethical Aide-de-Camp," *The Academy of Management Executive* (August 1987): 176.

[27] Ibid., 177.

ETHICS AND BUSINESS DECISIONS

The entrepreneur is challenged by business decisions each day. Many of these decisions are complex and raise ethical considerations.

Complexity of Decisions

The business decisions of entrepreneurs are so complex for five reasons. First, ethical decisions have extended consequences. They often have a ripple effect in that the consequences are felt by others outside the venture. For example, the decision to use inexpensive but unsafe products in operations will affect both workers and consumers of the final good.

Second, business decisions involving ethical questions have multiple alternatives. It is not always "do" or "don't do." Many decisions have a wide range of alternatives that may allow a mixture of less-important decisions. In reference to the first example about the use of unsafe products, the entrepreneur may have the alternative of using still less expensive but nevertheless safe products.

Third, ethical business decisions often have mixed outcomes. Social benefits as well as costs are involved with every major business decision, as are financial revenues and expenses.

Fourth, most business decisions have uncertain ethical consequences. It is never absolutely certain what actual consequence(s) a decision will have even when it appears logical; in other words, a decision is never without ethical risk.

Finally, most ethical business decisions have personal implications. It is difficult for an entrepreneur to divorce himself or herself from a decision and its potential outcome. Venture success, financial opportunity, and new-product development are all areas that may be affected by decisions having ethical consequences. The entrepreneur often will find it impossible to make a purely impersonal decision.[28]

These five statements about business decisions need to be considered when an entrepreneur is developing a new venture. They indicate the need to grasp as much information as possible about each major decision. One ethicist, who believes this implies understanding the characteristic features of a venture's activities, which in turn allows for a stronger sensitivity to the outcomes, has noted that "Someone in business needs to know its general tendencies—the special tracks it leaves—to anticipate points of crisis, and of special concern to us, to increase the possibility of intelligent moral actions."[29]

Some of the pertinent questions that can be used to examine the ethics of business decisions are listed here:

1. Have you defined the problem accurately?

2. How would you define the problem if you stood on the other side of the fence?

3. How did this situation occur in the first place?

4. To whom and to what do you give your loyalty as a person and as a corporation member?

5. What is your intention in making this decision?

---

[28] LaRue T. Hosmer, *The Ethics of Management* (Homewoood, IL: Irwin, 1987). 13–15.

[29] Wade L. Robison, "Management and Ethical Decision-Making," *Journal of Business Ethics* (spring 1984): 287.

6. How does this intention compare with the probable results?

7. Whom could your decision or action injure?

8. Can you discuss the problem with the affected parties before you make your decision?

9. Are you confident your position will be as valid over a long period of time as it seems now?

10. Could you disclose without qualm your decision or action to your boss, your CEO, the board of directors, your family, and society as a whole?

11. What is the symbolic potential of your action if understood? If misunderstood?

12. Under what conditions would you allow exceptions to your stand?[30]

Although this is not a conclusive list, it does provide a frame of reference for entrepreneurs wrestling with the complexity of decisions concerning their venture.

Ethics, as we have seen, is extremely difficult to define, codify, and implement because of its surfacing of personal values and morality. Yet the importance of ethics when initiating new enterprises must be stressed. As one writer has noted, "The singular importance of enterprises to our daily lives and our collective future demands our careful attention and finest efforts."[31]

THE SOCIAL RESPONSIBILITY CHALLENGE

Over the past three decades, social responsibility has emerged as a major issue. Although it takes different forms for different industries and companies, the basic challenge exists for all.

Social responsibility consists of obligations a business has to society. These obligations extend to many different areas. Table 6.4 (on page 165) presents some of them. The diversity of social responsibility opens the door for questions concerning the *extent* corporations should be involved.

An examination of the stages or levels of social responsibility behavior corporations exhibit reveals that distinct differences exist in the way corporations respond. S. Prakesh Sethi, a researcher in social responsibility, has established a framework that classifies the social actions of corporations into three distinct categories: social obligation, social responsibility, and social responsiveness (see Table 6.5 on page 166).

This framework illustrates the range of corporate intensity about social issues. Some firms simply react to social issues through obedience to the laws—**social obligation;** others respond more actively, accepting responsibility for various programs—**social responsibility;** still others are highly proactive and are even willing to be evaluated by the public for various activities—**social responsiveness.**

Another way to examine this concept is through a social responsibility scale (see Figure 6.3 on page 167). This scale extends from 0 (minimum social responsibility response)

---

[30] Laura L. Nash, "Ethics without the Sermon," *Harvard Business Review* (November/December 1981). Copyright © 1981 by the President and Fellows of Harvard College; all rights reserved. For additional questions, see Diane E. Kirrane, "Managing Values: A Systematic Approach to Business Ethics," *Training & Development Journal* (November 1990): 53–60.

[31] Henderson, "The Ethical Side," 46.

CONTEMPORARY ENTREPRENEURSHIP

Social Responsibility Pays Off

Social responsibility. Ethics. These are buzzwords in the business biosphere of the 1990s. Many companies are putting forth great efforts to treat people more fairly, to be responsible to all stakeholders, and to conduct business with an open sense of morality. Others are only talking about it. Maybe it's because they fear appearing "too soft" or "too nice" compared to the competition. Is being socially responsible and ethical worth that risk? Can companies afford to be more caring? According to Alfred Marcus, professor of strategic management at the University of Minnesota's Carlson School of Management in Minneapolis, the answer is yes. As a matter of fact, Marcus claims that a company stands to *lose* money if it is not socially responsible or displaying ethical behavior.

Marcus studied the 13 most significant studies available on this subject and found that a definite correlation exists between higher profits and more responsible corporate behavior. Seven of the 13 studies revealed a positive relationship between financial performance and social responsibility, while only 2 showed the opposite. His analysis "clearly didn't find that unethical behavior pays," Marcus says. In most cases irresponsible or unethical behavior is costly. Much evidence indicates that a wrong decision by a company can have extreme impact on the bottom line as well as the ability of that company to market its products and services in the future. The fact ethical behavior creates fatter profits is proven not only by surveys but also by countless ex-amples throughout corporate America. Want further proof? Here are five ways caring pays off.

Workplace

Most employers realize work is hindered when employees feel unappreciated, are working 50-plus hours per week, or have family and personal problems to deal with. But many of them don't know how to address these issues to make work more satisfying and enjoyable for their employees. In addition, much employee mistreatment still exists in corporations today. Deborah Anderson at Respond 2 Inc., a consulting firm, found in a survey that 95 percent of the people they surveyed experience more mistreatment at work than at home, and on average 26 percent experience or witness psychological abuse of employees several times a day. These types of mistreatment have a significant impact on employee productivity, job satisfaction, errors, and morale. For companies that create an employee-friendly atmosphere, the rewards are phenomenal. One example is Staple Companies, a property casualty insurer in St. Paul, Minnesota. It offers employees support groups, on-site day care, assistance programs, and above-industry-average wages and benefits. The company's bottom line proves that caring pays off. Its employee assistance program saved Staple $1.8 million in 1994, and the company enjoys a turnover rate of less than 8 percent, which is the lowest in the industry.

Supporting a Cause

A great marketing idea. A great cause. One is not much good without the other, but when they are integrated great things can happen for everyone involved, especially the company. A 1995 study by Cone Communications in Boston and Roper Starch Worldwide in New York found that of those surveyed, 54 percent said they would pay more for a product that supported a cause they cared about, 31 percent viewed a company's sense of social responsibility as a key factor when making a purchase, and 66 percent said they would switch brands and 62 percent would switch retailers in favor of a socially responsible firm. Three years ago Avon Products, Inc., a cosmetics company, founded the Avon Worldwide Fund for Women's Health. The fund's biggest program is the Breast Cancer Awareness Crusade that raised $16.5 million to help finance community-based breast cancer education and early-detection services. While these programs Avon initiated literally help save lives, they also have helped the company's sales and image. Avon was the subject of more than 400 major media stories about the Breast Cancer Awareness Crusade during just the first two years of its operation. The media attention, combined with the sales force's effort to persistently deliver the awareness message, helped to boost company sales.

Environment

Environmental issues vary from the use of chemicals and nonrenewable sources to the safeness and biodegradability of products. Many companies are finding it pays to think environmentally. According to several studies, including the 1995 study by the Investor Responsibility Research Center, just the act of reducing pollution can boost profits. In eight of ten cases, low-polluting companies outperform their high-polluting competitors. In addition, firms with a high number of environmental lawsuits earn a lower level of return on assets and return on equity than others in their industry.

Community Relations

For some companies community relations is just another form of public relations or a marketing tool that adds little real value to the community. But many companies are finding the real value in taking their community and civic involvement seriously. Sincere corporate/community ties increase employee morale and customer loyalty, which leads to tangible financial gains for the company. One example of how community relations can not only benefit a company but also possibly save it from ruins is the World Eye Bookstore in Greenfield, Massachusetts. After the store was wiped out by a fire, community members who appreciated over the years World Eye's products and community service rebuilt the store. On a larger scale, the Dayton Hudson Corp., based in Minneapolis, was the first publicly known U.S. company to donate 5 percent of its pretax profits to various charities. In 1987, it avoided a hostile takeover because state officials who were pleased with its community involvement passed antitakover legislation to protect it.

CONTINUED

Employee Ownership

Today, employee stock ownership plans (ESOP) are an effective tool to keep high-quality workers in a company and to let employees feel they have some say in their work lives. However, Corey Rosen, executive director of the National Center for Employee Ownership (NSEO) in Oakland, California, warns that an ESOP is not enough by itself. If ownership is combined with actual employee participation in management planning, company profits will increase. According-ing to a U.S. General Accounting Office study, productivity grew 52 percent after employee ownership was created at firms that practice participative management. According to a NSEO study, a company will grow 6 to 11 times faster than its competitors if it combines employee ownership and participatory management.

SOURCE: Dale Kurschner, "5 Ways Ethical Business Creates Fatter Profits," *Business Ethics* 10, no. 2 (March/April 1996): 20–23. Adapted with permission from *Business Ethics*, P. O. Box 8439, Minneapolis, MN 55408.

to 10 (maximum social responsibility response). Number *1* represents the reactive form of obedience and *10* the proactive form of social support.

Only a few studies have examined different features of social responsibility by entrepreneurs.[32] For example, one researcher examined the perspectives of 180 small-business owners on social responsibility and found that 88 percent recognized social responsibility as part of their business role.[33] In another study, the researchers used a random telephone survey to explore the general public's perceptions of social responsibility in big versus small businesses. Their findings indicated that entrepreneurs were more critical of their own performance than was the general public.[34]

Environmental Awareness

The decade of the 1990s has been one of greater environmental concern. This reawakening of the need to preserve and protect our natural resources has motivated businesses into a stronger **environmental awareness.** As illustrated in Table 6.4, the environment stands out as one of the major challenges of social responsibility. In June 1992, 140 world leaders, along with 30,000 additional participants, gathered in Rio de Janeiro for the Earth Summit to discuss worldwide environmental problems. Our recent "throwaway" culture has endangered our natural resources from soil to water to air.

Researchers Paul Hawken and William McDonough state: "Industry is being told that if it puts its hamburgers in coated-paper wrappers, eliminates emissions, and plants two trees for every car sold, we will be on the way to an environmentally sound world. Nothing could be further from the truth. The danger lies not in the half measures but in the illusions

[32] Judith Kenner Thompson and Howard L. Smith, "Social Responsibility and Small Business: Suggestions for Research," *Journal of Small Business Management* (January 1991): 30–44.

[33] Erika Wilson, "Social Responsibility of Business: What Are the Small Business Perspectives?" *Journal of Small Business Management* (July 1980): 17–24.

[34] James J. Chrisman and Fred L. Fry, "Public versus Business Expectations: Two Views on Social Responsibility for Small Business," *Journal of Small Business Management* (January 1982): 19–26.

TABLE 6.4	WHAT IS THE NATURE OF SOCIAL RESPONSIBILITY?
Environment	Pollution control Restoration or protection of environment Conservation of natural resources Recycling efforts
Energy	Conservation of energy in production and marketing operations Efforts to increase energy efficiency of products Other energy-saving programs (for example, company-sponsored car pools)
Fair Business Practices	Employment and advancement of women and minorities Employment and advancement of disadvantaged individuals (disabled, Vietnam veterans, ex-offenders, former drug addicts, mentally retarded, and hardcore unemployed) Support for minority-owned businesses
Human Resources	Promotion of employee health and safety Employee training and development Remedial education programs for disadvantaged employees Alcohol and drug counseling programs Career counseling Child day-care facilities for working parents Employee physical fitness and stress management programs
Community Involvement	Donations of cash, products, services, or employee time Sponsorship of public health projects Support of education and the arts Support of community recreation programs Cooperation in community projects (recycling centers, disaster assistance, and urban renewal)
Products	Enhancement of product safety Sponsorship of product safety education programs Reduction of polluting potential of products Improvement in nutritional value of products Improvement in packaging and labeling

SOURCE: Richard M. Hodgetts and Donald F. Kuratko, *Management*, 3rd ed. (San Diego: Harcourt Brace Jovanovich, 1991), 670.

they foster, the belief that subtle course corrections can guide us to a good life that will include a 'conserved' natural world and cozy shopping malls."[35]

This quote illustrates the enormous challenges entrepreneurs confront as they attempt to build socially responsible organizations for the future. Of the 100 million enterprises worldwide, a growing number are attempting to redefine their social responsibilities because they no longer accept the notion that the business of business is business. Because of an international ability to communicate information widely and quickly, many entrepreneurs are beginning to recognize their responsibility to the world around them. Entrepreneurial organizations, the dominant inspiration throughout the world, are beginning the arduous task of addressing social-environmental problems.

Entrepreneurs need to take the lead in designing a new approach to business in which everyday acts of work and life accumulate as a matter of course into a better world. One

[35] Paul Hawken and William McDonough, "Seven Steps to Doing Good Business," *Inc.*, November 1993, 79–92.

TABLE 6.5   **CLASSIFYING CORPORATE SOCIAL BEHAVIOR**

Dimension of Behavior	Stage One: Social Obligation	Stage Two: Social Responsibility	Stage Three: Social Responsiveness
Response to social pressures	Maintains low public profile, but if attacked, uses PR methods to upgrade its public image; denies any deficiencies; blames public dissatisfaction on ignorance or failure to understand corporate functions; discloses information only where legally required	Accepts responsibility for solving current problems; will admit deficiencies in former practices and attempt to persuade public that its current practices meet social norms; attitude toward critics conciliatory; freer information disclosures than stage one	Willingly discusses activities with outside groups; makes information freely available to public; accepts formal and informal inputs from outside groups in decision making; is willing to be publicly evaluated for its various activities
Philanthropy	Contributes only when direct benefit to it clearly shown; otherwise, views contributions as responsibility of individual employees	Contributes to noncontroversial and established causes; matches employee contributions	Activities of stage two, *plus* support and contributions to new, controversial groups whose needs it sees as unfulfilled and increasingly important

SOURCE: Excerpted from S. Prakash Sethi, "A Conceptual Framework for Environmental Analysis of Social Issues and Evaluation of Business Response Patterns," *Academy of Management Journal* (January 1979): 68.

theorist has developed the term "ecovision" as a leadership style for innovative organizations.[36] **Ecovision** encourages open and flexible structures that encompass the employees, the organization, and the environment, with attention to evolving social demands.

The environmental movement consists of many initiatives connected primarily by values rather than by design. A plan to create a sustainable future should realize its objectives through a practical, clearly stated strategy. Some of the key steps recommended by Hawken and McDonough follow:[37]

1. Eliminate the concept of waste. Seek newer methods of production and recycling.

2. Restore accountability. Encourage consumer involvement in making companies accountable.

3. Make prices reflect costs. Reconstruct the system to a "green fee" where taxes are added to energy, raw materials, and services to encourage conservation.

4. Promote diversity. Continue researching the needed compatibility of our ever-evolving products and inventions.

[36] Reginald Shareef, "Ecovision: A Leadership Theory for Innovative Organizations," *Organizational Dynamics* 20 (summer 1991): 50–63.

[37] Hawken and McDonough, "Seven Steps," 81–88.

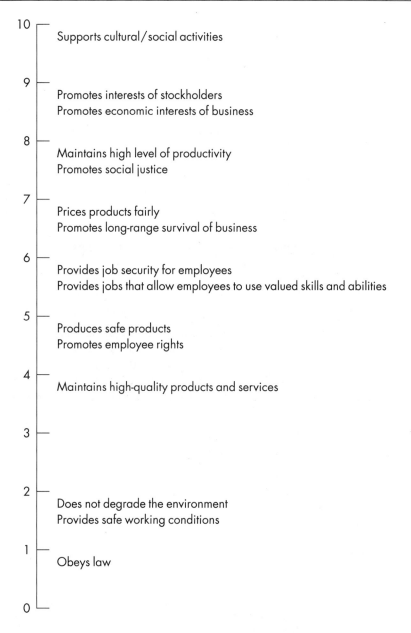

FIGURE 6.3   **A SOCIAL RESPONSIBILITY SCALE**

10 — Supports cultural/social activities

9 —
Promotes interests of stockholders
Promotes economic interests of business

8 —
Maintains high level of productivity
Promotes social justice

7 —
Prices products fairly
Promotes long-range survival of business

6 —
Provides job security for employees
Provides jobs that allow employees to use valued skills and abilities

5 —
Produces safe products
Promotes employee rights

4 — Maintains high-quality products and services

3 —

2 —
Does not degrade the environment
Provides safe working conditions

1 — Obeys law

0 —

SOURCE: Adapted from Kimberly B. Boal and Newman Peery, "The Cognitive Structure of Corporate Social Responsibility," *Journal of Management* (fall/winter 1985): 71–82.

5. Make conservation profitable. Rather than demanding "low prices" to encourage production shortcuts, allow new costs for environmental stewardship.

6. Insist on accountability of nations. Develop a plan for every trading nation of sustainable development enforced by tariffs.

TABLE 6.6   ISSUES VIEWED BY SMALL-BUSINESS OWNERS

Demands Strong Ethical Stance	Greater Tolerance Regarding Ethical Position
Faulty investment advice	Padded expense account
Favoritism in promotion	Tax evasion
Acquiescing in dangerous design flaw	Collusion in bidding
Misleading financial reporting	Insider trading
Misleading advertising	Discrimination against women
Defending healthfulness of cigarette smoking	Copying computer software

SOURCE: Justin G. Longenecker, Joseph A. McKinney, and Carlos W. Moore, "Ethics in Small Business," *Journal of Small Business Management* (January 1989): 30.

Even though the studies specific to ethics, social responsibility, and entrepreneurs are still emerging, a number of views are agreed on. The research is showing differences in ethical environment, ethical precepts and ethical perceptions between large firms and small firms. The reasons center around the structure of smaller firms, which have fewer professional specialists, less formality, and a stronger influence by the owner-entrepreneur.

THE OPPORTUNITY FOR ETHICAL LEADERSHIP BY ENTREPRENEURS

Even though ethics and social responsibility present complex challenges for entrepreneurs, the value system of an owner-entrepreneur is the key to establishing an ethical organization. An owner has the unique opportunity to display honesty, integrity, and ethics in all key decisions. The owner's actions serve as a model for all other employees to follow.

In small businesses the ethical influence of the owner is more powerful than in larger corporations because his or her leadership is not diffused through layers of management. Owners are easily identified, and usually employees constantly observe them in a small business. Therefore, entrepreneurs possess a strong potential to establish high ethical standards in all business decisions.

To illustrate, one study examined the ethical concern of owner-entrepreneurs regarding specific business issues.[38] Table 6.6 provides a list of the issues owners believed needed a strong ethical stance, as well as the issues the same entrepreneurs viewed with greater

---

[38] Justin G. Longenecker, Joseph A. McKinney, and Carlos W. Moore, "Ethics in Small Business," *Journal of Small Business Management* (January 1989): 27–31.

tolerance in regard to demanding ethics. It verifies that ethical decision making is a complex challenge due to the nature and personal perception of various issues.[39]

Overall, entrepreneurs must realize that their personal integrity and ethical example will be the key to their employees' ethical performance. Their values can permeate and characterize the organization. This unique advantage creates a position of ethical leadership for entrepreneurs.[40]

✳ SUMMARY

Ethics is a set of principles prescribing a behavioral code that explains right and wrong; it also may outline moral duty and obligations. Because it is so difficult to define the term, it is helpful to look at ethics more as a process than as a static code. Entrepreneurs face many ethical decisions, especially during the early stages of their new ventures.

Decisions may be legal without being ethical and vice versa. As a result, entrepreneurs can make four types of decisions: legal and ethical, legal and unethical, illegal and ethical, and illegal and unethical. When making decisions that border on the unethical, entrepreneurs commonly rationalize their choices. These rationalizations may be based on morally questionable acts committed "against the firm" or "on behalf of the firm" by the managers involved. Within this framework are four distinct types of managerial roles: nonrole, role failure, role distortion, and role assertion.

Sometimes the entrepreneur must make decisions that involve economic trade-offs. In some situations the company will make a profit but others in society may suffer. To establish ethical strategies, some corporations create codes of conduct. A code of conduct is a statement of ethical practices or guidelines to which an enterprise adheres. Codes are becoming more prevalent in organizations today, and they are proving to be more meaningful in their implementation.

Some ethicists have attempted to provide a clearer view of morality by examining organizational behavior along a continuum that includes immoral, amoral, and moral management. However, entrepreneurs need to focus on a holistic approach that places ethics in perspective and that allows personnel to understand what they can and cannot do. In this way the blurred line between ethical and unethical behavior becomes clearer.

It is also important for entrepreneurs to realize that many decisions are complex and that it can be difficult to deal with all of a decision's ethical considerations. Some of them may be overlooked, and some may be sidestepped because the economic cost is too high. In the final analysis, ethics are sometimes judgment calls, and what is unethical to one entrepreneur is viewed as ethical to another.

The challenge of social responsibility has emerged as a major issue for entrepreneurs. Social responsibility consists of obligations a business has to society. The social actions of corporations are classified into three categories: social obligation, social responsibility, and

[39] Neil Humphreys, Donald P. Robin, R. Eric Reidenbach, and Donald L. Moak, "The Ethical Decision Making Process of Small Business Owner/Managers and Their Customers," *Journal of Small Business Management* (July 1993): 9–22; and Douglas W. Naffziger, Jeffrey S. Hornsby, Donald F. Kuratko, William R. LaFollette, and Richard M. Hodgetts, "The Ethical Perceptions of Small Business Owners: A Factor Analytic Study," *Journal of Small Business Management* (October 1994): 9–16.

[40] G. Lynn Shostack, "Stand Up for Ethics," *Journal of Business Strategy* (May/June 1990): 48–50; Justin G. Longenecker, Joseph A. McKinney, and Carlos W. Moore, "Do Smaller Firms Have Higher Ethics?" *Business and Society Review* (fall 1989): 19–21; Paul J. Serwinek, "Demographic and Related Differences in Ethical Views among Small Businesses," *Journal of Business Ethics* (July 1992): 555–66; and Donald F. Kuratko, "The Ethical Challenge for Enterpreneurs," *Enterpreneurship, Innovation, and Change* (December 1995): 291–94.

social responsiveness. Studies have revealed that entrepreneurs recognize social responsibility as part of their role and that the structure of smaller firms allows entrepreneurs to more personally influence the organization. This opportunity for entrepreneurs to exert ethical influence on their ventures creates a unique challenge of ethical leadership for all entrepreneurs. Despite the ever-present lack of clarity and direction in ethics, however, ethics will continue to be a major issue for entrepreneurs during the late 1990s.

Key Terms and Concepts

Amoral management	Rationalizations
Code of conduct	Role assertion
Ecovision	Role distortion
Environmental awareness	Role failure
Ethics	Social obligation
Immoral management	Social responsibility
Moral management	Social responsiveness
Nonrole	

Review and Discussion Questions

1. In your own words, what is meant by the term *ethics?*
2. Ethics must be based more on a process than on a static code. What does this statement mean? Do you agree? Why or why not?
3. A small pharmaceutical firm has just received permission from the Food and Drug Administration (FDA) to market its new anticholesterol drug. Although the product has been tested for five years, management believes serious side effects may still result from its use, and a warning to this effect is being printed on the label. If the company markets this FDA-approved drug, how would you describe its actions from an ethical and legal standpoint? Use Figure 6.1 to help you.
4. Marcia White, the leading salesperson for a small manufacturer, has been giving purchasing managers a kickback from her commissions in return for their buying more of the company's goods. The manufacturer has a strict rule against this practice. Using Figure 6.1, how would you describe Marcia's behavior? What would you suggest the company do about it?
5. Explain the four distinct roles managers may take in rationalizing morally questionable acts "against the firm" or "on behalf of the firm." Be complete in your answer.
6. What is a code of conduct, and how useful is it in promoting ethical behavior?
7. Describe carefully the differences between immoral, amoral, and moral management. Use Table 6.3 in your answer.
8. Why do complex decisions often raise ethical considerations for the entrepreneur?
9. Social responsibility can be classified into three distinct categories. Describe each category, and discuss the efforts of entrepreneurs to become more socially responsible.
10. Describe the critical threat to our environment as a major challenge of social responsibility.
11. What is "ecovision"? Outline some specific recommendations for entrepreneurs to consider that promote environmental awareness.
12. How can entrepreneurs develop a position of ethical leadership in business today?

13. Cal Whiting believes entrepreneurs need to address the importance of ethics in their organizations. However, in his own company he is unsure of where to begin because the entire area is unclear to him. What would you suggest? Where can he begin? What should he do? Be as practical as you can in your suggestion.

Experiential Exercise   *Knowing the Difference*

Most entrepreneurial actions are ethical and legal. Sometimes, however, they are unethical and/or illegal. The four categories of ethical/legal actions and a list of examples of each category (*a* through *h*) follow. Match them up by placing the number of the category next to appropriate examples from the list (two are given for each category).

1. Ethical and legal
2. Unethical and legal
3. Ethical and illegal
4. Unethical and illegal

_____ *a)* Giving a gift of $50,000 to a foreign minister to secure a business contract with his country (a customary practice in his country) and then writing off the gift as a tax-deductible item

_____ *b)* Knowing that 1 percent of all tires have production defects but shipping them anyway and giving mileage allowances to anyone whose tires wear out prematurely

_____ *c)* Manufacturing a new fuel additive that will increase gas mileage by 10 percent

_____ *d)* Offering a member of the city council $100,000 to vote to give the entrepreneur the local cable television franchise

_____ *e)* Publishing a newspaper story that wrongly implies but does not openly state that the governor (a political opponent of the newspaper) is deliberately withholding state funds for education in the newspaper's effort to win nomination support for its candidate from the state teachers union

_____ *f)* Obtaining inside information from another brokerage that results in the entrepreneur netting more than $2 million

_____ *g)* Producing a vaccine, already approved by the Food and Drug Administration, that will retard the growth of bone cancer

_____ *h)* Producing and selling a drug that will reduce heart attacks but failing to complete all of the paperwork that must be filed with the government prior to selling the product

Answers   *a)* 3   *e)* 2
b) 2   *f)* 4
c) 1   *g)* 1
d) 4   *h)* 3

 **CASE 6.1**

Letting the Family In

When Carmine Guion started his retail company three years ago, he had more than enough working capital to keep operations going. This abundance of money helped him grow rapidly, and today he has outlets in 16 states. In order to become larger, however, he is going to have to secure outside funding. Carmine has decided to issue stock. The investment house advising him has suggested he float an issue of 1 million shares at $5 each. After all expenses, he will clear $4.50 per share. Carmine and his wife intend to hold onto 250,000 shares and sell 750,000. Carmine feels that with his shares and those that will be bought by his relatives and friends, he need have little concern about the firm's being taken over by outside investors.

Carmine talked to his father, who agreed to buy 10,000 shares at $5. Carmine's two uncles are each buying 5,000 shares at $5. A group of 20 other relatives is going to buy an additional 5,000 shares.

Earlier this week Carmine received some good news from his accountant. His profit estimate for next year is going to be at least double what he estimated. When Carmine shared this information with the investment brokers, they were delighted. "When this news gets out," one of them told him, "your stock will rise to $13 to $15 a share. Anyone who gets in on the original offering at $5 will do very well indeed."

Carmine has told only his father and two uncles the good news. Based on this information, the three of them have decided to buy three times as much stock as previously planned. "When it rises to around $12," his father said, "I'll sell 10,000 shares and hang on to the other 5,000." His uncles intend to do the same thing. Carmine is delighted. He also intends to tell some of his other relatives about the improved profit picture prior to the time the initial stock offering is made.

Questions

1. Has Carmine been unethical in his conduct? What is your reasoning?
2. Is it ethical for Carmine to tell his other relatives the good news? Why or why not?
3. If you were advising Carmine, what would you tell him? Why?

 **CASE 6.2**

A Friend for Life

The Glades Company is a small manufacturer. It has produced and marketed a number of different toys and appliances that have done very well in the marketplace. Late last year the product designer at the company, Tom Berringer, told the president, Paula Glades, that he had invented a small, cuddly, talking bear that might have a great deal of appeal. The bear is made of fluffy brown material that simulates fur and has a tape inside that contains 50 messages.

The Glades Company decided to find out exactly how much market appeal the bear would have. Fifty of them were produced and placed in kindergartens and nurseries around town. The results were better than the firm had hoped. One of the nurseries reported: "The bear was so popular that most of the children wanted to take it home for an evening." Another said the bear was the most popular toy in the school.

Based on these data, the company decided to manufacture and market 1,000 of the bears. At the same time, a catchy marketing slogan was formulated: "A Friend for Life." The bear was marketed as a product a child could play with for years and years. The first batch of 1,000 bears sold out within a week. The company then scheduled another production run. This one was for 25,000 bears. Last week, in the middle of the production run, a problem was uncovered. The process of making the bear fur is much more expensive than had been anticipated. The company is faced with two options: It can absorb the extra cost and have the simulated fur produced, or it can use a substitute fur that will not last as long. Specifically, the original simulated fur will last for up to seven years of normal use; the less-expensive simulated fur will last for only eight months.

Some of the managers at Glades believe most children are not interested in playing with the same toy for more than eight months, so substituting the less-expensive simulated fur for the more-expensive fur should be no problem. Others believe the company will damage its reputation if it opts for the substitute fur. "We are going to have complaints within eight months, and we are going to rue the day we agreed to a cheaper substitute," the production manager argues. The sales manager disagrees, contending that "The market is ready for this product, and we ought to provide it." In the middle of this crisis, the accounting department issued its cost analysis of the venture. If the company goes with the more-expensive simulated fur, it will lose $2.75 per bear. If it chooses the less-expensive simulated fur, it will make a profit of $4.98 per bear.

The final decision on the matter rests with Paula Glades. People on both sides of the issue have given her their opinion. One of the last to speak was the vice president of manufacturing, who said, "If you opt for the less-expensive fur, think of what this is going to do to your marketing campaign of 'A Friend for Life.' Are you going to change this slogan to 'A Friend for Eight Months'?" But the marketing vice president urged a different course of action: "We have a fortune tied up in this bear. If you stop production now or go to the more-expensive substitute, we'll lose our shirts. We aren't doing anything illegal by substituting the fur. The bear looks the same. Who's to know?"

Questions

1. Is the recommendation of the marketing vice president legal? Is it ethical? Why or why not?
2. Would it be ethical if the firm used the less-expensive simulated fur but did not change its slogan of "A Friend for Life" and did not tell the buyer about the change in the production process? Why or why not?
3. If you were advising Paula, what would you recommend?

PART 2

ENTREPRENEURIAL CASE ANALYSIS

"Sportin' Life": A Minority Entrepreneur's Creation

The Creator's Vision

In February 1988, a board of venture capitalists and private investors on the Emerging Business Forum in Indianapolis listened intently to artist/entrepreneur George Huggins describe his new cartoon creation—"Sportin' Life."

> . . . an idea whose time has come. "Sportin' Life" is an all-sports, anti-drug, pro-ethics mascot. It is essential today that our children be continuously exposed to good sportsmanship, honesty, ethics, fair play, and, of course, the avoidance of drugs. "Sportin' Life" offers our youth a role model in cartoon characterization to address the needed values lacking in so many sports heroes. Children can become a "teammate" with "Sportin' Life" and learn that competition should always be fun and yet ethical. It's an individual effort to be all you can be, and it's best accomplished through unity. "Sportin' Life" is the ideal innovation to bring children together as part of a team that focuses on the highest values of sports and, in addition, works carefully to instill an antidrug atmosphere.
>
> In order to establish "Sportin' Life" in the marketplace, I am seeking to strategically place the concept in a toy doll format as well as posters for endorsement of anti-drug or other virtuous themes. Eventually, I would like to license the character into other products if the market demands.
>
> Ladies and gentlemen, I need your support to launch this character.

The Forum's Reaction

The investors were impressed with the concept and the sincerity with which George Huggins presented it. However, a detailed business plan outlining the marketing, production, and financial projections would have to be developed before any of the investors would commit capital.

In the words of David C. Clegg, the president of the Indiana Institute for New Business Ventures, which sponsors the Emerging Business Forum, "One critical test for an entrepreneur's idea is the development of a complete business plan. It acts as a road map for outlining the venture's direction amid its opportunities. Thus, George must develop the concept further and attempt to substantiate the potential of the new character. If that can be done, I believe George will find capital sources more willing to commit to this project."

George realized then that he needed a complete business plan before seeking any more sources for seed capital. Even though he did not have the business background to understand a comprehensive business plan, George began the process of researching and developing information needed to confirm the viability of his idea. The following sections represent the pertinent segments researched and developed for the "Sportin' Life" character.

George Huggins: Artist/Entrepreneur

The place to start understanding the development of "Sportin' Life" is a little background on George

---

SOURCE: This case was prepared by Dr. Donald F. Kuratko of the College of Business at Ball State University as a basis for class discussion rather than to illustrate either effective or ineffective handling of an administrative situation. Presented to the Midwest Society for Case Research Workshop, 1989. All rights reserved to the author and to the Midwest Society for Case Research. Copyright © 1989 by Donald F. Kuratko.

Huggins. George is a black entrepreneur whose artistic talents are known in the Muncie, Indiana, area. He is currently an art teacher for the local high school. In addition, George owns and operates Geo-Graphic Art Productions, a small company that provides artwork of various kinds to agencies needing posters, banners, fliers, and so forth. Although not very profitable due to low volume (mostly caused by George's limited time in the promotion of the business), the business has provided George another outlet to become known, especially in the black business community. On numerous occasions George has been the recipient of the community's minority achievement award for artistic talent.

Previous to his teaching and business operation, George spent ten years as a designer for the Ball Stores clothing department, also located in Muncie. This not only developed his artistic talents but also increased his visibility in the community.

George is 44 years old, married, and the father of four children. He holds a bachelor's degree in art education and has pursued graduate-level courses in computer art and journalism.

Since 1983 George has worked in his spare time developing this new cartoon character. A complete storyboard exists that depicts the beginning of "Sportin' Life" and why it has become an all-sports mascot representing sound values, good sportsmanship, and antidrugs.

> For the first time in my life I have used my teaching and artistic talent to create a concept needed in my community. The sports world is so pervasive in the lives of young children, and today that world is fraught with scandals, drugs, cheating, and coverups. Especially in the black community, young children seek to emulate the sports heroes and yearn to be part of a team. "Sportin' Life" offers a membership on a team that represents the values and ethics we need to develop in our children. In addition, he leads the team against the use of drugs. Thus, my character teaches the children what is missing from actual sports in the media. I believe this character represents everything I would like to accomplish in life. I believe in "Sportin' Life," and I want our children to become Teammates! (See Figure A for sketches of "Sportin' Life.")

The Development of "Sportin' Life" (Niche, Competition, and Market)

The character "Sportin' Life" has some aspects no other character possesses. The idea that the character represents antidrugs is not the only outstanding quality. Being a sports figure gives the character a special identity, as do the values it represents. No other entity representing the antidrug campaign is a sports character; thus "Sportin' Life," the antidrug character, will be a special figure with its sports theme. In addition, the goals of the "Sportin' Life" concept are unprecedented because they address three specific areas: drug-free living, good sportsmanship, and moral/ethical behavior.

Although "Sportin' Life," as a doll, has no direct competition, it will have a great deal of indirect competition. The Hulk Hogan doll represents one sport, wrestling. Because this doll is small and made of plastic, it does not compete directly with the soft-bodied "Sportin' Life." Other indirect competitors are any soft or plastic dolls. These could be teddy bears, Cabbage Patch Kids, Barbies, or any stuffed animals. A consumer might consider any of these alternatives when purchasing a toy or present for a child instead of "Sportin' Life."

If "Sportin' Life" were to represent the drug-free theme, it would be up against three major competitors. The first major competitor is McGruff. McGruff has narrowed his anticrime campaign to the antidrug campaign. McGruff will be a tough competitor. He has prime TV advertising time plus a short video and theme song that have been out for almost two months as of this writing. Although McGruff is on the antidrug bandwagon, he does not represent the "Say No to Drugs" organization. According to a survey, which will be discussed later in this plan, people still think McGruff is an anticrime figure, not the new antidrug character. Thus "Sportin' Life" still has a chance to hit the market representing the drug-free theme and still be recognized as such. The second major competitor to "Sportin' Life" is Woodsy Owl. His new campaign against drugs follows the same direction as McGruff with the same advantages. The last major competitor is Ronald McDonald. When Ronald goes around to different towns to give his show, he presents safety, health, and antidrug themes. Because Ronald is a character and not a real person, children identify with him. Also, Ronald has been seen by

FIGURE A ALL THE WAY "LIVE"

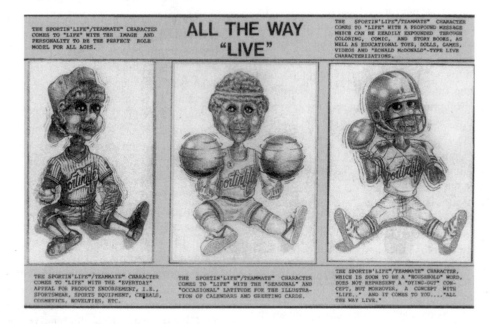

many children over and over in the fast-food commercials. Being in the public eye, Ronald has quite a degree of credibility, like McGruff and Woodsy Owl. This strength would carry over if Ronald would decide to pursue the role of being a spokesperson for the drug-free campaign.

Two minor competitors to "Sportin' Life" are the characters Snoopy and Garfield. Although they are not full-time contenders to the "Say No to Drugs" program, they can get public awareness and could be competitors in the future. To find out more in this area, the "Just Say No" foundation was contacted. From its point of view, the drug-free program should be approached by letting children see actual people instead of characters saying no to drugs. People supporting this idea are Nancy Reagan, Isiah Thomas, and Dr. J. In the music industry, groups saying no to drugs are the Jets and Rock Against Drugs (RAD). They have an advantage over "Sportin' Life" because they are humans who communicate *with* children, not characters who speak *at* children. Using real persons as spokespeople for the "Say No to Drugs" program makes the topic more credible to children. Although, in this society, children identify with a character more often than with a real person, especially with "Come to Life" human dolls fashioned

in toddler proportions and acting out everyday activities.

"Sportin' Life" would have an opportunity to widen its niche if his image were reproduced on a poster. For example, in the elementary schools no standard program represents the antidrug theme. However, individual teachers advocate the drug-free theme, but it is on their own accord and sporadic throughout the area schools. "Sportin' Life" could be introduced to the school system as a school-wide mascot for the antidrug theme through a poster campaign.

Basically, the market for the doll and the antidrug campaign character is targeted at the same group. The target market for the antidrug character that will promote antidrugs and good sportsmanship campaigns will be elementary-level boys and girls 5 to 11 years of age. At these ages, children can be influenced not to use drugs and to participate in good sportsmanship. Also, "Sportin' Life," being a cartoon character, would probably appeal to elementary-aged children. The target market for the doll is slightly different in the respect that George wants to start to market the doll toward black elementary-aged children. Also, the doll will be marketed to families that have the discretionary income to purchase a doll like "Sportin'

Life." Because "Sportin' Life" has black facial features and a dark complexion, the targeting of the doll at black children will be a good beginning. George plans to see if the concept of the doll will be accepted or rejected before expanding to all elementary-aged children. The idea is to start out small and move to a larger market.

Three main regions are currently being targeted: The first is Delaware County (located in central Indiana), the second is the state of Indiana, and the third is the Midwest. Delaware County has 9,871 children from the ages of 5 to 11 (kindergarten through the fifth grade), of which approximately 950 are black children. This information is from the 1988 statistics obtained from the Delaware County Planning Commission and from the public and private schools. Within the state of Indiana are 58,135 black children in the same age group. The last region is midwestern states consisting of Iowa, Illinois, Kentucky, Michigan, Minnesota, Ohio, Pennsylvania, West Virginia, and Wisconsin. Excluding Indiana, 6,468,800 children exist, and 786,763 of these are black children within the targeted age group. With all the regions combined, the total market is 7,083,910 children, and, of that, 826,763 were black children.

The Survey

A survey was conducted to gain insight into the consumers' reaction to the "Sportin' Life" character as spokesperson for an antidrug campaign and also to the "Sportin' Life" doll. The survey took place at three sites in Muncie. The reason for three different sites was to gain a wide range of income levels and also racial status. One hundred four adults responded, as did a disappointing number of 6 children in the targeted age group. The survey showed a good reaction to the concept of the doll and the character to be used for antidrug campaigns. (Appendix A contains complete survey results.)

The first question received a 94 percent affirmative response on whether the idea of a sports character advocating good sportsmanship and antidrugs is a good idea. The biggest answer why it is not a good idea is that drug problems are exploited by the media in the professional sports ranks as well as the amateur and college ranks. The character would be appealing to both boys and girls as indicated by an 88 percent affirmative response.

The biggest response for what sport it should represent was basketball. The main reason for this was because of the dominant influence of basketball in Indiana. The next highest response was baseball, followed by football, and the fourth highest was for "Sportin' Life" to represent all sports. Many respondents said that the sports portrayed should depend on the area in which you are marketing (for example, basketball for Indiana). Eighty-eight percent of the people responded that "Sportin' Life" would be a good spokesperson for an antidrug theme, and of the 104 surveyed, 96 percent said that it would be effective within the target market age group. When the respondents were asked where they had noticed antidrug campaigns, television received 89 responses. Radio and billboards both received 24 responses, and the school setting followed with 12 responses. The newspaper, Nancy Reagan, posters, and magazines all had 8 responses or fewer.

A 79 percent affirmative response was given to the ability of the character to appeal to children if made into a doll; also, 72 percent said a need existed for a doll that represents antidrugs and good sportsmanship within the targeted age group. When asked if they knew of any doll to compete with "Sportin' Life," 88 percent of the surveys said no. In regard to competitive dolls, the responses included Teddy Ruxpin, Cabbage Patch, My Buddy, and, simply, all dolls.

The color of the character should pose no problem, since 79 percent responded favorably to the current color. Many responded that the uniform colors could be brighter. If the character is going to be successful it has to get in the public eye and be a memorable product. When asked in the survey if they heard about McGruff the dog, 73 percent responded yes. However, only 50 percent knew he represented anticrime, and only 11 percent knew of his campaigns against drug use. George must establish his character like McGruff and his campaign against crime. Because the public does not realize McGruff is against drugs, a gap exists in the public's perception of a character of this nature.

The results from the survey showed a possible modification of the target market for the doll. The antidrug sports character for promotion of an antidrug campaign would remain the same for all elementary children. The target market for the doll concept was aimed primarily at black children in elementary school. However, 90 percent of the people who responded to the two concepts of the doll and anti-drug promotion were white, and the 10 percent that were black had parallel answers.

"Sportin' Life": Doll Manufacture

The most common dolls of today are made either of plastic or cloth. The plastic dolls can be either hard or soft. The cloth dolls can be all cloth, such as the Cabbage Patch dolls, or they can be a combination of cloth and plastic, such as the Teddy Ruxpin doll. The cloth dolls are not feasible for "Sportin' Life" because the distinctive facial features would be unattainable. Thus, attention was centered on the manufacturing of a plastic doll. Three manufacturing processes are available for plastic doll manufacturing. They are injection molding, blow molding, and rotational molding. Rotational molding would be the best for the "Sportin' Life" doll.

Three possible alternatives to manufacture the "Sportin' Life" doll are (1) set up a manufacturing site in the Muncie area, (2) license the doll to another manufacturing company, and (3) manufacture the doll overseas in the Orient.

The ideal doll George Huggins would manufacture has the following characteristics:

- 14 inches in height
- The doll will come in three possible outfits: basketball, baseball, and football.
- The head and all of the accessories will be constructed from a plastic material.
- The body will be made of a cloth and stuffed with a soft, cottonlike material.
- The outfits will be made out of a cottonlike material.
- The eyes will be painted on.
- The hands will have Velcro in them to hold onto the sports equipment

After deciding on the type of doll he wanted to manufacture, George looked into the alternatives. He first examined a suitable manufacturing facility for that purpose and calculated all of the costs involved in the process. (See Table 1.) The cost figures are based on the average costs for the industry and related resources. The labor costs were derived from the average labor costs for the area according to the related jobs. The utility costs were based on past utility ex-

penses at the facility and on the average utility costs for similar manufacturing facilities. The machinery costs were compiled from three different price lists obtained from equipment dealers. The mold costs were derived in the same manner.

After obtaining all of the necessary estimated production costs, George broke down the costs per doll. The estimated production cost for a local manufacturing site figured out to be approximately $38 per doll. This price could fluctuate a couple of dollars either way according to the accuracy of the estimates and according to the actual production output per day.

The second alternative was to license the doll to a doll manufacturer for production. Only a few places do this type of production, so the possibilities of an in-country manufacturing firm are limited. George contacted a doll manufacturing company in Ohio. After several weeks of discussion, it gave him an estimated price for the doll. The price range was $20–$25 per doll. This price would be according to the production amount desired, but the manufacturer believed at this point that its price per doll would be closer to the $20 amount. This doll would meet the same specifications mentioned earlier, and it would be shipped fully assembled and packaged.

The third alternative was to manufacture the doll overseas. Most of the dolls sold in the United States were produced in the Orient. However, the limited number of doll producers in America leads one to believe this is an inexpensive alternative. Because of George's lack of adequate connections to overseas producers, at this time, he has no estimated price per doll for this alternative.

A final alternative for manufacturing the "Sportin' Life" doll based on the information George was able to obtain was to license the doll to the Ohio Doll Company. While a doll may be produced fairly inexpensively, the concept of licensing creates an entirely new set of legal considerations.

"Sportin' Life": Poster Production

The printing of posters may be an easy way to promote this idea. "Sportin' Life" needs to become a recognizable character to children and their parents. Therefore, posters may be a viable method for accomplishing that goal.

Several advantages to creating "Sportin' Life" posters exist. First, when George receives a sponsor-

TABLE 1	LOCAL MANUFACTURING FACILITY COSTS

Assumptions

1. Average daily production will be 100 dolls.
2. Production facility will be 5,000 square feet.
3. Average production will be 22 days per month.
4. Equipment will be amortized over 5 years.

	Monthly	Yearly
Rent	$ 416.67	$ 5,000.00
Utilities		
Gas (heat)	400.00	4,800.00
Electric	2,500.00	30,000.00
Sewage	80.00	960.00
Water	220.00	2,640.00
Phone	100.00	1,200.00
Total	$ 3,300.00	$ 39,600.00
Labor Costs		
Rotation molder (1) @ $10.34	1,819.00	21,828.00
Injection molder (1) @ 10.34	1,819.00	21,828.00
Sewers (6) @ 6.52	6,885.00	82,620.00
Painters (3) @ 7.69	4,060.00	48,720.00
Assemblers (3) @ 6.52	3,442.00	41,304.00
Pattern cutters (2) @ 5.60	1,971.00	23,652.00
Secretary @ 6.25	1,100.00	13,200.00
Operations manager's salary	2,166.00	26,000.00
Total	$ 23,262.00	$ 279,152.00
Material Costs		
Cloth	24,000.00	288,000.00
Plastic stock	16,000.00	192,000.00
Paints	600.00	7,200.00
Hair material	3,000.00	36,000.00
Body stuffing	6,000.00	72,000.00
Glue	600.00	7,200.00
Velcro	800.00	9,600.00
Packaging	2,200.00	26,400.00
Total	$ 53,200.00	$ 638,400.00

	One-Time Cost
Equipment Costs	
Rotation molding machine	$ 60,000.00
Injection molding machine	45,000.00

(Continued)

TABLE 1	LOCAL MANUFACTURING FACILITY COSTS *(continued)*

Pattern cutters (2)	8,000.00
Sewing machines (6)	12,000.00
Set-up cost	20,000.00
Tables, chairs, storage bins	8,000.00
Office equipment/supplies	7,000.00
Total	$160,000.00

Mold Costs

Head	$ 18,000.00
Baseball glove	6,000.00
Baseball cap	3,500.00
Baseball bat	2,500.00
Football helmet	7,000.00
Football mask	4,000.00
Football	4,000.00
Basketball	4,000.00
Football cleats	6,000.00
Baseball cleats	6,000.00
Basketball shoes	6,000.00
Total	$ 67,000.00

	Monthly	Yearly
Total Costs		
Rent	$ 416.67	$ 5,000.00
Utilities	3,300.00	39,600.00
Labor	23,262.00	279,152.00
Raw materials	53,200.00	638,400.00
Amortized machine/mold costs (5 years)	3,783.33	45,400.00
Total	$ 83,962.00	$1,007,552.00
Break-even price per doll	$ 38.16	

	Monthly	Yearly
Total Capital Needed for Manufacturing Start-Up and First Month's/Year's Expenses without Any Income		
Rent	$ 416.67	$ 5,000.00
Utilities	3,300.00	39,600.00
Labor	23,262.00	279,152.00
Materials	53,200.00	638,400.00
Equipment	160,000.00	160,000.00
Molds	67,000.00	67,000.00
Total	$307,178.67	$1,189,152.00

ship, his posters will have a message. This message is "say no to drugs." The adult consumer will support the idea of the poster, while children will love the actual "Sportin' Life." Because the poster appeals to both the parents and the children, it will have a high sales volume.

Also, the posters would be available in two different sizes. The 8½-inch × 11-inch poster is on high-quality paper, so it can be framed. The other poster, 11 inches × 17 inches, would be more appropriate for walls. "Sportin' Life" could be a positive image on a child's wall at home as well as on the walls at school (especially in the sport locker rooms).

Finally, "Sportin' Life" posters could be sold in literally hundreds of places. Unlike some products and services, posters are bought by almost all age groups. Several printing shops in the area were contacted to estimate the cost of the posters. The following depicts the costs:

300 (100 × 3 poses) 8½ inch × 11 inch	$ 36.95
1,500 (500 × 3 poses) 11 inch × 17 inch	83.80
3,000 (1,000 × 3 poses) 11 inch × 17 inch	132.50
	$253.25

Unit Cost Breakdown

300 total of 8½ inch × 11 inch	$.37
1,500 total of 11 inch × 17 inch	.17
3,000 total of 11 inch × 17 inch	.13

For a small investment of $253.25, "Sportin' Life" could be well on his way to becoming a poster character.

Pricing (Doll and Posters)

The doll market is an extremely tough market. Many different types, styles, and characteristics exist within the doll market. The doll prices range from $5.00 to $90.00 depending on the style and the type. The research done by George divided the doll market into three categories: low-priced, medium-priced, and high-priced dolls.

The low-priced dolls have the following characteristics. The prices range from $5.00 to $15.00. The dolls that fit into this range are Bert and Ernie, Nosy Bear, and Noid. The Bert and/or Ernie doll is a 10-inch × 5-inch doll dressed in Sesame Street clothes. The small amount of hair on the dolls does not appear authentic. The next doll that fits into this category is Nosy Bear. Priced at $13.00 and dressed in very bright colors, this doll looks like a bear and is 8 inches × 6 inches in size. The third and last doll to fit into this category is the Noid, which is the Domino's Pizza representative. This doll has hair and has the dimensions of 12 inches × 6 inches. It also has

average clothing and a few facial features. The following characteristics are apparent when observing the low-priced dolls: They all have little hair; none is very soft; none has real facial features; and none comes with accessories.

The medium-priced doll range appeared to have many more dolls and many more features. The first is the Couch Potato. This doll resembles a potato and sits in a brown gunny sack. The doll is very soft and has a size of 12 inches × 6 inches. The next doll is called the Puffalumps. This doll is priced at $20.00 and comes with clothing. It is very soft and has dimensions of 12 inches × 8 inches. The next doll that fell into this range is Baby Talks Back. This doll is priced at $25.00 and has teeth and hair, is very soft, and has dimensions of 18 inches × 8 inches. Alf, another very popular medium-priced doll, is priced at $29.95. This doll is 20 inches × 9 inches and is big, soft, and hairy. The last doll is the Cabbage Patch Cornsilk Kids. This doll is priced at $35.00 and is approximately 18 inches × 9 inches. It is very soft, has nice clothes, has a full head of hair, and appears to be more appealing than the other dolls. The general noticeable characteristics in the medium-priced doll range are the higher cost, some accessories, and softer and larger dolls.

The dolls within the high-priced range are priced from $50.00 and up. Currently only the Cabbage Patch doll with the artificial intelligence fits into this category. The characteristics this doll has follow: talks, sings, nice clothing, beautiful hair, facial features, shoes, and adoption papers. This doll sells for $90.00 and appears to be the most popular doll of all the ones within these three categories.

In compliance with the production requirements of the "Sportin' Life" doll, George found the best fit was the medium-priced range. If the doll is subcontracted out, the doll will run a production cost of $25.00. With this in mind, the "Sportin' Life" doll would have to establish a market price between $45.00 and $50.00. Although "Sportin' Life" would be at the high end of the medium-price range, the size of the doll, its facial features, and its clothing may support a $50.00 price sticker.

In examining the poster market, George found that the market prices of posters are dependent on size as compared to the popularity of any one character. The poster market is divided into three categories broken

TABLE 2	PROFIT MARGINS

Doll

Low	Medium	High
$35.00	$45.00	$55.00
40% markup over production costs	80% markup over production costs	120% markup over production costs

Posters: 8½" x 11"

Low	Medium	High
$1.00	$1.50	$1.75
170% markup over production costs	305% markup over production costs	372% markup over production costs

Posters: 11" × 17"

Low	Medium	High
$2.00	$2.50	$2.75
1,000% markup	1,300% markup	1,500% markup

Dolls	Prices
Cabbage Patch 1	$89.99
Couch Potato	24.99
Bert/Ernie	7.99
Puffalump	19.99
Nosy Bear	12.99
Alf	29.99
Cabbage Patch 2	34.99
Noid (Domino's Pizza)	13.00
Baby Talks Back	22.00

Posters	8½" × 11"	11" × 17"	22" × 18"
Alf	$1.50	$2.50	$3.99
Bud-Lite Dog	1.50	2.50	3.99
Alf 2	1.50	2.50	3.99
California Raisin	1.50	none	3.99
Noid (Domino's Pizza)	1.50	2.50	3.99
Argus	1.50	2.50	none
Garfield	1.50	2.95	none

TABLE 3	PRO FORMA INCOME STATEMENT FOR "SPORTIN' LIFE"		
	Year 1	**Year 2**	**Year 3**
Sales Revenue			
A. Gross sales	$ 64,157	$292,179	$602,127
B. Discounts, returns, ½ allowance	(930)	(4,382)	(9,031)
C. Net sales	$ 63,227	$287,797	$593,096
D. Cost of Goods Sold			
Dolls	25,950	107,675	177,100
Posters 8½" × 11"	841	5,384	12,040
Posters 11" × 17"	989	4,920	14,167
Total cost of goods sold	$ 27,780	$117,979	$203,307
Gross profit	$ 35,447	$169,818	$389,789
Operating Expenses			
E. Advertising	1,325	2,920	$ 6,020
F. Wages	57,600	68,200	82,000
G. Office supplies	3,660	4,250	4,250
H. Rent	3,000	3,000	4,200
I. Legal	1,000	3,000	3,000
J. Telephone	875	1,200	1,600
K. Miscellaneous	600	1,200	1,200
Total operating expenses	$ 71,068	$ 83,770	$102,270
Operating income/loss	$(35,621)	$ 86,048	$287,519
L. Other income	2,400	2,400	2,400
Other expenses			
Profit before taxes	$(33,221)	$ 88,448	$289,919
Taxes			95,673
M. Net income/loss	$(33,221)	$ 59,063	$194,246

down by size. A small poster has a size of 8½ inches × 11 inches; a medium, 11 inches × 17 inches; and a large, 22 inches × 18 inches. The characters found on the posters were Alf, Bud-Lite Dog, Alf 2, California Raisins, Argus, and Garfield. The small posters sold for $1.50, the medium-sized posters sold for $2.50, and the large posters sold for $4.00. (See Table 2 for full results.)

Financial Segment

Table 3 provides a rough projection of the pro forma income statement developed by George Huggins for the first three years. Explanations are also provided to show how George estimated many of the figures. This section attempts to give some actual financial numbers to work with.

Income Statement First Year (Explanations)

- The pro forma income statement gross sales for the first year were obtained by combining the sales of dolls with the sales of both sizes of posters for the Delaware County area. The doll and poster sales were estimated, respectively, to be 10 percent and 50 percent of the 9,871 Delaware County children between the ages of 5 and 11. (Dolls: 10% × 9,871 = 987 × $45.00; posters: 50% × 9,871 = 4,935 × $1.50 and 4,935 × $2.50.) These figures may seem high, but the expectation is that sales will overflow into surrounding counties by the end of the year. It is also estimated that the posters will be sold to schools and other organizations that wish to promote antidrugs and sportsmanlike conduct.

The gross monthly sales totals for the first year are established at 10 percent per month with the sixth and seventh months being the average. The gross sales for the year do not include an increase for the Christmas season because the business will still be in the early growth stage and have no real momentum.

- The discounts, returns, and allowances were estimated at about 1.5 percent of the year's gross sales. This figure is extremely safe compared with other industry figures.
- It is estimated that net sales for the first year will be $63,227.
- The manufacturing cost of the dolls was estimated to be $25 for each doll for the first three years; poster manufacturing costs were $.17 for the 8-inch × 11-inch size and $.20 for the 11-inch × 17-inch size.

The operating expenses follow:

- *Advertising*—an initial cost of $50 is estimated plus an additional outlay of $75 a month thereafter.
- *Wages*—for the first year estimates came to $57,600 for three employees. The three employees will be a manager (George Huggins), an accountant, and a graphic artist.
- *Office supplies*—including furniture, art supplies, a personal computer, ledgers, paper, and so on; these were estimated to be $3,000. (Depreciation was calculated on the balance sheet.)
- *Rent*—$250 a month includes utilities, and it will be paid three months in advance
- *Legal fees*—These will cost approximately $1,000 a year.

- *Phone*—This is expected to run $200 for initial hookup and the first month's calls. Subsequent months are estimated to be between $50 and $75.
- *Miscellaneous*—$50 a month will be included for unforeseen expenses.
- Other income of $200 a month will come from such sources as sponsorship, videos, and miscellaneous sales. These sales minus the expenses and manufacturing costs will put the company at a loss.
- The company will recognize a $33,221 loss for the first year, and this is why it is estimated that an initial investment of $50,000 will be necessary to get started and an additional $25,000 loan will be needed after the first year.

Income Statement, Second Year

The plan for the second year is to expand the market area to include the entire state of Indiana. The marketing area would be enlarged to 615,110 children between the ages of 5 and 11. Projecting a market share of 0.5 percent of 615,110, now 3,075 additional children would purchase the doll priced at $45.00. Also projecting a market share for posters of 4 percent of 615,110, 24,604 additional children would purchase the two posters.

The second year's gross sales will have the first and fourth quarters showing the average, with the second quarter showing 20 percent more sales because of the Christmas trade and the third quarter showing a 20 percent decline because of the after-Christmas slump.

Estimated sales figures for the second year are hoped to be about half of those of an established firm within the industry.

Advertising expenses for the second year are established at 1 percent of sales.

Wage increases will be given yearly to each employee assuming that the maximum number of staff remains at three. The yearly increases will be based on the amount of increased responsibilities these employees have taken on.

Income Statement, Third Year

In the third year the marketing area will be expanded to include ten states in the Midwest. This will increase the market area to 7,083,910 children in the current age group. This would give "Sportin' Life" an increase of 0.1 percent of that entire market for doll sales and a 1 percent share of that market for poster sales. In order to achieve this demand, the prices for the products for the first three years will remain constant.

The gross sales in the third year will have the first and fourth quarters showing the average, with the second quarter showing 20 percent more sales because of the Christmas trade and the third quarter showing a 20 percent decline because of the after-Christmas slump.

Estimated sales figures by the end of the third year are projected to be $602,127, which is the industry average.

Advertising expenses for the third year are established at 1 percent of sales.

Operating expenses in the third year will increase because of plans for expansion into a ten-state Midwest area.

A projected net income of $194,246 is expected by the end of the third year. This should be enough to pay off debts and expand into new areas.

In conclusion, some important facts to note are that accounts receivable and inventory turnover will initially be three months, but, thereafter, the turnover rate will be reduced to one month. Possibly, beginning expenses for renovation will include carpeting, blinds, and so forth.*

Critical Risks (Product Safety and Liability)

A final consideration was given to the critical risks faced by George. Product liability was an immediate concern. Accidents involving consumer products cause 20 million injuries per year—110,000 causing permanent disability, 30,000 resulting in death. In facing these statistics, entrepreneurs must take responsibility for product safety and liability.

The existence and potential of product liability litigation are of great concern; the number of generous awards given to successful plaintiffs is rapidly increasing. A product-safety failure can have a potentially adverse effect on a new venture's reputation and

sales. The need to comply with federal and state safety standards, as well as the need to monitor any potentials for safety risks, are also concerns facing George.

No product is completely without risks, though, and George must judge whether his product's determined level of risk is acceptable on legal, political, moral, and economic grounds. For example, George may be more concerned with potential risks because he cannot bear the cost of litigation as easily as a multimillion-dollar corporation.

Many impediments and trends exist today concerning product safety that George should remain aware of. These impediments and trends are listed here:

Impediments to Improving Product-Safety Efforts:

1. Regulations and regulators
2. Altering company attitudes
3. Increasing product complexity
4. Lack of proper organization
5. Product testing and evaluation
6. Costs and staffing problems
7. Product liability problems
8. Miscellaneous technical problems

Trends:

1. Continued proliferation of product safety regulations
2. Additional increase in volume of product liability litigation
3. Increased management attention to financial impact of product failure

"Sportin' Life" Dilemma

George has prepared partial research needed to develop a business plan for his character. The dilemma he faces is threefold: First, is the information complete enough to structure a clear business plan for investors? Second, what investors should be approached—debt sources such as banks and other loan agencies or equity sources such as venture capitalists and informal investors? And, third, how can the sources be found to submit the "Sportin' Life" plan for consideration?

---

*Though these expenses do not appear on the income statement, they have been considered.

George sits back in his chair and ponders the future of "Sportin' Life." It's a concept he's worked on for two years, and still the actual commercialization seems so far off. George says, "I believe in this character as a real tool for teaching our children. There must be a source of capital that would support it. It truly is an idea whose time has come. . . ."

Questions

1. As a consultant to George Huggins, what exactly would you recommend as the most viable opportunity and why?
2. Do entrepreneurial opportunities exist that George has not considered? What are they?
3. For developing a complete business plan, what information is needed or should be expanded for this product concept?
4. What other sources of capital should George pursue?

Appendix A

"Sportin' Life" Survey (Adults)

1. Is the idea of an all-sports character advocating good sportsmanship and antidrugs a good idea?
2. Do you believe that a character of this nature would appeal to both boys and girls?
3. What sports do you think children would like the character to represent?
4. Would you like to see this character as a spokesperson for the antidrug theme?
5. Would it be effective on children ages 5–11?
6. If not, what ages should the idea concentrate on?
7. Where have you noticed antidrug campaigns? (TV, radio, billboard, etc.)
8. If this idea were made into a doll, do you think it would appeal to children?
9. Is there a need by children for a doll like this?
10. Do you know of any doll to compete with this one? If so, what is it?
11. Do you feel like the color of the character is appealing to all kids?
12. Have you ever heard of McGruff? If so, what do you think he represents?
13. Would you buy the character if it were made into a doll?
14. What size and type of doll would you prefer?
15. How much would you be willing to pay for the doll?
16. What range is your income in?

$0–9,999	_____
$10,000–24,999	_____
$25,000–34,999	_____
$35,000–above	_____

Survey Results

1. yes—94%
2. yes—88%
3.

Vball.	Footbl.	Bsktbl.	Basebl.	Bowl.	Gym.	Soc.	Ten.	All	Other
4	19	66	2	1	1	3	1	7	2

4. yes—88%
5. yes—96%
6. Teenagers
7.

TV	Radio	Billbds.	Posters	Newspr.	Nancy R.	Mag.	School
89	24	24	3	8	5	2	12

8. yes—79%
9. yes—72%
10. no—88%
11. yes—79%
12. yes—73% (over 50% assoc. with crime, only 11% with "Say No to Drugs")
13. yes—63%   no—36%   maybe—1%

14.

0–10 in.	11–15 in.	16–20 in.	21–25 in.	26+ in.
11%	3%	22%	4%	1%

Mostly soft and cuddly with hard plastic head.

15.

<$10	$10–15	$15–20	$25	$30+	(28% no answer)
8%	31%	18%	5%	10%	

16.

$0–9,999	25%
$10,000–24,999	8
$25,000–34,999	15
$35,000+	13
No Answer	39

PART 2

EXERCISE

How Ethical Are You?

Directions: Please read the business situations described below and write the number in the blank which shows the degree to which you personally feel they are ethically acceptable.

Never Acceptable			Indifferent		Always Acceptable	
1	2	3	4	5	6	7

1. An executive earning $50,000 a year padded his expense account by almost $1,500 a year. _____

2. In order to increase profits, a general manager used a production process which exceeded legal limits for environmental pollution. _____

3. Because of pressure from his brokerage firm, a stockbroker recommended a type of bond which he did not consider to be a good investment. _____

4. A small business received one-fourth of its gross revenue in the form of cash. The owner reported only one-half of the cash receipts for income tax purposes. _____

5. A company paid a $350,000 "consulting" fee to an official of a foreign country. In return, the official promised assistance in obtaining a contract which should produce a $10 million profit for the contracting company. _____

6. A company president found that a competitor had made an important scientific discovery which would sharply reduce the profits of his own company. He then hired a key employee of the competitor in an attempt to learn the details of the discovery. _____

7. A highway building contractor deplored the chaotic bidding situation and cutthroat competition. He, therefore, reached an understanding with other major contractors to permit bidding which would provide a reasonable profit. _____

8. A company president recognized that sending expensive Christmas gifts to purchasing agents might compromise their positions. However, he continued the policy since it was common practice and changing it might result in loss of business. _____

9. A corporate director learned that his company intended to announce a stock split and increase its dividend. On the basis of this information, he bought additional shares and sold them at a gain following the announcement. _____

10. A corporate executive promoted a loyal friend and competent manager to the position of divisional vice president in preference to a better-qualified manager with whom he had no close ties. _____

11. An engineer discovered what he perceived to be a product design flaw which constituted a safety hazard. His company declined to correct the flaw. The engineer decided to keep quiet, rather than taking his complaint outside the company. _____

12. A comptroller selected a legal method of financial reporting which concealed some embarrassing financial facts which would otherwise have become public knowledge.
_____

13. An employer received applications for a supervisor's position from two equally qualified applicants but hired the male applicant be-

SOURCE: Adapted from Donald F. Kuratko, Douglas W. Naffziger, and Jeffrey S. Hornsby, "Managing Ethics: Why 'Hoping for the Best' Doesn't Work,". *Small Business Forum,* (Winter 1994/1995), pp. 36–43.

cause he thought some employees might resent being supervised by a female. _____

14. As part of the marketing strategy for a product, the producer changed its color and marketed it as "new and improved" even though its other characteristics were unchanged. _____

15. A cigarette manufacturer launched a publicity campaign challenging new evidence from the Surgeon General's office that cigarette smoking is harmful to the smoker's health. _____

16. An owner of a small firm obtained a free copy of a copyrighted computer software program from a business friend rather than spending $500 to obtain his own program from the software dealer. _____

SURVEY RESULTS: HERE IS HOW 240 SMALL-BUSINESS OWNERS RESPONDED

1. Mean response = 2.0
2. Mean response = 1.5
3. Mean response = 1.7
4. Mean response = 2.7
5. Mean response = 3.3
6. Mean response = 3.9
7. Mean response = 3.2
8. Mean response = 3.2
9. Mean response = 2.8
10. Mean response = 3.5
11. Mean response = 2.3
12. Mean response = 4.1
13. Mean response = 3.1
14. Mean response = 3.2
15. Mean response = 3.5
16. Mean response = 3.6

DEVELOPING THE ENTREPRENEURIAL PLAN

Chapter 7

$\mathscr{E}$NVIRONMENTAL ASSESSMENT: PREPARATION FOR A NEW VENTURE

CHAPTER OBJECTIVES

1. To examine some of the major ways of assessing the economic environment

2. To review the regulatory environment within which a new venture must exist

3. To examine the industry environment from a competitive market analysis and strategic point of view

4. To present the community environmental perspective for a local impact understanding

5. To examine community support in terms of reliance and deservedness

6. To review the nature of business incubators and their importance to emerging ventures

Coping with the constantly changing environment is probably the most important determinant of a company's success or failure in a free enterprise system.

Alan J. Rowe, Richard O. Mason, and Earl E. Dickel,
Strategic Management and Business Policy

THE ENVIRONMENT FOR NEW VENTURES

Many ways of making an **environmental assessment** for a new venture exist.[1] In the main, however, these approaches are neither highly sophisticated nor heavily quantitative. As neither an economist nor a quantitative analyst, the average new-venture entrepreneur will stay within the confines of what he or she can understand and use for conducting this assessment. This often entails evaluating the general economic environment and determining what governmental regulations, both national and local, will impact the venture. A more detailed evaluation of the industry is then made, with primary consideration given to such areas as common industry characteristics, barriers to entry, and competitive analysis. The overall economic method of analysis is from general considerations to specific considerations.

The last part of the analysis focuses on the community perspective, that is, local conditions. The entrepreneur will examine location factors, the fit between the business and the local environment, and, if the situation warrants, the use of a business incubator. Throughout the analysis the entrepreneur will concentrate on gathering practical and useful information that will help answer the question What do I need to know in getting ready for this new venture?

Environmental Scanning

Environmental scanning refers to the efforts an owner-entrepreneur uses for examining the external and internal environments before making a decision.[2]

The *external environment* consists of variables (opportunities and threats) that are outside the organization and not typically within the short-run control of the entrepreneur (see Figure 7.1). These variables form the context within which the venture exists. The external environment has two parts: task environment and societal environment. The **task environment** includes elements or groups that directly affect and are affected by an organization's

[1] Arnold C. Cooper, Timothy B. Folta, and Carolyn Woo, "Entrepreneurial Information Search," *Journal of Business Venturing* (March 1995): 95–106.

[2] See Sumaria Indra Mohan-Neill, "The Influence of Firm's Age and Size on Its Environmental Scanning Activities," *Journal of Small Business Management* (October 1995): 10–21.

FIGURE 7.1   **ENVIRONMENTAL VARIABLES**

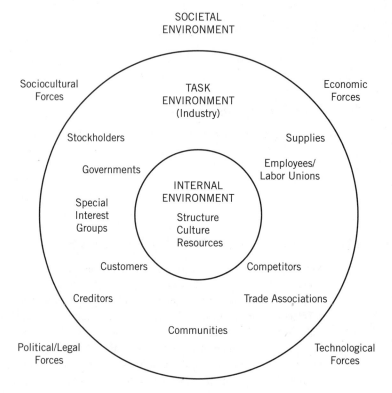

SOURCE: Thomas L. Wheeler and J. David Hunger, *Strategic Management and Business Policy,* 4th ed., 14, Figure 1.3. © 1997 Addison-Wesley Publishing Company, Inc. Reprinted by permission of Addison-Wesley Longman, Inc.

major operations. Some of these are stockholders, governments, suppliers, local communities, competitors, customers, creditors, labor unions, special interest groups, and trade associations. The task environment of a venture is often referred to as its *industry.* The **societal environment** includes more general forces—those that do not directly touch the short-run activities of the organization but can, and often do, influence its long-run decisions.

The *internal environment* of a venture consists of variables (strengths and weaknesses) that are within the organization itself and are not usually within the short-run control of the entrepreneurs. These variables form the context in which work is done. They include the venture's structure, culture, and resources. The venture structure is the way a venture is organized in terms of communication, authority, and work flow. It is often referred to as the "chain of command" and is graphically described in an organizational chart. The organization's **culture** is the pattern of beliefs, expectations, and values shared by the organization's members. In a firm norms typically emerge that define the acceptable behavior of people from top management down to the operative employees. Resources are the assets that form the raw material for the production of an organization's products or services. These assets include people and managerial talent as well as financial assets, plant facilities, and the skills and abilities within functional areas.

The research for answers usually begins with a general macroview of the economic and industry environments.

A MACROVIEW: THE ECONOMIC AND INDUSTRY ENVIRONMENTS

Two major areas of the macroview warrant consideration: (1) the overall economic environment and (2) the specific industry environment.

Assessing the Economic Environment

The economic environment plays a vital role in the success or failure of any new venture. Too often it becomes obvious that an entrepreneur made little effort to determine whether the economic environment was friendly or hostile to his or her specific venture.[3] Additionally, entrepreneurs often commit funds to a business without adequate preliminary investigation. An assessment of the economic environment can help them avoid these pitfalls. Some of the most important questions to be answered follow: How many firms are in this industry? Do the firms vary in size and general characteristics, or are they all similar? What is the geographic concentration of firms in the industry; that is, are they in one area, or are they widely dispersed? Do the firms serve only the domestic market? Do opportunities to serve foreign markets exist as well? What federal, state, and local government regulations affect this type of business? What is the competitive nature of this business?

Answers to these questions provide an overall picture of the business climate within which a new venture will operate. In addition, entrepreneurs with emerging new ventures must realize that certain attitudes and skills are needed for proper assessment of the environment. These are the most important, presented from a management point of view:

- A broadened awareness of influences in the external environment that affect the corporation and management decision making
- The ability to integrate traditional business concerns about influences from the external environment into a comprehensive decision-making framework based on a holistic view of business and its relationship to the larger society in which it functions
- Political skills (compromise, negotiation) to resolve the conflicting interests among different constituencies that have diverse values and objectives
- Communication skills to articulate a business position on a very complex public issue and to persuade people that this position has merit and deserves serious consideration
- Intellectual skills to analyze and understand complex public issues—the ability to think clearly about these issues and exchange ideas with the various business publics.[4]

UNDERSTANDING THE REGULATORY ENVIRONMENT   A business must comply with governmental rules and regulations. Costs and profits can be affected as much by a

---

[3] See Andrew H. Van de Ven, "The Development of an Infrastructure for Entrepreneurship," *Journal of Business Venturing* (May 1993): 211–30.

[4] Rogene A. Buchholz, *Business Environment and Public Policy: Implications for Management & Strategy Formulation,* 4th ed. (1992), 15. Reprinted by permission of Prentice-Hall, Inc., Englewood Cliffs, New Jersey.

government directive as by a management decision from the front office or a customer decision at the checkout counter. Fundamental entrepreneurial decisions—such as what lines of business to go into, what products and services to produce, which investments to finance, how and where to make goods and how to market them, and what prices to charge—are increasingly subject to governmental control.[5]

Over the past decade, government has become a partner to small business. The administrators in Washington have begun to establish new ground rules by which small-business ventures have as equal a chance to survive and prosper as large ventures. A coalition to advocate the interests of small firms and new ventures is now emerging, and a network of state commerce departments, trade and professional associations, the National Chamber of Commerce, the Small Business Administration (SBA), and certain universities is developing a stronger voice for the small businessperson/entrepreneur.

Over the past few decades many legislators focused their attention on big business and expected little firms to fall into line. Although some aid and benefits were provided to small-business entrepreneurs, most governmental efforts were directed at regulation. In the process the small firm became saddled with the same amount of regulatory red tape as the giant corporation. Today it appears the tide has turned. The past few years have seen a shift in the attitudes and actions of legislators.[6] A number of reasons can be cited for this shift: an awareness of the need to strengthen the small-business sector of the economy; an effort by Washington to increase national employment by promoting small-business interests; and the growth of foreign multinationals in the United States, which unleashed a renewed pride in the country's innovative and entrepreneurial spirit. *Nation's Business* captured the essence of this new attitude when it stated:

> Everywhere you look in America there is a small business—the corner drugstore, the auto dealer, the barbershop, the dry cleaner, the grocer, and every entrepreneur you meet will rail against the same problems—restrictive regulation, burdensome taxes, lack of capital, flagging innovation. . . .
>
> Despite conflicting theories and policies, everyone agrees on one thesis: Unless something is done to help small business survive successfully as an American institution, it will become as rare as the buffalo, with effects as severe on the American economy as the vanishing of that species had on the American Indian.[7]

Governmental regulation is one of the most discernible influences on businesses today. Since it encompasses so many regulatory acts and agencies, this aspect of the environment is the first new ventures must consider (see Figure 7.2).

Governmental regulations affect smaller ventures in a variety of ways:

- *Prices:* Small businesses are often forced to raise their prices to absorb the costs of regulatory compliance.
- *Cost inequities:* Financially, small companies feel the brunt of regulatory burdens more than large corporations.
- *Competitive restriction:* Putting a greater burden on small business tends to favor big business, thereby subtly encouraging big while discouraging small.

---

[5] Ronald G. Cook and David Barry, "When Should the Small Firm Be Involved in Public Policy?" *Journal of Small Business Management* (January 1993): 39–50.

[6] William F. Doescher, "Recognition at Last," *D & B Reports* (March/April 1993): 10–11.

[7] "Beset, Bothered and Beleaguered," *Nation's Business,* February 1980, 22.

FIGURE 7.2   **IMPACT OF REGULATORY AGENCIES ON THE TYPICAL BUSINESS**

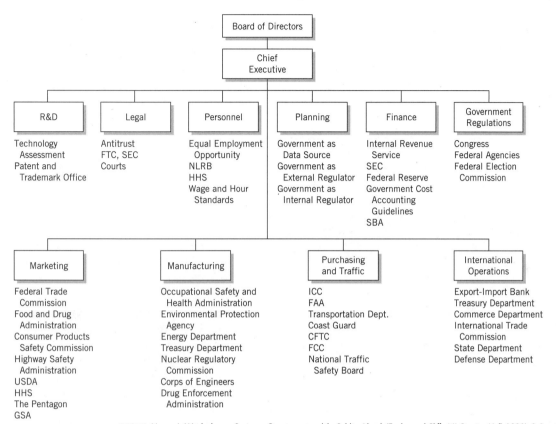

SOURCE: Murray L. Weidenbaum, *Business, Government and the Public,* 4th ed. (Englewood Cliffs, NJ: Prentice-Hall, 1990), 9. Reprinted by permission of Prentice-Hall, Englewood Cliffs, New Jersey.

- *Managerial restriction:* Due to time devoted to paperwork-imposed duties, the small-business person must sacrifice valuable managerial time in complying with governmental regulations.
- *Mental burden:* Postponed projects, wasted time, and managerial failure due to lack of time and energy all begin to take their toll on the small-business person. Frustration leading to depression may spell failure for the business.

Public-policy experts agree that one of the most serious consequences of federal regulation of business is the threat to the continued existence of the small firm.[8] Regulatory burdens may surface not only in compliance costs but also in the paperwork burden that becomes the ancillary aspect of governmental policies:

> The small firm, unlike its large firm counterpart, does not have a professional staff to respond to heavy paperwork and reporting requirements. Often the owner/entrepreneur is the only individual with sufficient knowledge to respond to an agency's

[8] See Murray L. Weidenbaum, *Business, Government, and the Public,* 4th ed. (Englewood Cliffs: Prentice-Hall, 1990); and George A. Steiner and John F. Steiner, *Business, Government, and Society* (New York: Random House, 1986).

requirement for information. Reporting costs, like the other more severe burdens of federal regulation, are not proportioned to the size of the firm.[9]

Some outside observers have suggested that small businesses simply ignore governmental compliance orders. The penalties for such actions are stiff, however, and the consequences are serious. Noncompliance can result in the failure of the entire venture.[10] A more reasonable approach is for entrepreneurs to turn to the public sector and demand assistance with easing the regulatory burden. This is now being done. Figure 7.3 illustrates an entrepreneur's contingency decision model for identifying and assessing key issues affecting the venture.

TRENDS IN POLICY FORMATION   The political influence of entrepreneurs has been steadily growing over the past decade. Indeed, it appears to be the growing trend in the political structure today. Any regulator or congressperson who ignores this group does so at personal peril. One report stated, "Politicians of every stripe are rushing to get out in front on the entrepreneurial issue. . . . New companies are being formed at record rates even without federal involvement, and a partisan debate revolves around the degree to which government should encourage new business activity."[11] As a result, regulatory reform legislation has established milestone laws that offer small businesses some objective considerations. Three of these acts are highlighted in the following section.

The Regulatory Flexibility Act   The **Regulatory Flexibility Act** (Reg. Flex) recognizes that the size of a business has a bearing on its ability to comply with federal regulation. The law puts the burden of review on the government to ensure that legislation does not unfairly impact small business. According to the SBA (1982), the major goals of this act are (1) to increase agency awareness and understanding of the impact of agency regulations on small business, (2) to require that agencies communicate and explain their findings to the public, and (3) to encourage agencies to provide regulatory relief to small entities. The chief council for advocacy is the Small Business Administration, which monitors the agencies for compliance.

The Equal Access to Justice Act   The **Equal Access to Justice Act** (Equal Access) provides greater equity between small businesses and regulatory bodies. According to this new act, if a small business challenges a regulatory agency and wins, the regulatory agency must pay the legal costs of the small business. Equal Access has five stipulations that help ensure equal justice for small business: (1) The government or the small business may initiate litigation; (2) bad faith by the governmental agency does *not* have to be proven; (3) substantially justified actions must be demonstrated by the agency; (4) to receive an award, the business does not have to prevail on all issues; and (5) no dollar limit to the awards exists.

The Prompt Payments Act   The **Prompt Payments Act** was enacted in 1982 to help small businesses doing work for the federal government to collect their money. The act

[9] Kenneth Chilton and Murray Weidenbaum, "Government Regulation: The Small Business Burden," *Journal of Small Business Management* (January 1982): 4–10.

[10] Robert F. Scherer, Daniel J. Kaufman, and M. Fall Ainina, "Complaint Resolution by OSHA in Small and Large Manufacturing Firms," *Journal of Small Business Management* (January 1993): 73–82.

[11] Kevin Farrell, "Entrepreneurial Economics," *Venture*, January 1983, 33.

FIGURE 7.3 AN ENTREPRENEUR'S CONTINGENCY DECISION MODEL FOR PUBLIC POLICY

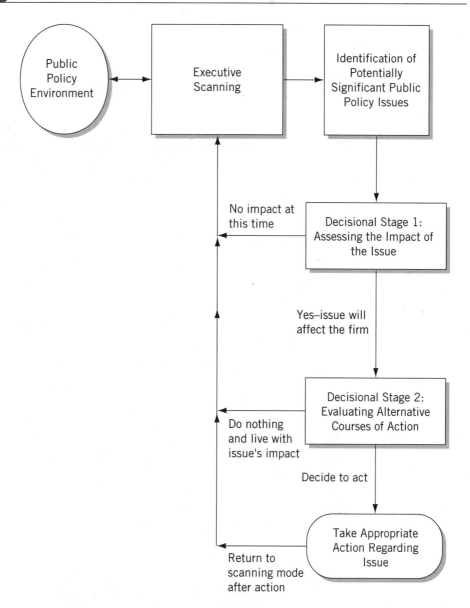

SOURCE: Ronald G. Cook and David Barry, "When Should the Small Firm Be Involved in Public Policy?" *Journal of Small Business Management* (January 1993): 44.

requires that bills be paid in 30 days with an additional 15-day grace period. Interest penalty charges become retroactive from the 30-day point. In addition, if any partial contractual disputes occur, the federal agency cannot withhold the entire contracted amount. Only the disputed monies may be withheld; the remaining bills must be paid. Moreover, all penalties (interest charges) must be paid out of the agency's current funds with no allowance for additional appropriations to cover late payment charges.

CONTEMPORARY ENTREPRENEURSHIP

Competition among States: The Real Winners Are Small Businesses

State legislatures have never been known for their small-business friendliness, but that may change. During the 1996 election campaign, welfare, education, and crime were on top of the priorities list. But according to a recent study by *Expansion Management* magazine, it seems many of these issues have been addressed, and legislators are starting to focus on business matters such as worker's compensation, tort reform, wages, and industry regulations.

In addition to these traditional areas of business legislation, many state governments are exploring innovative ways to create a favorable business environment. Due to increased competition among the states, many are looking for methods to earn a reputation as a great place to do business. And this trend leads to creating new and innovative ways of attracting small companies. States are trying to attract new businesses by lowering taxes, offering training or cash grants, and lowering utility costs, among other efforts. For the past two years, Texas has been at the top of the list of states where residents can take home more of the money they make, thanks to having zero corporation and personal taxes. Also, according to Jack Wimer, *Expansion Management*'s editor, "More businesspeople and educators—people who want to create jobs—are getting into legislatures. In the 1997 sessions, we should see a lot more business-related legislation."

So, which cities and states are making these kind of efforts? Dun & Bradstreet Information Services conducts an annual ranking of the nation's top cities for small businesses. The cities are evaluated based on categories: risk, business performance, economic growth, quality of life, and state attitude toward small businesses. Because business performance and state attitudes toward small businesses are important indicators of a city's economy, they were given extra weight in the evaluation. The categories are defined as follows:

- *Risk* is the probability of a company becoming insolvent within the next two years. Risk includes such factors as the company's financial health, how it pays suppliers, and how long it has been in business. Cities with a low percentage of high-risk firms rank higher than those with a higher percentage of high-risk firms.

- *Business performance* includes company failure rates and payment delinquencies, where high failure rates and delinquencies lowered a city's ranking.

- *Economic growth* is based on changes in business incorporations and in the number of nonagricultural jobs, where high growth in incorporations and employment increased a city's ranking.

- *Quality of life* is based on per capita income and cost-of-living data.

- *State attitude toward small business* is based on the 1996 Development Report Card for the States, which was developed by the Corporation for Economic Development. This report measures economic performance, business vitality, and developmental capacity. In addition, the corporate income-tax rates and the quality of small-business support programs were considered.

The cities are put into three categories: large cities, midsized cities, and small cities. These are the top five Best Cities in the large category for 1996.

1. **Portland, Oregon.** This is the second year in a row that Portland has topped the Best Cities list. Portland's economy is booming with a new crowd of high-tech businesses that have contributed nearly $12 billion in capital investment to its economy. The Portland environment is very small-business friendly. Oregon is the home of the first Small Business Development Center. Today, entrepreneurs also benefit from Venture Oregon, which presents start-up business plans to venture capitalists. But Portland's biggest asset is the unique mind-set of its entrepreneurs. Rather than making it big and cashing in, these entrepreneurs seem more interested in building companies that will endure the test of time.

2. **Denver, Colorado.** Business in the Mile High City just keeps getting better and better. Small boutiques and restaurants in Denver are finding plenty of customers as the trend of people moving inward around the country continues. Service-based companies are also doing well in this area, including desktop publishing and printing companies. In addition, Internet-related businesses are rapidly emerging in the Denver area. Looking to the future, with the opening of the Park Meadows Mall, the Coors Field Stadium, and the new Denver International Airport, Denver will likely become an even more attractive location for many different types of businesses.

3. **Minneapolis, Minnesota.** Minneapolis has a solid, diversified industry base that includes medical products, machining, printing and publishing, and computers. Minneapolis also hosts many giants, such as 3M, Honeywell, and General Mills, who desperately need suppliers. Minneapolis, named Moneyapolis by *Forbes* magazine, is known for its venture capital. Many of the major investors of Minneapolis's private equity community have a strong passion for helping small businesses. The city has the country's highest rates of Small Business Administration lending on volume as well. Minneapolis has several government support systems that offer assistance to entrepreneurs, such as Minnesota Technology Inc. Most businesses benefited from recent legislation that decreased worker's compensation costs. In addition, the Mall of America has fostered some of the most innovative retail concepts in the nation. And with plans for entertainment retailing downtown and the revitalization of the city's riverfront area, Minneapolis will continue to offer many opportunities for small and large businesses alike.

4. **Atlanta, Georgia.** According to a University of Georgia study, the businesses in the Atlanta area should reap rewards from the Olympics for the next 30 years, a noteworthy reason for local businesses to stay and for new ventures to come. Atlanta is the second biggest convention city in the United States, mostly due to its

CONTINUED

reputation for hospitality and a rich service sector. Service businesses that boom in Atlanta include hotels, food service, restaurants, and convention-based companies. High-tech firms and outsourcing firms also do well in this city. Factors that play a key role in Atlanta's continued attractiveness to businesses include some of the fastest growing counties in the country, reasonable operating costs, and plentiful labor.

5. **Indianapolis, Indiana.** Indianapolis's strong suit is its commitment to small businesses and its strategies to ensure their success. These include nurturing strong public-private collaborations, encouraging small firms to enter the global arena, and creating a competitive banking climate. Another attractive feature is the state's tax structure, which is one of the most favorable in the country. Indianapolis continues its commitment to growing its own businesses with its Value Added Committee. This committee is made of government, corporate, and small-business advocates who provide enterpreneurs with all types of services, including mentoring, troubleshooting, management assistance, and networking. And the future looks promising for Indianapolis because a recently developed study will help determine what needs to be done to create more entrepreneurial growth over the next 20 years.

SOURCES: Janean Chun, "Law Review," *Entrepreneur,* July 1996, 14. Karen Axelton, Janean Chun, Debra Phillips, Cynthia E. Griffin, Heather Page, Lynn Beresford, and Holly Celeste Fisk, "30 Best Cities for Small Businesses," *Entrepreneur,* October 1996, 120–25.

OTHER SIGNIFICANT PUBLIC POLICY DEVELOPMENTS   During the 1990s, the U.S. government has been grappling with some of the major policy issues of our lifetime. Trade, taxes, regulations, the environment, job training, immigration, and health care reform are among the issues on which governmental decisions will affect U.S. businesses.

Health care reform may have the most significant consequence for American businesses. Medical care in the United States commands 14 percent of the nation's gross domestic product, with predictions suggesting it will exceed 19 percent by 1999.

In 1980 the White House inaugurated a special small-business conference, which eventually led to a breakfast series that began in November 1982. The major objective of these meetings was to analyze the unique problems confronting small businesses. These meetings included entrepreneurs, small-business people, and small-business lobbyists, brought together by the administration to begin formulating entrepreneurial policy. In 1986 another White House conference convened to reassess the policies of the previous five years and to make recommendations for future policy decisions. These conferences have been successful because they have encouraged an informal exchange of ideas *before* overall policy was officially decided. In June 1995 the third White House Conference on Small Business revisited the concerns of small firms.[12]

These newly instituted conferences and meetings should create an atmosphere of respect and understanding for the entrepreneur/small businessperson in future federal and state policies. Certainly, they are a step in the right direction.

---

[12] Marcia Bradford, "Conference Call," *Entrepreneur,* February 1994, 148–51.

Examining the Industry Environment

Noted strategic consultant Michael E. Porter has suggested that at its root, environmental assessment involves asking two critical questions. "First, what is the structure of your industry, and how is it likely to evolve over time?" If the business the entrepreneur is in is not very attractive—and we will soon show how to measure its attractiveness—then the person may want to get out of it or redefine it.

Second, what is the company's relative position in the industry? No matter how attractive the game is, entrepreneurs will not do well if their company does not hold a good position in it. Conversely, the business can be in a lackluster industry with low average profitability, yet if it occupies exactly the right niche, it can perform very well.

"Most small companies, of course, cannot change an industry's structure. What they can do, however, is establish a good position in the industry, a position based on sustainable competitive advantage," Porter says.[13]

Evaluation of the industry environment is the second critical step in the overall economic assessment of a new venture. A number of major elements of industry structure exist, as depicted in Figure 7.4.[14] As this diagram shows, the process of assessing the entire industry structure is detailed and comprehensive. For our purposes here, however, we shall examine only those segments of which entrepreneurs need to be aware.

COMMON INDUSTRY CHARACTERISTICS   Although industries vary in size and development, certain characteristics are common to new and emerging industries. The most important of these are discussed next.

Technological Uncertainty   A great deal of uncertainty usually exists about the technology in an emerging industry: What product configuration will ultimately prove to be the best? Which production technology will prove to be the most efficient? How difficult will it be to develop this technology? How difficult will it be to copy technological breakthroughs in the industry?

Strategic Uncertainty   Related to technological uncertainty is a wide variety of strategic approaches often tried by industry participants. Since no "right" strategy has been clearly identified, industry participants will formulate different approaches to product positioning, advertising, pricing, and the like, as well as different product configurations or production technologies.

First-Time Buyers   Buyers of an emerging industry's products or services are perforce first-time buyers. The marketing task is thus one of substitution, or getting the buyer to make the initial purchase of the new product or service.

Short Time Horizons   In many emerging industries the pressure to develop customers or produce products to meet demand is so great that bottlenecks and problems are dealt with

---

[13] Michael E. Porter, "Knowing Your Place—How to Assess the Attractiveness of Your Industry and Your Company's Position in It," *Inc.*, September 1991, 90.

[14] See, for example, Michael E. Porter, *Competitive Strategy* (New York: Free Press, 1980); Michael E. Porter, *Competitive Advantage* (New York: Free Press, 1985); and Michael E. Porter, "From Competitive Advantage to Corporate Strategy," *Harvard Business Review* (May/June 1987): 43–59.

FIGURE 7.4   **ELEMENTS OF INDUSTRY STRUCTURE**

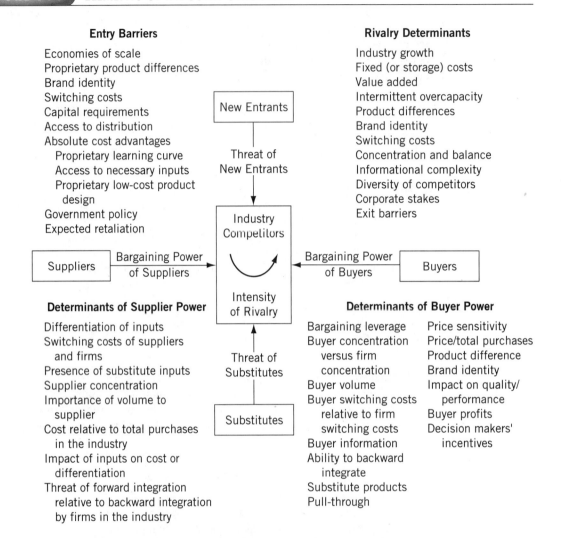

Entry Barriers

Economies of scale
Proprietary product differences
Brand identity
Switching costs
Capital requirements
Access to distribution
Absolute cost advantages
  Proprietary learning curve
  Access to necessary inputs
  Proprietary low-cost product
  design
Government policy
Expected retaliation

Rivalry Determinants

Industry growth
Fixed (or storage) costs
Value added
Intermittent overcapacity
Product differences
Brand identity
Switching costs
Concentration and balance
Informational complexity
Diversity of competitors
Corporate stakes
Exit barriers

Determinants of Supplier Power

Differentiation of inputs
Switching costs of suppliers
  and firms
Presence of substitute inputs
Supplier concentration
Importance of volume to
  supplier
Cost relative to total purchases
  in the industry
Impact of inputs on cost or
  differentiation
Threat of forward integration
  relative to backward integration
  by firms in the industry

Determinants of Buyer Power

Bargaining leverage
Buyer concentration
  versus firm
  concentration
Buyer volume
Buyer switching costs
  relative to firm
  switching costs
Buyer information
Ability to backward
  integrate
Substitute products
Pull-through

Price sensitivity
Price/total purchases
Product difference
Brand identity
Impact on quality/
  performance
Buyer profits
Decision makers'
  incentives

Determinants of Substitution Threat

Relative price performance of substitutes
Switching cost
Buyer propensity to substitute

SOURCE: Adapted with permission of The Free Press, a division of Simon & Schuster, from *Competitive Advantage: Creating and Sustaining Superior Performance* by Michael E. Porter, 6. Copyright © 1985 by Michael E. Porter.

expediently rather than on the basis of an analysis of future conditions.[15] Short-run results are often given major attention, while long-run results are given little consideration.

[15] For a detailed discussion of this topic, see Porter, *Competitive Strategy;* and Michael E. Porter and Victor E. Millar, "How Information Gives You Competitive Advantage," *Harvard Business Review* (July/August 1985): 149–60.

TABLE 7.1	POSSIBLE CONSTRAINTS TO INDUSTRY DEVELOPMENT
Constraint	**Explanation**
Inability to obtain raw materials and components	The development of an emerging industry requires that new suppliers be established or existing suppliers expand output or modify raw materials and components to meet the industry's needs. In the process, severe shortages of raw materials and components are very common.
Period of rapid escalation of raw materials prices	Because of burgeoning demand and inadequate supply, prices for key raw materials often skyrocket in the early phases of an emerging industry. This situation is partly simple economics of supply and demand and partly the result of suppliers realizing the value of their products to the desperate industry.
Absence of infrastructure	Emerging industries are often faced with difficulties, such as those of material supply, caused by the lack of appropriate infrastructure: distribution channels, service facilities, trained mechanics, complementary products.
Perceived likelihood of obsolescence	An emerging industry's growth will be impeded if buyers perceive that second- or third-generation technologies will significantly make currently available products obsolete. Buyers will wait instead for the pace of technological progress to slow down and prices to fall as a consequence.
Erratic product quality	For many newly established firms, the lack of standards and technological uncertainty often cause erratic product quality in emerging industries. This erratic quality, even if caused by only a few firms, can negatively affect the image and credibility of the entire industry.
Image and credibility with the financial community	As a result of newness, the high level of uncertainty, customer confusion, and erratic quality, the emerging industry's image and credibility with the financial community may be poor. This result can affect not only the ability of firms to secure low-cost financing but also the ability of buyers to obtain credit.

SOURCE: Adapted with permission of The Free Press, a division of Simon & Schuster, from *Competitive Strategy: Techniques for Analyzing Industries and Competitors* by Michael E. Porter, 221–24. Copyright © 1980 by The Free Press.

BARRIERS TO ENTRY   In addition to the structural components of an emerging industry, **barriers to entry** exist. These barriers may include proprietary technology (expensive to access), access to distribution channels (limited or closed to newcomers), access to raw materials and other inputs (e.g., skilled labor), cost disadvantages due to lack of experience (magnified with the technological and competitive uncertainties), or risk (which raises the effective opportunity cost of capital). Other barriers to entry are presented in Table 7.1. Some of these barriers will decline or disappear as the industry develops. However, it is still important for entrepreneurs to be aware of these barriers.

COMPETITIVE ANALYSIS   Another important area is the analysis of the competition in the industry. Both the quality and quantity of the competition must be carefully scrutinized. This **competitive analysis** involves consideration of the number of competitors as well as the strength of each. Figure 7.5 provides an illustrative grid that can be used to analyze the competition.

In assessing the competition, it is important to keep in mind the various elements that will affect the profile. Figure 7.6 illustrates the components of a competitive analysis from the standpoint of (1) what drives the competition and (2) what the competition can do. The

FIGURE 7.5 **COMPETITIVE PROFILE ANALYSIS**

Instructions
Place an *X* to denote any competitive factor that a competitor has or can provide/perform better than you.

Competitive Factor	Competitive Firms			
	Company A	Company B	Company C	Your Company
Product uniqueness				
Relative product quality				
Price				
Service				
Availability/convenience				
Reputation/image				
Location				
Advertising and promotional policies/ effectiveness				
Product design				
Caliber of personnel				
Raw material cost				
Financial condition				
Production capability				
R&D position				
Variety/selection				

competition's current strategy and future goals will help dictate its response. So too will the assumptions that each competitor has about itself as well as its perceived strengths and weaknesses.

Figure 7.6 provides a framework that allows an entrepreneur to better assess the competition. A good competitive analysis is vital to the ultimate success of any new venture.

FIGURE 7.6   COMPONENTS OF A COMPETITIVE ANALYSIS

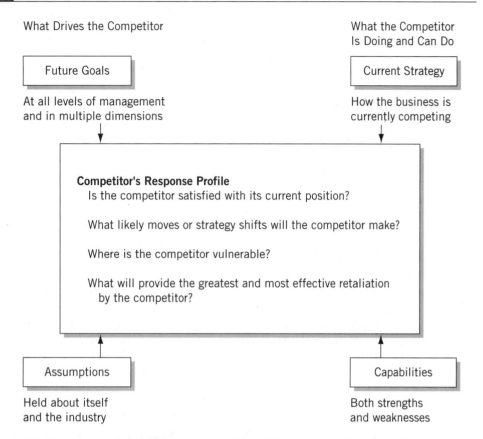

What Drives the Competitor

What the Competitor
Is Doing and Can Do

Future Goals

Current Strategy

At all levels of management
and in multiple dimensions

How the business is
currently competing

Competitor's Response Profile
Is the competitor satisfied with its current position?

What likely moves or strategy shifts will the competitor make?

Where is the competitor vulnerable?

What will provide the greatest and most effective retaliation
by the competitor?

Assumptions

Capabilities

Held about itself
and the industry

Both strengths
and weaknesses

SOURCE: Adapted with permission of The Free Press, a division of Simon & Schuster, from *Competitive Strategy: Technique for Analyzing Industries and Competitors* by Michael E. Porter, 49. Copyright © 1980 by The Free Press.

Taking the Right Steps   In addition to Figure 7.6, a number of useful steps can assist an entrepreneur with examining the industry. The following are five of the most helpful:

1. *Clearly define the industry for the new venture.* The key here is to develop a *relevant* definition that describes the focus of the new venture. Definitions will vary, of course, depending on the venture and its specific target market. The more clearly the entrepreneur can define the industry for the new venture, the better the chance the venture will get off to a sound start.

2. *Analyze the competition.* An analysis of the number, relative size, traditions, and cost structures of direct competitors in the industry can help establish the nature of the competition. Will competition become more or less intense as the number and characteristics of competitors change over time? This question also can be answered through detailed analysis. For instance, what will happen to the degree of competition if *(a)* market growth increases rapidly, *(b)* direct competitors equalize in size, *(c)* one or two direct competitors become substantially larger in size, or *(d)* product/service differentiation slows down?

3. *Determine the strength and characteristics of suppliers.* The important factor here is to establish the stance of the venture in relation to the suppliers. How will the new firm be treated compared to other, more established firms? Do many suppliers offering diverse services exist, or must the new venture be prepared to accept limited services from a few?

4. *Establish the value-added measure of the new venture.* The concept of **value added** is a basic form of contribution analysis in which sales minus raw material costs equals the value added. The purpose behind this measure is to determine how much value the entrepreneur is adding to the product or service. This introduces the concept of *integration*—backward or forward. Backward integration is the movement of a buyer to acquire supplier services. Forward integration is the movement of a supplier to absorb the duties of a buyer. The likelihood of integration occurring is determined substantially by the degree to which the value added is essential to the final processing and user consumption.

5. *Project the market size for the particular industry.* Markets are dynamic and prone to change over time. Therefore, it is important to examine the historical progression of the market, establish its present size, and extrapolate the data to project the market growth potential. This can be done in terms of the industry life cycle, consumers (numbers and trends), product/service developments, and competitive analysis.

These five key points are not all-inclusive. However, they do represent an initial analysis of the industry environment a new venture faces. This type of macroanalysis is important for establishing the framework within which a venture will start, grow, and, it is hoped, prosper. Once this analysis is complete, attention can be turned to the microenvironment, which provides a community perspective.

A MICROVIEW: THE COMMUNITY PERSPECTIVE

After analyzing the macroenvironment of the economy and the industry, the entrepreneur needs to focus on **microenvironmental assessment.** This analysis is directed toward the community where the new venture is to be launched.[16]

Researching the Location

Assessing the local community environment is as vital to the success of a new venture as is the assessment of the regulatory economy and the industry. We shall now discuss a number of major community facets to consider.

COMMUNITY DEMOGRAPHICS   A study of **community demographics** helps entrepreneurs determine the composition or makeup of consumers who live within the community. These data typically include such statistics as community size; the residents' purchasing power (disposable income), average educational background, and types of occupation; the percentages of residents who are professionals and nonprofessionals; and the extent of entrepreneurial activity in the community.

[16] William H. Hudnut III, "The Rise of the Entrepreneurial City: An Urban Agenda for the 1990s," *Hudson Institute Briefing Paper,* November 1993, 158; see also John Case, "Place Matters," *Inc.: The State of Small Business,* 1996 Special Issue, 94–95.

A few factors may be of special concern in this data analysis. One is the size of the new venture relative to the community itself and to other businesses in the community. Analysis of this factor helps the entrepreneur evaluate the new venture's potential in terms of sales, growth, employment, and attraction of customers. Each variable is directly related to the size factor, and all variables are interrelated. For example, a new venture may actually increase the total sales of all competitive firms in the community. A new furniture store located opposite an established furniture store often will serve to increase overall sales by drawing more business to the locale. People from other communities will come to comparison shop and will stay to buy. People from the local community will be more likely to purchase their furniture from one of these two stores than to drive to other communities to do so. The major reason is that furniture is a comparison good, and most people like to look at the offerings of at least two stores before they buy.

Another important demographic characteristic is the amount of entrepreneurial activity in the community. To assess this factor, it is important to count the number of entrepreneurs in the community, to examine their types of business ventures, and to establish their track records with suppliers (within and outside the region), their success with local banks, and their customer base. If the community has a lot of entrepreneurial activity, it will be more receptive to new ventures, and doors will be more easily opened. For example, local banks will be more accustomed to reviewing entrepreneurial loan applications and will have developed expertise in evaluating such applications and dealing with follow-up business.

ECONOMIC BASE   The extent of an entrepreneur's opportunity may be determined, in part, by the **economic base** of the community. This base includes the nature of employment, which influences the size and distribution of income, and the purchasing trends of consumers in the area. Additionally, it is wise to examine any community dependence on one large firm or industry that may be affected by seasonal or cyclical fluctuations.

POPULATION TRENDS   It is important to examine population trends in order to identify expanding communities as opposed to long-term declining or static populations. Growth usually indicates solid, aggressive civic leadership with opportunities available for budding entrepreneurial ventures. Favorable signs of a growing community typically include chain or department store branches throughout the area, branch plants of large industrial firms, a progressive chamber of commerce, a good school system, transportation facilities (air, rail, highway), construction activity, and an absence of vacant buildings. In addition, many entrepreneurs supplement this information with selected sources of environmental data. Table 7.2 describes some of these sources.

OVERALL BUSINESS CLIMATE   A summary view of the community from the business perspective includes consideration of transportation, banking, professional services, the economic base, growth trends, and the solidity of the consumer income base. It is important to make an assessment of the general business climate before deciding on the location of a new venture. (See the "Experiential Exercise: A Sample Community Analysis" for more on this subject.)

Determining Reliance and Deservedness

Another method of evaluating a community is in terms of **reliance** and **deservedness.** In such an evaluation the following questions are particularly important:

TABLE 7.2   **SELECTED SOURCES OF ENVIRONMENTAL DATA**

Source	Description
The Census of Population (Census Bureau)	Taken every ten years, these data present information on age, race, sex, marital status, family status, ethnic origin, migration, education, income, occupation, employment, and other characteristics of the population. This information is available for states and counties and for every city, town, or village. For cities of 50,000 or more, inhabitants' data have been tabulated by census tracts—small areas with an average population of 4,000 or 5,000; summary information is available for the entire metropolitan area in which such a city is located, as well as for individual blocks within the city.
The Census of Manufacturers (Census Bureau)	Taken every four years, these data include the number of manufacturing establishments, the number of production and other employees, value added by manufacture, cost of materials, value of shipments, and recent capital expenditures for each of the nation's manufacturing industries. These data also are compiled for each of the states, and much of the information is available for counties as well.
The Census of Business (Census Bureau)	Taken every four years, this census provides information on all types of retail and wholesale trade and services. Included are data on the number of establishments, gross annual sales or receipts, the number of employees, annual payroll, and the number of active proprietors of unincorporated enterprises. These data are compiled for each state and county and for all communities with a population of 2,500 or more.
Department of Commerce publications	Each state's department of commerce has various publications that track the business activity of counties and cities, as well as state employment and industry data.
Sales Management magazine's "Buying Power Index"	Published annually, this publication contains a wealth of information helpful in setting sales quotas, planning distribution, locating warehouses, and studying sales potential. It includes information on population and income for every state by county and city, including per capita and per household incomes. Retail sales estimates are also made for every state by county and city. This information is combined and weighted to produce a buying power index useful for predicting sales in a particular locality.

1. How familiar is the entrepreneur with the community where the venture will be located?

2. Will the proposed venture make any special positive or negative impacts on the community during the prestart-up period or during the start-up period?

3. Does the entrepreneur have special skills in human relations with which to nurture key local contacts?

4. What active steps can be taken to strengthen local support and maximize local opportunities during the start-up period?

5. What active steps can be taken to reduce local opposition and minimize local problems during the start-up period?

Answers to these questions help determine the level of support likely to exist in a given community. Entrepreneurs can gain exceptional community support in two major ways.

FIGURE 7.7 RELIANCE VERSUS COMMITMENT: DEVELOPMENT OF EXCEPTIONAL COMMUNITY SUPPORT

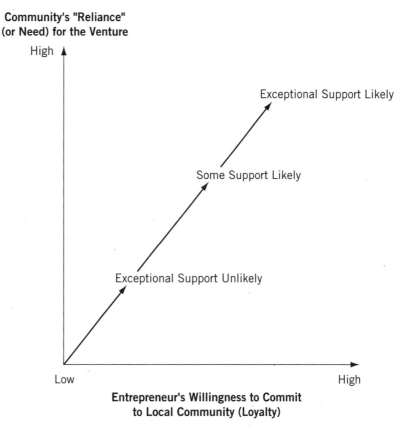

Community's "Reliance" (or Need) for the Venture

High

Exceptional Support Likely

Some Support Likely

Exceptional Support Unlikely

Low　　　　　　　　　　　　　　High

Entrepreneur's Willingness to Commit to Local Community (Loyalty)

SOURCE: Adapted from Robert C. Ronstadt, *Entrepreneurship* (Natick, MA: Lord Publishing, Inc., 1984), 84. Reprinted with permission.

The first is based on (1) the strength of the community's reliance on or need for the entrepreneur's venture and (2) the entrepreneur's willingness to make a commitment to the community. Figure 7.7 illustrates this idea.

The second way entrepreneurs may gain exceptional community support is through the community perception of their "deservedness." People generally identify with those who they think deserve their support. Thus, the strength of the relationship between this perceived deservedness and the community's identification with the new venture will influence the possibility of exceptional community support. Figure 7.8 illustrates this relationship.

Examining the Use of Business Incubators

In some locales, it is possible for a new venture to use an incubator approach in getting started. Although many definitions of the term **business incubator** exist, most agree it is a facility with adaptable space that small businesses can lease on flexible terms and at reduced rents. Support services—financial, managerial, technical, and administrative—are available and shared, depending on the size and nature of tenants' needs. Most incubators

FIGURE 7.8   **DESERVEDNESS VERSUS IDENTIFICATION: DEVELOPMENT OF EXCEPTIONAL COMMUNITY SUPPORT**

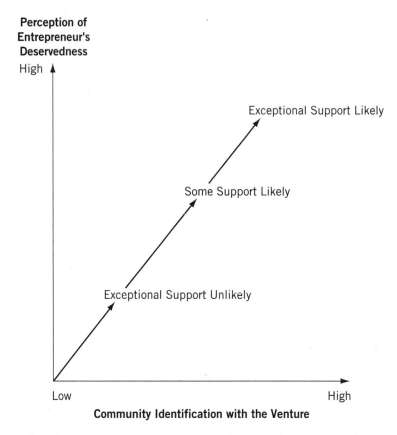

SOURCE: Adapted from Robert C. Ronstadt, *Entrepreneurship* (Natick, MA: Lord Publishing, Inc., 1984), 85. Reprinted with permission.

limit the amount of time, ranging from two to five years, a small business may occupy space in the facility.

The basic purpose of an incubator is to increase the chances of survival for new start-up businesses.[17] Four major types of incubators exist, and the objectives of each type tend to vary:

1. *Publicly sponsored:* These incubators are organized through city economic development departments, urban renewal authorities, or regional planning and development commissions. Job creation is the main objective of the publicly sponsored incubator.

2. *Nonprofit sponsored:* These incubators are organized and managed through industrial development associations of private industry, chambers of commerce, or community-based organizations with broad community support or a successful record in real es-

[17] Fred L. Fry, "The Role of Incubators in Small Business Planning," *American Journal of Small Business* (summer 1987): 51–62.

tate development. Area development is the major objective of nonprofit-sponsored incubators.

3. *University related:* Many of these incubator facilities are spin-offs of academic research projects. Most are considered science and technology incubators. The major goal of university-related incubators is to translate the findings of basic research and development into new products or technologies.

4. *Privately sponsored:* These incubators are organized and managed by private corporations. The major goal is to make a profit and, in some cases, to make a contribution to the community.[18]

Regardless of type, however, most incubators provide the following kinds of services:

- Below-market-rate rental space on flexible terms. The rates are negotiable but usually range from $.50 to $4.00 per square foot.
- Elimination of building maintenance responsibilities. This allows new entrepreneurs freedom from maintenance of furniture and equipment and of such areas as loading docks, lunch areas, conference rooms, and reception areas.
- Sharing of equipment and services that would otherwise be unavailable or unaffordable. Such services are typically divided into three major categories: (1) offices and communications services such as typing, photocopying, and phone answering; (2) business services such as business planning and financial planning; and (3) facilities and equipment services, including a reception area, conference rooms, and computers.
- Additional information on and access to various types of financial and technical assistance
- Provision of an environment where small businesses are not alone, thereby reducing the anxiety of starting a new venture
- Increased business tenants' visibility to the community

Figure 7.9 shows how an incubator works. Differences do exist between publicly sponsored and privately sponsored incubators. Table 7.3 gives some statistics on incubators.

Incubators are targeted toward providing benefits for small businesses that are incapable of generating their own managerial, technical, financial, or administrative services. A less obvious but recently realized focus is the community benefits from establishing incubators. The latest research in this area reveals the following important community benefits:

- Transformation of underused property into a center of productivity
- Creation of opportunities for public/private partnerships
- Diversification of the local economic base
- Enhancement of the locality's image as a center of innovation and entrepreneurship
- Increased employment opportunities[19]

Thus business incubators have become appealing to small businesses and community developers alike. Public, private, and nonprofit groups have all demonstrated a willingness

[18] See Mihailo Temali and Candace Campbell, *Business Incubator Profiles* (Minneapolis: Institute for Public Affairs, University of Minnesota, 1984).

[19] See the following for a detailed discussion of incubators: David N. Allen and Syedur Rahman, "Small Business Incubators," *Journal of Small Business Management* (July 1985): 12–22; Donald F. Kuratko and William R. LaFollette, "Examining the Small Business Incubator Explosion," *Mid-American Journal of Business* (September 1986): 29–34; and Richard Steffens, "What Incubators Have Hatched," *Planning* (May 1992): 28–30.

FIGURE 7.9 HOW DOES THE INCUBATOR WORK?

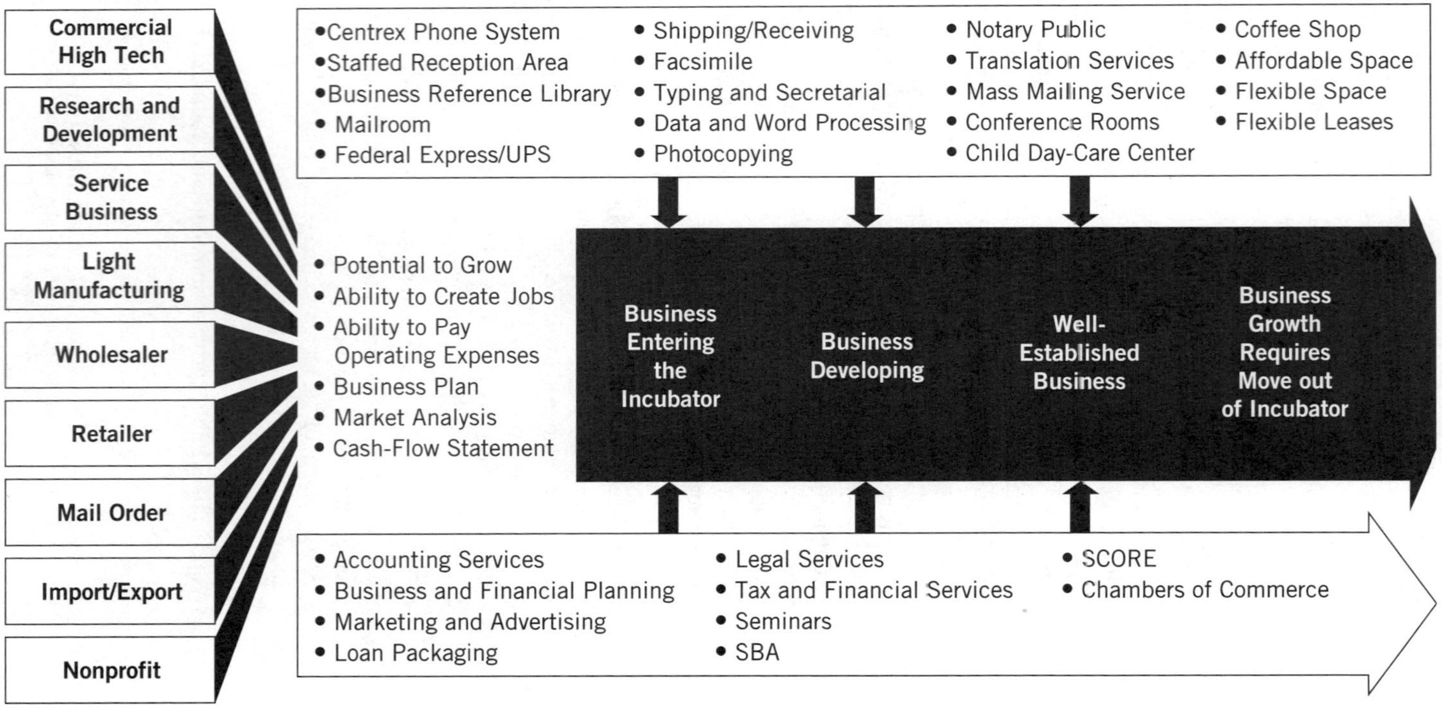

TABLE 7.3	PRIVATELY AND PUBLICLY SPONSORED INCUBATORS: A COMPARISON

Characteristic	Differences
Size and tenant capacity	Privately sponsored facilities are twice the size of publicly sponsored facilities and have a median tenant capacity of 45 compared to 14 for public initiatives.
Incubator governance	Publicly sponsored incubators have executive or advisory boards, while privately sponsored do not.
Tenant selection	The criterion of publicly sponsored incubators is job creation potential with strict entry standards, while privately sponsored incubators seek profit potential in their tenants and thus do not have strict entry barriers.
Exit policy	Public facilities have a time limit on tenant residency, while private incubators tend to allow residents to stay or grow out of the facility.
Rent	Private incubators charge higher rents (usually two or three times more than public facilities) per square foot.
Services	While both sectors have centralized services, the concentration is different. Privately sponsored incubators tend to provide physical and human services (i.e., space, secretarial, maintenance, conference rooms, etc.), whereas publicly sponsored facilities concentrate more on financial and business services.
Financial sources	Privately sponsored incubators have a majority of the financing sources in the private sector, whereas the publicly sponsored initiatives are widely distributed among private, governmental, and industrial development financial sources.
Operating revenue	Both types of incubators use the revenue from rent and services for their operating income. The difference arises in the nonrent revenue that is needed to operate the incubator. Publicly sponsored incubators receive most of this revenue from government sources. Privately sponsored incubators rely to a great extent on private sources, which allows them to receive, on average, more money.
Staff	Privately sponsored incubators have larger staffs than do publicly sponsored facilities (mean size of 5 as opposed to 1.7). Consulting staff size tends to be about the same; however, the incubator managers of privately sponsored facilities possess more business experience than do their public counterparts.
Growth patterns	Publicly sponsored incubators place a greater emphasis on job creation and have registered a higher level of growth in employment (157%) than privately sponsored incubators (31%). However, in sales growth the privately sponsored facilities, which emphasize net profit of the tenants, have demonstrated a larger increase (75%) than the publicly sponsored facilities (35.2%).

SOURCE: Data from David N. Allen and Syedur Rahman, "Small Business Incubators: A Positive Environment for Entrepreneurship," *Journal of Small Business Management* (July 1985): 12–22; also see Mihailo Temali and Candace Campbell, *Business Incubator Profiles* (Minneapolis: Institute for Public Affairs, University of Minnesota, 1984).

to develop this concept. In the process, supporters have arisen among the public, the media, and the financial community. In particular, the goal of this communal positioning of new businesses under one roof for the purpose of providing low rent and shared on-site services will increase entrepreneurial success and thus enhance the economic development of local communities.

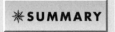

In assessing a new venture, entrepreneurs consider a number of different environments. Typically, they begin with the macro and then move on to the micro, focusing on data that help them decide how to establish the venture. Two major macro areas warrant their consideration. One is the overall economic environment; the other is the specific industry environment. The overall economic environment analysis covers the nature of the industry and the regulatory environment that exists there. The specific industry environment entrepreneurs address includes common industry characteristics, barriers to entry, and competitive analysis.

The microanalysis focuses on examining the location, determining reliance and deservedness, and studying the feasibility of using business incubators. When examining the location, entrepreneurs consider areas such as community demographics, the economic base, population trends, and the overall business climate. "Experiential Exercise: A Sample Community Analysis" provides additional information on this topic. To determine reliance and deservedness, entrepreneurs look for a right fit between the business and the community. When exploring business incubators, they focus attention on the presence of these facilities in the local area and the benefits they would hold for the specific enterprise.

Key Terms and Concepts

Barriers to entry	Equal Access to Justice Act
Business incubator	Microenvironmental assessment
Community demographics	Prompt Payments Act
Competitive analysis	Regulatory Flexibility Act
Culture	Reliance
Deservedness	Societal environment
Economic base	Task environment
Environmental assessment	Value added

Review and Discussion Questions

1. To assess the economic environment of a venture, an entrepreneur would like a number of questions answered. Identify and discuss five of these questions.
2. Briefly discuss each of the following effects of governmental regulations on small ventures: prices, cost inequities, competitive restrictions, managerial restrictions, mental burdens.
3. How does each of the following legislative acts affect small ventures? *(a)* the Regulatory Flexibility Act, *(b)* the Equal Access to Justice Act, *(c)* the Prompt Payments Act.
4. Of what value is Figure 7.5 to helping an entrepreneur make a new-venture assessment?
5. What are barriers to entry? How do they affect new-venture assessment?
6. How could an entrepreneur use Figure 7.6 to conduct a competitive profile analysis? What would the results provide? What types of decisions could the individual make from the analysis?
7. Identify and describe four of the steps to take when making an industry assessment.

8. How can an entrepreneur go about researching the location for a venture? What information can community demographics and population trends provide?

9. Discuss this statement: One method of evaluating a community is in terms of reliance and deservedness.

10. What is a business incubator? What are the four major types of incubators?

11. Of what value is a business incubator to a new venture? Explain in detail.

Experiential Exercise   *A Sample Community Analysis*

Assume you are in the process of opening a small retail hardware store. Choose a site location in your community, and then answer the following questions about the community, potential customers, competition, and location.

Potential of the Trading Area

1. How big is the trading area? _____ sq. mi.

2. What is the customer potential within five miles? _____ customers

3. What is the density of population? _____ people per sq. mi.

4. Is transportation adequate for supplies? _____ yes _____ no

5. What is the income level of the trading area? _____ per capita

6. What is the local employment pattern, based on number of people employed?
   _____ % people employed

7. What is the general makeup of the community? _____ residential _____ old
   _____ growing

8. What are the trends in population and income? _____ up _____ down

9. Is new construction on the increase? _____ yes _____ no

10. Are school enrollments up? _____ yes _____ no

11. Are retail sales on the increase? _____ yes _____ no

12. Have average business improvements been made recently? _____ yes _____ no

13. Does business property have a high vacancy rate? _____ yes _____ no

14. Have shopping patterns changed drastically in recent years? _____ yes _____ no

15. Are customers moving to or away from the potential location? _____ to
    _____ from

16. What are the present zoning restrictions? _____
    _____

Can Customers Get to the Location?

1. Is the area served by adequate public transportation? _____ yes _____ no

2. How broad an area does the transportation service encompass? _____ sq. mi.

3. Is the area generally attractive to shoppers? _____ yes _____ no

4. Can it be easily reached by automobile? _____ yes _____ no

5. Is public parking adequate and relatively inexpensive? _____ yes _____ no

6. How many spaces in the available nearby parking lot are taken up by all-day parkers? _____ many _____ few

7. If located on a highway, is the location easily accessible from the main traffic flow? _____ yes _____ no

8. What are restrictions on signs and store identification? _____

9. If the location is on a limited access road, how close is the nearest interchange? _____ miles

10. Is the location accessible to delivery trucks? _____ yes _____ no

11. Is the traffic speed too fast to encourage entrance by automobile? _____ yes _____ no

12. Are most customers who drive past the location on their way to work or on shopping trips? _____ on way to work _____ on shopping trips

13. Will nearby stores help you? Are the other stores in the shopping center, neighborhood, or highway location of a nature that will attract customers who also will become patrons of your store? _____ yes _____ no _____ maybe _____ likely

14. What are the prospects for changes in traffic flow in the near future? _____ slight _____ likely

15. Will anticipated changes improve or damage the location? _____ improve _____ damage

16. Are zoning changes planned that would affect accessibility of the location? _____ yes _____ no

Judging the Competition

1. How many other businesses of the same kind exist between the prospective location and the most highly populated area? _____ stores

2. Is this spot the most convenient store location in the area? _____ yes _____ no

3. How many other stores of the same kind are in this trading area? _____ stores

4. How many of them will compete with you for customers? _____ stores

5. Do these other stores have better parking facilities? _____ yes _____ no

6. Do these other stores offer the same type of merchandise? _____ yes _____ no

7. Do you consider these other stores more aggressive or less aggressive than your own operation will be? _____ more _____ less

8. What other competing stores are planned for this trading area in the near future?

9. Are other potential sites that are closer to the majority of customers likely to be developed in the near future? _____ yes _____ no

10. Are your major competitors well-known, well-advertised stores? _____ yes _____ no

11. Does a need for another store of this kind in the area actually exist? _____ yes _____ no

12. How well is the demand for this product being met in the area? _____ very well _____ moderately well

13. If any empty stores or vacant lots are near the location, is a competitive store planned for them? _____ yes _____ no

Can the Location Attract New Business?

1. Is the location in an attractive district? _____ yes _____ no

2. Do numerous stores exist that will draw potential customers for you into the area? _____ yes _____ no

3. Is the location near well-known and well-advertised stores? _____ yes _____ no

4. Is this location the most attractive one in the area? _____ yes _____ no

5. Is the location on the side of the street with the busiest customer traffic? _____ yes _____ no

6. Is the location nearer to the general parking area than locations of competing firms? _____ yes _____ no

7. Is the location in the center of or on the fringe of the shopping district? _____ center _____ fringe

8. Is it near common meeting places for people, such as public offices? _____ yes _____ no

9. Are most of the people passing the store prospective customers? _____ yes _____ no

10. Are the people who pass usually in a hurry, or are they taking time to shop? _____ in a hurry _____ taking time to shop

Cost of the Location

1. What will your rent be? $_____ per month

2. Who will pay the utility costs? _____ you _____ others

3. Who pays additional costs, such as taxes, public services, and costs of improvements? _____ you _____ others

4. What are the possibilities for eventual expansion? _____ good _____ poor

5. Are good employees available? _____ yes _____ no

6. Will your potential income justify your costs? _____ yes _____ no

Based on your analysis, is this a good community in which to open a retail hardware store? Explain.

 **CASE** **7.1**

An Incubator Investigation

For the past four years Darlene Danforth has worked for a large office-fixture and supply company. The local area sales representative for one of the company's major suppliers recently announced he was retiring. The man had had a heart attack and had decided to find a less strenuous job. Unexpectedly one day, Darlene received a call from the supplier. "For the past ten years we have been selling your company a lot of office fixtures and supplies," the supplier told Darlene. "And for the past two years we've been working directly with you. We now have an opening for a sales rep in your city. If you take the job, we can guarantee you'll make 25 percent more money than you're making now. Your job will be to call on other office-fixture and supply companies in the state, in addition to your present company, of course. We pay 2 percent on all sales and have 125 active accounts you would be taking over. In addition, we know that more than 2,000 companies in the state are potential customers. So there's plenty of room for growth. Would you like the job?"

Darlene thought about the offer for a week, talked it over with her employer, and decided to take the job. Because her state is not very large, she can reach most of her customers in two to three hours. This means she has little likelihood of being away from home very often. However, she will need to set up an office, maintain records, and have some general office functions performed for her. Since Darlene has never had to run her own business before, she is concerned about her ability to manage the operation. Her boss has suggested she look into a business incubator. "For your particular needs, this can be exactly what you need. It will provide you an office, a secretary, and some support help while you are on the road selling." The idea sounds fine to Darlene, but she really does not know much about incubators. She has decided the first place to start is by investigating what incubators are all about and what functions they can perform for her.

Questions

1. Give a detailed description of a business incubator.
2. Identify and describe three benefits a business incubator would offer Darlene.
3. Would an incubator be of value to Darlene? Why or why not?

Chapter 8

MARKETING RESEARCH FOR NEW VENTURES

CHAPTER OBJECTIVES

1. To review the importance of marketing research for new ventures

2. To present factors that inhibit the use of marketing

3. To examine the marketing concept: philosophy, segmentation, and consumer orientation

4. To establish the areas vital to marketing planning

5. To highlight the questions concerning hazards in marketing

6. To characterize the marketing stages of growing ventures

7. To introduce telemarketing as an emerging tool for marketing

8. To discuss the key features of a pricing strategy

The generation and use of market research enables a management team to learn *about* changes *in the market* faster *than the competition, making it a major component of competitive rationality and competitive advantage.*

Peter R. Dickson,
Marketing Management

A **market** is a group of consumers (potential customers) who have purchasing power and unsatisfied needs.[1] A new venture will survive only if a market exists for its product or service.[2] This is so obvious that it would seem every entrepreneur would prepare thoroughly the market analysis needed for establishing a target market. However, many entrepreneurs know very little about their market, and some even attempt to launch new ventures without identifying any market. (See Table 8.1 concerning the marketing skills of great entrepreneurs.)

A number of techniques and strategies can assist entrepreneurs with effectively analyzing a potential market. By using them, entrepreneurs can gain in-depth knowledge about the specific market and can translate this knowledge into a well-formulated business plan. Effective marketing analysis also can help a new venture position itself and make changes that will result in increased sales. The key to this process is marketing research.

MARKETING RESEARCH

Marketing research involves the gathering of information about a particular market, followed by analysis of that information.[3] A knowledge and understanding of the procedures involved in marketing research can be very helpful to the entrepreneur in gathering, processing, and interpreting market information.

Defining the Research Purpose and Objectives

The first step in marketing research is to define precisely the informational requirements of the decision to be made. Although this may seem too obvious to mention, the fact is needs

[1] For a discussion of markets, see E. Jerome McCarthy and William D. Perreault, *Basic Marketing: A Managerial Approach,* 8th ed. (Homewood, IL: Irwin, 1984), Chapter 2; and Peter R. Dickson, *Marketing Management* (Fort Worth: The Dryden Press, 1994).

[2] Harriet Buckman Stephenson, "The Most Critical Problem for the Fledgling Small Business: Getting Sales," *American Journal of Small Business* (summer 1984): 26–33.

[3] For a thorough presentation, see Stephen W. McDaniel and A. Parasuraman, "Practical Guidelines for Small Business Marketing Research," *Journal of Small Business Management* (January 1986): 1–7.

222

TABLE 8.1	COMMON ELEMENTS IN THE MARKETING SKILLS OF GREAT ENTREPRENEURS

1. They possess unique environmental insight, which they use to spot opportunities others overlook or view as problems.

2. They develop new marketing strategies that draw on their unique insights. They view the status quo and conventional wisdom as something to be challenged.

3. They take risks that others, lacking their vision, consider foolish.

4. They live in fear of being preempted in the market.

5. They are fiercely competitive.

6. They think through the implications of any proposed strategy, screening it against their knowledge of how the marketplace functions. They identify and solve problems others do not even recognize.

7. They are meticulous about details and are always in search of new competitive advantages in quality and cost reduction, however small.

8. They lead from the front, executing their management strategies enthusiastically and autocratically. They maintain close information control when they delegate.

9. They drive themselves and their subordinates.

10. They are prepared to adapt their strategies quickly and to keep adapting them until they work. They persevere long after others have given up.

11. They have clear visions of what they want to achieve next. They can see further down the road than the average manager can see.

SOURCE: Peter R. Dickson, *Marketing Management* (Fort Worth: The Dryden Press, 1994), 8.

are too often identified without sufficient probing. If the problem is not defined clearly, the information gathered will be useless.

In addition, specific objectives should be established. For example, one study has suggested the following set of questions for establishing objectives for general marketing research:

- Identify where potential customers go to purchase the good or service in question.
- Why do they choose to go there?
- What is the size of the market? How much of it can the business capture?
- How does the business compare with competitors?
- What impact does the business's promotion have on customers?
- What types of products or services are desired by potential customers?[4]

Gathering Secondary Data

Information that has already been compiled is known as **secondary data.** Generally speaking, secondary data are less expensive to gather than new, or primary, data. The entrepreneur should exhaust all the available sources of secondary data before going further into the research process. Marketing decisions often can be made entirely with secondary data.

---

[4] Robert T. Justis and Bill Jackson, "Marketing Research for Dynamic Small Business," *Journal of Small Business Management* (October 1978): 10–20; see also Timothy M. Baye, "Relationship Marketing: A Six-Step Guide for the Business Start-Up," *Small Business Forum* 13, no. 1 (spring 1995): 26–41.

Secondary data may be internal or external. Internal secondary data consist of information that exists within the venture. The records of the business, for example, may contain useful information. External secondary data are available in numerous periodicals, trade association literature, and government publications.

Unfortunately, several problems accompany the use of secondary data. One is that such data may be outdated and, therefore, less useful. Another is that the units of measure in the secondary data may not fit the current problem. Finally, the question of validity is always present. Some sources of secondary data are less valid than others.

Gathering Primary Data

If the secondary data are insufficient, a search for new information, or **primary data,** is the next step. Several techniques can be used to accumulate primary data. These are often classified as observational methods and questioning methods. Observational methods avoid contact with respondents, whereas questioning methods involve respondents in varying degrees. Observation is probably the oldest form of research in existence. Observational methods can be used very economically. Furthermore, they avoid a potential bias that can result from a respondent's awareness of his or her participation under questioning methods. A major disadvantage of observational methods, however, is that they are limited to descriptive studies.

Surveys and experimentation are two questioning methods that involve contact with respondents. **Surveys** include contact by mail, telephone, and personal interviews. Mail surveys are often used when respondents are widely dispersed; however, these are characterized by low response rates. Telephone surveys and personal interview surveys involve verbal communication with respondents and provide higher response rates. Personal interview surveys, however, are more expensive than mail and telephone surveys. Moreover, individuals often are reluctant to grant personal interviews because they feel a sales pitch is forthcoming. (Table 8.2 illustrates the major survey research techniques.)

Experimentation is a form of research that concentrates on investigating cause-and-effect relationships. The goal is to establish the effect an experimental variable has on a dependent variable. For example, what effect will a price change have on sales? Here the price is the experimental variable, and sales volume is the dependent variable. Measuring the relationship between these two variables would not be difficult if it were not for the many other variables involved.[5]

DEVELOPING AN INFORMATION-GATHERING INSTRUMENT   The questionnaire is the basic instrument for guiding the researcher and the respondent through a survey. The questionnaire should be developed carefully before it is used. Several major considerations for designing a questionnaire are listed here:

- Make sure each question pertains to a specific objective in line with the purpose of the study.
- Place simple questions first and difficult-to-answer questions later in the questionnaire.
- Avoid leading and biased questions.

[5] Thomas J. Callahan and Michael D. Cassar, "Small Business Owners' Assessments of Their Abilities to Perform and Interpret Formal Market Studies," *Journal of Small Business Management* (October 1995): 1–9.

TABLE 8.2

COMPARISON OF MAJOR SURVEY RESEARCH TECHNIQUES

Criteria	Direct/Cold Mailing	Mail Panels	Telephone	Personal In-Home	Mall Intercept
Complexity and versatility	Not much	Not much	Substantial, but complex or lengthy scales difficult to use	Highly flexible	Most flexible
Quantity of data	Substantial	Substantial	Short, lasting typically between 15 and 30 minutes	Greatest quantity	Limited, 25 minutes or less
Sample control	Little	Substantial, but representativeness may be a question	Good, but nonlisted households can be a problem	In theory, provides greatest control	Can be problematic; sample representativeness may be questionable
Quality of data	Better for sensitive or embarrassing questions; however, no interviewer present to clarify what is being asked		Positive side, interview can clear up any ambiguities; negative side, may lead to socially accepted answers	In addition, there is the chance of cheating	In addition, unnatural testing environment can lead to bias
Response rates	In general, low; as low as 10%	70–80%	60–80%	Greater than 80%	As high as 80%
Speed	Several weeks; completion time will increase with follow-up mailings	Several weeks with no follow-up mailings, longer with follow-up mailings	Large studies can be completed in 3 to 4 weeks	Faster than mail but typically slower than telephone surveys	Large studies can be completed in a few days
Cost	Inexpensive; as low as $2.50 per completed interview	Lowest	Not as low as mail; depends on incidence rate and length of questionnaire	Can be relatively expensive, but considerable variability	Less expensive than in-home, but higher than telephone; again, length and incidence rate will determine cost
Uses	Executive, industrial, medical, and readership studies	All areas of marketing research, particularly useful in low-incidence categories	Particularly effective in studies that require national samples	Still prevalent in product testing and other studies that require visual cues or product prototypes	Pervasive-concept tests, name tests, package tests, copy test

SOURCE: Reproduced with permission from William Dillon, Thomas J. Madden, and Neil H. Firtle, *Marketing Research in a Marketing Environment* (Homewood, IL: Richard D. Irwin, 1990), 201. Reproduced with permission of The McGraw-Hill Companies.

ENTREPRENEURIAL

EDGE

Smaller Markets Equals Bigger Payoffs

Mass marketing is a practice of the past. Traditionally, marketing targets were very broad and somewhat generic. Typical markets included everyone who was between the ages of 18 and 49, and advertising was rather bland, encouraging everyone to drink the same soda, buy the same couch, and wear the same pants. The influence of baby boomers, the awakening of ethnic and cultural pride, the growth of the senior market, and the invasion of the Information Age have changed all that. The successful marketers of the 1990s realize that for any marketing effort to hit the bull's eye, it must set its sights on a smaller target. This means entrepreneurs must become fluent in *niche marketing* to stay ahead.

This change in marketing strategy to more narrowly defined markets is a result of the enormous changes the marketplace has experienced. The consumer marketplace has become differentiated, and these marketing-savvy consumers resent being lumped together in groups based only on their age or status. This is why it is so important for marketers to know who their consumers are on a number of different levels. What are their motivations? How does a particular product or service fit into their lives? What are they looking for? What options are available?

Going one step further, marketers must realize that consumer markets need to be analyzed to a microscopic level. Even a relatively narrow market should be broken down into smaller parts. This need to dissect potential markets could be attributed to the changing life cycles of today's consumers. Traditionally, people would go from one stage to the next and marketers felt a significant degree of certainty about which age people would do certain activities. But now life cycles are circular with people repeating stages—raising a family, getting a divorce, and raising another family. For example, of two 65-year-old men, one could be retired and traveling the world, and the other could be recently remarried and raising a small child.

Studying the consumer market can generate unlimited opportunities for finding new niches for marketing a product or service. Market niches can be based on gender, region, socioeconomic status, technological sophistication, education level, or even lifestyle. And the list goes on and on. The following science mar-

- Ask "How could this question be misinterpreted?" Reword questions to reduce or eliminate the possibility they will be misunderstood.
- Give concise but complete directions in the questionnaire. Succinctly explain the information desired, and route respondents around questions that may not relate to them.
- When possible, use scaled questions rather than simple yes/no questions in order to measure intensity of an attitude or frequency of an experience. For example, instead

keting statistics illustrate the precision of consumer marketing:

- Female baby boomers influence 80 percent of leisure decisions. They also conduct 44 percent of all business travel.
- Black adults under the age of 25 are three times more likely to buy a pager than the average U.S. adult.
- Only 40 percent of U.S. Latinos watched the 1995 Superbowl, while 70 percent of U.S. Latinos watched the 1994 World Cup finals.

According to Geoffrey Meredith, president of Lifestage Matrix Marketing, the consumer characteristics used to define markets and how the consumers are grouped into niches also have changed the marketing strategies of the 1990s. During the 1980s generational marketing emerged. Generations are usually formed from birth dates that span 20 to 25 years. Generational marketing, which already has become dated, usually defines consumers not only by age but also by economic, social, psychological, and demographic factors. The trend today seems to lie in *cohort marketing*, which is often dictated by what was popular during the cohort's coming-of-age period. Cohorts are formed from historical events that influence the group's taste in music, apparel, and food, as well as its attitudes on money and sexuality. Other factors that should be considered

in defining markets are life stages, such as getting married, buying a home, or retiring, and physiographics or physical conditions related to age, such as menopause, vision impairments, or arthritis.

All of these characteristics and factors should play an essential role when entrepreneurs define a niche and effectively market to that niche. Although niche marketing may seem somewhat complicated and costly, it is not any more so than traditional types of marketing. The main difference between traditional mass marketing and today's niche marketing is in the results. Niche marketing produces much more targeted and effective results.

Even the smallest of companies can use these techniques to find a niche and really go after a market and own it. The Internet is going to play an important role in developing niche marketing, especially for small companies. "It will allow companies to provide customized, individual, one-on-one, interactive marketing," Cheryl Russell, the editor in chief of New Strategist Publications in New York, says. As competition continues to escalate, it is going to be crucial that marketing efforts not aim for somewhere on the target but hit the bull's eye.

SOURCE: Janean Chun, "Direct Hit," *Entrepreneur*, October 1996, 140–49.

of asking, "Do we have friendly sales clerks?" (yes/no), ask, "How would you evaluate the friendliness of our sales clerks?" Have respondents choose a response on a 5-point scale ranging from "Very unfriendly" (1) to "Very friendly" (5).[6]

---

[6] McDaniel and Parasuraman, "Practical Guidelines," 5.

Interpreting and Reporting the Information

After the necessary data have been accumulated, they should be developed into usable information. Large quantities of data are only facts. They must be organized and molded into meaningful information. The methods of summarizing and simplifying information for users include tables, charts, and other graphic methods. Descriptive statistics, such as the mean, mode, and median, are most helpful in this step of the research procedure.

Marketing Research Questions

The need for marketing research before and during a venture will depend on the type of venture. However, typical research questions might include the following, divided by subject.

SALES

1. Do you know all you need to know about your competitors' sales performance by type of product and territory?

2. Do you know which accounts are profitable and how to recognize a potentially profitable one?

3. Is your sales power deployed where it can do the most good, maximizing your investment in selling costs?

DISTRIBUTION

1. If you are considering introducing a new product or line of products, do you know all you should about distributors' and dealers' attitudes toward it?

2. Are your distributors' and dealers' salespeople saying the right things about your products or services?

3. Has your distribution pattern changed along with the geographic shifts of your markets?

MARKETS

1. Do you know all that would be useful about the differences in buying habits and tastes by territory and kind of product?

2. Do you have as much information as you need on brand or manufacturer loyalty and repeat purchasing in your product category?

3. Can you now plot, from period to period, your market share of sales by products?

ADVERTISING

1. Is your advertising reaching the right people?

2. Do you know how effective your advertising is in comparison to that of your competitors?

3. Is your budget allocated appropriately for greater profit—according to products, territories, and market potentials?

PRODUCTS

1. Do you have a reliable quantitative method for testing the market acceptability of new products and product changes?

2. Do you have a reliable method for testing the effect on sales of new or changed packaging?

3. Do you know whether adding higher or lower quality levels would make new profitable markets for your products?

INHIBITORS TO MARKETING RESEARCH

Despite the fact most entrepreneurs would benefit from marketing research, many fail to do it. A number of reasons for this exist, among them cost, complexity, level of need for strategic decisions, and irrelevancy. A number of articles have dealt with the lack of marketing research by entrepreneurs in the face of its obvious advantages and vital importance to the success of small businesses.[7]

Cost

Marketing research can be expensive, and some entrepreneurs believe that only major organizations can afford it. Indeed, some high-level marketing research is expensive, but also very affordable marketing techniques can be used by smaller companies.

Complexity

A number of marketing research techniques involve sampling, surveying, and statistical analysis. This complexity, especially the quantitative aspects, is frightening to many entrepreneurs, and they shun it. The important point to remember is that the key concern is interpretation of the data, and an entrepreneur always can obtain the advice and counsel of those skilled in statistical design and evaluation by calling on the services of marketing research specialists or university professors trained in this area.

Strategic Decisions

Some entrepreneurs feel that only major strategic decisions need to be supported through marketing research. This idea is tied to the cost and complexity issues already mentioned. The contention is that because of the cost and statistical complexity of marketing research, it should be conducted only when the decisions to be made are major. The problem is not only in the misunderstanding of cost and complexity but also in the belief that marketing research's value is restricted to major decisions. Much of the entrepreneur's sales efforts could be enhanced through the results of such research.

---

[7] As an example, see Alan R. Andreasen, "Cost-Conscious Marketing Research," *Harvard Business Review* (July/August 1983): 74–75.

Irrelevancy

Many entrepreneurs believe marketing research data will contain either information that merely supports what they already know or irrelevant information. Although it is true that marketing research does produce a variety of data, some of which may be irrelevant, it is also a fact that much of the information is useful. In addition, even if certain data merely confirm what the entrepreneur already knows, it is knowledge that has been tested and thus allows the individual to act on it with more confidence.

As indicated by these inhibitors, most of the reasons for entrepreneurs not using marketing research center either on a misunderstanding of its value or on a fear of its cost. However, the approach to marketing does not have to be expensive and can prove extremely valuable.

DEVELOPING THE MARKETING CONCEPT

Effective marketing is based on three key elements: marketing philosophy, market segmentation, and consumer behavior. A new venture must integrate all three elements when developing its marketing concept and its approach to the market. This approach helps set the stage for how the firm will seek to market its goods and services.

Marketing Philosophy

Three distinct types of marketing philosophies exist among new ventures: production driven, sales driven, and consumer driven.

The **production-driven philosophy** is based on the belief "produce efficiently and worry about sales later." Production is the main emphasis; sales follow in the wake of production. New ventures that produce high-tech, state-of-the-art output sometimes use a production-driven philosophy. A **sales-driven philosophy** focuses on personal selling and advertising to persuade customers to buy the company's output. When an overabundance of supply occurs in the market, this philosophy often surfaces. New auto dealers, for example, rely heavily on a sales-driven philosophy. A **consumer-driven philosophy** relies on research to discover consumer preferences, desires, and needs *before* production actually begins. This philosophy stresses the need for marketing research in order to better understand where or who a market is and to develop a strategy targeted toward that group. Of the three philosophies, a consumer-driven orientation is often most effective, although many ventures do not adopt it.

Three major factors influencing the choice of a marketing philosophy follow:

1. *Competitive pressure.* The intensity of the competition will many times dictate a new venture's philosophy. For example, strong competition will force many entrepreneurs to develop a consumer orientation in order to gain an edge over competitors. If, on the other hand, little competition exists, the entrepreneur may remain with a production orientation in the belief that what is produced will be sold.

2. *Entrepreneur's background.* The range of skills and abilities entrepreneurs possess varies greatly. While some have a sales and marketing background, others possess production and operations experience. The entrepreneur's strengths will influence the choice of a market philosophy.

3. *Short-term focus.* Sometimes a sales-driven philosophy may be preferred due to a short-term focus on "moving the merchandise" and generating sales. Although this focus appears to increase sales (which is why many entrepreneurs pursue this philosophy), it also can develop into a hard-selling approach that soon ignores customer preference and contributes to long-range dissatisfaction.

Any one of the three marketing philosophies can be successful for an entrepreneur's new venture. It is important to note, however, that over the long run the consumer-driven philosophy is the most successful. This approach focuses on the needs, preferences, and satisfactions of the consumer and works to serve the end user of the product or service.

Market Segmentation

Market segmentation is the process of identifying a specific set of characteristics that differentiate one group of consumers from the rest. For example, although many people eat ice cream, the market for ice cream can be segmented based on taste and price. Some individuals prefer high-quality ice cream made with real sugar and cream because of its taste; many others cannot tell the difference between high-quality and average-quality ingredients and, based solely on taste, are indifferent between the two types. The price is higher for high-quality ice cream such as Häagen-Daz or Ben & Jerry's, so the market niche is smaller for these offerings than it is for lower-priced competitors. This process of segmenting the market can be critical for new ventures with very limited resources.

In order to identify specific market segments, entrepreneurs need to analyze a number of variables. As an example, two major variables that can be focused on are demographic and benefit variables. Demographic variables include age, marital status, sex, occupation, income, location, and the like. These characteristics are used to determine a geographic and demographic profile of the consumers and their purchasing potential. The benefit variables help to identify unsatisfied needs that exist within this market. Examples may include convenience, cost, style, trends, and the like, depending on the nature of the particular new venture. Whatever the product or service, it is extremely valuable to ascertain the benefits a market segment is seeking in order to further differentiate a particular target group.

Consumer Behavior

Many types and patterns of consumer behavior have been identified for new-venture purposes. However, entrepreneurs can focus their attention on only two considerations: personal characteristics and psychological characteristics. Table 8.3 provides an example by tying these characteristics to the five types of consumers: innovators, early adopters, early majority, late majority, and laggards.

In the table the differences in social class, income, occupation, education, housing, family influence, and time orientation are illustrated. So, too, are the psychological characteristics labeled as needs, perceptions, self-concept, aspiration groups, and reference groups. This breakdown can provide an entrepreneur with a visual picture of the type of consumer to target for the sales effort.

The next step is to link the characteristic makeup of potential consumers with buying trends in the marketplace. Table 8.4 on page 235 shows the changing priorities shaping buying decisions during the 1990s. Each of these factors relates to consumer attitudes and behaviors based on education, the economy, the environment, and/or societal changes. By

CONSUMER CHARACTERISTICS

TABLE 8.3

Personal Characteristics

	Innovators (2–3%)	Early Adopters (12–15%)	Early Majority (33%)	Late Majority (34%)	Laggards (12–15%)
1. Social class	Lower upper	Upper middle	Lower middle	Upper lower	Lower lower
2. Income	High income (inherited)	High income (earned from salary and investment)	Above-average income (earned)	Average income	Below-average income
3. Occupation	Highest professionals Merchants Financiers	Middle management and owners of medium-sized businesses	Owners of small businesses Nonmanagerial office and union managers	Skilled labor	Unskilled labor
4. Education	Private schooling	College	High school Trade school	Grammar school, some high school	Very little—some grammar school
5. Housing	Inherited property Fine mansions	Large homes—good suburbs or best apartments	Small houses Multiple-family dwellings	Low-income housing in urban-renewal projects	Slum apartments
6. Family influence	Not family oriented Children in private school or grown	Children's social advancement important Education important	Child centered and home centered	Children taken for granted	Children expected to raise themselves
7. Time orientation	Present oriented, but worried about impact of time	Future oriented	Present oriented	Present (security) oriented	Tradition oriented, live in the past

Psychological Characteristics

	Self-actualization needs (realization of potential)	Esteem needs (for status and recognition by others)	Belonging needs (with others and groups)	Safety needs (freedom from fear)	Survival needs (basic needs)
1. Nature of needs	Self-actualization needs (realization of potential)	Esteem needs (for status and recognition by others)	Belonging needs (with others and groups)	Safety needs (freedom from fear)	Survival needs (basic needs)
2. Perceptions	Cosmopolitan in outlook	Prestige Status conscious Aspire to upper class	Local aspirations and local social acceptance	Home and product centered	Live from day to day
3. Self-concept	Elite	Social strivers, peer group leaders, venturesome	Respectability from own reference groups and home	Security, home centered, aggressive, apathetic, no hope	Fatalistic, live from day to day
4. Aspiration groups	British upper class	Innovator class	In own social strata, dissociated from upper lower	Others in this classification and in early majority, dissociated from lower lower	Don't aspire
5. Reference groups	Sports, social, and travel groups	Dominate industry and community organizations Golf, college, and fraternity	Social groups of this strata: chambers of commerce, labor unions, family, church, P.T.A., auxiliaries	Family, labor unions	Ethnic group oriented

SOURCE: Roy A. Lindberg and Theodore Cohn, *The Marketing Book for Growing Companies That Want to Excel* (New York: Van Nostrand Reinhold, 1986), 80–81. Reprinted with permission.

CONTEMPORARY ENTREPRENEURSHIP

Out-Marketing the Giants

In today's business world everything appears to be focused on the "superstore" concept. The Wal-Marts, Kmarts, Lowes, and Meijers are all mass marketing and, of course, are *all* the "lowest price guaranteed!" How does an entrepreneur compete within this multimedia blitz of supersize and compressed prices? It's not easy, but, as always, the entrepreneurial spirit devises opportunities to capitalize on. Here are a few tips for outwitting the giants.

- Tap your database: Use purchase data to customize incentives, and use direct mail based on demographics, location, product preference, and price.
- Excel at "guerrilla marketing": Use local promotions to get close to customers and break through advertising clutter.
- Create store-specific marketing pro-

grams: Win retailer loyalty, differentiate your product, and build local sales.
- Search for missed opportunities: Small marketers can often focus on a relatively neglected product—such as duct tape or dental floss—and take share from a bigger player or increase sales in a tired category.
- Apply the personal touch: Small-business marketers can get a big payoff when top executives pay personal attention to customers' letters, retailers' queries, and sales staffs' suggestions.
- Utilize today's technology: The cost of database technology is dropping, making direct-mail marketing a viable tactic for small-business marketers with tight budgets.

SOURCE: Christopher Power, "How to Get Closer to Your Customers," *Business Week*, Enterprise Issue, 1993, 42–45.

tying together the data in Tables 8.3 and 8.4, the entrepreneur can begin to examine consumer behavior more closely.

An analysis of the way consumers view the venture's product or service provides additional data. Entrepreneurs should be aware of five major consumer classifications:

1. *Convenience goods*—whether staple goods (foods), impulse goods (checkout counter items), or emergency goods and services—consumers will want these goods and services but will not be willing to spend time shopping for them.

2. *Shopping goods* are products consumers will take time to examine carefully and compare for quality and price.

3. *Specialty goods* consist of products or services consumers make a special effort to find and purchase.

4. *Unsought goods* are items consumers do not currently need or seek. Common examples are life insurance, encyclopedias, and cemetery plots. These products require explanation or demonstration.

TABLE 8.4	CHANGING PRIORITIES AND PURCHASES IN THE FAMILY LIFE CYCLE

Stage	Priorities	Major Purchases
Fledgling: teens and early 20s	Self; socializing; education	Appearance products, clothing, automobiles, recreation, hobbies, travel
Courting: 20s	Self and other; pair bonding; career	Furniture and furnishings, entertainment and entertaining, savings
Nest building: 20s and early 30s	Babies and career	Home, garden, do-it-yourself items, baby-care products, insurance
Full nest: 30–50s	Children and others; career; midlife crisis	Children's food, clothing, education, transportation, orthodontics, career and life counseling
Empty nest: 50–75	Self and others; relaxation	Furniture and furnishings, entertainment, travel, hobbies, luxury automobiles, boats, investments
Sole survivor: 70–90	Self; health; loneliness	Health care services, diet, security and comfort products, TV and books, long-distance telephone services

SOURCE: Peter R. Dickson, *Marketing Management* (Fort Worth: The Dryden Press, 1994), 91.

5. *New products* are items that are unknown due to lack of advertising or are new products that take time to be understood. When microcomputers were first introduced, for example, they fell into this category.

Understanding these classifications is important both for selling to consumers and for choosing distribution channels. Figure 8.1 illustrates the relationship between the consumer classification of items and the distribution channels followed.

MARKETING STAGES FOR GROWING VENTURES

Most emerging ventures will evolve through a series of marketing stages. In each stage the marketing functions will differ; thus each requires a specific type of marketing strategy.[8]

A growing venture has four distinct stages: entrepreneurial marketing (Stage 1), opportunistic marketing (Stage 2), responsive marketing (Stage 3), and diversified marketing (Stage 4).[9] Table 8.5 provides a breakdown of each stage in relation to marketing strategy, marketing organization, marketing goals, and critical success factors. Notice that the strategy in each stage relates closely to the marketing goals. For example, entrepreneurial marketing (Stage 1) has a strategy of developing a market niche and a goal of attaining credibility in the marketplace. Stage 2, opportunistic marketing, seeks a strategy of market penetration for the purpose of attaining sales volume, thereby demonstrating the logical progression depicted in the table. Stage 3, responsive marketing, seeks to develop the

[8] Richard B. Robinson Jr. and John A. Pearce II, "Product Life-Cycle Considerations and the Nature of Strategic Activities in Entrepreneurial Firms," *Journal of Business Venturing* (spring 1986): 207–24.

[9] Tyzoon T. Tyebjee, Albert V. Bruno, and Shelby H. McIntyre, "Growing Ventures Can Anticipate Marketing Stages," *Harvard Business Review* (January/February 1983): 62–66.

FIGURE 8.1   **USING CLASSIFICATION OF GOODS TO SELECT CHANNEL INTERMEDIARIES**

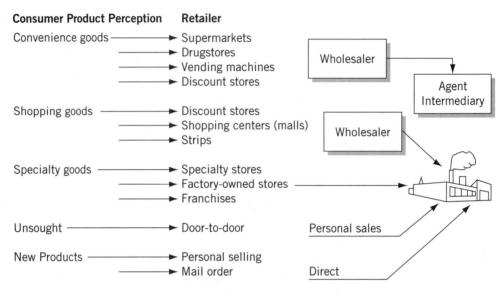

SOURCE: William A. Cohen and Marshall E. Reddick, *Successful Marketing for Small Business* (New York: Amacom, 1981), 128.

TABLE 8.5   **THE EVOLUTION OF THE MARKETING FUNCTION**

	Stage 1: Entrepreneurial Marketing	Stage 2: Opportunistic Marketing	Stage 3: Responsive Marketing	Stage 4: Diversified Marketing
Marketing Strategy	Market niche	Market penetration	Product-market development	New-business development
Marketing Organization	Informal, flexible	Sales management	Product-market management	Corporate and divisional levels
Marketing Goals	Credibility in the marketplace	Sales volume	Customer satisfaction	Product life-cycle and portfolio management
Critical Success Factors	A little help from your friends	Production economies	Functional coordination	Entrepreneurship and innovation

SOURCE: Reprinted by permission of the *Harvard Business Review* (exhibit 1) from "Growing Ventures Can Anticipate Marketing Stages," by Tyzoon T. Tyebjee, Albert V. Bruno, and Shelby H. McIntyre, January/February 1983, 64. Copyright © 1983 by the President and Fellows of Harvard College; all rights reserved.

product market and create customer satisfaction. Stage 4, diversified marketing, focuses on new-business development and seeks to manage the product life cycle.

The progression of the marketing organization from an informal level to a divisional level is a little more difficult to develop. Table 8.6 illustrates the evolution of a marketing

TABLE 8.6	THE EVOLUTION OF A MARKETING ORGANIZATION	
Problem	**Diagnosis**	**Prescription**
Top management suddenly finds itself unable to provide needed attention to marketing.	Stage 1 business is ready for transition to Stage 2.	Hire a sales manager. Continue to hold top management responsible for product planning and pricing and for providing sales support in initial contact with new customers.
There are too many products or markets for top management to coordinate all business functions for each.	Stage 2 company is ready for transition to Stage 3.	Hire product managers and give them support in sales, advertising, and market intelligence. Delegate all marketing responsibility to product managers. Put top management in charge of strategic planning.
Growth opportunities are limited in current product-market scope.	Stage 3 business is ready for transition to Stage 4.	Decentralize marketing activities to divisional level. Establish a corporate marketing group that: Reviews division marketing plans. Furnishes specialized skills in planning and research. Manages corporate-level marketing communication.

SOURCE: Reprinted by permission of the *Harvard Business Review* (exhibit 11) from "Growing Ventures Can Anticipate Marketing Stages," by Tyzoon T. Tyebjee, Albert V. Bruno, and Shelby H. McIntyre, January/February 1983, 64. Copyright © 1983 by the President and Fellows of Harvard College; all rights reserved.

organization through the four stages. The movement from an informal setting to the hiring of sales management personnel to the establishment of a marketing division is depicted in a problem/diagnosis/prescription format in the table.

It is important to realize that these stages are developed with a growing venture in mind. The idea of growth as a strategic planning factor, discussed in Chapter 15, is also presented here as a marketing factor.

MARKETING PLANNING

Marketing planning is the process of determining a clear, comprehensive approach to the creation of customers. For developing this plan, the following elements are critical:

- *Marketing research:* determining who the customers are, what they want, and how they buy
- *Sales research:* promoting and distributing products according to marketing research findings
- *Marketing information system:* collecting, screening, analyzing, storing, retrieving, and disseminating marketing information on which to base plans, decisions, and actions
- *Sales forecasting:* coordinating personal judgment with reliable market information

- *Marketing plans:* formulating plans for achieving long-term marketing and sales goals
- *Evaluation:* identifying and assessing deviations from marketing plans[10]

Marketing Research

The purpose of marketing research is to identify customers—target markets—and to fulfill their desires. For marketing research, the following areas warrant consideration:

- *The company's major strengths and weaknesses.* These factors offer insights into profitable opportunities and potential problems and provide the basis for effective decision making.
- *Market profile.* A market profile helps a company identify its current market and service needs: How profitable are existing company services? Which of these services offer the most potential? Which (if any) are inappropriate? Which will customers cease to need in the future?
- *Current and best customers.* Identifying the company's current clients allows management to determine where to allocate resources. Defining the best customers enables management to more directly segment this market niche.
- *Potential customers.* By identifying potential customers, either geographically or with an industry-wide analysis of its marketing area, a company increases its ability to target this group, thus turning potential customers into current customers.
- *Competition.* By identifying the competition, a company can determine which firms are most willing to pursue the same basic market niche.
- *Outside factors.* This analysis focuses on changing trends in demographics, economics, technology, cultural attitudes, and governmental policy. These factors may have substantial impact on customer needs and, consequently, expected services.
- *Legal changes.* Marketing research performs the important task of keeping management abreast of significant changes in governmental rates, standards, and tax laws.[11]

Marketing research need not be extremely expensive. Presented next are some useful tips regarding low-cost research. These tips can be valuable to entrepreneurs needing research but lacking the funds for sophisticated measures.

Tip 1: Establish a contest requiring entrants to answer a few simple questions about the quality of your products or services. The entry form is dropped into a convenient deposit box at the exit door of your store or service department with the drawing at month's end.

Tip 2: Piggyback a questionnaire about the quality of your products or services onto a company catalog or sales brochure. Be sure also to ask what other items the customer would like to see the organization offering. Such a system functions as an ongoing program of organizational evaluation.

Tip 3: Every organization receives the occasional complaint from a disgruntled customer. Instead of treating such situations casually, many organizations now adopt a management-by-exception philosophy and give grievances a high priority. Management follow-up with an in-depth interview often results in the revelation of unsuspected problems.

---

[10] "Marketing Planning," *Small Business Reports* (April 1986): 68–72.

[11] Ibid., 70.

Tip 4: Develop a standard set of questions regarding the quality of your organization's product and services suitable for administration by telephone. Have a secretary or part-time employee set aside a half-day a month in which 20 to 30 customers are called. Such a program often reminds customers to place an order. Many clients feel flattered their opinions are sought.

Tip 5: Some organizations have succeeded by including research questionnaires in various products' packages. In this way they attempt to determine how a buyer heard about an item, why it was purchased from the firm, and so on. The only difficulty with this approach is that it focuses on customers and neglects research about the potential of sales to those who have not bought.[12]

Sales Research

An entrepreneur needs continually to review the methods employed for sales and distribution in relation to the market research that has been conducted. Matching the correct customer profile with sales priorities is a major goal in sales research. The following is a list of potential questions to be answered by this research:

- Do salespeople call on their most qualified prospects on a proper priority and time-allocation basis?
- Does the sales force contact decision makers?
- Are territories aligned according to sales potential and salespeople's abilities?
- Are sales calls coordinated with other selling efforts, such as trade publication advertising, trade shows, and direct mail?
- Do salespeople ask the right questions on sales calls? Do sales reports contain appropriate information? Does the sales force understand potential customers' needs?
- How does the growth or decline of a customer or a prospect's business affect the company's own sales?

Marketing Information System

A marketing information system compiles and organizes data relating to cost, revenue, and profit from the customer base. This information can be useful for monitoring the strategies, decisions, and programs concerned with marketing. As with all information systems design, the key factors affecting the value of such a system are (1) data reliability, (2) data usefulness or understandability, (3) reporting system timeliness, (4) data relevancy, and (5) system cost.

Sales Forecasting

Sales forecasting is the process of projecting future sales through historical sales figures and the application of statistical techniques. The process is limited in value due to its reliance on historical data, which many times fail to reflect current market conditions. As a segment of the comprehensive marketing-planning process, however, sales forecasting can be very valuable.

---

[12]*Marketing Tactics Master Guide for Small Business,* by Gerald B. McCready, © 1982, 8. Reprinted by permission of the publisher, Prentice-Hall, a division of Simon & Schuster, Englewood Cliffs, New Jersey.

Marketing Plans

Marketing plans are part of a venture's overall strategic effort.[13] To be effective, these plans must be based on the venture's specific goals. Here is an example of a five-step program designed to help entrepreneurs follow a structured approach to developing a market plan:

Step 1: Appraise marketing strengths and weaknesses, emphasizing factors that will contribute to the firm's "competitive edge." Consider product design, reliability, durability, price/quality ratios, production capacities and limitations, resources, and need for specialized expertise.

Step 2: Develop marketing objectives along with the short- and intermediate-range sales goals necessary to meet those objectives. Next, develop specific sales plans for the current fiscal period. These goals should be clearly stated, measurable, and within the company's capabilities. To be realistic, these goals should require only reasonable efforts and affordable expenditures.

Step 3: Develop product/service strategies. The product strategy begins with identifying the end users, wholesalers, and retailers, as well as their needs and specifications. The product's design, features, performance, cost, and price then should be matched to these needs.

Step 4: Develop marketing strategies. Strategies are needed to achieve the company's intermediate- and long-range sales goals and long-term marketing objectives. These strategies should include advertising, sales promotion campaigns, trade shows, direct mail, and telemarketing. Strategies also may be necessary for increasing the size of the sales force or marketing new products. Contingency plans will be needed in the event of technological changes, geographic market shifts, or inflation.

Step 5: Determine pricing structure. A firm's pricing structure dictates which customers will be attracted, as well as the type or quality of products/services that will be provided. Many firms believe the market dictates a "competitive" pricing structure. But this is not always the case—many companies with a high price structure are very successful. Regardless of the strategies, customers must believe that the product's price is appropriate. The price of a product or service, therefore, should not be set until marketing strategies have been developed.[14]

Evaluation

The final critical factor in the marketing planning process is evaluation. Since a number of variables can affect the outcome of marketing planning, it is important to evaluate performance. Most important, reports should be generated from a customer analysis—attraction or loss of customers with reasons for the gain or loss, as well as established customer preferences and reactions. This analysis can be measured against performance in sales volume, gross sales dollars, or market share. It is only through this type of evaluation that flexibility and adjustment can be incorporated into marketing planning.

TELEMARKETING

Telemarketing is the use of telephone communications to sell merchandise directly to consumers. It is one of the fastest-growing direct market channels available to entrepreneurs and has become a direct-marketing tool.

---

[13] Avraham Shama, "Marketing Strategies during Recession: A Comparison of Small and Large Firms," *Journal of Small Business Management* (July 1993): 62–72.

[14] "Marketing Planning," 71.

Revenues generated by telephone sales are growing at an annual rate of 25 percent to 35 percent, according to the Direct Marketing Association. In fact, in 1991 marketers spent an estimated $234 billion in telephone charges to increase sales of their products and services. It is estimated that the average household receives at least 19 telemarketing calls per year and places 16 orders for products and services via the telephone.

In many cases, firms have switched to fully automated telemarketing systems. Telemarketing systems now can use automatic-dialing and recorded-message players (ADRMPs) to dial numbers and play advertising messages that are voice activated and even that record orders from customers or forward the call to an operator.[15]

Advantages

A telemarketing program can assist a venture in its marketing functions in a number of ways. A firm may be able to increase potential customer sales, upgrade sales or encourage multiple orders, reactivate old accounts, and support the current sales staff through an effective telemarketing program. Some of the specific advantages of telemarketing follow:

- *Receptiveness.* Most prospects are more receptive to telephone calls than to personal contact. This is true, in part, because potential customers expect less sales pressure over the phone.
- *Impressions.* First impressions, although often biased, can affect sales success. The telephone can help reduce many of the prospect's biases, since prejudgments can be based only on the caller's voice.
- *More presentations.* A conscientious field salesperson may obtain one high-quality prospect out of four contacts, while a telemarketer may reach only one high-quality prospect out of 8 calls. However, a telephone salesperson can make 30 to 40 calls per hour, resulting in four to five presentations.
- *Unlimited geographic coverage.* Telephone salespeople can penetrate markets anywhere in the world where telephones are available.
- *Better time management.* The average field salesperson spends only three out of eight hours actually selling. The balance of the day is occupied in traveling or waiting for appointments. The telemarketer, on the other hand, uses the majority of the workday to sell. When a potential customer is unavailable, the salesperson simply makes a note to call later and dials another prospect.
- *Immediate feedback.* Telemarketing is the quickest means of assessing new sales strategies and allows them to be readily tested, adjusted, and retested before they are applied in the field. Some firms take advantage of telephone sales' immediate feedback by including marketing research questions in sales presentations.
- *Better control.* An inside sales force can be supervised more easily than a field staff. Typically, one supervisor for every five telephone salespeople monitors the sales team's performance.
- *Less "piracy."* Since inside sales personnel do not meet the customers or the competition's salespeople, they are less likely to receive job offers.
- *Lower salary and commissions.* Typically, compensation for a telemarketer is approximately 50 percent that of a field salesperson.

[15] Philip Kotler, *Marketing Management,* 9th ed. (Upper Saddle River, NJ: Prentice-Hall, 1997), 729–30.

ENTREPRENEURIAL
EDGE

Deregulation Creates Opportunities

One of the most recent telecommunications reforms could create much more than lower rates. The Telecommunications Act of 1996 could create many new opportunities. The bill deregulates communication, allowing one company to handle all types of communication. For example, cable companies will be able to offer cable television, long-distance and local calling, and even access to the Internet. What does this mean for savvy entrepreneurs? The sky's the limit!

A significant provision of the act establishes the Telecommunications Development Fund. This gives entrepreneurs low-interest loans to create telecommunication ventures. The fund will be financed with interest generated by license deposits, which are expected to be as high as $100 million within one year. Loans could be used for working capital, start-ups, acquisitions, and upgrading facilities.

With venture funding in process, many entrepreneurs are wondering what types of businesses could be created from this new array of opportunities. According to Andrew D. Ory, owner of Priority Call Management Inc., the best opportunities exist in the cellular area. Ory's company soon will be working with wire-based and wireless telephone service providers wanting to link networks of wire-based and cellular telephone services. Before the act, only two cellular providers were allowed in each market, creating a duopoly that nearly eliminated incentives to offer services. The deregulation will increase competition for obtaining consumers and will create more business for companies like Ory's that can provide the infrastructure needed.

Entrepreneurs could find other opportunities in creating small phone companies. For example, a small phone company could be set up for an apartment complex. The phone company would do the billing and could be maintained with one technician. The service through the small company would be less expensive because it would not have the large overhead costs of big companies. These small companies also could convince large phone companies to lease or sell their less-profitable services in rural communities.

Looking into the future, many believe the day will come when every home in America will have a PC hooked to the Internet. This will offer unlimited opportunities for entrepreneurs. One example is

---

- *Other lower expenses.* A telemarketer can perform such diverse duties as handling marginal accounts, canvassing, and simple order taking more quickly than an outside salesperson by generating more customer calls per hour. The resulting savings in both expenses and time is telemarketing's greatest advantage.[16]

[16] "Telemarketing: Designing a Profitable Program," *Small Business Reports* (August 1987): 23–24.

a virtual grocery store where the consumers can place their order on line, as well as specifying when it should be delivered.

The Telecommunications Act of 1996 also has a provision that mandates the Internet hookup fees for schools, libraries, and public health facilities. This provision requires that hookup fees be affordable to enable these entities to access the information superhighway. This provision offers another array of opportunities for entrepreneurs. Lower rates will increase the incentive for schools, libraries, and health facilities to get connected to the Internet, creating a huge market. Because of their low overhead costs, small businesses could serve these budget-conscious customers better than a large company. Business owners also should consider providing a low-cost series of seminars on how to use the Internet. These new markets also can increase business for companies selling hardware, software, and printers.

More specifically, schools present a number of opportunities for entrepreneurs. The U.S. Department of Education has a goal to connect every public school and classroom to the Internet by the year 2000. In the meantime, according to the Department of Education, only 50 percent of U.S. public schools have access to the Internet, and only 10 percent have been wired correctly, leaving plenty of potential for entrepreneurs. Also, Janet Reeder, library media specialist at Pinckney Elementary School in Lawrence, Kansas, believes that most parents want their children to have access to computer education and are willing to pay for it. To tap into this market, a mobile for-profit computer club could be created to teach students about the Internet and keep them up to date on new developments. An increase will occur in the demand for developing computer networks that combine the educational applications of the Internet with the school's curriculum. And, finally, the possibility of intranets, mini in-school Internets, creates another opportunity for entrepreneurs.

The medical field also presents another facet of new opportunities. The biggest opportunities are in creating software for medical facilities to interface with the Internet, in creating home pages and in other related activities. By forming local area networks on the Internet, entrepreneurs would enable doctors, hospitals, clinic operators, and others to quickly share patient information. Consultants also will be in high demand to help medical personnel understand how technology can be integrated into their work.

SOURCE: Cynthia E. Griffin, "Electric Avenues," *Entrepreneur*, June 1996, 134–41.

Pitfalls

Although telemarketing has numerous advantages, an entrepreneur also should be aware of potential pitfalls. First, poor telephone techniques can defeat the telemarketing strategy. Bad habits such as vagueness, impersonal attitude, overaggressiveness, rudeness, dishonesty, and long-winded discussions have to be avoided. This can be done through effective training programs.

Second, dissension between the field sales staff and the telephone sales personnel can arise. In order for the two groups to cooperate and work together effectively, both groups must have clear guidelines as well as open lines of communication between them. In addition, current customers need to be aware of the sales force's joint effort so they never feel discontent when the field representatives turn an account over to the telephone staff. A venture's management needs to address the coordination of leads, sales calls, follow-ups, and resulting commissions.

Finally, entrepreneurs must be aware of the ever-present problem of rapid turnover of telephone staff. The work can be very monotonous, with people frequently leaving to find more interesting, challenging work. Additionally, the stigma of "phone peddling" often makes the workers feel their jobs are unimportant. To overcome these problems, management must make a sincere effort to create a professional, satisfied, and well-trained telemarketing staff.

PRICING STRATEGIES

One final marketing issue that needs to be addressed is that of pricing strategies. Many entrepreneurs, even after marketing research is conducted, are unsure of how to price their product or service. A number of factors affect this decision: the degree of competitive pressure, the availability of sufficient supply, seasonal or cyclical changes in demand, distribution costs, the product's life-cycle stage, changes in production costs, prevailing economic conditions, customer services provided by the seller, the amount of promotion done, and the market's buying power. Obviously, the ultimate price decision will balance many of these factors and, usually, will not satisfy *all* conditions. However, awareness of the various factors is important.

Other considerations, sometimes overlooked, are psychological in nature:

- The quality of a product in some situations is interpreted by customers by the level of the item's price.
- Some customer groups shy away from purchasing a product where no printed price schedule is available.
- An emphasis on the monthly cost of purchasing an expensive item often results in greater sales than an emphasis on total selling price.
- Most buyers expect to pay even-numbered prices for prestigious items and odd-numbered prices for commonly available goods.
- The greater the number of meaningful customer benefits the seller can convey about a given product, generally the less will be the price resistance.[17]

Pricing procedures differ depending on the nature of the venture—retail, manufacturing, or service. The general procedural outline presented in Table 8.7, however, might be applied to any type of business. The table demonstrates the basic steps in adopting a pricing system and how that system should relate to the desired pricing goals. All ten procedures taken together result in the four specific pricing goals most ventures seek.

With this general outline in mind, potential entrepreneurs can formulate the most appropriate pricing strategy. Table 8.8 provides a thorough analysis of pricing strategies, outlining when each strategy is generally used, what the procedures are, and the advantages and

---

[17] McCready, *Marketing Tactics,* 79.

TABLE 8.7	A GENERAL PRICE DETERMINATION PROCEDURE LEADING TO GENERAL PRICING GOALS	

Steps in Price Determination	Pricing Goals
1. Research the competitive product offerings. 2. Estimate the total market demand. 3. Calculate the available sales potential. 4. Determine the volume objective. 5. Set the company's or department's profit goal. 6. Select an appropriate price strategy. 7. Decide on the most effective distribution method. 8. Establish costs of promotion. 9. Anticipate the required discount structures. 10. Determine a specific list price.	• The organization will maintain the highest price possible on a product, as long as the market share is held constant or is growing. • The organization will maintain prices at a level consistent with competitive activity and market acceptance. • The organization will maintain prices that reflect an adequate return on investment. • The organization will maintain prices according to prevailing market conditions except where a greater profit might be attained from a unique market opportunity.

SOURCE: *Marketing Tactics Master Guide for Small Business*, by Gerald B. McCready, © 1982, 79, 81–82. Adapted by permission of the publisher, Prentice-Hall, a division of Simon & Schuster, Englewood Cliffs, New Jersey.

disadvantages associated with each. This checklist can provide entrepreneurs with reference points for establishing and evaluating pricing strategies for their ventures.

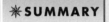

✳ SUMMARY

Marketing research involves the gathering of information about a particular market followed by analysis of that information. The marketing research process has five steps: (1) Define the purpose and objectives of the research, (2) gather secondary data, (3) gather primary data, (4) develop an information-gathering instrument (if necessary), and (5) interpret and report the information.

Entrepreneurs do not carry out marketing research for four major reasons: (1) cost, (2) complexity of the undertaking, (3) belief that only major strategic decisions need to be supported through marketing research, and (4) belief that the data will be irrelevant to company operations. Usually they misunderstand the value of marketing research or fear its cost.

Developing a marketing concept has three important areas. One is the formulation of a marketing philosophy. Some entrepreneurs are production driven, others are sales driven, and still others are consumer driven. The entrepreneur's values and the market conditions will help determine this philosophy. A second area is market segmentation, which is the process of identifying a specific set of characteristics that differentiate one group of consumers from the rest. Demographic and benefit variables are often used in this process. A third area is an understanding of consumer behavior. Since many types and patterns of consumer behavior exist, entrepreneurs need to focus on the personal and psychological characteristics of their customers. In this way they can determine a tailor-made, consumer-oriented strategy. This customer analysis focuses on such important factors as general

PRICING STRATEGY CHECKLIST

TABLE 8·8

Strategy Objective	When Generally Used	Procedure	Advantages	Disadvantages
Skim the cream of the market for high short-term profit (without regard for long term).	No comparable competitive products Drastically improved product or new product innovation Large number of buyers Little danger of competitor entry due to high price, patent control, high R&D costs, high promotion costs, and/or raw material control Uncertain costs Short life cycle Inelastic demand	Determine preliminary customer reaction. Charge premium price for product distinctiveness in short run, without considering long-run position. Some buyers will pcy more because of higher present value to them. Then gradually reduce price to tap successive market levels (i.e., skimming the cream of a market that is relatively insensitive to price). Finally, tap more sensitive segments.	Cushions against cost overruns Requires smaller investment Provides funds quickly to cover new-product promotion and initial development costs Limits demand until production is ready Suggests h gher value in buyer's mind Emphasizes value rather than cost as a guide to pricing Allows initial feeling out of demand before full-scale production	Assumes that a market exists at high price Results in ill will in early buyers when price is reduced Attracts competition Likely to underestimate ability of competitors to copy product Discourages some buyers from trying the product (connotes high profits) May cause long-run inefficiencies
Slide down demand curve to become established as efficient manufacturer at optimum volume before competitors become entrenched, without sacrificing long-term objective (e.g., obtain satisfactory share of market).	By established companies launching innovations Durable goods Slight barriers to entry by competition Medium life span	Tap successive levels of demand at highest prices possible. Then slide down demand curve faster and further than forced to in view of potential competition. Rate of price change is slow enough to add significant volume at each successive price level, but fast enough to prevent large competitor from becoming established on a low-cost volume basis.	Emphasizes value rather than cost as a guide to pricing Provides rapid return on investment Provides slight cushion against cost overruns	Requires broad knowledge of competitive product developments Requires much documented experience Results in ill will in early buyers when price is reduced Discourages some buyers from buying at initial high price

Strategy	Conditions	Method	Advantages	Disadvantages
Compete at the market price to encourage others to produce and promote the product to stimulate primary demand.	Several comparable products Growing market Medium to long product life span Known costs	Start with final price and work back to cost. Use customer surveys and studies of competitors' prices to approximate final price. Deduct selling margins. Adjust product, production, and selling methods to sell at this price and still make necessary profit margins.	Requires less analysis and research Existing market requires fewer promotion efforts Causes no ill will in early buyers since price will not be lowered soon	Limited flexibility Limited cushion for error Slower recovery of investment Must rely on other differentiating tools
Market penetration to stimulate market growth and capture and hold a satisfactory market share at a profit through low prices. Become strongly entrenched to generate profits over long term.	Long product life span Mass Market Easy market entry Demand is highly sensitive to price Unit costs of production and distribution decrease rapidly as quantity of output increases Newer product No "elite" market willing to pay premium for newest and best	Charge low prices to create a mass market resulting in cost advantages derived from larger volume. Look at lower end of demand curve to get price low enough to attract a large customer base. Also review past and competitor prices.	Discourages actual and potential competitor inroads because of apparent low profit margins Emphasizes value more than cost in pricing Allows maximum exposure and penetration in minimum time May maximize long-term profits if competition is minimized	Assumes volume is always responsive to price reductions, which isn't always true Relies somewhat on glamour and psychological pricing, which doesn't always work May create more business than production capacity available Requires significant investment Small errors often result in large losses.
Preemptive pricing to keep competitors out of market or eliminate existing ones	Used more often in consumer markets Manufacturers may use this approach on one or two products, with other prices meeting or higher than those of competitors.	Price at low levels so that market is unattractive to possible competitors. Set prices as close as possible to total unit cost. As increased volume allows lower cost, pass advantage to buyers via lower prices. If cost declines rapidly with increases in volume, can start price below cost. (Can use price approaching variable costs)	Discourages potential competitors because of apparent low profit margins Limits competitive activity and expensive requirements to meet them	Must offer other policies which permit lower price (limited credit, delivery, or promotions) Small errors can result in large losses Long-term payback period

SOURCE: Roy A. Lindberg and Theodore Cohn, *The Marketing Book for Growing Companies That Want to Excel* (New York: Van Nostrand Reinhold, 1986), 116–17. Reprinted with permission.

buying trends in the marketplace, specific buying trends of targeted consumers, and the types of goods and services being sold.

Most emerging ventures go through the four marketing stages of entrepreneurial marketing, opportunistic marketing, responsive marketing, and diversified marketing. Each stage requires a different strategy, and the entrepreneur must adjust accordingly.

Marketing planning is the process of determining a clear, comprehensive approach to the creation of customers. For developing this plan, the following elements are critical: marketing research, sales research, a marketing information system, sales forecasting, marketing plans, and evaluation.

Two additional critical areas in marketing for new ventures are telemarketing and pricing. Telemarketing is the use of telephone communications to directly contact and sell merchandise to consumers. The cost/benefit ratio of telecommunications is so high that it is likely to be one of the most important marketing tools of the late 1990s. Pricing strategies are a reflection of marketing research and must consider such factors as market competitiveness, consumer demand, life cycle of the goods or services being sold, costs, and prevailing economic conditions.

Key Terms and Concepts

Consumer-driven philosophy	Production-driven philosophy
Experimentation	Sales-driven philosophy
Market	Secondary data
Market segmentation	Surveys
Marketing research	Telemarketing
Primary data	

Review and Discussion Questions

1. In your own words, what is a market? How can marketing research help an entrepreneur identify a market?
2. What are the five steps in the marketing research process? Briefly describe each.
3. Which is of greater value to the entrepreneur, primary or secondary data? Why?
4. Identify and describe three of the primary inhibitors to marketing research.
5. How would an entrepreneur's new-venture strategy differ under each of the following marketing philosophies: production driven, sales driven, consumer driven? Be complete in your answer.
6. In your own words, what is market segmentation? What role do demographic and benefit variables play in the segmentation process?
7. Identify and discuss three of the most important personal characteristics that help an entrepreneur identify and describe customers. Also, explain how the product life cycle will affect the purchasing behavior of these customers.
8. Identify and discuss three of the psychological characteristics that help an entrepreneur identify and describe customers. Also, explain how the product life cycle will affect the purchasing behavior of these customers.
9. How does the way consumers view a venture's product or service affect strategy? For example, why would it make a difference to the entrepreneur's strategy if the consumers viewed the company as selling a convenience good as opposed to a shopping good?
10. Identify and describe four of the major forces shaping buying decisions in the 1990s.

11. Most emerging ventures will evolve through a series of marketing stages. What are these stages? Identify and describe each.

12. What does the entrepreneur of an emerging venture need to know about sales research and a marketing information system?

13. For developing a marketing plan, what are the five steps that are particularly helpful? Identify and describe each.

14. How can the entrepreneur evaluate the marketing planning process? Be complete in your answer.

15. How does telemarketing work? What are its advantages? What are its pitfalls? Why is it likely to be a major marketing tool of the late 1990s?

16. What are some of the major environmental factors that affect pricing strategies? What are some of the major psychological factors that affect pricing? Identify and discuss three of each.

Experiential Exercise   *Identifying the Customer*

One of the most important activities of entrepreneurs is identifying their customers. A list of the five basic types of consumers (*A* through *E*) and a list of descriptions of these types (*a* through *o*) follow. Identify the order in which people adopt new goods by ranking the first list from *1* (first adopters) to *5* (last adopters). Then match the descriptions with the types of consumer by placing a *1* next to those that describe initial adopters on down to a *5* next to those that describe final adopters. (Three descriptions are listed for each of the five types of consumer.) Answers are provided at the end of the exercise.

_____   A. Early adopters

_____   B. Early majority

_____   C. Laggards

_____   D. Innovators

_____   E. Late majority

_____   *a)* High-income people who have inherited their wealth

_____   *b)* Future oriented

_____   *c)* Below-average-income wage earners

_____   *d)* Present (security) oriented

_____   *e)* High-income people who have incomes from salary and investment

_____   *f)* Highest professionals, including merchants and financiers

_____   *g)* Present oriented

_____   *h)* Average-income wager earners

_____   *i)* Middle managers and owners of medium-sized businesses

_____   *j)* Above-average-income wage earners

_____   *k)* Present oriented, but worried about the impact of time

_____ *l)* Unskilled labor

_____ *m)* Skilled labor

_____ *n)* Owners of small businesses; nonmanagerial office and union managers

_____ *o)* Tradition-oriented people who often live in the past

Answers

A. 2	*a)* 1	*f)* 1	*k)* 1
B. 3	*b)* 2	*g)* 3	*l)* 5
C. 5	*c)* 5	*h)* 4	*m)* 4
D. 1	*d)* 4	*i)* 2	*n)* 3
E. 4	*e)* 2	*j)* 3	*o)* 5

VIDEO CASE **8.1**

Rogaine: Marketing an Accidental Miracle

For baby boomers struggling to grow old gracefully in a society that places a lot of emphasis on appearance, hair loss is a nightmare. But, in the early 1970s, Upjohn stumbled across a treatment that offers hope and new hair to the growing ranks of men and women who are losing their hair. "Back in the early 70s, we were testing a product in the laboratories to see if it was effective, and one of the side effects we found in a high percentage of the people who were using it was excessive hair growth all over their body," Tim Thieme, Upjohn's director of product management, recalls. "We were very disappointed at first because this was a drug for hypertension and it wasn't supposed to grow hair. But then we stood back and said, 'Well, let's take a look at it.' Nobody had ever done tests before to determine whether or not a product grew hair."

Upjohn conducted a study involving 2,300 men in 27 tests throughout the United States and discovered the product they dubbed Rogaine did indeed grow hair. Upjohn submitted its data to the federal Food and Drug Administration and waited for approval to begin marketing Rogaine. Approval was granted, and, suddenly, Upjohn had the first legitimate hair-*grow* product in history.

Although Rogaine is now available as an over-the-counter treatment in millions of grocery markets and drugstores, the FDA first branded Rogaine as a prescription treatment that only could be obtained from physicians. "We knew this was going to be a consumer-driven product," Thieme admits. "We didn't want consumers to come in and ask for Rogaine if the doctors didn't know anything, so we had to go to the medical community first—the doctors, nurses, pharmacists—to let them know about the product. When we achieved a certain level of awareness in the medical community, then we could go to the consumer. We had to determine internally whether we would advertise to the consumer. Once that decision was made, we had other hurdles we had to overcome before we could reach the consumer and that dealt with the Food and Drug Administration and what they were going to let us say or not say about the product."

In the beginning, the FDA allowed Upjohn to say very little about Rogaine. Upjohn's first television commercials for the product were soft-sell spots that simply encouraged consumers to consult their physicians about hair loss and treatment options. They included a toll-free telephone number viewers could call to acquire a list of doctors in their area who had been briefed about Rogaine. Upjohn wasn't allowed to mention Rogaine by name.

"The objective of that commercial was to inform consumers that if they were indeed concerned about hair loss, there was a legitimate place they could go and find out what options they had available to them," Eldon Eby, director of consumer promotion, explains. Later, as the FDA became more comfortable with Rogaine, Upjohn was able to launch a more-aggressive campaign comprised of more-specific television commercials and newspaper and magazine ads. Each piece of media provided toll-free numbers consumers could call for more information. Callers then were sent an informational video, along with a brochure listing doctors who offered Rogaine, and a $10 gift certificate redeemable with their first prescription.

More than 2 million people have called Rogaine's toll-free number—many of them women. Early on, Upjohn's research revealed that a significant number of women suffer from hair loss, and these women have an even harder time accepting hair loss than their male counterparts. "We understood that there was a different segment here that we had to address, and we had to get to them in the most efficient way," Eby says. "Buying unisex media didn't really work. We needed to go into women's magazines. Women wanted more information, in many cases, than men and different kinds of information." Upjohn established toll-free numbers specifically for women. Female callers received a free informational video, featuring testimonials from women who had experienced success with Rogaine, and a list of area doctors offering the product to their patients.

More than 20 years after Upjohn's discovery, diligent consumer analysis and strategic target marketing have enabled the company to not only transform a failed treatment for hypertension into one of its most lucrative products but also to be a pioneer in this new market.

Quesions

1. What key marketing research questions were answered by Upjohn in the development of Rogaine?
2. Is there a marketing philosophy that best describes Upjohn's approach to the market with Rogaine?
3. Using Table 8.3, what consumer characteristics could be used to define Rogaine's market segment?

 **CASE 8.2**

Dealing with the Competition

Six months ago Roberta O'Flynn opened a small office supply store. Roberta sells a wide range of general office merchandise, including photocopying and typing paper, writing tablets, envelopes, writing instruments, and computer diskettes, as well as a limited range of office desks, chairs, and lamps.

Several office supply stores in the local area are, in Roberta's opinion, competitors. In an effort to better understand the competition, Roberta has visited four of these stores and pretended to be a customer so she could get information regarding their prices, product offerings, and service. Each has a different strategy. For example, one of them sells strictly on price. It is the customer's responsibility to pick up the merchandise and carry it away. Another relies heavily on service, including a 90-day credit plan for those purchasing equipment in excess of $500. This company's prices are the highest of the four stores

Roberta visited. The other two stores use a combination of price and service strategies.

Roberta believes that in order to get her new venture off the ground, she must develop a marketing strategy that helps her effectively compete with these other firms. Since her store is extremely small, Roberta believes that a certain amount of marketing research could be of value. On the other hand, her budget is extremely limited, and she is not sure how to collect the information. Roberta believes that what she needs to do is develop a market niche that will be loyal to her. In this way, no matter how extensive the competition, she always will have a group of customers who buy from her. Roberta also believes that the focus of this research has to be in two general directions. First, she has to find out what customers look for from an office supply store. How important is price? Service? Quality? Second, she has to determine the general strategy of each of her major competitors so she can develop a plan of action for preventing them from taking away her customers. Right now, however, her biggest question is How do I go about getting the information I need?

Questions

1. Will the information Roberta is seeking be of value to her in competing in this market? Why or why not?
2. How would you recommend Roberta put together her marketing research plan? What should be involved? Be as complete as possible in your answer.
3. How expensive will it be for Roberta to follow your recommendations for her marketing research plan? Describe any other marketing research efforts she could undertake in the near future that would be of minimal cost.

 **CASE**   **8.3**

For Cooks Only

When Phil Hartrack was a young man, he already knew what he wanted to be: a salesperson. His mother was delighted. "Salespeople make great money," she explained to him, "and with your appetite, you're going to need all of the money you can make. You've got the biggest appetite in the family."

After graduating from college, Phil took a job with a consumer-goods firm. For the next ten years, he was one of its leading salespeople every year. At the end of this time, however, Phil admitted to himself that although he enjoyed selling, what he really wanted to do was sell books. "I want to own my own bookstore," he told his wife. "I know it sounds silly because I have had no experience in bookstore selling, but I've always loved books, and I'm a terrific salesperson." After researching the market, Phil and his wife had to face a very important fact: The competition in this business is extremely aggressive. Most small bookstores do not last more than three years, and the majors such as Walden and Doubleday dominate the industry.

Phil refused to admit defeat. "There has to be a market niche somewhere in this field that the majors are not addressing. I'm going to find that niche and go after it," he told his banker. Six months ago, Phil concluded that he had found this niche. "Cookbooks are the wave of the future," he explained to his wife. "The average person today buys twice as many cookbooks as ten years ago. It is the fastest-growing segment of the book market. Moreover, with your cooking skills and my appetite, we're a natural for this market. We love food, and we have sales skills."

Taking all of their savings, Phil and his wife opened their bookstore in a popular suburban mall. It is called For Cooks Only and sells only cookbooks. By the end of the first month, the Hartracks realized they had made the right choice. Their wide selection of cookbooks and their familiarity with many of the books helped them build a loyal clientele. They even installed a photocopying machine. If someone wants a recipe but does not want to buy the book, a photocopy of it is made for the individual. This service has resulted in many people coming by to get a recipe—and then returning within a couple of weeks to buy the book.

Although Phil is quite happy over the business's success, he realizes that his limited market niche could dry up in a short period of time. He feels that the best way to prevent this from happening is by conducting marketing research, seeing if he can add any additional books or services to the line, and developing the strongest possible clientele loyalty. The first place to begin, in his opinion, is by examining the current purchasing habits of customers and then using this as a foundation for deciding where to go from here.

Questions

1. From the customer's viewpoint, what type of good is a cookbook? Defend your answer.
2. Why is Phil's store doing so well? Include in your answer his philosophy of marketing.
3. In his marketing research efforts, what type of information would you suggest Phil collect? How can he go about doing this? Be complete in your answer.

Chapter 9

FINANCIAL PREPARATION FOR ENTREPRENEURIAL VENTURES

CHAPTER OBJECTIVES

1. To explain the principal financial statements needed for any entrepreneurial venture: balance sheet, income statement, and cash-flow statement

2. To outline the process of preparing an operating budget

3. To discuss the nature of cash flow and to explain how to draw up such a document

4. To describe how pro forma statements are prepared

5. To explain how capital budgeting can be used in the decision-making process

6. To illustrate how to use break-even analysis

7. To describe ratio analysis and illustrate some of the important measures and meanings

8. To describe the value of decision support systems in the management of financial resources

Small company managers are too inclined to delegate to outside accountants every decision about their companies' financial statements. Indeed, it is most unfair to suppose that accountants can produce—without management's advice and counsel—the perfect statement for a company. Instead, I contend, top managers of growing small companies must work with their independent accountants in preparing company financial statements to ensure that the right message is being conveyed. . . .

James McNeill Stancill,
"Managing Financial Statements: Image and Effect,"
Growing Concerns (New York: Wiley, 1984)

Today's entrepreneur operates in a competitive environment characterized by the constraining forces of governmental regulation, competition, and resources. In regard to the latter, no firm has access to an unlimited amount of resources. So in order to compete effectively, the entrepreneur must allocate resources efficiently. Three kinds of resources are available to the entrepreneur: human, material, and financial. This chapter focuses on financial resources in the entrepreneurial environment, beginning with a discussion of financial statements as a managerial planning tool. How the budgeting process translates into the preparation of pro forma statements is presented, and attention is also given to break-even analysis and ratio analysis as profit-planning tools. Finally, we discuss the value of decision support systems in small-business financial planning.

THE IMPORTANCE OF FINANCIAL INFORMATION FOR ENTREPRENEURS

Financial information pulls together all the information presented in the other segments of the business: marketing, distribution, manufacturing, and management. It quantifies all the assumptions and historical information concerning business operations.[1]

Some of the questions that should be answered in a typical financial segment follow:

What is your total estimated income for the first year?
What is your estimated monthly income for the first year?

---

[1] See Richard G. P. McMahon and Leslie G. Davies, "Financial Reporting and Analysis Practices in Small Enterprises: Their Association with Growth Rate and Financial Performance," *Journal of Small Business Management* (January 1994): 9–17.

What will it cost you to open the business?

What will be your monthly cash flow during the first year?

What will your personal monthly financial needs be?

What sales volume will you need in order to make a profit during the first three years?

What will be your break-even point?

What will be your projected assets, liabilities, and net worth on the day before you expect to open?

What will your potential funding sources be?

How will you use the money from lenders or investors?

How will the loan be secured?

The entrepreneur or small-business owner should consider the following financial information significant for financial management:

- The legal form of organization, including its tax implication
- The importance of ratio analysis in planning
- Techniques and uses of projected financial statements
- Techniques and approaches for designing a cash-flow schedule
- Reasons and approaches for developing a business plan
- Techniques and approaches for evaluating the capital budget
- Inventory management considerations
- Accounts receivable management considerations
- Cash and temporary investment management issues
- Liability management considerations
- Capital structure planning approaches
- Evaluating a closely held firm
- Business plan outline[2]

The key component of the financial segment is the *balance sheet,* which represents the financial condition of a company at a certain date. It details the items the company owns (assets) and the amount the company owes (liabilities). It also shows the net worth of the company and its liquidity. The balance sheet must follow the traditional accounting equation:

$$\text{Assets} = \text{Liabilities} + \text{Owner's Equity}$$

Another key component is the *income statement,* commonly referred to as the *P & L (profit and loss) statement,* which provides the owner/manager with the results of operations. It measures the success of the business.

The *statement of cash flow* is an analysis of the cash availability and cash needs of the business. The projected cash flow is a planning tool to allow management to make borrowing and investing decisions. Because of swings in the business cycles, collection experiences, timing of expenditures, purchase of capital items and various other transactions that generate or deplete cash, an owner/manager must manage the cash resources of his or her

---

[2] Donald E. Vaughn, *Financial Planning for the Entrepreneur* (Upper Saddle River, NJ: Prentice Hall, 1997), 3.

business. A successful business manager invests idle cash and appropriately finances cash shortages (short-term financing for temporary fluctuations and long-term financing for capital improvements).[3]

It should be remembered that entrepreneurs make assumptions to explain how numbers are derived and correlate with information presented in other parts of the business operations. The set of assumptions on which projections are based should be clearly and precisely presented. Numbers without these assumptions will have little meaning. It is only after carefully considering such assumptions that the entrepreneur will be able to assess the validity of financial projections. Because the rest of the financial plan is an outgrowth of these assumptions, they are the most integral part of any financial segment. (See Table 9.1 for a financial glossary for entrepreneurs.)

In order for entrepreneurs to develop the key components of a financial segment, they should follow a clear process, described in the next section.

PREPARING FINANCIAL STATEMENTS

One of the most powerful tools the entrepreneur can use in planning financial operations is a **budget.**[4] The *operating budget* is a statement of estimated income and expenses over a specified period of time. Another common type of budget is the *cash budget,* which is a statement of estimated cash receipts and expenditures over a specified period of time. It is typical for a firm to prepare both types of budgets by first computing an operating budget and then constructing a cash budget based on the operating budget. A third common type of budget is the *capital budget,* which is used to plan expenditures on assets whose returns are expected to last beyond one year. This section examines all three of these budgets: operating, cash flow, and capital. Then the preparation of pro forma financial statements from these budgets is discussed.

The Operating Budget

Typically, the first step in creating an operating budget is the preparation of the **sales forecast.**[5] An entrepreneur can prepare the sales forecast in several ways. One way is to implement a statistical forecasting technique such as *simple linear regression.* Simple linear regression is a technique in which a linear equation states the relationship among three variables:

$$Y = a + bx$$

Y is a dependent variable (it is dependent on the values of a, b, and x), x is an independent variable (it is not dependent on any of the other variables), a is a constant (in regression analysis, Y is dependent on the variable x, all other things held constant), and b is the slope of the line (the change in Y divided by the change in x). For estimating sales, Y is the

---

[3] See Clyde P. Stickney and Roman L. Weil, *Financial Accounting,* 7th ed. (Fort Worth: The Dryden Press, 1994), 8–14.

[4] Neil C. Churchill, "Budget Choice: Planning vs. Control," *Harvard Business Review* (July/August 1984): 151.

[5] Fred A. Shelton and Jack C. Bailes, "How to Create an Electronic Spreadsheet Budget," *Management Accounting* (July 1986): 42.

TABLE 9.1   A FINANCIAL GLOSSARY FOR THE ENTREPRENEUR

Accrual system of accounting A method of recording and allocating income and costs for the period in which each is involved, regardless of the date of payment or collection. For example, if you were paid $100 in April for goods you sold in March, the $100 would be income for March under an accrual system. (Accrual is the opposite of cash system of accounting.)

Asset Anything of value that is owned by you or your business.

Balance sheet An itemized statement listing the total assets and liabilities of your business at a given moment. It is also called a *statement of condition*.

Capital (1) The amount invested in a business by the proprietor(s) or stockholders. (2) The money available for investment or money invested.

Cash flow The schedule of your cash receipts and disbursements.

Cash system of accounting A method of accounting whereby revenue and expenses are recorded when received and paid, respectively, without regard for the period to which they apply.

Collateral Property you own that you pledge to the lender as security on a loan until the loan is repaid. Collateral can be a car, home, stocks, bonds, or equipment.

Cost of goods sold This is determined by subtracting the value of the ending inventory from the sum of the beginning inventory and purchases made during the period. Gross sales less cost of goods sold gives you gross profit.

Current assets Cash and assets that can be easily converted to cash, such as accounts receivable and inventory. Current assets should exceed current liabilities.

Current liabilities Debts you must pay within a year.

Depreciation Lost usefulness; expired utility; the diminution of service yield from a fixed asset or fixed asset group that cannot or will not be restored by repairs or by replacement of parts.

Equity An interest in property or in a business, subject to prior creditors. An owner's equity in his business is the difference between the value of the company's assets and the debt owed by the company. For example, if you borrow $30,000 to purchase assets you pay $50,000 for, your equity is $20,000.

Expense An expired cost; any item or class of cost of (or loss from) carrying on an activity; a present or past expenditure defraying a present operating cost or representing an irrecoverable cost or loss; an item of capital expenditures written down or off; or a term often used with some qualifying expression denoting function, organization, or time, such as a selling expense, factory expense, or monthly expense.

Financial statement A report summarizing the financial condition of a business. It normally includes a balance sheet and income statement.

Gross profit Sales less the cost of goods sold. For example, if you sell $100,000 worth of merchandise you paid $80,000 for, your gross profit would be $20,000. To get net profit, however, you would have to deduct other expenses incurred during the period in which the sales were made, such as rent, insurance, and sales staff salaries.

Interest The cost of borrowing money. It is paid to the lender and is usually expressed as an annual percentage of the loan. That is, if you borrow $100 at 12%, you pay 1% (.01 × $100 = $1) interest per month. Interest is an expense of doing business.

Income statement Also called *Profit-and-loss statement*. A statement summarizing the income of a business during a specific period.

Liability Money you owe to your creditors. Liabilities can be in the form of a bank loan, accounts payable, etc. It represents a claim against your assets.

Loss When a business's total expenses for the period are greater than the income.

Net profit Total income for the period less total expenses for the period. (See *Gross profit*.)

Net worth The same as *equity*.

Personal financial statement A report summarizing your personal financial condition. Normally it includes a listing of your assets, liabilities, large monthly expenses, and sources of income.

Profit (See *Net profit* and *Gross profit*.) "Profit" usually refers to net profit.

Profit-and-loss statement Same as *Income statement*.

Variable cost Costs that vary with the level of production on sales, such as direct labor, material, and sales commissions.

Working capital The excess of current assets over current liabilities.

variable used to represent the expected sales, and x is the variable used to represent the factor on which sales are dependent. Some retail stores may believe their sales are dependent on their advertising expenditures, whereas other stores may believe their sales are dependent on some other variable, such as the amount of foot traffic past the store.

When using regression analysis, the entrepreneur will draw conclusions about the relationship between, for example, product sales and advertising expenditures. Presented next is an example of how Mary Tindle, owner of a clothing store, used regression analysis.

Mary began with two initial assumptions: (1) If no money is spent on advertising, total sales will be $200,000, and (2) for every dollar spent on advertising, sales will be increased by two times that amount. Relating these two observations yields the following simple linear regression formula:

$$S = \$200{,}000 + 2A$$

where
$$S = \text{Projected Sales}$$
$$A = \text{Advertising Expenditures}$$

(Note that it is often easier to substitute more meaningful letters into an equation. In this case, the letter S was substituted for the letter Y simply because the word *sales* starts with that letter. The same is true for the letter A, which was substituted for the letter X.) In order to determine the expected sales level, Mary must insert different advertising expenditures and complete the simple linear regression formula for each different expenditure. The following data and Figure 9.1 demonstrate results.

Simple Linear Regression ($000)

A	2A	S = $200 + 2A
$ 50	$100	$300
100	200	400
150	300	500
200	400	600
250	500	700
300	600	800

Another commonly used technique for the preparation of a sales forecast is the estimation that current sales will increase a certain percentage over the prior period's sales. This percentage is based on a trend line analysis that covers the five preceding sales periods and assumes that the seasonal variations will continue to run in the same pattern. Obviously, since it needs five preceding sales periods, trend line analysis is used for more established ventures. It is nevertheless an important tool entrepreneurs should be aware of as the venture grows and becomes more established. Here is an example of how John Wheatman, owner of Wheatman's Market, used trend line analysis to forecast sales for his retail store:

After considerable analysis of his store's sales history, John Wheatman decided to use trend line analysis and estimated that sales would increase 5 percent during the next year, with the seasonal variations remaining in roughly the same pattern. Since he has a personal computer with an electronic spreadsheet program, John chose to use the input

FIGURE 9.1   **REGRESSION ANALYSIS**

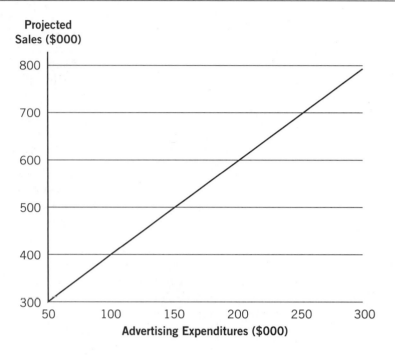

TABLE 9.2   **WHEATMAN'S MARKET: SALES FORECAST FOR 19XX** ($000)

	Jan.	Feb.	Mar.	Apr.	May	June
Sales	$300	$350	$400	$375	$500	$450
× 1.05	315	368	420	394	525	473

	July	Aug.	Sept.	Oct.	Nov.	Dec.
Sales	$475	$480	$440	$490	$510	$550
× 1.05	499	504	462	515	536	578

of last year's sales figures in the spreadsheet and to instruct the computer to increase each month by 5 percent. The results are shown in Table 9.2.

After a firm has forecast its sales for the budget period, **expenses** must be estimated. The first type of expenses that should be estimated are the cost of goods sold, which follows sales on the income statement. For retail firms this is a matter of projecting purchases and the corresponding desired beginning and ending inventories. Many firms prefer to have a certain percentage of the next month's sales on hand in inventory. Here is how John Wheatman determines his store's expected purchases and inventory requirements:

| TABLE 9.3 | WHEATMAN'S MARKET: PURCHASE REQUIREMENTS BUDGET FOR 19XX ($000) |

	Jan.	Feb.	Mar.	Apr.	May	June	July	Aug.	Sept.	Oct.	Nov.	Dec.
Sales revenue	$315	$368	$420	$394	$525	$473	$499	$504	$462	$515	$536	$578
Cost of goods sold												
Beginning inventory	$ 63	$ 74	$ 84	$ 79	$105	$ 95	$100	$101	$ 92	$103	$107	$116
Purchases	263	305	331	341	410	383	400	395	380	416	437	413
Cost of goods available	$326	$379	$415	$420	$515	$478	$500	$496	$472	$519	$544	$529
Ending inventory	74	85	79	105	95	100	101	92	102	107	116	66
Cost of goods sold	$252	$294	$336	$315	$420	$378	$399	$403	$370	$412	$428	$462
Gross profit	$ 63	$ 74	$ 84	$ 79	$105	$ 95	$100	$101	$ 92	$103	$108	$116

Cost of goods sold = Current period sales × .80

Ending inventory = Next month's sales × (.80)(.25) (since inventory is carried at cost)

Cost of goods available = Cost of goods sold + Ending inventory

Beginning inventory = Prior month's ending inventory or current month's sales × (.80)(.25)

Purchases = Cost of goods available − Beginning inventory

Gross profit = Sales − Cost of goods sold

For determining his purchase requirements, John Wheatman believes his gross profit will represent 20 percent of his sales dollar. This is based on analysis of the past five years' income statement. Consequently, cost of goods sold will represent 80 percent of the sales for the current month. In addition, John wants to have approximately one week's inventory on hand. Thus the ending inventory is estimated to be 25 percent of next month's sales. The results are shown in Table 9.3.

A manufacturing firm, on the other hand, will need to establish its production budget, a material purchases budget based on the product budget, and the corresponding direct labor budget. The production budget is management's estimate of the number of units that need to be produced in order to meet the sales forecast. This budget is prepared by working backward through the cost of goods sold section. First, the predicted number of units that will be sold during that month is determined. Then the desired ending-inventory-level balance is added to this figure. The sum of these two figures is the number of units that will be needed in inventory. Once the inventory requirements have been determined, the entrepreneur must determine how many of these units will be accounted for by the beginning inventory (which is the prior month's ending inventory) and how many units will have to be produced. The production requirement is calculated by subtracting the period's beginning inventory from the inventory needed for that period. For example:

Tom B. Good, president and founder of General Widgets, has decided to implement a budget in order to help plan for his company's growth. After receiving the unit sales forecast from his sales manager, Tom examined last year's product movement reports and determined that he would like to have 10 percent of the next month's sales on hand as a buffer against possible fluctuations in demand. He has also received a report from

TABLE 9.4	GENERAL WIDGETS: PRODUCTION BUDGET WORKSHEET FOR 19XX (000)											
	Jan.	**Feb.**	**Mar.**	**Apr.**	**May**	**June**	**July**	**Aug.**	**Sept.**	**Oct.**	**Nov.**	**Dec.**
Projected sales (units)	125	136	123	143	154	234	212	267	236	345	367	498
Desired ending inventory	14	12	14	15	23	21	27	24	35	37	50	26
Available for sale	139	148	137	158	177	255	239	291	271	382	417	524
Less: Beginning inventory	12	14	12	14	15	23	21	27	24	35	37	50
Total production requirements	127	134	125	144	162	232	218	264	247	347	380	474

his production manager that his ending inventory this year is expected to be 12,000 widgets, which will also be the beginning inventory for the budget period. Table 9.4 shows the results.

After the production budget has been calculated, the materials required for producing the specified number of units can be determined from an analysis of the bill of materials for the product being manufactured. In addition, by examining the amount of direct labor needed to produce each unit, management can determine the amount of direct labor that will be needed during the forthcoming budget period.

The last step in preparing the operating budget is to estimate the operating expenses for the period. Three of the key concepts in developing an expense budget are fixed, variable, and mixed costs. A **fixed cost** is one that does not change in response to changes in activity for a given period of time. Rent, depreciation, and certain salaries are examples. A **variable cost** is one that changes in the same direction as and in direct proportion to changes in operating activity. Direct labor, direct materials, and sales commissions are examples. **Mixed costs** are a blend of fixed and variable costs. An example is utilities, since part of this expense would be responsive to change in activity, and the rest would be a fixed expense, remaining relatively stable over the budget period. Mixed costs can present a problem for management in that it is sometimes difficult to determine how much of the expense is variable and how much is fixed.

After the expenses have been budgeted, the sales, cost of goods, and expense budget are combined to form the operating budget. Table 9.5 outlines Wheatman's Market's anticipated expenses for the budget year and the completed operating budget for the period. Each month represents the pro forma, or projected, income and expenses for that period.

The Cash-Flow Budget

After the operating budget has been prepared, the entrepreneur can proceed to the next phase of the budget process, the **cash-flow budget.** This budget, which is often prepared with the assistance of an accountant, provides an overview of the cash inflows and outflows

| TABLE 9.5 | WHEATMAN'S MARKET: EXPENSE AND OPERATING BUDGETS |

In order to identify the behavior of the different expense accounts, John Wheatman decided to analyze the past five years' income statements. Following are the results of his analysis:

- Rent is a constant expense and is expected to remain the same over the next year.
- Payroll expense changes in proportion to sales, since the more sales the store has, the more people it must hire to meet increased consumer demands.
- Utilities are expected to remain relatively constant over the budget period. This is because the food coolers will be running at the same level even though the sales levels may vary.
- Taxes are based primarily on sales and payroll and are therefore considered a variable expense.
- Supplies will vary in proportion to sales. This is because most of the supplies (cash register tape, vegetable trays, meat trays, and plastic meat and vegetable bags) will be used to support sales.
- Repairs are relatively stable and are a fixed expense. John has maintenance contracts on the equipment in the store, and the cost is not scheduled to rise during the budget period.

WHEATMAN'S MARKET: EXPENSE BUDGET FOR 19XX ($000)

	Jan.	Feb.	Mar.	Apr.	May	June	July	Aug.	Sept.	Oct.	Nov.	Dec.
Operating expenses												
Rent	$ 2	$ 2	$ 2	$ 2	$ 2	$ 2	$ 2	$ 2	$ 2	$ 2	$ 2	$ 2
Payroll	32	37	42	39	53	47	50	50	46	51	54	58
Utilities	5	5	5	5	5	5	5	5	5	5	5	5
Taxes	3	4	4	4	5	5	5	5	5	5	5	6
Supplies	16	18	21	20	26	24	25	25	23	26	27	29
Repairs	2	2	2	2	2	2	2	2	2	2	2	2
Total expenses	$ 60	$ 68	$ 76	$ 72	$ 93	$ 85	$ 89	$ 89	$ 83	$ 91	$ 95	$102
Sales revenue	$315	$368	$420	$394	$525	$473	$499	$504	$462	$515	$536	$578
Cost of goods sold												
Beginning inventory	$ 63	$ 74	$ 84	$ 79	$105	$ 95	$100	$101	$ 92	$103	$107	$116
Purchases	263	305	331	341	410	383	400	395	380	416	437	413
Cost of goods available	$326	$379	$415	$420	$515	$478	$500	$496	$472	$519	$544	$529
Ending inventory	74	85	79	105	95	100	101	92	102	107	116	66
Cost of goods sold	$252	$294	$336	$315	$420	$378	$399	$403	$370	$412	$428	$462
Gross profit	$ 63	$ 74	$ 84	$ 79	$105	$ 95	$100	$101	$ 92	$103	$108	$116
Operating expenses												
Rent	$ 2	$ 2	$ 2	$ 2	$ 2	$ 2	$ 2	$ 2	$ 2	$ 2	$ 2	$ 2
Payroll	32	37	42	39	53	47	50	50	46	51	54	58
Utilities	5	5	5	5	5	5	5	5	5	5	5	5
Taxes	3	4	4	4	5	5	5	5	5	5	5	6
Supplies	16	18	21	20	26	24	25	25	23	26	27	29
Repairs	2	2	2	2	2	2	2	2	2	2	2	2
Total expenses	$ 60	$ 68	$ 76	$ 72	$ 93	$ 85	$ 89	$ 89	$ 83	$ 91	$ 95	$102
Net profit	$ 3	$ 6	$ 8	$ 7	$ 12	$ 10	$ 11	$ 12	$ 9	$ 12	$ 12	$ 14

during the period. By pinpointing cash problems in advance, management can make the necessary financing arrangements.[6]

[6] Fred Waedt, "Understanding Cash Flow Statements, or What You Need to Know before You Ask for a Loan," *Small Business Forum* (spring 1995): 42–51.

| TABLE 9.6 | | WHEATMAN'S MARKET: CASH-FLOW BUDGET |

John Wheatman has successfully completed his operating budget and is now ready to prepare his cash-flow worksheet. After analyzing the sales figures and the cash receipts, John has determined that 80 percent of monthly sales are in cash. Of the remaining 20 percent, 15 percent is collected in the next month, and the final 5 percent is collected in the month following (see cash receipts worksheet below). Wheatman's purchases are typically paid for the week following the purchase. Therefore, approximately one-fourth of the purchases are paid for in the following month. Rent expense is paid for a month in advance. However, since it is not expected to go up during the budget period, the monthly cash outlay for rent remains the same. All the other expenses are paid for in the month of consumption (see cash disbursements worksheet below). Finally, the cash-flow worksheet is constructed by taking the beginning cash balance, adding the cash receipts for that month, and deducting the cash disbursements for the same month.

WHEATMAN'S MARKET: CASH RECEIPTS WORKSHEET FOR 19XX ($000)

	Jan.	Feb.	Mar.	Apr.	May	June	July	Aug.	Sept.	Oct.	Nov.	Dec.
Sales	$315	$388	$420	$394	$525	$473	$499	$504	$462	$515	$536	$578
Current month	$252	$294	$336	$315	$420	$378	$399	$403	$370	$412	$428	$462
Prior month	82	47	55	63	59	79	71	75	76	69	77	80
Two months back	26	28	16	18	21	19	26	24	24	25	24	26
Cash receipts	$360	$369	$407	$396	$500	$476	$496	$502	$470	$506	$529	$568

WHEATMAN'S MARKET: CASH DISBURSEMENTS WORKSHEET FOR 19XX ($000)

	Jan.	Feb.	Mar.	Apr.	May	June	July	Aug.	Sept.	Oct.	Nov.	Dec.
Purchases	$263	$305	$331	$341	$410	$383	$400	$395	$380	$416	$437	$413
Current month	$197	$228	$248	$256	$307	$287	$300	$296	$285	$312	$328	$309
Prior month	98	66	76	83	85	102	96	100	99	95	104	109
Purchase payments	$295	$294	$324	$339	$392	$396	$396	$396	$384	$407	$432	$419
Operating expenses	$ 60	$ 68	$ 76	$ 72	$ 93	$ 85	$ 89	$ 89	$ 83	$ 91	$ 95	$102
Cash payments	$355	$362	$400	$412	$485	$481	$485	$485	$467	$498	$527	$521

WHEATMAN'S MARKET: CASH-FLOW WORKSHEET FOR 19XX ($000)

	Jan.	Feb.	Mar.	Apr.	May	June	July	Aug.	Sept.	Oct.	Nov.	Dec.
Beginning cash	$122	$127	$134	$141	$127	$141	$143	$154	$170	$173	$181	$184
Add: Receipts	360	369	407	396	500	476	496	502	470	506	529	568
Cash available	$482	$496	$541	$537	$627	$617	$639	$656	$640	$679	$710	$752
Less: Payments	355	362	400	411	485	481	485	485	467	498	527	521
Ending cash	$127	$134	$141	$126	$142	$136	$154	$171	$173	$181	$183	$231

The first step in the preparation of the cash-flow budget is the identification and timing of cash inflows. For the typical business, cash inflows will come from three sources: (1) cash sales, (2) cash payments received on account, and (3) loan proceeds. Not all of a firm's sales revenues are cash. In an effort to increase sales, most businesses will allow some customers to purchase goods on account. Consequently, part of the funds will arrive

TABLE 9.7	SUMMARY OF ACCOUNT CHANGES FOR PRO FORMA BALANCE SHEET

Cash. Begin with the original cash balance, and add (or subtract) the change in cash as depicted on the cash-flow budget.

Accounts receivable. Examine the last couple of months on the cash-flow budget to determine what charges will be included in the accounts receivable. Also, be sure all of the original receivables have been accounted for.

Inventory. This figure can be picked up from the cost-of-goods budget.

Fixed assets. This number will probably remain the same; however, any changes can be picked up on the cash-flow budget from an analysis of the loan proceeds.

Accounts payable. Again, examine the last couple of months on the cash-flow budget, this time analyzing the purchases to determine what purchases will not have been paid for.

Loans/notes payable. Analyze the loan proceeds. In addition, interest will have to be accrued in a separate interest-payable account.

Capital. The major item to be included here is the projected net income for the budget period.

in later periods and will be identified as cash payments received on account. Loan proceeds represent another form of cash inflow that is not directly tied to the sales revenues. A firm may receive loan proceeds for several reasons—for example, the planned expansion of the firm (new building and equipment) or meeting cash-flow problems stemming from an inability to pay current bills.

Some businesses have a desired minimum balance of cash indicated on the cash-flow budget, highlighting the point at which it will be necessary to seek additional financing. Table 9.6 provides an example of how Wheatman's Market prepared its cash-flow budget.

PRO FORMA STATEMENTS

The final step in the budget process is the preparation of **pro forma statements,** which are projections of a firm's financial position over a future period (pro forma income statement) or on a future date (pro forma balance sheet). In the normal accounting cycle, the income statement is prepared first and then the balance sheet. Similarly, in the preparation of pro forma statements, the pro forma income statement is followed by the pro forma balance sheet.

In the process of preparing the operating budget, the firm will have already prepared the pro forma income statements for each month in the budget period. Each month presents the anticipated income and expense for that particular period, which is what the monthly pro forma income statements do. In order to prepare an annual pro forma income statement, the firm combines all months of the year.

The process for preparing a pro forma balance sheet is more complex. The last balance sheet prepared before the budget period began, the operating budget, and the cash-flow budget are needed in preparing a pro forma balance sheet. Starting with the beginning balance sheet balances, the projected changes as depicted on the budgets are added to create the projected balance sheet totals. Table 9.7 provides a summary of the changes that should be added to the appropriate accounts.

TABLE 9.8　　　　　**WHEATMAN'S MARKET: PRO FORMA STATEMENTS**

At this point in the budget process, John Wheatman has the information necessary to prepare pro forma financial statements. The first set he has decided to prepare are the pro forma income statements. To do this, John simply copies the information from the operating budget (see comparative income statements below and compare with operating budget). The next set of pro forma statements is the pro forma balance sheets. In order to compile these, John uses the following information along with the operating budget and the cash-flow worksheet he has prepared:

Cash: the ending cash balance for each month from the cash-flow worksheet

Accounts receivable: 20 percent of the current month's sales plus 5 percent of the preceding month's sales

Inventory: the current month's ending inventory on the pro forma income statements

Prepaid rent: The $2,000 is expected to remain constant throughout the budget period and is always paid one month in advance.

Building and equipment: No new acquisitions are expected in this area, so the amount will remain constant.

Accumulated depreciation: Since no new acquisitions are anticipated, this will stay the same; all buildings and equipment are fully depreciated.

Accounts payable: 25 percent of current purchases

Capital: prior month's capital balance plus current month's net income

WHEATMAN'S MARKET: COMPARATIVE PRO FORMA INCOME STAEMENTS FOR 19XX ($000)

	Jan.	Feb.	Mar.	Apr.	May	June	July	Aug.	Sept.	Oct.	Nov.	Dec.
Sales	$315	$388	$420	$394	$525	$473	$499	$504	$462	$515	$536	$578
Cost of goods sold												
Beginning inventory	$ 63	$ 74	$ 84	$ 79	$105	$ 95	$100	$101	$ 92	$103	$107	$116
Purchases	263	305	331	341	410	383	400	395	380	416	437	413
Cost of goods available	$326	$379	$415	$420	$515	$478	$500	$496	$472	$519	$544	$529
Ending inventory	74	85	79	105	95	100	101	92	102	107	116	66
Cost of goods sold	$252	$294	$336	$315	$420	$378	$399	$403	$370	$412	$428	$462
Gross profit	$ 63	$ 74	$ 84	$ 79	$105	$ 95	$100	$101	$ 92	$103	$108	$116

After preparing the pro forma balance sheet, the entrepreneur should verify the accuracy of his or her work with the application of the traditional accounting equation:

$$\text{Assets} = \text{Liabilities} + \text{Owner's Equity}$$

If the equation is not in balance, the work should be rechecked. Table 9.8 provides a brief account of the process of preparing pro forma financial statements for Wheatman's Market.

CAPITAL BUDGETING

Entrepreneurs may be required to make several investment decisions in the process of managing their firms. The impact of some of these decisions will be felt primarily within one year. On other investments, however, the returns are expected to extend beyond one year. Investments that fit into this second category are commonly referred to as capital

| **TABLE 9.8** | WHEATMAN'S MARKET: PRO FORMA STATEMENTS *(continued)* |

	Jan.	Feb.	Mar.	Apr.	May	June	July	Aug.	Sept.	Oct.	Nov.	Dec.
Operating expenses												
Rent	$ 2	$ 2	$ 2	$ 2	$ 2	$ 2	$ 2	$ 2	$ 2	$ 2	$ 2	$ 2
Payroll	32	37	42	39	53	47	50	50	46	51	54	58
Utilities	5	5	5	5	5	5	5	5	5	5	5	5
Taxes	3	4	4	4	5	5	5	5	5	5	5	6
Supplies	16	18	21	20	26	24	25	25	23	26	27	29
Repairs	2	2	2	2	2	2	2	2	2	2	2	2
Total expenses	$ 60	$ 68	$ 76	$ 72	$ 93	$ 85	$ 89	$ 89	$ 83	$ 91	$ 95	$102
Net profit	$ 3	$ 6	$ 8	$ 7	$ 12	$ 10	$ 11	$ 12	$ 9	$ 12	$ 12	$ 14

WHEATMAN'S MARKET: COMPARATIVE PRO FORMA BALANCE SHEETS FOR 19XX ($000)

	Jan.	Feb.	Mar.	Apr.	May	June	July	Aug.	Sept.	Oct.	Nov.	Dec.
Assets												
Cash	$127	$134	$141	$126	$142	$136	$154	$171	$173	$181	$183	$231
Accounts receivable	91	89	102	100	125	121	123	126	117	126	133	142
Inventory	74	84	79	105	95	100	101	92	103	107	116	66
Prepaid rent	2	2	2	2	2	2	2	2	2	2	2	2
Building and equipment	350	350	350	350	350	350	350	350	350	350	350	350
Less: Accumulated depreciation	−350	−350	−350	−350	−350	−350	−350	−350	−350	−350	−350	−350
Total assets	$294	$309	$324	$333	$364	$359	$380	$391	$395	$416	$434	$441
Liabilities												
Accounts payable	$ 66	$ 76	$ 83	$ 85	$102	$ 96	$100	$ 99	$ 95	$104	$109	$103
Capital	228	234	242	249	261	270	280	292	300	312	326	339
Total liabilities and equity	$294	$310	$325	$334	$363	$366	$380	$391	$395	$416	$435	$442

investments or capital expenditures. A technique the entrepreneur can use to help plan for capital expenditures is the concept of **capital budgeting.**[7]

The first step in capital budgeting is to identify the cash flows and their timing. The inflows, or returns as they are commonly called, are equal to net operating income before deduction of payments to the financing sources but after the deduction of applicable taxes and with depreciation added back, as represented by the following formula:

$$\text{Expected Returns} = X(1 - T) + \text{Depreciation}$$

X is equal to the net operating income, and T is defined as the appropriate tax rate. An illustration follows.

---

[7] See Eugene F. Brigham and Louis C. Gapenski, *Financial Management,* 7th ed. (Fort Worth: The Dryden Press, 1994), 383–512.

John Wheatman is faced with a dilemma. He has two mutually exclusive projects, both of which require an outlay of $1,000. The problem is that he can afford only one of the projects. After discussing the problem with his accountant, John discovered that the first step he needs to take is to determine the expected return on each project. In order to gather this information, he has studied the probable effect on the store's operations and has developed the data shown in Table 9.9.

Thus Table 9.9 provides a good illustration of the expected returns of John Wheatman's two projects. At this point, however, the cash inflows of each year are shown without consideration of the time value of money. The cash outflow is used to refer to the initial cash outlay that must be made in the beginning (the purchase price). When gathering data to estimate the cash flows over the life of a project, it is imperative to obtain reliable estimates of the savings and expenses associated with the project.

The principal objective of capital budgeting is to maximize the value of the firm. It is designed to answer two basic questions:

1. Which of several mutually exclusive projects should be selected? (Mutually exclusive projects are alternative methods of doing the same job. If one method is chosen, the other methods will not be required.)

2. How many projects, in total, should be selected?[8]

The three most common methods used in capital budgeting are the payback method, the net present value (NPV) method, and the internal rate of return (IRR) method. Each has certain advantages and disadvantages. In this section, the same proposal will be used under each method to more clearly illustrate each technique.

Payback Method

One of the easiest capital-budgeting techniques to understand is the **payback method** or, as it is sometimes called, the payback period. In this method the length of time required to "pay back" the original investment is the determining criterion. The entrepreneur will select a maximum time frame for the payback period. Any project that requires a longer period will be rejected, and projects that fall into the time frame will be accepted. Here is an example of the payback method used by Wheatman's Market:

John Wheatman has a decision to make. He would like to purchase a new cash register for his store but is unsure which of two proposals to accept. Each machine costs $1,000. An analysis of the projected returns reveals the following information:

Year	Proposal A	Proposal B
1	$500	$100
2	400	200
3	300	300
4	20	400
5	10	500

After careful consideration, John decides to use the payback method with a cutoff period of 3 years. In this case he discovers that Proposal A would be paid back in 2⅓ years;

[8] Ibid., 403.

| TABLE 9.9 | | WHEATMAN'S MARKET: EXPECTED RETURN WORKSHEET | | | |

Proposal A

Year	X	(1 − T) (T = .40)	X(1 + T)	Depreciation	X(1 − T) + Depreciation
1	$ 500	$0.60	$ 300	$200	$500
2	333	0.60	200	200	400
3	167	0.60	100	200	300
4	−300	0.60	−180	200	20
5	−317	0.60	−190	200	10

Proposal B

Year	X	(1 − T) (T = .40)	X(1 − T)	Depreciation	X(1 − T) + Depreciation
1	$−167	$0.60	$−100	$200	$100
2	0	0.60	0	200	200
3	167	0.60	100	200	300
4	333	0.60	200	200	400
5	500	0.60	300	200	500

X = Anticipated change in net income

T = Applicable tax rate (.40)

Depreciation = Depreciation (computed on a straight-line basis) 1 Cost/Life = 1,000/5

$900 of the original investment will be paid back in the first 2 years and the last $100 in the third year. Proposal B, on the other hand, will require 4 years for its payback. Using this criterion John chooses Proposal A and rejects Proposal B.

One of the problems with the payback method is that it ignores cash flows beyond the payback period. Thus, it is possible for the wrong decision to be made. Nevertheless, many companies, particularly entrepreneurial firms, continue to use this method for several reasons: (1) It is very simple to use in comparison to other methods, (2) projects with a faster payback period normally have more favorable short-term effects on earnings, and (3) if a firm is short on cash, it may prefer to use the payback method because it provides a faster return of funds.

Net Present Value

The **net present value (NPV) method** is a technique that helps to minimize some of the shortcomings of the payback method by recognizing the future cash flows beyond the payback period. The concept works on the premise that a dollar today is worth more than a dollar in the future. How much more depends on the applicable cost of capital for the firm. The cost of capital is the rate used to adjust future cash flows to determine their value in present period terms. This procedure is referred to as discounting the future cash flows, and the discounted cash value is determined by the present value of the cash flow.

To use this approach, the entrepreneur must find the present value of the expected net cash flows of the investment, discounted at the appropriate cost of capital, and subtract from it the initial cost outlay of the project. The result is the net present value of the proposed project. Many financial accounting and finance textbooks have tables (called present value tables) that list the appropriate discount factors to multiply by the future cash flow to determine the present value. In addition, financial calculators are available that will compute the cash flow given the cost of capital, future cash flow, and the year of the cash flow. Finally, given the appropriate data, electronic spreadsheet programs can be programmed to determine the present value. After the net present value has been calculated for all of the proposals, the entrepreneur can select the project with the highest net present value. Here is an example of the NPV method used by Wheatman's Market:

Not really satisfied with the results he has obtained from the payback method, John Wheatman has decided to use the NPV method to see what result it would produce. After conferring with his accountant, John learned that the cost of capital for his firm is 10 percent. He then prepared the following tables:

Proposal A

Year	Cash Flow	Discount Factor	Present Value
1	$500	0.9091	$ 454.55
2	400	0.8264	330.56
3	300	0.7513	225.39
4	20	0.6830	13.66
5	10	0.6209	6.21
			$1,030.37
Less: Initial outlay			−1,000.00
Net present value			$ 30.37

Proposal B

Year	Cash Flow	Discount Factor	Present Value
1	$100	0.9091	$ 90.91
2	200	0.8264	165.28
3	300	0.7513	225.39
4	400	0.6830	273.20
5	500	0.6209	310.45
			$1,065.23
Less: Initial outlay			−1,000.00
Net present value			$ 65.23

Since Proposal B has the higher net present value, John selected Proposal B and rejected Proposal A.

Internal Rate of Return

The **internal rate of return (IRR) method** is similar to the net present value method in that the future cash flows are discounted. However, they are discounted at a rate that makes the net present value of the project equal to zero. This rate is referred to as the internal rate of return of the project. The project with the highest internal rate of return is then selected. As it would seem, a project that would be selected under the NPV method also would be selected under the IRR method.

One of the major drawbacks to the use of the IRR method is the difficulty that can be encountered when using the technique. Under the NPV method, it is quite simple to look up the appropriate discount factors in the present value tables. When using the IRR concept, however, the entrepreneur must begin with a net present value of zero and work backward through the tables. What this means, essentially, is that the entrepreneur must estimate the approximate rate and eventually try to track the actual internal rate of return for the project. Although this may not seem too difficult for projects with even cash flows (that is, cash flows that are fairly equal over the business periods), projects with uneven cash flows (fluctuating periods of cash inflow and cash outflow) can be a nightmare. Unfortunately, reality dictates that most projects will probably have uneven cash flows. Fortunately, electronic calculators and spreadsheet programs are available that can determine the actual internal rate of return, given the cash flows, initial cash outlays, and the appropriate cash-flow periods. Here is an example of the IRR method used by Wheatman's Market:

Having obtained different results from the payback period and the NPV method, John Wheatman is confused about which alternative to select. To alleviate this confusion, he has decided to use the internal rate of return to evaluate the two proposals and has decided that the project with the higher IRR will be selected (after all, it would win two out of three times). Accordingly, he has prepared the following tables with the help of his calculator:

	Proposal A (11.83% IRR)		
Year	Cash Flow	Discount Factor	Present Value
1	$500	0.8942	$ 447.10
2	400	0.7996	319.84
3	300	0.7151	214.53
4	20	0.6394	12.80
5	10	0.5718	5.73
			$ 1,000.00
Less: Initial outlay			−1,000.00
Net present value			$ 0.00

Proposal B (12.01 IRR)

Year	Cash Flow	Discount Factor	Present Value
1	$100	0.8928	$ 89.27
2	200	0.7971	159.42
3	300	0.7117	213.51
4	400	0.6354	254.15
5	500	0.5673	283.65
			$1,000.00
Less: Initial outlay			−1,000.00
Net present value			$ 0.00

Proposal B is selected because it has the higher IRR. This conclusion supports the statement that the project with the higher NPV will also have the higher IRR.

The Wheatman's Market examples illustrate the use of all three capital-budgeting methods. Even though Proposal A was chosen by the first method (payback), under the other two methods (net present value and internal rate of return) Proposal B surfaced as the better proposal. It is important for entrepreneurs to understand all three methods and to use the one that best fits their needs. If payback had been John Wheatman's *only* consideration, then Proposal A would have been selected. When future cash flows beyond payback are to be considered, the NPV and the IRR are the methods to determine the best proposal.

The budgeting concepts discussed so far are extremely powerful planning tools. But how can entrepreneurs monitor their progress during the budget period? How can they use the information accumulated during the course of the business to help plan for future periods? Can this information be used for pricing decisions? The answer to the third question is yes, and the rest are answered in the following sections.

BREAK-EVEN ANALYSIS

In today's competitive marketplace, entrepreneurs need relevant, timely, and accurate information that will enable them to price competitively and yet be able to earn a fair profit. **Break-even analysis** supplies this information.

Break-Even Point Computation

Break-even analysis is a technique commonly used to assess expected product profitability. It helps determine how many units must be sold in order to break even at a particular selling price.

CONTRIBUTION MARGIN APPROACH   A common approach to break-even analysis is the **contribution margin approach.** Contribution margin is the difference between the selling price and the variable cost per unit. It is the amount per unit that is contributed to covering all other costs.[9] Since breakeven is the point at which income equals expenses, the contribution margin approach formula is this:

[9] Don R. Hansen and Maryanne M. Mowen, *Management Accounting,* 2d ed. (Cincinnati: Southwestern, 1992), 360–84.

$$0 = (SP - VC)S - FC \ \text{ or } \ FC = (SP - VC)S$$

where

SP = Unit selling price
VC = Variable costs per unit
S = Sales in units
FC = Fixed cost

This model also can be used for profit planning by including the desired profit as part of the fixed cost.

GRAPHIC APPROACH   Another approach to break-even analysis among entrepreneurial firms is the graphic approach. In order to use this approach, the entrepreneur needs to graph at least two numbers: total revenue and total costs. The intersection of these two lines (i.e., where total revenues are equal to the total costs) is the firm's break-even point. Two additional costs—variable costs and fixed costs—also may be plotted. Doing so enables the entrepreneur to visualize the various relationships in the firm's cost structure.

HANDLING QUESTIONABLE COSTS   Although the first two approaches are adequate for situations in which costs can be broken down into fixed and variable costs, some firms have expenses that are difficult to assign. For example, are repairs and maintenance expenses fixed or variable expenses? Can firms facing this type of problem use break-even analysis for profit planning? The answer is yes, thanks to a new technique designed specifically for entrepreneurial firms. This technique calculates break-even points under alternative assumptions of fixed or variable costs to see if a product's profitability is sensitive to cost behavior. The decision rules for this concept follow: If expected sales exceed the higher break-even point, then the product should be profitable, regardless of the other break-even point; if expected sales do not exceed the lower break-even point, then the product should be unprofitable; and only if expected sales are between the two break-even points is further investigation of the questionable cost's behavior needed.[10]

The concept works by substituting the cost in question *(QC)* first as a fixed cost and then as a variable cost. The break-even formulas presented earlier would have to be modified to determine the break-even levels under the two assumptions. Under the fixed-cost assumption, the entrepreneur would use the following equation:

$$0 = (SP - VC)S - FC - QC$$

To calculate the breakeven assuming *QC* is variable, the following equation would be used:

$$0 = [SP - VC - (QC/U)]S - FC$$

U is the number of units for which the questionable cost normally would be appropriate. What the entrepreneur is determining is the appropriate unit cost that should be used if the

---

[10] Kenneth P. Sinclair and James A. Talbott Jr., "Using Break-Even Analysis when Cost Behavior Is Unknown," *Management Accounting* (July 1986): 53.

CONTEMPORARY ENTREPRENEURSHIP

Going Public without a Product?

Traditionally, a company looking to go public to raise capital had to accomplish two things. First, the business would have to take its show on the road. Traveling from one location to another, owners/managers would present their company to potential investors, emphasizing the company's proven history with charts revealing increasingly profitable quarters. Second, the business had to have $4 million in assets and $2 million in net worth for an underwriter to even consider taking the business public. But today all that has changed. Private and institutional investors are looking for ways to increase their returns. Many of them are turning to companies that promise tremendous gains, regardless of whether they meet the old requirements of underwriters.

As a matter of fact, these investors are taking chances on companies that haven't even begun to collect revenues or, more surprising, do not even have a finished product yet! Audrey Contente is a prime example. Contente had spent millions of dollars to develop a new product that promised to revolutionize the femi-

nine hygiene market. The product, called Instead, is a new soft-plastic tampon that molds to each individual and can be worn twice as long as a regular tampon. Knowing it would take even more money, millions of dollars, to finish the development of her new product and distribute it nationwide, she decided to go public. She made 76 presentations in 22 days. She only had her management team, some testimonials from financial experts, and product samples to show potential investors. But in spite of having no final product and no revenues, Contente's company, Ultrafem Inc. of New York City, was able to raise $39 million.

Contente is only one example of how entrepreneurial companies are going public at earlier stages than ever before. In 1995, 575 companies sold $29 billion worth of new stock, and the 1996 figures are expected to surpass these. How long this investment frenzy will continue is unpredictable, so businesses still in the start-up mode are rushing to gain funding through the public market.

With investors looking for big returns, the types of businesses open to public of-

cost is a variable cost. Given next is an example of how an entrepreneur could use the technique:

Tim Goodman, president of Goodman Industries, a small manufacturer of round widgets, has decided to use break-even analysis as a profit-planning tool for his company. He believes using this technique will enable his firm to compete more effectively in the marketplace. From an analysis of the operating costs, Tim has determined that the variable cost per unit is $9, while fixed costs are estimated to be $1,200 per month. The anticipated selling price per unit is $15. He also has discovered he is unable to classify one cost as either variable or fixed. It is a $200 repair and maintenance expense allocation. This $200 is appropriate for an activity level of 400 units; therefore, if the cost were

ferings without revenues or profitability are limited. Investors look for hot categories where returns seem most promising. Early-stage public offerings first began in the late 1980s. The hot category then was biotech companies. These companies typically were powerful on applications and technology but lacked the funds to sustain them. Although these companies spent millions on research and development, investors were willing to bet on the possibility of the staggering returns these companies often produced. Today, some of the most promising fields include biotech, health care, and especially software and Internet companies. The software and Internet-related companies seem to have the most potential for early-stage public funding. In the first quarter of 1996, five Internet-related companies went public. Within one week of their public offerings, these companies' stocks averaged a trading price of 36 percent above their opening price.

One of these firms was founded by Bill Melton. He started his company, Cyber-Cash, Inc., in 1994 after he discovered a way to securely exchange money on the Internet. Melton developed a plan to conduct bank transactions electronically and software to provide security for cash, check, and credit-card services. Even though revenues are not expected until late 1997, the shares opened at a price of $17, and, 2.4 million shares later, the closing price for that first day was $28.25.

The types of businesses likely to go public are not the only changes in regard to public funding. Traditionally, underwriters are hired, usually at a fee of 10 percent of the offering, to facilitate the public offering. Today, companies are going public, without the expense of an underwriter, on the Internet. For companies requiring less than $5 million, the Internet can be a valuable source of funds. Spring Street Brewing Co. made headlines when it raised $1.6 million during its first offering on the Internet. Many others have followed suit although market pros warn businesses and investors to be cautious about Internet offerings.

As some of these riskier ventures begin to fail, the current frenzy for start-up investments may slow down, and some investors and underwriters may return to their more conservative practices. But right now the market is outstanding for entrepreneurs who can take advantage of its demand for companies with promising futures and big returns.

SOURCE: Gianna Jacobson, "Early-Stage IPOs," *Success*, August 1996, 15–20.

variable, it would be $.50 per unit ($200/400). Finally, sales are projected to be 400 units during the next budget period.

The first step in this process is to determine the break-even point assuming the cost in question is fixed. Consequently, Tim would use the following equation:

$$
\begin{aligned}
0 &= (SC - VC)S - FC - QC \\
&= (15 - 9)S - 1{,}200 - 200 \\
&= 6S - 1{,}400 \\
1{,}400 &= 6S \\
234 &= S
\end{aligned}
$$

FIGURE 9.2   **GOODMAN INDUSTRIES: FIXED-COST ASSUMPTION**

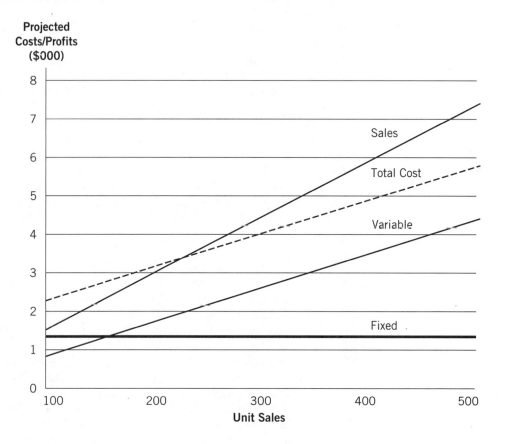

Figure 9.2 provides a graphic illustration. Notice that the final quantity was rounded up to the next unit, because business normally will not sell part of a unit.

The next step in the process is to calculate the break-even point assuming the cost in question is a variable cost. Tim would use the following equation to ascertain the second break-even point:

$$
\begin{aligned}
0 &= [SC - VC - (QC/U)]S - FC \\
  &= [15 - 9 - (200/400)]S - 1{,}200 \\
  &= (6 - .50)S - 1{,}200 \\
1{,}200 &= 5.50S \\
219 &= S
\end{aligned}
$$

Figure 9.3 presents a graphic illustration.

Now that the two possible break-even points have been established, Tim must compare these to his projected sales. These variable-cost sales of 400 units are greater than the larger break-even point of 234 units. Therefore, the product is assumed to be

FIGURE 9.3 GOODMAN INDUSTRIES: VARIABLE-COST ASSUMPTION

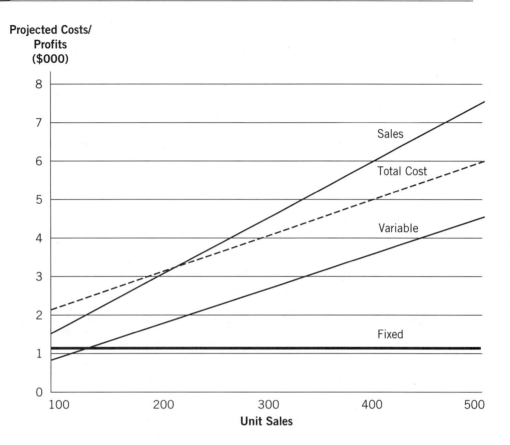

profitable regardless of the cost behavior of the repair and maintenance expense. It does not matter whether the cost is variable or fixed; the firm still will be profitable.

RATIO ANALYSIS

Financial statements report both on a firm's position at a point in time and on its operations over some past period. However, the real value of financial statements lies in the fact they can be used to help predict the firm's earnings and dividends. From an investor's standpoint, predicting the future is what financial statement analysis is all about; from an entrepreneur's standpoint, financial statement analysis is useful both as a way to anticipate conditions and, more important, as a starting point for planning actions that will influence the course of events.

An analysis of the firm's ratios is generally the key step in a financial analysis. The **ratios** are designed to show relationships among financial statement accounts. For example, Firm A might have a debt of $6,250,000 and interest charges of $520,000, while Firm B might have a debt of $62,800,000 and interest charges of $5,840,000. Which company is stronger? The true burden of these debts, and the companies' ability to repay them, can be ascertained (1) by comparing each firm's debt to its assets and (2) by comparing the

TABLE 9.10		FINANCIAL RATIOS	
Ratio	**Formula**	**What It Measures**	**What It Tells You**
Owners			
Return on investment (ROI)	$\dfrac{\text{Net income}}{\text{Average Owner's Equity}}$	Return on owner's capital; when compared with return on assets, it measures the extent financial leverage is being used for or against the owner.	How well is this company doing as an investment?
Return on assets (ROA)	$\dfrac{\text{Net Income}}{\text{Average Total Assets}}$	How well assets have been employed by management	How well has management employed company assets? Does it pay to borrow?
Managers			
Net profit margin	$\dfrac{\text{Net Income}}{\text{Sales}}$	Operating efficiency; the ability to create sufficient profits from operating activities	Are profits high enough, given the level of sales?
Asset turnover	$\dfrac{\text{Sales}}{\text{Average Total Assets}}$	Relative efficiency in using total resources to produce output	How well are assets being used to generate sales revenue?
Return on assets	$\dfrac{\text{Net Income}}{\text{Sales}} \times \dfrac{\text{Sales}}{\text{Total Assets}}$	Earning power on all assets; ROA ratio broken into its logical parts; turnover and margin	How well has management employed company assets?
Average collection period	$\dfrac{\text{Average Accounts Receivable}}{\text{Annual Credit Sales}} \times 365$	Liquidity of receivables in terms of average number of days receivables are outstanding	Are receivables coming in too slowly?
Inventory turnover	$\dfrac{\text{Cost of Goods Sold Expense}}{\text{Average Inventory}}$	Liquidity of inventory; the number of times it turns over per year	Is too much cash tied up in inventories?
Average age of payables	$\dfrac{\text{Average Accounts Payable}}{\text{Net Purchases}} \times 365$	Approximate length of time a firm takes to pay its bills for trade purchases	How quickly does a prospective customer pay its bills?

interest each must pay to the income it has available for interest payment. Such comparisons are made by ratio analysis.[11]

Table 9.10 has been prepared as an entrepreneur's guide to understanding the various ratios. Note that this outline presents the ratio's importance to owners, managers, and creditors. More important than the simple calculation of formulas are the categories that explain what each ratio *measures* and what each ratio *tells* an entrepreneur.

Ratio analysis can be applied from two directions. **Vertical analysis** is the application of ratio analysis to one set of financial statements. Here, an analysis "up and down" the statements is done to find signs of strengths and weaknesses. **Horizontal analysis** looks at financial statements and ratios over time. In horizontal analysis, the trends are critical: Are

[11] See Eugene F. Brigham, *Fundamentals of Financial Management,* 6th ed. (Fort Worth: The Dryden Press), 1992.

TABLE 9.10		FINANCIAL RATIOS *(continued)*	
Ratio	**Formula**	**What It Measures**	**What It Tells You**
Short-Term Creditors			
Working capital	Current Assets − Current Liabilities	Short-term debt-paying ability	Does this customer have sufficient cash or other liquid assets to cover its short-term obligations?
Current ratio	$\dfrac{\text{Current Assets}}{\text{Current Liabilities}}$	Short-term debt-paying ability without regard to the liquidity of current assets	Does this customer have sufficient cash or other liquid assets to cover its short-term obligations?
Quick ratio	$\dfrac{\text{Cash} + \text{Marketable Securities} + \text{Accounts Receivable}}{\text{Current Liabilities}}$	Short-term debt-paying ability without having to rely on inventory sales	Does this customer have sufficient cash or other liquid assets to cover its short-term obligations?
Long-Term Creditors			
Debt-to-equity ratio	$\dfrac{\text{Total Debt}}{\text{Total Equity}}$	Amount of assets creditors provide for each dollar of assets owner(s) provide	Is the company's debt load excessive?
Times interest earned	$\dfrac{\text{Net Income} + (\text{Interest} + \text{Taxes})}{\text{Interest Expense}}$	Ability to pay fixed charges for interest from operating profits	Are earnings and cash flows sufficient to cover interest payments and some principal repayments?
Cash flow to liabilities	$\dfrac{\text{Operating Cash Flow}}{\text{Total Liabilities}}$	Total debt coverage; general debt-paying ability	Are earnings and cash flows sufficient to cover interest payments and some principal repayments?

SOURCE: Kenneth M. Macur and Lyal Gustafson, "Financial Statements as a Management Tool," *Small Business Forum* (fall 1992): 24.

the numbers increasing or decreasing? Are particular components of the company's financial position getting better or worse?[12]

DECISION SUPPORT SYSTEMS

For most entrepreneurial firms, financial analysis is of critical importance. One technique a firm can use to manage its financial resources is a **decision support system (DSS).** Computer-based DSS tools add a new dimension to the analysis of pro forma financial

[12] Kenneth M. Macur and Lyal Gustafson, "Financial Statements as a Management Tool," *Small Business Forum* (fall 1992): 23–34.

ENTREPRENEURIAL

EDGE

Ratio Name	How to Calculate	What It Means in Dollars and Cents
Balance Sheet Ratios		
Current	$\dfrac{\text{Current Assets}}{\text{Current Liabilities}}$	Measures solvency: the number of dollars in current assets for every $1 in current liabilities *Example:* A current ratio of 1.76 means that for every $1 of current liabilities, the firm has $1.76 in current assets with which to pay it.
Quick	$\dfrac{\text{Cash + Accounts Receivable}}{\text{Current Liabilities}}$	Measures liquidity: the number of dollars in cash and accounts receivable for each $1 in current liabilities *Example:* A quick ratio of 1.14 means that for every $1 of current liabilities, the firm has $1.14 in cash and accounts receivable with which to pay it.
Cash	$\dfrac{\text{Cash}}{\text{Current Liabilities}}$	Measures liquidity more strictly: the number of dollars in cash for every $1 in current liabilities *Example:* A cash ratio of 0.17 means that for every $1 of current liabilities, the firm has $0.17 in cash with which to pay it.
Debt-to-worth	$\dfrac{\text{Total Liabilities}}{\text{Net Worth}}$	Measures financial risk: the number of dollars of debt owed for every $1 in net worth *Example:* A debt-to-worth ratio of 1.05 means that for every $1 of net worth the owners have invested, the firms owes $1.05 of debt to its creditors.
Income Statement Ratios		
Gross margin	$\dfrac{\text{Gross Margin}}{\text{Sales}}$	Measures profitability at the gross profit level: the number of dollars of gross margin produced for every $1 of sales *Example:* A gross margin ratio of 34.4% means that for every $1 of sales, the firm produces 34.4 cents of gross margin.
Net margin	$\dfrac{\text{Net Profit before Tax}}{\text{Sales}}$	Measures profitability at the net profit level: the number of dollars of net profit produced for every $1 of sales *Example:* A net margin ratio of 2.9% means that for every $1 of sales, the firm produces 2.9 cents of net margin.

Ratio Name	How to Calculate	What It Means in Dollars and Cents
Overall Efficiency Ratios		
Sales-to-assets	$\dfrac{\text{Sales}}{\text{Total Assets}}$	Measures the efficiency of total assets in generating sales: the number of dollars in sales produced for every $1 invested in total assets *Example:* A sales-to-assets ratio of 2.35 means that for very $1 dollar invested in total assets, the firm generates $2.35 in sales.
Return on assets	$\dfrac{\text{Net Profit before Tax}}{\text{Total Assets}}$	Measures the efficiency of total assets in generating net profit: the number of dollars in net profit produced for every $1 invested in total assets *Example:* A return on assets ratio of 7.1% means that for every $1 invested in assets, the firm is generating 7.1 cents in net profit before tax.
Return on investment	$\dfrac{\text{Net Profit before tax}}{\text{Net Worth}}$	Measures the efficiency of net worth in generating net profit: the number of dollars in net profit produced for every $1 invested in net worth *Example:* A return on investment ratio of 16.1% means that for every $1 invested in net worth, the firm is generating 16.1 cents in net profit before tax.
Specific Efficiency Ratios		
Inventory turnover	$\dfrac{\text{Cost of Goods Sold}}{\text{Inventory}}$	Measures the rate at which inventory is being used on an annual basis *Example:* An inventory turnover ratio of 9.81 means that the average dollar volume of inventory is used up almost ten times during the fiscal year.
Inventory turn-days	$\dfrac{360}{\text{Inventory Turnover}}$	Converts the inventory turnover ratio into an average "days inventory on hand" figure *Example:* An inventory turn-days ratio of 37 means that the firm keeps an average of 37 days of inventory on hand throughout the year.
Accounts receivable turnover	$\dfrac{\text{Sales}}{\text{Accounts Receivable}}$	Measures the rate at which accounts receivable are being collected on an annual basis *Example:* An accounts receivable turnover ratio of 8.00 means that the average dollar volume of accounts receivable are collected eight times during the year.
Average collection period	$\dfrac{360}{\text{Accounts Receivable Turnover}}$	Converts the accounts receivable turnover ratio into the average number of days the firm must wait for its accounts receivable to be paid *Example:* An average collection period ratio of 45 means that it takes the firm 45 days on average to collect its receivables.

CONTINUED

Ratio Name	How to Calculate	What It Means in Dollars and Cents
Accounts payable turnover	$\dfrac{\text{Cost of Goods Sold}}{\text{Accounts Payable}}$	Measures the rate at which accounts payable are being paid on an annual basis *Example:* An accounts payable turnover ratio of 12.04 means that the average dollar volume of accounts payable are paid about 12 times during the year.
Average payment period	$\dfrac{360}{\text{Accounts Payable Turnover}}$	Converts the accounts payable turnover ratio into the average number of days a firm takes to pay its accounts payable *Example:* An accounts payable turnover ratio of 30 means that it takes the firm 30 days on average to pay its bills.

statements and break-even points.[13] Management information that has previously been beyond the reach of the entrepreneur now can be readily synthesized to aid in evaluating the effects of various conditions on, for example, a business cash lifeline or comparing alternative investments.

A DSS can facilitate the financial planning process through the use of integrated pro forma financial statements and the generation of alternatives that can be quickly explored. This technique allows the entrepreneur to specify the desired minimum cash balance and determine the minimum level of sales to meet this requirement for all periods of the business plan or for the budget period. In addition, net income can be calculated at various points to see how it compares with the targeted profits. If a conflict does exist between the targeted net income and the generated minimum cash-balance profits, the manager can easily rerun the model, modifying some of the variables, such as borrowings, sales, and expenses. Finally, the entrepreneur can use the DSS to perform a sensitivity analysis for other levels of sales and expenses. Armed with this information, the individual can formulate a plan of action based on a more complete view of the financial characteristics and interactions of the business.[14]

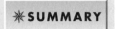

✳ SUMMARY

Three principal financial statements are important to entrepreneurs: the income statement, the balance sheet, and the cash-flow statement. The budgeting process facilitates financial statement preparation. Some key budgets entrepreneurs should prepare are the operating

[13] Roger L. Hayen, "Applying Decision Support Systems to Small Business Financial Planning," *Journal of Small Business Management* (July 1982): 35; see also Frederic J. Herbert and John H. Bradley, "Expert Systems Development in Small Business: A Managerial Perspective," *Journal of Small Business Management* (July 1993:) 23–34.

[14] Hayen, "Applying Decision Support Systems," 36.

budget, the cash-flow budget, and the capital budget. The operating budget typically begins with a sales forecast, followed by an estimation of operating expenses. A cash-flow budget provides an overview of the inflows and outflows of cash during a specific period. Pro forma financial statements then are prepared as projections of the firm's financial position over a future period (pro forma income statement) or on a future date (pro forma balance sheet). The operating and cash-flow budgets often are used to prepare these pro forma statements. The capital budget is used to help entrepreneurs make investment decisions. The three most common methods of capital budgeting are the payback period, the net present value method, and the internal rate of return method.

Another commonly used decision-making tool is break-even analysis, which tells how many units must be sold in order to break even at a particular selling price. It is possible to use this analysis even when fixed or variable costs only can be estimated. Ratio analysis was discussed as an analytical tool for entrepreneurs. Ratios are designed to show relationships between financial statement accounts.

The last part of the chapter examined decision support systems. Computer-based DSS tools are adding a new dimension to the analysis of pro forma financial statements and break-even points and are helping entrepreneurs deal more effectively with financial decision making.

Key Terms and Concepts

Break-even analysis	Mixed costs
Budget	Net present value (NPV) method
Capital budgeting	Operating budget
Cash-flow budget	Payback method
Contribution margin approach	Pro forma statements
Decision support system (DSS)	Ratios
Expenses	Sales forecast
Fixed cost	Simple linear regression
Horizontal analysis	Variable cost
Internal rate of return (IRR) method	Vertical analysis

Review and Discussion Questions

1. What is the importance of financial information for entrepreneurs? Briefly describe the key components.
2. What are the benefits of the budgeting process?
3. How is the statistical forecasting technique of simple linear regression used in making a sales forecast?
4. Describe how an operating budget is constructed.
5. Describe how a cash-flow budget is constructed.
6. What are pro forma statements? How are they constructed? Be complete in your answer.
7. Describe how a capital budget is constructed.
8. One of the most popular capital-budgeting techniques is the payback method. How does this method work? Give an example.
9. Describe the net present value method. When would an entrepreneur use this method? Why?

10. Describe the internal rate of return method. When would an entrepreneur use this method? Why?
11. When would an entrepreneur be interested in break-even analysis?
12. If an entrepreneur wants to use break-even analysis but has trouble assigning some costs as either fixed or variable, can break-even analysis still be used? Explain.
13. What is ratio analysis? How is horizontal analysis different from vertical analysis?
14. What is a decision support system? How can it be of value in helping entrepreneurs manage their financial resources?

Experiential Exercise   *The Project Proposal*

Bill Sergent has just received a request for proposal (RFP) from a large computer firm. The firm is looking for a supplier to provide it with high-tech components for a supercomputer being built for the Department of Defense. Bill's firm, which is only eight months old, was founded by a group of scientists and engineers whose primary expertise is in the area of computers and high technology. Bill is thinking about making a reply to the RFP, but first he wants to conduct a break-even analysis to determine how profitable the venture will be. Here is the information he will be using in his analysis:

- The computer firm wants 12 different components built, and the purchase price will be $10,000 per component.
- The total cost of building the first component will be $20,000.
- The cost of building each of the 11 other components will be $8,000, $6,000, $5,000, $4,000, $5,000, $6,000, $8,000, $10,000, $28,000, $40,000, and $40,000, respectively.
- Bill's company will not accept any proposal that will give it less than a 10 percent return on sales.

On the basis of this information, complete the following break-even chart, and then answer the two questions.

Revenues ($000)

```
$150 _____
 140 _____
 130 _____
 120 _____
 110 _____
 100 _____
  90 _____
  80 _____
  70 _____
  60 _____
  50 _____
  40 _____
  30 _____
  20 _____
  10 _____
       1    2    3    4    5    6    7    8    9   10   11   12
                                                        Units
```

1. Should Bill bid on the contract? Why or why not? _____

_____

_____

2. If Bill has some room for negotiation with the computer firm, what would you recommend he do? Why? _____

_____

_____

 **CASE** **9.1**

It's All Greek to Her

When Regina McDermott opened her auto repair shop, she thought her 15 years of experience with cars was all she would need. To a degree she was right. Within six months her shop had more work than it could handle, thanks to her widening reputation. At the same time, however, Regina has found it necessary to spend more and more time dealing with financial planning.

Three weeks ago her accountant came by to see her to discuss a number of finance-related matters. One of these is the need for cash budgeting. "I can work up a cash budget for you," he explained. "However, I think you should understand what I'm doing so you will realize the importance of the cash budget and be able to visualize your cash inflows and outflows. I think you also need to make a decision regarding the new equipment you are planning to purchase. This machinery is state of the art, but, as we discussed last week, you can buy a number of different types of machinery. You are going to have to decide which is the best choice."

Regina explained to her accountant that she was indifferent about which equipment to buy. "All of this machinery is good. Perhaps I should purchase the cheapest." At this point the accountant explained to her that she could use a number of ways to evaluate this type of decision. "You can base your choice on the payback method—how long it takes to recover your investment in each of these pieces of equipment. You can base it on net present value by discounting future cash flows to the present. Or you can base it on internal rate of return, under which the cash flows are discounted at a rate that makes the net present value of the project equal to zero."

Regina listened quietly and when the accountant was finished, she told him, "Let me think about the various ways of evaluating my capital investment and I'll get back to you. Then, perhaps, you and I can work out the numbers together." Her accountant said this sounded fine to him and he left. Regina began to wish she had taken more accounting courses while in college. As she explained to her husband, "When the accountant begins to talk, it's all Greek to me."

Questions
1. What is the purpose of a cash-flow budget? What does it reveal? Of what value would it be to Regina?
2. How does the payback method work? How does the net present value method work? How would you explain each of these methods to Regina?
3. How does the internal rate of return method work? How would you explain it to Regina?

 **CASE 9.2**

The Contract Proposal

Dennis Darby owns a small manufacturing firm that produces electronic components for use in helicopters. Most of his business is a result of military and aircraft manufacturer contracts, although 10 percent of revenues come from firms that own or rent helicopters. The latter are typically large *Fortune* 500 companies or leasing/rental firms that work on a contractual basis for clients.

Dennis would like to increase his revenues from sales to private corporations that own their own helicopters. Specifically, he would like to do more business with oil companies that maintain helicopter fleets for ferrying people to and from oil rigs in the Gulf of Mexico and other offshore locations. Early this week Dennis received a request from an oil company for 120 electronic components. He turned the order over to his chief estimator, who estimates that the fixed costs associated with producing these components will be $35,000, the unit variable cost will be $400, and the unit selling price will be $800.

Dennis will not accept any order on which return on sales is less than 20 percent. Additionally, the estimator has told him that a $1,000 expense can be classified as either fixed or variable. Dennis intends to take this information and make a decision whether or not to accept the contract from the oil company. He has to make a decision within the next three days.

Questions

1. What is the break-even point for this project? Will the company make money if it manufactures the components? Show your calculations.
2. If the project will be profitable, will it provide Dennis the desired 20 percent? Explain.
3. Of what value is break-even analysis to Dennis? Be complete in your answer.

Chapter 10

DEVELOPING AN EFFECTIVE BUSINESS PLAN

CHAPTER OBJECTIVES

1. To examine the critical factors that should be addressed in planning

2. To explore the planning pitfalls that plague many new ventures

3. To outline the importance of a business plan and describe the benefits derived from it

4. To set forth the viewpoints of those who read a business plan and illustrate the six steps followed in the reading process

5. To emphasize the importance of coordinating the business plan segments

6. To review key recommendations by venture-capital experts for the development of a plan

7. To present a complete outline of an effective business plan and a discussion of each segment

8. To present some helpful hints for writing an effective business plan

9. To highlight points to remember in the presentation of a business plan

It is well established that you can't raise money without a business plan. . . . a business plan is a work of art in its own right. It's the document that personifies and expresses your company. Each plan, like every snowflake, must be different. Each is a separate piece of art. Each must be reflective of the individuality of the entrepreneur. Just as you wouldn't copy someone else's romancing techniques, so should you seek to distinguish your plan for its differences.

Joseph R. Mancuso,
How to Write a Winning Business Plan

Planning is essential to the success of any undertaking. Planning entails the formulation of goals and directions for the future of a venture.[1] A number of critical factors must be addressed when planning:

1. *Realistic goals.* These must be specific, measurable, and set within time parameters.

2. *Commitment.* The venture must be supported by all involved—family, partners, employees, team members.

3. *Milestones.* Subgoals must be set for continual and timely evaluation of progress.

4. *Flexibility.* Obstacles must be anticipated, and alternative strategies must be formulated.

The comprehensive business plan, which should be the result of meetings and reflections on the direction of the new venture, is the major tool for determining the essential operation of a venture. It also is the primary document for managing the venture. One of the major benefits of this plan is that it helps the enterprise avoid common pitfalls that often undo all previous efforts. The following section describes these pitfalls.

PITFALLS TO AVOID IN PLANNING

A number of pitfalls in the business plan process should be avoided. The five pitfalls presented in this section represent the most common errors committed by entrepreneurs. To make these danger areas more easily recognizable, certain indicators or warning signs

---

[1] See Douglas W. Naffziger and Donald F. Kuratko, "An Investigation into the Prevalence of Planning in Small Business," *Journal of Business and Entrepreneurship* (fall 1991): 99–110.

are presented. Each pitfall then has a possible solution introduced that will help entrepreneurs avoid the particular trap that limits a new venture's opportunity to succeed.

PITFALL 1: NO REALISTIC GOALS   Although this pitfall may sound self-explanatory, these particular indicators demonstrate how common and disguised it can be: lack of any attainable goals, lack of a time frame to accomplish things, lack of priorities, and lack of action steps.

One way to avoid this pitfall is to set up a timetable with specific steps to be accomplished during a specific period.

PITFALL 2: FAILURE TO ANTICIPATE ROADBLOCKS   One of the most common pitfalls occurs when the entrepreneur is so immersed in his or her idea that objectivity goes out the window. In other words, the person does not recognize the possible problems that may arise. Indicators are no recognition of future problems, no admission of possible flaws or weaknesses in the plan, and no contingency or alternative plans.

The best way to avoid this pitfall is to list (1) the possible obstacles that may arise and (2) the alternatives that state what might have to be done to overcome the obstacles.

PITFALL 3: NO COMMITMENT OR DEDICATION   Too many entrepreneurs appear to lack real commitment to their ventures. Although ventures may have started from a hobby or part-time endeavor, entrepreneurs must be careful to avoid the impression they do not take their ventures seriously. Indicators are excessive procrastination, missed appointments, no desire to invest personal money, and appearance of making a "fast buck" from a hobby or a "whim."

The easiest way to avoid this pitfall is to act quickly and to be sure to follow up all professional appointments. Also, be ready and willing to demonstrate a financial commitment to the venture.

PITFALL 4: LACK OF DEMONSTRATED EXPERIENCE (BUSINESS OR TECHNICAL)
Since many investors weigh very heavily the entrepreneur's actual experience in a venture, it is important entrepreneurs demonstrate what background they possess. Because too many beginners attempt to promote ideas they really have no true knowledge of, they are doomed to fail simply because they are perceived as ignorant of the specifics in the proposed business. Indicators are no experience in business, no experience in the specific area of the venture, lack of understanding of the industry in which the venture fits, and failure to convey a clear picture of how and why the venture will work and who will accept it.

To avoid this pitfall, entrepreneurs need to give evidence of personal experience and background for this venture. If they lack specific knowledge or skills, they should obtain assistance from those who possess this knowledge or these skills. Demonstrating a team concept about those who will be helping out also may be useful.

PITFALL 5: NO MARKET NICHE (SEGMENT)   Many entrepreneurs propose an idea without establishing who the potential customers will be. Just because the entrepreneur likes the product or service does not mean others will buy it. Numerous inventions at the U.S. Patent Office never reached the marketplace because no customers were targeted to buy them—no market was ever established. Indicators are uncertainty about who will buy the basic idea(s) behind the venture, no proof of a need or desire for the good or product proposed, and assumption that customers or clients will purchase just because the entrepreneur thinks so.

ENTREPRENEURIAL

EDGE

Low-Cost Ideas, Strategies, and Research

Business Plan

- Get in touch with the Small Business Administration: 800-827-5722; FAX, 800-697-4636; Web site, http://www.sbaonline.sba.gov.
- Get the number for the local SBA, Small Business Development Center, and other relevant state agencies.
- Get a copy of *Small Business Success*. Published by Pacific Bell and the SBA, it is available for free at 800-848-8000.
- Use local resources such as colleges and universities to write a thorough business plan.
- Access The Ed Lowe Small Business Network at http://lowe.org., or access other small-business bulletin boards.
- Find appropriate discussion groups on-line: Compuserve, Working From Home or Entrepreneur forums; America Online, Small Business Center.
- Use Yahoo's Business Resources to narrow the on-line search.

Equipment

- Look for serviceable office components at home.
- Contact local office buildings that may change tenants periodically, leaving unwanted equipment, furniture, and so forth.
- Attend auctions and tag sales, which are often advertised in the classifieds.

- Get the *Ergonomics and Office Design Workbook* (800-344-2600) and *Lighting in the Healthy Office* (800-777-0330) so health is not sacrificed for an inexpensive office.

Advertising

- Request media kits from local newspapers and radio and television stations.
- Consider leafleting as an effective, low-cost advertising option (most effective when you know where most of the customers are coming from).
- Consider advertising in magazines. Remnant ads can be inexpensive.
- Visit http://www.garlic.com/rfwilson/web-mrkt.htm to create a Web site for under $1,000.
- Phone messages should say something about the business or tell about a new product or special price.
- Visit http://www.missouri.edu/internet-advertising-guide.html for information on advertising on the Internet.

Sales and Marketing

- Use do-it-yourself market research whenever possible (talk with businesspeople, and interact with potential customers).
- Give customers a chance to provide feedback (surveys, comment cards, etc.).

- Team up with related, noncompeting businesses for joint marketing.
- Ask existing customers for verbal or written referrals.
- Find marketing answers and information on American Online or CompuServe, including http://www.gmarketing.com.
- Call the National Marketing Federation (800-2-SOLVE-IT) for answers to marketing questions.
- Visit the Web Digest for Marketers at http://www.advert.com/webdigest/wdfm2.4html for Web site ideas.
- Request a free subscription to *@issue,* a free quarterly newsletter to help design sales and marketing materials. Fax a subscription request to 617-451-6355.

Finances

- To find out what type of money is available through SBA, contact the National Business Association (NBA; 800-456-0440) for a free copy of *First Step Review.*
- For private investors, visit http://www.texel.com and Venture Connect, a Web site that links investors and entrepreneurs looking for cash, or run an ad in the Business Opportunity section of the local newspaper.
- Explore the state's economic development programs by contacting the nearest Small Business Development Center (for the local number call 703-448-6124).
- Use credit cards creatively to manage expenses (e.g., low-interest introductions).
- Institute a system to flag unpaid invoices to improve collection or receivables.

Supplies

- Ask for better terms from suppliers.
- Barter.
- Use buying alliances to lower costs.
- Ask vendors for free samples of products.
- Contact Avery (800-252-8379) and Post-it Products (fax, 612-633-7092).

Communications

- Do your own public relations (offer to write an article for a newspaper, or teach a free class).
- Use E-mail aggressively.
- Send mail early in the day.
- Ask for a phone number that translates into letters that correspond to the business.
- Get 800 numbers for all vendors.
- Send faxes after 5 P.M.
- Talk to the nearest Postal Business Center for information on rate discounts.

Staff

- Consider student interns.
- Don't overlook family for help.
- Pay only commission to sales help.
- Provide inexpensive employee training by giving staff free introductory members to on-line services, and direct them to appropriate forums.

SOURCE: Stephen J. Simurda, *Small Business Computing,* "Launching or Growing Your Business on a ShoeString," (April 1996): 59–63

The best possible way to avoid this pitfall is to have a market segment specifically targeted and to demonstrate why and how the specific product or service will meet the needs or desires of this target group. (More specific information on market research was developed in Chapter 8.)

The five pitfalls detailed here represent the most common points of failure entrepreneurs experience *before* their business plan ever gets reviewed. In other words, these critical areas must be carefully addressed before developing a business plan. If these pitfalls can be avoided, then the entire business plan will be written more carefully and thus will be reviewed more thoroughly. This preparation helps entrepreneurs establish a solid foundation on which to develop an effective business plan.

WHAT IS A BUSINESS PLAN?

A **business plan** is the written document that details the proposed venture. It must illustrate current status, expected needs, and projected results of the new business.[2] Every aspect of the venture needs to be described: the project, marketing, research and development, manufacturing, management, critical risks, financing, and milestones or a timetable. A description of all of these facets of the proposed venture is necessary to demonstrate a clear picture of what that venture is, where it is projected to go, and how the entrepreneur proposes it will get there. The business plan is the entrepreneur's road map for a successful enterprise.[3]

In some professional areas the business plan is referred to as a venture plan, a loan proposal, or an investment prospectus. Whatever the name, the business plan is the minimum document required by any financial source. The business plan allows the entrepreneur entrance into the investment process. Although it should be used as a working document once the venture is established, the major thrust of the business plan is to encapsulate the strategic development of the project in a comprehensive document for outside investors to read and understand.

The business plan describes to investors and financial sources all of the events that may affect the proposed venture. Details are needed for various projected actions of the venture, with associated revenues and costs outlined. It is vital the assumptions on which the plan is based are explicitly stated. For example, increases/decreases in the market or upswings/downswings in the economy during the start-up period of the new venture should be stated.

The emphasis of the business plan always should be the final implementation of the venture. In other words, it's not just the writing of an effective plan that is important but also the translation of that plan into a successful enterprise.[4]

BENEFITS OF A BUSINESS PLAN

The entire business planning process forces the entrepreneur to analyze all aspects of the venture and to prepare an effective strategy to deal with the uncertainties that arise. Thus a business plan may help an entrepreneur avoid a project doomed to failure. As one researcher states, "If your proposed venture is marginal at best, the business plan will show

---

[2] Fred L. Fry and Charles R. Stoner, "Business Plans: Two Major Types," *Journal of Small Business Management* (January 1985): 1–6.

[3] Donald F. Kuratko and Arnold Cirtin, "Developing a Business Plan for Your Clients," *National Public Accountant* (January 1990): 24–28.

[4] James W. Henderson, *Obtaining Venture Financing* (Lexington, MA: Lexington Books, 1988), 13–14.

you why and may help you avoid paying the high tuition of business failure. It is far cheaper not to begin an ill-fated business than to learn by experience what your business plan could have taught you at a cost of several hours of concentrated work."[5]

It is important entrepreneurs prepare their own business plan. If an entrepreneurial team is involved, then all of the key members should be part of writing the plan; in this case it is important the lead entrepreneur understand the contribution of each team member. If consultants are sought to help prepare a business plan, the entrepreneur must remain the driving force behind the plan. Seeking the advice and assistance of outside professionals is always wise, but entrepreneurs need to understand every aspect of the business plan, since it is they who come under the scrutiny of financial sources. Thus the business plan stands as the entrepreneur's description and prediction for his or her venture, and it must be defended by the entrepreneur—simply put, it is the entrepreneur's responsibility.[6]

Other benefits are derived from a business plan for both the entrepreneur and the financial sources that read it and evaluate the venture. Specifically for the entrepreneur, the following benefits are gained:

- The time, effort, research, and discipline needed to put together a formal business plan force the entrepreneur to view the venture critically and objectively.
- The competitive, economic, and financial analyses included in the business plan subject the entrepreneur to close scrutiny of his or her assumptions about the venture's success.
- Since all aspects of the business venture must be addressed in the plan, the entrepreneur develops and examines operating strategies and expected results for outside evaluators.
- The business plan quantifies objectives, providing measurable benchmarks for comparing forecasts with actual results.
- The completed business plan provides the entrepreneur with a communication tool for outside financial sources as well as an operational tool for guiding the venture toward success.[7]

The financial sources that read the plan derive the following benefits from the business plan:

- The business plan provides for financial sources the details of the market potential and plans for securing a share of that market.
- Through prospective financial statements, the business plan illustrates the venture's ability to service debt or provide an adequate return on equity.
- The plan identifies critical risks and crucial events with a discussion of contingency plans that provide opportunity for the venture's success.
- By providing a comprehensive overview of the entire operation, the business plan gives financial sources a clear, concise document that contains the necessary information for a thorough business and financial evaluation.
- For a financial source with no prior knowledge of the entrepreneur or the venture, the business plan provides a useful guide for assessing the individual entrepreneur's planning and managerial ability.[8]

[5] Joseph R. Mancuso, *How to Write a Winning Business Plan* (Englewood Cliffs: Prentice-Hall, 1985), 44.

[6] See Donald F. Kuratko, "Demystifying the Business Plan Process: An Introductory Guide," *Small Busines Forum* (winter 1990/1991): 33–40.

[7] Adapted from Henderson, *Obtaining Venture Financing,* 14–15; and Mancuso, *How to Write,* 43.

[8] Henderson, *Obtaining Venture Financing,* 15.

DEVELOPING A WELL-CONCEIVED BUSINESS PLAN

Most investors agree that only a well-conceived and well-developed business plan can gather the necessary support that will eventually lead to financing. The business plan must describe the new venture with excitement and yet with complete accuracy.

Who Reads the Plan?

It is important to understand the audience for whom the business plan is written. Although numerous professionals may be involved with reading the business plan, such as venture capitalists, bankers, investors, potential large customers, lawyers, consultants, and suppliers, entrepreneurs need to clearly understand three main viewpoints when preparing the plan.[9]

The first viewpoint is, of course, the entrepreneur's, since he or she is the one developing the venture and clearly has the most in-depth knowledge of the technology or creativity involved. This is the most common viewpoint in business plans and it is essential. However, too many plans emphasize this viewpoint and neglect the viewpoints of potential customers and investors.

More important than high technology or creative flair is the marketability of a new venture. Referred to as "market-driven," this type of enterprise convincingly demonstrates the benefits to users—the particular group of customers it is aiming for—and the existence of a substantial market. This viewpoint—that of the marketplace—is the second critical emphasis with which an entrepreneur must write a business plan. Yet although the actual value of this information is considered high, too many entrepreneurs tend to de-emphasize in-depth marketing information in their business plans.[10] Establishing an actual market (determining who will buy the product or use the service) and documenting that the anticipated percentage of this market is appropriate for the venture's success are valuable criteria for the business plan.

The third viewpoint is related to the marketing emphasis just discussed. The investor's point of view is concentrated on the financial forecast. Sound financial projections are necessary if investors are to evaluate the worth of their investment. This is not to say an entrepreneur should fill the business plan with spreadsheets of figures. In fact, many venture-capital firms employ a "projection discount factor," which merely represents the belief of venture capitalists that successful new ventures usually reach approximately 50 percent of their projected financial goals.[11] However, a three- to five-year financial projection is essential for investors to use in making their judgment of a venture's future success.

These three viewpoints have been presented in an order of decreasing significance to point out the emphasis needed in a well-conceived business plan. If they are addressed carefully in the plan, then the entrepreneur has prepared for what experts term the **five-minute reading.** The following six steps represent the typical business plan reading process many venture capitalists use (less than a minute is devoted to each step).

Step 1: Determine the characteristics of the venture and its industry.

---

[9] Stanley R. Rich and David E. Gumpert, "How to Write a Winning Business Plan," *Harvard Business Review* (May/June 1985): 156–66.

[10] Gerald E. Hills, "Market Analysis in the Business Plan: Venture Capitalists' Perceptions," *Journal of Small Business Management* (January 1985): 38–46.

[11] Rich and Gumpert, "How to Write," 159.

Step 2: Determine the financial structure of the plan (amount of debt or equity investment required).

Step 3: Read the latest balance sheet (to determine liquidity, net worth, and debt/equity).

Step 4: Determine the quality of entrepreneurs in the venture (sometimes *the* most important step).

Step 5: Establish the unique feature in this venture (find out what is different).

Step 6: Read the entire plan over lightly (this is when the entire package is paged through for a casual look at graphs, charts, exhibits, etc.).[12]

These steps provide insight into how the average business plan is read. It appears somewhat unjust that so much of the entrepreneur's effort is put into a plan that is given only a five-minute reading. However, that's the nature of the process for many venture capitalists. Other financial or professional sources may devote more time to analyzing the plan. But keep in mind that venture capitalists read through numerous business plans; thus, knowing the steps in their reading process is valuable for developing any plan. Related to this process of venture capitalists is a quote that links male entrepreneurs and venture capitalists: "The men who manage men manage men who manage things, *but* the men who manage money manage the men who manage men."[13]

Putting the Package Together

When presenting a business plan to potential investors, the entrepreneur must realize the entire package is important. Presented next is a summary of key issues that the entrepreneur needs to watch for if the plan is going to be viewed successfully.

A business plan gives financiers their first impressions of a company and its principals.

Potential investors expect the plan to look good, but not too good; to be the right length; to clearly and concisely explain early on all aspects of the company's business; and not to contain bad grammar and typographical or spelling errors.

Investors are looking for evidence that the principals treat their own property with care—and will likewise treat the investment carefully. In other words, form as well as content is important, and investors know that good form reflects good content and vice versa.

Among the format issues we think most important are the following:

Appearance: The binding and printing must not be sloppy; neither should the presentation be too lavish. A stapled compilation of photocopied pages usually looks amateurish, while bookbinding with typeset pages may arouse concern about excessive and inappropriate spending. A plastic spiral binding holding together a pair of cover sheets of a single color provides both a neat appearance and sufficient strength to withstand the handling of a number of people without damage.

Length: A business plan should be no more than 40 pages long. The first draft will likely exceed that, but editing should produce a final version that fits within the 40-page ideal. Adherence to this length forces entrepreneurs to sharpen their ideas and results in a document likely to hold investors' attention.

---

[12] Mancuso, *How to Write,* 52.

[13] Ibid., 65.

Background details can be included in an additional volume. Entrepreneurs can make this material available to investors during the investigative period after the initial expression of interest.

The cover and title page: The cover should bear the name of the company, its address and phone number, and the month and year in which the plan is issued. Surprisingly, a large number of business plans are submitted to potential investors without return addresses or phone numbers. An interested investor wants to be able to contact a company easily and to request further information or express an interest, either in the company or in some aspect of the plan.

Inside the front cover should be a well-designed title page on which the cover information is repeated and, in an upper or a lower corner, the legend "Copy number" provided. Besides helping entrepreneurs keep track of plans in circulation, holding down the number of copies outstanding—usually to no more than 20—has a psychological advantage. After all, no investor likes to think that the prospective investment is shopworn.

The executive summary: The two pages immediately following the title page should concisely explain the company's current status, its products or services, the benefits to customers, the financial forecasts, the venture's objectives in three to seven years, the amount of financing needed, and how investors will benefit.

This is a tall order for a two-page summary, but it will either sell investors on reading the rest of the plan or convince them to forget the whole thing.

The table of contents: After the executive summary, include a well-designed table of contents. List each of the business plan's sections and mark the pages for each section.[14]

An attractive appearance, an effective length, an executive summary, a table of contents, proper grammar, correct typing, and a cover page—all are important factors when putting together a complete package. These points many times separate successful plans from unacceptable ones.

Guidelines to Remember

The following points are a collection of recommendations by experts in venture capital and new-venture development.[15] These guidelines are presented as tips for successful business plan development. Entrepreneurs need to adhere to them in order to understand the importance of the various segments of a business plan they are creating, which will be discussed in the next section.

KEEP THE PLAN RESPECTABLY SHORT Readers of business plans are important people who refuse to waste time. Therefore entrepreneurs should explain the venture not only

---

[14] Reprinted by permission of the *Harvard Business Review.* An exhibit from "How to Write a Winning Business Plan," by Stanley R. Rich and David E. Gumpert, May/June 1985, 162. Copyright © 1985 by the President and Fellows of Harvard College; all rights reserved.

[15] These guidelines are adapted from Jeffry A. Timmons, "A Business Plan Is More than a Financing Device," *Harvard Business Review* (March/April 1980): 25–35; W. Keith Schilt, "How to Write a Winning Business Plan," *Business Horizons* (September/October 1987): 13–22; Donald F. Kuratko and Ray V. Montagno, *The Entrepreneur's Guide to Venture Formation* (Muncie, IN: Center for Entrepreneurial Resources, Ball State University, 1986), 33–34; and Donald F. Kuratko, Ray V. Montagno, and Frank J. Sabatine, *The Entrepreneurial Decision* (Muncie, IN: The Midwest Entrepreneurial Education Center, Ball State University, 1997), 40–50.

carefully and clearly but also concisely. (The plan should be no more than 50 pages long, excluding the appendix.)

ORGANIZE AND PACKAGE THE PLAN APPROPRIATELY   A table of contents, an executive summary, an appendix, exhibits, graphs, proper grammar, a logical arrangement of segments, and overall neatness are elements critical to the effective presentation of a business plan.

ORIENT THE PLAN TOWARD THE FUTURE   Entrepreneurs should attempt to create an air of excitement in the plan by developing trends and forecasts that describe what the venture *intends* to do and what the opportunities are for the use of the product or service.

AVOID EXAGGERATION   Sales potentials, revenue estimates, and the venture's potential growth should not be inflated. Many times a best-case, worst-case, and probable-case scenario should be developed for the plan. Documentation and research are vital to the plan's credibility.

HIGHLIGHT CRITICAL RISKS   The critical-risks segment of the business plan is important in that it demonstrates the entrepreneur's ability to analyze potential problems and develop alternative courses of action.

GIVE EVIDENCE OF AN EFFECTIVE ENTREPRENEURIAL TEAM   The management segment of the business plan should clearly identify the skills of each key person as well as demonstrate how all such persons can effectively work together as a team in managing the venture.

DO NOT OVERDIVERSIFY   Focus the attention of the plan on one main opportunity for the venture. A new business should not attempt to create multiple markets nor pursue multiple ventures until it has successfully developed one main strength.

IDENTIFY THE TARGET MARKET   Substantiate the marketability of the venture's product or service by identifying the particular customer niche being sought. This segment of the business plan is pivotal to the success of the other parts. Market research has to be included to demonstrate how this market segment has been identified.

KEEP THE PLAN WRITTEN IN THE THIRD PERSON   Rather than continually stating "I," "we," or "us," the entrepreneur should phrase everything as "he," "they," or "them." In other words, avoid personalizing the plan, and keep the writing objective.

CAPTURE THE READER'S INTEREST   Because of the numerous business plans submitted to investors and the small percentage of business plans funded, entrepreneurs need to capture the reader's interest right away by stating the uniqueness of the venture. Use the title page and executive summary as key tools for capturing the reader's attention and creating a desire to read more.

These guidelines are helpful for entrepreneurs preparing to write a business plan. The following section analyzes the ten major segments of a business plan.

ELEMENTS OF A BUSINESS PLAN

A detailed business plan usually has ten sections. The ideal length of a plan is 50 pages, although depending on the need for detail, the overall plan can range from 40 to more than 100 pages (including appendix).[16] Table 10.1 provides an outline of a typical plan. The remainder of this section describes the specific parts of the plan. A complete business plan for the Roaring '20s Museum appears as an Entrepreneurial Case Analysis at the end of this chapter.

Summary

Many people who read business plans (bankers, venture capitalists, investors) like to see a summary of the plan that features its most important parts. Such a summary gives a brief overview of what is to follow, helps put all of the information into perspective, and should be no longer than three pages. The summary should be written only after the entire business plan has been completed. In this way particular phrases or descriptions from each segment can be identified for inclusion in the summary. Since the summary is the first, and sometimes the only, part of a plan read, it must present the quality of the entire report. The summary must be a clever snapshot of the complete plan.

The statements selected for a summary segment should briefly touch on the venture itself, the market opportunities, the financial needs and projections, and any special research or technology associated with the venture. And this should be done in such a way that the evaluator or investor will choose to read on. If this information is not presented in a concise, competent manner, the reader may put aside the plan or simply conclude the project does not warrant funding.

Business Description

First, the name of the venture should be identified, with any special significance related (e.g., family name, technical name, etc.). Second, the industry background should be presented in terms of current status and future trends. It is important to note any special industry developments that may affect the plan. If the company has an existing business or franchise, this is the appropriate place to discuss it. Third, the new venture should be thoroughly described along with its proposed potential. All key terms should be defined and made comprehensible. Functional specifications or descriptions should be provided. Drawings and photographs also may be included.

Fourth, the potential advantages the new venture possesses over the competition should be discussed at length. This discussion may include patents, copyrights, and trademarks, as well as special technological or market advantages.

Marketing Segment

In the **marketing segment** of the plan the entrepreneur must convince investors that a market exists, that sales projections *can be achieved,* and that the competition can be beaten.

This part of the plan is often one of the most difficult to prepare. It is also one of the most critical because almost all subsequent sections of the plan depend on the sales

---

[16] See Donald F. Kuratko, "Cutting through the Business Plan Jungle," *Executive Female* (July/August 1993): 17–27.

| TABLE 10.1 | COMPLETE OUTLINE OF A BUSINESS PLAN |

Section I: Summary

Section II: Business Description Segment
   A. General description of the venture (product or service)
   B. Industry background
   C. Company history or background
   D. Goals/potential of the venture and milestones (if any)
   E. Uniqueness of the product or service

Section III: Marketing Segment
   A. Research and analysis
      1. Target market (customers)
      2. Market size and trends
      3. Competition
      4. Estimated market share
   B. Marketing plan
      1. Marketing strategy: sales and distribution
      2. Pricing
      3. Advertising and promotions

Section IV: Research, Design, and Development Segment
   A. Development and design plans
   B. Technical research results
   C. Research assistance needs
   D. Cost structure

Section V: Manufacturing Segment
   A. Location analysis
   B. Production needs: facilities and equipment
   C. Suppliers/transportation factors
   D. Labor supply
   E. Manufacturing cost data

Section VI: Management Segment
   A. Management team: key personnel
   B. Legal structure: stock agreements, employment agreements, ownership, etc.
   C. Board of directors, advisers, consultants, etc.

Section VII: Critical-Risks Segment
   A. Potential problems
   B. Obstacles and risks
   C. Alternative courses of action

Section VIII: Financial Segment
   A. Financial forecast
      1. Profit and loss
      2. Cash flow
      3. Break-even analysis
      4. Cost controls
   B. Funding sources and usage
   C. Budgeting plans
   D. Financing stages

Section IX: Milestone Schedule Segment
   A. Timing and objectives
   B. Deadlines/milestones
   C. Relationship of events

Section X: Appendix and/or Bibliography

CONTEMPORARY ENTREPRENEURSHIP

Emerging Business Forums

A growing trend is formal business plan presentations in forums.

Business forums are developing in major cities all across the United States. Massachusetts Institute of Technology established its first business forum in 1978 in Boston. Since that time, Chicago, Milwaukee, and Indianapolis are examples of cities that have followed with similar forums.

One type of forum, known as Emerging Business Forum, offers entrepreneurs constructive critiques of their business plans by experienced business executives, venture capitalists, consultants, and fellow entrepreneurs.

Emerging Business Forums offer evaluation and counsel to growth enterprises. Entrepreneurs typically have 30 minutes to present their business plans before the review panel and a live audience. Members of the panel offer candid comments, pointing out both strengths and weaknesses of the plan. Audience participation follows. Presenters have the opportunity to respond to the evaluations and suggestions offered. They also receive written evaluations of the oral presentation from audience members. (The entrepreneur doesn't make the written plan available to the audience.) The Emerging Business Forum allows for individual contacts among the audience, panelists, and presenters.

SOURCE: Donald F. Kuratko, "Demystifying the Business Plan Process: An Introductory Guide," *Small Business Forum* (winter 1990/1991):34.

estimates developed here. The projected sales levels, based on the market research and analysis, directly influence the size of the manufacturing operation, the marketing plan, and the amount of debt and equity capital required.

Most entrepreneurs have difficulty preparing and presenting market research and analyses that will convince investors the venture's sales estimates are accurate and attainable. The following are aspects of marketing that should be addressed when developing a comprehensive exposition of the market.

MARKET NICHE AND MARKET SHARE   A **market niche** is a homogeneous group with common characteristics, that is, all the people who have a need for the newly proposed product or service. In describing this niche, the writer should address the bases of customer purchase decisions: price, quality, service, personal contacts, or some combination of these factors.

Next, a list of potential customers who have expressed interest in the product or service, together with an explanation for their interest, should be included. If it is an existing business, the current principal customers should be identified and the sales trend should be discussed. It is important to describe the overall potential of the market. Sales projections should be made for at least three years, and the major factors affecting market growth (industry trends, socioeconomic trends, governmental policy, and population shifts) should be discussed. A review of previous market trends should be included, and any differences between past and projected annual growth rates should be explained. The sources of all data and methods used to make projections should be indicated. Then, if any major customers are willing to make purchase commitments, they should be identified, and the extent of those commitments should be indicated. On the basis of the product or service advantages, the market size and trends, the customers, and the sales trends in prior years, the writer should estimate market share and sales in units and dollars for each of the next three years. The growth of the company's sales and its estimated market share should be related to the growth of the industry and the customer base.

COMPETITIVE ANALYSIS   The entrepreneur should make an attempt to assess the strengths and weaknesses of the competing products or services. Any sources used to evaluate the competition should be cited. This discussion should compare competing products or services on the basis of price performance, service, warranties, and other pertinent features. It should include a short discussion of the current advantages and disadvantages of competing products and services and why they are not meeting customer needs. Any knowledge of competitors' actions that could lead to new or improved products and an advantageous position also should be presented.

Finally, a review of competing companies should be included. Each competitor's share of the market, sales, and distribution and production capabilities should be discussed. Attention should be focused on profitability and the profit trend of each competitor. Who is the pricing leader? Who is the quality leader? Who is gaining? Who is losing? Have any companies entered or dropped out of the market in recent years?

MARKETING STRATEGY   The general marketing philosophy and strategy of the company should be outlined in the **marketing strategy.** These should be developed from market research and evaluation data and should include a discussion of (1) the kinds of customer groups to be targeted by the initial intensive selling effort; (2) the customer groups to be targeted for later selling efforts; (3) methods of identifying and contacting potential customers in these groups; (4) the features of the product or service (quality, price, delivery, warranty, etc.) to be emphasized to generate sales; and (5) any innovative or unusual marketing concepts that will enhance customer acceptance (e.g., leasing where only sales were previously attempted).

This section also should indicate whether the product or service will initially be introduced nationally or regionally. Consideration also should be given to any seasonal trends and what can be done to promote contraseasonal sales.

PRICING POLICY   The price must be "right" in order to penetrate the market, maintain a market position, and produce profits. In this discussion a number of pricing strategies should be examined, and then one should be convincingly presented. This pricing policy should be compared with the policies of the major competitors. The gross profit margin between manufacturing and final sales costs should be discussed, and consideration should be given as to whether this margin is large enough to allow for distribution, sales, warranty, and service expenses; for amortization of development and equipment costs; and for profit. Attention also should be given to justifying any price increases over competitive items on the basis of newness, quality, warranty, or service.

ADVERTISING PLAN   For manufactured products, the preparation of product sheets and promotional literature; the plans for trade show participation, trade magazine advertisements, and direct mailings; and the use of advertising agencies should be presented. For products and services in general, a discussion of the advertising and promotional campaign contemplated to introduce the product and the kind of sales aids to be provided to dealers should be included. Additionally, the schedule and cost of promotion and advertising should be presented, and, if advertising will be a significant part of the expenses, an exhibit showing how and when these costs will be incurred should be included.

These five subsets of the marketing segment are needed to detail the overall marketing plan, which should describe *what* is to be done, *how* it will be done, and *who* will do it.

Research, Design, and Development Segment

The extent of any research, design, and development in regard to cost, time, and special testing should be covered in this segment. Investors need to know the status of the project in terms of prototypes, lab tests, and scheduling delays.

In order to have a comprehensive section, the entrepreneur should have (or seek out) technical assistance in preparing a detailed discussion. Blueprints, sketches, drawings, and models are often important.

It is equally important to identify the design or development work that still needs to be done and to discuss possible difficulties or risks that may delay or alter the project. In this regard, a developmental budget that shows the costs associated with labor, materials consulting, research, design, and the like should be constructed and presented.

Manufacturing Segment

This segment always should begin by describing the location of the new venture.[17] The chosen site should be appropriate in terms of labor availability, wage rate, proximity to suppliers and customers, and community support. In addition, local taxes and zoning requirements should be sorted out, and the support of area banks for new ventures should be touched on.

Production needs should be discussed in terms of the facilities required to handle the new venture (plant, warehouse storage, and offices) and the equipment that needs to be acquired (special tooling, machinery, computers, and vehicles).

Other factors that might be considered are the suppliers (number and proximity) and the transportation costs involved in shipping materials. Also, the labor supply, wage rates, and needed skilled positions should be presented.

Finally, the cost data associated with any of the manufacturing factors should be presented. The financial information used here can be applied later to the financial projections.

Management Segment

This segment identifies the key personnel, their positions and responsibilities, and the career experiences that qualify them for those particular roles. Complete résumés should be provided for each member of the management team. Also, this section is where the entrepreneur's role in the venture should be clearly outlined. Finally, any advisers, consultants or members of the board should be identified and discussed.

The structure of payment and ownership (stock agreements, consulting fees, etc.) should be described clearly in this section. In summary, the discussion should be sufficient so

---

[17] Parts of this section may not apply to certain ventures.

investors can understand each of the following critical factors that have been presented: (1) organizational structure, (2) management team and critical personnel, (3) experience and technical capabilities of the personnel, (4) ownership structure and compensation agreements, and (5) board of directors and outside consultants and advisers.

Critical-Risks Segment

In this segment potential risks such as the following should be identified: effect of unfavorable trends in the industry, design or manufacturing costs that have gone over estimates, difficulties of long lead times encountered when purchasing parts or materials, and unplanned-for new competition.

In addition to these risks, it is also wise to cover the what-ifs. For example, what if the competition cuts prices, the industry slumps, the market projections are wrong, the sales projections are not achieved, the patents do not come through, or the management team breaks up?

Finally, suggestions for alternative courses of action should be included. Certainly, delays, inaccurate projections, and industry slumps all can happen, and people reading the business plan will want to know the entrepreneur recognizes these risks and has prepared for such critical events.

Financial Segment

The financial segment of a business plan must demonstrate the potential viability of the undertaking. In this part of the plan, three basic financial statements must be presented: the pro forma balance sheet, the income statement, and the cash-flow statement.

THE PRO FORMA BALANCE SHEET   *Pro forma* means projected, as opposed to actual. The pro forma balance sheet projects what the financial condition of the venture will be at a particular point in time. Pro forma balance sheets should be prepared at start-up, semi-annually for the first years, and at the end of each of the first three years. The *balance sheet* details the assets required to support the projected level of operations and shows how these assets are to be financed (liabilities and equity). Investors will want to look at the projected balance sheets to determine if debt/equity ratios, working capital, current ratios, inventory turnover, and so on are within the acceptable limits required to justify the future financings projected for the venture.

THE INCOME STATEMENT   The *income statement* illustrates the projected operating results based on profit and loss. The sales forecast, which was developed in the marketing segment, is essential to this document. Once the sales forecast (earnings projection) is in place, production costs must be budgeted based on the level of activity needed to support the projected earnings. The materials, labor, service, and manufacturing overhead (fixed and variable) must be considered, in addition to such expenses as distribution, storage, advertising, discounts, and administrative and general expenses—salaries, legal and accounting, rent, utilities, and telephone.

THE CASH-FLOW STATEMENT   In new-venture creation, the *cash-flow statement* may be the most important document since it sets forth the amount and timing of expected cash inflows and outflows. This section of the business plan should be carefully constructed.

CONTEMPORARY ENTREPRENEURSHIP

Writing the Business Plan

Your desk is covered with pieces of information that you want to put into your business plan. You've had your coffee. Your phone is off the hook. But you spend the next fifteen minutes staring out the window . . . unable to get going.

You're not alone. Most people experience some form of writer's block when faced with a particularly important or large-scale job.

Why? Most researchers who study the act of writing currently believe that many of our writing problems are caused by our approach. They say that all writers—whether they are conscious of it or not—go through a five-stage process when they write: prewriting, writing, revising, editing, and proofreading. The majority of writing problems are caused, the researchers say, when the writer tries to do all of the steps at once. Let's take a closer look at each of these steps:

Prewriting

This is the stage where you decide what you're going to say. You may write or review your notes, assemble facts, organize your thoughts, establish your goals, or draft an outline. The more you have to say, the more important this stage is. Generally, the more time you spend here, the less time you will spend in the revising stage.

Writing

After you know in broad terms what you need to say, you can start saying it. This is the stage where you just get it down. Resist the temptation to try to say everything perfectly. Don't correct grammar or punctuation. Don't stop after every sentence to critique yourself. Just keep going.

Revising

When you're done, you can start revising for clarity. Rework your sentences until you are sure that your reader will understand them.

Then, take a break from the project. At the very least, return a phone call or

Given a level of projected sales and capital expenditures over a specific period, the cash-flow forecast will highlight the need for and the timing of additional financing and will indicate peak requirements for working capital. Management must decide how this additional financing is to be obtained, on what terms, and how it is to be repaid. The total amount of needed financing may be supplied from several sources: part by equity financing, part by bank loans, and the balance by short-term lines of credit from banks. This information becomes part of the final cash-flow forecast.

A detailed cash flow, if understood properly, can direct the entrepreneur's attention to operating problems before serious cash crises arise.

In the financial segment it is important to mention any assumptions used for preparing the figures. Nothing should be taken for granted. Also, it should include how the statements

stand up and stretch. The next stage will require you to switch gears dramatically, and it will be much easier if you approach it from a fresh perspective.

Editing

This is the most crucial—and most difficult—stage of the writing process. At this point, you should take a very objective look at your business plan and ask yourself:

- Does it do what it should do?
- Is it convincing?
- Do I need to include more information? Less?
- Have I supported all of my most important statements?
- Is it well organized?
- Is it readable?
- Is the tone appropriate? Is the style appropriate?

Proofreading

All that is left to do now is to look for typographical errors, minor grammatical errors, and to make sure that the business plan is spaced correctly on the page. It helps if someone else can take a look. Keep in mind that minor errors

could undermine the impact of the whole business plan.

The most important applications of the process approach are: Don't correct yourself while you write, and don't wait for "the perfect opening sentence" to come to you.

Speaking from my own experience as a professional writer (who hates to write), this process approach makes a lot of sense. I consciously go through the steps about 90 percent of the time. While I taught this at University of Wisconsin—Milwaukee, about 75 percent of my students said that this approach saved them time and was especially helpful when they had tight deadlines.

SOURCE: Catherine Stover, "A Common Stumbling Block: The Writing Process," *Small Business Forum* (winter 1990/1991): 35.

were prepared (by a professional CPA or by the entrepreneur) and who will be in charge of managing the business's finances.

The final document that should be included in the financial segment is a break-even chart, which shows the level of sales (and production) needed to cover all costs. This includes costs that vary with the production level (manufacturing labor, materials, sales) and costs that do not change with production (rent, interest charges, executive salaries).

Milestone Schedule Segment

The *milestone schedule segment* provides investors with a timetable for the various activities to be accomplished. It is important to demonstrate that realistic time frames have been planned and that the interrelationship of events within these time boundaries is understood. Milestone scheduling is a step-by-step approach to illustrating accomplishments in a piece-meal fashion. These milestones can be established according to any appropriate time frame, such as quarterly, monthly, or weekly. It is important, however, to coordinate the time frame not only with such early activities as product design and development, sales projections, establishing the management team, production and operations scheduling, and market planning but with other activities as well:

- Incorporation of the venture
- Completion of design and development
- Completion of prototypes
- Hiring of sales representatives
- Product display at trade shows
- Signing up distributors and dealers
- Ordering production quantities of materials
- Receipt of first orders
- First sales and first deliveries (dates of maximum interest because they relate directly to the venture's credibility and need for capital)
- Payment of first accounts receivable (cash in)

These items are examples of the types of activities that should be included in the milestone schedule segment. The more detailed the schedule, the better the chance the entrepreneur can persuade potential investors he or she has thought things out and is therefore a good risk.

Appendix and/or Bibliography Segment

The final segment is not mandatory, but it allows for additional documentation that is not appropriate in the main parts of the plan. Diagrams, blueprints, financial data, vitae of management team members, and any bibliographical information that supports the other segments of the plan are all examples of material that can be included. It is up to the entrepreneur to decide which, if any, items to put into this segment. However, the material should be limited to relevant and supporting information.

Table 10.2 provides an important recap of the major segments of a business plan, using helpful hints as practical reminders for entrepreneurs. By reviewing this, entrepreneurs can gain a macroview of the planning process. Table 10.3 on pages 309–310 is a personal checklist that gives entrepreneurs the opportunity to evaluate their business plan for each segment. The step-by-step evaluation is based on coverage of the particular segment, clarity of its presentation, and completeness.

PRESENTATION OF THE BUSINESS PLAN

Once a business plan is prepared, the next major challenge is presenting the plan to either a single financial person or, in some parts of the country, a forum where numerous financial investors have gathered.[18] In any situation the oral presentation is a key step in selling the business plan to potential investors.

[18] For example, the Massachusetts Institute of Technology sponsors a business plan forum in Boston, and the Venture Club of Indiana sponsors a monthly meeting with presentations.

TABLE 10.2	HELPFUL HINTS FOR WRITING THE BUSINESS PLAN

The Summary

No more than three pages

This is the most crucial part of your plan because it must capture the reader's interest.

What, how, why, where, etc., must be summarized.

Complete this part *after* the finished business plan has been written.

The Business Description Segment

The name of the business

A background of the industry with history of the company (if any) should be covered here.

The potential of the new venture should be described clearly.

Any unique or distinctive features of the venture should be spelled out.

The Marketing Segment

Convince investors that sales projections and competition can be met.

Market studies should be used and disclosed.

Identify target market, market position, and market share.

Evaluate *all* competition and specifically cover why and how you will be better than the competitors.

Identify all market sources and assistance used for this segment.

Demonstrate pricing strategy, since your price must penetrate and maintain a market share to *produce profits*. Thus the lowest price is *not* necessarily the "best" price.

Identify your advertising plans with cost estimates to validate the proposed strategy.

The Research, Design, and Development Segment

Cover the *extent* of and *costs* involved in needed research, testing, or development.

Explain carefully what has been accomplished *already* (prototype, lab testing, early development).

Mention any research or technical assistance provided for you.

The Manufacturing Segment

Provide the advantages of your location (zoning, tax laws, wage rates).

List the production needs in terms of facilities (plant, storage, office space) and equipment (machinery, furnishings, supplies).

Describe the access to transportation (for shipping and receiving).

Explain proximity to your suppliers.

Mention the availability of labor in your location.

Provide estimates of manufacturing costs—be careful; too many entrepreneurs underestimate their costs.

The Management Segment

Provide résumés of all key people in the management of the venture.

Carefully describe the legal structure of the venture (sole proprietorship, partnership, or corporation).

Cover the added assistance (if any) of advisers, consultants, and directors.

Provide information on how everyone is to be compensated (how much, also).

(Continued)

TABLE 10.2 **HELPFUL HINTS FOR WRITING THE BUSINESS PLAN** *(continued)*

The Critical-Risks Segment

Discuss potential risks *before* investors point them out. Some examples follow:
    Price cutting by competitors
    Potentially unfavorable industry-wide trends
    Design or manufacturing costs in excess of estimates
    Sales projections not achieved
    Product development schedule not met
    Difficulties or long lead times encountered in the procurement of parts or raw materials
    Larger-than-expected innovation and development costs to stay competitive

Name alternative courses of action.

The Financial Segment

Provide statements.

Describe the needed sources for your funds and the uses you intend for the money.

Provide a budget.

Create stages of financing for the purpose of allowing evaluation by investors at various points.

The Milestone Schedule Segment

Provide a timetable or chart to demonstrate when each phase of the venture is to be completed. This shows the relationship of events and provides a deadline for accomplishment.

SOURCE: Donald F. Kuratko, Ray V. Montagno, and Frank J. Sabatine, *The Entrepreneurial Decision* (Muncie, IN: The Midwest Entrepreneurial Education Center, Ball State University, 1997), 45–46. Reprinted with permission.

The presentation should be organized, well prepared, interesting, and flexible. Entrepreneurs should develop an outline of the significant highlights that will capture the audience's interest. Although the outline should be followed, they also must feel free to add or remove certain bits of information as the presentation progresses—a memorized presentation lacks excitement, energy, and interest.

Suggestions for Preparation

The following steps in preparing an oral presentation are suggested for entrepreneurs:

1. Know the outline thoroughly.

2. Use key words in the outline that help recall examples, visual aids, or other details.

3. Rehearse the presentation in order to get the feel of its length.

4. Be familiar with any equipment to be used in the presentation—such as an overhead projector, a slide projector, or a VCR.

5. The day before, practice the complete presentation using all visual aids and equipment.

6. The day of the presentation, arrive early in order to set up, test any equipment, and organize notes and visual aids.[19]

---

[19] For more on oral presentations, see Norman B. Sigband and Arthur H. Bell, *Communication for Management and Business,* 4th ed. (Glenview, IL: Scott, Foresman, 1986), 458–66.

TABLE 10.3	BUSINESS PLAN CHECKLIST: A PERSONAL STEP-BY-STEP EVALUATION

	Have You Covered This in the Plan?	Is the Answer Clear? (Yes/No)	Is the Answer Complete? (Yes/No)

Business Description Segment

1. What type of business are you planning?
2. What products or services will you sell?
3. What type of opportunity is it (new, part-time, expansion, seasonal, year-round)?
4. Why does it promise to be successful?
5. What is the growth potential?
6. What uniqueness exists?

(Discuss strengths and weaknesses in this segment.)

Marketing Segment

1. Who are your potential customers?
2. How big is the market?
3. Who are your competitors? How are their businesses prospering?
4. How will you promote sales?
5. What market share do you anticipate?
6. How will you price your product or service?
7. What advertising and promotional strategy are you using?

(Discuss strengths and weaknesses in this segment.)

Research, Design, and Development Segment

1. Have you carefully described your design or development?
2. Have you received any technical assistance?
3. What research needs do you anticipate?
4. Are the costs involved in research and design reasonable?

(Discuss strengths and weaknesses in this segment.)

Manufacturing Segment

1. Where will the business be located?
2. What factors have influenced the choice of location?
3. Have you described the needs for production facilities and equipment?
4. Who will be your suppliers?
5. What type of transportation is available?
6. What is the supply of available labor?

(Discuss strengths and weaknesses in this segment.)

Management Segment

1. Who will manage the business?
2. What qualifications do you have?
3. How many employees will you need? What will they do?
4. What are your plans for employee salaries, wages, benefits?
5. What consultants or specialists will you need? Why will you need them?
6. What legal form of ownership will you choose? Why?
7. What licenses and permits will you need?
8. What regulations will affect your business?

(Discuss strengths and weaknesses in this segment.)

(Continued)

TABLE 10.3	BUSINESS PLAN CHECKLIST: A PERSONAL STEP-BY-STEP EVALUATION *(continued)*		
	Have You Covered This in the Plan?	**Is the Answer Clear? (Yes/No)**	**Is the Answer Complete? (Yes/No)**

Critical-Risks Segment

1. What potential problems have you identified?
2. How many obstacles do you foresee?
3. Have you calculated the risks?
4. What alternative courses of action are there?

(Discuss strengths and weaknesses in this segment.)

Financial Segment

1. What is your total estimated business income for the first year? Monthly income for the first year? Quarterly income for the second and third years?
2. What will it cost you to open the business?
3. What will be your monthly cash flow during the first year?
4. What will be your personal monthly financial needs?
5. What sales volume will you need in order to make a profit during the first three years?
6. What will be the break even point?
7. What will be your projected assets, liabilities, and net worth on the day before you expect to open?
8. What will be your total financial needs?
9. What will be your potential funding sources?
10. How will you use the money from lenders or investors?
11. How will the loan be secured?

(Discuss strengths and weaknesses in this segment.)

Milestone Schedule Segment

1. What timing have you projected for this project?
2. How have you set your objectives?
3. Have you set deadlines for each stage of your venture?
4. Does a relationship exist among events in this venture?

(Discuss strengths and weaknesses in this segment.)

Appendix Segment

1. Have you included any documents, drawings, agreements, or other materials needed to support the plan?
2. Do you have any names of references, advisers, or technical sources you should include?
3. Do you have any other supporting documents?

(Discuss any strengths and weaknesses in this segment.)

What to Expect

Entrepreneurs should realize the audience reviewing their business plan is antagonistic. The venture-capital sources pressure them in order to test their venture as well as the entrepreneurs. Thus, entrepreneurs must expect and prepare for a critical, sometimes skep-

TABLE 10.4	WHAT TO DO WHEN A VENTURE CAPITALIST TURNS YOU DOWN: TEN QUESTIONS

1. *Confirm the decision:* "That means you do not wish to participate at this time?"

2. *Sell for the future:* "Can we count you in for a second round of financing, after we've completed the first?"

3. *Find out why you were rejected:* "Why do you choose not to participate in this deal?" (Timing? Fit? All filled up?)

4. *Ask for advice:* "If you were in my position, how would you proceed?"

5. *Ask for suggestions:* "Can you suggest a source who invests in this kind of deal?"

6. *Get the name:* "Whom should I speak to when I'm there?"

7. *Find out why:* "Why do you suggest this firm, and why do you think this is the best person to speak to there?"

8. *Work on an introduction:* "Who would be the best person to introduce me?"

9. *Develop a reasonable excuse:* "Can I tell him that your decision to turn us down was based on _____?"

10. *Know your referral:* "What will you tell him when he calls?"

SOURCE: Joseph R. Mancuso, *How to Write a Winning Business Plan* (Englewood Cliffs: Prentice-Hall, 1985), 37.

tical audience of financial sources. As an example, the following comments from Joseph R. Mancuso, president of the Center for Entrepreneurial Management, illustrate the reality of what entrepreneurs face:

> When you finally do hand over your plan, the venture source will glance at it briefly and begin his preliminary comments. No matter how good you think your plan is, he's not going to look at it and say, "This is the greatest plan I've ever seen!" so don't go in looking for praise. It's highly likely that his remarks will be critical, and even if they aren't, they'll seem that way. Don't panic. Even if it seems like an avalanche of objections, bear in mind that Digital Equipment Corporation (DEC) was turned down by everyone before American Research & Development (AR&D) in Boston decided to take a $70,000 chance on them. That might not seem like much now, but at the time it made all the difference. And Fred Adler didn't put $25,000 into Data General until all of the other established venture capitalists had turned down the deal. These are two of the best venture capital deals of all time and they almost didn't happen, so don't expect results in the first twenty minutes.[20]

Entrepreneurs must be prepared to handle the questions from the evaluators and learn from the criticism. They should never feel defeated but rather should make a commitment to improving the business plan for future review. Table 10.4 outlines some of the key questions that might be asked when a business plan is turned down. Entrepreneurs should use the answers to these questions to revise, rework, and improve their business plan. The goal is not so much to succeed the *first* time as it is to *succeed*.

[20] Mancuso, *How to Write,* 34.

SUMMARY

This chapter has provided a thorough examination of an effective business plan. The critical factors in planning and the pitfalls to be avoided were discussed. Indicators of these pitfalls and ways to avoid them were also presented.

Next, a business plan was defined, and benefits for both entrepreneurs and financial sources were discussed. Developing a well-conceived plan was presented from the point of view of the audience for whom the plan is written. The typical six-step reading process of a business plan was presented in order for entrepreneurs to better understand how to put the business plan together. Ten guidelines in developing a business plan were provided, collated from the advice of experts in venture capital and new-business development.

The next section illustrated some of the major questions that must be answered in a complete and thorough business plan. The business plan was outlined with every major segment addressed and explained.

The chapter then presented some helpful hints for preparing a business plan, along with a self-analysis checklist for doing a careful critique of the plan before it is presented to investors.

Finally, the chapter closed with a review of how to present a business plan to an audience of venture capital sources. Some basic presentation tips were listed, together with a discussion of what to expect from the plan evaluators.

Key Terms and Concepts

Balance sheet	Market niche
Business plan	Marketing segment
Cash-flow statement	Marketing strategy
Five-minute reading	Milestone schedule segment
Income statement	Pro forma

Review and Discussion Questions

1. What are the critical factors to be considered when preparing a business plan?
2. Describe each of the five planning pitfalls entrepreneurs often encounter.
3. Identify an indicator of each pitfall named in number 2. What would you do about each?
4. Identify the benefits of a business plan (a) for an entrepreneur and (b) for financial sources.
5. What are the three major viewpoints to be considered when developing a business plan?
6. Name the six-step process that venture capitalists follow when reading a business plan.
7. What are some components to consider in the proper packaging of a plan?
8. Identify five of the ten guidelines to be used for preparing a business plan.
9. Briefly describe each of the major segments to be covered in a business plan.
10. Why is the summary segment of a business plan written last? Why not first?
11. What are five elements included in the marketing segment of a business plan?
12. What are some critical factors covered in the management segment of a business plan?

13. What is the meaning of the term *critical risks?*
14. Describe each of the three financial statements that are mandatory for the financial segment of a business plan.
15. Why are milestones important to a business plan?

Experiential Exercise   *Putting Together a Business Plan*

The ten major segments of a business plan are listed in the following left column. Identify the order in which each segment will appear in the plan by placing a 1 next to the first part on down to a 10 next to the last part.

Then match each of the 20 items or descriptions on the right with the segment in which it would appear. For example, if an item would appear in the first segment, put a 1 next to this description. Two items or descriptions are listed for each segment of the report.

Answers are provided at the end of the exercise.

Segments of the Report	Contents of the Segments
_____ A. Financial segment	_____ a) Describes the potential of the new venture
_____ B. Marketing segment	_____ b) Discusses the advantages of location
_____ C. Management segment	_____ c) Discusses price cutting by the competition
_____ D. Summary	_____ d) Provides bibliographical information
_____ E. Manufacturing segment	_____ e) Most crucial part of the plan
_____ F. Business description segment	_____ f) Describes any prototypes developed
_____ G. Critical-risks segment	_____ g) Analyzes case if any sales projections are not attained
_____ H. Appendix	_____ h) Shows the relationship between events and deadlines for accomplishment
_____ I. Research, design, and development segment	_____ i) Provides résumés of all key personnel
_____ J. Milestone schedule segment	_____ j) Contains support material such as blueprints and diagrams
	_____ k) Discusses pricing strategy
	_____ l) Should be written after the business plan is completed
	_____ m) Provides a budget
	_____ n) Explains proximity to suppliers
	_____ o) Sets forth timetables for completion of major phases of the venture
	_____ p) Provides industry background
	_____ q) Explains costs involved in testing
	_____ r) Identifies target markets
	_____ s) Describes legal structure of the venture
	_____ t) Provides balance sheet and income statement

Answers

A. 8	F. 2	a) 2	f) 4	k) 3	p) 2
B. 3	G. 7	b) 5	g) 7	l) 1	q) 4
C. 6	H. 10	c) 7	h) 9	m) 8	r) 3
D. 1	I. 4	d) 10	i) 6	n) 5	s) 6
E. 5	J. 9	e) 1	j) 10	o) 9	t) 8

 **CASE**

CASE 10.1

It's Just a Matter of Time

Pedro Santini has been a computer analyst for five years. In his spare time he has developed a word processing software program that is more comprehensive and powerful than any on the market. Since he does not have a great deal of money, Pedro believes the first step in producing and marketing this product should be to get the necessary venture capital.

The software program has been written and trial-tested by Pedro and a handful of friends to whom he gave the material. Two of these friends are full-time typists who told him that the program is faster and easier to use than anything on the market. Pedro believes that these kinds of testimonials point out the profit potential of the product. However, he still needs to get financial support.

One of Pedro's friends has suggested a meeting with a venture capitalist, "These guys have all sorts of money to lend for new ventures," the friend told Pedro. "All you have to do is explain your ideas and sell them on giving you the money. They are always looking to back a profitable idea, and yours is certain to be one of the best they have seen in a long time."

Pedro agrees with his friend but believes he should not discuss the matter with a venture capitalist until he has thought through answers to the various types of questions likely to be asked. In particular, Pedro believes he should be able to provide the venture capitalist with projected sales for the first three years and be able to explain the types of expenses that would be incurred. Once he has done this, Pedro feels he will be ready to talk to the individual. "Right now," he told his friend, "it's just a matter of time. I'd think that within seven to ten days I'll be ready to present my ideas and discuss financial needs."

Questions

1. In addition to financial questions, what other questions is the venture capitalist likely to ask Pedro?
2. Would a business plan be of any value to Pedro? Why or why not?
3. How would you recommend Pedro get ready for his meeting with the venture capitalist? Be complete in your answer.

 **CASE**

CASE 10.2

The Incomplete Plan

When Joan Boothe drew up her business plan, she was certain it would help her get venture capital. Joan is in the throes of putting together a monthly magazine directed toward executive women in the workplace. The objective of the periodical is to provide information useful to women who are pursuing careers. The first issue is scheduled to go to press in 90 days. Some of the articles included in this issue are "Managing Your Time for Fun and Profit," "What You Need to Know about Dressing for Success," and "Money Management: Do It Like the Experts." A section also is devoted to successful women at work. It is titled "Women in the News." Other features include a question-and-answer section that responds to letters and inquiries from readers (the first issue's questions were submitted by a group of women executives, each of whom had been asked to help get the column started by sending in a question); a stock market section that reviews industries or companies and points out the benefits and risks associated with investing in them; and a column on the state of the economy and the developments or trends expected over the next 12 months.

Joan's business plan consisted of six parts: a summary, a business description, a manufacturing segment, a management segment, a milestone schedule segment, and an appendix. When it was returned to her with the rejection letter, the venture-capital firm wrote, "Without a marketing segment, attention to critical risks, and a financial segment, this plan is incomplete and cannot be favorably reviewed by us. If you would provide us with this additional information and submit the rewritten plan within the next 60 days, we will be happy to review the plan and give you our opinion within 10 working days."

Questions

1. What should Joan put in the marketing segment? What types of information will she need?
2. For the critical-risks assessment segment, what key areas does Joan have to address? Discuss two of these.
3. For the financial segment, what suggestions would you make to Joan regarding the kinds of information to include? Be as specific as possible.

PART 3

ENTREPRENEURIAL CASE ANALYSIS

A BUSINESS PLAN

The Roaring '20s Museum

436 West Ontario Street
Chicago, Illinois 60610

Introduction

This case analysis presents the complete business plan for the Roaring '20s Museum, created by Michael Y. Graham. This plan was the *international award-winning* business plan at the University of Miami International Business Plan Competition. The business plan represents the hard work, vision, and perseverance of an entrepreneur.

Michael Yore Graham personified a college professor's dream come true: a student dedicated to doing whatever it takes to research, write, present, and defend an award-winning business plan, the Roaring '20s Museum.

As you read Mike's plan, try to resist concluding that he must be a magician, creating the plan out of smoke and mirrors. The plan's critical mass is Mike's vision, energy, and commitment blended with his resourcefulness and willingness to adjust preconceived notions to the realities of business.

There's an old saying, "Fail to plan; plan to fail." Mike Graham planned to win the University of Miami's International Business Plan Competition, and he plans to open the Roaring '20s Museum in the near future.

Will you join him on opening day?

James R. Paradiso
Professor of Management
College of Lake County
Grayslake, Illinois

This plan was prepared and written by Michael Yore Graham, 345 Cleveland Avenue, Libertyville, IL 60048. Reprinted with permission.

Business Plan Outline

I. Summary

A. STATEMENT OF PURPOSE: THE ROARING '20S MUSEUM, AN ILLINOIS LIMITED PARTNERSHIP

The following business plan has been formulated to obtain $650,000 in venture capital to establish Chicago's first and only Prohibition/gangster era museum. It will also serve as a formal outline for the first five years of the museum's operation. A limited partnership business structure has been chosen to maintain limited liability for investors, combined with various tax advantages. Twenty-five limited partnership units (LPUs) will be offered for sale at a price of $26,000 each, yielding a $650,000 capital fund. The general partner, Era Management, Inc., will contribute $200,000 in equity interest, yielding an adjusted capital fund of $850,000. The financial forecasts (pages 336–349), though conservative, show that this investment has significant promise.

In the beginning of the sixth year of operation, it is the intention of the limited partnership to sell the museum at three times the gross sales of the fifth year, yielding a projected capital gain on each LPU of $93,423. Total projected ROI per LPU before tax: (Cash payout) $39,520 + (Capital gain) $93,423 = $132,943 or 511 percent. See Table A.1.

This offering involves a high degree of risk for an untried business venture. Each potential investor should thoroughly examine this business plan before making any investment decision.

B. DESCRIPTION OF THE ROARING '20S MUSEUM

The Roaring '20s is a commercial Prohibition/gangster era museum designed to allow each visitor an opportunity to step back in time and relive Chicago's most rowdy, roaring, and colorful era. By participating and interacting with the museum's displays and multimedia presentations, the visitors will meet Al Capone, sit in his custom Cadillac, participate in a raid led by Elliott Ness, and truly understand the nature and motivation of the gangsters who lived and died during Chicago's bloody past. The museum will also examine the political and social characters and events of the era, based on an easy-to-follow chronological sequence.

The museum has three primary goals. The first is to thoroughly entertain the visitors during their stay. The second is to educate them on this important segment of Chicago's and the nation's history. The third is to meet and exceed the projected return on investment (ROI) for the limited partnership.

C. SUMMARY OF PROPOSED MARKETING STRATEGY

1. Roaring '20s Market   The thrust of the proposed marketing strategy is to attract potential visitors who most readily associate Chicago with its gangster past. The potential market for the museum is composed of Chicago's annual attraction of:

1. 2.8 million conventioneers

TABLE A.1   **PROJECTED CASH PAYMENT AND ROI FOR EACH LPU ($26,000) BEFORE TAX**

Fiscal Year	Cash Payout	ROI
2nd Year Operation	$ 6,080.00	23%
3rd Year Operation	6,080.00	23
4th Year Operation	9,120.00	35
5th Year Operation	18,240.00	70
Total	$39,520.00	151%

FIGURE A.1　**MAP OF ATTRACTIONS OF RIVER NORTH NEIGHBORHOOD**

SOURCE: *Chicago Tribune,* July 18, 1986.

2. 900,000 foreign tourists

3. 3.1 million out-of-state tourists

4. 3.5 million Chicagoland residents

2. Channel of Distribution　The Roaring '20s Museum will use a direct retailer-to-visitor/buyer channel of distribution in its attraction of potential visitors. The location of the museum, 436 W. Ontario Street, is in the very heart of Chicago's eating and entertainment district (see Figure A.1).

D.　SUMMARY OF FINANCIAL ESTIMATES

1. Sales Forecast　Table A.2 is a five-fiscal-year gross sales projection for the Roaring '20s Museum.

2. Profit Forecast　Table A.3 is a profit (loss) projection for the first five years of operation.

3. Capital Needed　Preopening expenses for renovation of the museum's interior, start-up costs, first-year operating expenses, and unforeseen expenses will require $650,000.

TABLE A.2	PROJECTED GROSS SALES, FIVE FISCAL YEARS	

Year	Gross Sales	Percentage Increase of Gross Sales
1st	$ 420,000	
2nd	547,000	25%
3rd	707,100	30
4th	850,980	20
5th	1,024,374	20

TABLE A.3	PROJECTED PROFIT (LOSS), FIVE FISCAL YEARS	

Year	Profit (Loss)
1st	$ (41)
2nd	75,081
3rd	191,478
4th	263,837
5th	355,369

II. BUSINESS DESCRIPTION

A. STATEMENT OF THE DESIRABILITY OF A ROARING '20S MUSEUM

1. Advantages   The museum's unique and enduring advantage, in regard to safeguarding against potential competition and protecting the limited partners' investment, is the nature and scope of its historical collection. It is the most extensive and interesting historical assemblage of material in the country related to Chicago and the nation's history during Prohibition, one that can never be duplicated.[1] Each piece was chosen for its visual impact, historical importance, uniqueness, and educational significance. The collection has been seen on national television during "The Mystery of Al Capone's Vaults." A large number of pieces were used in Paramount Pictures' making of *The Untouchables,* and the collection has been the subject of feature articles in the *Chicago Tribune, Chicago Sun-Times,* Associated Press releases, and four other newspapers and magazines (see accompanying boxes).

Through the combination of the use of the 2,000-piece, one-of-a-kind collection containing everything from the doors of Al Capone's bedroom to a working bootleg whiskey still and the use of state-of-the-art multimedia technology, the visitors will enter a historical time warp and *relive* Chicago's most colorful and violent era.

---

[1] Lori Rotenberk, "Chicago's Gangster Era Lives in Libertyville," *Chicago Sun-Times,* November 4, 1986, 25.

Hollywood Finds Graham Hoard

Michael Graham's collection of Chicago Prohibition Era memorabilia is being used in a Brian De Palma movie, *The Untouchables,* being filmed this summer and fall in Chicago.

Graham, 23, of Libertyville, worked as a researcher for WGN-TV's "The Mystery of Al Capone's Vaults" last spring.

The Untouchables, with Robert de Niro and Sean Connery, will be shot in locations in Chicago and Galena, said Graham. A warehouse off Roosevelt Road on the west side is being converted into a studio. About 40 of Graham's pieces will be used in a speakeasy scene scheduled for shooting on Aug. 18, he said.

The movie company is using beer barrels, whiskey bottles, old Police Gazettes, federal badges, documents, sheet music from the 1920s, saloon licenses, an old-time radio, a 50-gallon copper vat, an Al Smith poster, Big Bill Thompson poster, "Repeal the 18th Amendment" license plates, a team photo of the 1919 Chicago White Sox (the Black Sox) and other items from Graham's collection. "They took almost everything," he said. Graham stores his stuff at home and in self-storage units in the area.

Graham said he expects to get "a couple of thousand dollars" from Paramount for the use of his stuff over six weeks.

The Untouchables is scheduled for release sometime next year.

Graham also has been contacted by producers from what he called "The 60 Minutes of Japan" for an interview.

Graham's latest find is a June 3, 1930 copy of the *Chicago Daily News.* That day's paper published a lengthy account of the "Fox Lake Massacre." Around midnight, June 2, a carload of gunmen crept up, lights out, to Manning's Hotel near Fox Lake and sprayed a group of late night revelers with machine gun, rifle, and automatic pistol fire. Three men, all said to be gangsters, were killed and several men and women were wounded. The *News Sun's* account said police found a total of 52, .38 and .45 caliber slugs or shells in and around the hotel after the slaughter.

Graham, the son of Libertyville Township Supervisor F. T. "Mike" Graham, has made himself an expert on the Prohibition Era in Chicago over the past two years and he hopes to establish a museum on the subject. Nearly a million foreign tourists visit Chicago each year and most of them are interested in Chicago's old gangland history, he observed. The museum will be a serious one, "nothing like Ripley's Believe It Or Not (in Chicago's Old Town)," he said.

SOURCE: "Hollywood Finds Graham Hoard," *Chicago Tribune,* May 9, 1986.

2. Short- and Long-Term Objectives   The short-term objective of the Roaring '20s Museum is to carve out a significant niche within the convention and tourism industry in Chicago within the first two years of operation, leading to over 200,000 visitors by the end of the second year. The long-term goal, within the third through fifth years of operation, will be to meet and exceed the projected cash payouts to the limited partnership and be in a position to attract over 350,000 visitors in the fifth year of operation. This will allow the limited partnership to sell the museum in the sixth year at its highest obtainable price.

3. Proprietor's Background   Michael Y. Graham has shown entrepreneurial tendencies from early on in his life. At the age of 11, Graham opened a miniature golf course adjacent to his parents' property in Libertyville, Illinois. While in high school, Mike successfully invested in stock and real estate ventures, allowing him the financial resources to pay for college and to take a seven-month trip throughout Asia. Graham has set up a national network of antique dealers for the collection of historic material for his museum and is a published authority and appraiser for historic memorabilia from this era. From 1983 to 1986 Graham held the position of Park Supervisor for Libertyville Township and supervised the planning and development of new park facilities for Libertyville, with a capital expenditure of over $200,000. Mike graduated from Western Illinois University in the spring of 1982 with a B.S. degree in political science and history and a 3.9/4.0 grade point average in his majors. Graham is the only student in the history of Illinois state colleges to complete a B.S. degree in two years. Mike graduated magna cum laude and was admitted to three scholastic honor societies while attending Western. Upon his return from a seven-month tour through Asia, Graham began his three-year research into Chicago and the nation's history during National Prohibition (1920–1933). In December of 1985, Graham was hired as the Chicago researcher for the television show "The Mystery of Al Capone's Vault." After completing his work on the television production, Graham was hired as a historical consultant for Paramount Pictures' filming of *The Untouchables*. In 1986 Graham appeared on PBS, CBS, WGN, Dutch National Television, and WBBM AM Radio in regard to his collection and area of historical expertise. Currently Graham is lecturing to both colleges and historical societies on U.S. and Chicago history during Prohibition. Mike is considered the definitive expert on Chicago and the nation's history during Prohibition.[2] In conjunction with historical research, Graham has thoroughly immersed himself in the study of the convention and tourism industry in Chicago as well as the day-to-day operations of a commercial museum. (See Figure A.2.)

4. The Image of the Roaring '20s   The entertainment value of the museum must and will be compatible with its educational qualities. Through the use of state-of-the-art multimedia technology in combination with the reconstruction of historical events and places utilizing the historical collection, the viewer will interact, participate, and be both entertained and educated in one process. It will be a museum that positively reflects the character and reputation of the city of Chicago and its people.

B. BACKGROUND OF PROPOSED BUSINESS

1. State of the Art for Commercial Museums in the United States   The commercial museum industry in the United States has been confined to four areas of exhibition material: Ripley's Believe It Or Not Odditoriums, wax, auto, and local historic eclectic museums. The museums are generally located in highly frequented tourist areas of major cities and resorts. After their fifth year of operation, the museums have shown a longevity of 15 to 40 years and a high sustained profitability rate.[3]

2. Roaring '20s Place in State of the Art
a) Projections and Trends for Convention and Tourism Industry in Chicago   Never has there been a more opportune time for a commercial museum such as the Roaring '20s to become a reality. The once prevalent de facto restrictions placed on the motion picture and television industry by former mayor Richard J. Daley regarding the examination of our gangster past have been removed from city hall policy. Judson Minor, spokesman for the City of Chicago corporation counsel, has stated that there are no longer any restrictions prohibiting a museum of this nature. The convention and tourism industry in Chicago is poised for significant and long-term growth. In January of 1985, the state of Illinois increased funding from $850,000 to $10.5 million a year for the promotion of Chicago and Illinois as a major tourist destination. Illinois is now the number-one state in the allocation of funds for tourism promotion.[4] An Illinois Office of Tourism projection

---

[2] Ruth Silverman, Libertyville, Illinois, *Daily Herald*, April 6, 1986, sec. B, 2.

[3] Julie Polascek, Manager, Ripley's Chicago museum, oral quote September 7, 1986.

[4] Mitchell Locin, "Such a Deal," *Chicago Tribune*, February 2, 1986.

Chicago's Gangster Era Lives in Libertyville

Listen to Michael Yore Graham as his ire flares: "Know what bothers me the most? I have to buy Chicago's history off the street. And that is criminal."

Criminal?

There's a bit of irony in those words. They come from this young man who revels in the mustiness of empty buildings. Loiters in basements seeking that particular element. Flicks and blows layers of dust from papers and photos.

Graham searches for a Chicago past most everyone else seems to want to forget. He knocks on doors at dusk wearing not a Super Bowl Bears T-shirt, but one that makes onlookers swing their heads for a second reading. In black letters: WANTED, AL CAPONE.

"Hey," they tell him, "those days are long gone. Forgotten. Al Capone is kaput."

Maybe so, but not to Graham. That roaring and rowdy Chicago era is as real to him today as the Council Wars are to aldermen. Then, Big Bill Thompson was mayor. Chicago wrestled with Prohibition and spawned an international reputation for gruesome crime by the Al Capone gang and the Dion O'Bannion hoods.

Now the 1920s lives in a stack of crates in Graham's Libertyville home. Early next year, the 24-year-old will give Chicago its first museum encapsulating that colorful era.

In 2½ years, Graham—who used his life savings for the collection—has compiled 2,000 historic pieces dating from 1893 to 1947. They are valued at more than $100,000. His archives from this period are considered among the best in the country.

Just where the museum will be, Graham's not telling. However, finding the proper spot was difficult, as most buildings associated with that era now are parking lots. The late Mayor Richard Daley wanted anything linked with the gangster image of Chicago wiped out.

But so in demand is Graham's collection that two European countries have requested that he exhibit his items overseas.

SOURCE: Lori Rotenberk, "Chicago's Gangster Era Lives in Libertyville: City's Rowdy Past Is Fodder for a Museum for the Future," *Chicago Sun-Times,* November 4, 1986, 25.

shows a marked increase in every major tourism indicator. Hotel occupancy in Chicago is up 4 percent; summer festival attendance is up 27 percent. More important, visitor attendance at public museums in Chicago is up between 20 and 35 percent during the peak months from May through August.[5] Bipartisan support for the promotion of both Chicago and Illinois by the Illinois House and Senate ensures continued long-term funding for the Illinois Office of Tourism.[6]

The completion of the McCormick Place expansion in 1985 allowed Chicago to maintain its position as the convention center of the world. The doubling of actual convention floor space to 2.1 million square feet left New York City, with 750,000 square feet, far behind. Projections show an annual increase of conventioneer spending of $276 million, tied to a 9 percent increase in attendance of trade shows based on the McCormick

---

[5] Illinois Department of Commerce and Community Affairs, August 1986 tourism fact sheet.

[6] William Recktenwald, "Madigan Pushes for Tourism," *Chicago Tribune,* April 14, 1986, sec. 2, 4.

FIGURE A.2   **PROPRIETOR'S RÉSUMÉ**

MICHAEL Y. GRAHAM

345 Cleveland Avenue
Libertyville, Illinois 60048

AREAS OF EXPERTISE	Considered to be the definitive historical expert on the following: Chicago Criminal History 1911–1933 focusing on James Colosimo, John Torrio, Al Capone, Dion O'Bannion, Hymie Weiss, George "Bugs" Moran.
	Chicago Political History 1920–1933 specializing on Mayors William Hale Thompson, William E. Dever, Anton J. Cermak, and Cook County State's Attorney Robert E. Crowe.
PERSONAL	Birthdate: 6-20-62 Single 6'0", 175 lbs. Excellent health
EDUCATION	Western Illinois University, Macomb, Illinois—2 years B.S. Degree—May 1982 Major: History Major: Political Science
EDUCATIONAL HIGHLIGHTS	Through a combination of C.L.E.P tests and upper-level proficiency examinations, I completed my 4-year B.S. degree in 2 years, the only person to accomplish this in the history of Western Illinois University.
	While attending Western I achieved a 4.0 GPA in Political Science and a 3.8 GPA in History, with an overall GPA of 3.56.
WORK EXPERIENCE	WESTGATE PRODUCTIONS, Toluca Lake, California
	Position: Researcher
	Responsibilities: From December 1985 to April 1986 I was the Chicago researcher for the two-hour TV docudrama "The Mystery of Al Capone's Vault." Duties included primary research, interviewing and screening people from the era, site location, script rewrite for historical accuracy.
	PARAMOUNT PICTURES, Chicago, Illinois
	Position: Historical Consultant for set decorations. A large portion of my collection was rented by Paramount for five major scenes in the movie *The Untouchables*.
	Currently lecturing to colleges and historical societies on U.S. and Chicago history during the Prohibition.
	LIBERTYVILLE TOWNSHIP, Libertyville, Illinois, 1983–1986
	Position: Libertyville Township Park Superintendent
	Responsibilities: Supervision of all township park maintenance and renovation and construction of new park facilities.
REFERENCES	Available upon request.

Place expansion. In conjunction with the facility's physical expansion, the McCormick Place Convention Bureau has undertaken a program to actively recruit foreign trade shows, most notably from Japan and Western Europe.[7]

The International Terminal expansion at O'Hare Airport increased foreign flights to and from Chicago by 25 percent in 1987. In conjunction with the O'Hare modernization, in 1984 the CTA opened the O'Hare–Jefferson Park mass transit line. The line allows 10,000 daily commuters access to downtown Chicago from O'Hare, giving them the opportunity for half-day or one-day visits to the Chicago area to see the city and the Roaring '20s Museum. The museum will provide a shuttle bus in the summer between the Jefferson Park station and the museum in cooperation with Sieben's Brewing Company.

[7] Jerry C. Davis, "A Bonanza of Benefits, McCormick Expansion Detailed," *Chicago Sun-Times*, January 3, 1985, Business Section, 1.

b) Competition: Direct and Indirect   There is currently no direct competition for the museum, nor is it likely that there will be any in the future. The lack of direct competition is ensured by having the most extensive collection on the subject of Prohibition in Chicago, one that can never be fully reproduced. What the museum will encounter is indirect competition from four major public museums and tourist attractions in the city, most notably the following:

- *The American Police Museum,* located at 1130 S. Wabash Avenue, Chicago, offers the public an awareness of what it is like to be a Chicago police officer. It provides programs in public safety and drug abuse prevention as well as Chicago police history. Yearly attendance is 10,000 visitors. There is no admission charge. The museum is 3½ miles southeast of the Roaring '20s.
- *The Chicago Historical Society,* located at North Avenue and Clark Street, is the general depository for all of Chicago's history and offers excellent exhibitions on all aspects of Chicago history. However, there is only a 3-by-6-foot section of the museum pertaining to Chicago's history during Prohibition, with four historic articles. Yearly attendance is 200,000; general admission is $1.50. It is situated 1½ miles northeast of the Roaring '20s location.
- *Here's Chicago,* located at 163 E. Pearson, is a multimedia slide and movie presentation showcasing current Chicago history. Visitors are exposed to Chicago architecture, history, and ethnic diversity during a 40-minute presentation. Yearly attendance is approximately 350,000 and admission is $3.75. It is located 1 mile east of the Roaring '20s Museum.
- *Ripley's Believe It Or Not Museum,* located at 1500 N. Wells Street, exhibits the weird and unique activities of man throughout the ages. Yearly attendance is 200,000, with an admission charge of $3.00. It is located 1 mile northwest of the Roaring '20s Museum.

The Roaring '20s Museum will also have to compete with Chicago's leading public museums, including the Museum of Science and Industry, Art Institute, and Adler Planetarium, and any other form of public entertainment, for the limited amount of time each visitor will have to spend in Chicago.

c) Strategy for Meeting Competition   The Roaring '20s Museum will combat indirect competition by clearly distinguishing itself from other tourist attractions in the city. Its promotional campaign will emphasize the unique characteristics of its 2,000-piece collection, its multimedia presentations, and the visitors' intimate participation and involvement in reliving the era. It will be promoted as the most unique and the *only* Prohibition/gangster era museum in the world.

III. Marketing

A. RESEARCH AND ANALYSIS

1. Target Market   As stated earlier, the focus of both time and financial commitment will be to attract visitors who most readily associate Chicago with its gangster past. The market survey (page 330) shows that foreign visitors show the greatest interest in Chicago's gangster era. Sixty-seven percent of the 900,000 annual foreign visitors to Chicago are made up of six nationalities: Canadian, English, Japanese, Mexican, West German, and French. Following the foreign tourist, the next area of focus will be the attraction of Chicago's 2.8 million conventioneers and their annual expenditure of $87 million on tourist-entertainment activities. Out-of-state visitors, which total 3.1 million each year, are primarily from St. Louis, Indianapolis, Milwaukee, and Detroit and compose the third segment of our market. The last segment will be the local Chicago metropolitan market with a potential of 3.5 million visitors.

2. Channel of Distribution and Location of the Roaring '20s Museum   The channel the Roaring '20s Museum will use is direct retailer to buyer. The geographic location of the Roaring '20s Museum has been carefully selected to maximize access to its target markets. Situated at 436 W. Ontario (see Figure A.1) the museum is one block away from the city's highest traffic pattern, the Ohio/Ontario corridor. This corridor is Chicago's major artery linking the suburban and O'Hare Airport automobile traffic with the downtown area. According to a survey, 50,000 to 67,000 cars pass through this area each day: commuters, business travelers, and tourists.[8]

In addition to the area's heavy traffic pattern, Ontario Street itself has become Chicago's trendiest address for restaurants, nightclubs, and fast-food establishments. Four of the top ten volume restaurants in Chicago, according to industry surveys, are scattered along it: Pizzeria Due, Ed Debevic's, Carson's the Place for Ribs, and a McDonald's restaurant.[9] Other attractions on the thoroughfare, which one writer calls "Eat Street" and another "Action Alley," include the Limelight nightclub, Mike Ditka's Sport Bar, and the Hard Rock Cafe. All the above restaurants are no more than 6 blocks away from the Roaring '20s Museum site.

Locating the Roaring '20s Museum next to Chicago's first and only microbrewery restaurant, Sieben's Brewing Company, is the single strongest factor favoring the location on Ontario Street. The 165,000 annual patrons to the brewery restaurant are regarded as likely potential visitors to the Roaring '20s Museum, located only 75 feet away from the brewery's main entrance. Historically, Sieben's Brewing Company played an important role in the shaping of Chicago's history during Prohibition, and Al Capone was a verified part owner. Discussion on joint tours and advertising campaigns are currently being finalized with the brewery owners. According to a conversation with Dick Walsh, a 28-year veteran of the commercial real estate industry in Chicago's Loop and near north side, "This is the best location for a museum of this nature in Chicago today."

3. Expected Market Share   Based on expected sales projections for the first five years, Table A.4 is a breakdown of expected market share versus time for each market segment.

B. MARKETING PLAN: OUTLINE OF ACTIVITIES TO BE USED IN PROMOTING THE MUSEUM
1. Advertising Methods for the Roaring '20s Museum   Advertising methods for the attraction of visitors will focus on radio, print, billboards, and brochure distribution. The advertising campaign has been designed to reach each target market and to allow for overlap to ensure complete coverage.

For the attraction of conventioneers and foreign and out-of-state tourists, the museum has chosen to advertise in Chicago's two most popular and most circulated convention and tourism magazines. Half-page, black-and-white ads describing the museum and its location will be placed in the following magazines:

1. *Key* magazine, weekly circulation of 20,000. Half-page ads will run for 26 weeks, May through October.

2. *Where* magazine, monthly circulation of 80,000. Half-page ads will run for six months, May through October.

Both magazines are distributed to hotels, restaurants, tourist attractions, and local convention and trade shows.

Coupled with the above magazines' circulation, an annual allotment of 50,000 museum brochures will be made available to the Illinois Tourism Office for distribution to its 17 state and 4 national satellite tourist information booths. McCormick Place Convention Aid Tourism Bureau will receive 25,000 brochures for distribution at the convention center and its Water Tower tourist information booth on Michigan Avenue. An additional 20,000 brochures will be made available to the Chicago Tourism Council and the Greater State Street Association for distribution. The museum will also provide 10,000 each of brochures in Japanese, German, French, and Spanish. Additional brochures will be distributed to foreign consulates in Chicago.

Complementing the above advertising activity, eight 3½-by-5¼-foot transparency advertising posters will be set up at the following locations:

- 2 located at O'Hare International Airport
- 3 located at Midway National Airport

---

[8] Business Plan, Sieben's Brewing Company, July 1985, 7–8.

[9] Ibid.

TABLE A.4			**PROJECTED MARKET SHARE**			

Number of Visitors to Chicago	Type	Fiscal Year				
		1st	**2nd**	**3rd**	**4th**	**5th**
900,000	Foreign	3.00%	4.00%	5.00%	6.00%	6.50%
2.8 million	Convention	1.00	1.50	2.00	2.50	3.00
3.1 million	Out-of-state	0.75	0.75	1.00	1.50	2.00
3.5 million	Local	1.00	2.00	2.00	2.00	2.50

Projected Total Attendance

1st Year	120,000
2nd year	171,000
3rd year	202,000
4th year	240,000
5th year	292,000

- 1 located at Union Railroad Station
- 1 located at Northwestern Railroad Station
- 1 located at the Greyhound Bus Terminal

In addition to the above, a 9-by-12-foot sign promoting the museum will be placed on the roof of the museum building at 436 W. Ontario Street, facing the Ohio Street exit, where 66,000 vehicles pass daily.

To attract local visitors, the following print advertising will be implemented:

1. 3-inch column advertisement in the *Chicago Tribune's* "Friday" section, to run only on the first Friday of every month beginning in May and ending in October. The *Chicago Tribune's* Friday metropolitan circulation is 696,000 copies.

2. 3-inch column advertisement in the *Chicago Sun-Times's* "Stepping Out" section, to be run the last Friday of the month beginning in May and ending in October. The *Chicago Sun-Times* Friday metropolitan circulation is 510,000 copies.

During the peak tourist season (June, July, and August), 48 radio ads will be aired Friday mornings on the following radio stations:

1. WGN, Roy Leonard Show, 10 A.M. to 3 P.M. Listening audience age 25–54, 6.7 radio market share. Two 30-second ads each Friday.

2. WLUP, Jonathan Brandmeier Show, 5:30 to 10 A.M. Listening audience age 18–34, 8.0 radio market share, number-one morning radio show in city. Two 30-second ads each Friday morning.

The final component of the public relations campaign will be the cultivation of the local, national, and international media. The museum and management will be made available for newspaper and magazine articles as well as radio and television interviews. By discussing the idea of the museum with local media experts, the museum's opening should receive a large share of local media coverage as well as national and international coverage. The museum will systematically inform the media of the activities and special events planned for the Roaring '20s Museum through the use of bulletins and media kits. Special monthly tours and parties will be given for members of the local media as well as persons or groups connected with the travel, convention, and tourism industry. In addition to the above, the management will provide free lectures to organizations, high schools, and colleges on Chicago's history during this period.

2. Sample Advertisement for the Roaring '20s Museum   The following is the script for a 30-second radio advertisement:

> Announcer (with husky gangster voice): Were you one of the 43 million suckers who watched the two-hour TV special, "The Mystery of Al Capone's Vault," with Geraldo Rivera? Well, you won't be a sucker, or disappointed, when you visit the Roaring '20s Museum at 436 W. Ontario Street. At the Roaring '20s you will relive Chicago's gangster era, meet Al Capone, and find out what it was really like when the streets of Chicago echoed with machine-gun fire. (Background: machine-gun fire) Remember, we are just 3 blocks west of Mike Ditka's, right next to Sieben's Brewing Company, at 436 W. Ontario. Open 10 A.M. until 12 P.M. on weekends.

3. Supporting Data for the Roaring '20s Attendance   In the process of assembling the historical material and financial resources for the opening of the Roaring '20s Museum, knowledgeable persons in the convention and tourism industry and Chicago business community were asked to comment on the feasibility of the museum.

- *William Hartnett, coproducer and part owner of "Here's Chicago":* "It's an idea whose time has come. I would have liked to have incorporated the gangster era into 'Here's Chicago's' presentation, but ran into opposition from the City of Chicago, which is the landlord of our building."[10]
- *Jim Krejcie, president of Sieben's Brewing Company:* "The combination of your museum and our microbrewery could lead to Chicago's number-one commercial tourist attraction, rivaling the Hancock and Sears Tower."[11]
- *Joseph Hannon, former chairman (1979–86), McCormick Place Convention and Tourism Bureau:* "A historically accurate, civically responsible, and entertaining museum, given the right location and capital funding, can't miss."[12]
- *Nancy Caldwell, tourist information manager at the Water Tower Tourist and Information Center:* "I have literally thousands of foreign visitors each year who ask me where the museum is on Al Capone. I'm looking forward to telling them to go to the Roaring '20s Museum on Ontario Street."[13]
- *Marilyn D. Clancey, president of the Chicago Tourism Council:* "Though I'm hesitant to give support to any project that might reinforce our gangster-town stigma, it is obvious to anyone familiar with the

[10] Phone interviews held between September 7 and 13, 1986.

[11] Ibid.

[12] Ibid.

[13] Ibid.

convention and tourism industry that a museum of this nature has an excellent chance at being a commercial success."[14]

The market survey presented below shows a potential visitor market for the Roaring '20s Museum as follows:

Foreign tourists	650,160
Out-of-state visitors	4,063,920
Local residents	1,707,480
Total	6,421,560

Based on the market survey and comparisons drawn from other commercial tourist attractions in both Chicago and other large cities, the projection of 120,000 visitors in our first year of operation is a realistic, if not conservative, projection.

IV. Research Design and Development

A. TECHNICAL DESCRIPTION OF SERVICE

1. How Service Is Used   The purpose of the Roaring '20s Museum is to take visitors back in time and allow them to relive Chicago's most colorful and murderous era. At the Roaring '20s Museum the visitors will interact with the historical displays and presentations. Visitors will partake in everything from watching a home whiskey still being operated, to visiting Sieben's Brewing Company, to witnessing a multimedia re-creation of the St. Valentine's Day Massacre, to bellying up to a speakeasy bar, to having a casual conversation with a multimedia re-creation of Al Capone and "Bugs" Moran. The patrons will be able to see, touch, hear, smell, and even taste what it was like to live when the streets of Chicago echoed with machine-gun fire.

The basic floor plan of the museum (see Figure A.3) will follow a chronological sequence beginning with the birth of the Prohibition movement in 1873 and ending with the death of Al Capone in 1947. Eighty-five percent of the museum's exhibits and multimedia presentations will focus on the actual years of Prohibition (1919–33), exploring the criminal, political, and social events of the era. Included in the museum will be a 1920s-style theater where footage of the most famous gangster movies will be shown every 20 minutes. There will also be vintage cars from the era. Employees will wear vintage clothing, and the visitors will have an opportunity to have their photos taken wearing Roaring '20s fashions while in the company of Al Capone or "Bugs" Moran. Finally there will be four special sections that will examine the emergence of jazz, sports figures of the period, Roaring '20s fashions, and a look at Chicago as it is today.

2. Past Feasibility Tests   Over a period of two years (August 1984–August 1986), a survey of foreign and out-of-state tourists as well as Chicagoland residents was conducted to determine the feasibility of a Prohibition/gangster era museum. The survey was composed of the following five questions:

1. What is your first and second word association when you think of Chicago?

2. What do you know about Al Capone, Carrie Nation, or Prohibition?

3. Would you be interested in visiting a museum that examines the entire Prohibition era?

4. What admission would you be most willing to pay? $2.50, $3.50, $4.50, or $5.00?

5. What type of historical displays would you expect to find in a museum of this nature?

---

[14] Ibid.

FIGURE A.3   **FLOOR PLAN**

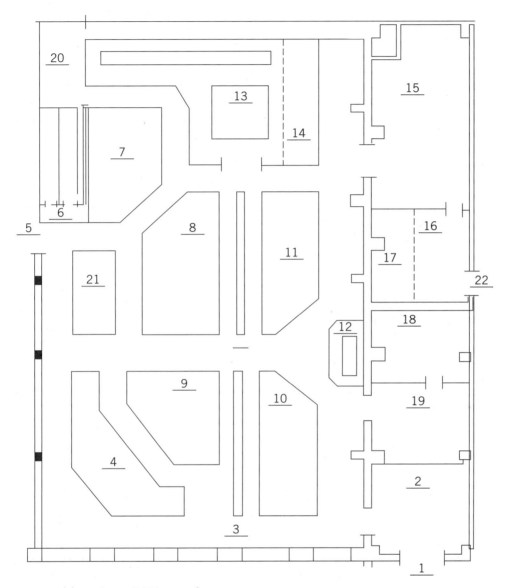

Museum Exhibition Space, 5,000 square feet
Offices, Archives, etc., 1,620 square feet

1. Main Entrance, Ontario Street
2. Ticket Sales Area
3. U.S. Temperance History
4. Sports Figures of the Era
5. Sieben's Brewing Company Tour
6. Rest Rooms
7. Chicago of the 1920s
8. Anatomy of a Gangster

9. Politicians of the Era
10. North Side Irish Gangsters
11. South Side Italian Gangsters
12. Capone's Cadillac
13. Capone's Office
14. St. Valentine's Day Massacre
15. Theater of the 1920s

16. Chicago Today
17. Souvenir Area
18. Archives
19. Offices
20. Storage Area
21. Fashions of the 1920s
22. Exit, Ohio Street

The three most important results of the survey are:

1. Out of the 750 foreign visitors questioned, 84 percent responded that they would visit a Prohibition-era museum, provided that a tour brochure was written in their native language; and 72 percent responded that they would pay $3.50 for admission.

2. Of out-of-state visitors surveyed 82 percent (including tourists and conventioneers) responded that they would visit the museum, and 69 percent stated that they would pay a $3.50 admission price. A total of 600 persons were surveyed.

3. Of Chicago-area residents surveyed 68 percent responded that they would likely· visit the museum, and 55 percent responded that they would pay a $3.50 admission price. There were 1,600 persons surveyed.

3. Future Tests   Future tests will be conducted daily by having customers fill out survey forms to determine their likes or dislikes concerning the multimedia presentations and the exhibition of historical material. Modification of exhibits will be made after specific trends have developed. Tests will also be conducted in the first two years of operation to determine the most effective promotional tools for attracting visitors. Surveys will be conducted on actual customers about how they became aware of the museum's existence and what made them want to visit it.

4. Follow-up Services   The Roaring '20s Museum is currently negotiating with Gray Line, Chicago Coach, and the City of Chicago Bus Tours to become a point of destination on their package tours of Chicago. In conjunction with the above, plans have been made for the third year of operation for the Roaring '20s Museum to conduct citywide tours of Chicago's historic gangster sites, under a joint arrangement with either Gray Line or Chicago Coach. The production and distribution of a video tour of the museum narrated in French, Spanish, Italian, German, English, and Japanese for international sale is planned for the third year of operation. Current discussions with Anheuser Busch, Inc., and the Miller Brewing Company call for franchising parts of the museum's archives relating to Prohibition and in particular to the brewing industry. The Roaring '20s Museum will allow one of the brewing companies exclusive access to its historical collection and museum exhibition space for a corporate display. In exchange for the above, a joint national advertising campaign promoting the museum will be required of the brewing company.

B. FACILITIES AND SPACE REQUIRED

The exterior of the museum will resemble a glamorized version of a Prohibition-era speakeasy (see Figure A.4). The decor of the entire museum, from Graham's office down to the cash register, will be made up of historic material from the 1920s. Special lighting, climate controls, and preservation methods in displaying the material will be taken into account when constructing the museum's interior. Display cabinets, counters, glass wall enclosures, and the framing of historical documents will be used throughout the museum for the display of historical material. Re-creations of historic scenes (the St. Valentine's Day Massacre, Dion O'Bannion's murder, etc.) will use a multimedia approach. Other special sections will include Al Capone's office, a re-creation of a speakeasy, a jazz section, as well as other special historic sections. The above special sections will be incorporated throughout the chronological sequence design of the museum. Also included will be a scaled-down version of a 1920s movie theater with seating for 75 people. The amount of floor space required for the exhibition of historic material and the re-creation of historic scenes is 5,000 square feet. An additional 1,500 square feet will be used for ticket and souvenir sales, office and research facilities, and public rest rooms (see Figure A.3). A state-of-the-art fire and burglar alarm system will be installed.

C. RESEARCH FACILITIES

Adjacent to the office will be a minilibrary and historical research area. This area will be the archives for the storage of historic material that is not on display and will also serve as a place for research on the era. Material in the museum will be made available for legitimate scholarly research on a conditional basis.

FIGURE A.4 **SKETCHES OF INTERIOR AND EXTERIOR OF THE MUSEUM**

V. Management

The legal and business structure of the Roaring '20s Museum will be established and operated as an Illinois Limited Partnership. The Roaring '20s Museum, Ltd., will be composed of the Roaring '20s Limited Partners, receiving a 76 percent equity interest, and the general partner, Era Management, Inc., which will receive the remaining 24 percent equity in the limited partnership. The general partner (Era Management, Inc.) is owned by the following four stockholders: Michael Yore Graham, William Hartnett, Joseph Hannon, and Burton Natarus. All aspects of the operation and management of the limited partnership will be conducted by Era Management, Inc. The four stockholders will constitute the board of directors and act in the following capacities:

Michael Y. Graham, President and General Operations Manager of Era Management, Inc. (See Figure A.2 for résumé.) Graham will be responsible for the overall operation of the museum, overseeing the construction of the museum's interior, the display and preservation of the historical material, hiring of personnel, supervising day-to-day operations and sales, and implementing major policy decisions made by the board of directors.

Immediately under Graham's charge will be a full-time museum manager who will work with Graham in the operation of the museum and gift shop and will assume Graham's responsibilities in his absence. Because of Graham's key role in the operation of the museum, and as the definitive historical expert on the era, a $350,000 key-man life insurance policy will be purchased to protect the limited partners' interests. In addition, two full-time ticket clerks and tour guides will be hired, as well as one full-time security guard and one full-time custodian. The museum will be very selective when hiring employees in order to ensure a friendly, enthusiastic, and responsible staff. All employees will be required to have a working knowledge of the history of Chicago during Prohibition, as it pertains to the museum.

Joseph Hannon, Vice President of Marketing Hannon is the former chairman of the McCormick Place Convention and Tourism Bureau. As the chairman of the world's largest convention center for six years, Hannon has acquired intimate firsthand knowledge of the convention and tourism industry in Chicago and will be responsible for coordinating our marketing and sales program.

William Hartnett, Vice President of Finance Hartnett is both a CPA and a successful real estate developer who was instrumental in developing Lake Point Towers. In addition, Hartnett is coproducer and part owner of "Here's Chicago," and he has three years of experience in the financial operation of Chicago's leading commercial tourist attraction.

Alderman Burton S. Natarus Natarus is the alderman for the 42nd ward, where the museum will be located. Alderman Natarus has served on the city council for 10 years and will serve as the museum's liaison with city hall. He will help expedite any city license or any zoning problems that may arise.

In return for their services, each member of the board of directors will receive a 1.3 percent interest in Era Management, Inc. The following is the equity structure for the limited partnership: General Partner, Era Management, Inc., 24 percent equity interest; Roaring '20s Museum limited partners, 76 percent equity interest. (See Figure A.5.)

VI. Critical Risks

This is a new business venture with no operating history and involving a high degree of risk, as any start-up business will meet. In analyzing this business plan, prospective investors should contact their financial advisers and carefully consider the following risk factors, which could adversely affect business.

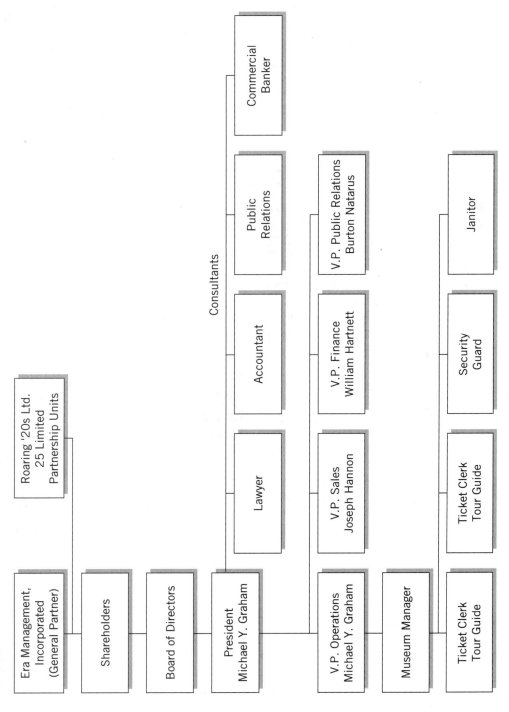

Era Management, Incorporated (General Partner)

Roaring '20s Ltd. 25 Limited Partnership Units

Shareholders

Board of Directors

President Michael Y. Graham

Consultants

Lawyer

Accountant

Public Relations

Commercial Banker

V.P. Operations Michael Y. Graham

V.P. Sales Joseph Hannon

V.P. Finance William Hartnett

V.P. Public Relations Burton Natarus

Museum Manager

Ticket Clerk Tour Guide

Ticket Clerk Tour Guide

Security Guard

Janitor

A. DELAYS

The time required to raise necessary capital, improve the premises, acquire movie and television rights for multimedia presentations, and obtain permits and licenses could conceivably be longer than anticipated.

B. EQUIPMENT

The use of multimedia technology involves complex equipment. Faulty design and installation of the equipment may result in delays and substandard performance. In addition to renovating the museum's interior, costs for environmental controls designed to protect the historic material may conceivably be higher than anticipated.

C. MANAGEMENT EXPERIENCE

The Board of Directors for Era Management, Inc., the general partner, has expertise in the historical background of the era, along with marketing and financial skills, as well as intimate knowledge of the convention and tourism industry. They, however, lack experience in operating a commercial museum, and this may adversely affect the museum's operation.

D. PUBLIC ACCEPTANCE

All indications show a very positive public response to the concept of a museum, but this could change because of the violent criminal subject matter that will be examined.

E. COMPETITION

There is a possibility that other public museums and tourist attractions may try to capitalize on visitors' interest in the gangster era by opening sections dealing with Chicago's history during this period, thus adversely affecting our projected attendance figures.

F. RETURN ON INVESTMENT

For the above-related reasons, a limited partner's return on investment by income distribution or sale is uncertain. There might never be any income earned by the partnership, and losses could consume limited partners' capital contributions. Even if the partnership earns income and makes a profit, there is no public market for LPUs and their value and resale potential are uncertain.

VII. Financial Segment

A. NOTES AND EXPLANATIONS FOR THE INCOME STATEMENT

This section will explain how the figures on the projected income statement (Tables A.5 through A.7) were calculated and the detailed assumptions that were made in their support.

1. Sales from Admission   Sales for the first five years are based on attracting the four primary target markets. The first year's anticipated sales of $420,000 and the subsequent next four years' sales were based on market survey tests and public amusement industry analyses. Era Management, Inc., has projected a 134 percent increase in sales by the fifth year of operation. Based on our financial commitment to a sustained and effective marketing program, coupled with our prime location, and in addition to offering the public the most unique, entertaining, educational, and interesting commercial museum in Chicago, Era Management, Inc., anticipates the museum will be able to meet and exceed the five-year projected sales, subject to the risks identified previously.

2. Souvenir Sales   The souvenir sales projected for the second through fifth year of operation were estimated at 8 percent of the attendance sales. This number was based on using the public amusement industry's average.[15] The above sales projection is shown net of credit card expense.

---

[15] Julie Polascek, Manager, Ripley's Chicago museum, September 7, 1986.

MONTHLY PROJECTED INCOME STATEMENT, FIRST YEAR

	July	Aug.	Sept.	Oct.	Nov.	Dec.	Jan.	Feb.	Mar.	Apr.	May	June	Total
Sales	$42,000	$42,000	$42,000	$42,000	$25,200	$25,200	$25,200	$25,200	$25,200	$42,000	$42,000	$42,000	$420,000
Gross Profit	42,000	42,000	42,000	42,000	25,200	25,200	25,200	25,200	25,200	42,000	42,000	42,000	420,000
Operating Expenses:													
Advertising	10,500	10,500	10,500	4,500	4,500	4,500	4,500	4,500	4,500	10,500	10,500	10,500	90,000
Salaries	8,341	8,271	8,041	8,142	7,665	7,132	6,534	6,261	6,586	7,912	8,815	8,250	91,950
Payroll	813	802	772	785	712	632	542	501	550	749	809	800	8,467
Rent	2,900	2,900	2,900	2,900	2,900	2,900	2,900	2,900	2,900	2,900	2,900	2,900	34,800
Goodwill of Bldg. Loc.	1,750	1,750	1,750	1,750	1,750	1,750	1,750	1,750	1,750	1,750	1,750	1,750	21,000
Utilities	2,000	2,000	2,000	2,000	2,000	2,000	2,000	2,000	2,000	2,000	2,000	2,000	24,000
Insurance	417	417	416	416	416	416	417	417	417	417	417	417	5,000
Accounting/Legal	200	200	200	200	200	200	200	200	200	200	200	200	2,400
Office Supplies	100	100	100	100	100	100	100	100	100	100	100	100	1,200
Repairs	150	150	150	150	150	150	150	150	150	150	150	150	1,800
Telephone	120	120	120	120	120	120	120	120	120	120	120	120	1,440
Depreciation Acquisition Pieces	113	113	113	113	113	113	113	113	113	113	113	113	1,358
Leasehold Improve.	5,956	5,952	5,952	5,952	5,952	5,952	5,952	5,952	5,952	5,952	5,952	5,952	71,428
Collection	2,500	2,500	2,500	2,500	2,500	2,500	2,500	2,500	2,500	2,500	2,500	2,500	30,000
Start-Up Cost	837	833	833	833	833	833	833	833	833	833	833	833	10,000
Sales Tax, 6%	2,520	2,520	2,520	2,520	1,512	1,512	1,512	1,512	1,512	2,520	2,520	2,520	25,200
Total Expense	39,217	39,128	38,867	32,981	31,423	30,810	30,123	29,809	30,183	38,716	39,679	39,105	420,041
Net Profit/Loss	2,783	2,872	3,133	9,019	(6,223)	(5,610)	(4,923)	(4,609)	(4,983)	3,284	2,321	2,895	(41)

No tax computed.

TABLE A.6

QUARTERLY PROJECTED INCOME STATEMENT

	Second Year					Third Year				
	Sept.	Dec.	Mar.	June	Total	Sept.	Dec.	Mar.	June	Total
Sales	$183,750	$78,750	$78,750	$183,750	$525,000	$238,875	$102,375	$102,375	$238,875	$682,500
Souvenir Sales	14,000	6,000	6,000	14,000	40,000	18,200	7,800	7,800	18,200	52,000
Cost of Goods Sold	6,300	2,700	2,700	6,300	18,000	9,590	4,110	4,110	9,590	27,400
Gross Profit	191,450	82,050	82,050	191,450	547,000	247,485	106,065	106,065	247,485	707,100
Operating Expenses:										
Advertising	36,225	15,525	15,525	36,225	103,500	41,658	17,854	17,854	41,659	119,025
Salaries	26,647	22,941	19,383	24,979	91,950	24,647	22,941	19,383	24,979	91,950
Payroll	2,963	1,270	1,270	2,964	8,467	2,963	1,270	1,270	2,964	8,467
Rent	9,483	9,483	9,483	9,483	37,932	10,337	10,336	10,337	10,336	41,346
Goodwill of Bldg. Loc.	6,562	6,563	6,562	6,563	26,250	8,531	8,532	8,531	8,531	34,125
Utilities	6,600	6,600	6,600	6,600	26,400	7,260	7,260	7,260	7,260	29,040
Insurance	1,625	1,625	1,625	1,625	6,500	2,193	2,194	2,194	2,194	8,775
Accounting/Legal	660	660	660	660	2,640	726	726	726	726	2,904
Office Supplies	330	330	330	330	1,320	363	363	363	363	1,452
Repairs	495	495	495	495	1,980	544	545	544	545	2,178
Telephone	468	468	468	468	1,872	631	632	632	632	2,527
Depreciation										
Acquisition Pieces	945	945	945	945	3,780	1,583	1,582	1,583	1,582	6,330
Capital Improve.	17,857	17,857	17,857	17,857	71,428	17,857	17,857	17,857	17,857	71,428
Collection	11,000	11,000	11,000	11,000	44,000	10,500	10,500	10,500	10,500	42,000
Start-Up Cost	2,500	2,500	2,500	2,500	10,000	2,500	2,500	2,500	2,500	10,000
Sales Tax, 6%	11,865	5,085	5,085	11,865	33,900	15,424	6,610	6,611	15,425	44,070
Total Expense	129,225	98,347	94,788	129,559	451,919	142,717	106,702	103,145	143,053	495,617
Net Profit/Loss	62,225	(16,297)	(12,738)	61,891	75,081	104,768	(637)	2,920	104,432	211,483
No tax computed.										

| TABLE A.7 | YEARLY PROJECTED INCOME STATEMENT, FIVE FISCAL YEARS |

	First	Second	Third	Fourth	Fifth	Sales Ratio
Sales	$420,000	$525,000	$682,500	$819,000	$ 982,800	91.8%
Souvenir Sales		40,000	52,000	67,600	87,880	8.2
Cost of Goods Sold		18,000	27,400	35,620	46,306	4.3
Gross Sales	420,000	547,000	707,100	850,980	1,024,374	95.7
Operating Expenses:						
Advertising	90,000	103,500	119,024	142,829	171,395	16.0
Salaries	91,950	91,950	91,950	110,340	115,857	10.8
Payroll	8,467	8,467	8,467	10,160	10,668	1.0
Rent	34,800	37,932	41,346	45,067	49,123	4.6
Goodwill of Bldg. Loc.	21,000	26,250	34,125	40,950	49,140	4.6
Utilities	24,000	26,400	29,040	31,944	35,138	3.3
Insurance	5,000	6,500	8,775	11,408	14,830	1.4
Accounting/Legal	2,400	2,640	2,904	3,485	17,425	1.6
Office Supplies	1,200	1,320	1,452	1,597	1,757	0.2
Repairs	1,800	1,980	2,178	2,396	4,792	0.4
Telephone	1,440	1,872	2,527	3,293	4,281	0.4
Depreciation						
Acquisition Pieces	1,356	3,780	6,330	7,050	6,930	0.6
Leasehold Improve.	71,428	71,428	71,428	71,428	71,428	6.7
Collection	30,000	44,000	42,000	42,000	42,000	3.9
Start-Up Cost	10,000	10,000	10,000	10,000	10,000	0.9
Sales Tax, 6%	25,200	33,900	44,070	53,196	64,241	6.0
Total Expense	420,041	471,919	495,617	587,143	669,005	62.5
Net Profit/Loss	(41)	75,081	211,483	263,837	355,369	

No tax computed.

3. Cost of Goods Sold for Souvenir Sales   The cost projection for souvenirs was based on an oral estimate of wholesale souvenir costs provided by Chicago Etc., the leading supplier of souvenir items to the Chicago area.

4. Gross Profit   (line 1 + line 2) − line 3 = line 4.

5. Advertising   Expenses for advertising for the first three years of operation are based on written and oral estimates from the following advertising media. The first-year budget of $90,000 for advertising is broken down as follows:

$ 8,500	6 months (May through October), ½-page, black-and-white ad in *Where* magazine
7,900	26 weeks (May through October), ½-page, black-and-white ad in *Key* magazine
12,000	200,000 color museum brochures, $.06 per piece
6,720	24 commercial radio spots on WGN's Roy Leonard Show; two 30-second ads will be run every Friday during the months of June, July, and August; each spot costs $280 × 24 ads = $6,720
9,600	24 commercial radio spots on WLUP's Jonathan Brandmeier Show; two 30-second radio ads every Friday for the months of June, July, and August; each spot costs $400 × 24 ads = $9,600

8,520	3-inch column ads placed in the *Chicago Tribune* the first Friday of each month, May through October; $1,420 per ad × 6 months = $8,520
7,950	3-inch column ads placed in the *Chicago Sun-Times* the last Friday of each month, May through October; $1,325 per ad × 6 months = $7,950
6,234	One 43-by-63-inch sign placed at the O'Hare Airport International Terminal; yearly rent $6,234
4,200	Two 43-by-63-inch signs at Union Station; yearly rent for both signs $4,200
2,800	One 43-by-63-inch sign in the Greyhound Bus Terminal; yearly rent $2,800
2,900	One 43-by-63-inch sign placed at the Northwestern Railroad Station; yearly rent $2,900
4,250	One 43-by-63-inch sign placed at Midway Airport; yearly rent $4,250
2,500	Construction of lighted 9-by-12-foot sign for the roof of the museum building, $2,500
4,500	Catering of opening day party
1,236	Miscellaneous advertising expenses
$90,000	TOTAL ADVERTISING BUDGET

Era Management, Inc., has projected a 90 percent increase in advertising expenditure by the end of the fifth year of operation. This increase will allow us to continue reaching our target markets and to increase expenditures in those advertising media found most effective in drawing visitors to the museum. The museum's cultivation of public relations constitutes the 44 percent difference between the projected five-year sales increase of 134 percent and the projected five-year advertising budget increase of 90 percent.

6. Salaries Salary expense for the first three years of operation is broken down as follows: $30,000, general operation manager's salary; $18,000, museum manager's salary; $11,000 each for janitor and security guard; $10,000 each for two full-time ticket sales clerks. In the fourth year of operation, a 20 percent increase in all salaries will occur, followed by a 5 percent increase the fifth year. In addition to their salaries, bonuses ranging from 10 to 25 percent of their base salaries are projected to be paid to employees in all five years of operation. (See payroll expenses below.)

7. Payroll Expenses Payroll includes social security withholding, overtime, holiday pay, and yearly bonuses for employees. There is no projected increase in the first three years of operation, a 20 percent increase in the fourth year, and a 5 percent increase in the fifth year.

8. Rent Rent for the first year was taken from a written estimate from Walsh Realty, landlord of the building ($2,512 per month for 6,500 square feet). In addition, the lease calls for the museum to pay $388 per month to cover its share of the real estate tax, for a total of $2,900 per month. The lease calls for a 9 percent annual increase for the first five years of operation.

9. Goodwill Location In addition to the rent, the landlord will receive 5 percent of yearly gross sales. The 5 percent figure is based on the "goodwill" of the building's prime location for the attraction of visitors. Five percent of estimated first-year sales is $21,000. The 5 percent clause is an annual payment for the extent of the seven-year lease.

10. Utilities The monthly utility rate of $2,000 per month was based on the previous renter's utility bill of $1,200. The 67 percent increase in our utility projection accounts for the extended museum hours. It is anticipated that utility rates will increase 10 percent annually in the second through fifth years.

11. Insurance   The insurance premium of $5,000 per year was taken from an oral estimate by Safeco Insurance Company, for coverage of fire, theft, flood, and liability insurance. The majority of the insurance premium is for liability insurance. For this reason, I have increased my total insurance premium the same percent as the increase in attendance for the second through fifth years.

12. Accounting/Legal   The majority of legal and accounting expense will be incurred as a start-up cost prior to the first year of operation. Projections for accounting and legal expense were determined by oral estimates given by the partnership's accountant and attorney. The majority of this expense will be paid for tax preparation and the yearly auditing of the museum's books. The fifth year shows an increase of 500 percent in both the accounting and legal expense due to the sale of the museum in the sixth year.

13. Office Supplies   This expense projection is based on an oral estimate by an office forms supplier. The $1,200 estimate allows for stationery, envelopes, and other office expense incidentals. It is anticipated that there will be a large volume of written correspondence in the first year of operation. A 10 percent annual increase has been projected for the second through fifth years of operation.

14. Repairs   Repairs and maintenance supplies for daily cleaning have been projected at $1,800 in the first year. Supplies will be purchased jointly with Sieben's Brewing Company, significantly reducing the costs. The $1,800 includes city and outside service, inspection and repairs for heating, lighting, or anything else mechanically related. A 10 percent increase per year for the second through fifth years is anticipated.

15. Telephone   The first year telephone expense was computed by Illinois Bell Telephone after a description of the business was given to them. The cost for installation has been included in the capital leasehold improvements. The increase for the second through fifth years is proportional to the increase in sales.

16. Depreciation   Depreciation has been calculated using the five-year accelerated write-off formula for the historical collection and the acquisition of historic pieces capital accounts. The capital leasehold improvements were depreciated using a straight-line method with no salvage value for the length of the seven-year lease. Start-up costs have been amortized using a straight-line method over a seven-year write-off period.

17. Sales Tax   All sales tax was computed on a monthly basis of 6 percent of sales (lines 1 + 2).

18. Total Expense   Sum of lines 5 through 17.

19. Net Profit/Loss   Gross profit (line 4) less total expense (line 18).

20. Income Tax   The limited partnership structure allows "passing through" of losses and profits to investors; therefore no income tax has been computed in the income statement.

B. NOTES AND EXPLANATIONS FOR PROJECTED CASH FLOW STATEMENT

This section will explain how the figures for the projected cash flow statement were calculated and the assumptions that were made (Tables A.8 and A.9). It is assumed that projections will remain constant for all five years unless stated otherwise.

1. *Cash Receipts.* It is anticipated that 100 percent of all ticket sales will be on a cash basis payable at the time of admission.

TABLE A.8

FIRST-YEAR MONTHLY CASH FLOW PROJECTION

	July	Aug.	Sept.	Oct.	Nov.	Dec.	Jan.	Feb.	Mar.	Apr.	May	June	Total
Cash Receipts	$42,000	$42,000	$42,000	$42,000	$25,200	$25,200	$25,200	$25,200	$25,200	$42,000	$42,000	$42,000	$420,000
Cash Disbursements													
Advertising	10,500	10,500	10,500	4,500	4,500	4,500	4,500	4,500	4,500	10,500	10,500	10,500	90,000
Salary	8,341	8,271	8,041	8,142	7,665	7,132	6,534	6,261	6,586	7,912	8,815	8,250	91,950
Payroll Expense	813	802	772	785	712	632	542	501	550	749	809	800	8,467
Rent Expense	2,900	2,900	2,900	2,900	2,900	2,900	2,900	2,900	2,900	2,900	2,900	2,900	34,800
Goodwill of Bldg. Loc.	9,000						12,000						21,000
Utilities Expense	2,000	2,000	2,000	2,000	2,000	2,000	2,000	2,000	2,000	2,000	2,000	2,000	24,000
Insurance Expense	2,500						2,500						5,000
Accounting/Legal	1,200					1,200							2,400
Office Supplies	600						600						1,200
Repairs						300						1,500	1,800
Telephone	120	120	120	120	120	120	120	120	120	120	120	120	1,440
Acquisition Pieces	750	750	750	750	750	750	750	750	750	750	750	750	9,000
Sales Tax, 6%	2,520	2,520	2,520	2,520	1,512	1,512	1,512	1,512	1,512	2,520	2,520	2,520	25,200
Total Disbursements	41,244	27,863	27,603	21,717	20,159	21,046	33,958	18,544	18,918	27,451	28,414	29,340	316,257
Cash Flow	756	14,137	14,397	20,283	5,041	4,154	(8,758)	6,656	6,282	14,549	13,586	12,660	103,743
Opening Balance	80,000	80,756	94,893	102,290	129,573	134,614	138,768	130,010	136,656	142,948	157,497	171,083	
Ending Balance	80,756	94,893	102,290	129,573	134,614	138,768	130,010	136,666	142,948	157,497	171,083	183,743	

TABLE A.9

QUARTERLY CASH FLOW PROJECTIONS

	Second Year					Third Year				
	Sept.	Dec.	Mar.	June	Total	Sept.	Dec.	Mar.	June	Total
Cash Receipts	$183,750	$78,750	$78,750	$183,750	$525,000	$238,875	$102,375	$102,375	$238,875	$682,500
Souvenir Sales	14,000	6,000	6,000	14,000	40,000	18,200	7,800	7,800	18,200	52,000
Cost of Goods Sold	6,300	2,700	2,700	6,300	18,000	9,590	4,110	4,110	9,590	27,400
Gross Sales	191,450	82,050	82,050	191,450	547,000	247,485	106,065	106,065	247,485	707,100
Cash Disbursements										
Advertising	36,225	15,525	15,525	36,225	103,500	41,658	17,854	17,854	41,658	119,024
Salary	24,647	22,941	19,383	24,979	91,950	24,647	22,941	19,383	24,979	91,950
Payroll Expense	2,963	1,270	1,270	2,964	8,467	2,963	1,270	1,270	2,964	8,467
Rent Expense	9,483	9,483	9,483	9,483	37,932	10,337	10,336	10,337	10,336	41,346
Goodwill of Bldg. Loc.		13,125	13,125		26,250		17,063	17,062		34,125
Utilities Expense	6,600	6,600	6,600	6,600	26,400	7,260	7,260	7,260	7,260	29,040
Insurance Expense		3,250	3,250		6,500		4,387	4,388		8,775
Accounting/Legal			2,640		2,640			2,904		2,904
Office Supplies		660		660	1,320		726		726	1,452
Repairs	990			990	1,980	1,089			1,089	2,178
Telephone	468	468	468	468	1,872	634	633	633	633	2,533
Acquisition Pieces	3,000	3,000	3,000	3,000	12,000	3,000	3,000	3,000	3,000	12,000
Sales Tax, 6%	11,865	5,085	5,085	11,865	33,900	15,424	6,610	6,611	15,425	44,070
Payout to Limited Partners		200,000			200,000		200,000			200,000
Total Disbursements	96,241	281,407	79,829	97,234	554,711	107,012	292,080	90,702	108,070	597,864
Cash Flow	95,209	(199,357)	2,221	94,216	(7,711)	140,473	(186,015)	15,363	139,415	109,236
Opening Balance	183,743	278,953	79,595	81,816		176,032	316,505	130,490	145,853	
Ending Balance	278,952	79,596	81,816	176,032		316,505	130,490	145,853	285,268	

Continued

TABLE A.9

QUARTERLY CASH FLOW PROJECTIONS (continued)

	Fourth Year					Fifth Year				
	Sept.	Dec.	Mar.	June	Total	Sept.	Dec.	Mar.	June	Total
Cash Receipts	$286,650	$122,850	$122,850	$286,650	$819,000	$343,980	$147,420	$147,420	$343,980	$982,800
Souvenir Sales	23,660	10,140	10,140	23,660	67,600	30,758	13,182	13,182	30,758	87,880
Cost of Goods Sold	12,467	5,343	5,343	12,467	35,620	16,207	6,946	6,946	16,207	46,306
Gross Sales	297,843	127,647	127,647	297,843	850,980	358,531	153,656	153,656	358,531	1,024,374
Cash Disbursements										
Advertising	49,990	21,424	21,425	49,990	142,829	59,988	25,709	25,709	59,989	171,395
Salary	38,619	16,551	16,551	38,619	110,340	40,550	17,379	17,378	40,550	115,857
Payroll Expense	3,556	1,524	1,524	3,556	10,160	3,734	1,600	1,600	3,734	10,668
Rent Expense	11,267	11,267	11,267	11,266	45,067	12,280	12,281	12,281	12,281	49,123
Goodwill of Bldg. Loc.		20,475	20,475		40,950		24,570	24,570		49,140
Utilities Expense	7,986	7,986	7,986	7,986	31,944	8,784	8,784	8,784	8,785	35,138
Insurance Expense		5,704	5,704		11,408		7,415	7,415		14,830
Accounting/Legal			3,485		3,485			17,425		17,425
Office Supplies		798		799	1,597		878	879		1,757
Repairs	1,198			1,198	2,396	2,396			2,396	4,792
Telephone	823	823	823	824	3,293	1,070	1,070	1,070	1,071	4,281
Acquisition Pieces					0					0
Sales Tax, 6%	18,619	7,979	7,979	18,619	53,196	22,484	9,636	9,636	22,484	64,241
Payout to Limited Partners		300,000			300,000				600,000	600,000
Total Disbursements	132,058	394,531	97,219	132,857	756,665	151,286	109,322	126,748	751,290	1,138,647
Cash Flow	165,785	(266,884)	30,428	164,986	94,315	207,245	44,334	26,907	(392,759)	(114,273)
Opening Balance	285,268	451,053	184,169	214,597		379,583	586,828	631,162	658,069	
Ending Balance	451,053	184,169	214,597	379,583		586,828	631,162	658,069	265,310	

2. *Souvenir Sales.* It is expected that 15 percent of all souvenir sales will involve the use of credit cards, based on Sieben's Brewing Company souvenir credit card sales. This figure is shown net of credit card expenses. The balance of 85 percent will be cash sales.

3. *Cost of Goods Sold.* Souvenirs will be purchased on a quarterly basis, reflecting the seasonal increase in attendance.

4. *Gross Profit.* (Line 1 + line 2) − line 3.

5. *Advertising.* The cost of advertising has been projected to be paid monthly, in the month that it is incurred. Seventy percent of the advertising budget is disbursed during the months of April through September.

6. *Salaries.* Salaries will be disbursed when incurred.

7. *Payroll Expense.* The social security tax will be paid the month after the expense is incurred. Overtime, bonuses, and holiday pay will be paid in the month that they are incurred.

8. *Rent Expense.* Rent will be paid in the beginning of the month when it is incurred.

9. *Goodwill of Building Location.* The 5 percent is payable in semiannual payments in January and July.

10. *Utilities Expense.* The utility bill will be paid in the month that the expense is incurred.

11. *Insurance Expense.* Insurance premium is paid semiannually, January and July, in equal installments.

12. *Accounting/Legal Expenses.* The accountant and lawyer will be paid semiannually.

13. *Office Supplies.* Office supplies are paid for twice a year in July and December.

14. *Repairs and Maintenance Expense.* City and outside service inspection, as well as the purchase of maintenance supplies, is scheduled for the month of June. Additional maintenance supplies are scheduled to be purchased in December.

15. *Telephone Expense.* The telephone payment is made in the month after the expense is incurred.

16. *Acquisition.* A projected monthly expenditure of $750, based on past monthly purchases of historic material, has been estimated, although this figure could fluctuate each month depending on what historic material becomes available.

17. *Sales Tax.* Tax payments will be made monthly.

18. *Payout to Limited Partnership.* Payments for the second through fifth years of operation will be made in December.

19. *Total Cash Disbursements.* Sum of lines 5 through 18.

20. *Cash Flow.* Line 4 − line 19.

21. *Opening Cash Balance.* $80,000 working capital for the first year of operation. For the next four years, the opening balance equals the ending balance for preceding year.

22. *Ending Balance.* Cash flow plus opening balance.

C. EXPLANATIONS OF PROJECTED BALANCE SHEETS FOR FIVE YEARS

This section will explain how the figures for the projected balance sheets were calculated and the assumptions that were made (Table A.10).

1. *Cash on Hand.* Projected cash on hand reflects the end balance of projected cash flow statements for each of the five years.

BALANCE SHEET

First Year

Assets

Current		
Cash on Hand		$183,743
Total	$183,743	
Fixed		
Acquisition Pieces	$ 9,000	
Less Accum. Depreciation	1,356	$ 7,644
Capital Improvements	500,000	
Less Accum. Depreciation	71,428	428,572
Historic Collection	200,000	
Less Accum. Depreciation	30,000	170,000
Start-Up Cost	70,000	
Less Accum. Amort. Costs	10,000	60,000
Total		$666,216
Total Assets		$849,959

Capital

Partners' Equity		$850,000
Profit (Loss)		(41)
Capital Payout to Limited Partners		0
Net Worth		$849,959

Second Year

Assets

Current		
Cash on Hand		$176,032
Total	$176,032	
Fixed		
Acquisition Pieces	$ 21,000	
Less Accum. Depreciation	5,136	$ 15,864
Capital Improvements	500,000	
Less Accum. Depreciation	142,856	357,144
Historic Collection	200,000	
Less Accum. Depreciation	74,000	126,000
Start-Up Cost	70,000	
Less Accum. Amort. Costs	20,000	50,000
Total		$549,008
Total Assets		$725,040

Capital

Partners' Equity		$849,959
Profit (Loss)		75,081
Capital Payout to Limited Partners		200,000
Net Worth		$725,040

BALANCE SHEET (continued)

Third Year

Assets

Current		
Cash on Hand	$285,268	
Total		$285,268
Fixed		
Acquisition Pieces	$ 33,000	
Less Accum. Depreciation	11,466	$ 21,534
Capital Improvements	500,000	
Less Accum. Depreciation	214,284	285,716
Historic Collection	200,000	
Less Accum. Depreciation	116,000	84,000
Start-Up Cost	70,000	
Less Accum. Amort. Costs	30,000	40,000
Total		$431,250
Total Assets		$716,518

Capital

Partners' Equity	$725,040
Profit (Loss)	191,478
Capital Payout to Limited Partners	200,000
Net Worth	$716,518

Fourth Year

Assets

Current		
Cash on Hand	$379,583	
Total		$379,583
Fixed		
Acquisition Pieces	$ 33,000	
Less Accum. Depreciation	18,516	$ 14,484
Capital Improvements	500,000	
Less Accum. Depreciation	285,712	214,288
Historic Collection	200,000	
Less Accum. Depreciation	158,000	42,000
Start-Up Cost	70,000	
Less Accum. Amort. Costs	40,000	30,000
Total		$300,772
Total Assets		$680,355

Capital

Partners' Equity	$716,518
Profit (Loss)	263,837
Capital Payout to Limited Partners	300,000
Net Worth	$680,355

(Continued)

Fifth Year

Assets

Current			
Cash on Hand		$265,310	
Total			$265,310
Fixed			
Acquisition Pieces	$ 33,000		
Less Accum. Depreciation	25,446	$ 7,554	
Capital Improvements	500,000		
Less Accum. Depreciation	357,140	142,860	
Historic Collection	200,000		
Less Accum. Depreciation	200,000	0	
Start-Up Cost	70,000		
Less Accum. Amort. Costs	50,000	20,000	
Total			$170,414
Total Assets			$435,724

Capital

Partners' Equity		$680,355
Profit (Loss)		355,369
Capital Payout to Limited Partners		600,000
Net Worth		$435,724

Note: A select ratio analysis has been made on the limited partnership's profit before tax and the return on assets for the fifth year of operation. Prentice-Hall's *Almanac of Industrial Ratios* was used in analyzing the limited partners' ratios, as compared to the amusement and recreational service industry average. The analysis of the two above selections shows that the limited partnership's ratio is significantly higher than the industry average.

2. *Acquisition of Pieces.* $9,000 worth of historical pieces were purchased in the first year of operation. An additional $12,000 worth will be purchased each year in the second and third years. Depreciation has been calculated using the five-year accelerated write-off formula for the historical collection and the acquisition of historic pieces capital accounts.

3. *Capital Leasehold Improvements.* The capital leasehold improvements are the total amount spent for the renovation of the museum's interior. The capital leasehold improvements were depreciated using a straight-line method with no salvage value for the length of the seven-year lease.

4. *Historic Collection.* The current replacement cost for the collection is $200,000. It will be depreciated using the five-year accelerated write-off formula.

5. *Start-Up Costs.* Start-up costs for the museum are projected at $70,000 and have been amortized using a straight-line method over a seven-year period.

6. *Total Assets.* The sum of cash on hand plus fixed assets minus depreciation.

7. *Partners' Equity.* The sum of the general partner's historic collection ($200,000) plus the limited partners' capital investment of $650,000 equals $850,000.

8. *Profit (Loss).* Taken from the projected income statements for each of the previous five years.

9. *Capital Payout.* The balance sheets for the second through fifth years will show a cash payout that is taken from the December quarterly cash flow statement for each respective year.

10. *Net Worth.* Line 7 + line 8 − line 9 = line 10.

D. PROFESSIONAL SUPPORT

The following will act on a consulting basis for the Roaring '20s Museum.

- **Accountant/CPA:** Belinda Zorn, Libertyville, Illinois
- **Insurance:** Pete Thompson, Safeco Insurance Company, Libertyville, Illinois
- **Legal Counsel:** Dennis Ryan, Gardner, Carton & Douglas, Libertyville, Illinois
- **Commercial Banker:** David Weinberg, Harris Bank, Chicago, Illinois

E. DETAILED USE OF CAPITAL FUNDS OBTAINED FROM THE SALE OF TWENTY-FIVE LPUS

Amount	Use of Funds	Allocation Date
$ 10,000	Architectural design, city licenses, and building permits	February, 1st Year
300,000	Capital leasehold improvements, interior renovation of museum, heating, lighting, plumbing, construction of display fixtures, special historic sections	March and June, 1st Year
190,000	Multimedia re-creation of St. Valentine's Day Massacre, 75-seat theater, licensing for gangster and newsreel movie rights	April, 1st Year
70,000	5-year key-man life insurance, preopening advertising, legal and accounting fees, insurance and rent prior to opening, other misc. expenses	February–July, 1st Year
80,000	Operating fund to cover expected and unexpected costs in the first year of operation	July, 1st Year–June, 2nd Year
$650,000	Total	

An open line of credit will be established at the Harris Bank in Chicago to meet unexpected financial needs.

VIII. Conclusion and Summary

A. TOTAL CAPITAL NEEDED

The total capital required for the opening and first-year operation of the museum is $650,000. The capital will be used in the following manner: $500,000 for the total renovation of the museum's interior, $70,000 in start-up costs, and $80,000 for the first year's working capital fund. A $100,000 open line of credit will be established at the Harris Bank to cover unexpected capital needs.

It is anticipated that the capital will be raised by selling 25 LPUs at $26,000 each, giving the limited partners a 76 percent equity in the limited partnership. The general partner, Era Management, Inc., will contribute $200,000 (the current value of the historic collection) and receive in return a 24 percent equity position in the limited partnership.

In the event that the $100,000 open line of credit is insufficient to cover unexpected needs, the general partner, upon approval of the limited partners, will offer for sale additional LPUs. The loss of owner's equity, expressed as a percent of the total equity, due to the issuance of additional LPUs, will be divided on a 24 percent/76 percent ratio between the general partner and the limited partners.

B. RETURN ON INVESTMENT FOR LIMITED PARTNERS

The total limited partners' equity interest is 76 percent, and they will receive cash payments and proceeds from the sale of the museum based on this percentage. The projected total cash payout for each $26,000 LPU is computed as follows:

	Cash Payout	/ Investment	= ROI
2nd Year Operation	$ 6,080	$26,000	23%
3rd Year Operation	6,080	26,000	23
4th year Operation	9,120	26,000	35
5th Year Operation	18,240	26,000	70
Total Cash Payout	$39,520		151%

In the beginning of the sixth year of operation, it is anticipated that the museum will be sold at three times the gross sales of the fifth fiscal year ($1,024,374 $\times$ 3 = $3,073,122), which is the public amusement industry guide when selling businesses of this nature.[16] The sale of the museum will yield each LPU $93,423 capital gain. The total ROI for each LPU before tax equals (Cash payout) $39,520 + (Capital gain) $93,423 = $132,943, or 511 percent pretax return.

C. TIMETABLE FOR STARTING BUSINESS

Dec.	Jan.	Feb.	Mar.	Apr.	May	June	July
1.							
2.							
3.							
4.							

1. *December 15 to February 15.* Finish securing $650,000 start-up capital, complete architectural design, secure building permits.

2. *February 15 to March 15.* Finalize museum interior design, seek bids for museum's renovation, and award contracts.

3. *March 15 to July 3.* Begin construction of museum's interior to be completed by July 3 and acquire movie and newsreel licenses.

4. *March 15 to July 25.* Coordinate all publicity and advertising campaigns for the grand opening and take care of problems and details that will arise.

[16] G. Dearth, City Museums, Inc., Pittsburgh, conversation November 19, 1986.

PART 3

EXERCISES

Recognizing Financial Terminology

The Accounting Equation

Step A: Identify the accounting equation.

_____ = _____ + _____

Step B: Apply the accounting equation to find the missing number.

Total Assets	= $346,700
Total Liabilities	= 196,300
Owner's Equity	= _____

Step C: Apply the accounting equation again to find the missing number.

Total Assets	= $_____
Total Liabilities	= 110,000
Owner's Equity	= 57,400

FINANCIAL TERMINOLOGY

Directions: The following is a list of financial terms. Identify each as an asset (A), liability (L), owner's equity (OE), revenue (R), or expense (E). In addition, place the correct identification letter in the appropriate statement column (balance sheet or income statement).

Terms	Balance Sheet	Income Statement
Cash in bank		
Accounts receivable		
Accounts payable		
Inventory on hand		
Payroll deductions payable		
Notes payable		
Capital stock		
Sales (credit)		
Sales (cash)		
Payroll		
Taxes		
Supplies		
Rent		
Building		
Equipment		
Purchases		
Cost of goods sold		
Gross profit		
Retained earnings		

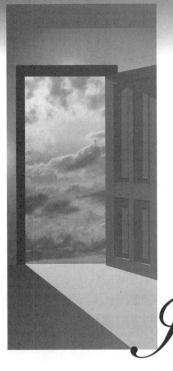

$\mathcal{I}$NITIATING ENTREPRENEURIAL VENTURES

Chapter 11

ASSESSMENT AND EVALUATION OF ENTREPRENEURIAL OPPORTUNITIES

CHAPTER OBJECTIVES

1. To explain the challenge of new-venture start-ups

2. To review common pitfalls in the selection of new-venture ideas

3. To present critical factors involved in new-venture development

4. To examine why new ventures fail

5. To study certain factors that underlie venture success

6. To analyze the evaluation process methods: profile analysis, feasibility criteria approach, and comprehensive feasibility method

7. To outline the specific activities involved in a comprehensive feasibility evaluation

To avoid all mistakes in the conduct of a great enterprise is beyond man's powers.... But, when a mistake has once been made, to use his reverses as lessons for the future is the part of a brave and sensible man.

Minicius (209 B.C.)

THE CHALLENGE OF NEW-VENTURE START-UPS

During the past few years, the number of new-venture start-ups has been consistently high. It is reported that more than 600,000 new firms have emerged in the United States every year since the mid-1980s.[1] That works out to approximately 1,500 business start-ups per day. In addition, the ideas for potential new businesses are also surfacing in record numbers; the U.S. Patent Office currently reviews more than 10,000 patent applications per month.

The reasons for entrepreneurs starting up new ventures are numerous. One study reported seven components of new-venture motivation: the need for approval, the need for independence, the need for personal development, welfare (philanthropic) considerations, perception of wealth, tax reduction and indirect benefits, and following role models.[2] These components are similar to the characteristics discussed in Chapter 4 concerning the "entrepreneurial perspective." Although researchers agree many reasons exist for starting a venture, the entrepreneurial motivations of individuals usually relate to the *personal characteristics* of the entrepreneur, the *environment*, and the *venture* itself. The complexity of these key factors makes the assessment of new ventures extremely difficult. One recent study examined the importance of start-up activities to potential entrepreneurs (those attempting to start a venture). Entrepreneurs who successfully started a business "were more aggressive in making their business real; that is, they undertook activities that made their businesses tangible to others: they looked for facilities and equipment, sought and got financial support, formed a legal entity, organized a team, bought facilities and equipment, and devoted full time to the business. Individuals who started businesses seemed to act with a greater level of intensity. They undertook more activities than those individuals who did not start their businesses. The pattern of activities seems to indicate that individuals who started firms put themselves into the day-to-day process of running an ongoing business as quickly as they could and that these activities resulted in starting firms that generated sales (94 percent of the entrepreneurs) and positive cash flow (50 percent of the

[1] *The State of Small Business: A Report of the President* (Washington, DC: Government Printing Office, 1995).

[2] Sue Birley and Paul Westhead, "A Taxonomy of Business Start-Up Reasons and Their Impact on Firm Growth and Size," *Journal of Business Venturing* (January 1994): 7–32.

FIGURE 11.1 **THE ELEMENTS AFFECTING NEW-VENTURE PERFORMANCE**

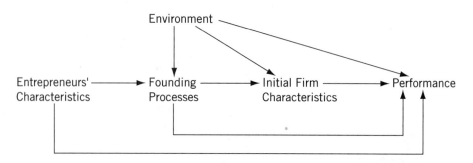

SOURCE: Arnold C. Cooper, "Challenges in Predicting New Firm Performance," *Journal of Business Venturing* (May 1993): 243. Reprinted with permission.

entrepreneurs)."[3] Another study examined the quantitative and qualitative managerial factors that contribute to the success or failure of a young firm. It was found that firms do not have equal resources starting out. More important, the successful firms made greater use of professional advice and developed more detailed business plans.[4] As researcher Arnold C. Cooper points out, the challenges to predicting new-firm performance include environmental effects (the risk of new products or services, narrow markets, and scarce resources); the entrepreneur's personal goals and founding processes (reasons for start-up); and the diversity of the ventures themselves (differing scales and potential).[5] (See Figure 11.1 for illustration.)

In addition to the complexity of the factors in new-venture performance, it is difficult to obtain reliable data concerning start-up, performance, and failure. Surveys by phone and mail have been used with owners, employees, and competitors to obtain measures of sales, profit, technology, market share, and so forth.[6] The results are not completely comparable to all ventures or all industries. It is from this pioneering work, however, that more and better data are being gathered for the evaluation of new ventures.

It should be understood that new-venture assessment begins with the idea and venture selection stage. However, most studies of new-venture development deal with established start-up businesses. Researchers Paul Reynolds and Brenda Miller describe a "fully developed new firm" as one that requires the full-time commitment of one or more individuals, is selling a product or service, has formal financial support, and has hired one or more individuals.[7]

Therefore, as ideas develop into new-venture start-ups, the real challenge is for those firms to survive and grow. In order to do this, they need to have a clear understanding of

[3] Nancy M. Carter, William B. Gartner, and Paul D. Reynolds, "Exploring Start-Up Event Sequences," *Journal of Business Venturing* (May 1996): 151–66.

[4] Robert N. Lussier, "A Nonfinancial Business Success versus Failure Prediction Model for Young Firms," *Journal of Business Management* (January 1995): 8–20.

[5] Arnold C. Cooper, "Challenges in Predicting New Firm Performance," *Journal of Business Venturing* (May 1993): 241–53.

[6] Candida G. Brush and Pieter A. Vanderwerf, "A Comparison of Methods and Sources for Obtaining Estimates of New Venture Performance," *Journal of Business Venturing* (March 1992): 157–70; see also Gaylen N. Chandler and Steven H. Hanks, "Measuring the Performance of Emerging Businesses: A Validation Study," *Journal of Business Venturing* (September 1993): 391–408.

[7] Paul Reynolds and Brenda Miller, "New Firm Gestation: Conception, Birth, and Implications for Research," *Journal of Business Venturing* (September 1992): 405–17.

the critical factors for selecting ventures, the known reasons for venture failure, and an effective evaluation process for new ventures.

PITFALLS IN SELECTING NEW VENTURES

The first key area of analysis is the selection of a new venture. This stage of transition from an idea to a potential venture can be the most critical for understanding new-venture development. Presented here are six of the most important pitfalls commonly encountered in the process of selecting a new venture.

Lack of Objective Evaluation

Many entrepreneurs lack objectivity. Engineers and technically trained people are particularly prone to falling in love with an idea for a product or service. They seem unaware of the need for the scrutiny they would give to a design or project in the ordinary course of their professional work. The way to avoid this pitfall is to subject all ideas to rigorous study and investigation.

No Real Insight into the Market

Many entrepreneurs do not realize the importance of a marketing approach in laying the foundation for a new venture. They show a managerial shortsightedness.[8] Also, they do not understand the life cycle that must be considered when introducing a new product or service.

No product is instantaneously profitable, nor does its success endure indefinitely. Entrepreneurs must not only project the life cycle of the new product, but they also must recognize that introducing the product at the right time is important to its success. Timing is critical. Action taken too soon or too late will often result in failure.

Inadequate Understanding of Technical Requirements

The development of a new product often involves new techniques. Failure to anticipate the technical difficulties with developing or producing a product can sink a new venture. Entrepreneurs cannot be too thorough when studying the project before initiating it. Encountering unexpected technical difficulties frequently poses time-consuming and costly problems.

Poor Financial Understanding

A common difficulty with the development of a new product is an overly optimistic estimate of the funds required to carry the project to completion. Sometimes entrepreneurs are ignorant of costs or are victims of inadequate research and planning. Quite often they tend to underestimate development costs by wide margins. It is not unusual for estimates to be less than half of what is eventually required.

---

[8] Theodore Levitt, "Marketing Myopia," *Harvard Business Review* (July/August 1960): 45–56.

Lack of Venture Uniqueness

A new venture should be unique. **Uniqueness** is the special characteristics and design concepts that draw the customer to the venture, which should provide performance or service that is superior to competitive offerings. The best way to ensure customer awareness of differences between the company's product and competitors' products is through product differentiation. Pricing becomes less of a problem when the customer sees the product as superior to its competitors. A product that is unique in a significant way can gain the advantage of differentiation.

Ignorance of Legal Issues

Business is subject to many legal requirements. One is the need to make the workplace safe for employees. A second is to provide reliable and safe products and services. A third is the necessity for patents, trademarks, and copyrights to protect one's inventions and products. When these legal issues are overlooked, major problems can result. (See the Contemporary Entrepreneurship box on world-class failures.)

CRITICAL FACTORS FOR NEW-VENTURE DEVELOPMENT

A number of **critical factors** are important for new-venture assessment. One way to identify and evaluate them is with a checklist (see Table 11.1). In most cases, however, such a questionnaire approach is too general. The assessment must be tailor-made for the specific venture.

A new venture goes through three specific phases: prestart-up, start-up, and poststart-up. The prestart-up phase begins with an idea for the venture and ends when the doors are opened for business. The start-up phase commences with the initiation of sales activity and the delivery of products and services and ends when the business is firmly established and beyond short-term threats to survival. The poststart-up phase lasts until the venture is terminated or the surviving organizational entity is no longer controlled by an entrepreneur.

The major focus in this chapter is on the prestart-up and start-up phases, since these are the critical segments for entrepreneurs. During these two phases five factors are critical: (1) the relative uniqueness of the venture, (2) the relative investment size at start-up, (3) the expected growth of sales and/or profits as the venture moves through its start-up phase, (4) the availability of products during the prestart-up and start-up phases, and (5) the availability of customers during the prestart-up and start-up phases.

Uniqueness

A new venture's range of uniqueness can be considerable, extending from fairly routine to highly nonroutine. What separates the routine from the nonroutine venture is the amount of innovation required during prestart-up. This distinction is based on the need for new process technology to produce services or products and on the need to service new market segments. Venture uniqueness is further characterized by the length of time a nonroutine venture will remain nonroutine. For instance, will new products, new technology, and new markets be required on a continuing basis? Or will the venture be able to "settle down" after the start-up period and use existing products, technologies, and markets?

CONTEMPORARY ENTREPRENEURSHIP

World-Class Failures

Ford's Diesel It had innovations galore—and quality problems from stuck hoods to defective power steering. Estimated loss per car was almost $1,117, or a total of $250 million.

DuPont's Corfam A synthetic leather supposed to do for shoes what nylon did for stockings. Leather was just better. Cost: $80 million to $100 million.

Polaroid's Polavision Edwin Land used Polaroid's wet-chemistry technology to develop an instant movie camera. But videotape technology was far better.

United Artists' *Heaven's Gate* Almost $30 million over budget, this Western movie bombed so badly it almost destroyed UA.

RCA's Videodisc This innovation was supposed to capture the video-recorder market, but it couldn't tape television shows. Loss: $500 million.

Time's TV-Cable Week This was a bid to compete with *TV Guide*. Cause of death: ballooning costs to customize editions for each cable system. Loss: $47 million.

IBM's PCjr The awkward Chiclet keyboard, the slow microprocessor, an unattractive price, and a late launch caused a major disaster. Cost: $40 million.

New Coke Coca-Cola's answer to Pepsi's sweeter formula provoked a national uproar from old-formula loyalists.

R. J. Reynolds' Premier This cigarette didn't burn or emit smoke, but it simply didn't taste good. Its failure persuaded CEO Ross Johnson to launch his equally disastrous buyout attempt.

NutraSweet's Simplesse This fat substitute was meant to change the way we eat. However, the market is swamped with substitutes, and many consumers like fat.

SOURCE: "Flops," *Business Week*, August 16, 1993, 80.

Investment

The capital investment required to start a new venture can vary considerably. In some industries less than $50,000 may be required, whereas in other industries millions of dollars are necessary. Moreover, in some industries only large-scale start-ups are feasible. For example, in the publishing industry one can start a small venture that can remain small or grow into a larger venture. By contrast, an entrepreneur attempting to break into the airline industry will need a considerable up-front investment.

Another finance-related critical issue is the extent and timing of funds needed to move through the venture process. To determine the amount of needed investment, entrepreneurs must answer questions such as these: Will industry growth be sufficient to maintain

TABLE 11.1   **A NEW-VENTURE IDEA CHECKLIST**

Basic Feasibility of the Venture

1. Can the product or service work?

2. Is it legal?

Competitive Advantages of the Venture

1. What specific competitive advantages will the product or service offer?

2. What are the competitive advantages of the companies already in business?

3. How are the competitors likely to respond?

4. How will the initial competitive advantage be maintained?

Buyer Decisions in the Venture

1. Who are the customers likely to be?

2. How much will each customer buy, and how many customers are there?

3. Where are these customers located, and how will they be serviced?

Marketing of the Goods and Services

1. How much will be spent on advertising and selling?

2. What share of market will the company capture? By when?

3. Who will perform the selling functions?

4. How will prices be set? How will they compare with the competition's prices?

5. How important is location, and how will it be determined?

6. What distribution channels will be used—wholesale, retail, agents, direct mail?

7. What are the sales targets? By when should they be met?

8. Can any orders be obtained before starting the business? How many? For what total amount?

Production of the Goods and Services

1. Will the company make or buy what it sells? Or will it use a combination of these two strategies?

2. Are sources of supplies available at reasonable prices?

3. How long will delivery take?

4. Have adequate lease arrangements for premises been made?

---

break-even sales to cover a high fixed-cost structure during the start-up period? Do the principal entrepreneurs have access to substantial financial reserves to protect a large initial investment? Do the entrepreneurs have the appropriate contacts to take advantage of various environmental opportunities? Do the entrepreneurs have both industry and entrepreneurial track records that justify the financial risk of a large-scale start-up?[9]

[9] Robert C. Ronstadt, *Entrepreneurship* (Dover, MA: Lord Publishing, 1984), 74.

TABLE 11.1	A NEW-VENTURE IDEA CHECKLIST *(continued)*

5. Can the needed equipment be available on time?

6. Do any special problems with plant setup, clearances, or insurance exist? How will they be resolved?

7. How will quality be controlled?

8. How will returns and servicing be handled?

9. How will pilferage, waste, spoilage, and scrap be controlled?

Staffing Decisions in the Venture

1. How will competence in each area of the business be ensured?

2. Who will have to be hired? By when? How will they be found and recruited?

3. Will a banker, lawyer, accountant, or other advisers be needed?

4. How will replacements be obtained if key people leave?

5. Will special benefit plans have to be arranged?

Control of the Venture

1. What records will be needed? When?

2. Will any special controls be required? What are they? Who will be responsible for them?

Financing the Venture

1. How much will be needed for development of the product or service?

2. How much will be needed for setting up operations?

3. How much will be needed for working capital?

4. Where will the money come from? What if more is needed?

5. Which assumptions in the financial forecasts are most uncertain?

6. What will be the return on equity, or sales, and how does it compare with the industry?

7. When and how will investors get their money back?

8. What will be needed from the bank, and what is the bank's response?

SOURCE: Karl H. Vesper, *New Venture Strategies*, copyright © 1990, 172. Adapted by permission of Prentice-Hall, Inc., Englewood Cliffs, New Jersey.

Sales Growth

The *growth of sales* through the start-up phase is another critical factor. Key questions are What is the growth pattern anticipated for new-venture sales and profits? Are sales and profits expected to grow slowly or level off shortly after start-up? Are large profits expected at some point with only small or moderate sales growth? Or are both high sales growth and high profit growth likely? Or will initial profits be limited with eventual high profit growth over a multiyear period? In answering these questions, it is important to remember that most ventures fit into one of the three following classifications.

ENTREPRENEURIAL
EDGE

A New Blend of Products and Services

What's the difference between a product and a service? It seems like a simple question, right? Well, consider the following: If a computer company lets you download "shareware" from its Web site that helps improve your business, is that a product or a service? Is Netscape a product or a service company? What once distinguished the two is diminishing as a new hybrid of products and services emerges. In an effort to offer customers and clients what they are looking for, companies are rebuilding their strategies as products become enhanced with services, "provices," and services become packaged with products, "serducts."

Where is this new hybrid coming from? Product companies and service companies alike are realizing that in order to satisfy the marketplace, they need to gen-

erate value-added innovation. Product companies fear that their once successful products are devolving into profitless commodities. Rather than finding ways to make better or cheaper products, they are searching for services to embrace their products. At the same time, service companies fear the notion that their most valuable assets go home every night. Rather than looking for more clever and innovative services, these companies are seeking ways to "productize" their expertise and sell it. This trend of hybridization is also being driven by the force of technology, particularly the World Wide Web, as was indicated here in the opening questions.

Oracle, a multibillion-dollar database company, has proven that this type of hybridization can be profitable—very prof-

Lifestyle ventures appear to have independence, autonomy, and control as their primary driving forces. Neither large sales nor profits are deemed important beyond providing a sufficient and comfortable living for the entrepreneur.

In **small profitable ventures,** financial considerations play a major role. Additionally, autonomy and control are important in the sense that the entrepreneur does not want venture sales (and employment) to become so large that he or she must relinquish equity or an ownership position and thus give up control over cash flow and profits, which, it is hoped, will be substantial.

In **high-growth ventures,** significant sales and profit growth are expected to the extent that it may be possible to attract venture capital money and funds raised through public or private placements.[10]

---

[10] Adapted from Ronstadt, *Entrepreneurship,* 75.

itable. Using its own product, Oracle has created a consulting firm, which is now one of the company's major sources of profit and growth. Another example is General Motors (GM), one of the world's largest auto companies. Automobiles come fully equipped with an assortment of services, including warranties, financing, and service guarantees. In addition, customers have the choice of buying a vehicle or leasing a vehicle. When purchasing a lease, are you purchasing a product or a service? All of these services play an important role in GM's profit objectives. And as new technology evolves, GM will have a whole new realm of personal services to offer within its "package" of products and services.

The way companies or even entire industries do business could be changed by hybridization. Automakers, for example, are considering a whole new approach to selling their product. Maybe they won't even sell a product anymore. Think about automakers selling a "com-

prehensive mobility package." This would consist of a contract that provides purchasers a series of vehicles. Purchasers would have access to different vehicles corresponding to different needs, although they would own none of them: an economical car through the week, a sports car for the weekend, and a luxury car for the evening. Is this arrangement a product or a service?

These new hybrids represent innovation at its best. The evolution from products and services to provices and serducts will allow companies to compete more as they strive to offer the marketplace what it wants—value. According to Michael Schrage, a research associate at MIT, "Indeed, provices and serducts will ultimately become the building blocks of tomorrow's business models. Tomorrow's business plans will revolve around product-service hybrids—not one or the other."

SOURCE: Michael Schrage, "Provices and Serducts," *Fast Company* (August/September 1996): 48–49.

Product Availability

Essential to the success of any venture is *product availability,* the availability of a salable good or service, at the time the venture opens its doors. Some ventures have problems in this regard because the product or service is still in development and needs further modification or testing. Other ventures find that because they bring their product to market too soon, it must be recalled for further work. A typical example is the software firm that rushes the development of its product and is then besieged by customers who find "bugs" in the program. Lack of product availability in finished form can affect the company's image and its bottom line.

Customer Availability

If the product is available before the venture is started, the likelihood of venture success is considerably better than otherwise. Similarly, venture risk is affected by *customer availability* for start-up. At one end of the risk continuum is the situation where customers are willing to pay cash for products or services before delivery. At the other end of the continuum is the enterprise that gets started without knowing exactly who will buy its product. A critical consideration is how long it will take to determine who the customers are and what their buying habits are. As Ronstadt notes:

> The decision to ignore the market is an extremely risky one. There are, after all, two fundamental criteria for entrepreneurial success. The first is having a customer who is willing to pay you a profitable price for a product or a service. The second is that you must actually produce and deliver the product or service. The farther a venture removes itself from certainty about these two rules, the greater the risk and the greater the time required to offset this risk as the venture moves through the prestart-up and start-up periods.[11]

WHY NEW VENTURES FAIL

Every year many millions of dollars are spent on starting new enterprises. Many of these newly established businesses vanish within a year or two; only a small percentage are successful. Most studies have found that the factors underlying the failure of new ventures are, in most cases, within the control of the entrepreneur. Some of the major reasons for the failure of new ventures follow.

Researchers Bruno, Leidecker, and Harder examined 250 high-tech firms and found three major categories of causes for failure: product/market problems, financial difficulties, and managerial problems.[12]

Product/market problems involved the following factors:

- *Poor timing.* In 40 percent of the cases studied, a premature entry into the marketplace contributed to failure.
- *Product design problems.* Although these may be related to timing, product design and development became a key factor at earlier stages of the venture, and when the essential makeup of the product or service was changed, failure resulted.
- *Inappropriate distribution strategy.* Whether it was based on commissioned sales representatives or direct sales at trade shows, the distribution strategy had to be geared toward the product and customer.
- *Unclear business definition.* Uncertainty about the "exact" business they were in caused these firms to undergo constant change and to lack stabilization.
- *Overreliance on one customer.* This resulted in a failure to diversify and brought about the eventual demise of some of the firms.

In the financial difficulties category were the following factors.

- *Initial undercapitalization.* In 30 percent of the case studies, undercapitalization contributed to failure.
- *Assuming debt too early.* Some of the firms attempted to obtain debt financing too soon and in too large an amount. This led to debt service problems.

[11] Ibid., 79.

[12] Albert V. Bruno, Joel K. Leidecker, and Joseph W. Harder, "Why Firms Fail," *Business Horizons* (March/April 1987): 50–58. For a more recent comparison, see Fahri Karakaya and Bulent Kobu, "New Product Development Process: An Investigation of Success and Failure in High Technology and Non-High Technology Firms," *Journal of Business Venturing* (January 1994): 49–66.

- *Venture capital relationship problems.* Differing goals, visions, and motivations of the entrepreneur and the venture capitalist resulted in problems for the enterprise.

Managerial problems involved two important factors.

- *Concept of a team approach.* These problems associated with the managerial team were found: (1) hirings and promotions on the basis of nepotism rather than qualifications, (2) poor relationships with parent companies and venture capitalists, (3) founders who focused on their weaknesses rather than on their strengths (though weakening the company, they supposedly were building their skills), and (4) incompetent support professionals (for example, attorneys who were unable to read contracts or collect on court judgments that already had been made).
- *Human resource problems.* Inflated owner ego, employee-related concerns, and control factors were all problems leading to business failure. The study also revealed such interpersonal problems as (1) kickbacks and subsequent firings that resulted in an almost total loss of customers, (2) deceit on the part of a venture capitalist in one case and on the part of a company president in another, (3) verbal agreements between the entrepreneur and the venture capitalists that were not honored, and (4) protracted lawsuits around the time of discontinuance.

In a more recent study of successful ventures (firms listed in the *Inc.* 500 group of fastest-growing privately held companies), the most significant problems encountered at start-up were researched in order to systematically sort them into a schematic. Table 11.2 lists the types and classes of problems identified during the first year of operation. The researcher also surveyed the current problems the owners of these successful firms encountered in order to explore the possible changes in problem patterns of new firms. It was found that dominant problems at **start-up** were sales/marketing (38 percent), obtaining external financing (17 percent), and internal financial management problems (16 percent). General management problems were also frequently cited in the start-up stage (11 percent). In the **growth stage,** sales/marketing remained the most dominant problem (22 percent), but it was less important than in the start-up stage. Internal financial management (21 percent) continued to be a dominant problem, as were human resource management problems (17 percent) and general management problems (14 percent). Additionally, more regulatory environment problems occurred in the growth stage (8 percent) than were mentioned in the start-up stage (1 percent). Finally, organizational structure/design (6 percent) emerged as a problem in the growth stage.[13]

It is important for entrepreneurs to recognize these problem areas at the outset because they remain challenges to the venture as it grows.

Another study of 645 entrepreneurs focused on the classification of start-up and growth problems experienced internally versus externally.[14] Figure 11.2 depicts the types of problems and the percentage of firms that reported these problems. **Internal problems** involved adequate capital, cash flow, facilities/equipment, inventory control, human resources, leadership, organizational structure, and accounting systems. **External problems** were related to customer contact, market knowledge, marketing planning, location, pricing, product considerations, competitors, and expansion. The researchers found that the

---

[13] David E. Terpstra and Philip D. Olson, "Entrepreneurial Start-up and Growth: A Classification of Problems," *Entrepreneurship Theory and Practice* (spring 1993): 5–20.

[14] H. Robert Dodge, Sam Fullerton, and John E. Robbins, "Stage of the Organizational Life Cycle and Competition as Mediators of Problem Perception for Small Businesses," *Strategic Management Journal* 15 (1994): 121–34.

TABLE 11.2 **TYPES AND CLASSES OF FIRST-YEAR PROBLEMS**

1. *Obtaining external financing*
   Obtaining financing for growth
   Other or general financing problems

2. *Internal financial management*
   Inadequate working capital
   Cash-flow problems
   Other or general financial management problems

3. *Sales/marketing*
   Low sales
   Dependence on one or few clients/customers
   Marketing or distribution channels
   Promotion/public relations/advertising
   Other or general marketing problems

4. *Product development*
   Developing products/services
   Other or general product development problems

5. *Production/operations management*
   Establishing or maintaining quality control

   Raw materials/resources/supplies
   Other or general production/operations management problems

6. *General management*
   Lack of management experience
   Only one person/no time
   Managing/controlling growth
   Administrative problems
   Other or general general management problems

7. *Human resource management*
   Recruitment/selection
   Turnover/retention
   Satisfaction/morale
   Employee development
   Other or general human resource management problems

8. *Economic environment*
   Poor economy/recession
   Other or general economic environment problems

9. *Regulatory environment*
   Insurance

SOURCE: David E. Terpstra and Philip D. Olson, "Entrepreneurial Start-up and Growth: A Classification of Problems," *Entrepreneurship Theory & Practice* (spring 1993): 19.

"intensity of competition" rather than life-cycle stages was more dominant in changing the relative importance of the problem areas. Thus, entrepreneurs need to recognize not only that start-up problems remain with the venture but also that the increasing competition will adjust the relative importance of the problems.

A third "failure" or problem study deals with a proposed **failure prediction model** based on financial data from newly founded ventures. The study assumed the financial failure process was characterized by too much initial indebtedness and too little revenue financing. As shown by the failure process schematic in Table 11.3, the risk of failure can be reduced by using less debt as initial financing and by generating enough revenue in the initial stages. Further, the study recognized the risk associated with the initial size of the venture being developed. Specific applications of the model included the following:[15]

1. *Role of profitability and cash flows.* The entrepreneur and manager should ensure that the products are able to yield positive profitability and cash flows in the first years.

[15] Erkki K. Laitinen, "Prediction of Failure of a Newly Founded Firm," *Journal of Business Venturing* (July 1992): 323–40.

FIGURE 11.2   **INTERNAL AND EXTERNAL PROBLEMS ENTREPRENEURS EXPERIENCE**

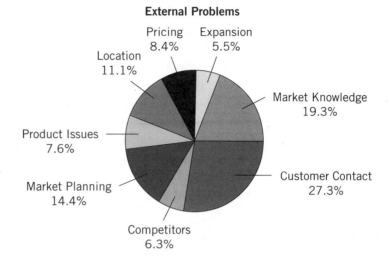

External Problems

- Pricing 8.4%
- Expansion 5.5%
- Location 11.1%
- Market Knowledge 19.3%
- Product Issues 7.6%
- Customer Contact 27.3%
- Market Planning 14.4%
- Competitors 6.3%

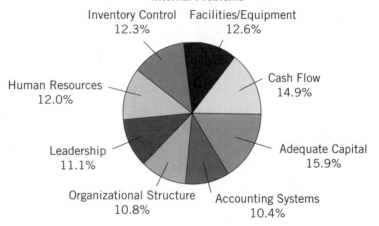

Internal Problems

- Inventory Control 12.3%
- Facilities/Equipment 12.6%
- Human Resources 12.0%
- Cash Flow 14.9%
- Leadership 11.1%
- Adequate Capital 15.9%
- Organizational Structure 10.8%
- Accounting Systems 10.4%

SOURCE: H. Robert Dodge, Sam Fullerton, and John E. Robbins, "Stage of Organizational Life Cycle and Competition as Mediators of Problem Perception for Small Businesses," *Strategic Management Journal,* 15 (1994): 129. Reprinted by permission of John Wiley & Sons, Ltd.

2. *Role of debt.* The entrepreneur and manager should ensure that enough stockholders' capital is in the initial balance sheet to buffer future losses.

3. *Combination of both.* The entrepreneur and manager should not start a business if the share of stockholders' capital in the initial balance sheet is low and if negative cash flows in the first years are probable.

4. *Role of initial size.* The entrepreneur and manager should understand that the more probable the negative cash flows and the larger the debt share in the initial balance sheet, the smaller the initial size of the business should be.

| TABLE 11.3 | THE FAILURE PROCESS OF A NEWLY FOUNDED FIRM |

1. Extremely high indebtedness (poor static solidity) and small size
2. Too slow velocity of capital, too fast growth, too poor profitability (as compared to the budget), or some combination of these
3. Unexpected lack of revenue financing (poor dynamic liquidity)
4. Poor static liquidity and debt service ability (dynamic solidity)

A. Profitability

1. Return on investment ratio defined on end-of-the-year basis

$$= \frac{\text{Net Profit} + \text{Interest Expenses}}{\text{Total Capital at the End of the Year}} \times 100$$

B. Liquidity

Dynamic

2. Cash flow to net sales

$$= \frac{\text{Net Profit} + \text{Depreciations}}{\text{Net Sales}} \times 100$$

Static

3. Quick ratio

$$= \frac{\text{Financial Assets}}{\text{Current Debt}}$$

C. Solidity

Static

4. Stockholders' capital to total capital

$$= \frac{\text{Total Capital} - \text{Debt Capital}}{\text{Total Capital}} \times 100$$

Dynamic

5. Cash flow to total debt

$$= \frac{\text{Net Profit} + \text{Depreciations}}{\text{Total Debt}} \times 100$$

D. Other Factors

Growth or Dynamic Size

6. Rate of annual growth in net sales

$$= \frac{\text{Net Sales in Year } t}{\text{Net Sales in Year } t - 1} \times 100$$

Size

7. Logarithmic net sales

$$= \ln(\text{Net Sales})$$

Velocity of Capital

8. Net sales to total capital

$$= \frac{\text{Net Sales}}{\text{Total Capital at the End of the Year}}$$

SOURCE: Erkki K. Laitinen, "Prediction of Failure of a Newly Founded Firm," *Journal of Business Venturing* (July 1992): 326–28. Reprinted with permission.

5. *Role of velocity of capital.* The entrepreneur and manager should not budget for fast velocity of capital in the initial years if the risk of negative cash flows is high. More sales in comparison to capital means more negative cash flows and poorer profitability.

6. *Role of control.* The entrepreneur and manager should monitor financial ratios from the first year, especially the cash-flow-to-total-debt ratio. Risky combinations of ratios (Z-scores), especially negative cash flows, a low stockholders'-capital-to-total-capital ratio, and a high velocity of capital should be monitored and compared with industrial standards. The entrepreneur should try to identify the reasons for poor ratios and pay special attention to keeping profitability at the planned level (with control ratios).

THE EVALUATION PROCESS

A critical task of starting a new business enterprise is solid analysis and evaluation of the feasibility of the product/service idea getting off the ground. Entrepreneurs must put their ideas through this analysis in order to discover if they contain any fatal flaws.

Asking the Right Questions

Many important evaluation-related questions should be asked. Ten sets of preliminary questions that can be used to screen an idea are presented here.

1. Is it a new product/service idea? Is it proprietary? Can it be patented or copyrighted? Is it unique enough to get a significant head start on the competition? Or can it be easily copied?

2. Has a prototype been tested by independent testers who try to blow the system or rip the product to shreds? What are its weak points? Will it stand up? What level of research and development should it receive over the next five years? If it is a service, has it been tested on guinea pig customers? Will they pay their hard-earned money for it?

3. Has it been taken to trade shows? If so, what reactions did it receive? Were any sales made? Has it been taken to distributors? Have they placed any orders?

4. Is the product or service easily understood by customers, bankers, venture capitalists, accountants, lawyers, and insurance agents?

5. What is the overall market? What are the market segments? Can the product penetrate these segments? Can any special niches be exploited?

6. Has market research been conducted? Who else is in the market? How big is the market? How fast is it growing? What are the trends? What is the projected life cycle of the product or service? What degree of penetration can be achieved? Are there any testimonials from customers and purchasing agents? What type of advertising and promotion plan will be used?

7. What distribution and sales methods will be used—jobbers, independent sales representatives, the company sales force, direct mail, door-to-door sales, supermarkets, service stations, company-owned stores? How will the product be transported: company-owned trucks, common carriers, postal service, or air freight?

8. How will the product be made? How much will it cost? For example, will it be produced in-house or by others? Will production be by job shop or continuous process? What is the present capacity of company facilities? What is the break-even point?

9. Will the business concept be developed and licensed to others or developed and sold away?

10. Can the company get—or has it already lined up—the necessary skills to operate the business venture? Who will be the workers? Are they dependable and competent? How much capital will be needed now? How much more in the future? Have major stages in financing been developed?[16]

Profile Analysis

A single strategic variable seldom shapes the ultimate success or failure of a new venture. In most situations a combination of variables influences the outcome. Thus it is important to identify and investigate these variables before the new idea is put into practice. The results of such a profile analysis enable the entrepreneur to judge the business's potential.

The internal profile analysis in the Experiential Exercise at the end of this chapter is one method of determining the resources available to a new venture. This checklist approach allows entrepreneurs to identify major strengths and weaknesses in the financial, marketing, organizational, and human resource factors needed for the venture to progress successfully. In this manner entrepreneurs can prepare for possible weaknesses that may inhibit the growth of their venture. More important, many of the reasons cited for venture failure earlier in this chapter can be avoided through a careful profile analysis.

Feasibility Criteria Approach

Another method, the **feasibility criteria approach,** was developed as a criteria selection list from which entrepreneurs can gain insights into the viability of their venture and is based on the following questions:

- *Is it proprietary?* The product does not have to be patented, but it should be sufficiently proprietary to permit a long head start against competitors and a period of extraordinary profits early in the venture to offset start-up costs.
- *Are the initial production costs realistic?* Most estimates are too low. A careful, detailed analysis should be made so no large, unexpected expenses arise.
- *Are the initial marketing costs realistic?* This answer requires the venture to identify target markets, market channels, and promotional strategy.
- *Does the product have potential for very high margins?* This is almost a necessity for a fledgling company. Gross margins are one thing the financial community understands. Without them, funding can be difficult.
- *Is the time required to get to market and to reach breakeven realistic?* In most cases, the faster the better. In all cases, the venture plan will be tied to this answer, and an error here can spell trouble later on.
- *Is the potential market large?* In determining the potential market, entrepreneurs must look three to five years into the future because some markets take this long to emerge. The cellular telephone, for example, had an annual demand of approxi-

[16] John G. Burch, *Entrepreneurship* (New York: Wiley, 1986), 68–69.

mately 400,000 units in 1982. However, by the late 1990s this market was estimated to grow by at least 45 percent annually.

- *Is the product the first of a growing family?* If it is, the venture is more attractive to investors. If they do not make a large return on the first product, they might on the second, third, or fourth.
- *Does an initial customer exist?* It is certainly impressive to financial backers when a venture can list its first ten customers by name. This pent-up demand also means the first quarter's results are likely to be good and the focus of attention can be directed to later quarters.
- *Are the development costs and calendar times realistic?* Preferably, they are zero. A ready-to-go product gives the venture a big advantage over competitors. If costs exist, they should be complete and detailed and tied to a month-by-month schedule.
- *Is this a growing industry?* This is not absolutely essential if the profits and company growth are there, but it means less room for mistakes. In a growing industry, good companies do even better.
- *Can the product and the need for it be understood by the financial community?* If the financiers can grasp the concept and its value, the chances for funding will increase. For example, a portable heart-monitoring system for postcoronary monitoring is a product many will understand. Undoubtedly, some of those hearing the presentation will have already had coronaries or heart problems of some sort.[17]

This criteria selection approach provides a means of analyzing the internal strengths and weaknesses that exist in a new venture by focusing on the marketing potential and industry potential critical to assessment. If the new venture meets fewer than six of these criteria, it typically lacks feasibility for funding. If the new venture meets seven or more of the criteria, it may stand a good chance of being funded. (See the Contemporary Entrepreneurship box.)

Comprehensive Feasibility Approach

A more comprehensive and systematic feasibility analysis, a **comprehensive feasibility approach,** incorporates external factors in addition to those in the criteria questions. Figure 11.3 presents a breakdown of the factors involved in a comprehensive feasibility study of a new venture—technical, market, financial, organizational, competitive. A more detailed feasibility analysis guide is provided in Table 11.4, which identifies the specific

FIGURE 11.3 **KEY AREAS FOR ASSESSING THE FEASIBILITY OF A NEW VENTURE**

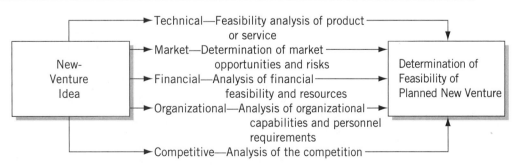

[17] Gordon B. Baty, *Entrepreneurship: Playing to Win* (Reston, VA: Reston Publishing, 1974), 33–34.

CONTEMPORARY ENTREPRENEURSHIP

Emerging Themes from Surviving Founders of Entrepreneurial Firms

1. **Know yourself.** Founders placed great importance on understanding their skills and deficiencies and recognizing what motive lay behind the urge to found a company. "Look in the mirror a lot."

2. **Love your product.** Several founders spoke in terms that suggested a service orientation: The function of the firm was to supply customers with something these customers literally had to have. This was particularly true of the smaller firms serving a primarily R&D or laboratory market.

3. **Honor your customer.** Many of these founders expressed a great deal of loyalty to the markets they served. They felt a personal responsibility to satisfy their customers.

4. **Treat your people well.** This was probably the one theme heard most often across the interviews. Over the long term, the partners one joined with, the people one hired, and the way these people were treated was

felt to be a critical success factor. "As long as you were fair with the people you were dealing with, and treated them right, you never had to worry." "You've got to really be an astute judge of people. That is by far the most important thing you can do: study people."

5. **Keep your integrity.** Several founders mentioned this point as a bedrock principle. Most had experience with other people or businesses that did not follow this injunction. Feelings ran high on this point.

These injunctions summarize the themes that emerged from surviving founders' answers to two questions: What have you learned over 20 years of successfully managing a new venture? and What advice would you give to someone starting a new venture today?

SOURCE: Albert V. Bruno, Edward F. McQuarrie, and Carol G. Torgrimson, "The Evolution of New Technology Ventures over 20 Years: Patterns of Failure, Merger, and Survival," *Journal of Business Venturing* (July 1992): 301. Adapted with permission.

activities involved in each feasibility area. Although all five of the areas presented in Figure 11.3 are important, two merit special attention: technical and market.

TECHNICAL FEASIBILITY The evaluation of a new-venture idea should start with identifying the technical requirements, the **technical feasibility,** for producing a product or service that will satisfy the expectations of potential customers. The most important of these follow:

- Functional design of the product and attractiveness in appearance
- Flexibility, permitting ready modification of the external features of the product to meet customer demands or technological and competitive changes

TABLE 11.4		SPECIFIC ACTIVITIES OF FEASIBILITY ANALYSES		
Technical Feasibility Analysis	**Market Feasibility Analysis**	**Financial Feasibility Analysis**	**Analysis of Organizational Capabilities**	**Competitive Analysis**
Crucial technical specifications	*Market potential*	*Required financial resources for:*	*Personnel requirements*	*Existing competitors*
Design	Identification of potential customers and their dominant characteristics (e.g., age, income level, buying habits)	Fixed assets	Required skills levels and other personal characteristics of potential employees	Size, financial resources, market entrenchment
Durability		Current assets		
Reliability		Necessary working capital		Potential reaction of competitors to newcomer by means of price cutting, aggressive advertising, introduction of new products, etc.
Product safety		*Available financial resources*	Managerial requirements	
Standardization	Potential market share (as affected by competitive situation)	Required borrowing		
Engineering requirements			Determination of individual responsibilities	
Machines	Potential sales volume	Potential sources for funds		
Tools		Cost of borrowing	Determination of required organizational relationships	Potential new competitors
Instruments	Sales price projections			
Work flow		Repayment conditions	Potential organizational development	
Product development	*Market testing*	Operation cost analysis		
Blueprints	Selection of test		Competitive analysis	
Models	Actual market test	Fixed costs		
Prototypes	Analysis of market	Variable costs		
Product testing	*Marketing planning issues*	Projected cash flow		
Lab testing		Projected profitability		
Field testing	Preferred channels of distribution, impact of promotional efforts, required distribution points (warehouses), packaging considerations, price differentiation			
Plant location				
Desirable characteristics of plant site (proximity to suppliers, customers), environmental regulations				

SOURCE: Hans Schollhammer and Arthur H. Kuriloff, *Entrepreneurship and Small Business Management*, 56. Copyright © 1979 by John Wiley & Sons, Inc. Reprinted by permission of John Wiley & Sons, Inc.

- Durability of the materials from which the product is made
- Reliability, ensuring performance as expected under normal operating conditions
- Product safety, posing no potential dangers under normal operating conditions
- Reasonable utility—an acceptable rate of obsolescence
- Ease and low cost of maintenance

- Standardization through elimination of unnecessary variety among potentially inter-changeable parts
- Ease of processing or manufacture
- Ease in handling and use[18]

The results of this investigation provide a basis for deciding whether a new venture is feasible from a technical point of view.

MARKETABILITY   Assembling and analyzing relevant information about the **marketability** of a new venture is vital for judging its potential success. Three major areas in this type of analysis are (1) investigating the full market potential and identifying customers (or users) for the goods or service, (2) analyzing the extent to which the enterprise might exploit this potential market, and (3) using market analysis to determine the opportunities and risks associated with the venture. To address these areas, a variety of informational sources must be found and used. For a market feasibility analysis, general sources would include these:

- *General economic trends:* various economic indicators such as new orders, housing starts, inventories, and consumer spending
- *Market data:* customers, customer demand patterns (e.g., seasonal variations in demand, governmental regulations affecting demand)
- *Pricing data:* range of prices for the same, complementary, and substitute products; base prices; and discount structures
- *Competitive data:* major competitors and their competitive strength

More attention is given to marketing issues in Chapter 8. At this point it is important to note the value of marketing research in the overall assessment and evaluation of a new venture.[19]

Thus, as demonstrated by Table 11.4, the comprehensive feasibility analysis approach is closely related to the preparation of a thorough business plan (covered in detail in Chapter 10). The approach clearly illustrates the need to evaluate each segment of the venture *before* initiating the business or presenting it to capital sources.

As a final example, one venture capitalist has stated, "The risks in entrepreneurship are you, your team, and any fundamental flaws in your venture idea. You must make a reasonable first evaluation of these risks." As an aid to this evaluation, Table 11.5 provides a list of representative functions that are keys to assessing a new venture.

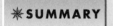
✳SUMMARY

The complexity of factors involved in new-venture start-up (as shown in Figure 11.1) makes it difficult to clearly assess and evaluate each one. In addition, the difficulty of obtaining reliable data on failed firms adds to this dilemma. Improvements are being made, however, and new-venture assessment is becoming a stronger process.

A number of pitfalls occur in the selection of a new venture: lack of an objective evaluation of the venture, lack of insight into the market, inadequate understanding of

[18] Hans Schollhammer and Arthur H. Kuriloff, *Entrepreneurship and Small Business Management* (New York: Wiley, 1979), 58.

[19] Gerald E. Hills, "Marketing Analysis in the Business Plan: Venture Capitalists' Perceptions," *Journal of Small Business Management* (January 1985): 38–46.

| TABLE 11.5 | REPRESENTATIVE FUNCTIONS TO EVALUATE FOR NEW VENTURES |

Marketing and Sales

- *Market research and evalution:* ability to design and conduct market research studies and to analyze and interpret study results; familiarity with questionnaire design and sampling techniques
- *Strategic sales:* experience in developing marketing strategies and establishing sales forces and then planning appropriate sales, advertising, and promotional programs and setting up an effective network distributor or sales representative organization
- *Sales management and merchandising:* ability to organize, supervise, motivate, and provide merchandising support to a direct sales force; ability to analyze territory and account sales potential and to manage a sales force to obtain target market share
- *Direct selling:* experience in identifying, meeting, and developing new customers; demonstrated success in closing sales
- *Service:* ability to perceive service needs of particular products; experience in determining service and spare parts requirements, handling customer complaints, and managing a service organization
- *Distribution management:* ability to organize and manage product flow from manufacturing through distribution channels to the ultimate customer, including familiarity with shipping costs, scheduling techniques, carriers, etc.
- *Overall marketing skills:* Give yourself a combined rating reflecting your skill level across all the marketing areas.

Operations

- *Manufacturing management:* knowledge of the product processes, machines, workforce, and space required to produce the product; experience in managing production to produce products within time, cost, and quality constraints
- *Inventory control:* familiarity with techniques of controlling in-process and finished-goods inventories of materials
- *Quality control:* ability to set up inspection systems and standards for effective quality control of incoming, in-process, and finished materials
- *Purchasing:* ability to identify appropriate supply sources, negotiate supplier contracts, and manage incoming flow of material into inventory; familiarity with economical order quantities and discount advantage
- *Overall operations skills:* Give yourself a combined rating reflecting your skill level across all the operations areas.

Research, Development, and Engineering

- *Direction and management of applied research:* ability to distinguish and keep a prudent balance between long-range projects at the frontiers of your technology, which attract the most creative individuals, and shorter-range research in support of current product development activity
- *Management of development:* ability to plan and direct work of development engineers and to use time and cost budgets so perfectionists do not ruin you and yet product performance, appearance, and production engineering needs can be met
- *Management of engineering:* ability to plan and direct engineers in the final design of a new product for manufacture and in the engineering and testing of the production process to manufacture that new product
- *Technical know-how:* ability to contribute personally to research, development, and engineering because of up-to-date, in-depth knowledge of the technologies in which your company is involved
- *Overall research, development, and engineering skills:* Give yourself a combined rating reflecting your skill level across the previous areas.

Financial Management

- *Raising capital:* ability to decide how best to acquire funds for start-up and growth; ability to forecast the need for funds and to prepare budgets; familiarity with sources and vehicles of short- and long-term financing
- *Money management:* ability to design, install, maintain, and use financial controls; familiarity with accounting and control systems needed to manage; ability to set up a project cost control system,

(Continued)

TABLE 11.5 **REPRESENTATIVE FUNCTIONS TO EVALUATE FOR NEW VENTURES *(continued)***

analyze overhead/contribution/absorption, prepare profit-and-loss and balance sheets, and manage a bookkeeper
- *Specfic skills:* cash-flow analysis; break-even analysis; contribution analysis; budgeting and profit-planning techniques; profit-and-loss, balance-sheet, and present-value analysis of return on investment and payback
- *Overall financial skills:* Give yourself a combined rating reflecting your skill level across all of the financial areas.

General Management and Administration

- *Problem solving:* ability to anticipate potential problems and plan to avoid them; ability to gather facts about problems, analyze them for *real* causes, and plan effective action to solve the problems; thoroughness in dealing with the details of particular problems and in follow-through
- *Communications:* ability to communicate effectively and clearly, both in speech and in writing, to the media, the public, customers, peers, and subordinates
- *Planning:* ability to set realistic and attainable goals, identify obstacles to achieving the goals, and develop detailed action plans to achieve those goals; ability to schedule own time systematically
- *Decision making:* ability to make decisions on your best analysis of incomplete data
- *Project management:* skill in organizing project teams, setting project goals, defining project tasks, and monitoring task completion in the face of problems and cost/quality constraints
- *Negotiating:* ability to work effectively in a negotiating situation; ability to quickly balance value given and value received
- *Personnel administration:* ability to set up payroll, hiring, compensation, and training functions
- *Overall administrative skills:* Give yourself a combined rating reflecting your skill level across all of the administrative areas.

Personnel Management

- *Leadership:* ability to understand the relationships among tasks, the leader, and the followers; ability to lead in situations where appropriate; willingness to manage actively, supervise, and control activities of others through directions, suggestions, inspiration, and other techniques
- *Listening:* ability to listen and understand without interrupting or mentally preparing your own rebuttal at the expense of hearing the message
- *Helping:* ability to ask for and provice help and to determine situations where assistance is warranted
- *Criticism:* ability to provide performance and interpersonal criticism to others that they find useful; ability to receive feedback from others without becoming defensive or argumentative
- *Conflict resolution:* ability to confront differences openly and to deal with them until resolution is obtained
- *Teamwork:* ability to work well with others in pursuing common goals
- *Selecting and developing subordinates:* ability to select and delegate responsibility to subordinates and to coach them in the development of their managerial capabilities
- *Climate building:* ability to create, by the way you manage, a climate and spirit conducive to high performance; ability to press for higher performance while rewarding work well done
- *Overall interpersonal skills:* Give yourself a combined rating reflecting your skills across all of the personnel management areas.

Legal and Tax Aspects

- *Corporate law:* familiarity with legal issues relating to stock issues, incorporation, distribution agreements, leases, etc.
- *Contract law:* familiarity with contract procedures and requirements (governmental and commercial), including default, warranty, and incentive provisions; fee structures; overhead, general, and administrative expenses allowable, and so forth
- *Patent law:* experience with preparation and revision of patent applications; ability to recognize a strong patent; familiarity with claim requirements
- *Tax law:* familiarity with general state and federal reporting requirements for businesses and with special provisions concerning Subchapter S corporations, tax shelters, fringe benefits, etc.
- *Overall legal and tax skills:* Give yourself a combined rating reflecting your skill level across all of the legal and tax areas.

SOURCE: *Pratt's Guide to Venture Capital Sources,* 8th ed. (Phoenix: Oryx Press, 1984), 13–15.

technical requirements, poor financial understanding, lack of venture uniqueness, and failure to be aware of legal issues.

When assessing a new venture, an entrepreneur needs to consider several critical factors: the uniqueness of the good or service, the amount of capital investment required to start the venture, the growth of sales, and the availability of the product.

Some major reasons new ventures fail are inadequate knowledge of the market, faulty product performance, ineffective marketing and sales effort, inadequate awareness of competitive pressures, rapid product obsolescence, poor timing, and undercapitalization. In drawing together these and other reasons, recent research reveals three major categories of causes for failure: product/market problems, financial difficulties, and managerial problems. In addition, the internal and external problems entrepreneurs face were discussed.

The feasibility of the entrepreneur's product or service can be assessed by asking the right questions, by making a profile analysis of the venture, and by carrying out a comprehensive feasibility study.

Key Terms and Concepts

Comprehensive feasibility approach	Internal problems
Critical factors	Lifestyle venture
Customer availability	Marketability
External problems	Product availability
Failure prediction model	Small profitable venture
Feasibility criteria approach	Start-up
Growth of sales	Technical feasibility
Growth stage	Uniqueness
High-growth venture	

Review and Discussion Questions

1. Explain the challenges involved in new-venture development.
2. Describe some of the key factors involved in new-venture performance (use Figure 11.1).
3. Many entrepreneurs lack objectivity and have no real insight into the market. In what way are these considered pitfalls of selecting new ventures?
4. Many entrepreneurs have a poor understanding of the finances associated with their new venture and/or have a venture that lacks uniqueness. In what way are these considered pitfalls of selecting new ventures?
5. Describe each of the five critical factors involved in the prestart-up and start-up phases of a new venture.
6. Identify and discuss three examples of product/market problems that can cause a venture to fail.
7. Identify and discuss two examples of financial difficulties that can cause a venture to fail.
8. Identify and discuss two examples of managerial problems that can cause a venture to fail.
9. List four major types of problems new ventures confront.
10. Describe the proposed "failure prediction" model for newly founded firms.
11. How can asking the right questions help an entrepreneur evaluate a new venture? What types of questions are involved?

12. Explain how a feasibility criteria approach works.
13. Explain how a comprehensive feasibility approach works.

Experiential Exercise   *Internal Profile Analysis*

Choose any emerging company with which you are familiar. If you are not familiar with any, consult magazines such as *Entrepreneur, Fortune,* and *Business Week,* and gather information on one firm. Then complete the following internal profile analysis by placing a check mark ($\checkmark$) in the appropriate column.

Internal Resource	Strong Weakness	Slight Weakness	Neutral	Slight Strength	Strong Strength
Financial					
Overall performance	_____	_____	_____	_____	_____
Ability to raise capital	_____	_____	_____	_____	_____
Working capital	_____	_____	_____	_____	_____
Position	_____	_____	_____	_____	_____
Marketing					
Market performance	_____	_____	_____	_____	_____
Knowledge of markets	_____	_____	_____	_____	_____
Product	_____	_____	_____	_____	_____
Advertising and promotion	_____	_____	_____	_____	_____
Price	_____	_____	_____	_____	_____
Distribution	_____	_____	_____	_____	_____
Organizational and Technical					
Location	_____	_____	_____	_____	_____
Production	_____	_____	_____	_____	_____
Facilities	_____	_____	_____	_____	_____
Access to suppliers	_____	_____	_____	_____	_____
Inventory control	_____	_____	_____	_____	_____
Quality control	_____	_____	_____	_____	_____
Organizational structure	_____	_____	_____	_____	_____
Rules, policies, and procedures	_____	_____	_____	_____	_____
Company image	_____	_____	_____	_____	_____
Human					
Number of employees	_____	_____	_____	_____	_____
Relevancy of skills	_____	_____	_____	_____	_____
Morale	_____	_____	_____	_____	_____
Compensation package	_____	_____	_____	_____	_____

Based on your analysis, what three recommendations would you make to the management?

1. _____
   _____

2. _____
   _____

3. _____
   _____

 **CASE 11.1**

Nothing Unique to Offer

Over the past four months, George Vazquez has been putting together his plan for a new venture. George wants to open a pizzeria near the local university. The area has three pizza enterprises, but George is convinced demand is sufficient to support a fourth.

The major competitor is a large national franchise unit that, in addition to its regular food-service menu of pizzas, salads, soft drinks, and desserts, offers door-to-door delivery. This delivery service is very popular with the university students and has helped the franchise unit capture approximately 40 percent of the student market. The second competitor is a "pizza wagon" that carries precooked pizzas. The driver circles the university area and sells pizzas on a first-come, first-served basis. The pizza wagon starts the evening with 50 pizzas of all varieties and sizes and usually sells 45 of them at full price. The last 5 are sold for whatever they will bring. It generally takes the wagon all evening to sell the 50 pizzas, but the profit markup is much higher than that obtained from the typical pizza sales at the franchise unit. The other competitor offers only in-house services, but it is well known for the quality of its food.

George does not believe it is possible to offer anything unique. However, he does believe that a combination of door-to-door delivery and high-quality, in-house service can help him win 15 percent to 20 percent of the local market. "Once the customers begin to realize that 'pizza is pizza,'" George told his partner, "we'll begin to get more business. After all, if there is no difference between one pizza place and another, they might just as well eat at our place."

Before finalizing his plans, George would like to bring in one more partner. "You can never have too much initial capital," he said. "You never know when you'll have unexpected expenses." But the individual whom George would like as a partner is reluctant to invest in the venture. "You really don't have anything unique to offer the market," he told George. "You're just another 'me too' pizzeria, and you're not going to survive." George hopes he will be able to change the potential investor's mind, but if he is not, George believes he can find someone else. "I have 90 days before I intend to open the business, and that's more than enough time to line up the third partner and get the venture under way," he told his wife yesterday.

Questions

1. Is there any truth to the potential investor's comment? Is the lack of uniqueness going to hurt George's chances of success? Explain.

2. If George were going to make his business venture unique, what steps might he take? Be complete in your answer.

3. In addition to the uniqueness feature, what other critical factors is George overlooking? Identify and describe three, and give your recommendations for what to do about them.

 **CASE** **11.2**

A Product Design Problem

When Billie Aherne learned the government was soliciting contracts for the manufacture of microcomputer components, she read the solicitation carefully. Billie's knowledge of microcomputers is extensive, and for the past five years she has been a university professor actively engaged in research in this area. If she could land this government contract, Billie felt certain she would be well on her way to going into business designing microcomputer components.

Billie asked for a leave of absence so she could bid on the microcomputer contract. She then worked up a detailed proposal and submitted it to the government. Eight months ago she learned she had been awarded the contract. For the next four months, Billie and two university colleagues who had joined her worked on completing their state-of-the-art components. When private firms learned of their contract, Billie was inundated with requests for components. She realized that as soon as she completed her government contract, she would be free to enter into contracts with private firms. Two months ago Billie shipped the components to the government. The next week she began signing contracts with firms in the private sector. In all, Billie signed agreements with six firms to provide each of them an average of $400,000 worth of components over the next four months. Last week the first shipment of components was delivered to one of the private firms.

In the mail earlier today Billie received a letter from the government. The communication informed her of quality problems with the components she had manufactured and shipped. Part of the letter read, "It took approximately four weeks of use before it became evident your components have a quality flaw. We believe the problem is in the basic design. We would like to meet with you at the earliest possible time to discuss your design and to agree on which steps must be taken in order for you to comply with the terms of your contract." Billie hoped to keep this news quiet until she could talk to the government representatives and find out what is going wrong. However, an hour ago she received a call from one of the private firms. "We hear that the microcomputer components you shipped to the government had a quality flaw," the speaker told Billie. "Could you tell us exactly what the problem is?"

Questions

1. What happened? What mistake did Billie make in terms of the new venture?
2. How could this problem have been prevented? Defend your answer.
3. What lesson about new-venture assessment does this case provide? Be complete in your answer.

Chapter 12

$\mathscr{S}$TRUCTURING THE NEW BUSINESS VENTURE

CHAPTER OBJECTIVES

1. To examine the legal forms of organization—sole proprietorship, partnership, corporation, and franchising

2. To illustrate the advantages and disadvantages of each of these four legal forms

3. To compare the characteristics and tax considerations of a partnership with those of a corporation

4. To explain the nature of the limited partnership

5. To examine how an S corporation works

6. To define the additional classifications of corporations

7. To review the costs and benefits associated with the corporate form of organization

8. To examine the franchise structure, benefits, and drawbacks

No one legal form of organization, or for that matter no combination of two or more of them, is suited to each and every small business. To try to say what is the best form for all enterprises would be like trying to select an all-purpose suit for a man.

In choosing a legal form of organization, consideration to the parties concerned must be made—their likes, dislikes and dispositions, their immediate and long-range needs and their tax situations. Seldom, if ever, does any one factor completely determine which is best.

U.S. Small Business Administration
"Selecting a Legal Structure for Your Firm"

IDENTIFYING LEGAL STRUCTURES

Before deciding how to organize an operation, prospective entrepreneurs need to identify the legal structure that will best suit the demands of the venture. The necessity for this is caused by changing tax laws, liability situations, the availability of capital, and the complexity of business formation.[1]

Three primary legal forms of organization are the sole proprietorship, the partnership, and the corporation. Because each form has specific advantages and disadvantages, it is impossible to recommend one form over the other. The entrepreneur's specific situation, concerns, and desires will dictate this choice.[2]

SOLE PROPRIETORSHIPS

A **sole proprietorship** is a business that is owned and operated by one person. The enterprise has no existence apart from its owner. This individual has a right to all of the profits and bears all of the liability for the debts and obligations of the business. The individual also has **unlimited liability,** which means his or her business and personal assets stand behind the operation. If the company cannot meet its financial obligations, the owner can be forced to sell the family car, house, and whatever assets that would satisfy the creditors.

---

[1] Kent Royalty, Robert Calhoun, Radie Bunn, and Wayne Wells, "The Impact of Tax Reform on the Choice of Small Business Legal Form," *Journal of Small Business Management* (January 1988): 9–17; and David S. Hulse and Thomas R. Pope, "The Effect of Income Taxes on the Preference of Organizational Form for Small Businesses in the United States," *Journal of Small Business Management* (January 1996): 24–35.

[2] For a detailed discussion of each form, see Kenneth W. Clarkson, Roger Leroy Miller, Gaylord A. Jentz, and Frank B. Cross, *West's Business Law,* 6th ed. (St. Paul: West, 1995): 748–63.

To establish a sole proprietorship, a person merely needs to obtain whatever local and state licenses are necessary to begin operations. If the proprietor should choose a fictitious or assumed name, he or she also must file a "certificate of assumed business name" with the county. Because of its ease of formation, the sole proprietorship is the most widely used legal form of organization.[3]

Advantages of Sole Proprietorships

Some of the advantages associated with sole proprietorships follow:

- *Ease of formation.* Less formality and fewer restrictions are associated with establishing a sole proprietorship than with any other legal form. The proprietorship needs little or no governmental approval, and it usually is less expensive than a partnership or corporation.
- *Sole ownership of profits.* The proprietor is not required to share profits with anyone.
- *Decision making and control vested in one owner.* No co-owners or partners must be consulted in the running of the operation.
- *Flexibility.* Management is able to respond quickly to business needs in the form of day-to-day management decisions as governed by various laws and good sense.
- *Relative freedom from governmental control.* Except for requiring the necessary licenses, very little governmental interference occurs in the operation.
- *Freedom from corporate business taxes.* Proprietors are taxed as individual taxpayers and not as businesses.

Disadvantages of Sole Proprietorships

Sole proprietorships also have disadvantages. Some of these follow:

- *Unlimited liability.* The individual proprietor is personally responsible for all business debts. This liability extends to *all* of the proprietor's assets.
- *Lack of continuity.* The enterprise may be crippled or terminated if the owner becomes ill or dies.
- *Less available capital.* Ordinarily, proprietorships have less available capital than other types of business organizations, such as partnerships and corporations.
- *Relative difficulty obtaining long-term financing.* Because the enterprise rests exclusively on one person, it often has difficulty raising long-term capital.
- *Relatively limited viewpoint and experience.* The operation depends on one person, and this individual's ability, training, and expertise will limit its direction and scope.

PARTNERSHIPS

A **partnership** is an association of two or more persons acting as co-owners of a business for profit. Each partner contributes money, property, labor, or skills, and each shares in the profits (as well as the losses) of the business.[4]

---

[3] For more on the sole proprietorship, see Roger LeRoy Miller and Frank B. Cross, *The Legal Environment Today* (St. Paul, MN: West, 1996), 365–66.

[4] For a good analysis of partnershps, see John R. Allison and Robert A. Prentice, *Business Law,* 6th ed. (Fort Worth: The Dryden Press, 1994), 659–716.

ENTREPRENEURIAL

EDGE

Advice You Should Take

Managing growth is a big challenge for large and small companies alike. An increasing number of small companies are looking to outsiders for help. By forming an advisory board of industry venterans, savvy entrepreneurs are able to map out growth plans, develop sophisticated management structures, and even venture into new markets. Even though no hard statistics on this trend exist, Charles Heller, the director at the Dingman Center for Entrepreneurship at the University of Maryland, will testify to the overwhelming popularity of advisory boards. "Of the 300 companies that we work with, more than half rely on outside advisers for direction today," Heller notes. Some professionals believe these boards, with their experience and expertise, can serve as "stealth business weapons that empower small companies to compete with their larger rivals," he says.

Wang Associates Health Communications, a New York City public relations firm, boasted nine consecutive years of tremendous growth. In 1992, the growth ceased. Julie Wang, chairperson, did not know how to keep her firm growing. She reached out to Louis Barnes, a professor of organizational behavior at the Harvard Business School. In compliance with his suggestions, she formed a three-member advisory board of experts. Together, they developed long-term plans for the company, an accounting system, human-resource policies, and a powerful management team. By 1995, Wang's revenues had skyrocketed to $5 million.

What do these professionals offer that is so valuable? Real-life experience. Advisers are usually respected entrepreneurs, corporate executives, and business school professors who have "been there and done that" and truly understand the challenges of running a business. Advisory boards are formed primarily to provide ambitious entrepreneurs with objective opinions and new perspectives. They are especially useful to small-business owners who cannot afford to hire high-priced consultants or seasoned managers. Such industry experts usually offer their services for a mere $500 to $1,000 per meeting per member (plus expenses). In addition, because advisers don't have the fiduciary responsibilities of a formal

The **Uniform Partnership Act** is generally followed by most states as the guide for legal requirements in forming a partnership.[5] Though not specifically required in the act, written articles of partnership are usually executed and are always recommended. This is because, unless otherwise agreed to in writing, the courts assume equal partnership, that is, equal sharing of profits, losses, assets, management, and other aspects of the business.

---

[5] The Uniform Partnership Act appears in full in Clarkson et al., *West's Business Law,* Appendix E, A-183–A-204; and also in Roger LeRoy Miller and Gaylord A. Jentz, *Business Law Today,* 4th ed. (St. Paul, MN: West, 1997), Appendix D, A-111–A-117.

board of directors, director and liability insurance are not required.

Although advisory boards can be very effective, a few precautions should be taken to protect both the company and the board from the risk of liability claims that could arise from their activities on behalf of the company. These include the following four steps:

1. Include provisions in the company's bylaws that outline the responsibilities and term of office for advisers.
2. Ask advisers to make no public statements for or about the company.
3. Advise the board to avoid undisclosed conflicts of interest.
4. Demand that proprietary information about the company, such as market research, be kept confidential.

The expertise and experience of advisers become particularly important when a business faces a major crisis or issue. But this should not be the only time to tap into this wealth of knowledge. After a business has survived the initial start-up aches and pains and is ready to pursue larger tasks, a well-connected board can really boost results. A knowledgeable board also can be critical when a business requires sophisticated management strategies to handle its growth. In addition, an effective group that insists on detailed financial and marketing information creates a good sounding board when making strategic plans. And, finally, their expertise can provide solutions to immediate problems, such as human-resource concerns, that may set long-term precedents.

Here are a few suggestions for recruiting advisory board members:

1. Explore your network of industry experts, fellow business owners, and civic leaders for referrals.
2. You may ask your accountant, attorney, or banker to be a member; however, they tend to think conservatively.
3. Make sure at least one member is familiar with your industry. The other members should be able to address your specific management issues.
4. Get to know your candidates before asking them to be advisers.
5. Assess their team skills to ensure the chemistry among members will be effective.
6. Prepare new members about the market and management challenges and issues your company faces before asking them to be an advisory board member.

SOURCE: Lester A. Picker "Hatch Ideas with Outside Advisors to Boost Profits," *Your Company* (June/July 1996): 32–35.

The articles of partnership clearly outline the financial and managerial contributions of the partners and carefully delineate the roles in the partnership relationship. The following are examples of the types of information customarily written into the agreement:

- Name, purpose, domicile
- Duration of agreement
- Character of partners (general or limited, active or silent)
- Contributions by partners (at inception, at later date)
- Division of profits and losses

- Draws or salaries
- Rights of continuing partner(s)
- Death of a partner (dissolution and windup)
- Release of debts
- Business expenses (method of handling)
- Separate debts
- Authority (individual partner's authority on business conduct)
- Books, records, and method of accounting
- Sale of partnership interest
- Arbitration
- Settlement of disputes
- Additions, alterations, or modifications of partnership
- Required and prohibited acts
- Absence and disability
- Employee management

In addition to the written articles, entrepreneurs must consider a number of different types of partnership arrangements. Depending on the needs of the enterprise, one or more of these may be used. It is important to remember that in a typical partnership arrangement at least one partner must be a general partner who is responsible for the debts of the enterprise and who has unlimited liability.[6]

Advantages of Partnerships

The advantages associated with the partnership form of organization follow:

- *Ease of formation.* Legal formalities and expenses are few compared with those for creating a more complex enterprise, such as a corporation.
- *Direct rewards.* Partners are motivated to put forth their best efforts by direct sharing of the profits.
- *Growth and performance facilitated.* In a partnership it often is possible to obtain more capital and a better range of skills than in a sole proprietorship.
- *Flexibility.* A partnership often is able to respond quickly to business needs in the form of day-to-day decisions.
- *Relative freedom from governmental control and regulation.* Very little governmental interference occurs in the operation of a partnership.
- *Possible tax advantage.* Most partnerships pay taxes as individuals, thus escaping the higher rate assessed against corporations.

Disadvantages of Partnerships

Partnerships also have disadvantages. Some of these follow:

- *Unlimited liability of at least one partner.* Although some partners can have limited liability, at least one must be a general partner who assumes unlimited liability.
- *Lack of continuity.* If any partner dies, is adjudged insane, or simply withdraws from the business, the partnership arrangement ceases. However, operation of the business

---

[6] For detailed coverage on limited partnership, see Miller and Jentz, *Business Law Today,* 683–86. For coverage of the Uniform Limited Partnership Act (ULPA), see Allison and Prentice, *Business Law,* 1179–87.

can continue based on the right of survivorship and the possible creation of a new partnership by the remaining members or by the addition of new members.

- *Relative difficulty obtaining large sums of capital.* Most partnerships have some problems raising a great deal of capital, especially when long-term financing is involved. Usually the collective wealth of the partners dictates the amount of total capital the partnership can raise, especially when first starting out.
- *Bound by the acts of just one partner.* A general partner can commit the enterprise to contracts and obligations that may prove disastrous to the enterprise in general and to the other partners in particular.
- *Difficulty of disposing of partnership interest.* The buying out of a partner may be difficult unless specifically arranged for in the written agreement.

Partnership Success

The desire and decision to form partnerships appear to be fairly well understood. However, very little information exists regarding the processes required to develop and nurture the partnership beyond the initial decision to establish the relationship. Given both the costs and risks associated with a failed partnership, insight into the factors affecting partnership success is quite useful. One research study attempted to shed light on these issues and to offer an improved understanding of the form and substance of the interaction between or among partners.

The study suggested that trust, the willingness to coordinate activities, and the ability to convey a sense of commitment to the relationship are key. Critical also are the communications strategies the trading parties use. (See Figure 12.1 for an illustration of the key factors.)

Joint participation enables all parties to better understand the strategic choices facing them. The researchers found that trust, commitment, communication quality, joint planning, and joint problem resolution all serve to better align partners' expectations, goals, and objectives. The challenge lies in developing a management philosophy or corporate culture under which independent trading parties can relinquish some control, while also engaging in planning and organizing that takes into account the needs of all parties.[7]

CORPORATIONS

A **corporation** is "an artificial being, invisible, intangible, and existing only in contemplation of the law" (Supreme Court Justice John Marshall, 1819). As such, a corporation is a separate legal entity apart from the individuals who own it. A corporation is created by the authority of state laws and is usually formed when a transfer of money or property by prospective shareholders (owners) takes place in exchange for capital stock (ownership certificates) in the corporation.[8] The procedures ordinarily required to form a corporation are (1) subscriptions for capital stock must be taken and a tentative organization created, and (2) approval must be obtained from the secretary of state in the state in which the corporation is to be formed. This approval is in the form of a charter for the corporation,

---

[7] Jakki Mohr and Robert Spekman, "Characteristics of Partnership Success: Partnership Attributes, Communication Behavior, and Conflict Resolution Techniques," *Strategic Management Journal* 15 (1994): 135–52.

[8] For detailed presentations of corporate laws and regulations, see Clarkson et al., *West's Business Law,* Appendix H, "The Revised Model Business Corporation Act," A-205–A-244.

FIGURE 12.1   **FACTORS ASSOCIATED WITH PARTNERSHIP SUCCESS**

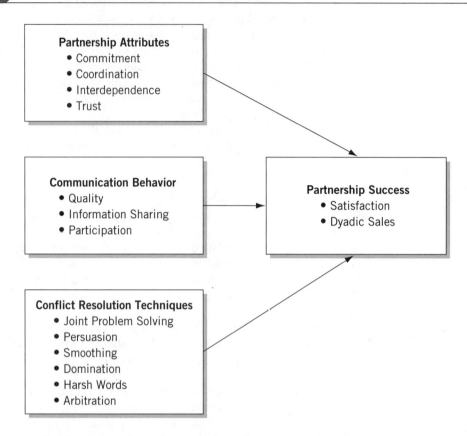

SOURCE: Jakki Mohr and Robert Spekman, "Characteristics of Partnership Success: Partnership Attributes, Communication Behavior, and Conflict Resolution Techniques," *Strategic Management Journal* 15 (1994): 137.

stating the powers and limitations of the particular enterprise. Corporations that do business in more than one state must comply with federal laws regarding interstate commerce and with the varying state laws that cover foreign (out-of-state) corporations.

Advantages of Corporations

Some of the advantages associated with corporations follow:

- *Limited liability.* The stockholder's liability is limited to the individual's investment. This is the most money the person can lose.
- *Transfer of ownership.* Ownership can be transferred through the sale of stock to interested buyers.
- *Unlimited life.* The company has a life separate and distinct from that of its owners and can continue for an indefinite period of time.
- *Relative ease of securing capital in large amounts.* Capital can be acquired through the issuance of bonds and shares of stock and through short-term loans made against the assets of the business or personal guarantees of the major stockholders.

- *Increased ability and expertise.* The corporation is able to draw on the expertise and skills of a number of individuals, ranging from the major stockholders to the professional managers who are brought on board.

Disadvantages of Corporations

Corporations also have disadvantages. Some of these follow:

- *Activity restrictions.* Corporate activities are limited by the charter and by various laws.
- *Lack of representation.* Minority stockholders are sometimes outvoted by the majority, who force their will on the others.
- *Regulation.* Extensive governmental regulations and reports required by local, state, and federal agencies often result in a great deal of paperwork and red tape.
- *Organizing expenses.* A multitude of expenses are involved in forming a corporation.
- *Double taxation.* Income taxes are levied both on corporate profits and on individual salaries and dividends.

Tables 12.1 and 12.2 compare the characteristics and the tax considerations of partnerships and corporations.

SPECIFIC FORMS OF PARTNERSHIPS AND CORPORATIONS

A number of specific forms of partnerships and corporations warrant special attention. The following examines these.

Limited Partnerships

Limited partnerships are used in situations where a form of organization is needed that permits capital investment without responsibility for management *and* without liability for losses beyond the initial investment. Such an organization allows the right to share in the profits with limited liability for the losses.

Limited partnerships are governed by the **Uniform Limited Partnership Act** (ULPA), which was formulated in 1916 and revised in 1976, with amendments added in 1985.[9] The act contains 11 articles and 64 sections of guidelines covering areas such as (1) general provisions, (2) formation, (3) limited partners, (4) general partners, (5) finance, (6) distributions and withdrawals, (7) assignment of partnership interest, (8) dissolution, (9) foreign limited partnerships, (10) derivative actions, and (11) miscellaneous. If a limited partnership appears to be the desired legal form of organization, the prospective partners must examine these ULPA guidelines.

The creation of a limited partnership is a formal proceeding, as opposed to the voluntary approach a general partnership uses. A limited partnership must involve two or more partners, and they must sign a certificate that sets forth, at a minimum, the following information:

[9] The complete Uniform Limited Partnership Act may be found in Clarkson et al., *West's Business Law,* Appendix E and F, A-183–A-204; and Allison and Prentice, *Business Law.*

TABLE 12.1   COMPARISON OF THE MAJOR FORMS OF BUSINESS

Characteristic	Sole Proprietorship	Partnership	Corporation
1. Method of Creation	Created at will by owner	Created by agreement of the parties	Charter issued by state—created by statutory authorization
2. Legal Position	Not a separate entity; owner is the business	Not a separate legal entity in many states	Always a legal entity separate and distinct from its owners—a legal fiction for the purposes of owning property and being a party to litigation
3. Liability	Unlimited liability	Unlimited liability (except for limited partners in a limited partnership)	Limited liability of shareholders—shareholders are not liable for the debts of the corporation
4. Duration	Determined by owner; automatically dissolved on owner's death	Terminated by agreement of the partners, by the death of one or more of the partners, by withdrawal of a partner, by bankruptcy, etc.	Can have perpetual existence
5. Transferability of Interest	Interest can be transferred, but individual's proprietorship then ends	Although partnership interest can be assigned, assignee does not have full rights of a partner	Share of stock can be transferred
6. Management	Completely at owner's discretion	Each general partner has a direct and equal voice in management unless expressly agreed otherwise in the partnership agreement	Shareholders elect directors who set policy and appoint officers
7. Taxation	Owner pays personal taxes on business income	Each partner pays *pro rata* share of income taxes on net profits, whether or not they are distributed	Double taxation—corporation pays income tax on net profits, with no deduction for dividends, and shareholders pay income tax on disbursed dividends they receive
8. Organizational Fees, Annual License Fees, and Annual Reports	None	None	All required
9. Transaction of Business in Other States	Generally no limitation	Generally no limitation	Normally must qualify to do business and obtain certificate of authority

SOURCE: Reprinted by permission from p. 751 of *West's Business Law*, 6th ed., by Kenneth W. Clarkson, Roger L. Miller, Gaylord A. Jentz, and Frank B. Cross. Copyright © 1995 by West Publishing Company. All rights reserved.

1. Name of the firm

2. Type of business

3. Location of the principal place of business

4. Name and place of residence of each member and whether each is a general or a limited partner

TABLE 12.2   **TAX ASPECTS OF PARTNERSHIPS AND CORPORATIONS**

Tax Aspect	Partnership	Corporation
1. Federal Income Tax	Partners are taxed on proportionate shares of partnership income, even if not distributed; the partnership files information returns only.	Income of the corporation is taxed; stockholders are also taxed on distributed dividends. The corporation files corporate income tax forms.
2. Accumulation	Partners are taxed on accumulated as well as distributed earnings.	Corporate stockholders are not taxed on accumulated earnings. There is, however, a penalty tax, in some instances, that the corporation must pay for unreasonable accumulations of income.
3. Capital Gains	Partners are taxed on their proportionate share of capital gains, which are taxed at ordinary income rate.	The corporation is taxed on capital gains and losses.
4. Exempt Income	Partners are not taxed on exempt income received from the firm.	Any exempt income distributed by a corporation is fully taxable income to the stockholders.
5. Pension Plan	Partners can adopt a Keogh plan, an IRA, or a 401-K plan.	Employees and officers who are also stockholders can be beneficiaries of a pension trust. The corporation can deduct its payments to the trust.
6. Social Security	Partners must pay a self-employment tax (in 1996, 12.4 percent on income up to 62,700, plus 2.9 percent Medicare tax with no limit on earnings that are subject to taxation).	All compensation to officers and employee stockholders is subject to Social Security taxation up to the maximum.
7. Death Benefits (excluding those provided by insurance)	There is no exemption for payments to partners' beneficiaries.	Benefits up to $5,000 can be received tax-free by employees' beneficiaries.
8. State Taxes	The partnership is not subject to taxes. State income taxes are paid by each partner.	The corporation is subject to state income taxes (although these taxes can be deducted on federal returns).

SOURCE: Reprinted by permission from p. 413 of *Business Law Today*, by Roger L. Miller and Gaylord A. Jentz. Copyright © 1997 by West Publishing Company. All rights reserved.

5. Duration of the partnership

6. Amount of cash and a description and agreed-on valuation of any other property contributed by each limited partner

7. Additional contributions (if any) each limited partner is to make and the times at which they are to make them

8. Methods for changes in personnel (if any) and subsequent continuance of the business

9. Share of profits or other compensation each limited partner is entitled to receive

The content of the certificate and the method of filing resembles that of the corporate charter. Additionally, private, informal agreements often are made covering matters not addressed in the certificate, such as the sharing of profits by the partners.[10]

Limited Liability Partnerships

The **limited liability partnership (LLP)** is a relatively new form of partnership that allows professionals the tax benefits of a partnership while avoiding personal liability for the malpractice of other partners. If a professional group organizes as an LLP, innocent partners are not personally liable for the wrongdoing of the other partners. The LLP is similar to the *limited liability company (LLC)* discussed later. The difference is that LLPs are designed more for professionals who normally do business as a partnership. As with limited liability companies, LLPs must be formed and operated in compliance with state statutes.

One of the reasons why LLPs are becoming so popular among professionals is that most LLP statutes make it relatively easy to establish an LLP. This is particularly true for an already formal partnership. For example, to become an LLP in Texas, all a partnership must do is fulfill the following requirements:

1. File the appropriate form with the secretary of state

2. Pay an annual fee of $200 per partner

3. Maintain at least $100,000 in professional liability insurance

4. Add either "L.L.P." or "Registered Limited Liability Partnership" to its name

Converting from a partnership to an LLP is easy also because the firm's basic organizational structure remains the same. Additionally, all of the statutory and common-law rules governing partnerships still apply (apart from those modified by the LLP statute). Normally, LLP statutes are simply amendments to a state's already existing partnership law.[11]

R&D Limited Partnerships

A form of partnership structure that has become a popular tool for funding the research and development expenses of entrepreneurial ventures is the **R&D** (research and development) **limited partnership.** This form of partnership is actually a limited partnership in many ways.

- The R&D partnership is *not* a taxable entity.
- Income the venture generates is distributed to the partners and taxed as personal income. (In the case of a loss, it may offset other earned income.)
- A general partner is responsible for managing operations and assuming business obligations.
- The limited partners are investors (provide capital) in the venture and do not actively participate in the management of the enterprise.

---

[10] For more detail on limited partnerships, see Roger E. Meiner, Al H. Ringleb, and Frances L. Edwards, *The Legal Environment of Business,* 5th ed. (St. Paul: West, 1994), 407–10.

[11] Miller and Jentz, *Business Law Today,* 686–87.

Under this structure, the venture developing a patentable idea is known as the "sponsoring company," and, in return for the investor's capital, it makes the technology (idea) available to the partnership through a licensing arrangement.

An R&D limited partnership has specific advantages and disadvantages. The advantages follow:

- Less dilution of stock ownership is expected than with any other equity source. The sponsoring company is able to retain greater control of the project.
- The risk of failure is borne by the partnership, because the partnership owns the technology. Thus, the sponsoring company pays only in the event of a successful development.
- If the contract is properly structured, the investment is "off balance sheet" financing; the funds do not show up as debt on the sponsoring company's financial statements. As a result, the company is likely to have an improved ability to borrow from conventional sources because of a substantially improved debt-to-equity ratio.
- The company's ability to generate cash is improved. Debt service on a typical loan begins immediately after the loan is received. Royalty payments under an R&D arrangement do not begin until the product is successfully marketed.[12]

The disadvantages follow:

- The cost of funds to the sponsoring company is high and is usually much more expensive than debt.
- The use of invested funds is restricted solely to R&D expenses.
- R&D partnerships are expensive to establish in terms of both time and money.[13]

S Corporations

Formerly termed a Subchapter S corporation, the **S corporation** takes its name from Subchapter S of the Internal Revenue Code, under which a business can seek to avoid the imposition of income taxes at the corporate level yet retain some of the benefits of a corporate form (especially the limited liability).

Commonly known as a "tax option corporation," an S corporation is taxed similarly to a partnership.[14] Only an information form is filed with the IRS to indicate the shareholders' income. In this manner the double-taxation problem of corporations is avoided. Corporate income is not taxed but instead flows to the personal income of shareholders of businesses and is taxable at that point.

Although this is very useful for small businesses, strict guidelines must be followed:

1. The corporation must be a domestic corporation.

2. The corporation must not be a member of an affiliated group of corporations.

3. The shareholders of the corporation must be individuals, estates, or certain trusts. Corporations, partnerships, and nonqualifying trusts cannot be shareholders.

4. The corporation must have 75 or fewer shareholders.

---

[12] James W. Henderson, *Obtaining Venture Capital* (Lexington, MA: Lexington Books, 1988), 270.

[13] Ibid.

[14] For details on S corporations, see Miller and Jentz, *Business Law Today,* pp. 720–21.

5. The corporation must have only one class of stock, although not all shareholders need have the same voting rights.

6. No shareholder of the corporation may be a nonresident alien.

BENEFITS FROM ELECTING S CORPORATIONS   The S corporation offers a number of benefits. For example, when the corporation has losses, Subchapter S allows the shareholders to use these losses to offset taxable income. Also, when the stockholders are in a tax bracket lower than that of the corporation, Subchapter S causes their entire income to be taxed in the shareholders' bracket, whether or not it is distributed. This is particularly attractive when the corporation wants to accumulate earnings for some future business purposes. The taxable income of an S corporation is taxable only to those who are shareholders at the end of the corporate year when that income is distributed.

The S corporation can choose a fiscal year that will permit it to defer some of its shareholders' taxes. This is important because undistributed earnings are not taxed to the shareholders until after the corporation's (not the shareholders') fiscal year. In addition, the shareholder in an S corporation can give some of his or her stock to other members of the family who are in a lower tax bracket. Finally, an S corporation can offer some tax-free corporate benefits. These benefits typically mean federal tax savings to the shareholders.

Limited Liability Companies

Since 1977, an increasing number of states have authorized a new form of business organization called the **limited liability company (LLC).** The LLC is a hybrid form of business enterprise that offers the limited liability of a corporation but the tax advantages of a partnership.

A major advantage of the LLC is that it does not pay taxes on an entity; rather, profits are "passed through" the LLC and paid personally by company members. Another advantage is that the liability of members is limited to the amount of their investments. In an LLC, members are allowed to participate fully in management activities, and, under at least one state's statute, the firm's managers need not even be LLC members. Yet another advantage is that corporations and partnerships, as well as foreign investors, can be LLC members. Also, no limit exists on the number of LLC shareholder members.

The disadvantages of the LLC are relatively few. Perhaps the greatest disadvantage is that LLC statutes differ from state to state, and thus any firm engaged in multistate operations may face difficulties. In an attempt to promote some uniformity among the states in respect to LLC statutes, the National Conference of Commissioners on Uniform State Laws drafted a uniform limited liability company statute for submission to the states to consider for adoption. Until all the states have adopted the uniform law, however, an LLC in one state will have to check the rules in the other states in which the firm does business to ensure it retains its limited liability.[15]

Other Corporation Classifications

Corporations also can be classified by location, fund sources, objectives, corporate activities, and ownership arrangements.

---

[15] Miller and Jentz, *Business Law Today,* 414; see also Mary Sprouse, "The Lure of Limited Liability Companies," *Your Company* (fall 1995): 19.

DOMESTIC AND FOREIGN CORPORATIONS   A corporation must be incorporated in a particular state. The corporation is referred to as a **domestic corporation** by its home state (the state in which it incorporated). By contrast, a corporation operating in any other state in the United States is known as a **foreign corporation.** (This discussion does not refer to international corporations; the terms *domestic* and *foreign* apply only to status within the United States.)

PUBLIC AND PRIVATE CORPORATIONS   A **public corporation** is one formed by the government to meet some political or governmental purpose. Cities and towns that incorporate are common examples. In addition, many organizations of the federal government are public corporations. **Private corporations** are created either wholly or in part for private benefit. Most business corporations are private. Private corporations can serve a public purpose, as a public utility does, for example, but they are nonetheless owned by private persons rather than by the government.

NONPROFIT CORPORATIONS   A familiar form of **nonprofit corporation** (or not-for-profit) is the religious, charitable, or educational corporation. Its purpose is not to make a profit, but it is permitted to do so if the profit is left within the corporation. Nonprofit corporations are organized under state statutes that usually provide for different formation and operating policies. Such corporations can issue shares of stock but cannot pay dividends to share owners. Most nonprofit corporations are private.

PROFESSIONAL CORPORATIONS   Most **professional corporations** are private corporations involving practitioners of professions such as law, accounting, or medicine. The professional corporation has become extremely popular because its tax benefits (pension plan, medical benefits, and so forth) are often more beneficial than those provided by a partnership form of organization.

CLOSE CORPORATIONS   The **close corporation,** or closely held corporation, is typically one in which all shares of stock are held either by a single shareholder or a small number of shareholders (the actual number is usually established by state law). These shares are not available for purchase by the general public. Close-corporation shareholders manage the firm directly.[16]

Costs Associated with Incorporation

Just about anyone can start a corporation. However, numerous expenses are associated with starting and running such a venture:

- *Lawyers' fees.* These can range from $1,000 to $5,000.
- *Accountants' fees.* It can cost from $500 to $1,000 to establish a bookkeeping system for a corporation.
- *Fees to the state.* The state can require an annual corporate fee of several hundred dollars.
- *Unemployment insurance taxes.* Even if the corporation has only one employee, it must still pay unemployment insurance taxes, either to the state in which it is registered or to the federal government.

[16] For a detailed account of close corporations, see Clarkson et al., *West's Business Law,* 806–8.

- *Employer's contribution to Social Security.* If a person is a salaried employee of some other company in addition to being an employee of his or her own corporation, he or she must pay an employer's "contribution" to Social Security. This contribution is nonrefundable.
- *Annual legal and accounting fees.* A variety of forms must be filed for corporations in different states. In addition, corporate records and minute books must be maintained. Typically, an accountant or a lawyer does this. Annual fees for such services can run into many hundreds of dollars.

FRANCHISING

Today, more than a third of all retail sales and an increasing part of the gross domestic product are generated by private franchises. A **franchise** is any arrangement in which the owner of a trademark, trade name, or copyright has licensed others to use it in selling goods or services. A *franchisee* (a purchaser of a franchise) is generally legally independent but economically dependent on the integrated business system of the *franchisor* (the seller of the franchise). In other words, a franchisee can operate as an independent businessperson but still obtain the advantages of a regional or national organization.[17]

Advantages of Franchising

A number of advantages are associated with franchising.[18]

TRAINING AND GUIDANCE   Perhaps the greatest advantage of buying a franchise, as compared to starting a new business or buying an existing one, is that the franchisor will usually provide both training and guidance to the franchisee. As a result, the likelihood of success is much greater for national franchisees who have received this assistance than for small-business owners in general. For example, it has been reported that the ratio of failure for small enterprises in general to franchised businesses may be as high as four or five to one.

BRAND-NAME APPEAL   An individual who buys a well-known national franchise, especially a big-name one, has a good chance to succeed. The franchisor's name is a drawing card for the establishment. People are often more aware of the product or service offered by a national franchise and prefer it to those offered by lesser-known outlets.

A PROVEN TRACK RECORD   Another benefit of buying a franchise is that the franchisor has already proved the operation can be successful. Of course, if someone is the first individual to buy a franchise, this is not the case. However, if the organization has been around for five to ten years and has 50 or more units, it should not be difficult to see how successful the operations have been. If all of the units are still in operation and the owners report they are doing well financially, one can be certain the franchisor has proved that the

---

[17] Clarkson et al., *West's Business Law,* 756.

[18] See Alden Peterson and Rajiv P. Dant, "Perceived Advantages of the Franchise Option from the Franchisee Perspective: Empirical Insights from a Service Franchise," *Journal of Small Business Management* (July 1990): 46–61; Richard M. Hodgetts and Donald F. Kuratko, *Effective Small Business Management,* 5th ed. (Fort Worth, TX: The Dryden Press, 1995), 125–155; and Scott A. Shane and Frank Hoy, "Franchising: A Gateway to Cooperative Entrepreneurship," *Journal of Business Venturing* (September 1996): 325–328.

layout and location of the store, the pricing policy, the quality of the goods or service, and the overall management system are successful.

FINANCIAL ASSISTANCE　Another reason a franchise can be a good investment is that the franchisor may be able to help the new owner secure the financial assistance needed to run the operation. In fact, some franchisors have personally helped the franchisee get started by lending money and not requiring any repayment until the operation is running smoothly. In short, buying a franchise is often an ideal way to ensure assistance from the financial community.

Disadvantages of Franchising

The prospective franchisee must weigh the advantages of franchising against the accompanying disadvantages. Some of the most important drawbacks follow:

1. Franchise fees

2. The control exercised by the franchisor

3. Unfulfilled promises by some franchisors

The following sections examine each of these disadvantages.

FRANCHISE FEES　In business, no one gets something for nothing. The larger and more successful the franchisor, the greater the franchise fee. For a franchise from a national chain, it is not uncommon to be faced with a fee of $5,000 to $100,000. Smaller franchisors or those who have not had great success charge less. Nevertheless, entrepreneurs deciding whether or not to take the franchise route into small business should weigh the fee against the return they could get putting the money into another type of business. Also, remember that this fee covers only the benefits discussed in the previous section. The prospective franchisee also must pay for building the unit and stocking it, although the franchisor may provide assistance in securing a bank loan. Additionally, a fee is usually tied to gross sales. Typically, the franchise buyer pays an initial franchise fee, spends his or her own money to build a store, buys the equipment and inventory, and then pays a continuing royalty based on sales, usually between 5 and 12 percent. Most franchisors require buyers to have 25 to 50 percent of the initial costs in cash. The rest can be borrowed, in some cases, from the franchising organization itself.[19] Table 12.3 presents a list of the costs involved in buying a franchise.

FRANCHISOR CONTROL　When one works in a large corporation, the company controls the employee's activities. If an individual has a personal business, he or she controls his or her own activities. A franchise operator is somewhere between these extremes. The franchisor generally exercises a fair amount of control over the operation in order to achieve a degree of uniformity. If entrepreneurs do not follow franchisor directions, they may not have their franchise license renewed when the contract expires.

---

[19] Bryce Webster, *The Insider's Guide to Franchising* (New York: Macmillan, 1986); and Lloyd T. Tarbutton, *Franchising: The How-To Book* (Englewood Cliffs: Prentice-Hall, 1986).

TABLE 12.3   **THE COSTS OF FRANCHISING**

Don't let the advantages of franchising cloud the fact that significant costs are involved. Although the franchise fee may be $75,000, the actual cost of "opening your doors for business" can be more than $200,000! Depending on the type of franchise, the following expenditures are possible:

1. **The Basic Franchise Fee**   For this, you may receive a wide range of services: personnel training, licenses, operations manuals, training materials, site selection and location preparation assistance, etc. Or you may receive none of these.

2. **Insurance**   You will need coverage for a variety of items, such as plate glass, office contents, vehicles, and others. You should also obtain so-called umbrella insurance. It is inexpensive and is meant to help out in the event of crippling million- or multimillion-dollar lawsuits.

3. **Opening Product Inventory**   If initial inventory is not included in your franchise fee, you will have to obtain enough to open your franchise.

4. **Remodeling and Leasehold Improvements**   In most commercial leases, you are responsible for these costs.

5. **Utility Charges**   Deposits to cover the first month or two are usually required for electricity, gas, oil, telephone, and water.

6. **Payroll**   This should include the costs of training employees before the store opens. You also should include a reasonable salary for yourself.

7. **Debt Service**   This includes principal and interest payments.

8. **Bookkeeping and Accounting Fees**   In addition to the services the franchisor may supply in this area, it is always wise to use your own CPA.

9. **Legal and Professional Fees**   The cost of hiring an attorney to review the franchise contract, file for and obtain any necessary zoning or planning ordinances, and handle any unforeseen conflicts must be factored into your opening-costs projections.

10. **State and Local Licenses, Permits, and Certificates**   These run the gamut from liquor licenses to building permits for renovations.

SOURCE: Donald F. Kuratko, "Achieving the American Dream as a Franchisee," *Small Business Network* (July 1987): 2.

UNFULFILLED PROMISES   In some cases, especially among less-known franchisors, the franchisees have not received all they were promised.[20] For example, many franchisees have found themselves with trade names that have no drawing power. Also, many franchisees have found that the promised assistance from the franchisor has not been forthcoming. For example, instead of being able to purchase supplies more cheaply through the franchisor, many operators have found themselves paying exorbitant prices for supplies. If franchisees complain, they risk having their agreement with the franchisor terminated or not renewed.

Franchise Law

The growth in franchise operations has outdistanced laws about franchising. A solid body of appellate decisions under federal or state laws relating to franchises has yet to be devel-

[20] Russell M. Knight, "Franchising from the Franchisor's and Franchisee's Points of View," *Journal of Small Business Management* (July 1986): 8–15.

oped.[21] In the absence of case law precisely addressed to franchising, the courts tend to apply general common-law principles and appropriate federal or state statutory definitions and rules. Characteristics associated with a franchising relationship are similar in some respects to those of principal/agent, employer/employee, and employer/independent-contractor relationships, yet a franchising relationship does not truly fit into any of these traditional classifications. (See the Contemporary Entrepreneurship box.)

Much franchise litigation has arisen over termination provisions. Because the franchise agreement is normally a form contract the franchisor draws and prepares, and because the bargaining power of the franchisee is rarely equal to that of the franchisor, the termination provisions of contracts are generally more favorable to the franchisor. This means the franchisee, who normally invests a substantial amount of time and money in the franchise operation to make it successful, may receive little or nothing for the business upon termination. The franchisor owns the trademark and hence the business.[22]

FINAL THOUGHTS

As mentioned earlier, an entrepreneur always should seek professional legal advice in order to avoid misunderstanding, mistakes, and, of course, added expenses.

The average entrepreneur encounters many diverse problems and stumbling blocks in venture formation. Since he or she does not have a thorough knowledge of law, accounting, real estate, taxes, and governmental regulations, an understanding of certain basic concepts in these areas is imperative.

The material in this chapter is a good start toward understanding the legal forms of organizations. It can provide entrepreneurs with guidelines for seeking further and more specific advice on the legal form that appears most applicable to their situation. (See Table 12.4 for a good review of an entrepreneur's options.)

The following key questions can be helpful for placing legal forms of business in perspective:

1. What is the size of the risk? What is the amount of the investor's liability for debts and taxes?

2. What would the continuity (life) of the firm be if something happened to the principal(s)?

3. What legal structure would ensure the greatest administrative adaptability for the firm?

4. What effects will federal, state, and local laws have on the operation?

5. What are the possibilities of attracting additional capital?

6. What are the needs for and possibilities of attracting additional expertise?

7. What are the costs and procedures associated with starting the operation?

8. What is the ultimate goal and purpose of the enterprise, and which legal structure can best serve this purpose?

[21] See Steven C. Michael, "To Franchise or Not to Franchise: An Analysis of Decision Rights and Organizational Form Shares," *Journal of Business Venturing* (January 1996): 59–71.

[22] Clarkson, et al., *West's Business.Law,* 1995.

CONTEMPORARY ENTREPRENEURSHIP

The Uniform Franchise Offering Circular

In 1979 the Federal Trade Commission established a Franchise Disclosure Rule requiring franchisors to make full presale disclosure nationwide. To comply with this ruling, the **Uniform Franchise Offering Circular** (UFOC) was developed.

The UFOC is divided into 23 items that provide different segments of information for prospective franchisees. In summary form, here are the major sections:

Sections I–IV: covers the franchisor, the franchisor's background, and the franchise being offered.

Sections V–VI: delineates the franchise fees, both initial and ongoing.

Section VII: sets forth all of the initial expenses involved to establish the entire franchise.

Sections VIII–IX: details the franchisee's obligation to purchase specific goods, supplies, services, and so forth from the franchisor.

Section X: provides information on any financing arrangements available to franchisees.

Section XI: describes in detail the contractual obligations of the franchisor to the franchisee.

Section XII: clearly outlines the geographic market within which the franchisee must operate.

Section XIII–XIV: discloses all pertinent information regarding trademarks, trade names, patents, and so forth.

Section XV: outlines the franchisor's expectations of the franchisee (day-to-day operations).

Section XVI: explains any restrictions or limitations.

Section XVII: sets forth the conditions for the franchise's renewal, termination, or sale.

Section XVIII: discloses the *actual* relationship between the franchise and any celebrity figure used in advertising for the franchise.

Section XIX: provides a factual description of any potential "earnings claims," including their assumptions and actual figures.

Section XX: lists the names and addresses of *all* existing franchises in the state where the proposed franchise is to be located.

Section XXI–XXIII: provides certified financial statements for the previous three fiscal years and a copy of the actual franchise contract.

The UFOC must be given to a prospective franchisee at least ten days prior to the payment of any fees or contracts signed. It is the responsibility of the franchisee to read and understand the various sections delineated in this document.

SOURCE: Adapted from David J. Kaufmann and David E. Robbins, "Now Read This," *Entrepreneur,* January 1991, 100–105.

| **TABLE 12.4** | **THE ENTREPRENEUR'S OPTIONS** |

Essential Characteristics

Major Traditional Business Forms

1. *Sole proprietorships:* the simplest form of business, used by anyone who does business without creating an organization. The owner is the business. The owner pays personal income taxes on all profits and is personally liable for all business debts.

2. *Partnerships*
   a) *General partnerships:* created by agreement of the parties; not treated as an entity except for limited purposes. Partners have unlimited liability for partnership debts, and each partner normally has an equal voice in management. Income is "passed through" the partnership to the individual partners, who pay personal taxes on the income.
   b) *Limited partnerships:* must be formed in compliance with statutory requirements. A limited partnership consists of one or more general partners, who have unlimited liability for partnership losses, and one or more limited partners, who are liable only to the extent of their contributions. Only general partners can participate in management.

3. *Corporations:* must be formed in compliance with statutory requirements: a legal entity separate and distinct from its owners that can have perpetual existence. The shareholder/owners elect directors, who set policy and hire officers to run the day-to-day business of the corporation. Shareholders normally are not personally liable for the corporation's debts. The corporation pays income tax on net profits; shareholders pay income tax on disbursed dividends.

Limited Liability Companies

The limited liability company (LLC) is a hybrid form of business organization that offers the limited liability feature of corporations but the tax benefits of partnerships. Unlike limited partners, LLC members participate in management. Unlike shareholders in S corporations, members of LLCs may be corporations or partnerships, are not restricted in number, and may be residents of other countries.

Other Organizational Forms

1. *Joint venture:* an organization created by two or more persons in contemplation of a limited activity or a single transaction; otherwise, similar to a partnership.

2. *Syndicate:* an investment group that undertakes to finance a particular project; may exist as a corporation or as a general or limited partnership.

3. *Joint stock company:* a business form similar to a corporation in some respects (transferable shares of stock, management by directors and officers, perpetual existence) but otherwise resembling a partnership.

4. *Business trust:* created by a written trust agreement that sets forth the interests of the beneficiaries and obligations and powers of the trustee(s). Similar to a corporation in many respects. Beneficiaries are not personally liable for the debts or obligations of the business trust.

5. *Cooperative:* an association organized to provide an economic service, without profit, to its members. May take the form of a corporation or a partnership.

Private Franchises

1. *Types of franchises*
   a) Distributorship (for example, automobile dealerships)
   b) Chain-style operation (for example, fast-food chains)
   c) Manufacturing/processing-plant arrangement (for example, soft-drink bottling companies, such as Coca-Cola)

2. *Laws governing franchising:* governed by contract law, occasionally by agency law, and by federal and state statutory and regulatory laws.

3. *The franchise contract*
   a) Ordinarily requires the franchisee (purchaser) to pay a price for the franchise license
   b) Specifies the territory to be served by the franchisee's firm
   c) May require the franchisee to purchase certain supplies from the franchisor at an established price
   d) May require the franchisee to abide by certain quality standards relating to the product or service offered but cannot set retail resale prices
   e) Usually provides for the date and conditions of termination of the franchise arrangement. Both federal and state statutes attempt to protect certain franchisees from franchisors who unfairly or arbitrarily terminate franchises.

SOURCE: Roger LeRoy Miller and Gaylord A. Jentz, *Business Law Today,* 4th ed. (St. Paul: West, 1997), 660–61.

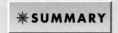

This chapter examined the three major forms of legal organization: sole proprietorship, partnership, and corporation. The advantages and disadvantages of each form were highlighted and compared. In addition, the characteristics and tax considerations of partnerships were compared with those of corporations.

The specific forms of partnerships and corporations were examined. In particular, the requirements and benefits of limited partnerships, limited liability partnerships, R&D limited partnerships, S corporations, and limited liability companies were presented.

Additional corporation classifications were reviewed, and a section was devoted to the corporate considerations of costs. Franchising also was discussed, with emphasis on the advantages and disadvantages as well as concerns over legal protections. Finally, a checklist of key questions for entrepreneurs to consider before structuring their venture was provided.

Key Terms and Concepts

Close corporation

Corporation

Domestic corporation

Foreign corporation

Franchise

Limited liability company (LLC)

Limited liability partnership (LLP)

Limited partnership

Nonprofit corporation

Partnership

Private corporation

Professional corporation

Public corporation

R&D limited partnership

S corporation

Sole proprietorship

Uniform Franchise Offering Circular (UFOC)

Uniform Limited Partnership Act

Uniform Partnership Act

Unlimited liability

Review and Discussion Questions

1. Identify the legal forms available for entrepreneurs structuring their ventures.
2. Define each of the following: sole proprietorship, partnership, and corporation.
3. What are the specific advantages and disadvantages associated with each primary legal form of organization?
4. Compare the major tax considerations of a partnership with those of a corporation.
5. What is the ULPA? Describe it.
6. Name three specific types of partners. How do they differ?
7. Explain the limited liability partnership.
8. What is the double taxation corporations face?
9. How does a limited partnership work? Give an example.
10. What is the nature of an S corporation? List five requirements for such a corporation.
11. Define each of the following: foreign corporation, nonprofit corporation, professional corporation, and close corporation.
12. What is a limited liability company?
13. What are the advantages and disadvantages of franchising?

14. Identify the UFOC. Explain why it is important in franchising.
15. What are four key questions to be considered by entrepreneurs before structuring their venture?

Experiential Exercise   *Get It Right*

The following list of advantages and disadvantages is associated with sole proprietorships, partnerships, and corporations. Place an *S* next to those that relate to sole proprietorships, a *P* next to those that relate to partnerships, and a *C* next to those that relate to corporations. If the advantage or disadvantage applies to more than one type of organizational form, put all answers on the accompanying line. Answers are provided at the end of the exercise.

Advantages	**Disadvantages**
1. Limited liability _____	1. Unlimited liability _____
2. Sole ownership of profits _____	2. Governmental regulation _____
3. Unlimited life _____	3. Lack of continuity _____
4. Ease of formation _____	4. Double tax _____
5. Flexibility _____	5. Difficulty obtaining large sums of
6. Transfer of ownership _____	capital _____
7. Relative freedom from	6. Organizing expenses _____
governmental control _____	7. Relatively limited viewpoint and
8. Increased ability and	experience _____
expertise _____	8. Activity restrictions _____

Answers	**Advantages**		**Disadvantages**	
	1. C	5. S, P	1. S, P	5. S, P
	2. S	6. C	2. C	6. C
	3. C	7. S, P	3. S, P	7. S
	4. S, P	8. C	4. C	8. C

 **CASE** **12.1**

Gina's Decision

When Gina Wilson opened her boutique six years ago, she had only one full-time employee. Since then Gina has added two general partners and greatly expanded the operation. Over the past year it has become obvious that the group could open another boutique that would be equally successful. The problem is money. The partnership lacks funds for expansion.

Gina's banker has suggested the company borrow $200,000 from the bank and pledge the firm's assets as collateral. "This will get you the money you need, and once you have the boutique going, you can repay the money," he told them. The idea sounds fine to the partners, although they are concerned about the risk involved. If the second boutique does not do well, it could affect the success of the first boutique by siphoning off funds to repay the loan.

Gina has been thinking about incorporating the business, selling stock, and using these funds for expansion purposes. She has not shared this idea with her banker because she wants to give it more thought, but she intends to talk it over with her partners later in the week. She is also pondering the value of an S corporation. She has heard her accountant talk about this type of corporation, although she is unsure of the type of legal arrangement it involves.

Questions

1. What are the benefits of the company's becoming a corporation? Is this a better idea than the banker's proposal of taking a $200,000 loan? Why or why not?
2. How does an S corporation work? Would this be a good idea for the firm? Why or why not?
3. What would you recommend to Gina? Explain in detail.

Chapter 13

LEGAL ISSUES RELATED TO EMERGING VENTURES

CHAPTER OBJECTIVES

1. To introduce the importance of legal issues to entrepreneurs

2. To examine patent protection, including definitions, preparation, and proper attorney selection

3. To review copyrights and their relevance to entrepreneurs

4. To study trademarks and their impact on new ventures

5. To present the major segments of the bankruptcy law that apply to business

6. To highlight some cost-saving legal tips

A major difficulty for the inexperienced entrepreneur is the host of strange terms and phrases which are scattered throughout most legal documents. The novice in this kind of reading should have some understanding not only of what *is contained in such documents, but also* why *these provisions have been included.*

If an entrepreneur cannot find the time or take the interest to read and understand the major contracts into which his company will enter, he should be very cautious about being an entrepreneur at all.

Patrick R. Liles,
Harvard Business School

Entrepreneurs cannot hope to have the legal expertise or background of a lawyer, of course, but they should be sufficiently knowledgeable about certain legal concepts that have implications for the business venture.[1]

Table 13.1 sets forth some of the major legal concepts that can affect entrepreneurial ventures. These concepts can be divided into three groups: (1) those that relate to the inception of the venture, (2) those that relate to the ongoing venture, and (3) those that relate to the growth and continuity of the venture. In this chapter the focus will be on the legal concepts related to the first and third groups. Specifically, we shall examine intellectual property protection (patents, copyrights, trademarks) and bankruptcy law.

PATENTS

A **patent** provides the owner with exclusive rights to hold, transfer, and license the production and sale of the product or process. Design patents last for 14 years; all others last for 17 years. The object of a patent is to provide the holder with a temporary monopoly on his or her innovation and thus to encourage the creation and disclosure of new ideas and innovations in the marketplace. Securing a patent, however, is not always an easy process.

A patent is an **intellectual property right.** It is the result of a unique discovery, and patent holders are provided protection against infringement by others. In general, a number of items can qualify for patent protection, among them processes, machines, products,

[1] Roger LeRoy Miller and Frank B. Cross, *The Legal Environment Today* (St. Paul, MN: West, 1996), 205–33.

TABLE 13.1	MAJOR LEGAL CONCEPTS AND ENTREPRENEURIAL VENTURES

I. Inception of an Entrepreneurial Venture

   A. Laws governing intellectual property
      1. Patents
      2. Copyrights
      3. Trademarks

   B. Forms of business organization
      1. Sole proprietorship
      2. Partnership
      3. Corporation
      4. Franchise

   C. Tax considerations

   D. Capital formation

   E. Liability questions

II. An Ongoing Venture: Business Development and Transactions

   A. Personnel law
      1. Hiring and firing policies
      2. Equal Employment Opportunity Commission
      3. Collective bargaining

   B. Contract law
      1. Legal contracts
      2. Sales contracts
      3. Leases

III. Growth and Continuity of a Successful Entrepreneurial Venture

   A. Tax considerations
      1. Federal, state, local
      2. Payroll
      3. Incentives

   B. Governmental regulations
      1. Zoning (property)
      2. Administrative agencies (regulatory)
      3. Consumer law

   C. Continuity of ownership rights
      1. Property laws and ownership
      2. Wills, trusts, estates
      3. Bankruptcy

plants, compositions of elements (chemical compounds), and improvements on already existing items.[2]

Securing a Patent

Because quite often the patent process is complex, careful planning is required. For pursuing a patent, the following basic rules are recommended by the experts:

Rule 1: Pursue patents that are broad, commercially significant, and offer a strong position. This means that relevant patent law must be researched in order to obtain

[2] Al H. Ringleb, Roger E. Meiners, and Frances L. Edwards, *Managing in the Legal Environment* (St. Paul, MN: West, 1996), 212–13; see also John R. Allison and Robert A. Prentice, *Business Law,* 6th ed. (Ft. Worth, TX: The Dryden Press, 1994), 194–97.

the widest coverage possible on the idea or concept. In addition, there must be something significantly novel or proprietary about the innovation. Record all steps or processes in a notebook and have them witnessed so that documentation secures a strong proprietary position.

Rule 2: Prepare a patent plan in detail. This plan should outline the costs to develop and market the innovation as well as analyze the competition and technological similarities to your idea. Attempt to detail the precise value of the innovation.

Rule 3: Have your actions relate to your original patent plan. This does not mean a plan cannot be changed. However, it is wise to remain close to the plan during the early stages of establishing the patent. Later, the path that is prepared may change, e.g., licensing out the patent versus keeping it for yourself.

Rule 4: Establish an **infringement budget.** Patent rights are only effective if potential infringers fear legal damages. Thus it is important to prepare a realistic budget for prosecuting violations of the patent.

Rule 5: Evaluate the patent plan strategically. The typical patent process takes three years. This should be compared to the actual life cycle of the proposed innovation or technology. Will the patent be worth defending in three years or will enforcement cost more than the damages collected?[3]

These rules relating to proper definition, preparation, planning, and evaluation can help entrepreneurs establish effective patent protection. In addition, they can help the patent attorney conduct the search process.

Patent applications must include detailed specifications of the innovation that any skilled person in the specific area can understand. A patent application has two parts:

1. **Specification** is the text of a patent and may include any accompanying illustrations. Because its purpose is to teach those fluent in this area of technology all they need to understand, duplicate, and use the invention, it may be quite long. The specification typically includes:

   a) An introduction explaining why the invention will be useful.

   b) Description of all prior art that you are aware of and that could be considered similar to the invention. The specification usually lists other patents, by number, with a brief description of each, but you can cite and describe unpatented technology as well.

   c) A summary of the invention that describes the essence of the new technology and emphasizes its difference from prior art, while including all its requisite features, whether novel or not.

   d) A detailed description of the invention, including anything that could be remotely relevant, reference to all reasonable variations, and number bounds. Take as much space as you like. Use as many numbers as reasonable, including close or tight limits based on experience, as well as loose ones based on what might be possible. This section should be detailed enough to really teach a skilled practitioner.

   e) Examples and/or experimental results, in full detail.

   f) The specification is inherently broad because its intent is to teach and also, as a practical matter, to allow some flexibility in the claims that are based on it.

---

[3] Reprinted by permission of the *Harvard Business Review.* An excerpt from "Making Patents Work for Small Companies," by Ronald D. Rothchild, July/August 1987, 24–30. Copyright © 1987 by the President and Fellows of Harvard College; all rights reserved.

2. **Claims** are a series of short paragraphs, each of which identifies a particular feature or combination of features that is protected by the patent. The entire claims section, at the end of the patent, is typically about one page long or less.

Claims define and limit the patented invention. The invention can be broad (a process requiring an "inorganic, nonmetal solid" would cover a lot of possibilities, for example) but sharply limited *not* to cover anything in prior art (other existing processes that use organics or metals).[4]

Once the application is filed with the **Patent and Trademark Office** of the Department of Commerce, an examiner will determine if the innovation qualifies for patentability. The examiner will do this by researching technical data in journals as well as previously issued patents. Based on the individual's findings, the application will be rejected or accepted.

Only a small percentage of issued patents are commercially valuable. Consequently, the entrepreneur must weigh the value of the innovation against the time and money spent to obtain the patent. Also, it is important to remember that many patents granted by the Patent and Trademark Office have been declared invalid after being challenged in court. This occurs for several reasons. One is that the patent holder waited an unreasonable length of time before asserting his or her rights. A second is that those bringing suit against the patent holder are able to prove the individual misused the patent rights, for example, by requiring certain purchases of other goods or services as part of the patent-use arrangement. A third is that other parties are able to prove the patent itself fails to meet tests of patentability and is therefore invalid.[5]

If, after careful review, an entrepreneur concludes that the innovation will withstand any legal challenge and is commercially worthwhile, a patent should be pursued. If a challenge is mounted, legal fees may be sizable, but a successful defense can result in damages sufficient to compensate for the infringement plus court costs and interest. In fact, the court may award damages of up to three times the actual amount. In addition, a patent infringer can be liable for all profits resulting from the infringement as well as for legal fees.[6]

COPYRIGHTS

A **copyright** provides exclusive rights to creative individuals for the protection of their literary or artistic productions. It is not possible to copyright an idea, but the particular mode for expression of that idea often can be copyrighted. This expression can take many forms, including books, periodicals, dramatic or musical compositions, art, motion pictures, lectures, sound recordings, and computer programs.

Any works created after January 1, 1978, and receiving a copyright are protected for the life of the author plus 50 years. The owner of this copyright may (1) reproduce the work, (2) prepare derivative works based on it (for example, a condensation or movie version of a novel), (3) distribute copies of the work by sale or otherwise, (4) perform the

[4] Reprinted by permission of the *Harvard Business Review.* An exhibit from "Making Patents Work for Small Companies," by Ronald D. Rothchild, July/August 1987, 28. Copyright © 1987 by the President and Fellows of Harvard College; all rights reserved.

[5] Robert A. Choate and William H. Francis, *Patent Law: Trade Secrets—Copyright—Trademarks* (St. Paul, MN: West, 1981), 1024–25; and Kenneth W. Clarkson, Roger LeRoy Miller, Gaylord A. Jentz, and Frank B. Cross, *West's Business Law,* 6th ed. (St. Paul, MN: West, 1995), 148–49.

[6] Roger LeRoy Miller and Gaylord A. Jentz, *Business Law Today* (St. Paul, MN: West, 1997), 168–69.

CONTEMPORARY ENTREPRENEURSHIP

Baby's Choice Diapers—A Legal Nightmare

Picture the following scenes for a potential entrepreneur: "You and two friends, all of you in your mid-twenties, hit on an idea for a business. Not just any idea—*the idea,* you feel it in your bones. And bingo, you're right. Capital is there for the asking. Sales rise so quickly your plant can't keep up. In the first six months of production you do $3 million, with profitability just about the corner.

"But somehow, in the same six months everything begins to go horribly awry: the dream that is right there, in your grasp, turns bit by bit into a nightmare. Relations with your investors sour. You and your partners are stripped of control. You stay on as an employee, only to be rudely dismissed less than two months later. Desperate, you try to figure out some way of capitalizing on your interest in the business, though you have no way of knowing, just then, what it's worth. When you run out of possibilities you settle for $63,800—with the very people who have booted you out.

"And then, within a month, they have organized a private placement, selling a hefty chunk of stock to outside investors. By the terms of the offering, the company is worth nearly $6 million.

"Once, 20 percent of that was to be yours. Now you have no company, no equity—and no job."

This is exactly what heppened to Tim Wagner, who had seen an opportunity for a new venture while working as a salesperson for National Starch and Chemical Corp. Wagner noticed the major disposable diaper companies—Procter & Gamble and Kimberly-Clark—were customers for National's glue. He learned about their business and decided to fill a niche with a low-priced disposable diaper. His idea was based on his research into new machinery from Europe that could cut production costs immensely.

Even though the two major corporations dominated the industry with 80 percent market share, Wagner believed 20 percent of the total $2.5 billion market was still available. And, with low-cost production, VMG (the name of Wagner's com-

---

work publicly, and (5) display the work publicly. Each of these rights, or a portion of each, also may be transferred.[7]

Understanding Copyright Protection

For the author of creative material to obtain copyright protection, the material must be in a tangible form so it can be communicated or reproduced. It also must be the author's own work and thus the product of his or her skill or judgment. Concepts, principles, processes, systems, or discoveries are not valid for copyright protection until they are put in tangible form—written or recorded.

---

[7] Ibid., 170–71; and Choate and Francis, *Patent Law,* 932–45.

pany) could undercut the national brands' wholesale price by 12 percent, allowing retailers to make more profit. The idea was right!

Unfortunately, the original legal agreement drawn up among Wagner, his two partners, and the investing limited partners was not so right. Weatherly Private Capital Co., an investment firm in Seattle, proposed a limited partnership agreement instead of establishing a corporation and selling stock. The three founders would be one of two general partners in the venture. Weatherly would be the other—acting in an administrative role, just to assuage investors. Neither half would put any significant cash into the deal; that would come from the limited partners. In return, the limiteds would be first in line for a payback, getting nearly all the net income from the diaper line until they recovered their original investment. Then their share would decline, stepwise, until they had earned seven times their capital. At that point the founders would get 60 percent of the partnership's income, the limiteds 30 percent, and Weatherly 10 percent. The idea was to work the venture from a 1 percent ownership share to the pro- posed 60 percent share over time. In this manner, Wagner and his partners could regain ownership later on.

The two major problems Wagner never realized were that limited partners usually want a fast payback on their investment, and they are in charge until that happens. Thus, when VMG's diapers—called Baby's Choice—began to expand rapidly in the marketplace in 1985, the limited partners refused to invest more money unless Wagner traded off more of his ownership. He refused and the fight was on.

After weeks of allegations, arguments, and legal maneuvering, the other partners removed Wagner. You can't dismiss a company founder without warning, Wagner thought. But they did. Suddenly, Tim Wagner was without a company, without a job, and without any money (except for the 1 percent partnership interest later settled on as $63,800).

"This is wrong," Wagner stated. But his control was gone and he cried for an hour. "This was my dream. I can't get it out of my mind."

SOURCE: John Case, "The Enemy Within," *Inc.*, April 1987, 32–38.

Formal registration of a copyright with the *Copyright Office of the Library of Congress* is a requirement before an author can begin a lawsuit for infringement. In addition, an author can find his or her copyright invalidated if proper notice isn't provided.

Anyone who violates an author's exclusive rights under a copyright is liable for infringement. However, because of the **"fair use" doctrine,** it is sometimes difficult to establish infringement. Fair use is described as follows:

[Reproduction of a copyrighted work for] purposes such as criticism, comment, news reporting, teaching (including multiple copies for classroom use), scholarship, or research is not an infringement of copyright. In determining whether the use made of a work in any particular case is a fair use, the factors to be considered shall include (1) the purpose and character of the use, including whether such use is of a commercial nature or is for nonprofit educational purposes; (2) the nature of the copyrighted work; (3) the amount and substantiality of the portion used in relation to the copyrighted work as a whole; and (4) the effect of the use upon the potential market for a value of the copyrighted work.[8]

If, however, an author substantiates a copyright infringement, the normal remedy is recovery of actual damages plus any profits the violator receives. The following guidelines for copyright protection are from a lawyer's point of view:

1. There is absolutely no cost or risk involved in protecting material which you generate by copyright. Therefore, as a matter of course, any writings that you prepare and spend a lot of time on should be copyrighted by putting the copyright notice © on it.

2. It is not necessary to register copyrights with the Copyright Office unless and until you want to sue somebody for infringement. Therefore, in the overwhelming majority of cases, assuming you are not in the publishing business, simply use the copyright notice and do not bother spending the time and effort necessary to register copyrights with the U.S. Copyright Office.

3. In buying material and using it yourself, I suggest that you take a commercial view of fair use. For example, if you buy a subscription to a periodical, you can duplicate various articles, or indeed, a complete issue on some occasions, for use within your own organization. There may be some technical arguments as to the extent of the fair use exception under the copyright laws, but I know of no case, nor any circumstance whatsoever, where a publisher has objected to a subscriber's making copies of something for internal use. At the other extreme, if you systematically make copies of other people's copyrighted material and thereby clearly deprive the copyright owner of additional subscriptions which he or she would otherwise have, or if you use copyrighted material in something you are going to sell for profit yourself, I think you are asking for trouble.

4. Be especially careful of catalogs and other similar materials which may have been compiled at some expense by other companies. Many times these catalogs will have so-called trap lines, which are fictitious items of information designed to trap someone who was simply copying the information. If a competitor of yours has put together an excellent catalog and spent a lot of time and money gathering the necessary information, you cannot simply copy it yourself and save all that time and money without running a risk under the copyright laws. This, of course, runs both ways, and that is why I suggest that you copyright everything that you spend a lot of time and money preparing. You may want to use trap lines also.

5. There may be some slight advantage in copyrighting advertisements. . . . In some situations it might be desirable to include the copyright notice on any advertisement you prepare if it seems possible to you that a competitor may want to try to use it. For example, a lawyer who was putting on seminars on product liability cases developed an excellent advertisement in the form of a very short article about the important aspects of minimizing product liability exposure. It was a mail-order-type advertisement consisting of a half a dozen pages or so, and I noticed it was copyrighted. The lawyer obviously had spent a lot of time in developing that ad, and did not want other people to be able to use his work to promote competitive seminars.

6. There are some things which cannot be copyrighted, such as U.S. government publications, which are in the public domain. Also, statutes, cases, congressional

---

[8] Clarkson et al., *West's Business Law,* 151.

history, congressional debates, and all such things which are generated by government agencies generally cannot be copyrighted. However, it is possible to copyright the arrangement of those things on a page. Thus, if a publisher has gone to the trouble of setting particular statutes in type, you cannot capitalize on this time and expense by simply cutting the page out of the published work and using that for duplication. You can, of course, retype the material and use it freely.

7. Ideas cannot be copyrighted. Therefore, if someone writes an article and copyrights it, you are certainly free to read that article, digest it, take the ideas from that article and other sources, and weave them into your own material without any copyright problems. On the other hand, if someone has copyrighted an article, you cannot simply rephrase it or change minor words and claim it as your own. Exactly where the line is to be drawn is not clear. However, a little common sense will give the appropriate answer in most of these cases.[9]

Protected Ideas?

The Copyright Act specifically excludes copyright protection for any "idea, procedure, process, system, method of operation, concept, principle or discovery, regardless of the form in which it is described, explained, illustrated, or embodied." Note that it is not possible to copyright an *idea*. The underlying ideas embodied in a work may be freely used by others. What is copyrightable is the particular way an idea is expressed. Whenever an idea and an expression are inseparable, the expression cannot be copyrighted.

Generally, anything that is not an original expression will not qualify for copyright protection. Facts widely known to the public are not copyrightable. Page numbers are not copyrightable because they follow a sequence known to everyone. Mathematical calculations are not copyrightable. Compilations of facts, however, are copyrightable. The Copyright Act defines a compilation as "a work formed by the collection and assembling of preexisting materials of data that are selected, coordinated, or arranged in such a way that the resulting work as a whole constitutes an original work of authorship."[10]

TRADEMARKS

A **trademark** is a distinctive name, mark, symbol, or motto identified with a company's product(s) and registered at the Patent and Trademark Office. Thanks to trademark law, no confusion should result from one venture's using the symbol or name of another.

Specific legal terms differentiate the exact types of marks. For example, trademarks identify and distinguish goods. Service marks identify and distinguish services. Certification marks denote the quality, materials, or other aspects of goods and services and are used by someone other than the mark's owner. Collective marks are trademarks or service marks members of groups or organizations use to identify themselves as the source of goods or services.[11]

---

[9] William A. Hancock, *The Small Business Legal Advisor* (New York: McGraw-Hill, 1982), 205–8. Copyright © 1982 McGraw-Hill Book Company. Reprinted with permission.

[10] Clarkson et al., *West's Business Law,* 149.

[11] See Thomas G. Field Jr., *Trademarks and Business Goodwill* (Washington, DC: Office of Business Development, Small Business Administration), 1990.

TABLE 13.2   **TRADEMARKS: PROTECTED AND UNPROTECTED**

Suggestive (Protected)	Descriptive (Unprotected)
Arch Rest (shoes)	After Tan (suntan lotion)
Holeproof (hosiery)	Breakfast Bread (bread)
Hour After Hour (deodorant)	Brilliant (flour)
Mr. Clean (cleaner)	Driverless (car rental)
Roach Motel (insect trap)	Faultless (bread)
Rusticide (rust remover)	5 Minute (glue setting in five minutes)
Soft Smoke (smoking tobacco)	Homemaker (calendar)
U-Drive-It (car rental)	Security (tires)
Wearever (cooking utensils)	Snap (ginger ale)

SOURCE: Reprinted by permission of *Harvard Business Review*. An excerpt from "How Can You Find a Safe Trademark?" by Thomas M. S. Hemnes, March/April 1985, 40–48. Copyright © 1985 by the President and Fellows of Harvard College; all rights reserved.

Usually, personal names or words that are considered generic or descriptive are not trademarked, unless the words are in some way suggestive or fanciful or the personal name is accompanied by a specific design. For example, English Leather may not be trademarked to describe a leather processed in England; however, English Leather is trademarked as a name for aftershave lotion, since this constitutes a fanciful use of the words. Consider also that even the common name of an individual may be trademarked if that name is accompanied by a picture or some fanciful design that allows easy identification of the product, such as Smith Brothers Cough Drops.[12] (See Table 13.2 for examples of protected and unprotected trademarks.)

In most cases the Patent and Trademark Office will reject an application for marks, symbols, or names that are flags or insignias of governments, portraits or signatures of living persons, immoral or deceptive, or likely to cause problems due to resemblance to a previously registered mark.[13] Once issued, the trademark is listed in the *Principal Register* of the Patent and Trademark Office. This listing offers several advantages: (1) nationwide constructive notice of the owner's right to use the mark (thus eliminating the need to show that the defendant in an infringement suit had notice of the mark); (2) Bureau of Customs protection against importers using the mark, and (3) incontestability of the mark after five years.[14]

In 1988, the Trademark Revision Act was passed by Congress. This act significantly altered the prior registration scheme, which required use of the mark before filing an application. The 1988 act, in contrast, allows a person to file on the basis either of use or of a bona fide intention to use the mark in commerce. This is the "intent-to-use" provision, which requires putting the mark into commerce within 6 months after filing with the U.S.

---

[12] Clarkson et al., *West's Business Law,* 144.

[13] For a complete discussion, see Choate and Francis, *Patent Law,* 992–1042.

[14] Dorothy Cohen, "Trademark Strategy," *Journal of Marketing* (January 1986): 61–74.

Patent and Trademark Office. At the end of the 6 months, the person must provide proof the mark was put into commerce and that the application was not opposed. Under extenuating circumstances, the 6-month period can be extended by 30 months, giving the applicant a total of 3 years from the date of notice of trademark approval to use the mark and file the required use statement. The new provision has considerably cut the costs of developing and marketing a new product. It has particularly benefited small companies.[15]

Historically, a trademark registration lasted 20 years; however, the current registrations are good for only 10 years with the possibility for continuous renewal every 10 years. It is most important to understand that a trademark may be invalidated in four specific ways:

1. **Cancellation proceedings** are a third party's challenge to the mark's distinctiveness within five years of its issuance.

2. **Cleaning-out procedure** refers to the failure of a trademark owner to file an affidavit stating it is in use or justifying its lack of use within six years of registration.

3. **Abandonment** is the nonuse of a trademark for two consecutive years without justification or a statement regarding the trademark's abandonment.

4. **Generic meaning** is the allowance of a trademark to represent a general grouping of products or services. For example, cellophane has come to represent plastic wrap, and scotch tape has come to represent adhesive tape. Xerox is currently seeking, through national advertising, to avoid having its name used to represent copier machines.

If a trademark is properly registered, used, and protected, the owner can obtain an injunction against any uses of the mark that are likely to cause confusion. (See the Part 4 Playboy case study on page 457 for an excellent example of a company seeking to protect its trademark.) Moreover, if infringement and damages can be proven in court, a monetary award may be given to the trademark holder.

Avoiding the Pitfalls

Trademark registration and search can be costly, sometimes ranging into thousands of dollars. Trademark infringement can be even more expensive. To avoid these pitfalls, one author has noted five basic rules entrepreneurs should follow when selecting trademarks for their new ventures.

Rule 1: Never select a corporate name or a mark without first doing a trademark search.
Rule 2: If your attorney says you have a potential problem with a mark, trust that judgment.
Rule 3: Seek a coined or a fanciful name or mark before you settle for a descriptive or a highly suggestive one.
Rule 4: Whenever marketing or other considerations dictate the use of a name or a mark that is highly suggestive of the product, select a distinctive logotype for the descriptive or suggestive words.

---

[15] Clarkson et al., *West's Business Law,* 147.

ENTREPRENEURIAL

EDGE

Nike vs. *Mike*: A Parody on Trademark Infringement

Mike Stanard had a great idea for his daughter to try during summer vacation: Establish an enterprise called "Just Did It" (a spoof on Nike's "Just Do It" slogan) and sell T-shirts with the famous swoosh design (identical to Nike's) but accompanied by the word "Mike" instead of Nike. The T-shirts would be sold for $19.95 and long-sleeved ones for $24.95. They would send out 1,400 brochures to college athletes and celebrities named Michael. What a great idea!

Nike did not think so. From 1971 to 1994, Nike had invested more than $300 million advertising its trademarks. Aggregate sales revenues from Nike trademarked apparel had exceeded $10 billion. The "Just Do It" slogan alone produced 1989–94 revenue exceeding $15 million. Nike sued Stanard for trademark infringement.

Stanard's defense was parody. A parody must convey two simultaneous and contradictory messages: that it is the original, but also that it is not the original and is instead a parody. The customer must be amused and not confused.

To assess whether a trademark infringement has occurred, the courts consider seven factors: (1) the degree of similarity between the trademarks, (2) the similarity of the products for which the name is used, (3) the area and manner of concurrent use, (4) the degree of care likely to be exercised by consumers, (5) the strength of the complainant's trademark, (6) whether actual product confusion exists among buyers, and (7) an intent on the part of the alleged infringer to palm off his or her products as those of another.

Since Stanard sold the shirts by mail (customers had to write a check to "Just Did It") and he had no apparent intent to copy Nike's products specifically, the court concluded no confusion existed. Thus, the parody defense succeeded. The parody defense doesn't always work, however. Marketers will have to decide whether the legal risk involved in parody marketing is worth unknown sales results.

Some examples of court rulings include these:

- Miami Mice was a valid parody of *Miami Vice*.
- Hard Rain Cafe was likely to confuse consumers regarding the Hard Rock Cafe.
- Enjoy Cocaine was not a valid parody of Enjoy Coca-Cola, where both used the familiar red-and-white logo.
- Stop the Olympic Prison, using the five-interlocking-rings logo, was considered not confusing with the Olympic Committee's trademark.
- Lardash was considered a valid parody of Jordache.
- Mutant of Omaha and the subtitle Nuclear Holocaust Insurance was not a valid parody of Mutual of Omaha.
- Bagzilla was a permissible pun of Godzilla and would not confuse consumers.
- Spy Notes was a valid parody of Cliff Notes.

SOURCE: Maxine S. Lans, "Parody as a Marketing Strategy," *Marketing News,* 3 January 1994, 20.

Rule 5: Avoid abbreviations and acronyms wherever possible, and when no alternative is acceptable, select a distinctive logotype in which the abbreviation or acronym appears.[16]

Trade Secrets

Certain business processes and information cannot be patented, copyrighted, or trademarked. Yet they may be protected as **trade secrets.** Customer lists, plans, research and development, pricing information, marketing techniques, and production techniques are examples of potential trade secrets. Generally, anything that makes an individual company unique and has value to a competitor could be a trade secret.[17]

Protection of trade secrets extends both to ideas and to their expression. For this reason, and because a trade secret involves no registration or filing requirements, trade-secret protection is ideal for software. Of course, the secret formula, method, or other information must be disclosed to key employees. Businesses generally attempt to protect their trade secrets by having all employees who use the process or information agree in their contracts never to divulge it. Theft of confidential business data by industrial espionage, such as stealing a competitor's documents, is a theft of trade secrets without any contractual violation and is actionable in itself.

The law clearly outlines the area of trade secrets: Information is a trade secret if (1) it is not known by the competition; (2) the business would lose its advantage if the competition were to obtain it; and (3) the owner has taken reasonable steps to protect the secret from disclosure.[18] Keep in mind that prosecution is still difficult in many of these cases.

BANKRUPTCY

Bankruptcy occurs when a venture's financial obligations are greater than its assets. No entrepreneur intentionally seeks bankruptcy. Although occasionally problems can arise out of the blue, here are several ways to foresee impending failure: (1) New competition enters the market, (2) other firms seem to be selling products that are a generation ahead, (3) the research and development budget is proportionately less than the competition's, and (4) retailers always seem to be overstocked.[19]

Other early warning signs of bankruptcy follow:

- Financial management is lax. No one knows how the company's money is spent.
- Company officers, too busy to keep tabs on the bookkeeping, have trouble providing information or documentation of corporate transactions to the accountant.
- Officers and family members make repeated emergency loans to the company. This usually means the business cannot get credit from banks.
- Customers are given large discounts if they pay more promptly. Products are put on sale to generate cash. This puts a faltering company in greater jeopardy by reducing needed markups.

---

[16] Thomas M. S. Hemnes, "How Can You Find a Safe Trademark?" *Harvard Business Review* (March/April 1985): 40–48; see also Michael Finn, "Everything You Need to Know about Trademarks and Publishing," *Publishers Weekly,* 6 January 1992, 41–44.

[17] Clarkson et al., *West's Business Law,* 156–57.

[18] Ringleb, Meiners, and Edwards, *Managing in the Legal Environment,* 213.

[19] Harlan D. Platt, *Why Companies Fail* (Lexington, MA: Lexington Books, 1985), 83.

CONTEMPORARY ENTREPRENEURSHIP

Using Bankruptcy as a Protective Strategy

Every year more and more companies are filing for Chapter 11 bankruptcy (more than 24,000 companies filed between July 1991 and June 1992). Although bankruptcy has long been considered a failure for entrepreneurs, in certain situations filing for Chapter 11 may be the best strategy for saving the business. If the problems are relatively short term, Chapter 11 bankruptcy protection provides temporary relief of the obligation to pay creditors, giving extra time to seek additional financing, to streamline the company, or to increase sales volume, and, in some cases, to actually emerge as a stronger company.

One example is Phil Akin. He opened the first Duds 'n Suds (a combination self-service laundry and bar) in 1983, when he was only 21 years old. The company expanded, selling more than 40 franchises and reaching annual sales of $5 million by 1987. Because the Duds 'n Suds franchise concept was a hit, Akin and his 28-person corporate staff decided to open several company-owned stores, franchising the expansion through a $6 million public stock offering.

In October 1987, after spending more than $600,000 on the legal, accounting, and printing costs associated with an initial public stock offering. Akin was ready for a successful offering, Two weeks later, the stock market crashed! Akin was left with a $600,000 bill for a public offering that never came off, which put him in violation of a previous lending agreement with his bank. When the bank called in its $350,000 note, Duds 'n Suds's debt grew to nearly $1 million.

By December, Akin had laid off 24 of the company's 28 employees, and by selling off some of the company's assets, he reduced his bank debt to $150,000 by early 1988. However, when it appeared that certain investors might take over the company, Akin filed for Chapter 11 protection and survived.

Remember, though, not all entrepreneurs find solace in Chapter 11. One of the primary reasons companies fail to survive a Chapter 11 is that the situation has passed a point of no return. For many small companies, Chapter 11 is simply a means of putting off the inevitable—a conversion to a Chapter 7 liquidation and the eventual breakup of the company.

SOURCE: Stephanie Barlow, "The 11th Hour," *Entrepreneur,* April 1993, 133–37.

- Contracts are accepted below standard price to generate cash. This is only a temporary—and eventually suicidal—answer to cash flow problems.
- The bank wants loans subordinated. If a business owner lends money to the company, the bank wants a guarantee the company will not pay back the owner before the bank. In other words, the bank suspects the business is in danger.
- Sales decrease without an accompanying cutback in the amount of inventory ordered. A business owner who lets this inequity mount will inevitably suffer big cash flow problems.

TABLE 13.3   **BANKRUPTCY-DETECTING FINANCIAL RATIOS**

	Derivation	Change to Watch For
Liquidity Ratios		
Net working capital (sometimes called risk)	Current assets less current liabilities	Fewer dollars
Cash flow versus current liabilities	Net income plus depreciation and other noncash expenses divided by current liabilities	Lower ratio
Debt Ratios		
Cash-flow coverage	Cash flow divided by fixed charges, including interest and dividends	Lower ratio
Times interest earned	Income before interest and taxes divided by interest charges	Lower ratio
Short-term debt to assets	Current liabilities divided by total assets	Higher ratio
Activity Ratios		
Inventory turn	Sales divided by inventory	Lower ratio
Average collection period	Accounts receivable divided by average daily sales	Higher ratio
Profitability Ratios		
Profit margin	Net income divided by sales	Lower ratio

SOURCE: Adapted from Harlan D. Platt, *Why Companies Fail* (Lexington, MA: Lexington Books, 1985), 86.

- Key personnel depart suddenly.
- An inadequate supply of materials delays or halts the company's product shipments. This may indicate suppliers have not received payment for some time and are not extending further credit.
- Payroll taxes are not paid. This, done in the belief the IRS's lag time in catching such delinquencies will give the business time to recover, spells disaster.[20]

In addition, specific financial ratios can assist in detecting impending bankruptcy. Table 13.3 lists these ratios, how they are derived, and what change to watch for.

In spite of many warning signs, numerous ventures are confronted with bankruptcy each year. In 1995 more than 70,000 business failures occurred (see Figure 13.1).[21] Although the trend has been decreasing over the past few years, entrepreneurs still need to understand some of the basic ideas involved in the bankruptcy codes.

[20] Reuben Abrams, "Warning Signs of Bankruptcy," *Nation's Business,* February 1987, 22.

[21] *The State of Small Business: A Report to the President* (Washington, DC: Government Printing Office, 1995), 39–41; and *The Business Failure Record* (Washington, DC: The Dun & Bradstreet Corp., 1995), 1–3.

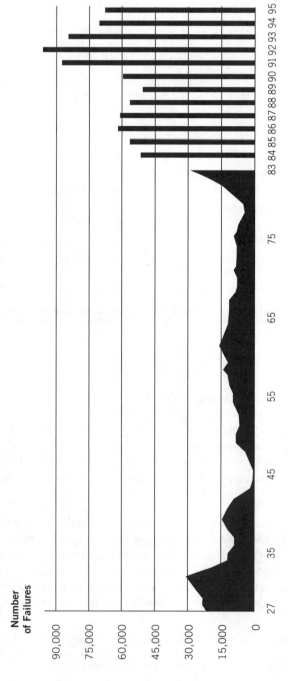

SOURCE: *Business Failure Record*, The Dun & Bradstreet Corporation, 1995, 2.

FIGURE 13.1   BUSINESS FAILURES THROUGH THE YEARS (1927–1995)

Number
of Failures

TABLE 13.4	BANKRUPTCY: A COMPARISON OF CHAPTERS 7, 11, 12, AND 13		
Issue	**Chapter 7**	**Chapter 11**	**Chapters 12 and 13**
Purpose	Liquidation	Reorganization	Adjustment
Who can petition	Debtor (voluntary) or creditors (involuntary)	Debtor (voluntary) or creditors (involuntary)	Debtor (voluntary) only
Who can be a debtor	Any "person" (including partnerships and corporations) except railroads, insurance companies, banks, savings and loan institutions, and credit unions; farmers and charitable institutions cannot be involuntarily petitioned	Any debtor eligible for Chapter 7 relief; railroads are also eligible	*Chapter 12:* any family farmer whose gross income is at least 50 percent farm dependent and whose debts are at least 80 percent farm related or any partnership or closely held corporation at least 50 percent owned by a farm family, when total debt does not exceed $1,500,000 *Chapter 13:* any individual (not partnerships or corporations) with regular income who owes fixed unsecured debt of less than $100,000 or secured debt of less than $350,000
Procedure leading to discharge	Nonexempt property is sold with proceeds to be distributed (in order) to priority groups; dischargeable debts are terminated	Plan is submitted; if it is approved and followed, debts are discharged	Plan is submitted (must be approved if debtor turns over disposable income for three-year period); if it is approved and followed, debts are discharged
Advantages	Upon liquidation and distribution, most debts are discharged, and debtor has opportunity for fresh start	Debtor continues in business; creditors can accept plan, or it can be "crammed down" on them; plan allows for reorganization and liquidation of debts over plan period	Debtor continues in business or possession of assets; if plan is approved, most debts are discharged after a three-year period

SOURCE: Kenneth W. Clarkson, Roger L. Miller, Gaylord A. Jentz, and Frank B. Cross, *West's Business Law*, 6th ed. (St. Paul, MN: West, 1995), 650.

The Bankruptcy Act

The **Bankruptcy Act** is a federal law that provides for specific procedures for handling insolvent debtors. An *insolvent debtor* is one who is unable to pay debts as they become due. The initial act of 1912 was amended in 1938 and then completely revised in 1978. Significant amendments were added in 1984. The purposes of the Bankruptcy Act are (1) to ensure that the property of the debtor is distributed fairly to the creditors, (2) to protect creditors from having debtors unreasonably diminish their assets, and (3) to protect debtors from extreme demands by creditors. The law was set up in order to provide assistance to both debtors and creditors.

Each of the various types of bankruptcy proceedings has its own particular provisions. For purposes of business ventures, the three major sections are called straight bankruptcy (Chapter 7), reorganization (Chapter 11), and adjustment of debts (Chapter 13). Table 13.4

provides a summary comparison of these three types of bankruptcies. The following section examines each type.

Chapter 7: Straight Bankruptcy

Sometimes referred to as **liquidation,** Chapter 7 bankruptcy requires the debtor to surrender all property to a trustee appointed by the court. The trustee then sells the assets and turns the proceeds over to the creditors. The remaining debts, with certain exceptions, are then discharged, and the debtor is relieved of his or her obligations.

A liquidation proceeding may be voluntary or involuntary. In a voluntary bankruptcy, the debtor files a petition with the bankruptcy court that provides a list of all creditors, a statement of financial affairs, a list of all owned property, and a list of current income and expenses. In an involuntary bankruptcy, the creditors force the debtor into bankruptcy. For this to occur, 12 or more creditors with at least 3 of them having a total of $5,000 of claims must exist; or if fewer than 12 exist, 1 or more creditors must have a claim of $5,000 against the debtor.[22]

Chapter 11: Reorganization

Reorganization is the most common form of bankruptcy. Under this format, a debtor attempts to formulate a plan to pay a portion of the debts, have the remaining sum discharged, and continue to stay in operation. The plan is essentially a contract between the debtor and creditors. In addition to being viewed as "fair and equitable," the plan must (1) divide the creditors into classes, (2) set forth how each creditor will be satisfied, (3) state which claims or classes of claims are impaired or adversely affected by the plan, and (4) provide the same treatment to each creditor in a particular class.

The same basic principles that govern Chapter 7 bankruptcy petitions also govern the Chapter 11 petitions. The proceedings may be either voluntary or involuntary, and the provisions for protection and discharge are similar to the Chapter 7 regulations.

Once an order for relief (the petition) is filed, the debtor in a Chapter 11 proceeding continues to operate the business as a **debtor-in-possession,** which means the court appoints a trustee to oversee the management of the business. The plan is then submitted to the creditors for approval. Approval generally requires that creditors holding two-thirds of the amount and one-half of the number of each class of claims impaired by the plan must accept it. Once approved, the plan goes before the court for confirmation. If the plan is confirmed, the debtor is responsible for carrying it out.[23]

Once the plan is confirmed by the creditors, it is binding for the debtor. This type of bankruptcy provides an alternative to liquidating the entire business and thus extends to the creditors and debtor the benefits of keeping the enterprise in operation.

Chapter 13: Adjustment of Debts

Under this arrangement individuals are allowed to (1) avoid a declaration of bankruptcy, (2) pay their debts in installments, and (3) be protected by the federal court. Individuals or sole proprietors with unsecured debts of less than $100,000 or secured debts of less than

---

[22] Clarkson et al., *West's Business Law,* 634–35.

[23] For a detailed discussion of Chapter 11 bankruptcy, see Clarkson et al., *West's Business Law,* 643–48.

$350,000 are eligible to file under a Chapter 13 procedure. This petition must be voluntary only; creditors are not allowed to file a Chapter 13 proceeding. In the petition the debtor declares an inability to pay his or her debts and requests some form of extension through future earnings (longer period of time to pay) or a composition of debt (reduction in the amount owed).

The individual debtor then files a plan providing the details for treatment of the debts. A Chapter 13 plan must provide for (1) the turnover of such future earnings or income of the debtor to the trustee as is necessary for execution of the plan, (2) full payment in deferred cash payments of all claims entitled to priority, and (3) the same treatment of each claim within a particular class (although the 1984 amendments permit the debtor to list codebtors, such as guarantors or sureties, as a separate class).[24] The plan must provide for payment within three years unless the court specifically grants an extension to five years.

Once the debtor has completed all payments scheduled in the plan, the court will issue a discharge of all other debts provided for in the plan. As always, some exceptions to the discharge exist, such as child support and certain long-term debts. In addition, the debtor also can be discharged even though he or she does not complete the payments within the three years if the court is satisfied that the failure is due to circumstances for which the debtor cannot justly be held accountable. During a Chapter 13 proceeding, no other bankruptcy petition (Chapter 7 or 11) may be filed against the debtor. Thus an individual has an opportunity to relieve a debt situation without liquidation or the stigma of bankruptcy. In addition, the creditors may benefit by recovering a larger percentage than through a liquidation.

Keeping Legal Expenses Down

Throughout these legal proceedings, the entrepreneur can run up a large legal bill. Presented next are some suggestions for minimizing these expenses:

- Establish the fee structure with an attorney before any legal matters are handled. This structure may be based on an hourly charge, a flat fee (straight contract fee), or a contingent fee (percentage of negotiated settlement).
- Always compromise and attempt to settle any dispute rather than litigate.
- Have your lawyer design forms that you can use in routine transactions.
- Use a less-expensive lawyer for small collections.
- Suggest cost-saving methods to your attorney for ordinary business matters.
- See your lawyer during normal business hours.
- Consult with your lawyer on several matters at one time.
- Keep abreast of legal developments in your field.
- Handle some matters yourself.
- Shop around, but don't lawyer-hop. Once you find a good lawyer, stick with that person. A lawyer who's familiar with your business can handle your affairs much more efficiently than a succession of lawyers, each of whom must research your case from scratch.[25]

---

[24] Clarkson et al., *West's Business Law,* 648.

[25] Adapted from Fred S. Steingold, "18 Ways to Cut Legal Costs," *Inc.,* special issue on small-business success, 1985.

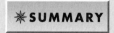

A patent is an intellectual property right that is a result of a unique discovery. Patent holders are provided protection against infringement by others. This protection is for 14 years in the case of design patents and for 17 years in all other cases.

Securing a patent can be a complex process, and careful planning is required. Some of the useful rules to follow in acquiring a patent were set forth in the chapter.

A patent may be declared invalid for several reasons: failure to assert the property right for an unreasonable length of time, misuse of the patent, and inability to prove the patent meets patentability tests. On the other hand, if a patent is valid, the owner can prevent others from infringing on it, and if they do infringe on it, the owner can bring legal action to prevent the infringement as well as, in some cases, obtain financial damages.

A copyright provides exclusive rights to creative individuals for the protection of their literary or artistic productions. This protection extends for the life of the author plus 50 years. In case of infringement, the author (or whoever holds the copyright) can initiate a lawsuit for infringement. This action can result in an end to the infringement and, in some cases, the awarding of financial damages.

A trademark is a distinctive name, mark, symbol, or motto identified with a company's product(s). When an organization registers a trademark, it has the exclusive right to use that mark. The registration before 1989 lasts for 20 years. However, after 1989 the registration is for 10 years and is renewable every 10 years thereafter. In case of infringement, the trademark holder can seek legal action and damages.

For more than a decade numerous business failures have occurred, but federal bankruptcy cases are decreasing the past few years after peaking in 1992. Three major sections of the Bankruptcy Act are of importance to entrepreneurs. Chapter 7 deals with straight bankruptcy and calls for a liquidation of all assets in order to satisfy outstanding debts. Chapter 11 deals with reorganization, a format wherein a business remains operating and attempts to formulate a plan to pay a portion of the debts, to have the remaining sum discharged, and to continue to pay the debt in installments. Chapter 13 deals with individual debtors who file a plan for adjustment of their debts. This would apply to sole proprietorships because they are individually owned. More business bankruptcies are handled under Chapter 11 than under the other two sections.

Key Terms and Concepts

Abandonment	Generic meaning
Bankruptcy Act	Infringement budget
Cancellation proceedings	Liquidation
Claims	Patent
Cleaning-out procedure	Patent and Trademark Office
Copyright	Specification
Debtor-in-possession	Trade secrets
Fair use doctrine	Trademark

Review and Discussion Questions

1. In your own words, what is a patent? Of what value is a patent to an entrepreneur? What benefits does it provide?

2. What are four basic rules entrepreneurs should remember about securing a patent?
3. When can a patent be declared invalid? Cite two examples.
4. If a patent is infringed on by a competitor, what action can the patent holder take? Explain in detail.
5. In your own words, what is a copyright? What benefits does a copyright provide?
6. How much protection does a copyright afford the owner? Can any of the individual's work be copied without paying a fee? Explain in detail. If an infringement of the copyright occurs, what legal recourse does the owner have?
7. In your own words, what is a trademark? Why are generic or descriptive names or words not given trademarks?
8. When may a trademark be invalidated? Explain.
9. What are three of the pitfalls individuals should avoid when seeking a trademark?
10. How can an entrepreneur find out if the business is going bankrupt? What are three early warning signs?
11. What type of protection does Chapter 7 offer to a bankrupt entrepreneur?
12. What type of protection does Chapter 11 offer to a bankrupt entrepreneur? Why do many people prefer Chapter 11 to Chapter 7?
13. What type of protection does Chapter 13 offer to a bankrupt entrepreneur? How does Chapter 13 differ from Chapter 7 or Chapter 11?

Experiential Exercise *Protecting Your Legal Interests*

Entrepreneurs need to know how to legally protect their interests in a property or work. The most effective way to gain legal protection is to obtain a copyright or a trademark. Two definitions are given here. Place a *C* next to the one that defines a copyright; place a *T* next to the one that defines a trademark. Then, on the list below (*a* through *j*), place a *C* next to each item that could be protected with a copyright and a *T* next to each item that could be protected with a trademark. Answers are provided at the end of the exercise.

_____ 1. A distinctive name, mark, symbol, or motto identified with a company's product

_____ 2. An exclusive protection of a literary or an artistic production

_____ *a)* Best-selling novel

_____ *b)* Logo

_____ *c)* Company's initials (such as IBM or ITT)

_____ *d)* Motion picture

_____ *e)* Word (such as Coke or Pepsi)

_____ *f)* Computer program

_____ *g)* Musical comedy

_____ *h)* Slogan

_____ *i)* Stage play

_____ *j)* Symbol

Answers   1. T   *a)* C   *c)* T   *e)* T   *g)* C   *i)* C
              2. C   *b)* T   *d)* C   *f)* C   *h)* T   *j)* T

 **CASE 13.1**

A Patent Matter

Technological breakthroughs in the machine industry are commonplace. Thus, whenever one company announces a new development, some of the first customers are that company's competitors. The latter will purchase the machine, strip it down, examine the new technology, and then look for ways to improve it. The original breakthroughs always are patented by the firm that discovers them, even though the technology is soon surpassed.

A few weeks ago Tom Farrington completed the development of a specialized lathe machine that is 25 percent faster and 9 percent more efficient than anything currently on the market. This technological breakthrough was a result of careful analysis of competitive products. "Until I saw some of the latest developments in the field," Tom told his wife, "I didn't realize how easy it would be to increase the speed and efficiency of the machine. But once I saw the competition's products, I knew immediately how to proceed."

Tom has shown his machine to five major firms in the industry, and all have placed orders with him. Tom has little doubt he will make a great deal of money from his invention. Before beginning production, however, Tom intends to get a patent on his invention. He believes his machine is so much more sophisticated and complex than any other machine on the market that it will take his competitors at least four years to develop a better product. "By that time I hope to have improved on my invention and continue to remain ahead of them," he noted.

Tom has talked to an attorney about filing for a patent. The attorney believes Tom should answer two questions before proceeding: (1) How long will it take the competition to improve on your patent? (2) How far are you willing to go in defending your patent right? Part of the attorney's comments were as follows: "It will take us about three years to get a patent. If, during this time, the competition is able to come out with something that is better than what you have, we will have wasted a lot of time and effort. The patent will have little value since no one will be interested in using it. Since some of your first sales will be to the competition, this is something to which you have to give serious thought. Second, even if it takes four years for the competition to catch up, would you be interested in fighting those who copy your invention after, say, two years? Simply put, we can get you a patent, but I'm not sure it will provide you as much protection as you think."

Questions
1. Given the nature of the industry, how valuable will a patent be to Tom? Explain.
2. If Tom does get a patent, can he bring action against infringers? Will it be worth the time and expense? Why or why not?
3. What do you think Tom should do? Why?

 **CASE 13.2**

All She Needs Is a Little Breathing Room

When Debbie Dawson started her business 12 months ago, she estimated it would be profitable within 8 months. That is not what happened. During the first 6 months she lost $18,000, and during the next 6 months she lost an additional $14,000. Debbie believes the business is going to get better during the next 6 months and that she will be able to break even by the end of the second year. However, her creditors are not sure. Debbie's business owes the two largest creditors a total of $48,000. The others are owed a total of $38,000.

Debbie believes that if she can postpone paying her creditors for a period of one year, her company will be strong enough to pay off all of its debts. On the other hand, if she has to pay the creditors now, she will be too weak financially to continue and will have to declare bankruptcy. "I really think it's in everyone's best interest to give me 12 months of breathing room," she explained to her husband. "If they will do this, everyone is going to come out on top. Otherwise, we are all going to take a financial bath."

Debbie has considered broaching the subject with her two major creditors. However, she is not sure whether this suggestion would be accepted or would be used as a basis for their bringing legal action against her. "If they think I am trying to stall them, they just might demand repayment immediately and force me into bankruptcy," she explained to a close friend. "Of course, if they see things my way, that's a different story. In any event, I'm reluctant to pursue this line of action without talking to my attorney."

Debbie hopes she and her lawyer, Juan, can work out a plan of action that will prevent her having to declare bankruptcy and liquidate the firm. During her phone call to set up a meeting with Juan, she commented, "If everyone remains calm and looks the situation over very carefully, I think they'll agree that my suggestion is a good one. After all, I'm not asking them to put any more money in the business, so the most they can lose is what they are owed currently. On the other hand, if they force my hand, they'll probably be lucky to get 40 cents on the dollar. If they wait, they could end up with all of their money. All I'm asking for is a little breathing room." Juan suggests they meet later this week to talk about it. "I'm sure we can think of something," he told her.

Questions

1. What type of bankruptcy agreement would you recommend? Why?
2. Why would you not recommend the other types of bankruptcy? Be complete in your answer.
3. When selling the creditors on your recommendation, what argument(s) would you use?

Chapter 14

♪ OURCES OF CAPITAL FOR ENTREPRENEURS

CHAPTER OBJECTIVES

1. To differentiate between debt and equity as methods of financing

2. To examine commercial loans and public stock offerings as sources of capital

3. To discuss private placements as an opportunity for equity capital

4. To study the market for venture capital and to review venture capitalists' evaluation criteria for new ventures

5. To discuss the importance of evaluating venture capitalists for a proper selection

6. To examine the existing informal risk-capital market

Money is like a sixth sense without which you cannot make a complete use of the other five.

William Somerset Maugham,
Of Human Bondage

Every entrepreneur planning a new venture confronts the dilemma of where to find start-up capital. Entrepreneurs usually are not aware that numerous possibilities and combinations of financial packages may be appropriate for new ventures.

It is important, therefore, to understand not only the various sources of capital but also the expectations and requirements of these sources. Without this understanding, an entrepreneur may be frustrated with attempts to find appropriate start-up capital.

Commercial loans, public offerings, private placements, convertible debentures, venture capital, and informal risk capital are some of the major terms used in the search for capital. But what exactly are they, and what is expected of an entrepreneur applying for these funds?

Studies have investigated the various sources of capital preferred by entrepreneurs.[1] Figure 14.1 illustrates the findings from one of those studies. At start-up the desire for venture capital was strongest, whereas five years later public offerings were preferred.

In this chapter we shall examine the various sources of capital available to new ventures, with some insights into the processes expected of the entrepreneur. We begin with an examination of the differences between debt and equity financing.

DEBT VERSUS EQUITY

The use of *debt* to finance a new venture involves a payback of the funds plus a fee (interest) for the use of the money. *Equity* financing involves the sale of some of the ownership in the venture. Debt places a burden of repayment and interest on the entrepreneur, while equity financing forces the entrepreneur to relinquish some degree of control. In the extreme, the choice for the entrepreneur is (1) to take on debt without giving up ownership in the venture or (2) to relinquish a percentage of ownership in order to avoid having to borrow. In most cases, a combination of debt and equity proves most appropriate.

Debt Financing

Many new ventures find that **debt financing** is necessary. Short-term borrowing (one year or less) is often required for working capital and is repaid out of the proceeds from sales.

---

[1] Albert V. Bruno and Tyzoon T. Tyebjee, "The Entrepreneur's Search for Capital," *Journal of Business Venturing* (winter 1985): 61–74; see also Howard E. Van Auken and Richard B. Carter, "Acquisitions of Capital by Small Business," *Journal of Small Business Management* (April 1989): 1–9.

FIGURE 14.1   **ENTREPRENEURS' PREFERRED FINANCING SOURCES**

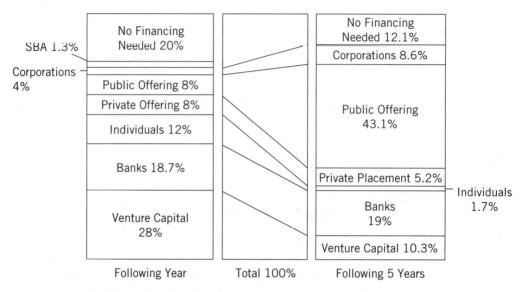

SOURCE: Reprinted by permission of the publisher from "The Entrepreneur's Search for Capital," by Albert V. Bruno and Tyzoon T. Tyebjee, *Journal of Business Venturing* (winter 1985): 71. Copyright 1985 by Elsevier Science Publishing Co., Inc.

Long-term debt (term loans of one to five years or long-term loans maturing in more than five years) is used to finance the purchase of property or equipment, with the purchased asset serving as collateral for the loans. The most common sources of debt financing are commercial banks.[2]

COMMERCIAL BANKS   About 11,000 commercial banks operate in the United States today.[3] Although some banks will make unsecured short-term loans, most bank loans are secured by receivables, inventories, or other assets. Commercial banks also make a large number of intermediate-term loans with maturities of one to five years. In about 90 percent of these cases, the banks require collateral, generally consisting of stocks, machinery, equipment, and real estate, and systematic payments over the life of the loan are required. Apart from real estate mortgages and loans guaranteed by the SBA or a similar organization, commercial banks make few loans with maturities greater than five years. Banks also may offer a number of services to a new venture, including computerized payroll preparation, letters of credit, international services, lease financing, and money market accounts.

To secure a bank loan, an entrepreneur typically will have to answer a number of questions. Five of the most common questions, together with descriptive commentaries, follow:

1. *What do you plan to do with the money?* Do not plan on using funds for a high-risk venture. Banks seek the most secure venture possible.

---

[2] *The State of Small Business: A Report of the President, 1995* (Washington, DC: Government Printing Office, June 1995), 277–80; see also Jerry Feigen, "Financing Sources for Small Businesses," *In-Business* (July/August 1990): 43–44.

[3] A complete listing can be found in the *American Bank Directory* (Norcross, GA: McFadden Business Publications, 1993).

2. *How much do you need?* Some entrepreneurs go to their bank with no clear idea of how much money they need. All they know is that they want money. The more precisely the entrepreneur can answer this question, the more likely the loan will be granted.

3. *When do you need it?* Never rush to the bank with immediate requests for money with no plan. Such a strategy shows that the entrepreneur is a poor planner, and most lenders will not want to get involved.

4. *How long will you need it?* The shorter the period of time the entrepreneur needs the money, the more likely he or she is to get the loan. The time at which the loan will be repaid should correspond to some important milestone in the business plan.

5. *How will you repay the loan?* This is the most important question. What if plans go awry? Can other income be diverted to pay off the loan? Does collateral exist? Even if a quantity of fixed assets exists, the bank may be unimpressed because it knows from experience that assets sold at a liquidation auction bring only a fraction of their value. Five to ten cents on the dollar is not unusual.[4]

Banks are not the only source of debt financing. Sometimes a new venture can obtain long-term financing for a particular piece of equipment from the manufacturer, which will take a portion of the purchase price in the form of a long-term note. Manufacturers are most willing to do this when an active market exists for their used equipment, so if the machinery must be repossessed, it can be resold. Also, new ventures sometimes can obtain short-term debt financing by negotiating extended credit terms with suppliers. However, this kind of trade credit restricts the venture's flexibility with selecting suppliers and may reduce its ability to negotiate supplier prices.

Debt financing has both advantages and disadvantages.

Advantages

- No relinquishment of ownership is required.
- More borrowing allows for potentially greater return on equity.
- During periods of low interest rates, the opportunity cost is justified since the cost of borrowing is low.

Disadvantages

- Regular (monthly) interest payments are required.
- Continual cash-flow problems can be intensified because of payback responsibility.
- Heavy use of debt can inhibit growth and development.

OTHER DEBT-FINANCING SOURCES In addition to commercial banks, other debt-financing sources include trade credit, accounts receivable factoring, finance companies, leasing companies, mutual savings banks, savings and loan associations, and insurance companies. Table 14.1 provides a summary of these sources, the business types they often finance, and their financing terms.

Trade credit is credit given by suppliers who sell goods on account. This credit is reflected on the entrepreneur's balance sheet as accounts payable, and in most cases it must

---

[4] A complete explanation can be found in Donald M. Dible, ed., *Winning the Money Game* (Santa Clara, CA: Entrepreneur Press, 1975), 276; see also Bruce G. Posner, "How to Finance Anything," *Inc.,* February 1993, 54–68.

TABLE 14.1	COMMON DEBT SOURCES				
	Business Type Financed		**Financing Term**		
Source	**Start-up Firm**	**Existing Firm**	**Short Term**	**Intermediate Term**	**Long Term**
Trade credit	Yes	Yes	Yes	No	No
Commercial banks	Sometimes, but only if strong capital or collateral exists	Yes	Frequently	Sometimes	Seldom
Finance companies	Seldom	Yes	Most frequent	Yes	Seldom
Factors	Seldom	Yes	Most frequent	Seldom	No
Leasing companies	Seldom	Yes	No	Most frequent	Occasionally
Mutual savings banks and savings-and-loan associations	Seldom	Real estate ventures only	No	No	Real estate ventures only
Insurance companies	Rarely	Yes	No	No	Yes

be paid in 30 to 90 days. Many small, new businesses obtain this credit when no other form of financing is available to them. Suppliers typically offer this credit as a way of attracting new customers.

Accounts receivable financing is short-term financing that involves either the pledge of receivables as collateral for a loan or the sale of receivables (factoring). Accounts receivable loans are made by commercial banks, whereas factoring is done primarily by commercial finance companies and factoring concerns.

Accounts receivable bank loans are made on a discounted value of the receivables pledged. A bank may make receivable loans on a notification or nonnotification plan. Under the notification plan, purchasers of goods are informed that their account has been assigned to the bank. They then make payments directly to the bank, which credits them to the borrower's account. Under the nonnotification plan, borrowers collect their accounts as usual and then pay off the bank loan.

Factoring is the sale of accounts receivable. Under this arrangement, the receivables are sold, at a discounted value, to a factoring company. Some commercial finance companies also do factoring. Under a standard arrangement the factor will buy the client's receivables outright, without recourse, as soon as the client creates them by its shipment of goods to customers. Factoring fits some businesses better than others, and it has become almost traditional in industries such as textiles, furniture manufacturing, clothing manufacturing, toys, shoes, and plastics.

Finance companies are asset-based lenders who lend money against assets such as receivables, inventory, and equipment. The advantage of dealing with a commercial finance company is that it often will make loans that banks will not. The interest rate varies from 2 percent to 6 percent over that charged by a bank. New ventures that are unable to raise money from banks and factors often turn to finance companies.

Other financial sources include equity instruments, (discussed in the next section) which give investors a share of the ownership. Examples of these follow:

- *Loan with warrants,* which provides the investor with the right to buy stock at a fixed price at some future date. Terms on the warrants are negotiable. The warrant customarily provides for the purchase of additional stock, such as up to 10 percent of the total issue at 130 percent of the original offering price within a five-year period following the offering date.
- *Convertible debentures,* which are unsecured loans that can be converted into stock. The conversion price, the interest rate, and the provisions of the loan agreement are all areas for negotiation.
- *Preferred stock,* which is equity that gives investors a preferred place among the creditors in the event the venture is dissolved. The stock also pays a dividend and can increase in price, thus giving investors an even greater return. Some preferred stock issues are convertible to common stock, a feature that can make them even more attractive.
- *Common stock,* which is the most basic form of ownership. This stock usually carries the right to vote for the board of directors. If a new venture does well, common-stock investors often make a large return on their investment. These stock issues often are sold through public or private offerings.

Equity Financing

Equity financing is money invested in the venture with no legal obligation for entrepreneurs to repay the principal amount or pay interest on it. The use of equity funding thus requires no repayment in the form of debt. It does, however, require sharing the ownership and profits with the funding source. Since no repayment is required, equity capital can be much safer for new ventures than debt financing. Yet the entrepreneur must consciously decide to give up part of the ownership in return for this funding.

Equity capital can be raised through two major sources: public stock offerings and private placements. In both cases, entrepreneurs must follow the state laws pertaining to the raising of such funds and must meet the requirements set forth by the Securities and Exchange Commission (SEC). This entire process can be difficult, expensive, and time consuming. The laws and regulations are complex and often vary from state to state. On the other hand, successful stock offerings can help a fledgling enterprise raise a great deal of money.

PUBLIC OFFERINGS *Going public* is a term used to refer to a corporation's raising capital through the sale of securities on the public markets. Here are some of the advantages to this approach:

- *Size of capital amount.* Selling securities is one of the fastest ways to raise large sums of capital in a short period of time.
- *Liquidity.* The public market provides liquidity for owners since they can readily sell their stock.
- *Value.* The marketplace puts a value on the company's stock, which in turn allows value to be placed on the corporation.
- *Image.* The image of a publicly traded corporation often is stronger in the eyes of suppliers, financiers, and customers.

In recent years many new ventures have had public offerings. In 1986, for example, 717 new issues—referred to as **initial public offerings,** or **IPOs**—occurred, which was a dramatic increase over 1980, when only 281 IPOs occurred. This surge in activity was

CONTEMPORARY ENTREPRENEURSHIP

The Small Corporate Offering Registration (SCOR)

The Small Corporate Offering Registration (SCOR) is a stock offering administered on the state rather than federal level. Currently, 26 states permit SCOR offerings, and another 11 give unofficial recognition, according to the North American Securities Administrators Association.

The new financing method is a way for small companies to sell stock to the general public without the costs of a Wall Street offering. Although it is similar in cost to a small private placement, this method has fewer sales restrictions. Unlike private placement stock, this stock may be advertised, freely traded, and sold to any type and number of buyers.

The process, sometimes called a ULOR (Uniform Limited Offering Registration) or SCOR offering, stems from a part of the federal securities law known as Rule 504 of Regulation D, adopted in the early 1980s. Among other things, Rule 504 exempts offerings of up to $1 million a year from federal registration, leaving their registration and regulation up to the state or states where they occur. However, it has two catches. The size of the offering is small: A company can raise only $1 million in a given year, although it can do multiple offerings. The company selling the stock also must be small, $25 million or less in annual revenues.

Companies must register with each state in which they want to offer stock. Apparently, small firms found the regulations and paperwork complex. Then, a study group from the American Bar Association (ABA) developed a special registration form. To protect investors yet keep costs affordable for small businesses, the ABA created a form that could be filled out by a competent CEO with a lawyer who is not a securities specialist. It would serve as a business plan, a state securities registration, and a prospectus to protect both the investor and the stock issuer.

The lawyers' form is known as U-7. After Washington state pioneered the form, the North American Securities Administration Association endorsed it in 1989. Since then 18 states have formally adopted the form, 4 informally accept its use, and 6 others are giving it serious consideration.

Most states have had only a few companies try the U-7. The main problem? Few businesspeople know about the changes. Lack of publicity isn't the only problem. Washington state, for example, has had a hard time finding securities dealers who think they can make money selling such small, risky offerings. All SCOR/ULOR offerings must be priced at $5 or more a share. That stipulation exempts them from the Securities and Exchange Commission's tough penny-stock rules and makes it more difficult to manipulate the price. Still, the stock has advantages for smaller companies. A SCOR offering is far less expensive than a regular initial private offering (IPO), and you don't need a high-paid underwriter. Its forms are relatively jargon free.

SOURCE: Martha E. Mangelsdorf, "Taking Stock," *Inc.*, September 1991, 24–26; and *Success*, December 1993, 30.

apparent during part of 1987. In August 1986 the average size of an initial public offering was $18 million. By August 1987 that average size had risen to $30.7 million, based on 63 deals that raised a total of $1.9 billion.[5] However, after the stock market crash in October 1987, the interest and activity in public offerings declined. As an example, in 1988, capital commitments fell 30 percent below the 1987 total. By 1989, the IPO market began to increase with 69 deals totaling $3.6 billion. In 1990, the number of initial public offerings rose to 98 deals while the dollar amount increased to $5.4 billion.[6] Then 1991 witnessed 121 IPOs with $3.8 billion. In 1992, 151 IPOs covered $4.4 billion. In 1993, 157 companies raised $4.58 billion through IPOs. Medical and health-related companies combined with biotechnology, consumer-related, telephone and data communications, and computer and software services to amass 273 IPOs over five years, representing 70 percent of the total market.[7] By 1995, the IPO market seemed to level off to approximately $2.5 billion annually.[8]

These figures reflect the tremendous *volatility* that exists within the stock market, and, thus, entrepreneurs should be aware of the concerns confronting them when pursuing the IPO market. In addition, for other reasons many new ventures have begun to recognize the disadvantages of going public. A few of these follow:

- *Costs.* The expenses involved with a public offering are significantly higher than for other sources of capital. Accounting fees, legal fees, and prospectus printing and distribution, as well as the cost of underwriting the stock, can result in high costs.
- *Disclosure.* Detailed disclosures of the company's affairs must be made public. New-venture firms often prefer to keep such information private.
- *Requirements.* The paperwork involved with SEC regulations, as well as continuing performance information, drains large amounts of time, energy, and money from management. Many new ventures consider these elements better invested in helping the company grow.
- *Shareholder pressure.* Management decisions are sometimes short term in nature in order to maintain a good performance record for earnings and dividends to the shareholders. This pressure can lead to a failure to give adequate consideration to the company's long-term growth and improvement.

The advantages and disadvantages of going public must be weighed carefully. If the decision is to undertake a public offering, then it is important the entrepreneur understand the process involved.

The SEC requires the filing of a registration statement that includes a complete prospectus on the company. The SEC then reviews the registration, ensuring that full disclosure is made before giving permission to proceed. (See Table 14.2 for a presentation of the registration process.)

The prospectus must disclose fully all pertinent information about a company and must present a fair representation of the firm's true prospects. All negative information must be clearly highlighted and explained. Some of the specific detailed information that must be presented follows:

- History and nature of the company
- Capital structure

---

[5] "Public Offerings," *Venture* (November 1987): 132.

[6] Rosalyn Retkwa, "Venture Capital Industry Now in Transition Period," *Pension World* (July 1990): 24–26.

[7] Michael F. Hinds, "Venture Capital," *U.S. Industrial Outlook, 1994* (Washington, DC: Department of Commerce), 46–48.

[8] *The State of Small Business: A Report of the President* (Washington, DC: Government Printing Office, 1995), 287.

TABLE 14.2	THE REGISTRATION PROCESS		
Event	**Participants**	**Agenda**	**Timetable**
Preliminary meeting to discuss issue	President, VP-Finance, independent accountants, underwriters, counsel	Discuss financial needs; introduce and select type of issue to meet needs	1 July (Begin)
Form selection	Management, counsel	Select appropriate form for use in registration statement	3 July (3 days)
Initial meeting of working group	President, VP-Finance, independent accountants, underwriter, counsel for underwriter, company counsel	Assign specific duties to each person in working group; discuss underwriting problems with this issue; discuss accounting problems with the issue	8 July (8 days)
Second meeting of working group	Same as for initial meeting	Review work assignments; prepare presentation to board of directors	22 July (22 days)
Meeting of board of directors	Board of directors, members of working group	Approve proposed issue and increase of debt or equity; authorize preparation of materials	26 July (26 days)
Meeting of company counsel with underwriters	Company counsel, counsel for underwriters, underwriters	Discuss underwriting terms and blue-sky problems	30 July (30 days)
Meeting of working group	Members of working group	Review collected material and examine discrepancies	6 Aug. (37 days)
Prefiling conference with SEC staff	Working group members, SEC staff, other experts as needed	Review proposed registration and associated problems: legal, financial, operative	9 Aug. (40 days)
Additional meetings of working group	Members of working group	Prepare final registration statement and prospectuses	12–30 Aug. (61 days)
Meeting with board of directors	Board of directors, members of working group	Approve registration statement and prospectuses; discuss related topics and problems	6 Sept. (68 days)

- Description of any material contracts
- Description of securities being registered
- Salaries and security holdings of major officers and directors and the price they paid for holdings
- Underwriting arrangements
- Estimate and use of net proceeds
- Audited financial statements
- Information about the competition with an estimation of the chances of the company's surviving

Some of the more important disclosure requirements for annual reports follow:

- Audited financial statements that include the balance sheets for the past two years and income and funds statements for the past three years
- Five years of selected financial data
- Management's discussion and analysis of financial conditions and results of operations

TABLE 14.2   **THE REGISTRATION PROCESS (continued)**

Event	Participants	Agenda	Timetable
Meeting of working group	Members of working group	Draft final corrected registration statement	10 Sept. (72 days)
Filing registration statement with SEC	Company counsel or representative and SEC staff	File registration statement and pay fee	12 Sept. (74 days)
Distribution of "red herring" prospectus	Underwriters	Publicize offering	16 Sept. (78 days)
Receipt of letter of comments	Members of working group	Relate deficiencies in registration statement	15 Oct. (107 days)
Meeting of working group	Members of working group	Correct deficiencies and submit amendments	21 Oct. (113 days)
"Due diligence" meeting	Management representatives, independent accountants, company counsel, underwriter's counsel, underwriters, other professionals as needed	Exchange final information and discuss pertinent problems relating to underwriting and issue	24 Oct. (116 days)
Pricing amendment	Management, underwriters	Add the amounts for the actual price, underwriter's discount or commission, and net proceeds to company to the amended registration statement	25 Oct. (117 days)
Notice of acceptance	SEC staff	Report from SEC staff on acceptance status of price-amended registration statement	28 Oct. (120 days)
Statement becomes effective			30 Oct. (122 days)

SOURCE: Reproduced from K. Fred Skousen, *An Introduction to the SEC*, 5th ed., 58–59, with the permission of South-Western Publishing Co. Copyright © 1991 by South-Western Publishing Co. All rights reserved.

- A brief description of the business
- Line-of-business disclosures for the past three fiscal years
- Identification of directors and executive officers, with the principal occupation and employer of each
- Identification of the principal market in which the firm's securities are traded
- Range of market prices and dividends for each quarter of the two most recent fiscal years
- An offer to provide a free copy of the 10-K report to shareholders on written request unless the annual report complies with Form 10-K disclosure requirements[9]

Some of the forms the SEC requires follow:

- Form S-1 (information contained in the prospectus and other additional financial data)

[9] K. Fred Skousen, *An Introduction to the SEC*, 5th ed. (Cincinnati: South-Western, 1991), 157.

- Form 10-Q (quarterly financial statements and a summary of all important events that took place during the three-month period)
- Form 8-K (a report of unscheduled material events or corporate changes deemed important to the shareholder and filed with the SEC within 15 days after the end of a month in which a significant material event transpired)
- Proxy statements (information given in connection with proxy solicitation)[10]

Entrepreneurs who pursue the public securities route should be prepared for these reporting requirements, disclosure statements, and the shared control and ownership with outside shareholders.

PRIVATE PLACEMENTS   Another method of raising capital is through the **private placement** of securities. Small ventures often use this approach.

The SEC provides **Regulation D,** which eases the regulations for the reports and statements required for selling stock to private parties—friends, employees, customers, relatives, local professionals. Regulation D defines four separate exemptions, which are based on the amount of money being raised. Along with their accompanying rule, these exemptions follow:

1. *Rule 504a—placements of less than $500,000:* No specific disclosure/information requirements and no limits on the kind or type of purchasers exist. This makes marketing offerings of this size easier than it was heretofore.

2. *Rule 504—placements up to $1,000,000:* Again, no specific disclosure/information requirements and no limits on the kind or type of purchasers exist.

3. *Rule 505—placements of up to $5 million:* The criteria for a public offering exemption are somewhat more difficult than those for smaller offerings. Sales of securities can be made to not more than 35 nonaccredited purchasers and to an unlimited number of accredited purchasers. If purchasers are nonaccredited as well as accredited, then the company must follow specified information disclosure requirements. Investors must have the opportunity to obtain additional information about the company and its management.

4. *Rule 506—placements in excess of $5 million:* Sales can be made to no more than 35 nonaccredited purchasers and an unlimited number of accredited purchasers. However, the nonaccredited purchasers must be "sophisticated" in investment matters. Also, the specific disclosure requirements are more detailed than those for offerings between $500,000 and $5 million. Investors must have the opportunity to obtain additional information about the company and its management.[11]

As noted in Rules 505 and 506, Regulation D uses the term **accredited purchaser.** Included in this category are the following:

- Institutional investors such as banks, insurance companies, venture capital firms, registered investment companies, and small-business investment companies (SBICs)

---

[10] For a complete listing, see ibid., 60; see also J. William Petty, Arthur J. Keown, David F. Scott Jr., and John D. Martin, *Basic Financial Management,* 6th ed. (Englewood Cliffs: Prentice-Hall, 1993), 696–99.

[11] A summary can be found in business law texts such as Kenneth W. Clarkson, Roger L. Miller, Gaylord A. Jentz, and Frank B. Cross, *West's Business Law,* 6th ed. (St. Paul, MN: West, 1995), 864–65.

- Any person who buys at least $150,000 of the offered security and whose net worth, including that of his or her spouse, is at least five times the purchase price
- Any person who, together with his or her spouse, has a net worth in excess of $1 million at the time of purchase
- Any person whose individual income was in excess of $200,000 in each of the past two years and who expects the same income for the current year
- Directors, executive officers, or general partners of the company or partnership selling the securities
- Certain tax-exempt organizations with more than $500,000 in assets

Everyone not covered in these descriptions is regarded as a nonaccredited purchaser.

"Sophisticated" investors are wealthy individuals who invest more or less regularly in new and early- and late-stage ventures. They are knowledgeable about the technical and commercial opportunities and risks of the businesses in which they invest. They know the kind of information they want about their prospective investment, and they have the experience and ability needed to obtain and analyze the data provided.

The objective of Regulation D is to make it easier and less expensive for small ventures to sell stock. However, many states have not kept pace with these rules. Consequently, many new ventures still find it costly and time consuming to try to clear their offerings in some states. In addition, many are discouraged by the disclosure requirements for offerings of $500,000 and over, which are cited under Rules 505 and 506. In spite of these difficulties, Regulation D does a lot to simplify small-company financing.[12] (See Contemporary Entrepreneurship on the Small Corporate Offering Registration.)

THE VENTURE CAPITAL MARKET

Venture capitalists are a valuable and powerful source of equity funding for new ventures. These are experienced professionals who provide a full range of financial services for new or growing ventures, including the following:

- Capital for start-ups and expansion
- Market research and strategy for businesses that do not have their own marketing departments
- Management-consulting functions and management audit and evaluation
- Contacts with prospective customers, suppliers, and other important businesspeople
- Assistance in negotiating technical agreements
- Help in establishing management and accounting controls
- Help in employee recruitment and development of employee agreements
- Help in risk management and the establishment of an effective insurance program
- Counseling and guidance in complying with a myriad of government regulations

Recent Developments

The 1991–1992 period marked a resurgence of the venture capital market. The venture capital industry disbursed $2.55 billion in venture fund investments in 1992, lifting the

---

[12] For a compilation of firms involved in private placements, see Robert J. Gaston, *Finding Private Venture Capital for Your Firm: A Complete Guide* (New York: Wiley, 1989).

TABLE 14.3	SOURCES OF VENTURE CAPITAL			
Item	1984	1990	1991	1992
Total	100.0%	100.0%	100.0%	100.0%
Individuals/families	14.6	11.0	12.2	11.0
Endowments	5.5	13.0	24.1	17.9
Insurance companies/banks	14.7	9.0	5.5	14.5
Foreign investors	16.7	7.0	11.7	11.1
Corporations	14.5	7.0	4.3	3.3
Pension funds	34.0	53.0	42.2	42.2

SOURCE: Michael F. Hinds, "Venture Capital," *U.S. Industrial Outlook, 1994* (Washington, DC: Department of Commerce), 46–48.

industry out of a slump that began in 1989. By 1995 the total funds raised by venture capital firms increased to $3.8 billion, a 52 percent increase over 1993.[13]

In addition to these developments, a number of major trends are occurring in the venture capital field today.

First, the predominant investor class is transforming from individuals, foundations, and families to pension institutions. Therefore, sources of capital commitments will continue to shift away from the less-experienced venture capital firm (less than three years) to the more-experienced firm (greater than three years). Table 14.3 illustrates this change in venture capital sources from 1984 to 1992. Second, funds are more specialized and less homogeneous. The industry has become more diverse, more specialized, and less uniform than is generally thought. Sharp differences are apparent in terms of investing objectives and criteria, strategy, and focusing on particular stages, sizes, and market technology niches.[14]

Third, feeder funds are emerging. Accompanying this specialization is a new farm team system. Large, established venture capital firms have crafted both formal and informal relationships with new funds as feeder funds. Often, one general partner of the established fund will provide time and know-how to the new fund. The team may share deal flow and coinvest in a syndicated deal. More often than not, these new funds focus on seed-stage or start-up deals that can feed later deals to the more conventional, mainstream venture capital firm with which they are associated.[15]

Fourth, small start-up investments are drying up. Many venture capital firms have numerous troubled ventures in their portfolios. As a result, general partners, who are often the most experienced and skillful at finding and nurturing innovative technological ventures, are allocating premium time to salvaging or turning around problem ventures. In addition, because start-up and first-stage investing demands the greatest intensity of in-

[13] *The State of Small Business: A Report of the President* (Washington, DC: Government Printing Office, 1995), 287.

[14] Edgar Norton and Bernard H. Tenenbaum, "Specialization versus Diversification as a Venture Capital Investment Strategy," *Journal of Business Venturing* (September 1993): 431–42.

[15] Edgar Norton and Bernard H. Tenenbaum, "Factors Affecting the Structure of U.S. Venture Capital Deals," *Journal of Small Business Management* (July 1992): 20–29.

TABLE 14.4	VENTURE CAPITAL DISBURSEMENTS BY STAGE, 1992			
Item	Dollars[a] Invested	Number of Companies	Number of Financings	Number of Investments
Total	$2,542	1,087	1,566	3,218
Expansion	1,400	600	806	1,718
LBO/acquisition	176	55	73	112
Other[b]	347	191	252	530
Other early stage	336	185	226	426
Seed	74	68	78	145
Start-up	209	108	131	287

[a] In millions of dollars.
[b] Bridge loans and the public purchases.

SOURCE: Michael F. Hinds, "Venture Capital," *U.S. Industrial Outlook, 1994* (Washington, DC: Department of Commerce), 46–49.

volvement by venture capital investors, this type of venture has felt the greatest effects. Finally, other venture capital funds lack professionals who have experience with start-ups and first-stage ventures. Consequently, the level of start-up and first-stage activity is down sharply. As Table 14.4 indicates, a large portion of the capital commitments are directed toward late-stage financing and away from early-stage financing.[16]

Fifth, the trend is for a new legal environment. The heated competition for venture capital in recent years has resulted in a more-sophisticated legal and contractual environment. The frequency and extent of litigation are rising. As an example, the final document governing the inventory/entrepreneur relationship—called the investment agreement—can be a few inches thick and can comprise two volumes. In this regard, legal experts recommend that the following provisions be carefully considered in the investment agreement: choice of securities (preferred stock, common stock, convertible debt, etc.), control issues (who maintains voting power), evaluation issues and financial covenants (ability to proceed with mergers and acquisitions), and remedies for breach of contract (rescission of the contract or monetary damages).[17]

Dispelling Venture Capital Myths

Because many people have mistaken ideas about the role and function of venture capitalists, a number of myths have sprung up about venture capitalists. Some of these, along with their rebuttals, follow.

[16] Adapted from Michael Gorman and William A. Sahlman, "What Do Venture Capitalists Do?" *Journal of Business Venturing* (July 1989): 231–48; and S. Michael Camp and Donald L. Sexton, "Trends in Venture Capital Investment: Implications for High Technology Firms," *Journal of Small Business Management* (July 1992): 11–19.

[17] Chislaine Bouillet-Cordonnier, "Legal Aspects of Start-Up Evaluation and Adjustment Methods," *Journal of Business Venturing* (March 1992): 91–102.

MYTH 1: VENTURE CAPITAL FIRMS WANT TO OWN CONTROL OF YOUR COMPANY AND TELL YOU HOW TO RUN THE BUSINESS   No venture capital firm intentionally sets out to own control of a small business. Venture capitalists have no desire to run the business. They do not want to tell entrepreneurs how to make day-to-day decisions and have the owner report to them daily. They want the entrepreneur and the management team to run the company profitably. They do want to be consulted on any major decision, but they want no say in daily business operations.[18]

MYTH 2: VENTURE CAPITALISTS ARE SATISFIED WITH A REASONABLE RETURN ON INVESTMENTS   Venture capitalists expect very high, exorbitant, unreasonable returns. They can obtain reasonable returns from hundreds of publicly traded companies. They can obtain reasonable returns from many types of investments not having the degree of risk involved in financing a small business. Because every venture capital investment involves a high degree of risk, it must have a correspondingly high return on investment.[19]

MYTH 3: VENTURE CAPITALISTS ARE QUICK TO INVEST   It takes a long time to raise venture capital. On the average, it will take six to eight weeks from the initial contact to raise venture capital. If the entrepreneur has a well-prepared business plan, the investor will be able to raise money in that time frame. A venture capitalist will see from 50 to 100 proposals a month. Out of that number, 10 will be of some interest. Out of those 10, 2 or 3 will receive a fair amount of analysis, negotiation, and investigation. Of the 2 or 3, 1 may be funded. This funneling process of selecting 1 out of 100 takes a great deal of time. Once the venture capitalist has found that one, he or she will spend a significant amount of time investigating possible outcomes before funding it.

MYTH 4: VENTURE CAPITALISTS ARE INTERESTED IN BACKING NEW IDEAS OR HIGH-TECHNOLOGY INVENTIONS—MANAGEMENT IS A SECONDARY CONSIDERATION   Venture capitalists back only good management. If an entrepreneur has a bright idea but a poor managerial background and no experience in the industry, the individual should try to find someone in the industry to bring onto the team. The venture capitalist will have a hard time believing that an entrepreneur with no experience in that industry and no managerial ability in his or her background can follow through on a business plan. A good idea is important, but a good management team is even more important.

MYTH 5: VENTURE CAPITALISTS NEED ONLY BASIC SUMMARY INFORMATION BEFORE THEY MAKE AN INVESTMENT   A detailed and well-organized business plan is the only way to gain a venture capital investor's attention and obtain funding. Every venture capitalist, before becoming involved, wants the entrepreneur to have thought out the entire business plan and to have written it down in detail.[20]

Venture Capitalists' Objectives

Venture capitalists have different objectives from most others who provide capital to new ventures. Lenders, for example, are interested in security and payback. As partial owners

---

[18] Ian C. MacMillan, David M. Kulow, and Roubina Khoylian, "Venture Capitalists' Involvement in Their Investments: Extent and Performance," *Journal of Business Venturing* (January 1989): 27–47.

[19] Gregory F. Chiampou and Joel J. Kallet, "Risk/Return Profile of Venture Capital," *Journal of Business Venturing* (January 1989): 1–10.

[20] David J. Gladstone, *Venture Capital Handbook* (Reston, VA: Reston, 1983), 21–24.

ENTREPRENEURIAL

EDGE

Tapping into the Investment Networks

Venture club networks are being established across the United States to provide investors and entrepreneurs with what they need most: each other. These networks create an environment in which business investors and entrepreneurs can make valuable contacts, exchange information, and create mutual business opportunities.

Venture club networks are helping facilitate and encourage the expansion of business and commercial investment activities. Membership in venture clubs is open to professional venture capitalists, private investors, investment bankers, commercial bankers, entrepreneurs, attorneys, accountants, consultants, and others involved in the investment community. Venture networks also provide entrepreneurs with the opportunity to find strategic partners who can supply noncash equities, such as space, manufacturing capabilities, equipment, customers, and support services.

The entrepreneur's continual dilemma is where to find the appropriate investment networks. Here are some sources:

- Center for Venture Research, University of New Hampshire, (603) 862-3369.
- Georgia Capital Network, Georgia Tech University, Atlanta, (404) 894-5344. Cost: free to investors; one-time $75 fee for entrepreneurs. About 45 investors and 40 entrepreneurs are listed.
- Investors' Circle, St. Charles, Illinois, (708) 876-1101. Cost: $150 to entrepreneurs. About 120 investors are listed; the number of entrepreneurs varies each month.

- Kentucky Investment Capital Network, University of Kentucky, Frankfort, (502) 564-7140. Cost: free. About 40 investors and 30 companies are listed.
- Northwest Capital Network, Portland, Oregon, (503) 282-6273. Cost: yearly fees of $250 for investors, $100 for entrepreneurs. About 60 investors and 200 entrepreneurs are listed.
- Private Investors Network, University of South Carolina at Aiken, (803) 648-6851, ext. 3518. Cost: a one-time $210 fee for investors, a one-year $100 fee for entrepreneurs.
- Technology Capital Network, Inc., Massachusetts Institute of Technology, Cambridge, Massachusetts, (617) 253-8214. Cost: $250 each for investors and entrepreneurs, listing on database for six months.
- Texas Capital Network, University of Texas, Austin, (512) 794-9398. Cost: one-time fees of $450 for individual investors, $950 for venture capitalists and corporate investors, $350 for entrepreneurs. The network lists about 300 investors, mostly individuals; and about 400 companies.
- Venture Capital Network of Minneapolis/St. Paul, University of St. Thomas, St. Paul, (612) 223-8663. Cost: free. The network is operating on a limited basis.
- Venture Club of Indiana, (317) 253-1244. Cost: $200. Contact Margo Jaqua.

SOURCE: Dale D. Buss, "Heaven Help Us," *Nation's Business*, November 1993, 34; and *The Venture Club Newsletter*, 1997.

FIGURE 14.2 **VENTURE CAPITALIST SYSTEM OF EVALUATING PRODUCT/SERVICE AND MANAGEMENT**

Level 4 Fully developed product/service Established market Satisfied users	4/1	4/2	4/3	4/4
Level 3 Fully developed product/service Few users as of yet Market assumed	3/1	3/2	3/3	3/4
Level 2 Operable pilot or prototype Not yet developed for production Market assumed	2/1	2/2	2/3	2/4
Level 1 Product/service idea Not yet operable Market assumed	1/1	1/2	1/3	1/4
	Level 1 Individual founder/ entrepreneur	**Level 2** Two founders Other personnel not yet identified	**Level 3** Partial management team Members identified to join company when funding is received	**Level 4** Fully staffed, experienced management team

Status of Product/Service (Riskiest)

◄─────────────── **Riskiest** ───────────────►

Status of Management

SOURCE: Stanley Rich and David Gumpert, *Business Plans That Win $$$*, 169. Reprinted by permission of Sterling Lord Literistic, Inc. Copyright © 1985 by Stanley Rich and David Gumpert.

of the companies they invest in, venture capitalists, however, are most concerned with return on investment. As a result, they put a great deal of time into weighing the risk of a venture against the potential return. They carefully measure both the product/service and the management. Figure 14.2 illustrates an evaluation system for measuring these two critical factors—status of product/service and status of management—on four levels. The figure demonstrates that ideas as well as entrepreneurs are evaluated when the viability of a venture proposal is determined.

TABLE 14.5   **RETURNS ON INVESTMENT VENTURE CAPITALISTS TYPICALLY SEEK**

Stage of Business	Expected Annual Return on Investment	Expected Increase on Initial Investment
Start-up business (idea stage)	60%+	10–15 × investment
First-stage financing (new business)	40%–60%	6–12 × investment
Second-stage financing (development stage)	30%–50%	4–8 × investment
Third-stage financing (expansion stage)	25%–40%	3–6 × investment
Turnaround situation	50%+	8–15 × investment

SOURCE: W. Keith Schilit, "How to Obtain Venture Capital," *Business Horizons* (May/June 1987): 78. Copyright © 1987 by the Foundation for the School of Business at Indiana University. Reprinted by permission.

Venture capitalists are particularly interested in making large returns on investments. Table 14.5 provides some commonly sought targets. Of course, these targets are flexible. They would be reduced, for example, in cases where a company has a strong market potential, is able to generate good cash flow, or the management has invested a sizable portion of its own funds in the venture.[21] However, an annual goal of 20 to 30 percent ROI would not be considered too high, regardless of the risks involved.

Criteria for Evaluating New-Venture Proposals

In addition to the evaluation of product ideas and management strength, numerous criteria are used to evaluate new-venture proposals. One group of researchers developed 28 of these, grouped into six major categories: (1) entrepreneur's personality, (2) entrepreneur's experience, (3) product or service characteristics, (4) market characteristics, (5) financial considerations, and (6) nature of the venture team.[22]

The study surveyed more than 100 venture capitalists regarding these criteria and found that they most frequently rated 10 of the criteria as essential when reviewing new-venture proposals (see Table 14.6). Six of these 10 relate to the entrepreneur personally, 3 deal with the investment in and growth of the project, and 1 relates to the venture's patent or copyright position.

The study also found that many venture capitalists would reject proposals when 2 of the just-mentioned criteria were missing. Table 14.7 reports the ten combinations that would produce rejections from 75 percent or more of the venture capitalists surveyed. In each of the combinations, an entrepreneurial trait was included, indicating that the entrepreneur is a critical factor in the evaluation process.

Other researchers have uncovered similar results. For example, John Hall and Charles W. Hofer examined the criteria venture capitalists use during a proposal screening and

[21] Keith Schilit, "How to Obtain Venture Capital," *Business Horizons* (May/June 1987): 76–81.

[22] Ian C. MacMillan, Robin Siegel, and P. N. Subba Narasimha, "Criteria Used by Venture Capitalists to Evaluate New Venture Proposals," *Journal of Business Venturing* (winter 1985): 119–28.

TABLE 14.6 **TEN CRITERIA MOST FREQUENTLY RATED ESSENTIAL IN NEW-VENTURE EVALUATION**

Criterion	Percentage
Capable of sustained intense effort	64
Thoroughly familiar with market	62
At least ten times return in 5–10 years	50
Demonstrated leadership in past	50
Evaluates and reacts to risk well	48
Investment can be made liquid	44
Significant market growth	43
Track record relevant to venture	37
Articulates venture well	31
Proprietary protection	29

SOURCE: Reprinted by permission of the publisher from "Criteria Used by Venture Capitalists to Evaluate New Venture Proposals," by Ian C. MacMillan, Robin Siegel, and P. N. Subba Narasimha, *Journal of Business Venturing* (winter 1985): 123. Copyright © 1985 by Elsevier Science Publishing Co., Inc.

evaluation. Table 14.8 outlines the factors used in the study.[23] Their results showed that venture capitalists reached a "go/no go" decision in an average of 6 minutes on the initial screening and less than 21 minutes on the overall proposal evaluation. They found that the venture capital firm's requirements and the long-term growth and profitability of the proposed venture's industry were the critical factors for initial screening. In the more-detailed evaluation the background of the entrepreneurs as well as the characteristics of the proposal itself were important.

In a study examining the "demand side" of venture capital, researchers surveyed 318 private entrepreneurs who sought out venture capital in amounts of $100,000 or more. The study found that entrepreneurs' success with acquiring funding is related to four general, variable categories: (1) characteristics of the entrepreneurs, including education, experience, and age; (2) characteristics of the enterprise, including stage, industry type, and location (e.g., rural or urban); (3) characteristics of the request, including amount, business plan, and prospective capital source; and (4) sources of advice, including technology, preparation of the business plan, and places to seek funding.[24] Table 14.9 illustrates some of the key results of these successful entrepreneurs.

The business plan is a critical element in a new-venture proposal and should be complete, clear, and well presented. Venture capitalists will generally analyze five major aspects of the plan: (1) the proposal size, (2) financial projections, (3) investment recovery, (4) competitive advantage, and (5) company management.

The evaluation process typically takes place in stages. The four most common stages follow:

[23] John Hall and Charles W. Hofer, "Venture Capitalist's Decision Criteria in New Venture Evaluation," *Journal of Business Venturing* (January 1993): 25–42.

[24] Ronald J. Hustedde and Glen C. Pulver, "Factors Affecting Equity Capital Acquisition: The Demand Side," *Journal of Business Venturing* (September 1992): 363–74.

TABLE 14.7

PERCENTAGE OF VENTURE CAPITALISTS WHO WOULD REJECT PROPOSALS THAT FAIL ON TWO CRITERIA

Pairs of Criteria	Percentage Who Reject the Proposal
1. Capable of effort Return of ten times within 5–10 years	84
2. Capable of effort Functionally balanced management team	80
3. Demonstrated leadership Familiar with target market	80
4. Capable of effort Demonstrated leadership	79
5. Able to evaluate risk Familiar with target market	77
6. Capable of effort Track record relevant to venture	77
7. Able to evaluate risk Return of ten times within 5–10 years	76
8. Capable of effort Significant growth rate of market	76
9. Demonstrated leadership Return of ten times within 5–10 years	75
10. Capable of effort Proprietary product	75

SOURCE: Reprinted by permission of the publisher from "Criteria Used by Venture Capitalists to Evaluate New Venture Proposals," by Ian C. MacMillan, Robin Siegel, and P. N. Subba Narasimha, *Journal of Business Venturing* (winter 1985): 123. Copyright © 1985 by Elsevier Science Publishing Co., Inc.

Stage 1: Initial screening. This is a quick review of the basic venture to see if it meets the venture capitalist's particular interests.

Stage 2: Evaluation of the business plan. This is where a detailed reading of the plan is done in order to evaluate the factors mentioned earlier.

Stage 3: Oral presentation. The entrepreneur verbally presents the plan to the venture capitalist.

Stage 4: Final evaluation. After analyzing the plan and visiting with suppliers, customers, consultants, and others, the venture capitalist makes a final decision.

This four-step process screens out approximately 98 percent of all venture plans. The rest receive some degree of financial backing.

Evaluating the Venture Capitalist

The venture capitalist will evaluate the entrepreneur's proposal carefully, and the entrepreneur should not hesitate to evaluate the venture capitalist. Does the venture capitalist understand the proposal? Is the individual familiar with the business? Is the person

TABLE 14.8	VENTURE CAPITALISTS' SCREENING CRITERIA

Venture Capital Firm Requirements

Must fit within lending guidelines of venture firm for stage and size of investment and kind of industries invested in or reject

Proposed business must be within geographic area of interest

Prefer proposals recommended by someone known to venture capitalist

Proposed industry must be kind of industry invested in by venture firm or reject

Nature of the Proposed Business

Projected growth should be relatively large within five years of investment

Economic Environment of Proposed Industry

Industry must be capable of long-term growth and profitability

Economic environment should be favorable to a new entrant

Proposed Business Strategy

Selection of distribution channel(s) must be feasible or reject

Product must demonstrate defendable competitive position

Financial Information on the Proposed Business

Financial projections should be realistic

Proposal Characteristics

Must have full information or reject

Should be a reasonable length, be easy to scan, have an executive summary, and be professionally presented

Proposal must contain a balanced presentation or reject

Use graphics, large print to emphasize key points

Entrepreneur/Team Characteristics

Relevant experience or reject

Should have a balanced management team in place

Management must be willing to work with venture partners

Entrepreneur who has successfully started previous business given special consideration

SOURCE: John Hall and Charles W. Hofer, "Venture Capitalists' Decision Criteria in New Venture Evaluation," *Journal of Business Venturing* (January 1993): 37.

---

someone with whom the entrepreneur can work? If the answers reveal a poor fit, it is best for the entrepreneur to look for a different venture capitalist.

One researcher found that venture capitalists *do* add value to an entrepreneurial firm beyond the money they supply, especially in high-innovation ventures. Because of this finding, entrepreneurs need to choose the appropriate venture capitalist at the outset, and, most important, they must keep the communication channels open as the firm grows.[25]

On the other hand, it is important to realize that the choice of a venture capitalist can be limited. Although funds are available today, they tend to be controlled by fewer groups, and the quality of the venture must be promising. Even though two and one-half times

---

[25] Harry J. Sapienza, "When Do Venture Capitalists Add Value?" *Journal of Business Venturing* (January 1992): 9–28.

	Characteristic (% of successful seekers)

TABLE 14.9

KEY RESULTS FROM ENTREPRENEURS SUCCESSFUL IN OBTAINING VENTURE CAPITAL

	Characteristic (% of successful seekers)
I. Business stage	
Seed	29%
Start-up	65
Expansion	38
Bridge financing	10
Other	12
II. Amount of dollars sought	44% have sought more than $1 million
III. Written business plan	98
Balance sheet	95
List of product competition	94
Marketing plan	98
Cash-flow projections for 3 years	94
IV. Where firms seek equity capital	
In-state venture capitalists	85
Out-of-state venture capitalists	58
In-state corporations	40
Out-of-state corporations	34
In-state private investors	79
Out-of-state private investors	47
In-state consultants/investment bankers	57
Out-of-state consultants/investment bankers	31

SOURCE: Ronald J. Hustedde and Glen C. Pulver, "Factors Affecting Equity Capital Acquisition: The Demand Side," *Journal of Business Venturing* (September 1992): 369–70.

more money is available today for seed financing than was available ten years ago, the number of venture capital firms is not increasing. In addition, a trend toward concentration of venture capital under the control of a few firms is growing.[26]

Nevertheless, the entrepreneur should not be deterred from evaluating prospective venture capitalists. The Contemporary Entrepreneurship selection (on page 451) provides a list of important questions a prospective venture capital firm should answer. Evaluating and even negotiating with the venture capitalist are critical to establishing the best equity funding:

> You may worry that if you rock the boat by demanding too much, the venture capital firm will lose interest. That's an understandable attitude; venture capital is hard to get and if you've gotten as far as the negotiating process, you're already among the lucky few.

[26] B. Elango, Vance H. Fried, Robert D. Hisrich, and Amy Polonchek, "How Venture Capital Firms Differ," *Journal of Business Venturing* (March 1995): 157–79.

But that doesn't mean you have to roll over and play dead. A venture capital investment is a business deal that you may have to live with for a long time. Although you'll have to give ground on many issues when you come to the bargaining table, there is always a point beyond which the deal no longer makes sense for you. You must draw a line and fight for the points that really count.[27]

INFORMAL RISK CAPITAL—"ANGEL" FINANCING

Not all venture capital is raised through formal sources such as public and private placements. Many wealthy people in the United States are looking for investment opportunities. They are referred to as **business angels** or **informal risk capitalists.** These individuals constitute a huge potential investment pool, as the following calculations show:

- The *Forbes* 400 richest people in America represent a combined net worth of approximately $125 billion (an average of $315 million per person).
- Forty percent of the 400 are self-made millionaires, with a combined net worth of approximately $50 billion.
- If 10 percent of the self-made wealth were available for venture financing, the pool of funds would amount to $5 billion.
- More than 500,000 individuals in America have a net worth in excess of $1 million. If 40 percent of these individuals were interested in venture financing, 200,000 millionaires would be available.
- Assuming only one-half of those 200,000 would actually consider investment in new ventures at a rate of $50,000 per person, 100,000 investors would provide a pool of $5 billion.
- If the typical deal took four investors with $50,000 each (from the pool of $5 billion), then a potential 25,000 ventures could be funded at $200,000 apiece.[28]

William E. Wetzel Jr., a noted researcher in the field of informal risk capital, has defined this type of investor as someone who has already made his or her money and now seeks out promising young ventures to support financially. "Angels are typically entrepreneurs, retired corporate executives, or professionals who have a net worth of more than $1 million and an income of more than $100,000 a year. They're self-starters. And they're trying to perpetuate the system that made them successful."[29] If entrepreneurs are looking for such an angel, Wetzel advises them, "Don't look very far away—within 50 miles or within a day's drive at most. And that's because this is not a full-time profession for them."[30]

Why would individuals be interested in investing in a new venture from which professional venture capitalists see no powerful payoff? It may be, of course, that the reduced investment amount reduces the total risk involved in the investment. However, informal investors seek other, nonfinancial returns, among them the creation of jobs in areas of high unemployment, development of technology for social needs (e.g., medical or energy),

---

[27] Harold M. Hoffman and James Blakey, "You Can Negotiate with Venture Capitalists," *Harvard Business Review* (March/April 1987): 16.

[28] William E. Wetzel Jr., "Informal Risk Capital: Knowns and Unknowns," in *The Art and Science of Entrepreneurship,* ed. Donald L. Sexton and Raymond W. Smilor (Cambridge, MA: Ballinger, 1986), 88.

[29] William E. Wetzel Jr., as quoted by Dale D. Buss, "Heaven Help Us," *Nation's Business* (November 1993): 29.

[30] William E. Wetzel Jr., "Angel Money," *In-Business* (November/December 1989): 44.

CONTEMPORARY ENTREPRENEURSHIP

Asking the Right Questions

There are a number of important questions that entrepreneurs should ask of venture capitalists. Here are seven of the most important along with their rationales.

1. Does the venture capital firm in fact invest in your industry? How many deals has the firm actually done in your field?

2. What is it like to work with this venture capital firm? Get references. (An unscreened list of referrals, including CEOs of companies that the firm has been successful with as well as those it has not, can be very helpful.)

3. What experience does the partner doing your deal have, and what is his or her clout within the firm? Check out the experiences of other entrepreneurs.

4. How much time will the partner spend with your company if you run into trouble? A seed-stage company should ask, "You guys are a big fund, and you say you can seed me a quarter

of a million dollars. How often will you be able to see me?" The answer should be at least once a week.

5. How healthy is the venture capital fund, and how much has been invested? A venture firm with a lot of troubled investments will not have much time to spare. If most of the fund is invested, there may not be much money available for your follow-on rounds.

6. Are the investment goals of the venture capitalists consistent with your own?

7. Have the venture firm and the partner championing your deal been through any economic downturns? A good venture capitalist won't panic when things get bad.

SOURCE: Reprinted from Marie-Jeanne Juilland, "What Do You Want from a Venture Capitalist?" 32, August 1987 issue of *Venture*, For Entrepreneurial Business Owners & Investors, by special permission. Copyright © 1987 Venture Magazine, Inc., 521 Fifth Ave., New York, NY 10175-0028.

---

urban revitalization, minority or disadvantaged assistance, and personal satisfaction from assisting entrepreneurs.[31]

How do informal investors find projects? Research studies indicate that they use a network of friends. Additionally, many states are formulating venture capital networks, which attempt to link informal investors with entrepreneurs and their new or growing ventures (see earlier Entrepreneurial Edge box).

The importance of understanding informal risk capital is illustrated by the fact that the pool of today's angel capital is 5 times the amount in the institutional venture capital market, providing money to 20 to 30 times as many companies. Angels invest more than

---

[31] William E. Wetzel Jr., "Angels and Informal Risk Capital," *Sloan Management Review* (summer 1983); see also John Freear, Jeffrey E. Sohl, and William E. Wetzel Jr., "Angels and Non-Angels: Are There Differences?" *Journal of Business Venturing* (March 1994): 109–23.

TABLE 14.10	"ANGEL STATS"	
Typical deal size	:	$250,000
Typical recipient	:	Start-up firms
Cash-out time frame	:	5 to 7 years
Expected return	:	35% to 50% a year
Ownership stake	:	Less than 50%

SOURCE: William E. Wetzel, University of New Hampshire's Center for Venture Research, as reported in *Small Business Reports* (April 1993): 39.

$10 billion a year in 30,000 to 40,000 companies nationwide, twice the amount of money and twice the number of companies ten years ago.[32]

Another important consideration for **angel capital** is that 60 percent of informal investment is devoted to seed a start-up business as opposed to 28 percent of venture capital. Of those initial deals, 82 percent were for less than $500,000 whereas only 13 percent of venture capital handled deals that small. The average size of an informal investment is $250,000, which indicates the importance of informal risk capital to entrepreneurs seeking small amounts of start-up financing.[33] (See Table 14.10 for some "Angel Stats.") Obviously, informal networks are a major potential capital source for entrepreneurs.

✳ SUMMARY

This chapter has examined the various forms of capital formation for entrepreneurs. Initial consideration was given to debt and equity financing in the form of commercial banks, trade credit, accounts receivable financing, factoring and finance companies, and various forms of equity instruments.

Public stock offerings have advantages and disadvantages as a source of equity capital. Although large amounts of money can be raised in short periods of time, the entrepreneur must sacrifice a degree of control and ownership. In addition, the Securities and Exchange Commission has myriad requirements and regulations that must be followed.

Private placements are an alternative means of raising equity capital for new ventures. This source is often available to entrepreneurs seeking venture capital in amounts under $500,000, although it is possible that up to $5 million could be raised with no more than 35 nonaccredited purchasers. The SEC's Regulation D clearly outlines the exemptions and requirements involved in a private placement. This placement's greatest advantage to the entrepreneur is limited company disclosure and only a small number of shareholders.

In recent years the venture capital market has grown dramatically. Billions of dollars are now invested annually to seed new ventures or help fledgling enterprises grow. The

---

[32] Dale D. Buss, "Heaven Help Us," *Nation's Business* (November 1993) 29–30; see also John Freear, Jeffrey E. Sohl, and William E. Wetzel Jr., "Angels: Personal Investors in the Venture Capital Market," *Entrepreneurship & Regional Development* 7 (1995): 85–94.

[33] Wetzel, "Angel Money," 42–44.

individuals who invest these funds are known as venture capitalists. A number of myths that have sprung up about these capitalists were discussed and refuted.

Venture capitalists use a number of different criteria when evaluating new-venture proposals. In the main these criteria focus on two areas: the entrepreneur and the investment potential of the venture. The evaluation process typically involves four stages: initial screening, business plan evaluation, oral presentation, and final evaluation.

In recent years informal risk capital has begun to play an important role in new-venture financing. Everyone with money to invest in new ventures can be considered a source for this type of capital. Some estimates put the informal risk capital pool at more than $5 billion. Entrepreneurs who are unable to secure financing through banks or through public or private stock offerings will typically turn to the informal risk capital market by seeking out friends, associates, and other contacts who may have (or know of someone who has) money to invest in a new venture.

Key Terms and Concepts

Accounts receivable financing	Finance companies
Accredited purchaser	Informal risk capitalists
Angel capital	Initial public offering (IPO)
Business angel	Private placements
Debt financing	Regulation D
Equity financing	Trade credit
Factoring	Venture capitalists

Review and Discussion Questions

1. Figure 14.1 shows that entrepreneurs prefer venture capital when getting started but five years later prefer to raise capital through public offerings. What is the logic behind this strategy?
2. What are the benefits and drawbacks of equity and of debt financing? Briefly discuss both.
3. Identify and describe four types of debt financing.
4. If a new venture has its choice between long-term debt and equity financing, which would you recommend? Why?
5. Why would a venture capitalist be more interested in buying a convertible debenture for $50,000 than in lending the new business $50,000 at a 10 percent interest rate?
6. What are some of the advantages of going public? What are some of the disadvantages?
7. Why do entrepreneurs look forward to the day when they can take their company public?
8. What is the objective of Regulation D?
9. If a person inherited $100,000 and decided to buy stock in a new venture through a private placement, how would Regulation D affect this investor?
10. How large is the venture capital pool today? Is it growing or shrinking?
11. Is it easier or more difficult to get new-venture financing today? Why?
12. Some entrepreneurs do not like to seek new-venture financing because they feel that venture capitalists are greedy. In your opinion, is this true? Do these capitalists want too much?
13. Identify and describe three objectives of venture capitalists.

14. How would a venture capitalist use Figure 14.2 to evaluate an investment? Use an illustration in your answer.
15. Identify and describe four of the most common criteria venture capitalists use to evaluate a proposal.
16. Of what practical value is Table 14.5 to new-venture entrepreneurs?
17. In a new-venture evaluation, what are the four stages through which a proposal typically goes? Describe each in detail.
18. An entrepreneur is in the process of contacting three different venture capitalists and asking each to evaluate her new business proposal. What questions should she be able to answer about each of the three?
19. An entrepreneur of a new venture has had no success in getting financing from formal venture capitalists. He now has decided to turn to the informal risk capital market. Who is in this market? How would you recommend the entrepreneur contact these individuals?
20. How likely is it that the informal risk capital market will grow during the next five years? Defend your answer.
21. Of all the sources of capital formation, which is ideal? Why?

Experiential Exercise   *Analyzing the Funding Sources*

For each funding source, write down what the text says about its usefulness for small firms. Then seek out and interview a representative of each source to find out the person's point of view of his or her relationship to small firms.

Source	What the Text Says	Source's Point of View
Banks		
Long-term loans		
Short-term loans		
Intermediate-term loans		
Private placement (Regulation D)		
Public offerings (IPO)		
Finance company		
Factor		
Trade credit		
State or local development companies		
Small Business Investment Company (SBIC)		
Informal risk capital (seed capital network)		
Venture capitalist		

 **CASE 14.1**

Looking for Capital

When Joyce and Phil Abrams opened their bookstore one year ago, they estimated it would take them six months to break even. Because they had gone into the venture with enough capital to keep them afloat for nine months, they were sure they would need no outside financing. However, sales have been slower than anticipated, and most of their funds now have been used to purchase inventory or meet monthly expenses. On the other hand, the store is doing better each month, and the Abramses are convinced they will be able to turn a profit within six months.

At present, Joyce and Phil want to secure additional financing. Specifically, they would like to raise $100,000 to expand their product line. The store currently focuses most heavily on how-to-do-it books and is developing a loyal customer following. However, this market is not large enough to carry the business. The Abramses feel that if they expand into an additional market such as cookbooks, they can develop two market segments that, when combined, would prove profitable. Joyce is convinced that cookbooks are an important niche, and she has saved a number of clippings from national newspapers and magazines reporting that people who buy cookbooks tend to spend more money per month on these purchases than does the average book buyer. Additionally, customer loyalty among this group tends to be very high.

The Abramses own all of their inventory, which has a retail market value of $280,000. The merchandise cost them $140,000. They also have at a local bank a line of credit of $10,000, of which they have used $4,000. Most of their monthly expenses are covered out of the initial capital with which they started the business ($180,000 in all). However, they will be out of money in three months if they are not to get additional funding.

The owners have considered investigating a number of sources. The two primary ones are a loan from their bank and a private stock offering to investors. They know nothing about how to raise money, and these are only general ideas they have been discussing with each other. However, they do have a meeting scheduled with their accountant, a friend, who they hope can advise them on how to raise more capital. For the moment, the Abramses are focusing on writing a business plan that spells out their short business history and objectives and explains how much money they would like to raise and where it would be invested. They hope to have the plan completed before the end of the week and take it with them to the accountant. The biggest problem they are having in writing the plan is that they are unsure of how to direct their presentation. Should they aim it at a banker or a venture capitalist? After their meeting with the accountant, they plan to refine the plan and direct it toward the appropriate source.

Questions

1. Would a commercial banker be willing to lend money to the Abramses? How much? On what do you base your answer?
2. Would this venture have any appeal for a venture capitalist? Why or why not?
3. If you were advising the Abramses, how would you recommend they seek additional capital? Be complete in your answer.

 **CASE** **14.2**

The $3 Million Venture

The Friendly Market is a large supermarket located in a city in the Southwest. "Friendly's," as it is popularly known, has more sales per square foot than any of its competitors because it lives up to its name. The personnel go out of their way to be friendly and helpful. If someone asks for a particular brand-name item and the store does not carry it, the product will be ordered. If enough customers want a particular product, it is added to the regular line. Additionally, the store provides free delivery of groceries for senior citizens, check-cashing privileges for its regular customers, and credit for those who have filled out the necessary application and have been accepted into the "Friendly Credit" group.

The owner, Charles Beavent, believes that his marketing-oriented approach can be successfully used in any area of the country. He is therefore thinking about expanding and opening two new stores, one in the northern part of the city and the other in a city located 50 miles east. Locations have been scouted, and a detailed business plan has been drawn up. However, Charles has not approached anyone about providing the necessary capital. He estimates he will need about $3 million to get both stores up and going. Any additional funding can come from the current operation, which throws off a cash flow of about $100,000 monthly.

Charles feels two avenues are available to him: debt and equity. His local banker has told him the bank would be willing to look over any business plan he submits and would give him an answer within five working days. Charles is convinced he can get the bank to lend him $3 million. However, he does not like the idea of owing that much money. He believes he would be better off selling stock to raise the needed capital. Doing so would require him to give up some ownership, but this is more agreeable to him than the alternative.

The big question now is How can the company raise $3 million through a stock offering? Charles intends to check into this over the next four weeks and make a decision within eight weeks. A number of customers have approached him over the past year and have asked him if he would consider making a private stock offering. Charles is convinced he can get many of his customers to buy into the venture, although he is not sure he can raise the full $3 million this way. The other approach he sees as feasible is to raise the funds through a venture capital company. This might be the best way to get such a large sum, but Charles wonders how difficult it would be to work with these people on a long-term basis. In any event, as he said to his wife yesterday, "If we're going to expand, we have to start looking into how we can raise more capital. I think the first step is to identify the best source. Then we can focus on the specifics of the deal."

Questions

1. What would be the benefits of raising the $3 million through a private placement? What would be the benefits of raising the money through a venture capitalist?
2. Of these two approaches, which would be best for Charles? Why?
3. What would you recommend Charles do now? Briefly outline a plan of action he can use to get the financing process started.

PART 4

ENTREPRENEURIAL CASE ANALYSIS

The Playboy Emblem: A Case of Trademark Infringement

The Letter

On August 26, 1982, a disturbing and almost unbelievable letter arrived certified mail (return receipt requested) at the tavern. The letter to John P. Browne stated:

Re: RABBIT HEAD Design Trademark Infringement—Bunny's Tavern, Brookfield, Illinois

Gentlemen:

It has been brought to our attention that Bunny's Tavern has painted on the outside wall of its establishment a rabbit head design virtually identical to our company's RABBIT HEAD Design trademark. The RABBIT HEAD Design is a trademark owned by Playboy Enterprises, Inc., and Bunny's unauthorized use of our mark constitutes trademark infringement and unfair competition. Bunny's continued use of our mark is likely to cause confusion to the general public, in that the public could consider Bunny's Tavern as being in some way sponsored by or otherwise associated with our company.

Unless Bunny's Tavern immediately and permanently ceases and desists its unauthorized use of our company's RABBIT HEAD Design trademark or any other mark or design similar thereto owned by or associated with our company within ten days of the date of this letter, we will recommend to management that legal action be taken against it to protect our company's rights.

Should Bunny's Tavern wish to avoid the possibility of future unpleasantness and the needless expense of litigation, please have an authorized

representative sign, date, and return the enclosed copy of this letter. Such signature will evidence Bunny's agreement to settle this matter according to the terms of this letter.

Should Bunny's Tavern continue its unauthorized use of our company's mark, it does so at its own risk.

Very truly yours,

PLAYBOY ENTERPRISES, INC.

Harriet E. Earle
Trademarks Coordinator

Background: John P. Browne and His Tavern

In November 1948 John P. Browne opened a neighborhood tavern of modest means. Located on 47th Street in Brookfield, Illinois (a western suburb of Chicago), the small building provided a room with 16 bar stools and no tables. A few arcade games (bowling and pinball) were available for entertainment of the clientele.

For over 34 years the tavern operated successfully (by standards of a lifestyle venture, that is, John P. Browne was able to make a profit and provide for his family). The customers were local neighborhood friends and workers from the surrounding factories located down the street (e.g., Electro-Motive and Materials Service). The clientele was loyal, and a strong rapport was established through the years with owner/operator John P. Browne and his customers,

SOURCE: This case was prepared by Dr. Donald F. Kuratko, College of Business, Ball State University, and is intended to be used as a basis for class discussion. Presented and accepted by the refereed Midwest Society for Case Research Workshop, 1986. All rights reserved to the author and to the Midwest Society for Case Research. Copyright © 1986 by Donald F. Kuratko.

since he handled most of the bartending duties himself. In his later years his father, Patrick J., also bartended, which provided the clientele with a family influence on the Browne establishment.

Throughout the continuous operation of this tavern business and loyal development of the clientele, John P. Browne became a well-liked and well-respected businessman in the local community. The Brookfield community (now with a population of 21,000) knew the purpose of his business and his clientele, which was to provide a local gathering spot for beer and alcohol consumption combined with a neighborhood atmosphere.

John P. Browne is known by all as "Bunny Browne" and has been all of his life. Sixty-three years ago a nurse in a Chicago hospital coined the nickname when she thought he was as "cute as a bunny." The nickname remained through his early years, and when John developed into a lightweight boxer in the Chicago area "Golden Gloves," the nickname characterized his bouncing style in the ring.

Thus, it was only fitting that John use his popular name for his neighborhood establishment in 1948. Therefore, "Bunny" Browne's Tap was named officially.

The Rabbit Head Emblem

The idea of painting an emblem on the side of Bunny Browne's tavern was conceived five years after the tavern opened. In 1954, one of the tavern's patrons, Joe Karasek, developed the idea as a gesture of friendship and gratitude to his friend Bunny Browne.

After discussing various caricatures that could be painted on the wall, both Bunny Browne and Joe Karasek agreed that a simple rabbit's head would be the easiest to distinguish from a distance and would clearly represent the nickname "Bunny."

Thus, in the summer of 1954 Joe began his task of painting the east side of the tavern black and then drawing the rabbit's head in white (see Figure 1).

Note: Playboy Enterprises developed its rabbit head design in 1953. It was designed by Arthur Paul, and it has stood for over 40 years as the Playboy symbol. In addition, Playboy had its emblem registered as a trademark that same year—1953. Thus, it became a protected property item of the Playboy domain (see Figure 2).

FIGURE 1

FIGURE 2

Bunny's Response

Bunny Browne was astounded that Playboy would ever consider his emblem any type of threat to its powerful sexual domain, especially considering that his type of tavern could never be misconstrued as a copy, replica, or even a poor imitation of the Playboy Clubs. Thus, how could a sole proprietor of a small local tavern in existence before Playboy started its empire in 1953 be guilty of "unfair competition" through a trademark infringement?

"I thought it was a joke," Bunny Browne said. "After all, it has been up there for nearly 30 years, and I am unaware of anyone ever having confused my establishment with the Playboy Club."

According to Bunny, he himself has never owned a copy of *Playboy* magazine, and, noting that at age 63 he is often the youngest person in the bar, his clientele wouldn't have any use for *that* kind of bunny. "Basically, I feel I'm absolutely no threat to their organization. They are simply nitpicking!" Bunny stated.

It seemed appropriate that a letter of clarification to Playboy's chief executive officer—Christine Hefner—would be the simplest approach. Surely there was a misunderstanding of Bunny Browne's tavern and once Christine Hefner understood, there would probably be no further action.

The return letter from Bunny Browne to Christine Hefner was sent on September 3, 1982. It read:

Dear Ms. Hefner:

Enclosed is a copy of a letter I received by certified mail from the office of your general counsel. As you see, it is addressed to Bunny's Tavern and says that my modest tavern, place of business, is guilty of unfair competition, and the use of a rather tired-looking emblem I have on the side wall could confuse the public, and cause the public to believe that my little tavern is associated with Playboy Enterprises, Inc.

In a way it is flattering to be considered a competitor of a giant enterprise, but it is disturbing to read the reference to expensive litigation and unpleasantness.

When you read what is involved (and I hope you will be given this letter), you too may feel that your lawyer's letter does not express your feeling and does not reflect favorably on Playboy Enterprises.

I was first called Bunny by a nurse in the hospital where I was born over 63 years ago. I have been known as Bunny all of my life. I have lived my life in Brookfield (pop. 21,000) and very few of the people in the village know me as John. I began my business as Bunny's in November 1948 and have operated it continuously since that time. My tavern is not large (16 stools and no tables). My trade is from Brookfield and the surrounding neighborhood. The emblem of Bunny has been on the wall since the 1950s. It is inconceivable that anyone would confuse my emblem and tavern with the Playboy Club. My patrons and the people of Brookfield would, I know, be astonished to learn of Playboy's fears and I am sure would be upset to learn that I have fears of future unpleasantness and expensive litigation.

Ms. Hefner, I hope you will inform me that you consider the action of your lawyers to be unnecessary and in this case not in the best interest of Playboy.

Sincerely,

John P. Browne
Bunny's Tavern
9536 W. 47th Street
Brookfield, Illinois 60513

Playboy's Response

The letter from John "Bunny" Browne did apparently reach Christine Hefner and, through her counsel Howard Shapiro, she replied in a letter dated September 13, 1982. It read:

Dear Mr. Browne:

Christine Hefner has asked me to reply to your letter to her of September 3, 1982.

Although our "Bunny" is not quite as old as you, we take quite a paternal interest in protecting it. Since 1953, when it was created for Playboy by Arthur Paul, it has become a symbol of our company and like an overprotective parent, we have gone to great lengths to keep it from harm.

It seems that a lot of our readers are also very protective of our Rabbit Head Design mark. Several of them, evidently, drove past your tavern and contacted us to inquire why our mark was on the side of your building. This is how your establishment came to our attention. It's obvious from this contact that people saw your "tired-looking personal emblem'' and thought of our company, and it is for this reason that Ms. Earle sent her letter.

It's obvious that you have a lot of pride in your tavern and in your reputation in the community. If someone else moved into your community, opened a tavern and utilized the name ''Bunny's,'' we would hope that you would feel that something that belonged to you was being taken away, just as we feel that the use of a Rabbit Head Design on the side of your building is taking something away from us.

Litigation is expensive and we have no desire to go that route unless it becomes absolutely necessary. It sounds as if this whole thing can be solved by a coat of paint rather than by lawyers and legal fees. If it's acceptable to you, we'd be willing to close our file on this matter on your representation that at some point within the next three to six months, your ''tired-looking personal emblem'' will be replaced with something that not only you can be proud of but we will be happy with too.

If this is acceptable to you, please sign a copy of this letter and return it to me.

Very truly yours,

PLAYBOY ENTERPRISES, INC.

Howard Shapiro

The Media Reaction

The case of Bunny Browne's problem with Playboy spread throughout the community of Brookfield, the surrounding suburbs, and finally into Chicago. The newspapers reviewed the disagreement as a simple ''attack'' by big business against the ''little guy.'' Articles quickly appeared in the local newspaper, and eventually editorials appeared by noted columnists Art Petacque and Hugh Hough of the *Chicago Sun-Times* and Mike Royko of the *Chicago Tribune*. (See excerpts here.)

Splitting Hares: Bunny's Tavern, a neighborhood bar in west suburban Brookfield, has never been mistaken for a Playboy Club by its beer-quaffing customers. But that didn't stop Playboy Enterprises from threatening legal action against the bar's owner, John P. ''Bunny'' Browne. (Petacque & Hough—*Chicago Sun-Times*)

There was a duel between Playboy Enterprises and a neighborhood tavern in Brookfield called Bunny's.

For three decades, the Bunny's tavern had a big painting of a rabbit head on the side of its building.

Then Playboy decided that the tavern's rabbit looked too much like Playboy's rabbit symbol and threatened to sue.

It seemed unfair, because the tavern sells booze, not Hefner's kinky fantasies. . . . (Royko—*Chicago Tribune*)

By October 1982 the news had traveled as far as Natchez, Mississippi, where Bunny Browne had friends and acquaintances in the likes of Ben Chase Callun and Mayor Tony Byrne. After years of visits, Bunny Browne was fondly dubbed an ''honorary citizen'' of Natchez. Thus, the Natchez paper carried an article concerning Playboy's squabble over Bunny's emblem.

It wasn't long before the local television stations sent their Minicams to film the tavern and interview Bunny over this incident with Playboy. While the television interviews were brief spots on the evening news, the interest in this little tavern in Brookfield, Illinois, was astounding.

Visitors came from all over the city and suburbs just to see this tavern and its rabbit head emblem that was upsetting Playboy Enterprises. To have a beer at Bunny's became something of a vogue—at least for a brief period of interest and curiosity.

Bunny's Dilemma

The fanfare subsided in a few weeks, and Bunny Browne's Tap returned to its normal routine and loyal clientele. They, being proud of Bunny's Tap in addition to being loyal, encouraged Bunny to take a stand against Playboy. ''Let's fight 'em all the way, Bunny!'' they shouted. Bunny retorted, ''Maybe I'll have to get in the ring and box with Playboy's best— like the old Golden Gloves days!'' The bar cheered and toasted Bunny.

But the reality Bunny Browne faced was a different dilemma from the old Golden Gloves days—and he knew it. As he closed up the tavern on this late

November evening, Bunny pondered about his rabbit head emblem that had for 30 years been a "friend" and now seemed to be the center of so much controversy. The now badly peeling painting had never been touched up in all those years. Bunny thought to himself that it never would be touched up if Playboy would simply let it fade away. Bunny said with an Irish grin, "I wish Playboy would just let my rabbit die a natural death—the way I'm doing." As he turned off the tavern lights, Bunny knew he must decide what to do.

Questions

1. If you were Bunny Browne, what exactly would you do? Why?

2. Explain what a trademark is and what rights it provides the owner.

3. Apply the "unfair competition" idea of trademark infringement to this case.

4. Do alternative solutions exist for Bunny Browne's tavern? If so, what are they?

5. What must a small business do to avoid infringing on the trademark rights of someone else?

6. Discuss the implications for Playboy Enterprises of pressuring a small business.

7. What lessons can be learned from Bunny Browne's situation?

8. Discuss the pros and cons of Bunny's decision (based on what you have recommended in question 1).

GROWTH AND DEVELOPMENT OF ENTREPRENEURIAL VENTURES

$\mathcal{S}$TRATEGIC PLANNING FOR EMERGING VENTURES

CHAPTER OBJECTIVES

1. To introduce the importance of planning for an entrepreneurial venture

2. To discuss the nature of strategic planning

3. To examine the key dimensions that influence a firm's planning process

4. To discuss some of the reasons why entrepreneurs do not carry out strategic planning

5. To relate some of the benefits of strategic planning

6. To examine four of the most common approaches entrepreneurs use to implement a strategic plan

7. To review the nature of operational planning for a venture

I have often heard it said that big companies, the corporate giants, are the ones that need to think about their business strategically. Smaller, more entrepreneurial companies, by contrast, do not need strategy; they can pursue other routes to business success. In my view, that is exactly backward. Unlike the giants, small businesses cannot rely on the inertia of the marketplace for their survival. Nor can they succeed on brute force, throwing resources at problems. On the contrary, they have to see their competitive environment with particular clarity, and they have to stake out and protect a position they can defend. That is what strategy is all about.

Michael E. Porter,
Inc., September 1991

THE NATURE OF PLANNING IN EMERGING FIRMS

Although most entrepreneurs do some form of planning for their ventures, it often tends to be informal and unsystematic.[1] The actual need for systematic planning will vary with the nature, size, and structure of the business. In other words, a small two-person operation may successfully use informal planning because little complexity is involved. But an emerging venture that is rapidly expanding with constantly increasing personnel size and market operations will need to formalize its planning because a great deal of complexity exists.

An entrepreneur's planning will need to shift from an informal to a formal systematic style for other reasons. First is the degree of uncertainty with which the venture is attempting to become established and to grow. With greater levels of uncertainty, entrepreneurs have a stronger need to deal with the challenges facing their venture, and a more formal planning effort can help them to do this. Second, the strength of the competition (in both numbers and quality of competitors) will add to the importance of more systematic planning in order for a new venture to monitor its operations and objectives more closely.[2] Finally, the amount and type of experience the entrepreneur has may be a factor in deciding the extent of formal planning. A lack of adequate experience, either technological or

[1] Douglas W. Naffziger and Donald F. Kuratko, "An Investigation into the Prevalence of Planning in Small Business," *Journal of Business and Entrepreneurship* (October 1991); see also Amar Bhide, "How Entrepreneurs Craft Strategies That Work," *Harvard Business Review* (March/April 1994): 150–61.

[2] Radha Chagnati, Rajeswararo Chagnati, and Vijay Mahajan, "Profitable Small Business Strategies under Different Types of Competition," *Entrepreneurship Theory and Practice* (spring 1989): 21–36.

465

business, may constrain the entrepreneur's understanding and thus necessitate formal planning to help determine future paths for the organization.

Formal planning is usually divided into two major types: strategic and operational. We shall begin by examining the nature of strategic planning, and then we will discuss operational planning.

STRATEGIC PLANNING

Strategic planning is the formulation of long-range plans for the effective management of environmental opportunities and threats in light of a venture's strengths and weaknesses. It includes defining the venture's mission, specifying achievable objectives, developing strategies, and setting policy guidelines.[3] Thus, strategic planning is the primary step in determining the future direction of a business. The "best" strategic plan will be influenced by many factors, among them the abilities of the entrepreneur, the complexity of the venture, and the nature of the industry. Yet, whatever the specific situation, five basic steps must be followed in strategic planning:

1. Examine the internal and external environments of the venture (strengths, weaknesses, opportunities, threats).

2. Formulate the venture's long-range and short-range strategies (mission, objectives, strategies, policies).

3. Implement the strategic plan (programs, budgets, procedures).

4. Evaluate the performance of the strategy.

5. Take follow-up action through continuous feedback.

(Figure 15.1 illustrates these basic steps in a flow diagram.)

The first step—examining the environment—can be one of the most critical for an emerging venture. A clear review of a venture's internal and external factors is needed, and both sets of factors must be considered when performing an environmental analysis. This analysis is often called a **SWOT analysis;** *SWOT* is an acronym for a venture's internal *s*trengths and *w*eaknesses and its external *o*pportunities and *t*hreats. The analysis should include not only the external factors most likely to occur and to have a serious impact on the company but also the internal factors most likely to affect the implementation of present and future strategic decisions. By focusing on this analysis, an emerging venture can proceed through the other steps of formulation, implementation, evaluation, and feedback.

It should be remembered that the greatest value of the strategic planning process is the "strategic thinking" it promotes among business owners. Although not always articulated formally, strategic thinking synthesizes the intuition and creativity of an entrepreneur into a vision for the future.[4]

This chapter now examines the different aspects of strategic planning for emerging ventures.

---

[3] See Thomas L. Wheelen and J. David Hunger, *Strategic Management and Business Policy,* 4th ed. (Reading, MA: Addison-Wesley, 1992); see also Michael A. Hitt, R. Duane Ireland, and Robert E. Hoskisson, *Strategic Management: Competitiveness and Globalization,* 2d ed. (St. Paul, MN: West, 1997).

[4] Henry Mintzberg, "The Fall and Rise of Strategic Planning," *Harvard Business Review* (January/February 1994): 107–14.

FIGURE 15.1 STRATEGIC MANAGEMENT MODEL

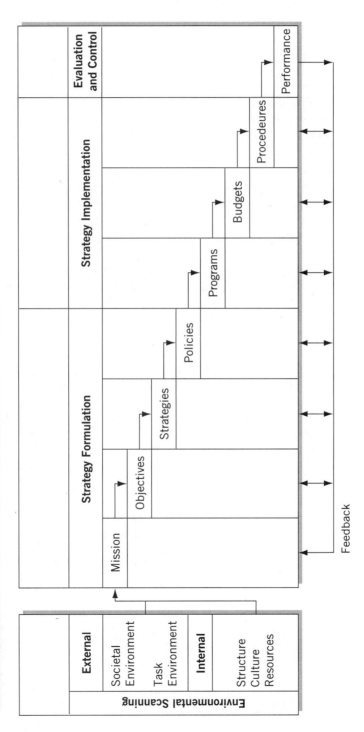

SOURCE: Thomas L. Wheelen and J. David Hunger, *Strategic Management and Business Policy*, 4th ed. (Reading, MA: Addison-Wesley, 1992), 13.

Key Dimensions Influencing a Firm's Strategic Planning Activities

Five factors shape the strategic management activities of growing companies: (1) demand on strategic managers' time, (2) decision-making speed, (3) problems of internal politics, (4) environmental uncertainty, and (5) the entrepreneur's vision.

DEMAND ON STRATEGIC MANAGERS' TIME   The increasing demand on key owner-managers' time that accompanies the complexity brought on by growth of the entrepreneurial firm brings about a need for more rigorous strategic management practices. This logically appealing proposition has been offered in the past by many researchers. From their perspective, increased strategic planning activity provides the means to accommodate owner-managers' needs to maintain control and direction of the enterprise, while giving up some activities in recognition of increased time pressures.

DECISION-MAKING SPEED   As the firm expands, the decisions to be made can be expected to increase both in number and frequency. These pressures are referred to as "delegation demands" on the growing firm's management. More systematic strategic planning practices are needed for entrepreneurs to guide and control the increasing decision making within the firm.

PROBLEMS OF INTERNAL POLITICS   Strategic planning practices are seen as one way to alleviate difficulties associated with the dysfunctional effects of internal politics on organizational decision making. By providing a formal process by which to channel partisan organizational priorities, strategic planning helps to control the politics that emerge as an entrepreneurial firm grows and develops organizational power seekers.

ENVIRONMENTAL UNCERTAINTY   Research has suggested that the need for strategic planning is greater in the presence of increased environmental uncertainty. Thus, it appears likely that environmental uncertainty is a key factor influencing the strategic management activities of entrepreneurial firms with an increasingly life-cycle-diverse product and market base.[5]

THE ENTREPRENEUR'S VISION   To a large degree, venture planning is an extension of the entrepreneurial ego. Planning is the process of transforming entrepreneurial vision and ideas into action. This process involves three basic steps:

Step 1: Commitment to an open planning process. Many entrepreneurs are suspicious of planning. They fear the loss of control and of flexibility. Quite often this fear is the chief obstacle to future success because it blinds the entrepreneur to the ideas of other knowledgeable people. This, in turn, closes the door on new ideas and greatly limits the benefits associated with an open planning process.

Step 2: Accountability to a corporate conscience. This often takes the form of an advisory board, which is a highly effective form of corporate conscience. It can substantially enhance the functioning of entrepreneurial ego. This committee differs from a board of directors by its lack of legal standing and the fact its primary objectives are to

---

[5] Richard B. Robinson Jr. and John A. Pearce II, "Product Life-Cycle Considerations and the Nature of Strategic Activities in Entrepreneurial Firms," *Journal of Business Venturing* (spring 1986): 207–24; see also Charles H. Matthews and Susanne G. Scott, "Uncertainty and Planning in Small and Entrepreneurial Firms: An Empirical Assessment," *Journal of Small Business Management* (October 1995): 34–52.

(1) increase the owner's sensitivity to larger issues of direction and (2) make the owner accountable, albeit on a voluntary basis.

Step 3: Establishment of a pattern of subordinate participation in the development of the strategic plan. The planning process can create organizational energy, especially if key members of the organization are instrumental in creating it. Interviews with key subordinates have revealed that the absence of the organizational and personal guideposts needed to chart and monitor a successful course of executive action tend to result in little support for the plan.[6]

These three steps may seem obvious to any entrepreneur attempting to translate his or her vision into a planning process. The fact remains, however, that such planning is too often lacking in many new small ventures.

THE LACK OF STRATEGIC PLANNING

The importance of new ventures to the economy is substantial in terms of innovation, employment, and sales, and effective planning can help these new firms survive and grow. Unfortunately, research has shown a distinct lack of planning on the part of new ventures. Five reasons for the lack of strategic planning have been found:

1. **Time scarcity.** Managers report that their time is scarce and difficult to allocate to planning in the face of day-to-day operating problems.

2. **Lack of knowledge.** Small firm owners/managers have minimal exposure to, and knowledge of, the planning process. They are uncertain of the components of the process and the sequence of those components. The entrepreneurs are also unfamiliar with many planning information sources and how they can be used.

3. **Lack of expertise/skills.** Small-business managers typically are generalists, and they often lack the specialized expertise necessary for the planning process.

4. **Lack of trust and openness.** Small firm owners/managers are highly sensitive and guarded about their businesses and the decisions that affect them. Consequently, they are hesitant to formulate a strategic plan that requires participation by employees or outside consultants.

5. **Perception of high cost.** Small-business owners perceive the cost associated with planning to be very high. This fear of expensive planning causes many business owners to avoid or ignore planning as a viable process.[7]

In addition to these reasons, other factors have been reported as difficulties of the planning process (see Table 15.1). For example, both high-performing and low-performing small ventures have problems with long-range planning. Both time and expense are major obstacles. Additionally, low-performing firms also report that a poor planning climate, inexperienced managers, and unfavorable economic conditions are problems.

---

[6] Richard L. Osborne, "Planning: The Entrepreneurial Ego at Work," *Business Horizons* (January/February 1987): 20–24.

[7] Richard B. Robinson Jr. and John A. Pearce II, "Research Thrusts in Small Firm Strategic Planning," *Academy of Management Review* (January 1984): 129; and Charles B. Shrader, Charles L. Mumford, and Virginia L. Blackburn, "Strategic and Operational Planning, Uncertainty, and Performance in Small Firms," *Journal of Small Business Management* (October 1989): 52.

TABLE 15.1   PERCEIVED DIFFICULTIES OF LONG-RANGE PLANNING

Difficulty	High-Performing Firms	Low-Performing Firms
Inadequately defined objectives	18%	25%
Securing commitment from employees	10	15
Insufficient time for planning	61	70
Generating enough alternatives	25	30
Unpredictable political environment	15	16
Coordinating the planning process	30	38
Unfavorable economic situation	31	40
Testing initial planning assumptions	16	19
Insufficient subordinate participation	32	39
Poor planning climate	10	29
Too expensive to do properly	66	71
Obtaining trustworthy data	16	16
Inexperienced managers	18	31

SOURCE: Christopher Orpen, "The Effects of Long-Range Planning on Small Business Performance: A Further Examination," *Journal of Small Business Management* (January 1985): 23.

Quite obviously, strategic planning is no easy chore for new ventures. On the other hand, many benefits can be gained from such planning.

THE VALUE OF STRATEGIC PLANNING

Does strategic planning pay off? Research shows it does. In one study in which the effects of planning on performance were examined, it was found that the extent of long-range planning was unrelated to company performance whether assessed by sales growth or by return on assets. However, when other factors, such as structure, attitude toward planning, implementation, time horizon, and the content of the planning were taken into consideration, the data strongly suggested that the smaller firms that performed financially better did a more thorough job in the planning process.[8] Although the time spent on planning may not have been apparent, the quality of planning was.

In another study, 357 Texas ventures were investigated.[9] Although only a minority of these firms reported engaging in detailed strategic planning, a large number did use some form of planning. The researchers were able to establish a five-level planning classification.

[8] Christopher Orpen, "The Effects of Long-Range Planning on Small Business Performance: A Further Examination," *Journal of Small Business Management* (January 1985): 16–23.

[9] Donald L. Sexton and Philip Van Auken, "A Longitudinal Study of Small Business Strategic Planning," *Journal of Small Business Management* (January 1985): 8.

CONTEMPORARY ENTREPRENEURSHIP

Mastering Competitive Intelligence

In general terms, competitive intelligence is defined as anything that could provide a competitive advantage. It is important for companies to learn competitors' information (and sometimes secrets) while protecting their own. Competitive intelligence can help a company in many ways, including the anticipation of a competitor's next move, learning from a competitor's successes and failures, and identifying new opportunities.

Planning is critical for competitive intelligence, which requires three strategic approaches:

1. Collecting readily available information through databases, trade journals, and public documents
2. Researching facts buried in secondary sources, which can include details on equipment and zoning
3. Gleaning secrets from intermediate sources, such as professionals, trade organizations, or a salesperson from a supplier within the industry

In the latter of the three approaches, entrepreneurs must think of three things when conducting an interview: offense, defense, and victory. They must think offensively when identifying competitor vulnerability, when exposing potential opportunities, and when assessing the impact their strategic actions might make on competitors. They must think defensively when identifying competitors' technological development, distribution channels, marketing tactics, and financial information. Finally, they must fight for victory by using the competitive intelligence they've gathered, ranking the competition, and preparing an attacking strategy.

When entrepreneurs choose a competitive intelligence methodology, information services should be their weapons. Appropriate on-line and hard-copy resources will require a focus with allowable time to process needed information. Professional consultants and/or the Society of Competitive Intelligence Professionals should be hired/contacted when help becomes necessary.

Access to competitive intelligence information can be found in numerous systems and forms. On-line databases will include information such as text articles or abstracts from journals, newspapers, and magazines. A few databases are Nexis, ABI Inform, and Dialog. *The Wall Street Transcript, Value Line,* and *Gales Encyclopedia of Associates* are examples of hard-copy resources. Finally, other agencies (federal) and services that will aid in competitive intelligence information gathering include organizations like the National Technical Information Services (NTIS), National Trade Data Bank CD-ROM, and the Broadcast Information Service reports.

On-line databases and the other resources listed are available by subscription but are often free in public and college business libraries.

SOURCE: Edward Parker, "The Spy Fighters," *Success,* April 1994, 33–39.

- *Strategy Level 0 (SL0):* no knowledge (predictive ability) of next year's sales, profitability, or profit implementation plans
- *Strategy Level 1 (SL1):* knowledge only of next year's sales, but no knowledge of upcoming industry sales, company profit, or profit implementation plans
- *Strategy Level 2 (SL2):* knowledge of next year's company and industry sales, but no knowledge of company profit or profit implementation plans
- *Strategy Level 3 (SL3):* knowledge of company and industry sales and anticipated profit, but no profit implementation plans
- *Strategy Level 4 (SL4):* knowledge of next year's company and industry sales, anticipated company profits, and profit implementation plans

When following this sample two years later, the researchers found that 20 percent of the firms that had no strategic planning (SL0) failed, while the same was true for only 8 percent of SL4 firms. The findings indicate a link between a small venture's success over time and its strategic planning. Yet the lack of strategic planning among small firms was prevalent in the early 1980s. Sexton and van Auken stated, "Strategic planning appears to be a scarce, fragile commodity in the small business environment. Most small firms do not engage in true strategic planning at all, and the rest may do so only sporadically or temporarily, despite the evidence that strategic planning can help firms to survive and prosper.[10]

However, other researchers have found planning among small firms increasing. Ackelsburg and Arlow, in a study of 732 U.S. firms, found that most of the small businesses did plan and that planning firms engaged in more goal-setting activities, forecasting, and other planning procedures than nonplanners.[11] Shuman, Shaw, and Sussman surveyed the planning practices of the *Inc.* 500 and found that a majority of the entrepreneurs did not have a business plan when they started their firms but as the firms grew the planning process became more prevalent and formalized.[12] CEO attitudes toward the impact of planning influenced the prevalence of strategic planning activities of this group. Seventy-two percent of the *Inc.* 500 CEOs surveyed perceived that planning leads to better decisions that in turn lead to increased profitability. The CEOs also believed that planning leads to increased time efficiency, company growth, and knowledge of the market.

A number of other studies have focused on the impact of planning on small firms.[13] These studies support the contention that strategic planning is of value to a venture. Most of the studies imply, if they do not directly state, that planning influences a venture's survival. As noted in Robinson and Pearce's study, a number of researchers found planning to be an important criterion for differentiating successful from unsuccessful firms.[14] In another study of 70,000 failed firms, lack of planning was identified as a major cause of failure,[15] and another investigation demonstrated that firms engaged in strategic planning outperformed those that were not.[16]

---

[10] Ibid., 15.

[11] Robert Ackelsburg and Peter Arlow, "Small Businesses Do Plan and It Pays Off," *Long Range Planning* (October 1985): 61–67.

[12] Jeffrey C. Shuman, John J. Shaw, and Gerald Sussman, "Strategic Planning in Smaller Rapid Growth Companies," *Long Range Planning* (December 1985): 48–53.

[13] Robinson and Pearce, "Research Thrusts," 132–33.

[14] Ibid.

[15] "The Business Failure Record," *Dun & Bradstreet,* 1995.

[16] Richard B. Robinson, "The Importance of Outsiders in Small Firm Strategic Planning," *Academy of Management Journal* (March 1982): 80–93.

CONTEMPORARY ENTREPRENEURSHIP

Objections to Planning

Dr. John L. Ward of Loyola University is one of the leading authorities on family business. He stresses the critical importance of strategic planning for growing firms that desire to continue through future generations. However, business owners have continual "objections" to the planning process. Here are some of those objections with responses to each.

Objection	Response
Planning is a "straitjacket" that limits flexibility.	Planning expands options and the ability to respond to change.
Too many uncertainties make planning impossible.	Planning generates more information and reduces uncertainty through better understanding.
Planning requires sharing sensitive information with others.	Planning motivates, increases the ability of the organization to understand how the business performs, and reduces unconstructive guessing as to what is going on.
Planning makes owners "go public" with ideas and prohibits them from changing their mind.	Planning allows others to better understand the need for change; "going public" increases the organization's ability to reach its goals.
Planning implies change from the comfortable (and successful) to the uncomfortable (and unknown).	Planning anticipates inevitable change and better implements required change.
Planning often increases "focus" on certain markets at the expense of a broader strategy.	Planning helps conserve valuable resources.
Planning suggests changes that may "cannibalize" past success.	Planning suggests options to minimize that possibility while encouraging the business to compete.
Planning identifies changes that require moving managers beyond their current skills; therefore, it increases their dependence on others who can contribute or teach those skills.	Planning helps perpetuate the institution beyond the lives of key managers.
Planning challenges business assumptions that contribute to clarity, consistency, and effectiveness.	Planning confirms many assumptions while addressing those that must change with the times.

SOURCE: Adapted from John L. Ward, *Keeping the Family Business Healthy* (San Francisco: Jossey-Bass Inc., 1987), 5–6. Adapted with permission.

TABLE 15.2	REPORTED BENEFITS OF LONG-RANGE PLANNING	
	High-Performance Firms	**Low-Performance Firms**
Cost savings	52%	50%
More efficient resource allocation	66	51
Improved competitive position	64	49
More timely information	42	31
More accurate forecasts	76	70
Better employee morale	31	32
Ability to explore alternatives	72	47
Reduced feelings of uncertainty	42	30
Faster decision making	49	46
Fewer cash-flow problems	36	30
Increased sales	65	50

SOURCE: Adapted from Christopher Orpen, "The Effects of Long-Range Planning on Small Business Performance: A Further Examination," *Journal of Small Business Management* (January 1985): 22.

In a more recent study of 220 small firms, Ibrahim established the importance of selecting an appropriate strategy (niche strategy) for a venture to build distinctive competence and a sustainable competitive advantage.[17] Another researcher, Mosakowski, examined the dynamic effects of strategies on company performance in the software industry. Her findings showed that when focus or differentiation strategies were established, performance by those firms was enhanced.[18]

One study tallied the benefits realized from long-range planning (see Table 15.2). In examining the responses from both high-performing firms and low-performing firms, researchers found a number of interesting similarities and differences. Both types of firms recognized cost savings, accurate forecasting, and faster decision making as a result of long-range planning. However, the high-performing firms also reported better resource allocation, an improvement of competitive position, a more thorough exploration of alternatives, and increased sales. Overall, it is clear that improved performance is often the result of better planning.

More specifically, a study conducted by Bracker and Pearson characterized the planning levels of small firms into structured strategic plans (SSP), structured operational plans (SOP), intuitive plans (IP), and unstructured plans (UP).[19] Table 15.3 illustrates the defini-

[17] A. Bakr Ibrahim, "Strategy Types and Small Firm's Performance: An Empirical Investigation," *Journal of Small Business Strategy* (spring 1993): 13–22.

[18] Elaine Mosakowski, "A Resource-Based Perspective on the Dynamic Strategy—Performance Relationship: An Empirical Examination of the Focus and Differentiation Strategies in Entrepreneurial Firms," *Journal of Management* 19, no. 4 (1993): 819–39.

[19] Jeffrey S. Bracker and John N. Pearson, "Planning and Financial Performances in Small Mature Firms," *Strategic Management Journal* 7 (1986): 503–22.

TABLE 15.3	STRATEGIC PLANNING LEVELS

Structured strategic plans (SSP): Formalized, written long-range plans covering the process of determining major outside interest focused on the organization; expectations of dominant inside interests; information about past, current, and future performance; environmental analysis; and determination of strengths and weaknesses of the firm and feedback. Typically 3–15 years in nature.

Structured operational plans (SOP): Written short-range operational budgets and plans of action for current fiscal period. The typical plan of action would include basic output controls, such as production quotas, cost constraints, and personnel requirements.

Intuitive plans (IP): These formal plans are developed and implemented based on the intuition and experience of the firm's owner. They are not written and are stored in the memory of the owner. They are of a short-term duration, no longer than one year in nature. They depend on objectives of the owner and the firm's present environment.

Unstructured plans (UP): No measurable structured planning in the firm.

SOURCE: Jeffrey S. Bracker and John N. Pearson, "Planning and Financial Performance of Small, Mature Firms," *Strategic Management Journal* 7 (1986): 507.

tions associated with these types of plans. The research concentrated on a sample of homogeneous, small, mature firms in the dry-cleaning industry and revealed that firms using structured strategic planning outperformed all other planning categories with regard to overall financial performance. In a later application of the same planning categories to a sample of growth-oriented firms in the electronics industry, the results supported the previous research by showing firms with structured strategic planning outperforming all others.[20]

In summary, all of the research indicates that firms that engage in strategic planning are more effective than those that do not. Most important, the studies emphasize the significance of the planning process, rather than merely the plans, as a key to successful performance.[21]

Fatal Vision in Strategic Planning

The actual execution of a strategy is almost as important as the strategy itself. Many entrepreneurs make unintentional errors while applying a specific strategy to their own specific venture. Competitive situations differ, and the particular application of known strategies must be tailored to those unique situations.

[20] Jeffrey S. Bracker, Barbara W. Keats, John N. Pearson, "Planning and Financial Performance among Small Firms in a Growth Industry," *Strategic Management Journal* 9 (1988): 591–603.

[21] Charles R. Schwenk and Charles B. Shrader, "Effects of Formal Strategic Planning on Financial Performance in Small Firms: A Meta Analysis," *Entrepreneurship Theory and Practice* (spring 1993): 53–64; see also Philip D. Olson and Donald W. Bokor, "Strategy Process—Content Interaction: Effects on Growth Performance in Small, Startup Firms," *Journal of Small Business Management* (January 1995): 34–44.

Researcher Michael E. Porter has noted five fatal mistakes entrepreneurs continually fall prey to in their attempt to implement a strategy.[22] Outlined next are these flaws and their explanation.

Flaw 1: Misunderstanding industry attractiveness. Too many entrepreneurs associate attractive industries with those that are growing the fastest, appear to be glamorous, or use the fanciest technology. This is wrong, because attractive industries have high barriers to entry and the fewest substitutes. The more high-tech or high-glamour a business is, the more likely a lot of new competitors will enter and make it unprofitable.

Flaw 2: No real competitive advantage. Some entrepreneurs merely copy or imitate the strategy of their competitors. That may be an easy tactic, and it is certainly less risky, but it means an entrepreneur has no competitive advantage. To succeed, new ventures must develop unique ways to compete.

Flaw 3: Pursuing an unattainable competitive position. Many aggressive entrepreneurs pursue a position of dominance in a fast-growing industry. However, they are so busy getting off the ground and finding people to buy their products that they forget what will happen if the venture succeeds. For example, a successful software program will be imitated quickly. So the advantage it alone gives cannot be sustained. Real competitive advantage in software comes from servicing and supporting buyers, providing regular upgrades, getting a company on-line with customers so their computer departments depend on the organization. That creates barriers to entry. Sometimes, small companies simply cannot sustain an advantage.

Flaw 4: Compromising strategy for growth. A careful balance must exist between growth and the competitive strategy that makes a new venture successful. If an entrepreneur sacrifices his or her venture's unique strategy in order to have fast growth, then the venture may grow out of business. Although fast growth can be tempting in certain industries, it is imperative entrepreneurs maintain and grow their strategic advantage also.

Flaw 5: Failure to explicitly communicate the venture's strategy to employees. It is essential for every entrepreneur to clearly communicate the company's strategy to every employee. Never assume employees already know the strategy. Always be explicit.

"One of the fundamental benefits of developing a strategy is that it creates unity, or consistency of action, throughout a company. Every department in the organization works toward the same objectives. But if people do not know what the objectives are, how can they work toward them? If they do not have a clear sense that low cost, say, is your ultimate aim, then all their day-to-day actions are not going to be reinforcing that goal. In any company, employees are making critical choices every minute. An explicit strategy will help them make the right ones," Porter says.[23]

IMPLEMENTING A STRATEGIC PLAN

New ventures can use a number of approaches to implement a strategic plan. The specific choice will be a function of the entrepreneur's personality and the environment in which

---

[22] Michael E. Porter, "Knowing Your Place—How to Assess the Attractiveness of Your Industry and Your Company's Position in It," *Inc.,* September 1991, 90–94.

[23] Ibid., 93.

FIGURE 15.2 THE OPPORTUNITY MANAGEMENT APPROACH

SOURCE: Adapted from Dean F. Olson and Omar L. Carey, *Opportunity Management: Strategic Planning for Smaller Businesses* (Reston, VA: Reston, 1985), 59.

the firm operates. Four basic approaches presented in this chapter are the opportunity management approach, the milestone planning approach, the strategic model approach, and the multistaged contingency approach. Each offers a comprehensive approach to strategic planning, although in practice entrepreneurs tend to draw the best elements from each rather than choose one and ignore the others.

Opportunity Management Approach

The **opportunity management approach** is based most heavily on environmental analysis.[24] The process begins with the construction of a strategic profile that considers (1) an evaluation of internal resources, (2) a forecast of external market conditions, (3) an evaluation of company strengths and weaknesses, and (4) a formulation of business objectives (see Figure 15.2). Quite often a formal worksheet is constructed to help the entrepreneur conduct a detailed analysis. Figure 15.3 provides an example of a form that can be used to evaluate company strengths and weaknesses. By saving these worksheets and comparing them on a year-by-year basis, the organization also can make a running analysis of opportunity management considerations over time and note the strategic changes influencing enterprise direction.

On the basis of this strategic profile, an opportunity profile is constructed. The latter is designed to help the enterprise gain maximum advantage from its resources. In this profile, action programs are designed, resources are allocated, and expected results are identified. Implementation and control steps follow, including organizing personnel, establishing budgets, formulating schedules, and analyzing financial statements. On the basis of the results, a new strategic profile and/or opportunity profile is constructed, and the process begins anew.

---

[24] For detailed information on this approach, see Dean F. Olson and Omar L. Carey, *Opportunity Management: Strategic Planning for Smaller Businesses* (Reston, VA: Reston, 1985); see also William Ming-Hone Tsai, Ian C. MacMillan, and Murray B. Low, "Effects of Strategy and Environment on Corporate Venture Success in Industrial Markets," *Journal of Business Venturing* (January 1991): 9–28.

FIGURE 15.3   **KEY STRENGTHS AND WEAKNESSES PROFILE**

KEY SUCCESS REQUIREMENTS   YEAR_____

Factor	Principal Market/Industry Success Requirements (Importance 1–10)	Company Compatibility Rating (1–10)
Marketing		
Production		
Innovation		
Finance		
Management		
Location		
Employee skills		

Company Strengths	**Company Weaknesses**

The opportunity management approach is popular because it is easy to understand and because implementation can be adjusted to meet changing conditions. The approach is based heavily on the first law of strategy: Lead from strength, which means doing what one does best.

Milestone Planning Approach

The **milestone planning approach** is based on the use of incremental goal attainment that takes a new venture from start-up through strategy reformulation.[25] Each important step is completed before moving on to the next one, and all are linked together into an overall strategic plan. Three major advantages of milestone planning are (1) the use of logical and practical milestones, (2) the avoidance of costly mistakes caused by failure to consider key parts of the plan, and (3) a methodology for replanning, based on continuous feedback from the environment.[26] Table 15.4 provides an example of a schedule that might be used in the milestone planning approach.

The milestone planning approach is popular with new ventures that are technical in nature, have multiple phases, or involve large sums of money. The approach is also used when close linkage between milestones or major objectives is needed. In contrast to opportunity management, milestone planning is more comprehensive and typically involves a greater investment of time and money.

[25] See Zenas Block and Ian C. MacMillan, "Milestones for Successful Venture Planning," *Harvard Business Review* (September/October 1985): 184–96.

[26] Ibid., 184.

TABLE 15.4   **A MILESTONE PLANNING APPROACH**

Milestone	Description	Key Questions
1	Formulation of the basic idea for the new venture	Has a need for the new venture been established?
2	Completion of a prototype (in this case, a new product)	What initial assumptions were made about development time and costs, and how have they changed? What has been learned about labor, material, and equipment, and how does this affect pricing plans? Do the product's characteristics still fit with the original concept and plan?
3	Raising the seed capital	Is the venture acceptable to investors? How is the venture being perceived in the marketplace?
4	Conducting a pilot operation	Have any of the venture's basic assumptions been challenged in the initial operations? Check specifically: • Suitability and costs of materials • Processing costs and skills • Training needs for production personnel • Reject percentages and costs and quality-control requirements
5	Market testing	Why are customers buying the product? Why are they not buying the product? Is the product different from or superior to the competition? How should estimates of achievable market share and size be modified?
6	Start-up of operations	Are selling and delivery commitments accurate? Do the market and financing requirements make sense?
7	Sale to first major account	How does the product compare with that of the competition? Should the initial selling method be continued or changed?
8	Reaction to the competition	What countermoves should be taken in response to the competition? What changes in advertising, promotion, sales, inventory, etc., are likely?
9	Redesign or redirection of strategy	What differences exist between the market and what the venture offers currently? What changes are needed in pricing, financing, design, marketing, etc.?

FIGURE 15.4   **NORMATIVE PLANNING MODEL**

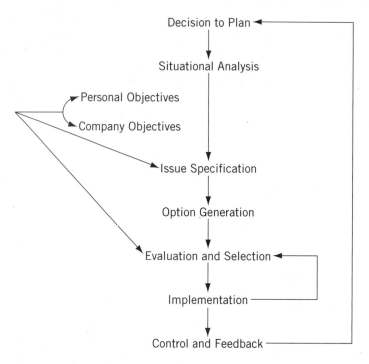

SOURCE: Jeffrey C. Shuman and John A. Seeger, "The Theory and Practice of Strategic Management in Smaller Rapid Growth Firms," *American Journal of Small Business* (summer 1986): 11.

Strategic Model Approach

Some new ventures follow a **strategic model approach,** which is also called *normative planning* because it represents the particular order in which strategic planning should be conducted.[27] Although the specific steps may vary slightly, Figure 15.4 provides a commonly used sequence. The biggest problem with this approach is that it tends to be more idealistic than realistic. Many new-venture planners find that the approach is not flexible enough for their needs. Additionally, it tends to be more valuable in large than in small undertakings. Nevertheless, an analysis of the steps is important to an understanding of how strategic planning can be used.

DECISION TO PLAN   The first step in normative strategic planning is a decision to commit time and money to formulating a strategic plan. For many entrepreneurs this is a major step, because they do not know a great deal about formal planning and must now learn how to use the process. At this stage the greatest burden falls on the entrepreneur, for although others may know some of the necessary inputs for the plan, the owner typically has the best overall understanding of the enterprise's mission and direction. The decision

[27] See Jeffrey C. Shuman and John A. Seeger, "The Theory and Practice of Strategic Management in Smaller Rapid Growth Firms," *American Journal of Small Business* (summer 1986): 7–18.

to plan is always based on anticipated positive results: The entrepreneur believes the venture will profit from planning.

SITUATIONAL ANALYSIS   This step enables the entrepreneur to gain an understanding of the venture, its current strategy, and potential thrusts or opportunities. This analysis helps define strengths and weaknesses and also helps the enterprise sidestep weaknesses that could result in financial setbacks.

PERSONAL AND COMPANY OBJECTIVES   In smaller companies the owner's personal objectives will influence company objectives. For example, if the individual is determined to develop a strong technological edge because, at heart, he or she is a scientist/inventor, this personal objective will play a major role in determining company objectives. To the extent personal objectives are good for the company, the company will prosper.

Company objectives are selected to exploit the strengths of the business and sidestep its weaknesses. Primary consideration typically is given to objectives such as return on investment, sales growth, productivity, cost containment, and personnel acquisition and development. Where possible, these objectives are quantified.

ISSUE SPECIFICATION   In issue specification the entrepreneur reviews the findings of the situational analysis in the context of both personal and company objectives in order to determine problem areas. A comparison of current performance and past plans is conducted, and a decision is made regarding whether or not to continue the current strategy.

OPTION GENERATION   At this point the entrepreneur identifies alternatives that might provide a solution to current major problems. In doing so, consideration is given to the company's competencies, resources, values, and financial capabilities.

EVALUATION AND SELECTION   The alternatives generated in the option stage are now compared in terms of relative effectiveness in dealing with key strategic issues. Careful consideration is given to the degree each alternative matches the company's competencies and resources, its relative competitive advantage, and management's overall goals. Factors judged to be of overriding importance are given priority, and decisions are then made.

IMPLEMENTATION   The next step is the establishment of timetables that spell out who will do what and by when. Strategic objectives are broken down into short-range goals so everyone knows what he or she is to do. The focus of operations is on efficiency-oriented matters such as profit and cost control and on day-to-day operational concerns.

CONTROL AND FEEDBACK LOOP   The control and feedback loop is used to ensure everything is being done according to plan. Actual performance is compared to expectations on a continuous basis. If something is going awry, steps are taken to correct the situation. Then, based on the results, new plans are formulated. This loop begins the process anew.

Multistage Contingency Approach

A final approach presented here is the **multistage contingency approach.** This process was developed by reviewing the various approaches to entrepreneurship. Three distinct variables are critical to any strategic analysis: the individual, the venture, and the

ENTREPRENEURIAL

EDGE

The Return of Corporate Culture

The buzzwords of the 1980s were "corporate culture." But the fierce competitive environment of the 1990s changed that. Success today comes from clinical, tough-minded action; hot new technology; savvy strategy and positioning; and brutal cost control. Or does it? Dozens of headline-making CEOs argue that corporate culture has never been needed more. They believe corporate culture truly does help companies get an edge in the most competitive business environment yet.

Amy Miller, founder of Amy's Ice Creams in Austin and Houston, Texas, faced a universal challenge: keeping her stores from becoming just another commodity. Her once safe niche of superpremium ice-cream stores soon became overpopulated. In order to distinguish herself from the other ice-cream shops, Miller knew she would have to do more than sell ice cream; she would have to sell an experience. She has done exactly that by planning, creating, and nurturing a culture that makes that experience inevitable. The culture succeeds in finding and developing the right people that behave in the right way at the right time. They juggle with their serving spades, breakdance on the freezer top, and toss scoops of ice cream to each other behind the counter. They even wear costumes and pop trivia questions. They create fun.

Although corporate culture was out of fashion for a decade, the right culture can become a competitive edge for both young businesses and more established entrepreneurial successes. What is corporate culture? "Culture refers to the values, beliefs, and attitudes that penetrate a business. It defines what the company considers important and what it considers unimportant. If strategy defines where a company wants to go, culture determines how—maybe whether—it gets there," *Inc.* writer John Case says. Although every business has some kind of culture, only a few have the strong, focused cultures that develop into real market-beating tools. These few have mission statements and values that mean something and that people take seriously.

environment. However, the stages of any venture (idea, pre-venture, start-up, early growth, harvest) are also critical to strategic analysis. In addition, a career perspective should be considered, which means the entrepreneur's career stage (early, middle, or late) can be a decisive factor when differentiating the variables within the venture development stages. Thus, it may be necessary to visualize entrepreneurial strategies as contingencies. In other words, all of the evolving and emerging conditions involved with any entrepreneurial pursuit cause a constant dynamism. If newly emerging entrepreneurial issues such as global expansion, the growth in numbers of women entrepreneurs, and corporate entrepreneurship are also introduced, then a model of entrepreneurial strategy would be multidimensional, multistage, and contingency based. Figure 15.5 attempts to capture all of these factors into

These few have a set of beliefs that serve as powerful guides for everyday actions and behaviors. Some of the classic examples include 3M's relentless focus on innovation and Disney's commitment to treating its theme-park customers as guests. For these companies, those vivid cultural values shape every move and decision their employees and managers make.

Here are two examples of corporations and their cultures that define them and their success:

- *GSD & M*, an advertising firm in Austin, boasts a client retention rate of 90 percent partly due to its emphasis on the client's goals. The campaign starts with the client's goals, and GSD&M follows them carefully and with great scrutiny. In fact, the agency hands out bonuses not when GSD&M reaches its goals but when the clients reach their goals. The client-centered culture is further demonstrated by the war rooms—entire rooms outfitted with the client's products, marketing statistics, and colors.

- *Black Diamond Equipment*, Salt Lake City, leads the pack of rock-climbing equipment companies by filling its workforce with rock-climbing enthusiasts. By employing individuals who use its products, the company is able to capitalize on the employee's passion and enthusiasm for the sport. "We breathe it, live it, think about it constantly," the vice president of human resources, Meredith Saarinen, says, "which makes the whole company a marketing and design resource."

Corporate culture is more important today than ever before. Today, customers expect nothing less than perfect quality, errorless service, and personalized relationships. And as organizations become flatter, the responsibility for company success is spreading to every employee in the organization. Every employee is making key decisions and judgments from the assembly line to the customer service desk. Every employee needs a set of beliefs and values to guide him or her in everyday actions. Disney, 3M, and others like them bring to life the type of corporate cultures that triumph over these and other business conditions that threaten the stability and profitability of all businesses.

SOURCE: John Case, "Corporate Culture," *Inc.* November 1996, 42–53.

a three-dimensional model that emphasizes the need for contingency strategies based on the evaluation and assessment of the various elements.[28]

Although all of these variables must be examined from a strategic perspective, the traditional strategic management process may provide assistance. As discussed earlier in the chapter, this perspective is summarized in the acronym SWOT (strengths, weaknesses, opportunities, and threats).[29] Thus, Figure 15.5 shows entrepreneurial contingency

[28] Donald F. Kuratko and Harold P. Welsch, *Entrepreneurial Strategy* (Fort Worth: The Dryden Press, 1994), 11–12.

[29] Wheelen and Hunger, *Strategic Management*, 47; see also William R. Sandberg, "Strategic Management's Potential Contribution to a Theory of Entrepreneurship," *Entrepreneurship Theory and Practice* (spring 1992): 73–90.

FIGURE 15.5 **ENTREPRENEURIAL STRATEGY: A CONTINGENCY MULTISTAGE APPROACH**

Strategic Entrepreneurial Assessment	New-Venture Initiation	Entrepreneurial Development and Continuation	Emerging Entrepreneurial Issues
Opportunity Evaluation	New-Venture Initiation	Entrepreneurial Growth and Development	Corporate Entrepreneurship
	• Creativity	• Understanding the Entrepreneurial Company	International: The Global Expansion
	• Assessment Evaluation		
	• Feasibility	Managing Paradox and Contradiction	Women Entrepreneurs
SWOT Analysis (Strengths/Weaknesses Opportunities/Threats)	The Business Plan Process	Acquisition of a Venture	Family Business
	• Definition		
	• Benefits	Valuation and Succession of Entrepreneurial Ventures	Entrepreneurial Careers
	• Business Plan Development	• Methods of Valuation	
		• Succession Strategy	

SOURCE: Donald F. Kuratko and Harold P. Welsch, *Entrepreneurial Strategy* (Fort Worth: The Dryden Press, 1994), 10.

issues for the purpose of entrepreneurial development and, eventually, entrepreneurial continuation.

THE NATURE OF OPERATIONAL PLANNING

Having examined the various factors and theories relating to strategic planning, we now shall review some of the basic concepts involved in operational planning.

Operational planning, also referred to as *short-range planning* or *functional planning,* consists of the specific practices established to carry out the objectives set forth in the strategic plan. The operational plan is thus an outgrowth or extension of the strategic planning process. In the areas of finance, marketing, production, and management, functional policies need to be established in order to implement the goals determined in the strategy.

Research shows that small-business managers more commonly perform operational planning than strategic planning. In addition, operational planning has been established as a critical component in the overall planning process of a small firm.[30]

Operational Planning Process

The overall planning process incorporates all of the factors involved in strategic planning and the implementation tools of operational planning (see Figure 15.6). Specifically, the tools applied in the functional areas of the business will be a key to implementation of the planning process. Some of the tools most widely known and used are budgets, policies, and procedures.

Budgets are planning devices used to establish future plans in financial terms. They are valuable tools in the operational sense, because they provide a set of measuring points by which the implemented plans can be evaluated. Effective budgeting is based on realistic estimates and appropriate allocations.

Policies are the fundamental guides for the venture as a whole. Each department or functional area needs to establish the policies that will guide its operations on a day-to-day basis. For example, sales policies, financial policies, credit policies, and manufacturing policies determine the daily course of business. Established policies allow entrepreneurs the freedom to work more on strategy since each specific functional problem does not have to be analyzed. Policies are guidelines to decision making and action. They delimit the area a decision is made in and ensure that the decision is consistent with objectives.[31]

Although procedures are similar to policies, they are usually policies that have been standardized as a continuing method. For example, credit approval may follow specific credit policies, but eventually the steps that are followed can be completely standardized. Thus procedures are often referred to as *standard operating procedures.*

Each of these operating tools represents methods for implementing and evaluating the goals of strategic planning. Thus operational planning becomes the ongoing phase that brings a venture's strategic plan to action.

---

[30] Charles B. Shrader, Charles L. Mumford, and Virginia L. Blackburn, "Strategic and Operational Planning, Uncertainty, and Performance in Small Firms," *Journal of Small Business Management* (October 1989): 45–60.

[31] Richard M. Hodgetts and Donald F. Kuratko, *Management,* 3d ed. (San Diego: Harcourt Brace Jovanovich, 1991), 171.

FIGURE 15.6 THE OVERALL PLANNING PROCESS FOR A VENTURE

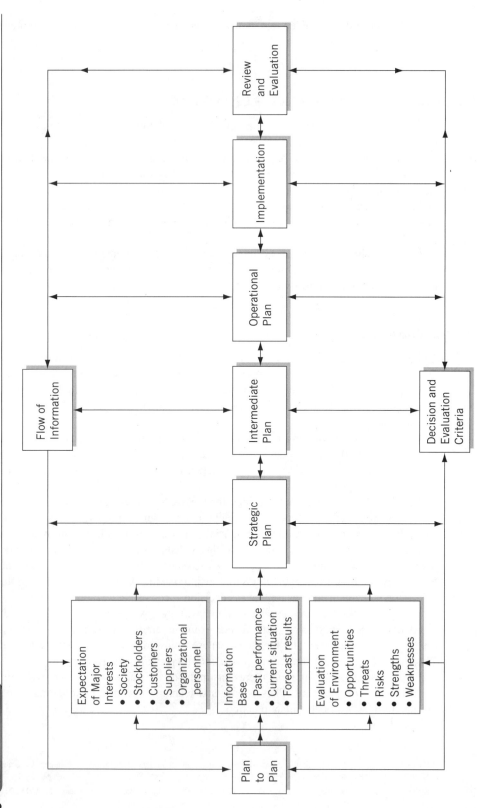

SOURCE: Richard M. Hodgetts and Donald F. Kuratko, *Management*, 3d ed. (San Diego: Harcourt Brace Jovanovich, 1991), 174.

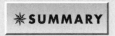

Summary

Although many ways of strategically planning a venture exist, all have one common element: Each is an extension of the entrepreneur's vision—each takes the owner's concept of the business and puts it into action.

Entrepreneurs do not use strategic planning for many reasons, among them scarcity of time, lack of knowledge about how to plan, lack of expertise in the planning process, and lack of trust in others.

A number of benefits to strategic planning exist. In particular, studies have shown that small firms that use this process tend to have better financial performance than those that do not. Other benefits are more efficient resource allocation, improved competitive position, higher employee morale, and more rapid decision making.

Four ways to carry out a strategic plan exist. The opportunity management approach relies heavily on environmental analysis. When using this approach, the entrepreneur will make an evaluation of the firm's internal resources, a forecast of external market conditions, and an evaluation of the company's strengths and weaknesses. Based on the results, objectives will be formulated and then pursued. The milestone planning approach is based on the use of incremental goal attainment that takes a new venture from start-up through strategy reformulation. Each major step is completed before moving on to the next one, and all are linked together in an overall strategic plan. The strategic model approach begins with the decision to plan, and then, after the environment is analyzed and objectives are formulated, a plan of action is set forth, implemented, and controlled via feedback. The latter approach is the one most commonly used by major corporations. Finally, the multistage contingency approach combines the stages of a venture with distinct variables that must be continually assessed for proper planning.

The operational plan is the implementation phase that includes specific tools for proper action. Sometimes referred to as functional planning, the operational plan uses budgets, policies, and procedures as methods for carrying out the objectives established in the strategic plan.

Key Terms and Concepts

Lack of expertise/skills

Lack of knowledge

Lack of trust and openness

Milestone planning approach

Multistage contingency approach

Operational planning

Opportunity management approach

Perception of high cost

Strategic model approach

Strategic planning

SWOT analysis

Time scarcity

Review and Discussion Questions

1. In what way does an entrepreneur's vision affect the company's strategic plan?
2. How is the strategy plan of an engineer/scientist entrepreneur likely to be different from that of an entrepreneur whose primary strength is in the manufacturing area? Be complete in your answer.
3. What are the three basic steps involved in transforming entrepreneurial vision and ideas into action?

4. Give three reasons why many entrepreneurs do not like to formulate strategic plans.

5. Describe five difficulties entrepreneurs face in long-range planning.

6. Does strategic planning really pay off for small ventures? Why or why not?

7. A new-venture entrepreneur is considering formulation of a strategic plan. However, he is concerned this effort will have little value for him. Is he right or wrong? Explain.

8. How can an entrepreneur use an opportunity management approach when formulating and implementing a strategic plan? Discuss the process.

9. What are the advantages of an opportunity management approach to strategic planning?

10. What types of ventures are most likely to profit from an opportunity management approach to strategic planning?

11. How does the milestone planning approach to strategic planning work?

12. What type of venture might profit from the use of a milestone planning approach? Defend your answer.

13. Why is the strategic model approach to planning not as popular as the opportunity management or milestone planning approach?

14. What benefits does the multistage contingency approach offer to new-venture entrepreneurs?

15. What is operational planning? What specific tools are used?

16. How does operational planning fit with strategic planning?

Experiential Exercise   *Strategic Planning in Action*

Go to the library and look through the past 12 issues of *Entrepreneur* or *Inc.* Pick out two stories of new or growing ventures that have been involved in formulating a strategic plan. Gather as much information as you can, and then for each firm answer the following questions:

Firm 1

What did the company's strategic plan involve? Describe it in detail._____

_____

_____

_____

How successful was the plan? Explain._____

_____

_____

_____

What conclusions can you draw regarding the value of strategic planning to this company? Be complete in your answer._____

_____

_____

_____

Firm 2

What did the company's strategic plan involve? Describe it in detail._____

_____

_____

_____

How successful was the plan? Explain. _____
_____
_____
_____

What conclusions can you draw regarding the value of strategic planning to this company?
Be complete in your answer. _____
_____
_____
_____

 **CASE 15.1**

The Banker's Request

Elizabeth Edwards opened her first restaurant three years ago. Since then she has opened
two more. Elizabeth caters to family dining and has developed a loyal following. Many
families come to her restaurant on a weekly basis. Friday, Saturday, and Sunday evenings
are so popular that reservations are not accepted.

Last year Elizabeth's three units grossed $1.2 million. Her accountant estimates that this
year the combined total will be in the neighborhood of $1.45 million.

The first restaurant was started with funds from her grandfather. Since then, internal
profits have been sufficient to handle most of her operating needs. However, her expansion
costs for the second and third restaurants were taken care of through a bank loan.

Elizabeth is now thinking of opening a fourth restaurant. Her banker is willing to lend
her the necessary funds but thinks this would also be a good time for her to draw up a
strategic plan. "You are getting too big to operate on a day-to-day basis," her banker said.
"You need a long-range plan that will help you manage your overall operations. You need
to start putting more focus on where you want to be in five years and how you are going to
get there." Her banker would like Elizabeth to submit this plan with her new loan application. "With this plan and your excellent record here at the bank," he assured her, "I am
sure your application will fly through the loan committee."

Elizabeth is not pleased with her banker's suggestion. First, she is unsure of how to
draw up a strategic plan. It seems to her it would take a great deal of effort and probably
not have any real value for her business. Second, she sees the banker's suggestion as
nothing more than an attempt to cover himself should the loan fall into default. "I suppose
when they lend you money they have to be able to justify the loan. In my case, they will
have loaned me a substantial amount of money, so they want to cover their actions with
the board of directors by showing that I have not only provided collateral for the loan but
have also provided them a detailed plan regarding the future operations of the enterprise.
I can't say that I blame them, but I really don't think that plan has any practical value for
me. Mostly it will be used to support the loan. Nevertheless, I want the loan, so I'll write
the plan."

Elizabeth has tentatively scheduled construction of the new restaurant to begin in 90
days. She would like to have all of the paperwork associated with the application completed
within 30 days. "I don't think it will be too difficult to write a strategic plan. I'll just pull
together some of my current financial statements, write a brief description of the firm and
its long-run objectives, and submit the plan along with the loan application sometime early
next month."

Questions

1. In Elizabeth's case, what approach would you recommend she use for writing her plan? Why?
2. What specific steps should Elizabeth take for writing the plan? Will her current idea of what to include in the plan be of any value?
3. What benefits would a strategic plan have for Elizabeth's firm? Be complete in your answer.

 **CASE 15.2**

A Two-Phase Approach

Since its founding six months ago, Diego Sanchez's electronics repair shop has been booming. Diego repairs electronic household appliances, including portable telephones, VCRs, televisions, radios, and stereo equipment. Usually it does not take a great deal of time to make the repairs. For example, most portable phones have battery-related problems. All the repairer has to do is replace the battery and recharge the unit. The cost of a battery is around $4 and the service charge is $35. So despite the fact the rent is high and the store has to keep a large supply of inventory on hand, profits are well over 40 percent.

Diego has been doing so well he has been thinking about opening a second store. However, he realizes that if this new venture does not pay off, he could be in financial straits. Before going any further, he has decided to sit down and plan his moves. The plan is going to have two major phases. The first phase will focus on areas such as where the store currently is heading, projected sales for the next two years, competitive counter-moves, responses to these countermoves, and overall financial performance. Diego believes it will not be long before competitors begin to move into his market niche. "You can't make tremendous return on investment without attracting serious competition," he has told his wife. "If I want to continue being successful, I have to figure out how to stop these guys from invading my market. I have to have a game plan." The second phase of the plan will incorporate the new store and will examine the impact of this expansion on overall operations.

Diego believes this two-phase approach will help him plan for current operations and future expansion. He also feels it will be easier to plan for the expansion if he first lays the groundwork with a basic strategic plan. Diego's biggest problem right now is that he does not know much about strategic planning for new ventures. He is thinking he might drop by the local university and talk to one of the professors who teaches entrepreneurship or business strategy and get some advice on how to proceed.

Questions

1. If you were advising Diego, what approach would you recommend he use for putting together his strategic plan? Why?
2. What advantages would your proposed approach have over other approaches? Compare and contrast at least three approaches.
3. How would your approach allow Diego to incorporate expansion planning into the overall plan?

Chapter 16

MANAGING ENTREPRENEURIAL GROWTH

CHAPTER OBJECTIVES

1. To discuss the five stages of a typical venture life cycle: development, start-up, growth, stabilization, and innovation or decline

2. To explore the elements involved with an entrepreneurial firm

3. To survey the ways entrepreneurs build adaptive firms

4. To examine the transition that occurs in the movement from an entrepreneurial style to a managerial approach

5. To explain the importance of the self-management concept in managing the growth stage

6. To identify the key factors that play a major role during the growth stage

7. To discuss the complex management of paradox and contradiction

8. To introduce the steps useful for breaking through the growth wall

The message here is straightforward. Old-fashioned entrepreneurship, not modern, profes-sional management, is the driving force of successful, high-growth companies. Indeed, the twentieth-century promise of the giant, rational corporation as the engine of prosperity comes up myth. The facts show that the real growth in all economies comes from younger, smaller, more entrepreneurial companies. Whether it's shareholder return, product innova-tion, or job creation, the performance differences can be downright shocking. Against all expert prediction, and the best intentions of managers, the world's great experiment in mass-produced enterprise is not working, anywhere!

Larry C. Farrell,
Searching for the Spirit of Enterprise
(Dutton Books, 1993)

Managing entrepreneurial growth may be the most critical tactic for the future success of business enterprises. After initiation of a new venture, the entrepreneur needs to develop an understanding of management change. This is a great challenge, because it often encompasses the art of balancing mobile and dynamic factors.[1]

Thus, the survival and growth of a new venture require that the entrepreneur possess both strategic and tactical skills and abilities. Which specific skills and abilities are needed depends in part on the venture's current development. Figure 16.1 illustrates the typical venture life cycle.

The purpose of this chapter is to examine the venture characteristics, managerial abili-ties, and entrepreneurial needs and drives in relation to the stages of the venture's devel-opment. Specifically, attention is concentrated on the growth stage, since this is the phase during which a venture usually reaches major crossroads in the decisions that affect its future. Managing growth can be a formidable challenge to the successful development of any venture.

DEVELOPMENT STAGES

As noted, Figure 16.1 presents the traditional **life-cycle stages** of an enterprise. These stages include new-venture development, start-up activities, growth, stabilization, and

---

[1] Jeanie Daniel Duck, "Managing Change: The Art of Balancing," *Harvard Business Review* (November/December 1993): 109–18.

FIGURE 16.1 **A VENTURE'S TYPICAL LIFE CYCLE**

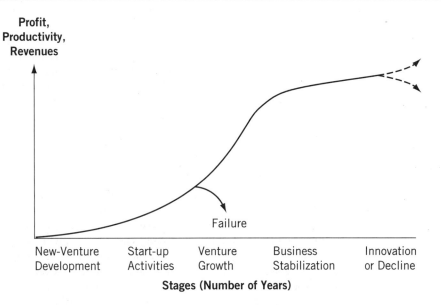

innovation or decline. Other authors have described these stages in different terms. For example, Alfred Chandler has presented a firm's evolution in the following stages:

1. Initial expansion and accumulation of resources

2. Rationalization of the use of resources

3. Expansion into new markets to assure the continued use of resources

4. Development of new structures to ensure continuing mobilization of resources[2]

These four phases are, in effect, the same major stages illustrated in Figure 16.1, with the exception of stabilization. In short, authors generally agree regarding a venture's life cycle. Presented next are the five major stages.

New-Venture Development

The first stage, **new-venture development,** consists of activities associated with the initial formulation of the venture. This initial phase is the foundation of the entrepreneurial process and requires creativity and assessment. In addition to the accumulation and expansion of resources, this is a creativity, assessment, and networking stage for initial entrepreneurial strategy formulation. The enterprise's general philosophy, mission, scope, and direction are determined during this stage.

[2] Alfred Chandler, *Strategy and Structure* (Cambridge, MA: MIT Press, 1962).

Start-Up Activities

The second stage, **start-up activities,** encompasses the foundation work needed for creating a formal business plan, searching for capital, carrying out marketing activities, and developing an effective entrepreneurial team. These activities typically demand an aggressive entrepreneurial strategy with maximum efforts devoted to launching the venture. This stage is similar to Chandler's description of the rationalization of the use of resources. It is typified by strategic and operational planning steps designed to identify the firm's competitive advantage and to uncover funding sources.[3] Marketing and financial considerations tend to be paramount during this stage.

Growth

The **growth stage** often requires major changes in entrepreneurial strategy. Competition and other market forces call for the reformulation of strategies. For example, some firms find themselves "growing out" of business because they are unable to cope with the growth of their ventures.[4] Highly creative entrepreneurs sometimes are unable, or unwilling, to meet the administrative challenges that accompany this growth stage. As a result, they leave the enterprise and move on to other ventures. Steven Jobs of Apple Computer was forced out of the firm during this stage. His creative ideas were detrimental to the growth of the venture. The firm needed a managerial entrepreneur to run the operation; Jobs had neither the expertise nor the desire to assume this role.[5]

This growth stage presents newer and more dominant problems than those the entrepreneur faced during the start-up stage.[6] These newer challenges force the entrepreneur into developing a different set of skills while maintaining an "entrepreneurial perspective" for the organization.[7] The growth stage is a transition from entrepreneurial one-person leadership to managerial team-oriented leadership.

Business Stabilization

The **stabilization stage** is a result of both market conditions and the entrepreneur's efforts. During this stage a number of developments commonly occur, including increased competition, consumer indifference to the entrepreneur's good(s) or service(s), and saturation of the market with a host of "me too" look-alikes. Sales often begin to stabilize, and the entrepreneur must begin thinking about where the enterprise will go over the next three to five years. This stage is often a "swing" stage in that it precedes the period when the firm either swings into higher gear and greater profitability or swings toward decline and failure. During this stage innovation is often critical to future success.

---

[3] Hugh M. O'Neill, "How Entrepreneurs Manage Growth," *Long Range Planning* (February 1983): 117.

[4] Donald F. Kuratko, "Managing Entrepreneurial Growth," *Entrepreneurship Development Review* (winter 1988): 1–5.

[5] For more on this example, see E. Bruce Peters, "The Conflict at Apple Was Almost Inevitable," *Research & Development* (December 1985): 58–60; Richard E. Crandall, "Company Life Cycles: The Effects of Growth on Structure and Personnel," *Personnel* (September 1987): 28–36; and Kenneth E. Marino and Marc J. Dollinger, "Top Management Succession in Entrepreneurial Firms," *Journal of Management Case Studies* (spring 1987): 70–79.

[6] David E. Terpstra and Philip D. Olson, "Entrepreneurial Start-up and Growth: A Classification of Problems," *Entrepreneurship Theory and Practice* (spring 1993): 5–20.

[7] See Jacqueline N. Hood and John E. Young, "Entrepreneurship's Requisite Areas of Development: A Survey of Top Executives in Successful Entrepreneurial Firms," *Journal of Business Venturing* (March 1993): 115–35.

FIGURE 16.2 THE ENTREPRENEURIAL MIND

Future Goals

		Change	Status Quo
Perceived Capability	Possible	Entrepreneur	Satisfied manager
	Blocked	Frustrated manager	Classic bureaucrat

Innovation or Decline

Firms that fail to innovate will die. Financially successful enterprises often will try to acquire other innovative firms, thereby ensuring their own growth. Also, many firms will work on new product/service development in order to complement current offerings.

All of a venture's life-cycle stages are important strategic points, and each requires a different set of strategies. However, this chapter concentrates specifically on the growth stage since entrepreneurs often ignore it. This happens not because of incompetence but rather because of the almost hypnotic effect a successful growth stage can cause. We shall now examine the key factors affecting the ability to manage this stage.

UNDERSTANDING THE ENTREPRENEURIAL COMPANY

It has been noted that entrepreneurs (1) perceive an opportunity, (2) pursue this opportunity, and (3) believe that success of the venture is possible.[8] This belief is often due to the uniqueness of the idea, the strength of the product, or some special knowledge or skill the entrepreneur possesses. These same factors must be translated into the organization itself as the venture grows.

The Entrepreneurial Mind

It is important for the venture's manager to maintain an entrepreneurial frame of mind. Figure 16.2 illustrates the danger of entrepreneurs evolving into bureaucrats who in turn stifle innovation.

In some cases, success will affect an entrepreneur's willingness to change and innovate. This is particularly true when the enterprise has developed a sense of complacency and the entrepreneur likes this environment. The person does not want to change. In fact, some entrepreneurs will create a bureaucratic environment where orders are issued from the top

---

[8] Howard H. Stevenson and Jose Carlos Jarillo-Mossi, "Preserving Entrepreneurship as Companies Grow," *Journal of Business Strategy* (summer 1986): 10.

down and change initiated at the lower levels is not tolerated.[9] As a result, no one in the venture is willing (or encouraged) to become innovative or entrepreneurial because the owner-founder stifles such activity.

One study found that the entrepreneur directly affects the firm's growth orientation as measured by profitability goals, product/market goals, human resource goals, and flexibility goals.[10] If the entrepreneur hopes to maintain the creative climate that helped launch the venture in the first place, specific steps or measures must be taken.

Building the Adaptive Firm

It is important for entrepreneurs to establish a business that remains flexible beyond start-up. An **adaptive firm** increases opportunity for its employees, initiates change, and instills a desire to be innovative. Entrepreneurs can build an adaptive firm in several ways.[11] The following are not inflexible rules, but they do enhance a venture's chance of remaining adaptive and innovative both through and beyond the growth stage.[12]

SHARE THE ENTREPRENEUR'S VISION   The entrepreneur's vision must be permeated throughout the organization in order for employees to understand the company's direction and share in the responsibility for its growth. The entrepreneur can communicate the vision directly to the employees through meetings, conversations, or seminars. It also can be shared through symbolic events or activities such as social gatherings, recognition events, and displays. Whatever the format, shared vision allows the venture's personnel to catch the dream and become an integral part of creating the future.[13]

INCREASE THE PERCEPTION OF OPPORTUNITY   This can be accomplished with careful job design. The work should have defined objectives for which people will be responsible. Each level of the hierarchy should be kept informed of its role in producing the final output of the product or service. This often is known as "staying close to the customer."[14] Another way to increase the perception of opportunity is through a careful coordination and integration of the functional areas. This allows employees in different functional areas to work together as a cohesive whole.

INSTITUTIONALIZE CHANGE AS THE VENTURE'S GOAL   This entails a preference for innovation and change rather than preservation of the status quo. If opportunity is to be perceived, the environment of the enterprise must not only encourage it but must also establish it as a goal. Within this context, a desire for opportunity can exist if resources are made available and departmental barriers are reduced.

[9] Ibid., 11.

[10] Vesa Routamaa and Jukka Vesalainen, "Types of Entrepreneurs and Strategic Level Goal Setting," *International Small Business Journal* (spring 1987): 19–29; see also Lanny Herron and Richard B. Robinson Jr., "A Structural Model of the Effects of Entrepreneurial Characteristics on Venture Performance," *Journal of Business Venturing* (May 1993): 281–94.

[11] Donald F. Kuratko, Jeffrey S. Hornsby, and Laura M. Corso, "Building an Adaptive Firm," *Small Business Forum* (spring 1996): 41–48.

[12] Stevenson and Jarillo-Mossi, "Preserving Entrepreneurship," 13–16.

[13] Steven H. Hanks and L. R. McCarrey, "Beyond Survival: Reshaping Entrepreneurial Vision in Successful Growing Ventures," *Journal of Small Business Strategy* (spring 1993): 1–12.

[14] Thomas J. Peters and Robert H. Waterman Jr., *In Search of Excellence* (New York: Harper & Row, 1982).

CONTEMPORARY ENTREPRENEURSHIP

Cabletron: Entrepreneurial Growth

Not every entrepreneur faces the dilemma to innovate or decline. In some cases entrepreneurs have gone through the cycle of "decline and then innovate." After they were knocked flat on their back, the entrepreneurs got up and went on to succeed.

Thirty-two-year-old S. Robert Levine experienced a number of failed ventures before he established Cabletron systems. He had tried a landscaping business, a biorhythm company, a limousine service, and even a real estate development firm. All of these ventures failed.

In 1983, Levine was working as a sales representative for a number of cable companies when he realized a great need existed for extra cable after corporations purchased their minicomputers. The extra cable was needed for rearranging floor plans to accommodate the new computers. However, Levine knew that such small amounts of cable were never kept in inventory by computer companies, and delivery usually would take six months.

Levine established Cabletron Systems to meet the needs of companies requesting small amounts of Teflon cable. Not only was the cable kept in stock, but also delivery within 48 hours was promised. The results? By 1985, Cabletron sales were $900,000, and the company was branching out into other computer supplies. In 1986, Levine moved from simply distribution to completely automated manufacturing, and sales grew in 1987 to $9 million.

After Cabletron moved into network testing devices, known as transceivers, its sales jumped to $25 million in 1988 and earned it the number-seven ranking on the *Inc. 500*. In 1990 sales climbed to $105 million, and Levine's continuing challenge is managing entrepreneurial growth.

SOURCE: Joshua Hyatt, "Born to Run," *Inc.*, January 1991, 36–50.

INSTILL THE DESIRE TO BE INNOVATIVE   The desire of personnel to pursue opportunity must be carefully nurtured. Words alone will not create the innovative climate. Specific steps such as the following should be taken:

- *A reward system.* Explicit forms of recognition should be given to individuals who pursue innovative opportunities. For example, bonuses, awards, salary advances, and promotions should be tied directly to the innovative attempts of personnel.
- *An environment that allows for failure.* The fear of failure must be minimized by the general recognition that often many attempts are needed before a success is achieved. This does not imply that failure is sought or desired. However, learning from failure, as opposed to expecting punishment for it, is promoted. When this type of environment exists, people become willing to accept the challenge of change and innovation.
- *Flexible operations.* Flexibility creates the possibility of change taking place and having a positive effect. If a venture remains too rigidly tied to plans or strategies, it

will not be responsive to new technologies, customer changes, or environmental shifts. Innovation will not take place because it will not "fit in."

- *The development of venture teams.* In order for the environment to foster innovation, **venture teams** and team performance goals need to be established. These must be not just work groups but visionary, committed teams that have the authority to create new directions, set new standards, and challenge the status quo.[15]

The Transition: From an Entrepreneurial Style to a Managerial Approach

The transitions between stages of a venture are complemented (or in some cases retarded) by the entrepreneur's ability to make a transition in style. A key transition occurs during the growth stage of a venture when the entrepreneur shifts into a managerial style. This is not easy to do. As Hofer and Charan have noted, "Among the different transitions that are possible, probably the most difficult to achieve and also perhaps the most important for organizational development is that of moving from a one-person, entrepreneurially managed firm to one run by a functionally organized, professional management team."[16]

A number of problems can occur during this transition, especially if the enterprise is characterized by factors such as (1) a highly centralized decision-making system, (2) an overdependence on one or two key individuals, (3) an inadequate repertoire of managerial skills and training, and (4) a paternalistic atmosphere.[17] These characteristics, although often effective in the new venture's start-up and initial survival, pose a threat to the firm's development during the growth stage. Quite often these characteristics inhibit development by detracting from the entrepreneur's ability to manage the growth stage successfully.

In order to bring about the necessary transition, the entrepreneur must carefully plan and then gradually implement the process. Hofer and Charan have suggested a seven-step process (see Figure 16.3):

1. The entrepreneur must want to make the change and must want it strongly enough to undertake major modifications in his or her own task behavior.

2. The day-to-day decision-making procedures of the organization must be changed. Specifically, participation in this process must be expanded. Greater emphasis also should be placed on the use of formal decision techniques.

3. The two or three key operating tasks that are primarily responsible for the organization's success must be institutionalized. This may involve the selection of new people to supplement or replace "indispensable" individuals who have performed these tasks in the past.

4. Middle-level management must be developed. Specialists must learn to become functional managers, while functional managers must learn to become general managers.

5. The firm's strategy should be evaluated and modified, if necessary, to achieve growth.

---

[15] Jon R. Katzenbach and Douglas K. Smith, "The Discipline of Teams," *Harvard Business Review* (March/April 1993): 111–20.

[16] Charles W. Hofer and Ram Charan, "The Transition to Professional Management: Mission Impossible?" *American Journal of Small Business* (summer 1984): 3; see also William Lowell, "An Entrepreneur's Journey to the Next Level," *Small Business Forum* (spring 1996): 68–74.

[17] Ibid., 4.

A SCHEMATIC REPRESENTATION OF THE TRANSITION PROCESS SHOWING ITS RELATIVE TIME DIMENSIONS

FIGURE 16.3

Activity	Time span (months)
Recognition and awareness of need to change	0–9
Entrepreneur wants to change	3–9
Entrepreneur tries to change his own day-to-day task behavior	6–42
Analyses of existing decision-making procedures	9–18
Stabilzation and formalization of decision-making procedures	12–21
Broadening of participation in decision making and use of consultative procedures	18–36
Identification of key tasks	9–15
Institutionalization of key tasks	15–36
Development of middle-level management	15–42
Assess adequacy of existing strategy	15–21
Implement new strategy	21–42
Evaluate original structure	21–27
Check with others	27–30
Implement new structure	30–39
Hire and fire new personnel	33–42
Develop board	33–42
Constant monitoring of change process through observation of key indicators	9–42

Time (Months): 0 3 6 9 12 15 18 21 24 27 30 33 36 39 42

SOURCE: Charles W. Hofer and Ram Charan, "The Transition to Professional Management: Mission Impossible?" *American Journal of Small Business* (summer 1984): 11. Reprinted with permission.

6. The organizational structure and its management systems and procedures must be slowly modified to fit the company's new strategy and senior managers.

7. The firm must develop a professional board of directors.[18]

[18] Ibid., 6.

The key factor in this process is found in the first step: the entrepreneur. Entrepreneurial self-management is the major area of concern.

Balancing the Focus (Entrepreneur and Manager)

In managing the growth stage, entrepreneurs must remember two important points. First, an adaptive firm needs to retain certain entrepreneurial characteristics in order to encourage innovation and creativity. Second, the entrepreneur needs to translate this spirit of innovation and creativity to his or her personnel while personally making a transition toward a more managerial style.[19] This critical entrepreneur/manager balance is extremely difficult to achieve. As Stevenson and Gumpert have noted, "Everybody wants to be innovative, flexible, and creative. But for every Apple, Domino's, and Lotus, there are thousands of new restaurants, clothing stores, and consulting firms that presumably have tried to be innovative, to grow, and to show other characteristics that are entrepreneurial in the dynamic sense—but have failed."[20]

Remaining entrepreneurial while making the transition to some of the more administrative traits is vital to the successful growth of a venture. Table 16.1 provides a framework for comparing the entrepreneurial and administrative characteristics and pressures relative to five major factors: strategic orientation, commitment to seize opportunities, commitment of resources, control of resources, and management structure. Each of these five areas is critical to the balance needed for managing entrepreneurially. At the two ends of the continuum (from entrepreneurial focus to administrative focus) are specific points of view. Stevenson and Gumpert have characterized these in question format:

The Entrepreneur's Point of View

- Where is the opportunity?
- How do I capitalize on it?
- What resources do I need?
- How do I gain control over them?
- What structure is best?

The Administrative Point of View

- What resources do I control?
- What structure determines our organization's relationship to its market?
- How can I minimize the impact of others on my ability to perform?
- What opportunity is appropriate?[21]

The logic behind the variance in the direction of these questions can be presented in a number of different ways. For example, the commitment of resources in the entrepreneurial frame of mind responds to changing environmental needs, whereas the managerial point of view is focused on the reduction of risk. In the control of resources, entrepreneurs will avoid ownership because of the risk of obsolescence and the need for more flexibility, whereas managers will view ownership as a means to accomplish efficiency and stability.

---

[19] John B. Miner, "Entrepreneurs, High Growth Entrepreneurs, and Managers: Contrasting and Overlapping Motivational Patterns," *Journal of Business Venturing* (July 1990): 221–34.

[20] Howard H. Stevenson and David E. Gumpert, "The Heart of Entrepreneurship," *Harvard Business Review* (March/April 1985): 85.

[21] Ibid., 86–87.

TABLE 16.1

THE ENTREPRENEURIAL CULTURE VERSUS THE ADMINISTRATIVE CULTURE

	Entrepreneurial Focus		Administrative Focus	
	Characteristics	**Pressures**	**Characteristics**	**Pressures**
Strategic Orientation	Driven by perception of opportunity	Diminishing opportunities Rapidly changing technology, consumer economics, social values, and political rules	Driven by controlled resources	Social contracts Performance measurement criteria Planning systems and cycles
Commitment to Seize Opportunities	Revolutionary, with short duration	Action orientation Narrow decision windows Acceptance of reasonable risks Few decision constituencies	Evolutionary, with long duration	Acknowledgment of multiple constituencies Negotiation about strategic course Risk reduction Coordination with existing resource base
Commitment of Resources	Many stages, with minimal exposure at each stage	Lack of predictable resource needs Lack of control over the environment Social demands for appropriate use of resources Foreign competition Demands for more efficient use	A single stage, with complete commitment out of decision	Need to reduce risk Incentive compensation Turnover in managers Capital budgeting systems Formal planning systems
Control of Resources	Episodic use or rent of required resources	Increased resource specialization Long resource life compared with need Risk of obsolescence Risk inherent in the identified opportunity Inflexibility of permanent commitment to resources	Ownership or employment of required resources	Power, status, and financial rewards Coordination of activity Efficiency measures Inertia and cost of change Industry structures
Management Structure	Flat, with multiple informal networks	Coordination of key noncontrolled resources Challenge to hierarchy Employees' desire for independence	Hierarchy	Need for clearly defined authority and responsibility Organizational culture Reward systems Management theory

SOURCE: Reprinted by permission of the *Harvard Business Review*. An exhibit from "The Heart of Entrepreneurship," by Howard H. Stevenson and David E. Gumpert, March/April 1985, 89. Copyright © 1985 by the President and Fellows of Harvard College; all rights reserved.

In terms of structure, the entrepreneurial emphasis is on a need for flexibility and independence, whereas the administrative focus is on ensuring integration with a complexity of tasks, a desire for order, and controlled reward systems.

These examples of differences in focus help establish the important issues involved at both ends of the managerial spectrum. Each point of view—entrepreneurial and administrative—has important considerations that need to be balanced if effective growth is going to take place.

THE SELF-MANAGEMENT CONCEPT   To help entrepreneurs manage the growth stage better, a **self-management concept** has been proposed by a group of researchers.[22] This concept consists of a variety of techniques designed to identify management behaviors requiring change and to assist the entrepreneur in making those changes. Figure 16.4 illustrates the process involved in a self-management concept.

The major focus of this approach is the concept of "self" applied to the action part of the process. The key steps in this process follow:

1. *Self-observation.* Entrepreneurs need to analyze their time and recognize how it is being used.

2. *Self-established goals.* After the analysis of time and apportionment of activities, the entrepreneur must set goals that can direct behavior. These goals need to be specific and challenging yet attainable.

3. *Cueing strategies.* The firm's environment must be arranged to have cues that remind personnel of the appropriate behaviors for effective performance.

4. *Rehearsal.* This step requires practice. The desired management behavior must be made part of the entrepreneur's everyday activity.

5. *Self-applied consequences.* This is the "what if" step in the process. What if the proper behavior is, or is not, accomplished? This step provides the rewards or punishment—self-induced—to encourage the proper actions. In this way, consequences are applied that reinforce the complete self-management approach.

Entrepreneurs can apply the self-management concept to improve their management abilities. This process follows the ideas of knowledge through analysis, of goal setting, and of reinforcement. It is a way for entrepreneurs to analyze their managerial style, to realign behaviors and time allotments, and to reinforce effective management techniques. Self-management can be especially useful for entrepreneurs whose enterprises are in the growth stage.

UNDERSTANDING THE GROWTH STAGE

The growth stage often signals the beginning of a metamorphosis from a personal venture to a group-structured operation. Domination by the lead entrepreneur gives way to a team approach based heavily on coordination and flexibility.

[22] Charles A. Snyder, Charles C. Manz, and Raymond W. LaForge, "Self-Management: A Key to Entrepreneurial Survival," *American Journal of Small Business* (July/September 1983): 20–26.

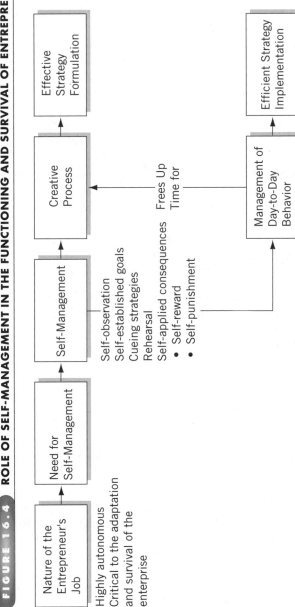

Nature of the Entrepreneur's Job

Highly autonomous
Critical to the adaptation and survival of the enterprise

Need for Self-Management

Self-Management

Self-observation
Self-established goals
Cueing strategies
Rehearsal
Self-applied consequences
• Self-reward
• Self-punishment

Creative Process

Frees Up Time for

Effective Strategy Formulation

Management of Day-to-Day Behavior

Efficient Strategy Implementation

SOURCE: Charles A. Snyder, Charles C. Manz, and Raymond W. laForge, "Self-Management: A Key to Entrepreneurial Survival," *American Journal of Small Business* (July/September 1983): 22. Reprinted with permission.

Key Factors during the Growth Stage

Entrepreneurs must understand four key factors about the specific managerial actions necessary during the growth stage. These factors are control, responsibility, tolerance of failure, and change.

CONTROL   Growth creates problems in command and control. When dealing with them, entrepreneurs need to answer three critical questions: Does the control system imply trust? Does the resource allocation system imply trust? Is it easier to ask permission than to ask forgiveness? These questions reveal a great deal about the control of a venture. If they are answered with yes, the venture is moving toward a good blend of control and participation. If they are answered with no, the reasons for each negative response should be closely examined.

RESPONSIBILITY   As the company grows, the distinction between authority and responsibility becomes more apparent. This is because authority always can be delegated, but it is most important to create a sense of responsibility. This action establishes flexibility, innovation, and a supportive environment. People tend to look beyond the job alone if a sense of responsibility is developed, so the growth stage is better served by the innovative activity and shared responsibility of all of the firm's members.

TOLERANCE OF FAILURE   Even though a venture has avoided the initial start-up pitfalls and has expanded to the growth stage, it is still important to maintain a tolerance of failure. The level of failure the entrepreneur experienced and learned from at the start of the venture should be the same level expected, tolerated, and learned from in the growth stage. Although no firm should seek failure, to continually innovate and grow it should tolerate a certain degree of failure as opposed to punishment for failure.

Three distinct forms of failure should be distinguished:

- *Moral failure.* This form of failure is a violation of internal trust. Since the firm is based on mutual expectations and trust, this violation is a serious failure that can result in negative consequences.
- *Personal failure.* This form of failure is brought about by a lack of skill or application. Usually responsibility for this form of failure is shared by the firm and the individual. Normally, therefore, an attempt is made to remedy the situation in a mutually beneficial way.
- *Uncontrollable failure.* This form of failure is caused by external factors and is the most difficult to prepare for or deal with. Resource limitations, strategic direction, and market changes are examples of forces outside the control of employees. Top management must carefully analyze the context of this form of failure and work to prevent its recurrence.

CHANGE   Planning, operations, and implementation are all subject to continual changes as the venture moves through the growth stage and beyond. Retaining an innovative and opportunistic posture during growth requires a sense of change and variation from the norm. It should be realized, however, that change holds many implications for the enterprise in terms of resources, people, and structure. It is therefore important during growth that the flexibility regarding change be preserved. This allows for faster managerial response to environmental conditions.

Managing Paradox and Contradiction

When a venture experiences surges in growth, a number of structural factors begin to present multiple challenges. Entrepreneurs constantly struggle over whether to organize these factors, such as cultural elements, staffing and development of personnel, and appraisal and rewards, in a rigid, bureaucratic design or a flexible, organic design. Table 16.2 depicts the conflicting designs for each element.

Research has shown that new-venture managers experiencing growth, particularly in emerging industries, need to adopt flexible, organic structures.[23] Rigid, bureaucratic structures are best suited for mature, stabilized companies. Thus, the cultural elements need to follow a flexible design of autonomy, risk taking, and entrepreneurship. This type of culture is a renewal of the entrepreneur's original force that created the venture. Although the entrepreneur's focus makes a transition toward a more administrative style, as mentioned earlier, the culture of the organization must be permeated with a constant renewal of the virtues of innovation and entrepreneurship.[24]

When designing a flexible structure for high growth, entrepreneurs must realize a number of contradictory forces are at work in certain other structural factors. Consider the following:

BUREAUCRATIZATION VERSUS DECENTRALIZATION Increased hiring stimulates bureaucracy: Firms formalize procedures as staffing doubles and triples. Employee participation and autonomy decline, and internal labor markets develop. Tied to growth, however, is also an increased diversity in product offering that favors less formalized decision processes, greater decentralization, and the recognition that the firm's existing human resources lack the necessary skills to manage the broadening portfolio.

ENVIRONMENT VERSUS STRATEGY High environment turbulence and competitive conditions favor company cultures that support risk taking, autonomy, and employee participation in decision making. Firms confront competitors, however, through strategies whose implementation depends on the design of formal systems that inhibit risk taking and autonomy.

STRATEGIC EMPHASES: QUALITY VERSUS COST VERSUS INNOVATION Rapidly growing firms strive to simultaneously control costs, enhance product quality, and improve product offerings. Minimizing costs and undercutting competitors' product prices, however, are best achieved by traditional hierarchical systems of decision making and evaluations. Yet these strategies conflict with the kinds of autonomous processes most likely to encourage the pursuit of product quality and innovation.[25]

These factors emphasize the importance of managing paradox and contradiction. Growth involves the multiple challenges of (1) the stresses and strains induced by attempts to control costs while simultaneously enhancing quality and creating new products to maintain competitive parity, and (2) centralizing to retain control while simultaneously decentralizing to encourage the contributions of autonomous, self-managed professionals

[23] Jeffrey G. Covin and Dennis P. Slevin, "New Venture Strategic Posture, Structure, and Performance: An Industry Life Cycle Analysis," *Journal of Business Venturing* (March 1990): 123–33.

[24] Ikujiro Nonaka and Tervo Yamanovchi, "Managing Innovation as a Self-Renewing Process," *Journal of Business Venturing* (September 1989): 299–315.

[25] Charles J. Fombrun and Stefan Wally, "Structuring Small Firms for Rapid Growth," *Journal of Business Venturing* (March 1989): 107–22.

ENTREPRENEURIAL

EDGE

From Entrepreneur to Manager

For many small-business owners, one of the most difficult tasks is to make the successful transition from a creative, task-juggling entrepreneur to a business-skill-applying manager. A dozen top small-business experts were asked their advice on making this transition successfully. Their answers were consolidated into the following list of key management strategies to help entrepreneurs grow their companies and boost their bottom line.

1. *Don't be the company handyperson.* When starting a new business, the entrepreneur must be able to do every job in the company. But as the company grows, it becomes essential that the entrepreneur learns to delegate. If he or she continues to do every little task, the business will certainly suffer. Jay Conrad Levinson, coauthor of *Guerrilla Marketing Online Weapons,* has some advice on how to escape from the do-it-yourself trap. He suggests that the owner keep a log of all the things he or she does. "You'll see there are things you must do and things you don't have to do. Never do anything you can delegate," Levinson says. By delegating, the entrepreneur will have more time to concentrate on essential leadership functions, such as setting long-term strategic goals.

2. *Hire to your shortcomings.* Oftentimes the strong entrepreneurial characteristics of a small-business owner, such as willingness to take risks, can become a hazard to an established business, according to Ned Herrmann, author of *The Whole Brain Business Book.* "Many business owners keep entrepreneuring when they should be focusing on the quality of product, competition, receivables, the kind of stuff that's boring," Herrmann says. The best remedy is to hire managers that complement the owner by filling in knowledge gaps. Herrmann explains that "Entrepreneurs tend to hire in their own image, so you get people who all think alike. But if you hire people who are different, it will lead to more innovative ideas."

3. *But don't overhire.* Today's labor market offers numerous staffing alternatives, such as temps, part-timers, and contract workers, that enable small businesses to keep taxes and insurance costs low. These alternatives also give businesses the flexibility to match their labor costs to the demand of their services, according to Irving Grousbeck, consulting professor of management at the Stanford Business School and cofounder of Continental Cablevision. In addition, "If one of your key people is sick or out for some other reason, you can bring in a trained person on an as-needed basis," Grousbeck says.

4. *Call out the "SWOT" team.* David H. Bangs Jr., author of *The Business Planning Guide,* suggests that a SWOT meeting should be held at least once a year to keep an ongoing business on track. The meeting would evaluate the company's strengths, weaknesses, opportunities, and threats (SWOT) in order to set goals and objectives

for the company. SWOT meetings should encourage frank, open discussions to be most productive. In addition, all employees should be required to attend, and the meeting should be facilitated by someone who is not involved in the company's day-to-day operations.

5. *Give employees a stake in the company's success.* In a small, lean business it is important to keep core employees motivated and loyal. "If you only have a small number of people working for you, obviously you count on these people for the success of the company," Joanna T. Lau, president of Lau Technologies in Acton, Massachusetts, says. Lau, also Ernst & Young's 1995 Turnaround Entrepreneur of the Year award winner, adds, "You might want to provide some of those people with the opportunity for equity in the business to create better loyalty."

6. *Hold down expenses.* The math is simple. Regardless of how much business is done, if a company's costs are outweighing its revenues, hard times are sure to follow. William F. Williams, president and CEO of Glory Foods Inc. in Columbus, Ohio, which is *Black Enterprise* magazine's Emerging Company of the Year for 1996, makes a conscious effort to keep his costs down by consistently pressing for better deals from suppliers and service providers. "The most important thing is to negotiate the best possible cost reductions you can at the outset of every business relationship," Williams claims. Cost-cutting opportunities are everywhere, such as bargaining rent space and shopping for interest rates.

7. *Go global.* "If you have an established business and you're not pursuing the international market, you're probably missing out on potential sales," Tammy L. Flor, president and CEO of Laurel Engineering Inc. in Chula Vista, California, and the SBA's 1995 Exporter of the Year, says. Although many small businesses may be intimidated by the thought of global competition, real opportunities do exist in these markets for even the smallest of companies.

8. *Scratch the customer's itch.* All types of business, regardless of what they sell, should adopt a cradle-to-grave approach toward their customers. Tom Hopkins, author of *Selling for Dummies,* describes this as a commitment to a follow-up system that starts by figuring out the "itch cycle" for the company's customers and product. The itch cycle is Hopkins's term for the period of time after a purchase from a company during which the customer is particularly receptive to making another commitment to that company. Hopkins's suggestion for benefiting from this cycle is to contact customers with handwritten letters expressing the company's hope that they are happy with their recent purchase. An example of this type of approach is a car salesperson who knows which customers usually buy a new car about every 30 months. "After about 28 months, the salesperson gets the latest model, drives it over to where the customer works, and invites him to drive it for a few days," Hopkins says. "And 85 percent of those cars are sold."

9. *Adapt to change.* "If customers want us to do things differently, we'll try to accommodate them. In fact, we ask them for suggestions," Peter Mendoza Jr., president of MBE

CONTINUED

Electric, a contracting business in Riverside, California, says. Peter and his vice-president brother, Brian, agree that one of their biggest challenges in customer relations is staying abreast of changes. In 1994, when the earthquake destroyed the Santa Monica Freeway, the Mendozas were asked to design a new electrical system—promptly. Although changes were made in the original contract twice and the scope of the work tripled, the job was completed in 66 days. Adapting to change has paid off for the Mendoza brothers. MBE Electric has grown from $2.6 million in sales to $5.5 million in three years, and the Mendozas were named the SBA's Young Entrepreneurs of the Year in 1996.

10. *Seek customer advice.* According to Susan RoAne, author of *How to Work a Room* and *The Secrets of Savvy Networking*, "Small-business owners fail when they have no relationship with the people who buy their products." She suggests calling or sending personal notes (via regular or E-mail) to key customers at least once every three months to gather their advice. Another suggestion is to ask customers to fill out a customer survey. According to RoAne, the survey should be no longer than one page, it should offer a discount on customers' next purchase if it is completed, and it should ask customers to tell what the company does or does not do well, in addition to providing space to include specific examples.

11. *Sniff out the silver linings.* The former president of Ben & Jerry's Ice Cream and author of *Ben & Jerry's: The Inside Scoop,* Fred Lager, says, "If I had one piece of advice, it would be to look for opportunities in the face of adversity." In his book, Lager describes the 1984 incident in which Pillsbury Co., owners of Häagen-Dazs, attempted to stop independent ice-cream dealers from offering Ben & Jerry's ice cream. "We were able to turn it to our advantage by asking 'What's the doughboy afraid of?' We got a lot of publicity. The result was that we got tremendous brand recognition—way beyond what we could have afforded with paid advertising," Lager recalls.

12. *Mix family and business with care.* Ross Nager, executive director of the Arthur Andersen Center for Family Business in Houston, Texas, says. "Don't forget your family." Small businesses can take advantage of the many roles family members can provide, such as a teenager's custodial work in the summers or the extended family's sales leads. Nager does suggest that to make the experience a positive one for everyone, relatives should be required to work somewhere else first, so their first job is not in the family business. This allows them to gain valuable outside experience, including realistic expectations, as well as increases their credibility among the other employees.

SOURCE: Stephen J. Simurda, "Instant MBA," *Small Business Computing* (February 1997): 60–63.

TABLE 16.2	CONFLICTING DESIGNS OF STRUCTURAL FACTORS	
	Flexible Design	**Bureaucratic Design**
Cultural Elements	Autonomous	Formalized
	Risk taking	Risk averse
	Entrepreneurial	Bureaucratic
Staffing and Development	Technical skills	Administrative skills
	Specialists	Generalists
	External hiring	Internal hiring
Appraisal and Rewards	Participative	Formalized
	Subjective	Objective
	Equity based	Incentive based

SOURCE: Charles J. Fombrun and Stefan Wally, "Structuring Small Firms for Rapid Growth," *Journal of Business Venturing* (March 1989): 109.

to the embryonic corporate culture. Rapidly growing firms are challenged to strike a balance among these multiple pulls when designing their managerial systems.

Confronting the Growth Wall

In attempting to develop a managerial ability to deal with venture growth, many entrepreneurial owners confront a **growth wall** that seems too gigantic to overcome. Thus, they are unable to begin the process of handling the challenges that growth brings about.

Researchers have identified a number of fundamental changes that confront rapid-growth firms, including instant size increases, a sense of infallibility, internal turmoil, and extraordinary resource needs. In addressing these changes that can build a growth wall, growth-oriented firms have exhibited a few consistent themes:

- The entrepreneur is able to envision and anticipate the firm as a larger entity.
- The team needed for tomorrow is hired and developed today.
- The original core vision of the firm is constantly and zealously reinforced.
- New "big-company" processes are introduced gradually as supplements to, rather than replacements for, existing approaches.
- Hierarchy is minimized.
- Employees hold a financial stake in the firm.[26]

These themes are important for entrepreneurs to keep in mind as they develop their abilities to manage growth.

One researcher found that internal constraints such as lack of growth capital, limited spans of control, and loss of entrepreneurial vitality occur in growth firms that struggle to survive versus those that successfully achieve high growth. In addition, fundamental

[26] Donald C. Hambrick and Lynn M. Crozier, "Stumblers and Stars in the Management of Rapid Growth," *Journal of Business Venturing* (January 1985): 31–45.

differences exist in the firms' approach to environmental changes and trends.[27] A six-step program was recommended as a process for breaking through the inability to handle environmental change or trends. These steps follow:

1. *Get the facts.* Develop an information base through competitor profiles, market studies, and technological analysis.

2. *Create a growth task force.* Develop a cross-functional team to organize and interpret the environmental data, to identify the venture's strengths and weaknesses, to brainstorm new ideas that leverage the firm's strengths, and to recommend key ideas that should be developed further.

3. *Plan for growth.* Develop a comprehensive plan for the recommended ideas that would be organized around four critical components: reasons for the stall in growth, the strategies to resolve the stall, a set of potential results, and identification of the necessary resources.

4. *Staff for growth.* Move beyond only the owner and key executives having responsibility for growth. Every manager needs to be charged with the constant challenge of responding to growth.

5. *Maintain a growth culture.* Create a corporate culture that encourages and rewards a growth-oriented attitude. Develop a core value statement that articulates the entrepreneur's commitment to growth.

6. *Use an advisory board.* Establish an outside board of advisors (directors) to become an integral part of the venture's growth. This board should help determine, design, and implement an organizational structure to enhance the desire for growth.[28]

Growth and Decision Making

The decision-making process is a critical issue in the growth stage of emerging ventures. The focus and style of decision making are distinctive from the earlier or later stages a venture goes through. Table 16.3 illustrates the primary decision-making focus for the growth stage compared to the early and later stages. Also, as depicted in the table, the organizational characteristics of successful early-stage firms and of successful mature firms are quite different. Indicative are differences in the problems they face. Early-stage firms usually face undefined tasks, such as technology or market development, characterized by high levels of uncertainty. As a result, their organizations typically demonstrate little structure in the form of job specialization, rules, or formality. Decision making is, in many instances, based solely on the owner communicating informally and face-to-face. The owner-founder integrates people, functions, and tasks in many instances through his or her own direct contact.

In contrast, mature firms that have attained a size of several hundred employees can no longer manage in such a fashion. They require some elements of formality, structure, and specialization to control and direct their organization effectively and efficiently. The transition of the decision-making process from that described for early-stage firms to that of

---

[27] Richard L. Osborne, "Second Phase Entrepreneurship: Breaking Through the Growth Wall," *Business Horizons* (January/February 1994): 80–86.

[28] Ibid., 82–85.

TABLE 16.3 **DECISION-MAKING CHARACTERISTICS AND GROWTH STAGES**

	Early Stage(s)	Growth Stage	Later Stage(s)
Primary Focus	Product business Definition Acquisition of resources Development of market position	Volume production Market share Viability	Cost control Profitability Future growth opportunity
Decision-Making Characteristics	Informal Centralized Nonspecialized Short time horizon	Transitional	Formal Decentralized Specialized Long and short time horizon

SOURCE: Thomas N. Gilmore and Robert K. Kazanjian, "Clarifying Decision Making in High Growth Ventures: The Use of Responsibility Charting," *Journal of Business Venturing* (January 1989): 71.

later-stage firms must be effected during the growth stage. Timing is critical. Premature introduction of structure and formalities may dampen the venture's creative, entrepreneurial climate. However, if formality and structure are not adopted soon enough, management may lose control of the organization as its size increases, leading to major dislocations of the firm and even failure.[29]

Therefore, entrepreneurs need to recognize the important transition of decision-making style during growth and to learn to authorize others to make necessary decisions in order to address the simultaneous challenges of rapid growth. Methods for entrepreneurs to consider when handling decisions during growth have been suggested.

One method concentrates on the use of **external resources** through networking.[30] In other words, networking entails the establishment of external personal relationships that the entrepreneur may use for professional assistance. The idea is to gain a competitive advantage by extending decision making and resource availability beyond the assets under the domain and control of the venture. One example of such resource use is a firm that obtains a license to use a well-known name to market a product that could not achieve recognition otherwise and that does so by promising a royalty on future sales. This is obviously taking advantage of a series of resources—all the resources normally needed to create a national brand—that it does not own. "External resources" are assets—physical or otherwise—a firm uses in its pursuit of growth and over which it has no direct ownership.[31] Another example would be the use of outside consulting assistance in the areas of administrative or operating problems. Strategic planning, security financing, marketing,

[29] Thomas N. Gilmore and Robert K. Kazanjian, "Clarifying Decision Making in High Growth Ventures: The Use of Responsibility Charting," *Journal of Business Venturing* (January 1989): 69–83.

[30] J. Carlos Jarillo, "Entrepreneurship and Growth: The Strategic Use of External Resources," *Journal of Business Venturing* (March 1989): 133–47.

[31] Ibid., 135.

TABLE 16.4	STEPS OF RESPONSIBILITY CHARTING

1. Establishment of initial parameters:
   Decision rules
   Common language
   Creating the matrix of key decisions and roles

2. Individual balloting and tabulation of patterns

3. Discussion, clarification, negotiation

4. Agreement on allocation of responsibility

5. Monitoring and renegotiation as needed

SOURCE: Thomas N. Gilmore and Robert K. Kazanjian, "Clarifying Decision Making in High Growth Ventures: The Use of Responsibility Charting," *Journal of Business Venturing* (January 1989): 73.

and day-to-day operational assistance are all areas in which emerging firms may seek outside assistance.[32]

Another method suggested to entrepreneurs for consideration when handling decisions during growth is **responsibility charting.**[33] The process assumes decision making involves multiple roles that participate in various ways at different points of time. Therefore, its three major components are decisions, roles, and types of participation. These three components are combined to form a matrix, so a respondent can assign a type of participation to each of the roles (at the top) for a specific decision (on the left). Responses are then analyzed either in a group setting with all participants present or by a facilitator alone when group size makes processing of the data unwieldy. The steps of responsibility charting are listed in Table 16.4.

When reporting the value of this process, Gilmore and Kazanjian stated, "Responsibility charting enables better discussions of power and authority because it allows a rich range of potential solutions, rather than the win-lose dynamics that result from discussing these issues in terms of boxes and lines of a new structure.

"In growth-stage ventures, team building often fails because of the influx of new executives. Once responsibility charting has been used to clarify major decisions, the results are a powerful way to orient new executives who step into key roles. Unlike a job description that only communicates one's duties, the chart shows how the role fits into many critical processes."[34]

Whether it's networking or responsibility charting, entrepreneurs need to develop methods for handling the increasing complexities of decision making in the growth stage. The key to any system may be the ability of the entrepreneur to delegate.

---

[32] James J. Chrisman and John Leslie, "Strategic, Administrative, and Operating Problems: The Impact of Outsiders on Small Firm Performance," *Entrepreneurship Theory and Practice* (spring 1989): 37–48.

[33] Thomas N. Gilmore and Robert K. Kazanjian, "Clarifying Decision Making in High Growth Ventures: The Use of Responsibility Charting," *Journal of Business Venturing* (January 1989): 69–83.

[34] Ibid., 81.

Effective Delegation

For making the transition from the owner dominance of an entrepreneurial venture to the diversity of operations in a growth stage, **effective delegation** is a key component to success. This process entails three steps: (1) assigning specific duties, (2) granting authority to carry out these duties, and (3) creating the obligation of responsibility for necessary action.[35]

Why is delegation so essential to growth-oriented ventures? Because to continue growth and innovation, the entrepreneur needs to free up his or her time and to rely on others in the enterprise to carry on the day-to-day activities.[36] Timothy W. Firnstahl, an executive with a small growth-oriented firm, states:

> In start-up companies, the visions are usually the entrepreneurs'—they have the clear ideas about the product or service they plan to offer. Moreover, they often have to be in all places at all times, taking care of every detail. Unfortunately, this 100 percent hands-on management does not permit an entrepreneur's staff to mature. Why think, if the boss has all the answers? Inadvertently, an entrepreneur usurps employees' responsibilities. Worse, people often perform well because they know the owner is right there.[37]

In addition to the three steps just outlined, two other delegation-related responsibilities arise.[38] The first is to hire the best employees—the basis of any effective entrepreneurial team. As a small venture grows into a larger enterprise, hiring becomes a major area of consideration. The organization needs to determine the proper skill so it can hire those who have the necessary skills (or abilities to learn these skills) to fill newly created jobs.

The second responsibility is to use delegation to free up time for thinking effectively. The entrepreneur needs to continually consider the basic philosophy and direction of the firm. Firnstahl put it this way:

> Thinking is not reading, meeting, routine reporting, listening, observing, or working. In a sense, thinking is dreaming the organization's future. It's the ability to see tomorrow and construct the company's ideal state. It's the ability to get excited about the possibilities of the future.[39]

In addition to the ideas presented thus far, other suggestions for thinking about the venture's future follow:

1. *View thinking as a strategy.* Thinking is the best way to resolve difficulties. The entrepreneur needs to maintain faith in his or her ability to think through problems. The individual also must recognize the difference between worrying and thinking. Worrying is repeated, needless problem analysis, whereas thinking is solution generation.

2. *Schedule large blocks of uninterrupted time.* Because thinking takes time, it must be scheduled. By carving out large blocks of uninterrupted time during periods when he or she is most productive, the entrepreneur makes effective use of time.

---

[35] See Richard M. Hodgetts and Donald F. Kuratko, *Management,* 3d ed. (San Diego: Harcourt Brace Jovanovich, 1991), 279–82.

[36] Wayne C. Shannon, "Empowerment: The Catchword of the 90's," *Quality Progress* (July 1991): 62–63.

[37] Timothy W. Firnstahl, "Letting Go," *Harvard Business Review* (September/October 1986): 15.

[38] Ibid., 15–16.

[39] Ibid., 16.

3. *Stay focused on relevant topics.* The entrepreneur must be prepared to work hard mentally until his or her mind produces the necessary quality. The ideas are there; it is a matter of ferreting them out.

4. *Record, sort, and save thoughts.* Ideas are the product of work; they should be recorded, sorted, and saved. Effective entrepreneurs write them on three-inch by five-inch cards, one idea per card, so they remain "mobile." Another approach is to use a handheld recorder to capture thoughts while driving and then to have these ideas written down. Files of ideas about the organization's future are a major source of information.[40]

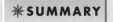

✻ SUMMARY

A typical life cycle of a venture has five stages: development, start-up, growth, stabilization, and innovation or decline. The focus of this chapter has been on maintaining an entrepreneurial frame of mind while making the necessary adjustments for dealing with the growth phase.

In building the desired adaptive firm, entrepreneurs need to be concerned with three important responsibilities: (1) increasing the perception of opportunity, (2) institutionalizing change as the venture's goals, and (3) instilling the desire to be innovative.

The transition from an entrepreneurial style to a managerial approach was then reviewed. A seven-step process for achieving this transition was described. The balance between the entrepreneurial and the administrative focus was then considered. This balance was demonstrated by illustrating five major factors: strategic orientation, commitment to seize opportunities, commitment of resources, control of resources, and management structure. This differentiation of major factors is important for analyzing aspects of the venture that need either more administrative or more entrepreneurial emphasis.

A self-management concept was introduced as an example of how entrepreneurs can assimilate more managerial aspects into their style. A self-applied process of observation, goals, cues, rehearsal, and consequences was discussed as a way of applying an action-oriented approach to the process of transition.

The chapter then examined the importance of a venture's growth stage. Underscoring the metamorphosis a venture goes through, four factors were discussed: control, responsibility, tolerance of failure, and change.

In addition, the challenge of managing paradox and contradiction was presented. The myriad challenges resulting from entrepreneurial growth involve the conflicts between rigid, bureaucratic designs and flexible, organic designs. The focus and style of decision making differ in the early stages from those of the later stages of a venture. Networking for external resources may be one solution to the need for simultaneous decisions during rapid growth. Another solution for handling decisions during growth is responsibility charting, which involves assigning a type of participation to a particular role for a specific decision. Finally, the managerial skill of delegation was examined to emphasize the importance of giving up specific managerial duties to free up the entrepreneur's time to think and to plan.

[40] Adapted from Firnstahl, "Letting Go," 18.

Key Terms and Concepts

Adaptive firm	New-venture development
Effective delegation	Responsibility charting
External resources	Self-management concept
Growth stage	Stabilization stage
Growth wall	Start-up activities
Life-cycle stages	Venture teams

Review and Discussion Questions

1. Briefly identify and describe the stages of development for a new venture.
2. Firms that fail to innovate will die. What does this statement mean in the context of new ventures?
3. What are the dangers of an entrepreneur evolving into a bureaucrat?
4. How can entrepreneurs build an adaptive firm? Be complete in your answer.
5. Successful ventures balance entrepreneurial characteristics with managerial style. What does this statement mean?
6. Comparing the entrepreneurial focus with the administrative focus involves five major areas of consideration. What are these areas?
7. How can the self-management concept be of value to entrepreneurs managing the growth stage?
8. Identify and describe the four key factors that need to be considered during the growth stage.
9. What is meant by managing paradox and contradiction?
10. Identify some examples of conflicting designs of structural factors. (Use Table 16.2.)
11. Describe the concepts of networking and responsibility charting, and explain their potential for improving entrepreneurs' decision-making abilities.
12. Why is delegation so important to entrepreneurs making the transition from an entrepreneurial venture to the diversified operations of the growth stage? Explain in detail.

Experiential Exercise   *The Venture Life Cycle*

At the top are the five basic phases or stages of the typical life cycle of a venture, labeled *A* through *E*. Rank these from *1* to *5*, beginning with the first phase and continuing to the last. Then examine the list of activities *(a* through *j),* and place a *1* next to those that happen during the first phase of the venture, on down to a *5* next to those that occur during the last phase. Answers are provided at the end of the exercise.

_____ A. Growth

_____ B. Innovation or decline

_____ C. Start-up

_____ D. Stabilization

_____ E. New-venture development

_____ *a)* Transition from one-person leadership to team management leadership

_____ *b)* New-product development

_____ *c)* Search for capital

_____ *d)* Increased competition

_____ *e)* Venture assessment

_____ *f)* Attempts to acquire other firms

_____ *g)* Consumer indifference to the entrepreneur's goods or services

_____ *h)* Accumulation of resources

_____ *i)* Major changes in entrepreneurial strategy

_____ *j)* Development of an effective entrepreneurial team

Answers

A. 3	*a)* 3	*f)* 5
B. 5	*b)* 5	*g)* 4
C. 2	*c)* 2	*h)* 1
D. 4	*d)* 4	*i)* 3
E. 1	*e)* 1	*j)* 2

VIDEO CASE 16.1

Baby Boomers and Beyond: Centex Looks Forward

Survey the American landscape and you're bound to see the distinctive mark of the Centex Corporation. For nearly 50 years, Centex has been constructing quality homes, dramatic skyscrapers, world-class symphony halls, art museums, and some of the country's most recognizable landmarks—including the Library of Congress and Disney World. Centex is the nation's largest and most geographically diverse home builder, as well as the fifth largest general building contractor. Its financial services division ranks in the top ten retail mortgage originators in the country—approving approximately 45,000 loans every year. Founded in 1950, the company went public in 1969 and has experienced dramatic growth ever since. Today, Centex is a multi-industry conglomerate operating in four related business segments: home building, financial services, contracting, and construction products.

With revenues totaling $3.1 billion, Centex's stellar growth has been built on a foundation of careful planning and analysis. "Every year, we complete a review of all our assumptions involving our business, our positioning, our product, and our placement," Tim Eller, president and CEO of Centex Homes, says. "In addition, our operating divisions invest a great deal of time and feasibility into diligence analysis before acquiring any land that will be developed."

Executive vice president and chief financial officer David Quinn reveals, "Our planning process uses quantitative analysis, of course, but, in addition, we look at strategic issues such as capital allocation to those businesses that are generating our target return. We also look at issues like people resources. Where do we have the people to fit the needs of a new business or expand into a new market?"

Recently, environmental factors have made it crucial for Centex to identify new business opportunities that will carry the company into the future. "Centex, being in the construction business and mortgage business, is the quintessential company that is affected by interest rates," Larry Hirsch, chair and CEO of the Centex Corporation, explains. "Over the last 24 months, we have been much more hesitant to enter new markets because we saw the environmental factors changing in the home building business. The banks and savings and loans started to provide more money to small- and medium-sized home builders, which increased competition even as the economy was continuing to expand. This meant the margins were coming down. Since there was more competition for land, the price of land was going up. The combination of those two factors said that we had to change our philosophy."

Centex conducted a number of focus groups using a cross section of its own employees. Led by Hirsch, this series of brainstorming sessions, titled "Baby Boomers and Beyond—Products, Services and Ideas," yielded some valuable insights for the company. "There was a recognition that as our population continues to age, it's going to be difficult for our society to utilize the traditional products and services to solve the problems of the aging population. And that energized an effort in Centex to say, 'How can we look at these areas in more detail?'" This feedback was incorporated into Centex's formal planning process. A task force was formed to evaluate how Centex's core competencies could translate into other profitable products and services with continuing sources of income. The result led Centex to launch two new business initiatives: senior housing and services and Centex Home Services, which offers Centex home buyers monthly home security and pest extermination services. "We recognize that businesses that have continuing sources of income are more productive to the company over time," Hirsch says.

An openness to new ideas, coupled with well-defined goals and carefully executed strategic plans, always have been among Centex's strengths. This kind of leadership has consistently earned Centex a place among *Fortune* magazine's list of most-admired companies. As Centex continues to construct new successes in the twenty-first century, it is likely to be admired for a long time to come.

Questions

1. How would Centex Corporation fit into the Life Cycle of a Venture?
2. Describe the elements of building an adaptive firm that apply to Centex.
3. What indications are there that Centex's management team balances entrepreneurial and administrative focus?

 **CASE 16.2**

Hendrick's Way

When Hendrick Harding started his consumer products firm, he was convinced he had a winning product. His small, compact industrial drill was easier to use than any other on the market and cost 30 percent less than any of the competitors' drills. The orders began to pour in, and within 6 months Hendrick's sales surpassed his first year's estimate. At the end of the first 12 months of operation his firm was grossing more than $50,000 a month, and he had a six-week backlog in filling orders.

The rapid growth of the firm continued for two years. Beginning about 4 months ago, however, Hendrick began to notice a dip in sales. The major reason appears to be a competitive product that costs 10 percent less than Hendrick's drill and offers all the same benefits and features. Hendrick believes that with a couple of minor adjustments he can improve his product and continue to dominate the market.

On the other hand, Hendrick is somewhat disturbed by the comments of one of his salespeople, George Simonds. George spends most of his time on the road and gets to talk to a great many customers. Here is what he had to say to Hendrick: "Your industrial drill has really set the market on its ear. And we should be able to sell a modified version of it for at least another 36 months before making any additional changes. However, you need to start thinking about adding other products to the line. Let's face it; we are a one-product company. That's not good. We have to expand our product line if we are to grow. Otherwise, I can't see much future for us."

The problem with this advice is that Hendrick does not want to grow larger. He is happy selling just the industrial drill. He believes that if he continues to modify and change the drill, he can maintain a large market share and the company will continue to be profitable. As he explained to George, "I see the future as more of the past. I really don't think there will be a great many changes in this product. There will be modifications, sure, but nothing other than that. I think this firm can live off the industrial drill for at least the next 25 years. We've got a great thing going. I don't see any reason for change. And I certainly don't want to come out with a second product. There's no need for it."

Questions

1. What is the danger in Hendrick's thinking? Explain in detail.
2. Could the self-management concept be of any value to Hendrick? Why or why not?
3. Using Table 16.1 as your point of reference, how would you describe Hendrick's focus? Based on your evaluation, what recommendations would you make to him?

 **CASE   16.3**

Keeping Things Going

The Clayton Company has grown 115 percent in the past year and 600+ percent in the past three years. A large portion of this growth is attributable to Jan Clayton's philosophy of hiring the best possible computer systems people and giving them the freedom they need to do their jobs.

Most of Jan's personnel operate out of work teams that analyze, design, and implement computer systems for clients. The way the process works is this: First, the company will get a call from a potential client indicating that it needs to have a computer system installed or a special software written for its operations. Jan will send over one of her people to talk to the client and analyze the situation. If it turns out that the Clayton Company has the expertise and personnel to handle the job, the client will be quoted a price. If this price is acceptable, a Clayton group will be assigned the project.

An example of a typical project is the client who called three weeks ago and wanted to purchase five personal computers for the firm's engineering staff. The company wanted these machines hooked up to the main computer. Additionally, the firm wanted its computer-aided design software to be modified so the engineers could see their computer-generated drawings in a variety of colors, not just in monochrome. The Clayton group installed the entire system and modified the software in ten working days.

Jan realizes that the growth of her enterprise will be determined by two factors. One is the creativity and ingenuity of her workforce. The other is the ability to attract talented personnel. "This business is heavily labor intensive," she explained. "If someone wants a computer system installation, that may take 100 labor hours. If I don't have the people to handle the project, I have to turn it down. My expansion is heavily dependent on hiring and training talented people. Additionally, I need more than just hard workers. I need creative people who can figure out new approaches to handling complex problems. If I can do these two things, I can stay a jump ahead of the competition. Otherwise, I won't be able to survive."

In dealing with these key factors for success, Jan has initiated three changes. First, she has instituted a bonus system tied to sales; these bonuses are shared by all of the personnel. Second, she gives quarterly salary increases, with the greatest percentages going to employees who are most active in developing new programs and procedures for handling client problems. Third, she has retreats every six months in which the entire staff goes for a long weekend to a mountain area where they spend three days discussing current work-related problems and ways of dealing with them. Time is also devoted to social events and to working on developing an esprit de corps among the personnel.

Questions

1. In what phase of the venture life cycle is Jan's firm currently operating? Defend your answer.
2. How are Jan's actions helping to build an adaptive firm? Give three specific examples.
3. If Jan's firm continues to grow, what recommendations would you make for future action? What else should Jan be thinking about doing in order to keep things moving smoothly? Be specific in your answer.

Chapter 17

GLOBAL OPPORTUNITIES FOR ENTREPRENEURS

CHAPTER OBJECTIVES

1. To introduce the new international developments that have expanded opportunities for the global market

2. To examine how entrepreneurs can take advantage of importing opportunities

3. To explore the entrepreneurial benefits of exporting

4. To discuss the advantages and disadvantages of entrepreneurial joint ventures

5. To examine the benefits of direct foreign investment by entrepreneurs

6. To explain how licensing arrangements work and to review their advantages and disadvantages

7. To set forth the five key steps for entering the international marketplace

Today, thanks to a thriving world economy, global telecommunications, and expanding travel, exchange among Europe, North America, and the Pacific Rim is happening at an unparalleled pace. In the urban centers of the developing world signs of the international youth culture are almost everywhere. . . .

For the companies that sell these new international products, that understand the world as one single market, it is an economic bonanza.

John Naisbitt and Patricia Aburdene,
Megatrends 2000, 1990

One of the most exciting and promising ways an entrepreneur can expand his or her business is to participate in the international market. Each year thousands of small-business enterprises are actively engaged in the international arena. Two of the primary reasons for this emerging opportunity are the decline in trade barriers, especially among major trading nations, and the emergence of major trading blocs that have been brought about by the North American Free Trade Agreement and the European Union. In addition, over the past decade Asia has become a hotbed for entrepreneurial opportunity, with China growing at a particularly rapid rate.[1]

In this chapter we shall discuss new developments in the global marketplace that directly affect entrepreneurial opportunities. We also shall examine the various methods of international participation. Finally, we shall consider the steps to be taken when going international: the required research, the feasibility study, and the implementation of the plan.

THE INTERNATIONAL ENVIRONMENT

"Global thinking" is important because today's consumers can select products, ideas, and services from many nations and cultures. Entrepreneurs who expand into foreign markets must be global thinkers in order to design and adopt strategies for different countries.

---

[1] For some examples, see Fred Luthans, Richard R. Patrick, and Brett C. Luthans, "Doing Business in Central and Eastern Europe: Political, Economic, and Cultural Diversity," *Business Horizons* (September/October 1995): 9–16; Charles H. Matthews, Xiaodong Qin, and Geralyn McClure Franklin, "Stepping toward Prosperity: The Development of Entrepreneurial Ventures in China and Russia," *Journal of Small Business Management* (July 1996): 75–85; and Y. Fan, N. Chen, and D. A. Kirby, "Chinese Peasant Entrepreneurs: An Examination of Township and Village Enterprises in Rural China," *Journal of Small Business Management* (October 1996): 73–75.

Doing business globally is rapidly becoming a profitable and popular strategy for many entrepreneurial ventures.[2] The myth that international business is the province of giant multinational enterprises long since has been disproven by capable and opportunistic entrepreneurs. According to the Small Business Administration, 25 percent of all firms that now export goods or services have fewer than 100 employees.[3] A number of factors are contributing to the continued increase of small ventures participating in the global marketplace. Four that warrant a brief look include (1) the World Trade Organization, (2) the North American Free Trade Agreement, (3) the European Union, and (4) developments in Asia.

The World Trade Organization

For many years the General Agreement on Tariffs and Trade (GATT) was the major trade liberalization organization whose objectives were to create a basic set of rules under which trade negotiations took place and to provide a mechanism for monitoring the implementation of those rules. In the early 1990s new agreements under GATT resulted in a tariff reduction of 38 percent worldwide. Consequently, the percentage of products entering the United States duty-free eventually rose from 10 percent to 40 percent, and, for industrialized countries worldwide, the percentage was scheduled to rise from 22 percent to 40 percent.

On January 1, 1995, GATT was replaced by the **World Trade Organization (WTO).** This newly created organization has more power to enforce rulings on trade disputes and to create a more efficient system for monitoring trade policies. In particular, it provides the principal contractual obligations determining how governments frame and implement domestic trade legislation and regulations.[4] Additionally, it is the platform from which trade relations among countries evolve through collective debate, negotiation, and adjudication. Most important, however, is that a large percentage of former GATT members have agreed to join the WTO. This includes world economic powers such as the United States, Japan, members of the European Union, and Canada. By early 1997 some 130 governments had joined the WTO, and applications from 29 more were being processed. Collectively, those who have joined account for more than 80 percent of all world trade.

The North American Free Trade Agreement

The **North American Free Trade Agreement (NAFTA)** is an international agreement between Canada, Mexico, and the United States whereby eventually no trade barriers will exist among the three nations. Additionally, it is likely that within the next decade Chile and other South American countries will join NAFTA. This, in turn, will create one of the largest trading blocs in the world, second only to the European Union. This new market is composed of 400 million consumers, and the total gross domestic product for the three countries is close to $7 trillion. Thus, new opportunities will occur for entrepreneurs in North America. The importance of the agreement can be clearly seen when exports and imports among the three partners are examined. Tables 17.1 and 17.2 show the importance of Canadian and Mexican trade for the United States. In all, these two countries account for more than 28 percent of all U.S. exports and more than 25 percent of all U.S. imports.

---

[2] Kenneth Chilton, "How American Manufacturers Are Facing the Global Marketplace," *Business Horizons* (July/August 1995): 10–19.

[3] *State of Small Business: A Report to the President* (Washington, DC: Government Printing Office, 1992), 15–16.

[4] "About the WTO," World Trade Organization release, March 1997. Available from World Wide Web @ http://www.

TABLE 17.1	THE TEN LARGEST U.S. EXPORT MARKETS

Country/Region	Value (billions of $)	Percent of World Trade
Canada	$133.7	22.9%
Japan	67.5	11.6
Mexico	56.8	9.7
United Kingdom	30.9	5.3
South Korea	26.6	4.6
Germany	23.5	4.0
Taiwan	18.4	3.2
Singapore	16.7	2.9
Netherlands	16.6	2.8
France	14.4	2.5
Subtotal	$405.1	69.5%
World	$583.9	

SOURCE: Reported in the *New York Times*, 2 March 1997, 8.

TABLE 17.2	THE TEN LARGEST U.S. IMPORT MARKETS

Country/Region	Value (billions of $)	Percent of World Trade
Canada	$156.5	20.3%
Japan	115.2	15.0
Mexico	73.0	9.5
China	51.5	6.7
Germany	38.9	5.1
Taiwan	29.9	3.9
United Kingdom	28.9	3.8
South Korea	22.7	3.0
Singapore	20.3	2.6
France	18.8	2.4
Subtotal	$555.5	72.3%
World	$770.6	

SOURCE: Reported in the *New York Times*, 2 March 1997, 8.

As NAFTA begins to take shape and trade barriers are reduced, the amount of trade among the three partners will increase. Perhaps even more important, the competition that will be created by the removal of trade barriers will force more and more small firms to increase their quality and overall competitiveness. In turn, this will make the firms more competitive when doing business in Asia, Europe, and other international markets.

Of particular importance to entrepreneurs is the fact potential markets will increase for both exports and imports.[5] The most efficient firms will find themselves able to provide higher quality and lower prices than their competitors, and no tariffs or quotas will keep out their goods.[6] At the same time, entrepreneurs in all three countries will find themselves protected from foreign competition because of local content laws. For example, all automobiles must have 60 percent of the net cost of the car produced in Canada, the United States, or Mexico. So Japanese manufacturers will not be able to take advantage of NAFTA by shipping most of the auto parts into Mexico, assembling them there, and then transporting them to the United States, since these cars do not meet the 60 percent net cost rule. However, cars made in the United States can be shipped to Mexico and Canada because they do meet the local content rule. Other industries that will profit from the NAFTA agreement include agriculture, banking, communications, construction, energy, insurance, publishing, and transportation. In addition, NAFTA will offer strong protection of patents, copyrights, industrial design rights, trade secret rights, and other forms of intellectual property.[7] Many entrepreneurs will find that their success in this market bloc will prepare them to do business elsewhere, including the European Union.

The European Union

The **European Union (EU)** was founded in 1957 as the European Economic Community and in 1992 became a full-fledged economic union. The objectives of the EU include (1) the elimination of custom duties among all member states; (2) the free flow of goods and services among all members; (3) the creation of common trade policies toward all countries outside the EU; (4) the free movement of capital and personnel within the bloc; (5) the encouragement of economic development throughout the bloc; and (6) monetary and fiscal coordination among all members.

The EU remains one of the major markets for American goods and services as well as for foreign direct investment. Like the North American trading bloc, the goal of many entrepreneurs is to gain admission into this market so that the benefits that accrue to insiders can be realized. Another potential strategy is to work with EU partners in the American market by helping them extend their worldwide coverage. This reason is best explained in terms of triad trade. Research reveals that approximately 60 percent of all international trade is conducted by three groups: the United States, EU countries, and Japan.[8] These three, commonly referred to as the triad, have dominated world trade for decades, and during the 1980s and 1990s they have managed to maintain the lion's share of international trade despite that during this period the amount of worldwide imports and exports more than doubled! This helps explain why entrepreneurs now are looking for emerging opportunities in the EU and EU-based firms. They also are casting their eyes to Japan and Asia.

---

[5] See Gregory K. Stephens and Charles R. Green, "Doing Business in Mexico: Understanding Cultural Differences," *Organizational Dynamics* (summer 1995): 39–55.

[6] William C. Symonds, Geri Smith, and Stephen Baker, "Border Crossings," *Business Week,* 22 November 1993, 40–42.

[7] For more on this, see "NAFTA: The Future of Free Trade in North America," *U.S./Latin Trade,* September 1993.

[8] Alan M. Rugman and Richard M. Hodgetts, *International Business* (New York: McGraw-Hill Book Company, 1995), 586.

Japan and Asia

Japan, the richest country in Asia, saw its wealth increase sharply during the 1980s. One reason was the major gains achieved in world markets. For example, Japanese automakers garnered 30 percent of the U.S. market. The only reason this dramatic success was not repeated in Europe was that some EU countries placed limits on the amount of market share foreign firms could capture. A second reason for the increase in Japanese wealth was the rising value of the yen. During the late 1980s and early 1990s, the yen's value increased by almost 50 percent; although by 1997 the yen had lost much of this value as it fell sharply against the dollar.

Additionally, since 1992, Japan's economy has been stalled, and its trade walls have been weakened. In particular, many countries, most notably the United States, are demanding that Japan work to erase its large trade balances by allowing more foreign competition and by purchasing more goods and services from nations to which it is selling its output. In recent years, the United States has had a large trade deficit (imports minus exports) with Japan, and the Americans want steps taken to prevent this from continuing. These developments mean that it should get progressively less difficult to enter the Japanese market.[9] Additionally, as more and more entrepreneurs pry open the trade door, competition will increase, prices will drop, and demand will rise. So Japan promises to be a lucrative market for entrepreneurs who are able to exploit it.

Other Asian countries that offer entrepreneurial opportunities include China, India, and South Korea, to name but three.[10] The economy in China, which has the largest population in the world, in recent years has done much better than many casual observers realize.[11] During the 1980s the average annual growth of its gross domestic product was 10 percent, which was higher than that achieved by more economically advanced countries such as Hong Kong, Singapore, and Taiwan. The market in China for both industrial and consumer goods is rapidly growing, and, as the government continues to open its trade door to outsiders, a dramatic increase in entrepreneurial opportunities is likely to occur there. India is also an investment target for entrepreneurs, since the government has changed its political stance and is taking steps to attract foreign investment. Most important, perhaps, is that India realizes that if it does not make significant strides during the 1990s, the country will fall far behind most other countries in Asia. South Korea has had a long and rapid economic growth. By the beginning of the decade, its gross domestic product per capita was $5,400, which made it one of the more affluent countries in Southeast Asia. As its economy continues to grow, South Korea will become an increasingly attractive market for entrepreneurs looking to do business in Asia. In particular, it has a strong U.S. presence, reducing the cultural barriers that often are forbidding to Americans.[12]

These events illustrate the powerful economic forces creating new opportunities for entrepreneurs in the global marketplace. Entrepreneurs should not only be aware of these opportunities, but they also should prepare for the best method to do international business and learn the proper procedure for entering the international marketplace.[13]

---

[9] James C. Morgan and J. Jeffrey Morgan, *Cracking the Japanese Market* (New York: Free Press, 1991).

[10] Richard M. Hodgetts and Fred Luthans, *International Management,* 3d ed. (New York: McGraw-Hill Book Company, 1997), 25–28.

[11] Joyce Barnathan et al., "China: The Emerging Economic Powerhouse of the 21st Century," *Business Week,* 17 May 1993, 54–65.

[12] For more on doing business in Asia, see Rugman and Hodgetts, *International Business,* Chapter 19.

[13] See Esmond D. Smith Jr. and Cuong Pham, "Doing Business in Vietnam: A Cultural Guide," *Business Horizons* (May/June 1996): 47–51.

FIGURE 17.1   **RISK OF ENTERING GLOBAL MARKETS**

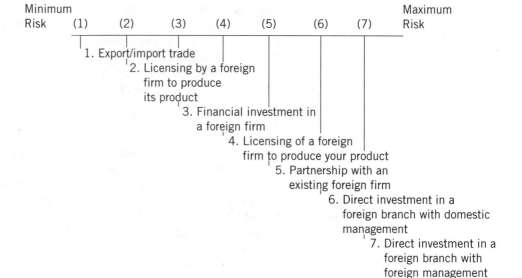

SOURCE: Roger D. Blackwell and Kristina Stephan, ''Growing Profits for Small Business through Global Expansion,'' *Small Business Forum* (winter 1990): 41.

METHODS OF GOING INTERNATIONAL

The entrepreneur can actively engage in the international market in five ways: importing, exporting, joint ventures, direct foreign investment, and licensing.[14] Each of these methods involves increasing levels of risk. Figure 17.1 illustrates the continuum of risk each method falls within. The final choice will depend on the organization's needs and the risk it is willing to take.

Importing

Importing is buying and shipping foreign-produced goods for domestic consumption. Each year the United States imports an increasing amount of goods. During the 1980s, the United States imported more goods than it exported, marking the first time this country became a net debtor nation since World War II. This situation continues today, and several factors have played a role in this change of trade status. One has been the rising cost of energy. A second, and complementary, reason is the low labor costs in other countries, which make their products financially attractive. A third reason is that some products are not available or produced domestically. (Diamonds, for example, are not mined in the United States but in Africa. As a result, American jewelry companies must import diamonds.)

How does an entrepreneur become aware of import opportunities? One way is to attend trade shows and fairs where firms gather to display their products and services. Some of these shows are international in flavor, with firms from different countries exhibiting their

[14] Richard M. Hodgetts and Donald F. Kuratko, *Management,* 3d ed. (San Diego: Harcourt Brace Jovanovich, 1991), 96–100.

products and services. Basically, the trade show gives the prospective customer the opportunity to window-shop. Another way is to monitor trade publications. Often, firms will advertise in trade publications to make themselves known to potential customers.

Exporting

When an entrepreneurial firm decides to participate actively in the international arena as a seller, rather than a buyer, it becomes an exporter. **Exporting** is the shipping of a domestically produced good to a foreign destination for consumption. Exporting is important for entrepreneurs because it often means increased market potential. Instead of limiting its market to the United States, the firm now has a broader sales sphere. According to the **learning curve concept,** increased sales will lead to greater efficiencies along the cost curve, which in turn will lead to increased profits. (The learning curve essentially states that as more and more units are produced, the firm becomes more efficient at production of the units, thereby lowering the cost per unit. The lower unit cost thus enables the firm to compete more effectively in the marketplace.)[15] It should be pointed out, however, that exporting normally will take three to five years to become profitable. Even if the firm is producing more units efficiently, it will take time to learn the intricacies and efficiencies of international business.[16]

Exporting has been increasing as a method for venture growth and increased profitability among small firms. One study examined the types of export strategies small firms use to gain a competitive edge in their market.[17] It identified four key competitive strategies. The first involves market differentiation through competitive pricing, through the development of brand identification, or through innovation in marketing techniques. The second type is a focus strategy involving specialty products for particular customers or involving new product development. The third strategy is achieving technological superiority of certain products. And the fourth key strategy is a product-oriented emphasis using the elements of customer service and high quality.[18] In order to pursue any of these strategies, entrepreneurs need to understand some of the ways to become involved in exporting that are presented in the following sections.

EXPORT MANAGEMENT COMPANY Participation in the export market takes a variety of forms. One of the simplest is to engage the services of an **export management company.** An export management company is a private firm that serves as an export department for several manufacturers. The company solicits and transacts export business on behalf of its clients in return for a commission, salary, or retainer plus commission.[19] In addition, some export management companies will purchase the product and sell it themselves to foreign customers. Export management companies can facilitate the export process by handling all of the details—from making the shipping arrangements to locating the customers.[20] When approaching an export management company, however, entrepreneurs

[15] See Peter Gumbel, "Western Europe Finds That It's Pricing Itself out of the Job Market," *Wall Street Journal,* 9 December 1993, 1, 10.

[16] For more on this, see Michael R. Czinkota and Ilkka A. Ronkainen, *International Marketing,* 3d ed. (Fort Worth: The Dryden Press, 1993), 260.

[17] Nabuaki Namiki, "Export Strategy for Small Business," *Journal of Small Business Management* (April 1988): 32–37.

[18] Ibid., 35.

[19] *A Basic Guide to Exporting* (Washington, DC: Government Printing Office, 1992), viii.

[20] Czinkota and Ronkainen, *International Marketing,* 445–49.

should exercise caution. Presented here is a list of questions that should be answered before they make a commitment:

1. What is the reputation of the firm? Is it financially sound?

2. How long has the company been in business?

3. What expertise does the firm have in the specific product line the entrepreneur is offering? How many product lines does it have? Are they related?

4. What experience does the company have as an export management company?

5. What is its track record as an export management company?

6. Is it a full-time or part-time operation?

7. Does it have an adequate number of personnel to satisfactorily service all its clients, and what is the expertise of each?

8. What foreign language capability does it have?

9. What services does it offer, that is, can it buy and sell for its own account, or does it want to act only as a representative or agent to bring buyer and seller together?

10. Will it accept a nonexclusive contract?

11. Can it handle documentation and shipping requirements?

12. Is the company equally familiar with selling in all areas of the world, or does it concentrate in certain areas, such as Latin America, Europe, or the Middle East?

13. Who are its clients? Is the entrepreneur permitted to contact them?

14. What is the minimum term of contract it will accept?

15. What about a performance clause? Will it accept one in a contractual arrangement?

16. Do its personnel make trips overseas on behalf of its clients?

17. Does it participate in trade shows or fairs overseas?

18. What overseas marketing data can the company provide regarding the entrepreneur's product or products?

19. Does it have representatives overseas?[21]

One of the dangers the entrepreneur encounters when using an export management company is the possibility of losing control of the export function. It is easy for the novice exporter to permit the export management company to exercise complete control over the export function. In fact, often the exporter is unaware of the destination of the products. If the firm should ever decide to start exporting on its own, the entrepreneur would have no idea where its products have been successful. In addition, the firm may be unaware of the proper documentation that needs to be filed. As a result, the exporter becomes heavily dependent on the export management company. To prevent this problem, the entrepreneur

---

[21] *Seven Steps to Exporting* (Indianapolis: Indiana District Export Council, 1990), 15A.

CONTEMPORARY ENTREPRENEURSHIP

The International Decision—Asking the Right Questions

If entrepreneurs are going to pursue the international marketplace, then a number of issues should be explored before they expand globally. The strategic options for small firms seeking to enter the international arena include three specific types: (1) Firms can choose to export products from the United States to foreign markets, (2) firms can establish a direct presence by setting up sales offices or manufacturing facilities in the foreign country they are interested in, and (3) firms can forge strategic alliances with foreign businesses.

Each of these options requires special preparations by the entrepreneur. However, general questions entrepreneurs need to answer in preparation for any global strategy include the following:

1. Is the product/service unique?
2. Is the entrepreneur flexible?
3. Who can use the product/service?
4. What are the costs?
5. What demands will international expansion place on the company's personnel?
6. Does serving the new foreign market fit with the company goals for growth and development?
7. Is the entrepreneur personally committed to international expansion?
8. Is the entrepreneur willing to invest enough money to initiate operations?
9. What analysis has been done on the competitors?
10. Can the entrepreneur be patient until global expansion begins to pay off?

SOURCES: Ronaleen Roha, "Taking Your Small Business Global," *Changing Times,* December 1989, 103–8; Gary L. Keefe, "Helping Clients Prepare for Global Markets," *Journal of Accountancy* (July 1989): 54–64; Charles W. L. Hill, *International Business: Competing in the Global Marketplace* (Burr Ridge, IL: Irwin, 1994), Chapter 17; and Hodgetts and Luthans, *International Management,* Chapter 8.

should receive reports detailing the activities performed on its behalf by the export management company.

FREIGHT FORWARDER   Another method of exporting entrepreneurs commonly use is to employ the services of a **freight forwarder.** A freight forwarder is an independent business that handles export shipments in return for compensation.[22] Some of the services a freight forwarder can provide follow:

- Quoting inland, ocean, and air shipping costs
- Arranging inland shipping and reserving necessary space aboard an ocean vessel
- Advising on the requirements of international packing
- Preparing the necessary export documentation
- Seeing to it that the goods reach the port and tracing lost shipments[23]

[22] *A Basic Guide to Exporting,* 93.

[23] *Seven Steps to Exporting,* 16.

Using a freight-forwarding service has several advantages. One is that this type of service does not cost as much as the service of an export management company. That is because an export management company handles all of the export-related activities, whereas the freight forwarder simply arranges for product shipment. Another advantage is that a freight forwarder can save the exporting firm many headaches. Shipping a product can be complex and confusing to the company. Arrangements must be made to ensure safe transportation from the departure point to the destination point, usually requiring more than one transportation mode. In addition, each country requires special forms and documentation when products are imported. If the forms are filled out incorrectly, payment, and quite possibly release of the goods, may be delayed indefinitely. The freight forwarder can obviate these potential nightmares by carefully monitoring the shipping process.

When selecting a freight forwarder, entrepreneurs should follow certain guidelines. First, if the cargo is to be shipped by sea, it is important that the freight forwarder be licensed by the Federal Maritime Commission. Such licensed freight forwarders are familiar with import rules and regulations, methods of shipping, U.S. government export regulations, and the documents connected with foreign trade.[24] Second, references should be obtained from past customers. Third, the services to be provided and the associated costs to the firm should be determined. Fourth, the entrepreneur should talk with experienced exporters as well as with the potential overseas distributors in order to solicit their opinions of particular freight forwarders.[25] Finally, the prospective exporter should check with current shippers of domestic products. Several freight companies are now expanding their operations into other countries and will handle all of the necessary shipping documentation and arrangements. This new service gives the entrepreneur the opportunity to contact a single shipper instead of maintaining information on many transportation companies.

FOREIGN SALES CORPORATION   Created by Congress as a replacement for the controversial **domestic international sales corporation (DISC),**[26] the **foreign sales corporation (FSC)** was enacted in 1984 to combat an increasingly unfavorable trade balance and apparent inequities in the tax treatment of U.S. exporters compared with the tax treatment other countries gave their exporters. The 1971 DISC regulation allowed companies to defer taxes on a portion of their export sales by forming a subsidiary called a domestic international sales corporation. By channeling export sales through the DISC, the organization could defer federal income taxes on 15 percent to 25 percent of its income from export sales.[27] In addition, as long as the firm kept the earnings in the DISC and they were reinvested in qualifying export assets, the deferral could become permanent. It was hoped this regulation would help spur additional export sales to improve the nation's balance of payments and to remove the incentive for U.S. companies to manufacture abroad.

U.S. trading partners objected to this legislation on the ground that it violated the General Agreement on Tariffs and Trade. Several GATT members contended that the DISC regulation was, in effect, a direct government subsidy on exports, which was prohibited by the agreement. After 12 years of discussion between the United States and the GATT Council, the Reagan administration sought to repeal the DISC legislation and replace it with the FSC regulation. The provisions of the FSC regulation were designed to comply

---

[24] *A Basic Guide to Exporting,* 39.

[25] Deloitte, Haskins, and Sells, *Exporting: Small and Growing Businesses* (New York: 1981).

[26] W. Timothy O'Keefe, Larry H. Beard, and Dana S. O'Keefe, "Are U.S. Exporters Benefiting from the FSC?" *Management Accounting* (May 1986): 43.

[27] Ibid.

more closely with the principal provisions of GATT.[28] Accordingly, in 1984 Congress passed the FSC legislation, which allows tax-exempt treatment to a portion of export income. To qualify for this treatment, the exporter must meet three conditions:

1. *It must have a foreign presence.* This requirement can be satisfied by incorporating in a qualified foreign country or eligible U.S. possession, maintaining an office outside the United States, and retaining a permanent set of books at that office. The FSC also must be managed outside of the United States, which can be accomplished by holding shareholder and board meetings outside the United States, maintaining a principal bank account outside the United States, and disbursing dividends as well as certain fees and salaries from this account.

2. *It must have economic substance.* Certain direct costs of a transaction are grouped into one of five categories: advertising, processing customer orders and arranging for delivery, transportation, determination of final invoice and receipt of payment, and assumption of credit risk. At least half of these costs the FSC incurs must be outside the United States. An alternative to this is that 85 percent of the direct costs for two categories must be outside the United States.

3. *It must perform activities relating to its exporting income outside the United States.* In order to meet this requirement, the exporter must perform certain processes outside the United States. These processes are related to the solicitation, negotiation, and creation of a contract. At least one of the activities must be performed by the FSC or its agent outside the United States.

The income of a firm that satisfies these requirements is considered foreign trade income and is partially exempt from federal income tax.

In order to provide relief for the small exporter, Congress enacted a provision for the "small FSC" and the "interest-charge DISC."[29] The small FSC is exempt from the foreign management and economic processes requirements, but it may take into consideration $5 million of export receipts for tax benefits. The interest-charge DISC is similar to the old DISC except that only $10 million of export receipts can be included, the amounts that qualify for shareholder distribution are different, and interest is charged on the amount of tax deferred by the interest-charge DISC.

OTHER USEFUL IDEAS   One last possibility the exporter should consider is that the customer may wish to arrange the transportation from the plant to the warehouse. Some companies have a carrier they prefer to do business with, particularly if the firms have developed a good relationship over the years. The customer may feel that this carrier will deliver the product to the warehouse more efficiently and with fewer problems than will other transport companies.

Simply because the entrepreneur has decided to export the firm's product does not guarantee additional profits.[30] Presented next is a list of the most common mistakes potential exporters make:

[28] Ibid.

[29] Ibid., 44.

[30] Yunus Kathawala et al., "Exporting Practices and Problems of Illinois Firms," *Journal of Small Business Management* (January 1989): 53–59.

- *Failure to obtain qualified export counseling and to develop a master international marketing plan before starting an export business.* To be successful, first clearly define the firm's goals and the problems it faces. Second, develop a plan to accomplish the objectives. Unless the firm has had experience in exporting, the first step will be difficult to take without qualified outside guidance.

- *Insufficient commitment by top management to overcome the initial difficulties and financial requirements of exporting.* It normally takes more time to establish the firm in a foreign market than it does in the domestic market. These early delays and costs may seem difficult to justify in comparison with the domestic operations. However, it is imperative to examine the long-range potential of the export program and to guide it through these early stages. If a firm foundation has been prepared by the entrepreneur, then the benefits should eventually outweigh the investment.

- *Insufficient care in selecting overseas distributors.* The selection of each foreign distributor is crucial. The complications of overseas communications and transportation require international distributors to act with greater independence than their domestic counterparts. In addition, the new exporter's history, trademarks, and reputation are usually unknown in the foreign market, causing the foreign customers to buy on the strength of the distributor. Consequently, a thorough evaluation of the personnel handling the firm's account, the distributor's facilities, and the management methods employed is critical.

- *Chasing orders from around the world instead of establishing a basis for profitable operations and orderly growth.* If the distributors are expected to actively promote the firm's account, they must be trained and assisted, and their performance must be monitored. This requires significant time and effort from the entrepreneur. Therefore, new exporters should concentrate their efforts in one or two geographic areas before attempting to expand into other areas.

- *Neglecting export business when the U.S. market booms.* Too many companies turn to exporting when business falls off in the United States. When domestic business starts to pick up again, they neglect their export trade or relegate it to a secondary place. Such neglect can cause serious damage to the firm's reputation and distributor's motivation, strangling the firm's export trade. Even if the domestic business remains strong, the company may eventually realize the neglect has succeeded only in shutting off a valuable source of additional profits.

- *Failure to treat international distributors on an equal basis with domestic counterparts.* Often companies carry out institutional advertising campaigns, special discount offers, sales incentive programs, special credit term programs, warranty offers, and so on in the U.S. market but fail to make similar assistance available to their international distributors. This is a mistake that can destroy the firm's overseas marketing efforts.

- *Unwillingness to modify products to meet regulations or cultural preferences of other countries.* Local safety and security codes, as well as import restrictions, cannot be ignored by foreign distributors. If necessary modifications are not made at the factory, the distributor must perform them, usually at a greater cost and, perhaps, not as well. It also should be noted that the small profit margin then makes the account less attractive.

- *Failure to print services, sales, and warranty messages in locally understood languages.* Although the firm's distributor's top management may speak English, it is unlikely all sales personnel will have this capability, thus creating an inconvenience for the overseas customer. Without a clear understanding of sales messages or service instructions, sales personnel will less effectively perform their functions.

- *Failure to consider use of an export management company.* If a firm decides it cannot afford its own export department, it should consider the possibility of securing the services of an export management company.
- *Failure to consider licensing or joint-venture agreements.* Import restrictions, insufficient personnel/financial resources, or a too-limited product line can cause companies to dismiss international marketing as simply not feasible. Yet nearly any product that competes on a national basis in the United States can be successfully marketed in most parts of the world. In general, what is needed for success is flexibility in using the proper combination of marketing techniques.[31]

This list is designed to help the entrepreneur profit from the mistakes of others. As the firm gains experience in exporting its product, it will become more proficient at the skills needed for success in the international marketplace and will increase its confidence in dealing with foreign customers.

After the entrepreneur has experienced success with product exports, he or she may be interested in establishing production facilities closer to the foreign market. Or it may not be economically feasible to ship a product to a country. In either type of scenario, the firm may want to investigate the possibility of a joint venture.

Joint Venture

Another alternative available to the entrepreneur in the international arena is the **joint venture.**[32] A joint venture occurs when two or more firms pool their resources and create a new entity to undertake productive economic activity. A joint venture thus implies the sharing of assets, profits, risks, and venture ownership with more than one firm.[33] A joint venture can take one of several different forms. In some countries, for example, it is not uncommon for a company to form a joint venture with the state or with a state-owned firm. This is particularly true in the case of petroleum companies with operations in the Middle East.

ADVANTAGES AND DISADVANTAGES   A firm may decide to participate in a joint venture for several reasons. One is that the firm would be able to gain an intimate knowledge of the local conditions and government where the facility is located.[34] Another is that each participant would be able to use the resources of the other firms involved in the venture. This allows participating firms a chance to compensate for weaknesses they may possess. Finally, both the initial capital outlay and the overall risk would be lower than if the firm were setting up the operation alone.

Additional advantages of a joint venture relate to the strategic fit of the domestic firm with the foreign firm. One study examined the strategic fit of domestic firms (D-type) with third world firms (TW-type) in a joint venture.[35] The dimensions of corporate-level advantages, operational-level advantages, and environmental advantages were all compared to

[31] *A Basic Guide to Exporting,* 84–85.

[32] For some useful joint-venture rules, see Carl F. Fey, "Success Strategies for Russian Foreign Joint Ventures," *Business Horizons* (November/December 1995): 49–54.

[33] Derrick E. D'Souza and Patricia P. McDougall, "Third World Joint Venturing: A Strategic Option for the Smaller Firm," *Entrepreneurship Theory and Practice* (summer 1989): 20.

[34] James C. Leontiades, *Multinational Corporate Strategy: Planning for World Markets* (Lexington, MA: Heath, 1985), 135.

[35] D'Souza and McDougall, "Third World Joint Venturing," 19–33.

TABLE 17.3 STRATEGIC FIT OF SMALL D-TYPE FIRMS IN THIRD-WORLD JOINT VENTURES

Dimension	Strategic Fit
Corporate-Level Advantages	
Relevant/complementary technology	Meeting developing country's specific technology needs in cost-efficient manner; easier to adopt and integrate technology with local technological infrastructure
Match with D-type firm's strategy and long-range plans	Being the recommended strategic alternative for D-type firm
Venture strategy	Flexible structure; informal control mechanism; tolerance of deviation from set guidelines
Ownership-control relationship	Not overly demanding on level of control; flexible and less lopsided control-ownership nexus
TW firm type and capabilities	Type of firm; capabilities of the TW firm: historical record distinctive competencies
Conflict of interest between partners	Product related; market related; technology information related
Operational-Level Advantages	
Managerial resource allocation	Relevant managerial resource; low cost of managerial services
Decision-making and reporting systems	Formality, structure and policies; ability to solve crisis-oriented problems; flexibility
Approaches to organizational functioning	Close-knit operations of the firm; tolerance to low level of responsibility and accountability by the joint venture
Cultural differences between the parent firms	At the societal level; at the business level; at the corporate level
Local vested interests	Extent of damage that they can cause
Size of the D-type firm	Similar in "size" to the TW firm; similar problem-solving approaches; easier day-to-day operations
Environmental Advantages	
Local government incentives/constraints	Identifying relevant incentives and constraints; government approval and incentives may be easier to obtain because the smaller D-type firm may not be perceived as a threat
Market structure and distribution channels	Demand-supply nexus; substitute products and new entrants; ability to transfer expertise
Perceived host-country business climate	Business climate perceived as being good or bad

SOURCE: Derrick E. D'Souza and Patricia P. McDougall, "Third World Joint Venturing: A Strategic Option for the Smaller Firm," *Entrepreneurship Theory and Practice* (summer 1989): 25. Reprinted with permission.

the strategic fit of the partners in the joint venture. Table 17.3 provides the complete listing of the advantages and their strategic fit.

One of the disadvantages associated with joint ventures is the problem of fragmented control. For example, a carefully planned logistics flow may be hampered if one of the firms decides to block the acquisition of new equipment. This type of problem can be avoided or diminished in a number of ways: (1) One party can control more than 50 percent of the voting rights. This will normally give formal control; however, even a minority opposing view can carry considerable influence. This can be particularly true if the differ-

CONTEMPORARY ENTREPRENEURSHIP

Preparing for Doing European Business

As the EC becomes a reality and the entire continent of Europe merges for economic trade, entrepreneurs need to be aware of the differences of doing business among the European countries. Even though they are unified for economic purposes, the countries in Europe maintain their respective cultures. Depending on the particular country an entrepreneur seeks to do business with, differences should be understood *before* expanding operations there. For example, even though many experts consider English the international language of business, the French, Germans, and Spanish have a strong bias for their own languages. It has been pointed out that you can always "buy" in English, but you will have to "sell" in the other country's language.

In addition, each country has a valued culture with customs that should not be ignored. The following examples illustrate the importance of being culturally prepared for European business:

- Suit jackets must stay on in offices, in restaurants, and on the street, even during the summer months in Europe.

- First names are seldom used without invitation in Europe.
- Lighter handshakes are a greeting standard except for southern and eastern Europe.
- For all business introductions the exchange of business cards is expected.
- In Italy, handshakes are a national pastime, yet the Italians seldom remember names on first introduction.
- In Greece, handshakes, embraces, and kissing are all forms of business greetings.
- Punctuality is a *must* in Europe.

As these examples illustrate, in Europe socializing, etiquette, patience, and protocol are integral parts of doing business. Entrepreneurs should contact the International Trade Administration (ITA) of the U.S. Department of Commerce in order to gain more information on specific countries.

SOURCES: Bob Weinstein, "Countdown to 1992," *Entrepreneur* (March 1991): 69–75; Donna Brown, "Strategies for Europe's New Market," *Small Business Reports* (January 1991): 36–42; and Alan M. Rugman and Richard M. Hodgetts, *International Business* (New York: McGraw-Hill, 1995), Chapter 17.

ences of opinion reflect different nationalities. (2) Only one of the parties is made responsible for the actual management of the venture. This may be complemented by a buyout clause. In case of a disagreement among the owners, one party can purchase the equity of the other. (3) One of the parties can control either the input or the output, exerting significant control over the venture decisions, despite voting and ownership rights.

The joint venture can be a powerful tool for growth in the international market. If used properly, it will effectively combine the strengths of the partners involved and thereby increase its competitive position.[36]

---

[36] See Kenneth J. Fedor and William B. Werther Jr., "Making Sense of Cultural Factors in International Alliances," *Organizational Dynamics* (spring 1995): 33–47.

Direct Foreign Investment

A **direct foreign investment** is a domestically controlled foreign production facility. This does not mean the firm owns a majority of the operation. In some cases, less than 50 percent ownership can constitute effective control because the stock ownership is widely dispersed. On the other hand, the entrepreneur may own 100 percent of the stock and not have control over the company. In some instances the government may dictate whom a firm may hire, what pricing structure the firm must use, and how earnings will be distributed. This causes some concern as to exactly who is in control of the organization. Because of the difficulty of identifying direct investments, governmental agencies have had to establish arbitrary definitions of the term. A direct foreign investment typically involves ownership of 10 percent to 25 percent of the voting stock in a foreign enterprise.[37]

A firm can make a direct foreign investment by several methods. One is to acquire an interest in an ongoing foreign operation. This initially may be a minority interest in the firm but enough to exert influence on the management of the operation. A second method is to obtain a majority interest in a foreign company. In this case the company becomes a subsidiary of the acquiring firm. Third, the acquiring firm may simply purchase part of the assets of a foreign concern in order to establish a direct investment. An additional alternative is to build a facility in a foreign country.

An entrepreneur may want to make a direct foreign investment for a number of reasons. One is the possibility of trade restrictions. Some countries have prohibitions or restrictive trade barriers on imports of certain products. These barriers can make exporting costly or impossible. In addition, foreign governments may grant tax incentives to a firm seeking direct investment in that country. These incentives can be attractive if the anticipated rate of return is estimated to be higher at the foreign location than domestically.

Direct investment can be an exciting venture for small firms making efforts to increase their sales and their competitive positions in the marketplace. However, it is sometimes not practical for a firm to make a direct investment in a foreign location. If the firm has a unique or proprietary product or manufacturing process, it may want to consider the concept of licensing.

Licensing

Licensing is a business arrangement in which the manufacturer of a product (or a firm with proprietary rights over certain technology or trademarks) grants permission to some other group or individual to manufacture that product in return for specified royalties or other payments. Foreign licensing covers myriad contractual arrangements in which the business (licenser) provides patents, trademarks, manufacturing expertise, or technical services to a foreign business (licensee).[38] Under such an arrangement, the entrepreneur need not make an extensive capital outlay to participate in the international market. Nor does the licenser have to be concerned with the daily production, marketing, technical, or management requirements; the licensee will handle all of this. The foreign firm merely looks to the

[37] Michael R. Czinkota, Ilkka A. Ronkainen, and Michael H. Moffett, *International Business,* 3d ed. (Fort Worth: The Dryden Press, 1994), 43–46.

[38] Donald Weinrauch and Arthur Langlois, "Guidelines for Starting and Operating an International Licensing Program for Small Business," *Journal of Small Business Management* (October 1983): 25.

domestic firm for expertise and, perhaps, an additional opportunity to sell a product owned by the licenser.[39]

For developing an international licensing program, three basic types of programs are available:

1. *Patents.* If the entrepreneur decides to use the patent approach, he or she should begin with a valid U.S. patent. Within one year, the entrepreneur should then file for patents in the countries where business will be transacted. Although this step can be expensive, it is essential because this action will give him or her a stronger bargaining position. Keep in mind that the United States is trying to adjust its patent system from "first to invent" to the international system of "first to file." It's being referred to as "patent harmonization" in order to be compatible with the international marketplace. The new system includes safeguards for small inventors, such as an inexpensive system for provisional patents. The goals are to make the patent process more efficient and to offer better foreign protection for inventors.[40]

2. *Trademarks.* Due to the difficulties that can occur in direct translations, it may be advisable for the entrepreneur to have more than one trademark licensed for the same product. The entrepreneur should keep in mind, however, that if the product is not well recognized in the international market, he or she will not be able to use it as a major incentive in the bargaining phase. Sometimes, licensees will want the patent rights but prefer to use their own trademarks. This can be particularly true if the foreign firm is well established.

3. *Technical Know-How.* This type of licensing is often the hardest to enforce since it depends on the security of secrecy agreements. (The licenser should sign an agreement to prevent the licensee from legally revealing trade secrets.) In some localities, governments have strict regulations governing the use of technical know-how licensing. Frequently, one may protect the technical capabilities for only five years before the licensee is free to use this know-how without paying royalties. However, keep in mind that this may differ from country to country, depending on their particular regulations. Because this is a complex process, the entrepreneur must continue to develop his or her technical capabilities to ensure an ongoing international need for the company's services.[41]

To arrange for licensing, these steps should be followed:

1. Obtain an enforceable and secured patent, trademark, or know-how position.

2. Allocate adequate resources for research, legal, and travel expenses.

3. Research interested foreign markets to be sure the product can be produced and marketed there.

4. Start with countries having a minimum of governmental regulation.

5. Make a tentative list of countries in order of preference.

[39] Ibid.

[40] Peter Coy, "The Global Patent Race Picks Up Speed," *Business Week,* 9 August 1993, 57–62; and "Patent Harmonization: Bad News for Inventors?" *Inc.,* November 1993, 34.

[41] See Shengliang Deng et al., "A Guide to Intellectual Property Rights in Southeast Asia and China," *Business Horizons* (November/December 1996): 43–56.

ENTREPRENEURIAL

EDGE

A World of Opportunities

Countries once at war are being brought together by entrepreneurship. With the rise of technology and the fall of European Communism, business owners have discovered a whole new world full of opportunities. This powerful movement by entrepreneurs into new markets is revitalizing ailing economies, and people who never had the chance before are building their own futures and their own prosperity. Entrepreneurs are shaping a new global economy. Economist Lester Thurow describes this new economy with one sentence in his book *The Future of Capitalism:* "For the first time in human history, anything can be made anywhere and sold everywhere."

With global opportunities also comes challenges: trade laws, governmental politics, currency fluctuations, cultural consumer preferences. These are only a few of the obstacles an entrepreneur may face when trudging into the international marketplace. But with a little research and persistence, most of these obstacles can be overcome. In addition, political stability and economic reform are making global markets more accessible to everyone.

The Clinton administration has identified ten countries as "Big Emerging Markets" (BEMs). These countries are considered the most attractive for U.S. exports and investments. According to Lauri Fitz-Pegado of the Department of Commerce, they are places where "the growth potential for export opportunities in the post-2000 period has been clearly identified." Companies deliberating going global should consider the following ten BEMs and the opportunities they present. (*GDP* is the gross domestic product.)

The People's Republic of China
Population: 1.2 billion
GDP: $418 billion
China, with the seventh largest economy, is the biggest of these commercial targets, although it is still Communist. The hottest sectors in this area include automobiles and parts, aircraft and parts, computers, chemicals, and electrical power systems.

Brazil   *Population: 162 million*
GDP: $508 billion
Brazil's newly acquired commercial stability and its tenth largest economy make it prime for newcomers. With 54 percent of its GDP from services and 35 percent from industry, its most attractive imports include security equipment, plastics, computer software, sporting goods, and computers and peripherals.

South Africa   *Population: 41 million*
GDP: $122 billion
South Africa's free market supplies many business and investment op-

portunities. Key areas include health care, telecommunications, electrification, and housing.

India *Population: 915 million*
GDP: $295 billion
More than 75 million people make up India's upper middle class, and they are desperately seeking U.S. products. The best opportunities are in information technology, food processing, telecommunications, transportation, power, and financial services.

Mexico *Population: 88 million*
GDP: $380 billion
Mexico, the third largest U.S. trading partner, has seen economic recovery fueled by a variety of forces, such as NAFTA. Hot markets in Mexico include telecommunications, auto parts, and pollution control.

Indonesia *Population: 193 million*
GDP: $166 billion
Indonesia was once primarily agricultural, but now 70 percent of its exports comprise airplanes, chemicals, electronics, and textiles. Key sectors for growth include health care, telecommunications, aerospace, and computer software and equipment.

South Korea *Population: 45 million*
GDP: $360 billion
South Korea's fast growth rate (goods and services are expected to grow 8 percent annually to the year 2000) and its advancement in manufacturing and technological innovation presents a market worth tapping into. Emerging markets include tele-

communications equipment, construction and engineering services, aircrafts and parts, architecture, and computers and peripherals.

Thailand *Population: 59 million*
GDP: $134 billion
Thailand is enjoying an economically stable free market that welcomes foreign investment and technological transfer as the keys to its economic growth. Thailand's fastest-growing industries include pollution control, transportation, energy, and telecommunications.

Argentina *Population: 34 million*
GDP: $280 billion
Argentina is boasting tremendous growth in GDP in addition to low inflation rates. Growth sectors include environmental and pollution control; wireless services and equipment, such as cellular phones; and electronic components and test equipment.

Poland *Population: 39 million*
GDP: $87 billion
Poland is central (geographically) and Eastern Europe's (politically) largest and fastest-growing country. The sector with the greatest potential is consumer goods, including household appliances and apparel. Other fast-growing areas include pollution control, automotive products, hospitality, banking, and telecommunications.

SOURCE: Frank McCoy, "Tapping into Emerging Markets," *Black Enterprise,* May 1996, 80–88.

6. Prepare attractive product catalogs and promotional brochures in different foreign languages.

7. Build a list of potential foreign licensees through consultation with trade associations, the U.S. Chamber of Commerce, the U.S. Department of Commerce, and commercial attachés at embassies in Washington, DC, or at U.S. embassies in foreign countries.

8. Contact the high-potential licensees and arrange visits for exploratory meetings.

9. Develop criteria for selecting firms to become licensees. Some factors to evaluate are marketing, production, customer base, channel strength, service support, reputation, and financial capabilities.

ADVANTAGES AND DISADVANTAGES   Licensing can be an extremely attractive way to enter the international arena. It requires a minimal capital outlay and can generate savings in tariffs and transportation costs. Another advantage is that licensing is a more realistic means of expansion than exporting, particularly for the high-tech firm. In addition, access to the market is easier in comparison with equity investments, and foreign governments are more likely to give their approval because technology is being brought into the country. Finally, a potential exists for the licensees to become partners and contributors in improving the "learning curve" of technology.

Disadvantages to licensing also exist. First, it is possible the licensee will become a competitor after the contract expires. Second, the licenser must get the licensee to meet contractual obligations and to adjust products or services to fit the licensee's market. Third, the licensing entrepreneur must manage the relationship's conditions and circumstances, as well as resolve conflicts or misunderstandings as they occur. Finally, the integrity and independence of both the licenser and licensee must be maintained.

To be competitive with larger firms, small businesses have to be on the cutting edge of bringing in new and innovative technology. Moreover, several small firms may not have the financial resources available to participate in the international marketplace by exporting, joint venture, or direct investment. For many of these firms, international licensing is a viable and exciting method of expanding operations.

ENTERING THE INTERNATIONAL MARKETPLACE: A PROCEDURAL OUTLINE

Thus far, five approaches for going international have been examined: importing, exporting, joint venture, direct investment, and licensing. In this section a procedural process for entering the international marketplace is presented. Figure 17.2 illustrates the process for an entrepreneur to follow when deciding whether to pursue a global expansion. In the following pages we have summarized the process into five distinct steps. This five-step process begins with research and moves into a feasibility study. From this point the financial arrangements are secured, the necessary documentation is prepared, and, finally, the plan is implemented.

Step 1: Conduct Research

One of the most difficult phases of entering the international arena is that of conducting research on the market. Unfortunately, not all countries have the marketing research capabilities that exist in the United States. Compounding this problem is the fact the entrepre-

FIGURE 17.2 **ANALYSIS OF GLOBAL EXPANSION DECISIONS**

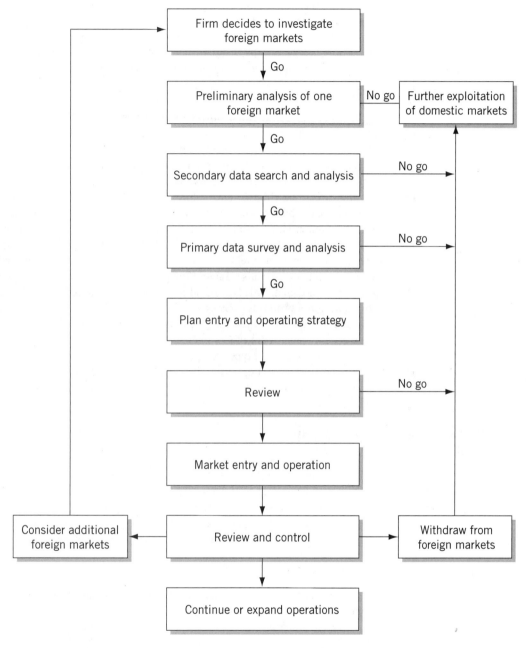

SOURCE: Roger D. Blackwell and Kristina Stephan, "Growing Profits for Small Business through Global Expansion," *Small Business Forum* (winter 1990): 55.

neur may be thousands of miles away from this market. As a result, the entrepreneur must often turn to methods and techniques other than marketing research to determine the most profitable markets.

One of the best places to start is the Federal Depository at a major library. This depository contains materials that can assist entrepreneurs searching for international markets. To determine the most profitable areas for the products, the entrepreneur must first identify the potential markets for those products. One way to do this is to ask at the Federal Depository for copies of publication FT 410, which is a listing of exports by product and by country. The products are classified in the Standard International Trade Classification codes. These data will help the potential exporter identify the markets with a strong historical demand for the product.

The next step is to conduct research in these markets. Again, the Federal Depository is an excellent source of information on target countries. Publications that should prove extremely useful to the entrepreneur are the Overseas Business Reports (OBR) and the Foreign Economic Trends (FET). The OBR evaluates various markets by analyzing pertinent marketing factors, presenting economic and commercial profiles, issuing semiannual outlooks for U.S. firms with the respective countries, and publishing selected statistical reports on the direction, volume, and nature of U.S. foreign trade. The FET provides information on current business conditions, current and near-term prospects, and the latest available data on the gross national product, foreign trade, wage and price indexes, unemployment rates, and construction starts. It is also helpful to gain insights into how to enter and do business in foreign markets. For example, how should an entrepreneurial firm go about negotiating business deals? Table 17.4 provides some answers in relation to the People's Republic of China. This type of information can be extremely helpful for opening doors and ensuring the venture's success.

Another marketing tool is the Trade Opportunities Program (TOP). TOP subscribers indicate to the U.S. Department of Commerce the products they wish to export, the countries of interest, and the desired types of opportunities. U.S. Foreign Service offices around the world then collect data on opportunities developing in their respective countries, and the TOP computer matches the opportunities with the subscriber and mails him or her the appropriate information.

Step 2: Prepare a Feasibility Study

A feasibility study should be undertaken to determine if the proposed project is capable of being carried out. Table 17.5 illustrates a format the study can take.

The feasibility study is a critical document of the entry procedure in that it helps demonstrate how realistic the project is. Because the first few years in the international markets typically will be nonprofitable, it is imperative the entrepreneur have sufficient foresight to look at both the long-term and the short-term prospects of the proposal.

Step 3: Secure Adequate Financing

Once it has been determined the project is feasible, arrangements should be made to secure proper financing. Quite often payments from overseas customers require special attention. Of course, if the customer has an excellent credit history, the entrepreneur may be willing to establish an open account with the business. If this is not the case, however, the seller may have to rely on an irrevocable letter of credit. This is a document the bank prepares, on the buyer's instructions, authorizing the seller to draw a specified sum of money under specified terms. This letter can be an extremely powerful form of financing since it guarantees payment of the account if all terms and conditions of the letter of credit are met.

Another form of financial assistance available to entrepreneurs is the financial guarantee. Several government agencies have programs that will guarantee payment. One such

TABLE 17.4	FACTORS RESPONSIBLE FOR SUCCESSFUL NEGOTIATIONS IN THE PEOPLE'S REPUBLIC OF CHINA (PRC)

Factors Responsible for Success	Average ranking by respondents (n = 168)[a]
Good personal relationship	6.006
Knowledge of business practices in the PRC	5.804
Clarity about the PRC's requirements	5.310
Use of the "old friend" approach	5.286
PRC's need for the product	5.256
Uniqueness of the product	5.107
Willingness to offer good financing	5.065
PRC's foreign-exchange availability	5.024
Willingness to sell at a good price	4.821
Preparation by the entrepreneurial team	4.458
Entrepreneurial firm's technical expertise	4.179
Familiarity with PRC social customs	3.940
Firm's past reputation for selling to the PRC	3.857
Knowledge of PRC's political and economic situation	3.768
Sincerity on the part of the entrepreneurial team	3.679
Use of an intermediary/agent	3.286
Use of a good interpreter	2.804
Willingness to arrange countertrade (e.g., a buyback)	2.750

[a] 7=extremely important; 1=not at all important.

SOURCE: Adapted from Thomas Leung and L. L. Yeung, "Negotiation in the People's Republic of China: Results of a Survey of Small Businesses in Hong Kong," *Journal of Small Business Management* (January 1995): 74.

agency is the Overseas Private Investment Corporation (OPIC), which also provides special insurance for overseas investments. OPIC insures against inconvertibility of funds, expropriation, and political violence. In addition, the Export-Import Bank (Eximbank) offers direct loans for large projects and equipment sales that require long-term financing as well as credit guaranteed to commercial banks that finance export sales. Through its Foreign Credit Insurance Association, the Eximbank also provides insurance to U.S. exporters, allowing them to extend credit to their foreign customers. Finally, the Small Business Administration can offer financial assistance in the form of loans to entrepreneurs for equipment that can be used to create exports. SBA loans are restricted to domestic firms only and therefore cannot be used for a direct foreign investment or a joint venture.

A final source of financing is the local banker. Most large banks have international banking divisions that can help the entrepreneur in his or her efforts to go international.

TABLE 17.5	FEASIBILITY STUDY OUTLINE

I. Identification of international project

II. Statement of feasibility

III. Summary and/or conclusion

IV. Entry selection (select one method and develop complete program)
- A. Methods of entry
  - 1. Exporting
    - a) Pros
    - b) Cons
  - 2. Joint venturing
    - a) Pros
    - b) Cons
  - 3. Direct investment
    - a) Pros
    - b) Cons
  - 4. Licensing
    - a) Pros
    - b) Cons
- B. Other considerations
  - 1. Financial considerations
    - a) Raw materials
    - b) Labor
    - c) Tax incentive and allowance
  - 2. Governmental considerations
    - a) Stability
    - b) Regulations
  - 3. Distribution
    - a) Modes of transportation
    - b) Channels

V. Market profile
- A. Overview: target market
  - 1. Population
  - 2. Major cities
  - 3. Language
  - 4. Climate
  - 5. Geography
  - 6. Imports
  - 7. Exports
  - 8. Exchange rate
  - 9. Transportation
  - 10. Communication
  - 11. Business practices
  - 12. Business hours
- B. Society/culture: background of society
- C. Major demographic factors
  - 1. Income
  - 2. Occupation
  - 3. Education
  - 4. Religion

TABLE 17.5	FEASIBILITY STUDY OUTLINE *(continued)*

    D. Political climate: background

    E. Economic climate

    F. Outlook for trade

    G. Opportunities and restraints

VI. Targeted consumer analysis

VII. Legal considerations

    A. Trade policy

    B. Registration of company

    C. Ownership of the business entity

    D. Governmental policy on foreign investment

    E. Industrial property protection

VIII. Risk identification and analysis

    A. Financial risk and property/business seizure

    B. Repatriation of capital

    C. Political risk

        1. Foreign relations with the United States

        2. Governmental stability

IX. Financial considerations

    A. Type of financing for proposed project

    B. Source of financing

        1. Internal

        2. World Bank

        3. Other

    C. Break-even analysis

        1. Return on investment

        2. Return on total assets employed

        3. Sales forecast

    D. Taxation considerations (U.S. and foreign)

    E. Policy on repatriation of profits

X. Labor and managerial considerations

    A. Organized labor

        1. Description

        2. Bargaining tools

    B. Work characteristics

        1. Hours worked

        2. Pay rates

    C. Recruitment

        1. Local

        2. Expatriate

        3. Third country

    D. Management

        1. Local

        2. Expatriate

        3. Compensation

Continued

TABLE 17.5   **FEASIBILITY STUDY OUTLINE *(continued)***

XI. Control strategies
   A. Difficulty of international control
      1. Distance
      2. Diversity
      3. Degree of certainty
   B. Centralized versus decentralized
   C. Policy

XII. Timetable for implementation

They can provide the names of freight forwarders, assistance with completing the necessary paperwork, and credit references on potential foreign customers. In fact, the international banker can be one of the most useful contacts for the entrepreneur participating in the global arena.

Step 4: File the Proper Documents

One of the most frustrating experiences for the exporter can be the documentation needed to export products to foreign countries. This task can be accomplished in several ways. One is to use the *Exporter's Encyclopedia* located in the reference section of many local libraries. This book lists all of the necessary documentation, as well as other vital information, for exporting to a particular country. The federal and state Departments of Commerce also can provide assistance in determining the required format and in completing the forms. In addition, several freight forwarders have programs wherein they help customers prepare the necessary documentation. Finally, some banks will provide similar assistance.

Step 5: Draw Up and Implement the Plan

The first step in implementing an international strategy is to define the firm's policy. Policy consists of guidelines for achieving the firm's objectives. The firm should define its international policy in accordance with its overall objectives. When it establishes these objectives, the company should ensure that they are realistic and attainable.

The next step is to ensure that the firm is efficiently organized for international operations. Normally with an exporting firm, the responsibility falls in two departments: marketing and finance. The marketing department is charged with creating export sales, and the finance department assumes the responsibility of fulfilling the documentation requirements and ensuring that the firm gets paid for its product. In order to provide export training for the affected departments, most firms also will send personnel to a seminar covering the basic aspects of exporting. In many states the U.S. Department of Commerce conducts several of these workshops each year to inform domestic businesses about opportunities in the international market.

Finally, after the plan has been drawn up, it must be put into effect. At the heart of this activity should be a timetable, or schedule, that indicates key tasks of the implementation process and who has responsibility for them. Many small firms use a Gantt chart to achieve this purpose. This chart displays the duration and timing of the activities related to a project—in this case, entering the international market.

Doing business globally is rapidly becoming a profitable and popular strategy for many entrepreneurial ventures. The North American Free Trade Agreement, between Canada, Mexico, and the United States, and the EU (European Union) are examples of the powerful economic forces creating opportunities for entrepreneurs in the international marketplace.

This chapter discussed five ways the entrepreneur can actively engage in the international market. One way is importing, which involves buying goods from other countries. Firms interested in importing can attend trade shows and fairs and gather information related to the various goods available for import.

A second way is exporting, which takes a variety of forms. A knowledge of export management companies, freight forwarders, and foreign sales corporations can be particularly helpful in this process.

A third way is through the use of joint ventures. These international arrangements offer many benefits for those looking to establish a presence in the international market. One study emphasized the importance of the strategic fit between domestic firms (D-type) and third-world firms (TW-type).

A fourth way is through direct foreign investment. Before entrepreneurs take this step, however, it is important they carefully evaluate the associated risks.

A fifth way is through licensing, which takes a number of different forms and has both advantages and disadvantages. The steps to follow when arranging for licensing were set forth.

The last part of the chapter examined the five steps for entering the international marketplace: (1) conduct research, (2) prepare a feasibility study, (3) secure adequate financing, (4) file the proper documents, and (5) draw up and implement the plan.

Key Terms and Concepts

Direct foreign investment	Importing
Domestic international sales corporation (DISC)	Joint venture
	Learning curve concept
European Union (EU)	Licensing
Export management company	North American Free Trade Agreement (NAFTA)
Exporting	
Foreign sales corporation (FSC)	World Trade Organization (WTO)
Freight forwarder	

Review and Discussion Questions

1. Describe some of the powerful economic forces that are creating global opportunities for entrepreneurs.
2. How can an entrepreneur become aware of import opportunities?
3. Of what value are an export management company and a freight forwarder to entrepreneurs who are seeking to export goods?

4. Before engaging the services of an export management company, an entrepreneur should ask what questions?
5. What is a foreign sales corporation? Of what value is it to entrepreneurs in the export business?
6. What are five of the most common mistakes potential exporters make?
7. How does a joint venture work? What are the advantages of this arrangement? What are the disadvantages?
8. How can a firm make a direct foreign investment?
9. How does a licensing arrangement work? What are the advantages and disadvantages of such an arrangement?
10. When entering the international marketplace, entrepreneurs should follow what five specific steps?

Experiential Exercise   *Going International*

When entrepreneurs decide to go international, they must take a number of steps—for example, hiring people to help them out, entering into agreements with overseas partners, and putting together a plan for conducting the venture. The following are ten groups or terms with which the entrepreneur should be familiar, labeled *A* through *J*. Match each of these groups or terms with its correct definition or description (*1* through *10*).

A. Export management company
B. Freight forwarder
C. Foreign sales corporation
D. Joint venture
E. Licensing
F. Direct foreign investment
G. Patents
H. Technical know-how
I. Conduct research
J. TOP

_____ 1. The first step taken to go international

_____ 2. A business arrangement in which the manufacturer of a product gives permission to some group or individual to manufacture the product in return for specified royalties or other payments

_____ 3. Can handle all the details for shipping goods overseas, although the cost can be high

_____ 4. Some of its income is exempt from federal taxes

_____ 5. A program for helping businesses identify overseas markets for their products

_____ 6. Foreign governments sometimes grant tax incentives for this

_____ 7. One of the basic types of international licensing programs

_____ 8. A company owned by two or more organizations

_____ 9. Another of the basic types of international licensing programs

_____ 10. Can arrange for shipment of the product to overseas markets

VIDEO CASE 17.1

Pier 1 Imports: Managing Worldwide Growth

More than 30 years after its Texas founders invited shoppers on an "affordable" adventure, Pier 1 Imports is enjoying the kind of growth and profitability other retailers only can dream about. "At Pier 1, we're fond of saying that our competitive advantage is there are no Pier 2s," Katie McAbee, vice president of communication, says. "We like to think of it in terms of we have product, we have presentations, and we have people. Our product is fabulous merchandise that you can't find anywhere else. Our presentation is a shopping experience that's discovery oriented. And we go out of our way to be friendly, helpful, and offer our customers the best."

Not so long ago, Pier 1 was best known for college-dorm beanbag chairs, incense, batik-print linens, and wicker *everything*. But like the baby boomers who first discovered Pier 1, the retail chain has grown up and become more sophisticated. With nearly 650 retail stores in the United States, Puerto Rico, Canada, and Mexico, Pier 1 is now one of the leading retail specialty stores in North America. In 1995, Pier 1 sold $712 million in decorative home furnishings, dinnerware, casual clothing, and unique gift items imported from more than 42 countries around the world—earning the company a record net income. "Our attitude is one of the primary things that have guided us on a course of productivity and helped us be an outstanding retailer," Steve Woodward, vice president of merchandise furniture, reveals. "This attitude permeates the company from the chairman to the president, all the way down through the associates on the sales floor. We're willing to take risks; we try things that other retailers might shy away from, but that's just a culturally accepted part of being with Pier 1."

Pier 1's can-do attitude has inspired the company to expand beyond domestic borders. "We realized that our product mix was a strong enough mix to sell worldwide," Jim Prucha, vice president of merchandise shelf goods, says. McAbee adds: "We've had people all over the globe approaching us and wanting to partner with us because our concept is so unique." In the early 1990s, Pier 1 invested in an extensive strategic planning process for worldwide growth. "Our strategy for profitable worldwide growth truly grew out of a vision," McAbee says. "It came out of our chairman and CEO, Clark Johnson, and our president, Marvin Girouard. They sincerely believe that as we begin to mature as a company in this country, we need to seek outside our own geographic boundaries and begin to look for opportunities for Pier 1 to be known beyond the United States and Canada." Recently, Pier 1 has formed lucrative partnerships with Sears de Mexico and Sears de Puerto Rico. It also teamed with an English company called The Pier in the United Kingdom and with a Japanese partner to open Pier 1 stores in Japan.

In a corporate document titled *A Strategy for Worldwide Growth,* Pier 1 clearly defines the major goals it plans to achieve by the year 2000. These goals include expanding the company's North American retail base to 900 stores doing $1.25 billion in sales and producing $475 million in net income by January 1, 2000. The company also plans to continue introducing Pier 1 stores internationally with direct investments in selected countries; to expand its market presence in Southeast Asia, Mexico, and Central and South America through master franchise agreements and joint ventures; to enter new specialty markets in North America; and to establish a major procurement, logistics, and distribution presence in Singapore to reinforce the company's international sourcing capacity. "We are lucky to have a very strong, very united team of senior management who were all involved not only in the development of our strategy but also how it would take shape and what it would take to get us there," McAbee says.

Prucha concludes: "We have been very, very good at importing for years and years. Now we have to become equally proficient at exporting. Exporting is a little different learning curve for us. But quite frankly, the only other obstacle we've encountered in international is we just can't keep up with the demand. We have people sending in letters and calling every day wanting to know if Pier 1's in their particular country. And we feel this is a very logical worldwide concept that can grow to who knows how large in the future."

Questions

1. As Pier 1 ships from importing to exporting what are some key points to remember?
2. What are the emerging global markets that Pier 1 should be seeking?
3. Discuss the advantages and disadvantages of a Joint Venture since it is Pier 1's strategy for expansion.

 **CASE   17.2**

A Foreign Proposal

Edgar Bruning left his job at a major computer manufacturing firm and started his own business five years ago, naming it Bruning Computer. Since then Edgar has secured five patents for computer-related equipment. His latest is a computer chip that can increase the speed of most personal computers by 35 percent. The cost of one of these computer chips is only $8, and the unit wholesales for $135. As a result, Bruning's profits have mushroomed.

Realizing that everything he developed can be copied by foreign competitors, Edgar entered into contractual arrangements with three European firms to market his product. These three firms have predetermined sales areas that cover all of Europe and the Middle East. Bruning ships 50 percent of its production output to these three firms, while the rest is sold to companies in the United States. Edgar recently has been thinking about increasing his production facilities. He is certain he could sell 40 percent more chips if he were able to make them.

Last week Edgar had a visit from the chief executive of a Japanese firm. The company has proposed a joint venture between itself and Bruning. The venture would work this way: Bruning would ship the company as many chips as are currently sent to the three firms in Europe. These chips would be paid for on a 90-day basis. The Japanese firm would act as Bruning's Far East sales representative during this part of the agreement. Then within 90 days the Japanese firm would purchase manufacturing equipment that would allow it to make the chips in Japan. "This will save us both labor and shipping costs," the Japanese executive pointed out. "And all profits will be divided on a 50/50 basis. Your only expenses will be your share of the manufacturing equipment, and we will apply your profits against those expenses. So you will have no out-of-pocket expenses."

The idea sounds very profitable to Edgar, but he is not sure he wants to give someone else the right to produce his product. "Technological secrecy is important in this business. It's the key to success," he noted to a colleague. On the other hand, Edgar realizes that without having someone to sell his product in the Far East, he is giving up a large potential market. Over the next ten days Edgar intends to make a decision about what to do.

Questions

1. What type of arrangement is Edgar using in his business dealings with the European firms? Be complete in your answer.
2. Is the Japanese business proposal a joint venture? Why or why not? Would you recommend that Edgar accept it? Why or why not?
3. If Edgar were looking for an alternative approach to doing business with the Japanese, what would you suggest? Defend your answer.

PART 5

ENTREPRENEURIAL CASE ANALYSIS

Acordia's "Little Giants"

Prologue

Overall, Acordia has redefined the notion of scale. Scale today is mostly associated with knowledge, not lumpy objects. The point of the individual Acordia company is to be a giant, not a dwarf. That is, within the collective heads of its 65 or so employees, an Acordia company will know more about its customers than bigger (total bodies, total assets) competitors. Moreover, through wise use of its overall network of inside and outside companies, it should be able to bring a wider set of resources to bear, more quickly, more efficiently, and more imaginatively than bigger competitors.

Tom Peters
Liberation Management (281–82)

Introduction

In 1986 The Associated Group (formerly known as Blue Cross/Blue Shield of Indiana) embarked on a critical 1,800-day strategic journey. During those days an ambitious transformation took place that changed one large, bureaucratic operation in health insurance into an entrepreneurial network of 50 companies involved with health insurance, life insurance, property and casualty insurance, insurance brokerage, government program administration, investment banking, computer software, and market research. This transformation took a company employing 2,800 people and serving only one state (Indiana) to a diversified "family" of companies that employs 7,000 people through 140 offices and serving 49 states. This re-markable restructuring strategy of "growing small" was made possible through the creation of new "Acordia" companies that would concentrate into specific market niches and operate as stand-alone entrepreneurial companies. It was an entrepreneurial vision transformed into entrepreneurial action, and the results have been an emotional, cultural, and financial success. In the fall of 1992 The Associated Group completed a successful Initial Public Offering of Acordia, Inc.

This strategic journey spanned five years but sought to accomplish so much that early in its inception critics were quick to point out the "overambitious" ideals of creating an entrepreneurial climate in a traditionally rigid, bureaucratic organization. Some execu-

---

SOURCE: This case was prepared by Dr. Donald F. Kuratko of the College of Business at Ball State University and Michael D. Houk, CEO of Acordia Corporate Benefits, Inc., 1996, as a basis for class discussion rather than to illustrate either effective or ineffective handling of an administrative situation. All rights reserved to the author. Copyright © 1996 by Donald F. Kuratko.

tives as well as some employees who didn't believe in the plan either left the company or took early retirement. Although the need to change was obvious to most of the employees, it was the dramatic challenge of restructuring into a network of entrepreneurial companies that scared away the weak of heart. Tearing away layer upon layer of bureaucracy is not easy in a well-entrenched, traditional culture. Yet the tearing away actually gave birth to a new breed of companies known as "Acordia." Through the creation of the Acordia concept, an actual network of companies was established that allowed an entrepreneurial structure to exist within a corporate giant. However, it is not the structure of Acordia that made such a difference as it is the vision and strategy behind it. The following section is intended to provide a short review of The Associated Group's past to better explain the present strategy of Acordia companies that is currently setting the stage for the future challenges.

Background: The Recent Past

One reason The Associated Group has been able to change and prosper when others in the insurance industry are struggling is that it has been different from the very beginning. It operated for many years as Blue Cross/Blue Shield of Indiana. Aggressiveness in the marketplace and conservative financial practices allowed it to become the largest health insurer in Indiana and the financially strongest Blue Cross/Blue Shield organization in the country. Unlike other Blue Cross and Blue Shield "Plans," it was chartered as two separate mutual-property and casualty-insurance companies without state tax or regulatory advantages. Indiana treated prepaid health care as insurance.

Another unusual element was the cooperative arrangement between Indiana Blue Cross and Indiana Blue Shield. Early on, a unique structure was developed to allow the then-separate companies to share expenses and concentrate on their individual areas of expertise. This cooperation continued until the companies' merger in 1985.

What looked at the time to be detriments and oddities proved instead integral to success. Since The Associated Group was competing with and being regulated as commercial insurance companies, the development of both financial strength and marketing skill was essential.

In the late 1970s and early 1980s, the health care market began to undergo permanent change, with costs skyrocketing and competition intensifying. In Indiana, population, employment, and personal income growth all slowed or flattened. The local economy was shifting from manufacturing to a new service base. The auto and steel industries—traditionally the largest Blue Cross/Blue Shield of Indiana customers—began to reduce employment. And the Blue Cross/Blue Shield System as a whole started to lose national accounts.

While these changes to the current customer base were occurring, rising health care costs and deepening cycles of profit and loss in the health insurance business were fostering new competitors and new managed-care products. These rapid and permanent changes on both the market and product sides of the business made the need for internal change clear. In order to enhance the long-term success of The Associated Group, it was imperative to change the strategic direction.

The New Strategic Direction

In 1986, a newly developed strategic plan was set in motion. Its three primary objectives were to strengthen the core health insurance business; to diversify into other lines of insurance and financial services that are noncyclical or countercyclical to health insurance; and to expand outside Indiana into growing markets that have economies countercyclical to those in the Midwest, particularly in the South, Southwest, and West.

In pursuing these objectives, the organization's core competencies were used by matching expertise with growth opportunities in other fields. As a successful health insurance company, it had a desire to expand into areas where marketing ability, administrative skill, and computer competence could provide market advantages. Familiarity and comfort with the assumption of actuarially predictable risk, as well as knowledge of how to work in regulated environments, provided existing strengths as the company set out its "enabling" objectives.

In order to meet the three original primary objectives stated earlier, the company had to set enabling objectives that would guide its efforts. These objectives included the following:

- Maintain a strong financial base and gain access to new sources of capital.
- Be recognized as an innovative product leader.
- Develop and maintain a strong management team.
- Make changes in corporate identity necessary to grow outside of Indiana and in new product lines.

However, as sincere as the enabling objectives sounded, the company still needed to *implement* the new direction, and two critical steps had to be taken. First, a restructuring through decentralizing operations had to occur, and, second, a new corporate culture would have to be developed. Thus, in 1986 the new course

---

| TABLE 1 | KEY HIGHLIGHTS OF BUILDING THE ACORDIA CONCEPT (YEAR BY YEAR) |

1986	1987
• The new strategic plan and corporate mission statement are conceived and adopted. • A new corporate identity, The Associated Group, is created. • To diversify product lines, Professional Administrator Limited, a Kentucky-based insurance group specializing in products for the construction industry, and Raffensperger, Hughes & Co., an Indiana-based investment banking firm, are acquired. • To strengthen the core health insurance business, Key Care Health Resources, a health care management company specializing in case management and wellness products, is formed. Partnerships are also formed with Caremark to provide case management, home health care, and mail-order pharmacy services and with American Biodyne to provide mental health services to health maintenance organization (HMO) customers.	• A newmarket-focused corporate culture is created by restructuring claims systems and forming dedicated service units in preparation for strategic decentralization. • A Department of Defense contract to provide utilization review and quality assurance for the Civilian Health and Medical Program of the Uniformed Services (CHAMPUS) is won. • Managed care becomes increasingly important. Health maintenance organization enrollment doubles. Premium income from managed care programs more than doubles. • Diversified insurance and financial services capabilities are demonstrated by providing risk management and employee benefits for the Tenth Pan Am Games, held in Indianapolis. • A decentralization plan is adopted.

1988	1989
• Market-focused strategic business units begin operating as independent companies, beginning decentralization. • A second CHAMPUS contract to administer benefits for 900,000 military personnel and their dependents in 17 states is received. • Digital Insurance Systems Corporation (DISCorp), a software development company, is acquired. • Health Networks of America is created to develop new health insurance products and provider networks.	• The purchase of American General Group Insurance Companies adds $600 million in health and life revenue and $750 million in assets, plus 17 sales offices in nine states. • The marketing and administrative operations of the Indiana health insurance business are organized into eight independent, customer-oriented subsidiaries called Acordia companies.

1990	1991
• American General Group Insurance Companies are renamed and placed in a holding company known as Anthem Companies, Inc.—the 3d largest health insurer in Florida, 8th largest in Texas, and 13th largest in California. • The Acordia companies begin selling products from several other insurance companies, becoming true insurance brokerage companies. Two new Acordia companies are created. • The holding company, Novalis, is created to provide systems technology, benefit design, and clinical expertise to the managed care industry.	• Robinson-Conner, the 21st largest property and casualty insurance brokerage firm in the United States, is acquired. Locations in ten states provide a total of $40 million annually in commissions and fees. • The Shelby Insurance Group, an Ohio-based property and casualty insurance underwriter with $197 million in revenue, is acquired. • Seven new Acordia companies are created. • Government services operations are consolidated in a company called AdminaStar and redirected for strategic expansion.

SOURCE: The Associated Group *Annual Report*, 1991, 7.

was set, and, as this case will illustrate, The Associated Group has never looked back.

RESTRUCTURING AND DECENTRALIZATION

The decentralization of operations and development of a more aggressive, entrepreneurial corporate culture were among the most challenging tasks, yet they were based on a few simple ideas: People do a better job when they are directly responsible for the results of their work; small work teams are more responsive than big organizations; customers have unique, definable needs; and service is more important than economies of scale.

These ideas are the antithesis of the assembly-line mentality that has dominated American business since the Industrial Revolution. As author and consultant Tom Peters has pointed out, assembly lines work in manufacturing, not in service businesses. Thus, instead of grouping employees by job function, the company divided them into smaller units organized around a specific type of customer with unique needs. These individual units became the nuclei for the Acordia companies, which today sell and service insurance and financial products to customers within specific industries, geographic areas, or demographic categories across the United States.

Restructuring went hand in hand with the philosophy of letting people do what they do best. Innovation was encouraged. The strategic plan was never a detailed route of how to get from here to there. It was a compass. As long as everyone moved in the same direction, each leader was free to find his or her own route, and every employee was free to be creative in fulfilling the requirements of his or her job. The Associated Group set about to attract a new breed of executive: experienced, well educated, aggressive, accustomed to taking risks. At The Associated Group, executives could run their own show with the spirit of an entrepreneur but have the resources and commitment of a large organization behind them.

The acquisition of new companies was an integral part of the restructuring, starting with Professional Administrators Limited and Raffensperger, Hughes & Co. and then American General Group Insurance Companies, a Texas-based life and health insurance company that instantly expanded the potential market into Florida, Texas, and California.

The diversification and expansion continued over the next two years with the addition of companies such as Novalis Corporation (a group of companies offering systems technology, software, and managed-care expertise to the insurance industry), Strategic Marketing and Research (a market research firm), and Robinson-Conner and The Shelby Insurance Group (acquired in 1991), which provided a strong presence in property and casualty brokerage and underwriting. (See Table 1 for year-by-year highlights of The Associated Group's development.)

The restructuring and diversification allowed The Associated Group to become a broad-based, diversified insurance and financial services company serving customers in 49 states with its business divided into seven major segments:

- *Health insurance and managed health care:* sold in Indiana under the trade name Blue Cross and Blue Shield of Indiana and in other states through Anthem Life, Anthem Health Plans, and Anthem Health Systems
- *Life insurance:* group policies provided through Anthem Life and personal life insurance and annuity products through The Shelby Insurance Group
- *Insurance brokerage and administration:* led by the growing network of Acordia companies
- *Property and casualty insurance:* provided by The Shelby Insurance Group, the latest acquisition
- *Government program administration:* provided by AdminaStar and its affiliates
- *Service industry products:* software, research, and managed care services through Novalis and its companies, including Health Networks of America and DISCorp, and strategic marketing and research
- *Financial services:* provided through Raffensperger-Hughes & Co., an investment banking firm headquartered in Indiana

The Acordia Strategy

The Acordia vision is to become the nation's largest supplier of insurance products to midmarket clients. This is implemented by targeting cities of 100,000 to 1,000,000 in population as well as by targeting employers with less than 5,000 employees and with $200,000 annually in property and casualty commissions and individuals with incomes greater than $50,000 and net worth greater than $500,000. Acordia seeks to become the "Wal-Mart" of insurance and brokerage administration. That vision, however, can become a reality only through the application of ten specific objectives.

OBJECTIVE 1

"Product Customization" is to demonstrate that Acordia adds value to an employer or an individual by *selecting* an insurance or financial service product, by *tailoring* it to the client's needs, and by *servicing* the product after the sale. This can be done by continuing to structure and restructure the Acordia companies to focus on tight client niches that demonstrate unique insurance and financial service needs. However, each Acordia company must reduce its overall cost of distribution and administration that is included in the price of insurance and financial services products, and each must use core health, property, and casualty insurance products to pay the base costs of distribution and use innovative, profitable products to create added value. Finally, each Acordia Operating Company should attempt to develop "pioneer customers" willing to experiment with new forms of packaging and new products and services.

OBJECTIVE 2

"Superior Performance" is to demonstrate superior financial performance to the shareholders in order to have capital available for expansion. This objective was expected to be achieved if each Acordia company could produce an average of 15 percent annual growth in earnings per share for 1992–1997 and maintain an above-average shareholder return on equity in the top half of comparable companies over the six-year period.

OBJECTIVE 3

"Limited Exposure" is to minimize the risk to investors' principal by diversifying sources of net income. This is accomplished by expanding horizontally (new insurance products to the employer) and vertically (new individual products to employees in the workplace setting). In addition, each Acordia must diversify sources of net income by product line and seek to produce 10 percent of the 1997 net income from a combination of new markets, including the following:

- New Acordia industrial companies should be created in specific markets generally based on SIC code and where a significant presence can be achieved and in-depth knowledge of the cli-

ent's business adds value to the products and services provided.
- New Acordia geographic markets should be created in "Main Street" cities where existing expertise can be leveraged and a significant presence can be achieved.

See Figure 1 for an illustration of the current Acordia structure.

OBJECTIVE 4

"Main Street" is to concentrate marketing efforts in high population growth areas in which competitors do not have a dominant presence (cities of 100,000 to 1 million population). These areas should be selected based on territories where Acordia's existing expertise can be leveraged to become one of the top three brokers and administrators as measured by revenue.

OBJECTIVE 5

"Mid-Market" clients are generally defined as employers with less than 5,000 employees and with $200,000 annually in property and casualty commissions and individuals with incomes greater than $50,000 annually and net worth greater than $500,000. The target customers are employers with 400–1,000 employees and $50,000–$100,000 in property and casualty commissions and individuals who are self-employed or new retirees. Markets are segmented by industries and geographic and demographic factors based on customer buying preferences and similarities of product need.

OBJECTIVE 6

"Concentrate and Divide" is to use a market segmentation strategy designed to continually refocus Acordia companies on increasingly specialized market segments. Thus, each Acordia company should be among the top three competitors in its market as measured by revenue. However, each Acordia should concentrate growth in a subsegment that can create an Acordia spin-off and provide stock options to employees for new spin-offs.

OBJECTIVE 7

"Targeted Acquisitions" is to target locations and product lines consistent with strategic diversification and growth objectives. Acquisitions will be made at the operating-company levels as well as by Acordia, Inc. However, acquired businesses must complement business in existing locations and product lines be-

FIGURE 1   **THE ACORDIA STRUCTURE**

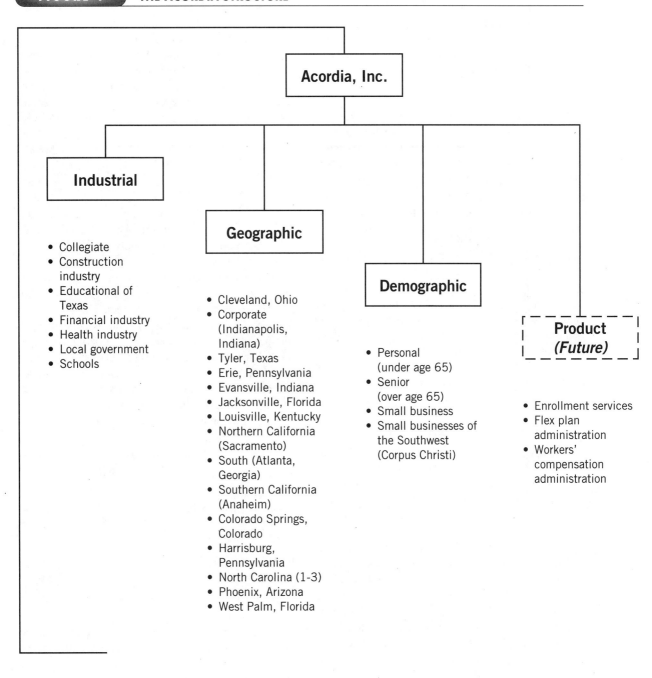

Acordia, Inc.

Industrial

- Collegiate
- Construction industry
- Educational of Texas
- Financial industry
- Health industry
- Local government
- Schools

Geographic

- Cleveland, Ohio
- Corporate (Indianapolis, Indiana)
- Tyler, Texas
- Erie, Pennsylvania
- Evansville, Indiana
- Jacksonville, Florida
- Louisville, Kentucky
- Northern California (Sacramento)
- South (Atlanta, Georgia)
- Southern California (Anaheim)
- Colorado Springs, Colorado
- Harrisburg, Pennsylvania
- North Carolina (1-3)
- Phoenix, Arizona
- West Palm, Florida

Demographic

- Personal (under age 65)
- Senior (over age 65)
- Small business
- Small businesses of the Southwest (Corpus Christi)

Product (Future)

- Enrollment services
- Flex plan administration
- Workers' compensation administration

fore expanding to new territories or product lines, and acquisitions should never dilute earnings per share. Thus, acquisitional searches should concentrate on candidates where the culture fits Acordia's strategy and culture.

OBJECTIVE 8

"Management System" is to maintain small, highly entrepreneurial, and expense-sensitive Acordia companies. This can be accomplished, and is being accomplished, if each Acordia company maintains only two levels of management with an "outside" board of directors and a maximum size of 200 employees. Also, the high-speed electronic network information systems for inter/intracompany communications and reporting should be in place with a fully decentralized computer system for each Acordia operating company.

OBJECTIVE 9

"Executive Talent" is to attract and retain the industry's best talent by offering the best benefits of being an entrepreneurial business owner and an executive with a large company. It is important to develop a program to recognize leaders among Acordia CEOs and to achieve a voluntary turnover of 5 percent or less among Acordia CEOs and vice presidents.

OBJECTIVE 10

"Strategic Compensation" is to develop powerful incentives for all employees to foster growth, increase shareholder value, and successfully execute the strategic plan. This may be the critical component in the Acordia strategy. A new cash compensation system tied directly to growth in earnings, an Acordia stock ownership plan, and a new performance-driven benefit plan all have been introduced. The next section describes this compensation plan in greater detail.

The Acordia Compensation Plan

The compensation system for executives and officers designed for the Acordia companies is an integral part of the strategic plan and is needed to implement the aggressive entrepreneurial approach of each Acordia. As designed, the compensation system is competitive (in comparison to the market) and yet challenging (incentives are a critical component).

The compensation plan has three major segments (see Figure 2). First, cash wages are positioned at the market average. However, the market average is achieved through a combination of target base plus an annual incentive. Although base pay will be at the low end of market ranges, the annual incentive is positioned at the high end so that total wage potential can be well above the market. Actual payment of wages is based on performance.

The incentive determination is based on three elements: the individual Acordia company's financial performance for the year; the individual Acordia company's board-of-directors assessment; and Acordia, Inc.'s discretionary input. Each board of directors

uses a worksheet similar to the one shown in Table 2 so that they have a clear understanding of the range of discretion to be applied. The goal is to create clear incentives tied directly to the firm's performance yet allowing for additional factors such as product and geographic diversification, customer satisfaction (identified through surveys), and employee satisfaction (identified through surveys). The second segment, aggressive long-term incentives, delivers significant compensation for performance *above* competitive levels, and the company's shareholders clearly benefit from such executive performance. The third segment involves benefits maintained at an appropriate competitive level and "directed executive compensation" (commonly known as "perks") designed in a cafeteria fashion, where each executive has a set pool of credits to apply toward his or her choice of items.

In addition, a stock option plan is designed to create long-term incentive and ownership opportunity for all Acordia companies' officers. The stock is, of course, Acordia, Inc., but its value is dependent on the performance of all the Acordia operating companies. The target pool is 1,800 shares of stock per year for each Acordia company, with a maximum individual officer award of 600 shares in any one year. Each Acordia company board of directors allocates the shares based on the following guidelines:

Individual Performance	Acordia Operating Company Growth Rate				
	12%		15%		16.5% and Above
Poor	0		0		0
Good	100	to	150	to	200
Excellent	200	to	400	to	500
Superior	300	to	500	to	600

This unique approach to compensation seeks to add value to the overall entrepreneurial strategy by fostering and supporting an ownership perspective among the officers in all Acordia companies.

Acordia Corporate Benefits, Inc.

As an example of the implementation of the Acordia strategy, the following section describes the develop-

| FIGURE 2 | ACORDIA COMPENSATION SYSTEM |

Cash Wages		Equity	Indirect Wages	
Base Pay	Annual Incentive	Long-Term Incentive	Directed Executive Compensation	Benefits

Compared to market by position   Compared to market for all employees

| TABLE 2 | ANNUAL INCENTIVE PLAN |

AWARD CALCULATION GUIDE   ($ EXPRESSED PER $10,000 OF TARGET AWARD)

Financial Result	Formula Award	Individual Acordia Co. Board Discretion Range[a]	Acordia, Inc., Discretion Range[b]	Total Maximum Award
Less than Threshold 0–11.9% growth	Not eligible for incentive based on formula. Shareholder retains right but has no obligation to consider an appropriate payout after reviewing compelling mitigating factors affecting performance.			
Threshold = 12%	$6,000 (60% of target award)	+/– $2,000 (40–80% of target award)	Up to $2,000 (0–20% of target award)	$10,000 (100% of target)
Target = 15%	$8,000 (80% of target award)	+/– $2,000 (60–100% of target award)	Up to $5,000 (0–50% of target award)	$15,000 (150% of target)
Outstanding = 16.5%	$10,000 (100% of target award)	+/– $2,000 (80–120% of target award)	Up to $6,000 (0–60% of target award)	$18,000 (180% of target)

[a] Should decrease only for significant variances or events or to give a message; not intended for fine-tuning and creating precision in awards.
[b] Shareholder cannot reduce but may increase board award; 100% is normal award for fully meeting expected results. Increase only for exceptional performance, exceptional service to Acordia, Inc., overall, etc.

ment and growth of one Acordia Company, Acordia Corporate Benefits, Inc.

Acordia Corporate Benefits, Inc., was incorporated as a Third Party Administrator and Insurance Agency in the State of Indiana effective December 1, 1990. Its approved mission was to market and administer insurance and insurance-related products to employers with 50 or more employees, excluding customers that fall within the missions of any other Acordia companies, such as schools, municipalities, and so forth (see Figure 1).

Generally speaking, employers in the manufacturing and service industries with fewer than 1,000 employees are targeted, while geographically it is restricted to employers located in the northern half of the United States.

Michael D. Houk, the company's new CEO, described the company's birth.

On December 1, 1990, 97 employees staffed the new company and prepared to move to a new facility February 1, 1991. During that 60-day period, we began to build our new culture . . . the culture of a company whose future was totally dependent upon the results it produced.

From the first day, we eliminated the multiple levels of management that employees had been accustomed to. Each employee was hired to a Vice President in our company who reported directly to the President . . . no more supervisors, managers, or directors to stagnate the communication channels. We also converted from a 37.5-hour work week to a 40-hour work week, added an Employee Profit Sharing Plan, a dress code, raised expectations, and set up our new facility with our new work flows in mind. . . . All these changes combined allowed us to eliminate over 30 positions from the operation that had been handling the business prior to December 1, 1990. Attitudes began to change, ever so slowly at first, but each day we saw some improvement. When we moved out of the old 15-story building to our new one-level facility on February 1, 1991, we realized a significant increase in the morale and excitement of our employees. Our employees began to take greater pride in where they worked and how they worked. . . . As a result, service to our customers improved! Our clients were no longer unknown employers and employees who generated work. . . . Now they were our clients upon whom our future would be built.

During that first year, we went on to add an Employee Advisory Committee that meets monthly with the President to continually refine our Corporate policies and practices . . . our culture! We've implemented a Weight Loss Program for our employees, a totally No Smoking facility, quarterly All-Employee meetings, dress-down day every payday, an annual family picnic, a Christmas Lunch, etc. . . . all organized and run by employees "elected" by their peers.

But have we been successful financially? In a word, . . . Yes!

During 1991, Revenues exceeded $10 million and Net Income before taxes exceeded $1.8 million . . . a pretax return on revenue of over 18 percent. The second full year was even better . . . and pretax net exceeded $2.2 million . . . a 22 percent increase over 1991! During 1992, over 40 percent of Net Income came from outside Indiana, and over 20 percent of our Net Income was from nonhealth sources. Acordia Corporate Benefits was now licensed as a Third Party Administrator and Life and Health Insurance Agency in over 20 states, concentrating in the Midwest.

Acordia Corporate Benefits began to consider diversification geographically, by product, or into nonhealth products. In 1993, the company added a new product line, Flexible Benefits Administration, which increased revenues by more than $1 million in the first year. Also, Acordia Corporate Benefits acquired a large Indianapolis-based property and casualty insurance agency during the first quarter of 1993, increasing revenue an additional $3.5 million.

By the end of 1993, annual revenue increased to more than $16 million, with pretax net income approaching $3 million and an employment base of approximately 160 employees—all in a span of three years.

What's more, this particular Acordia made the transition from a business totally dependent on the health insurance business and employers in Indiana alone to a business operating in more than 20 states with more than one-third of its revenue from nonhealth products.

"We have become an employer of empowered employees who look forward to change, new products, and a promising future," Houk says. "We are no longer totally reliant upon a single product and a single state. However, growth brings new challenges to our management team. The Acordia Strategy requires that the companies remain small and focused. Our newest challenge is to look inward to determine what unique marketing niche will be best suited to provide the base of a new Acordia company. It may be a geographic segment of our company, or industrial segment of our current clients."

Future Considerations

Although The Associated Group achieved many of its strategic goals, its commitment to growth and diversification continues. By late 1997, The Associated Group plans to be more diversified, to serve more markets, and to continue to build successful businesses from its core competencies. Each time another building block is added the future is enhanced. The first 1,800 days (from 1986) provided a strong base to build on for the following 1,800 days.

Of course, no one can predict exactly what lies ahead. But guideposts exist: trends, movements, signs of the times. The following section outlines some of the most pressing areas.

HEALTH CARE

President Bill Clinton's health care reforms, announced in 1993, are now under way. Managed care is the future of health care. The nonmanaged segments of the health benefits industry are becoming smaller each year. The unlimited choices people have had regarding their own providers and providers have enjoyed when prescribing given courses of therapy will become more ordered as the industry responds to pay or cost pressures. Everyone in the health care system, from hospitals and physicians to insurance companies to the patients themselves, will become more informed and more involved in health care economics and decisions. The only companies to survive and prosper will be those that understand and deliver effective managed care. The Associated Group is positioned at the forefront of technology and product innovation in the managed care industry.

With regard to public policy, the health care industry will see more changes in the next decade than in any of the previous three. The Associated Group is an active participant, at both the state and federal levels, in the debate on health care costs and access and reflects the potential for different policy outcomes through its business strategy.

Trends within the Blue Cross/Blue Shield System also deserve attention due to the national prominence of this product line. Recent years have seen some of the 73 licensees struggling to meet the needs of traditional customers and to remain financially sound, with one even reaching the point of insolvency.

AGING AMERICA

The retirement boom is coming, and the next 1,800 days will find the United States at its leading edge. The population of America is slowly growing older and living longer; the 1990s has seen increases in two-generation geriatric families, with adult children in their 60s and 70s caring for parents in their 90s. By the year 2000, the number of Americans over age 75 will have grown by nearly 35 percent.

The pressures on our health care system become even more critical as the U.S. population ages and requires more medical attention. As one of America's leading health insurers, The Associated Group says it is committed to finding new ways to finance and deliver effective health care to older Americans.

FINANCIAL SERVICES

Today, the lines separating the various segments of the financial services industry are more blurred than ever before. Institutions that once had little in common will continue to become more alike. Technological advances are changing the way people handle their money. Though a "checkless society" has been predicted since the 1960s, the idea is becoming reality. Electronic transactions are more efficient and accurate than paper transactions. And more people are gaining access to the technology required to completely automate their finances and investments. The Associated Group says it is committed to a future in financial services by continuing to successfully diversify operations to be in a position to offer a broader variety of products.

CONTINUED DEMASSIFICATION

The trend toward specialization in U.S. society that marked The Associated Group's 1,800 days since 1986, a trend predicted by futurists such as Alvin Toffler more than a decade ago, has shown no signs of slowing. On the contrary, it seems to be accelerating. As the things we do, the choices we have, and the information we process become more specialized, uniform, traditional solutions make less sense. We have fewer mass needs that can be addressed with cookie-cutter products and services.

The ability to tailor products and services to niche markets is one of The Associated Group's new core competencies. For its following 1,800 days, Acordia companies continues to focus on even more tightly defined industry, demographic, and geographic market segments to try to deliver what customers want and need with great expertise and efficiency.

THE CHANGING ROLE OF THE CORPORATION

The mirror image of the declining capability and credibility of government has meant a broadened role for corporations in meeting the noneconomic needs of U.S. society. Corporations, which must survive in increasingly competitive markets, have proven to be effective and highly adaptable entities. Not surprisingly, society has increasingly turned to the business community to solve problems traditionally viewed as public-sector issues.

The Associated Group has long acknowledged and accepted its obligations as a socially responsible corporation that is vitally interested in the communities where it does business.

Questions

1. Describe the significant changes that The Associated Group went through. And discuss how they are relevant to managing entrepreneurial growth.
2. What exactly is the Acordia strategy? How effective do you think it is?
3. Describe The Acordia Compensation Plan and how it helped the innovative strategy.

Part 6

CONTEMPORARY CHALLENGES IN ENTREPRENEURSHIP

CHAPTER 18
Valuation of Business Ventures

CHAPTER 19
Management Succession and Continuity: A Family Business Perspective

CHAPTER 20
Total Quality and the Human Factor: Continuous Challenges for Entrepreneurs

VALUATION OF BUSINESS VENTURES

CHAPTER OBJECTIVES

1. To describe four basic steps to follow when buying a business

2. To outline ten key questions to ask when buying an ongoing venture

3. To explain the importance of valuation

4. To examine the underlying issues involved in the valuation process

5. To outline the various aspects of analyzing a business

6. To present the major points to consider when establishing a firm's value

7. To highlight the available methods of valuing a venture

8. To examine the three principal methods currently used in business valuations

9. To consider additional factors affecting a venture's valuation

10. To discuss the leveraged buyout (LBO) as a method of purchasing a business

The real fair market value of anything is defined as the price and terms agreed on between a willing seller and a willing buyer. However, in interpreting this definition, give careful consideration to the circumstances of the buyer and seller.

Douglas E. Kellogg,
"How to Buy a Small Manufacturing Business,"
Harvard Business Review

BUYING A BUSINESS VENTURE

A prospective entrepreneur may seek to purchase a business venture rather than start up an enterprise. This can be a successful method of getting into business, but numerous factors need to be analyzed. Purchasing a business venture is a complex transaction, and the advice of professionals always should be sought. However, a few basic steps that can be easily understood are presented here, including the entrepreneur's personal preferences, examination of opportunities, evaluation of the selected venture, and key questions to ask.

Personal Preferences

Entrepreneurs need to recognize certain personal factors and to limit their choices of ventures accordingly. An entrepreneur's background, skills, interests, and experience are all important factors in selecting the type of business to buy. In addition, personal preferences for location and size of a business should guide the selection process. If an entrepreneur always has desired to own a business in the South or West, then that is exactly where the search should begin.

Examination of Opportunities

Entrepreneurs in search of a possible venture to buy need to examine the available opportunities through various sources:

- *Business brokers.* Professionals specializing in business opportunities often can provide leads and assistance in finding a venture for sale. However, the buyer should evaluate the broker's reputation, services, and contacts. The entrepreneur also should remember that the broker usually represents—and gets a commission on the sale from—the seller.
- *Newspaper ads.* "Business Opportunity" classified ads are another source. Because an ad often will appear in one paper and not another, it may be necessary to check the classified sections of all the papers in the area.

567

- *Trade sources.* Suppliers, distributors, manufacturers, trade publications, trade associations, and trade schools may have information about businesses for sale.
- *Professional sources.* Professionals such as management consultants, attorneys, and accountants often know of businesses available for purchase.

Evaluation of the Selected Venture

After the entrepreneur considers personal preferences and examines information sources, the next step is to evaluate specific factors of the venture being offered for sale:

- The *business environment:* The local environment for business should be analyzed to establish the potential of the venture in its present location.
- *Profits, sales, and operating ratios:* The business's profit potential is a key factor in evaluating the venture's attractiveness and in later determining a reasonable buying price. To estimate the potential earning power of the business, the buyer should review past profits, sales, and operating ratios and project sales and profits for the next one to two years. Valuation will be discussed further, later in the chapter.
- The *business assets:* The tangible (physical) and intangible (e.g., reputation) assets of the business need to be assessed. These assets should be examined:
  - •• Inventory (age, quality, salability, condition)
  - •• Furniture, equipment, fixtures (value, condition, leased or owned)
  - •• Accounts receivable (age of outstanding debts, past collection periods, credit standing of customers)
  - •• Trademarks, patents, copyrights, business name (value, how essential to business success, degree of competitive edge)
  - •• Goodwill (reputation, established clientele, trusted name)

Key Questions to Ask

In addition to evaluating the major points just presented, the entrepreneur should ask key questions to analyze the viability of the potential purchase. These questions range from the owner's reasons for selling to the degree of competition the business faces.[1] The following questions highlight some of the critical areas that need to be addressed.

1. *Why is this business being sold?* It is important to establish the owner's motivation for selling. Although the reason may be very good, such as retirement or ill health, an entrepreneur needs to investigate and verify it. If at any time the owner's reason for selling does not appear to be the prime motivation, then further research must be done on that particular business.

2. *What is the physical condition of the business?* The overall condition of the facilities needs to be carefully assessed in order to avoid major expenses after the purchase. Sometimes owners sell a business simply to avoid remodeling the entire location.

---

[1] See Richard M. Hodgetts and Donald F. Kuratko, *Effective Small Business Management,* 5th ed. (Fort Worth: The Dryden Press, 1995), 105–11.

3. *How many key personnel will remain?* In order to conduct a smooth transition, a purchasing entrepreneur needs to be sure of which personnel will remain after the sale. Certain key personnel may be extremely valuable to the continuity of the venture.

4. *What is the degree of competition?* The answer to this question must cover two distinct parts: the quantity and the quality of competitors. In other words, how many competitors are there, and how strong are they?

5. *What are the conditions of the lease?* When the business is being sold but not the building or property, it is vital to know all of the conditions of the present lease. In addition, the landlord's future plans should be established as far as future lease provisions are concerned.

6. *Do any liens against the business exist?* This refers to the position of creditors and the liabilities of the business. Entrepreneurs should check for any delinquent payments or outstanding debt of any kind by the business.

7. *Will the owner sign a covenant not to compete?* Legal restraint of trade is the actual purpose here, since a purchaser does not want the seller reopening a firm in direct competition. Thus, the law allows a reasonable covenant to cover the time and distance within which the seller agrees not to compete.

8. *Are any special licenses required?* The buyer needs to verify the federal, state, or local requirements, if any, that pertain to the type of business being purchased.

9. *What are the future trends of the business?* This is an overall look at the particular industry trends and how this business will fit into them. In addition, the financial health of the business needs to be projected.

10. *How much capital is needed to buy?* The final purchase price is not the only factor to consider. Repairs, new inventory, opening expenses, and working capital are just a few of the additional costs that should be considered. Table 18.1 illustrates how to calculate the total amount needed for buying a business venture.[2]

THE IMPORTANCE OF BUSINESS VALUATION

Every entrepreneur should be able to calculate the value of his or her business and also should be able to determine the value of a competitor's operation. Such **business valuation** is essential in these situations:

- Buying or selling a business, division, or major asset
- Establishing an employee stock option plan (ESOP) or profit-sharing plan for employees
- Raising growth capital through stock warrants or convertible loans.
- Determining inheritance tax liability (potential estate tax liability)
- Giving a gift of stock to family members
- Structuring a buy/sell agreement with stockholders
- Attempting to buy out a partner
- Going public with the company or privately placing the stock

[2] For additional insights, see Ted S. Front, "How to Be a Smart Buyer," *D & B Reports* (March/April 1990): 56–58.

TABLE 18.1	TOTAL AMOUNT NEEDED TO BUY A BUSINESS	
Family Living Expenses	From last paycheck to takeover day	$ _____
	Moving expense	_____
	For three months after takeover day	_____
Purchase Price	Total amount (or down payment plus three monthly installments)	_____
Sales Tax	On purchased furniture and equipment	_____
Professional Services	Escrow, accounting, legal	_____
Deposits, Prepayments, Licenses	Last month's rent (first month's rent in Operating Expense below)	_____
	Utility deposits	_____
	Sales tax deposit	_____
	Business licenses	_____
	Insurance premiums	_____
Takeover Announcements	Newspaper advertising	_____
	Mail announcements	_____
	Exterior sign changes	_____
	New stationery and forms	_____
New Inventory		_____
New Fixtures and Equipment		_____
Remodeling and Redecorating		_____
Three Months' Operating Expense	Including loan repayments	_____
Reserve to Carry Customer Accounts		_____
Cash	Petty cash, change, etc.	_____
	Total	$ _____

Note: Money for living and business expenses for at least three months should be set aside in a bank savings account and not used for any other purpose. This is a cushion to help get through the start-up period with a minimum of worry. If expense money for a longer period can be provided, it will add to peace of mind and help the buyer concentrate on building the business.

SOURCE: Reprinted with permission from Bank of America NT&SA, "How to Buy and Sell a Business or Franchise," *Small Business Reporter,* copyright © 1987, 9.

Equally important is the entrepreneur's desire to know the real value of the venture. This valuation can provide a scorecard for periodically tracking the increases or decreases in the business's value.

UNDERLYING ISSUES

Three issues underlie the valuation of a business: (1) the differing goals of the buyer and seller, (2) the emotional bias of the seller, and (3) the reasons for the acquisition.

Goals of the Buyer and Seller

It is important to remember one's reasons for valuing an enterprise. Both major parties to the transaction, buyer and seller, will assign different values to the enterprise because of their basic objectives. The seller will attempt to establish the highest possible value for the business and will not heed the realistic considerations of the market, the environment, or the economy. To the seller the enterprise may represent a lifetime investment—or at the very least one that took a lot of effort. The buyer, on the other hand, will try to determine the lowest possible price to be paid. The enterprise is regarded as an investment for the buyer, and he or she must assess the profit potential. As a result, a pessimistic view often is taken. An understanding of both positions in the valuation process is important.

Emotional Bias

The second issue in valuing a business is the **emotional bias** of the seller. Whenever someone starts a venture, nurtures it through early growth, and makes it a profitable business, the person tends to believe the enterprise is worth a great deal more than outsiders believe it is worth. Entrepreneurs therefore must try to be as objective as possible in determining a fair value for the enterprise (realizing this fair amount will be negotiable).

Reasons for the Acquisition

The third issue in valuing a business is the reasons an entrepreneur's business is being acquired. The following are some of the most common reasons for acquisition:

- Developing more growth-phase products by acquiring a firm that has developed new products in the company's industry
- Increasing the number of customers by acquiring a firm whose current customers will broaden substantially the company's customer base
- Increasing market share by acquiring a firm in the company's industry
- Improving or changing distribution channels by acquiring a firm with recognized superiority in the company's current distribution channel
- Expanding the product line by acquiring a firm whose products complement and complete the company's product line
- Developing or improving customer service operations by acquiring a firm with an established service operation, as well as a customer service network that includes the company's products
- Reducing operating leverage and increasing absorption of fixed costs by acquiring a firm that has a lower degree of operating leverage and can absorb the company's fixed costs
- Using idle or excess plant capacity by acquiring a firm that can operate in the company's current plant facilities
- Integrating vertically, either backward or forward, by acquiring a firm that is a supplier or distributor
- Reducing inventory levels by acquiring a firm that is a customer (but not an end user) and adjusting the company's inventory levels to match the acquired firm's orders
- Reducing indirect operating costs by acquiring a firm that will allow elimination of duplicate operating costs (e.g., warehousing, distribution, etc.)
- Reducing fixed costs by acquiring a firm that will permit elimination of duplicate fixed costs (e.g., corporate and staff functional groups)[3]

---

[3] "Acquisition Strategies—Part 1," *Small Business Reports* (January 1987): 34. Reprinted with permission from *Small Business Reports.*

ENTREPRENEURIAL

EDGE

"Due Diligence"

Hendrix F. C. Niemann was 37 years old, well educated, experienced in business, and out of work. He decided to use his severance pay and his savings to purchase a business of his own. For months Niemann analyzed numerous prospective businesses that were for sale: a hospital transcription service, a sandwich producer for vending machines, a sailboat dealership, and a food distribution company. None of these businesses seemed to be the opportunity Niemann wanted. He was married with three children, and this business opportunity *had* to be right.

Finally, he found an appropriate opportunity. Automatic Door Specialists, a manufacturer of security systems, had sales of $2 million, fairly good cash flow, a purchase price just above book value, and a 65-year-old owner ready to retire. After going through 17 business brokers, dozens of business ads, and four months of unemployment, Niemann believed this was it. He signed a letter of agreement contingent on a due-diligence process he would accomplish. (Due diligence is close examination of a firm's financial records, legal liabilities, and business questions.)

And what did the due-diligence inspec-tion produce? A $36,000 loss occurred the first half of the fiscal year; half of the accounts receivable were more than 90 days old, and the majority dated back over a year; an overstated inventory caused a *true* loss year to date closer to $80,000; sales were down 50 percent; half of the net worth of the company was gone; and once the debt from the acquisition was added to the books, no money would be left for Niemann to draw a salary! It got worse as Niemann met with the key employees to find out the "inside" story of Automatic Door Specialists. Key people had left the company to work for competitors, parts and tools were in short supply, promises had been made to customers and then forgotten, and the building was a firetrap with no hot water.

All of this bad news provided Niemann with enough facts to demand a 50 percent reduction in the purchase price or to call the deal off. The seller accepted the new purchase price, and Automatic Door Specialists had a new owner. The due-diligence process paid off for Hendrix Niemann.

SOURCE: Hendrix F. C. Niemann, "Buying a Business," *Inc.*, February 1990, 28–38.

In summary, it is important that the entrepreneur and all other parties involved objectively view the firm's operations and potential. An evaluation of the following points can assist in this process:

- A firm's potential to pay for itself during a reasonable period of time
- The difficulties the new owners face during the transition period

TABLE 18.2		TAX TREATMENTS OF ASSETS

Asset	Seller	Buyer
Goodwill	Capital gains	Deductible over 15-year period
Capital stock	Capital gains on price that exceeds basis	Not deductible, becomes new cost basis
Compensation	Earned income	Deductible
Covenant not to compete[a]	Ordinary income or capital gain if not separately valued	Deductible over 15-year period
Fixed assets	Possible recapture of investment credit	Not deductible (treated as ordinary capital asset); capitalized and then amortized over useful life
Depreciation	Ordinary income on proceeds that exceed basis and do not exceed original cost, then capital gains	Depreciation deductions over statutorily defined recovery periods

[a] Under the 1986 Tax Reform Act, the IRS may levy a 20 percent excise tax when a covenant not to compete exceeds 300 percent of an individual's average annual compensation for the preceding five years.

- The amount of security or risk involved in the transaction; changes in interest rates
- The effect on the company's value if a turnaround is required
- The number of potential buyers
- Whether current managers intend to remain with the firm[4]

In addition, it is important to evaluate the taxes associated with the purchase or sale of an enterprise. Table 18.2 presents some of the tax considerations for both the buyer and seller.

ANALYZING THE BUSINESS

In analyzing small, closely held businesses, entrepreneurs should not make comparisons with larger corporations. Many factors distinguish these types of corporations, and valuation factors that have no effect on large firms may be significantly important to smaller enterprises. For example, many closely held ventures have the following shortcomings:

- *Lack of management depth.* The degrees of skills, versatility, and competence are limited.
- *Undercapitalization.* The amount of equity investment is usually low (often indicating a high level of debt).
- *Insufficient controls.* Because of the lack of available management and extra capital, measures in place for monitoring and controlling operations are usually limited.
- *Divergent goals.* The entrepreneur often has a vision for the venture that differs from the investors' goals or stockholders' desires, thus causing internal conflicts in the firm.

[4] "Valuing a Closely Held Business," *The Small Business Report* (November 1986): 30–31.

These weaknesses indicate the need for careful analysis of the small business.

The checklist in Table 18.3, which is patterned after the information required for an effective business plan (see Chapter 10), provides a concise method for examining the various factors that differentiate one firm from another.

ESTABLISHING A FIRM'S VALUE

After using the checklist in Table 18.3, the entrepreneur can begin to examine the various methods used to valuate a business. It should be noted that the establishment of an actual value is more of an art than a science. Estimations, assumptions, and projections are all part of the process. The quantified figures are calculated based, in part, on such hidden values and costs as goodwill, personal expenses, family members on the payroll, planned losses, and the like.[5]

Several traditional valuation methods are presented here, each using a particular approach that covers these hidden values and costs. Employing these methods will provide the entrepreneur with a general understanding of how the financial analysis of a firm works. Remember, also, that many of these methods are used concurrently and that the *final* value determination will be the actual price agreed on by the buyer and seller.

Valuation Methods

Table 18.4 on pages 580–584 lists the various methods that may be used for business valuation. Each method listed is described and key points about them are presented. Specific attention here will be concentrated on the three methods that are considered the principal measures used in current business valuations: (1) adjusted tangible assets (balance sheet values), (2) price/earnings (multiple earnings value), and (3) discounted future earnings.

ADJUSTED TANGIBLE BOOK VALUE   A common method of valuing a business is to compute its net worth as the difference between total assets and total liabilities. However, it is important to adjust for certain assets in order to assess true economic worth, since inflation and depreciation affect the value of some assets.

In the computation of the **adjusted tangible book value,** goodwill, patents, deferred financing costs, and other intangible assets are considered with the other assets and deducted from or added to net worth. This upward or downward adjustment reflects the excess of the fair market value of each asset above or below the value reported on the balance sheet. Here is an example:

	Book Value	Fair Market Value
Inventory	$100,000	$125,000
Plant and equipment	400,000	600,000
Other intangibles		(50,000)
	$500,000	$675,000

Excess = $175,000

[5] Ibid., 30.

Remember that in industry comparisons of adjusted values, only assets used in the actual operation of the business are included.

Other significant balance sheet and income statement adjustments include (1) bad debt reserves; (2) low-interest, long-term debt securities; (3) investments in affiliates; and (4) loans and advances to officers, employees, or other companies. Additionally, earnings should be adjusted. Only true earnings derived from the operations of the business should be considered. One-time items (from the sale of a company division or asset, for example) should be excluded. Also, if the company has been using a net operational loss carryforward, so its pretax income has not been fully taxed, this also should be considered.

Upward (or downward) income and balance sheet adjustments should be made for any unusually large bad-debt or inventory write-off, and for certain accounting practices, such as accelerated versus straight-line depreciation.

PRICE/EARNINGS RATIO (MULTIPLE OF EARNINGS) METHOD   The **price/earnings ratio** (P/E) is a common method used for valuing publicly held corporations. The valuation is determined by dividing the market price of the common stock by the earnings per share. A company with 100,000 shares of common stock and a net income of $100,000 would have earnings per share of $1. If the stock price rose to $5 per share, the P/E would be 5 ($5 divided by $1). Additionally, since the company has 100,000 shares of common stock, the valuation of the enterprise now would be $500,000 (100,000 shares × $5).

The primary advantage of a price/earnings approach is its simplicity. However, this advantage applies only to publicly traded corporations. Closely held companies do not have prices in the open market for their stock and thus must rely on the use of a multiple derived by comparing the firm to similar public corporations. This approach has four major drawbacks.[6]

1. The stock of a private company is not publicly traded. It is illiquid and may actually be restricted from sale (i.e., not registered with the Securities and Exchange Commission). Thus any P/E multiple usually must, by definition, be subjective and lower than the multiple commanded by comparable publicly traded stocks.

2. The stated net income of a private company may not truly reflect its actual earning power. To avoid or defer paying taxes, most business owners prefer to keep pretax income down. In addition, the closely held business may be "overspending" on fringe benefits instituted primarily for the owner's benefit.

3. Common stock that is bought and sold in the public market normally reflects only a small portion of the business's total ownership. The sale of a large controlling block of stock (typical of closely held businesses) demands a premium.

4. It is very difficult to find a truly comparable publicly held company, even in the same industry. Growth rates, competition, dividend payments, and financial profiles (liquidity and leverage) rarely will be the same.

[6] Adapted from Thomas J. Martin, *Valuation Reference Manual* (Hicksville, NY: Thomar Publications, 1987), 7.

TABLE 18.3 CHECKLIST FOR ANALYZING A BUSINESS

History of the Business

The original name of business and any subsequent name changes

Date company was founded

Names of all subsidiaries and divisions; when they were formed and their function

States where company is incorporated

States where company is licensed to do business as a foreign corporation

Review of corporate charter, bylaws, and minutes

Company's original line of business and any subsequent changes

Market and Competition

Company's major business and market

Description of major projects

Sales literature on products

Growth potential of major markets in which company operates

Name, size, and market position of principal competitors

How does company's product differ from that of the competition?

Company's market niche

Information on brand, trade, product names

Sales pattern of product lines, i.e., are sales seasonal or cyclical?

Review of any statistical information available on the market, i.e., trade associations, government reports, Wall Street reports, etc.

Comparative product pricing

Gross profit margin on each product line (Analyze sales growth and profit changes for three years.)

Concentration of government business

Research and development expenditures—historical and projected

Sales and Distribution

How does company sell—own sales force or through manufacturer representatives?

Compensation of sales force

Details on advertising methods and expenditures

Details on branch sales offices, if any

Details on standard sales terms, discounts offered, return and allowance policies

Are any sales made on consignment?

Does company warehouse its inventory?

If company uses distributors, how are they paid, and what are their responsibilities? (For example, do they provide warranty services?)

Are company's products distributed nationwide or in a certain geographic area?

Names and addresses of company's principal customers

Sales volume of principal customers by product line for last few years

How long have customers been buying from company?

Credit rating of principal customers

Historical bad-debt experience of company

Details on private label business, if any

Do sales terms involve any maintenance agreements?

Do sales terms offer any express or implied warranties?

TABLE 18.3 **CHECKLIST FOR ANALYZING A BUSINESS (continued)**

Has company experienced any product liability problems?

Does company lease, as well as sell, any of its products?

What is the percentage of foreign business? How is this business sold, financed, and delivered?

Have any new products come on the market that would make company's products obsolete or less competitive?

Have any big customers been lost? If so, why?

Size and nature of market—fragmented or controlled by large companies?

Manufacturing

Full list of all manufacturing facilities

Are facilities owned or leased?

Does company manufacture from basic raw materials, or is it an assembly-type operation?

Types and availability of materials required to manufacture the product.

Time length of production cycle

Does company make a standard shelf-type product, manufacture to specification, or both?

How is quality control handled in the factory?

What is accounting system for work in process?

Are any licenses needed to manufacture product?

What is present sales capacity based on current manufacturing equipment?

Does company have a proprietary manufacturing process?

What is company's safety record in its factory operations?

Do any problems with OSHA or federal or state environmental regulations exist?

What is stability of company's supplier relationships?

Employees

Total number of employees by function

Does a union exist? If not, what is the probability of unionization? If a union exists, what have been its historical relations with company?

Any strikes or work stoppages?

Details on local labor market

Details on company's wage and personnel policies

Is employee level fixed, or can workforce be varied easily in terms of business volume?

What is company's historical labor turnover, especially in key management?

Analysis of working conditions

Analysis of general employee morale

Has the company ever been cited for a federal violation, e.g., OSHA, Pregnancy Discrimination Act, Fair Labor Practices, etc.?

What are fringe benefits, vacation time, sick leave, etc.?

Physical Facilities

List of all company-used facilities, giving location, square footage, and cost

Which facilities are owned? Which leased?

What is present condition of all facilities, including machinery and equipment?

If any facilities are leased, details of expiration term, cost, renewal options, etc.

Are current facilities adequate for current and projected needs?

Will any major problems occur if expansion is needed?

continued

TABLE 18.3 CHECKLIST FOR ANALYZING A BUSINESS *(continued)*

Is adequate insurance maintained?

Are facilities adequately protected against casualty loss, such as fire damage, through sprinkler systems, burglar alarms, etc.?

Are facilities modern and functional for work process and employees?

Are facilities air-conditioned and do they have adequate electric, heat, gas, water, and sanitary service?

Are facilities easily accessible to required transportation?

What is cost, net book value, and replacement value for company-owned buildings and equipment?

Ownership

List of all current owners of the company's common and preferred stock, by class if applicable

List of all individuals and the number of shares exercisable under stock option and warrant agreements with prices and expiration dates

Breakdown of ownership by shares and percentage: actual and pro forma (assuming warrants and stock options exercised)

Does common stock have preemptive rights or liquidation or dividend preference?

Do the shares carry an investment letter?

Do restrictions on the transferability of the shares or on their use as collateral exist?

Do any buy/sell agreements exist?

Does an employee stock ownership plan or stock bonus plan exist?

Are the shares fully paid for?

Are any shareholders' agreements outstanding?

Has any stock been sold below par or stated value?

Does cumulative voting exist?

With respect to the principal owner's stock, have any shares been gifted or placed in a trust?

How many shares does the principal stockholder own directly and beneficially (including family)?

If all stock options and warrants are exercised, will the principal stockholder still control 51 percent of the company?

If a business is being bought or sold, what percentage of the total outstanding shares is needed for approval?

Financial

Three years of financial statements

- Current ratio and net quick ratio
- Net working capital and net quick assets
- Total debt as a percent of stockholder's equity
- Source and application of funds schedules

Analysis of the company's basic liquidity and turnover ratios

- Cash as a percent of current liabilities
- Accounts receivable and inventory turnovers
- Age of accounts payable
- Sales to net working capital

If company has subsidiaries (or divisions), consolidating statements of profit and loss

Verification of the cash balance and maximum and minimum cash balances needed throughout year

If the company owns marketable securities, what is their degree of liquidity (salability) and current market values?

TABLE 18.3   **CHECKLIST FOR ANALYZING A BUSINESS** *(continued)*

Age of all accounts and notes receivable, any customer concentration, and the adequacy of bad debt reserve

Cost basis for recording inventories and any inventory reserves; age of inventory and relation to cost of sales (turnover)

Details on all fixed assets, including date of purchase, original cost, accumulated depreciation, and replacement value

Current market appraisals on all fixed assets, real estate, and machinery and equipment

Analysis of any prepaid expenses or deferred charges as to nature and as to amortization in or advance to affiliates; comparison of true value to book value; financial statements

Personal financial statements of principal stockholders

If company carries any goodwill or intangible items, such as patents or trademarks, what is their true value (to extent possible)? Does company have any intangible assets of value not carried on books (such as mailing lists in a publishing operation)?

Analysis of all current liabilities, including age of accounts payable, and details of all bank debt and lines of credit, including interest rate, term, and collateral; loan agreements

Details on all long-term debt by creditor, including loan agreement covenants that may affect future operations

Do any contingent liabilities or other outstanding commitments, such as long-term supplier agreements exist?

Details on franchise, lease, and royalty agreements

Income statement accounts for at least three years and analysis of any significant percentage variances, i.e., cost of sales as percent of sales

Company's tax returns—do they differ from its financial statements? Which years still may be open for audit?

Three-year projection of income and cash flow for reasonableness of future sales and profits and to establish financing needs

Pension, profit-sharing, and stock bonus plans for contractual commitments and unfunded past-service liability costs

Management

Details on all officers and directors—length of service, age, business background, compensation, and fringe benefits

Ownership positions: number of shares, stock options, and warrants

Similar details on other nonofficer/nondirector key management

Organizational chart

What compensation-type fringe benefits are offered to key management: bonuses, retirement-plan stock bonuses, company-paid insurance, deferred compensation?

What is management's reputation in its industry?

Does management have any personal interests in any other businesses? Does it have any other conflicts of interest?

Does key management devote 100 percent of its time to the business?

Any employment contracts—amount of salary, length of time, other terms

Has key management agreed to a noncompete clause and agreed not to divulge privileged information obtained while employed with company?

TABLE 18.4	METHODS FOR VENTURE VALUATION	
Method	**Description/Explanation**	**Notes/Key Points**
Fixed price	Two or more owners set initial value	Inaccuracies exist due to personal estimates
	Based on what owners "think" business is worth	Should allow periodic update
	Uses figures from any one or combination of methods	
	Common for buy/sell agreements	
Book value (known as balance sheet method) 1. Tangible 2. Adjusted tangible	1. *Tangible book value:* Set by the business's balance sheet Reflects net worth of the firm Total assets less total liabilities (adjusted for intangible assets)	Some assets also appreciate or depreciate substantially; thus, not an accurate valuation
	2. *Adjusted tangible book value:* Uses book value approach Reflects fair market value for certain assets Upward/downward adjustments in plant and equipment, inventory, and bad debt reserves	Adjustments in assets eliminate some of the inaccuracies and reflect a fair market value of each asset
Multiple of earnings	Net income capitalized using a price/earnings ratio (net income multiplied by P/E number)	Capitalization rates vary as to firm's growth; thus, estimates or P/E used must be taken from similar publicly traded corporation
	15% capitalization rate often used (equivalent to a P/E multiple of 6.7, which is 1 divided by 0.15)	
	High-growth businesses use lower capitalization rate (e.g., 5%, which is a multiple of 20)	
	Stable businesses use higher capitalization rate (e.g., 10%, which is a multiple of 10)	
	Derived value divided by number of outstanding shares to obtain per-share value	
Price/earnings ratio (P/E)	Similar to a return-on-investment approach	More common with public corporations
	Determined by price of common stock divided by after-tax earnings	Market conditions (stock prices) affect this ratio
	Closely held firms must multiply net income by an appropriate multiple, usually derived from similar publicly traded corporations	
	Sensitive to market conditions (prices of stocks)	
Discounted future earnings (discounted cash flow)	Attempts to establish future earning power in current dollars	Based on premise that cash flow is most important factor

TABLE 18.4	METHODS FOR VENTURE VALUATION *(continued)*	
Method	**Description/Explanation**	**Notes/Key Points**
	Projects future earnings (5 years), then calculates present value using a discounted rate Based on projected "timing" of future income	Effective method if (1) business being valued needs to generate a return greater than investment and (2) only cash receipts can provide the money for reinvesting in growth
Return on investment (ROI)	Net profit divided by investment Provides an earnings ratio Need to calculate probabilities of future earnings Combination of return ratio, present value tables, and weighted probabilities	Will *not* establish a value for the business Does not provide projected future earnings
Replacement value	Based on value of each asset if it had to be *replaced* at current cost Firm's worth calculated as if building from "scratch" Inflation and annual depreciation of assets are considered in raising the value above reported book value Does *not* reflect earning power or intangible assets	Useful for selling a company that's seeking to break into a new line of business Fails to consider earnings potential Does not include intangible assets (goodwill, patents, etc.)
Liquidation value	Assumes business ceases operation Sells assets and pays off liabilities Net amount after payment of all liabilities is distributed to shareholders Reflects "bottom value" of a firm Indicates amount of money that could be borrowed on a secured basis Tends to favor seller since all assets are valued as if converted to cash	Assumes each division of assets sold separately at auction Effective in giving absolute bottom value below which a firm should liquidate rather than sell
Excess earnings	Developed by the U.S. Treasury to determine a firm's intangible assets (for income tax purposes) Intent is for use only when no better method available Internal Revenue Service refers to this method as a last resort Method does not include intangibles with estimated useful lives (i.e., patents, copyrights)	Method of last resort (if no other method available) Very seldom used
Market value	Needs a "known" price paid for a similar business Difficult to find recent comparisons Methods of sale may differ—installment vs. cash Should be used only as a reference point	Valuable only as a reference point Difficult to find recent, similar firms that have been sold

CONTEMPORARY ENTREPRENEURSHIP

Buying a Business: Doing It Right

One reason entrepreneurs need to know how to valuate a business is that they may want to buy one someday. When this is the case, they should keep in mind a number of factors. Here are five of the most important:

1. Get a lawyer involved from the beginning. The purchase of assets often involves tax questions, unknown risks, and, in some cases, the assumption of liabilities. A lawyer can help the entrepreneur be aware of these issues before they become problems.

2. Be aware of hidden risks that may not surface for 12–18 months. For example, a customer who was injured by a company-made product before the firm was sold may end up suing the new entrepreneur.

3. Have the old owner sign a noncompete clause whereby the individual promises not to reenter the business for a certain number of years (at least not in the local area). Be sure this clause is reasonable in terms of what is being promised; otherwise, the courts may set it aside.

4. Have a certified public accountant or an outside financial expert confirm all income and expenses as well as asset accounts. In this way, the entrepreneur knows what he or she is buying.

5. Before closing the deal, check out the seller. Why is the individual selling? Additionally, is the individual honest in business dealings? If not, the person may end up trying to walk away from the deal before the purchase has been finalized.

SOURCE: "Buying a Business: What to Watch Out For," *Financial Enterprise* (summer 1987): 13–14.

When applied to a closely held firm, here is an example of how the multiple-of-earnings method could be used:

$$
\begin{aligned}
\text{Shares of common stock} &= 100{,}000 \\
\text{1997 net income} &= \$100{,}000 \\
\text{15\% capitalization rate assumed} &= 6.7 \text{ price/earnings multiple} \\
&\quad \text{(derived by dividing 1 into 15)} \\
\text{Price per share} &= \$6.70 \\
\text{Value of company} = 100{,}000 \times \$6.70 &= \$670{,}000
\end{aligned}
$$

DISCOUNTED EARNINGS METHOD   Most analysts agree that the real value of any venture is its potential earning power. The **discounted earnings method,** more than any other, determines the firm's true value. One example of a pricing formula using earning power as well as adjusted tangible book value is illustrated in Table 18.5.

The idea behind discounting the firm's cash flows is that dollars earned in the future (based on projections) are worth less than dollars earned today (due to the loss of purchasing power). With this in mind, the "timing" of projected income or cash flows is a critical factor.

TABLE 18.5	THE PRICING FORMULA

Step 1. Determine the adjusted tangible net worth of the business. (The total market value of all current and long-term assets less liabilities.)

Step 2. Estimate how much the buyer could earn annually with an amount equal to the value of the tangible net worth invested elsewhere.

Step 3. Add to this a salary normal for an owner-operator of the business. This combined figure provides a reasonable estimate of the income the buyer can earn elsewhere with the investment and effort involved in working in the business.

Step 4. Determine the average annual net earnings of the business (net profit before subtracting owner's salary) over the past few years.

This is before income taxes, to make it comparable with earnings from other sources or by individuals in different tax brackets. (The tax implications of alternate investments should be carefully considered.)

This trend of earnings is a key factor. Have they been rising steadily, falling steadily, remaining constant, or fluctuating widely? The earnings figure should be adjusted to reflect these trends.

Step 5. Subtract the total of earning power (2) and reasonable salary (3) from this average net earnings figure (4). This gives the extra earning power of the business.

Step 6. Use this extra earnings figure to estimate the value of the intangibles. This is done by multiplying the extra earnings by what is termed the "years-of-profit" figure.

This "years-of-profit" multiplier pivots on these points. How unique are the intangibles offered by the firm? How long would it take to set up a similar busines and bring it to this stage of development? What expenses and risks would be involved? What is the price of goodwill in similar firms? Will the seller be signing an agreement with a covenant not to compete?

If the business is well established, a factor of five or more might be used, especially if the firm has a valuable name, patent, or location. A multiplier of three might be reasonable for a moderately seasoned firm. A younger but profitable firm might merely have a one-year profit figure.

Step 7. Final Price equals Adjusted Tangible Net Worth plus Value of Intangibles (Extra Earnings times "Years of Profit").

Example	Business A	Business B
1. Adjusted value of tangible net worth (assets less liabilities).	$100,000	$100,000
2. Earning power at 10%[a] of an amount equal to the adjusted tangible net worth, if invested in a comparable risk business.	10,000	10,000
3. Reasonable salary for owner-operator in the business.	18,000	18,000
4. Net earnings of the business over recent years (net profit before subtracting owner's salary).	30,000	23,350
5. Extra earning power of the business (line 4 minus lines 2 and 3).	2,000	(4,650)
6. Value of intangibles—using three-year profit figure for moderately well-established firm (3 times line 5).	6,000	None
7. Final price (lines 1 and 6).	$106,000	$100,000 (or less)

In *example A,* the seller receives a value for goodwill because the business is moderately well established and earning more than the buyer could earn elsewhere with similar risks and effort.

In *example B,* the seller receives no value for goodwill because the business, even though it may have existed for a considerable time, is not earning as much as the buyer could through outside investment and effort. In fact, the buyer may feel that even an investment of $100,000—the current appraised value of net assets—is too much because it cannot earn sufficient return.

[a] This is an arbitrary figure, used for illustration. A reasonable figure depends on the stability and relative risks of the business and the investment picture generally. The rate of return should be similar to that which could be earned elsewhere with the same approximate risk.

SOURCE: Reprinted with permission from Bank of America NT&SA, "How to Buy and Sell a Business or Franchise," *Small Business Reporter,* copyright 1987, 17.

The next Contemporary Entrepreneurship selection provides a step-by-step example of the process of discounting cash flows. Basically, the method uses a four-step process:

1. Expected cash flow is estimated. For long-established firms, historical data are effective indicators, although adjustments should be made when available data indicate that future cash flows will change.

2. An appropriate discount rate is determined. The buyer's viewpoint has to be considered in the calculation of this rate. The buyer and seller often disagree, since each requires a particular rate of return and will view the risks differently. Another point the seller often overlooks is that the buyer will have other investment opportunities to consider. The appropriate rate, therefore, must be weighed against these factors.

3. A reasonable life expectancy of the business must be determined. All firms have a life cycle that depends on such factors as whether the business is one product/one market or multiproduct/multimarket.

4. The firm's value is then determined by discounting the estimated cash flow by the appropriate discount rate over the expected life of the business.[7]

OTHER FACTORS TO CONSIDER

After reviewing these valuation methods, the entrepreneur needs to remember that additional factors intervene in the valuation process and that these should be given consideration. Presented next are three factors that may influence the final valuation of the venture.

Avoiding Start-Up Costs

Some buyers are willing to pay more for a business than what the valuation methods illustrate its worth to be. This is because buyers often are trying to avoid the costs associated with start-up and are willing to pay a little more for an existing firm. The higher price they pay will be still less than actual start-up costs and also avoids the problems associated with working to establish a clientele. Thus, for some buyers a known commodity may command a higher price.

Accuracy of Projections

The sales and earnings of a venture are always projected on the basis of historical financial and economic data. Short histories, fluctuating markets, and uncertain environments are all reasons for buyers to keep projections in perspective. It is critical they examine the trends, fluctuations, or patterns involved in projections for sales revenues (higher prices or more customers?), market potential (optimistic or realistic assumptions?), and earnings potential (accurate cost/revenue/market data?), because each area has specific factors that need to be either understood or measured for the accuracy of the projection.

Control Factor

The degree of control an owner legally has over the firm can affect its valuation. If the owner's interest is 100 percent or such that the complete operation of the firm is under his or her influence, then that value is equal to the enterprise's value. If the owner does not

---

[7] "Valuing a Closely Held Business," 34.

possess such control, then the value is less. For example, buying out a 49 percent shareholder will not be effective in control against a 51 percent shareholder. Also, two 49 percent shareholders are equal until a 2 percent "swing vote" shareholder makes a move. Obviously, minority interests also must be discounted due to lack of liquidity—a minority interest in a privately held corporation is difficult to sell. Overall, it is important to look at the control factor as another facet in the purchase of any interest in a firm.

THE LEVERAGED BUYOUT: AN ALTERNATIVE FOR SMALL VENTURES

After the valuation procedures have been completed, the entrepreneur may have a problem securing the necessary cash for purchasing the business. One alternative allows the entrepreneur to finance the transaction by borrowing on the target company's assets. This method is the **leveraged buyout (LBO).**

Entrepreneurs have used the LBO for a number of years to purchase small privately held firms whenever they lacked the needed funds by borrowing against assets such as accounts receivable, inventory, and equipment.

Issues Involved with LBOs

A great deal of literature is available about leveraged buyouts of multibillion-dollar firms. The 1980s brought about a huge increase in LBOs as a powerful financial tool for acquisition. A number of researchers have examined the long-run benefits of firms involved with LBOs.[8] However, it is most important for the entrepreneur to understand the smaller-scale LBO where ownership is concentrated in the hands of relatively few owners.

The **entrepreneurial leveraged buyout (E-LBO)** is characterized as having (1) at least two-thirds of the purchase price generated from borrowed funds, (2) more than 50 percent of the stock after acquisition owned by single individuals or their family, and (3) the majority investors devoting themselves to the active management of the company after acquisition.[9]

Generally, a company selected for a leveraged buyout has dependable cash flow from operations, a high ratio of fully depreciated fixed assets (plant, equipment, etc.), an established product line, and low current and long-term debt. This is because the traditional asset-based leveraged buyout bases the transaction on the presence of enough assets to loan against, as well as on the company's current position to take on more debt.

However, a relatively new form of buyout is available called the **cash-flow leveraged buyout (LBO).**[10] This type is different because a cash-flow lender relies very heavily on the target company's cash receipts and on indicators of that positive cash flow continuing. These loans demand a higher yield than the traditional asset-based type, which are usually available at two or three points above the prime interest rate. In addition, many cash-flow lenders may require the current management team to remain with the business and retain some equity so that they have a vested interest in performance. The lender also may take some equity, leaving the purchasing entrepreneur paying high interest rates and giving up

---

[8] See, for example, Nancy Mohan, "Do LBOs Sustain Efficiency Gains?" *Akron Business and Economic Review* (fall 1990): 91–99; see also Tim Opler and Sheridan Titman, "The Determinants of Leveraged Buyout Activity: Free Cash Flow vs. Financial Distress Costs," *The Journal of Finance* (December 1993): 1985–99.

[9] J. M. Kelly, R. A. Pitts, and B. Shin, "Entrepreneurship by Leveraged Buyout: Some Preliminary Hypotheses," *Frontiers of Entrepreneurship Research* (Wellesley, MA: Babson Center for Entrepreneurial Studies, 1986), 281–92.

[10] James McNeill Stancill, "LBOs for Smaller Companies," *Harvard Business Review* (January/February 1988): 18–26; and Stanley L. Gaffin, "Evaluating Cash Flow: Key to a Successful Small Business LBO," *Credit and Financial Management* (December 1986): 16–20.

CONTEMPORARY ENTREPRENEURSHIP

What Is This Business Worth?

Let's look at a business you wish to acquire. You will do the following:

1. Present the *net* cash flow projections for this business for five years (1998 through 2002)
2. Change the format for presenting the data (You may find it easier to use.)
3. Use a present value rate of 24 percent

Assume you have an opportunity to buy a small division of a large company. Since you know the business intimately, you can accurately forecast the company's growth. Right now it's not profitable, but with your expertise and plans, you expect it can generate $380,000 net cash flow over five years and have a value (net worth) of $400,000 at the end of year five. (The $380,000 net cash flow is *after* all cash outlays.)

Question

Since you want to earn a minimum annual return of 24 percent on your invest-

ment (i.e., the purchase price), how much should you pay for the division?

Here are the facts: Assume the acquisition will occur on December 31, 1997, and the projected annual net cash flow (the excess of all cash inflow over all cash outflow) looks like this:

	1998	1999	2000	2001	2002
Net cash flow (thousands)	$0	$40	$80	$110	$150

Answer

Since you want an annual return of 24 percent on your money, simply compute the present value of the projected net cash-flow stream. You also must compute the value of the $400,000 net worth position (projected assets less liabilities) at the end of year five.

Referring to present value tables in financial handbooks (or using a calculator), you can obtain the following data:

---

too much equity (in some cases 70 percent).[11] Since asset-based LBOs have lower interest rates, allow control to be with the purchasing entrepreneur, and usually leave all the stock with the entrepreneur, they remain the most popular form of leveraged buyouts.

The results of small-firm or entrepreneurial leveraged buyouts are interesting. One research study examined the current state of small-firm LBOs and what changes occurred after the LBO took place.[12] The results indicated that most of the small-company LBOs occured in industries far different from the high-growth, high-technology environments of the glamorous start-up. The cash-flow requirements of the high-debt component seemed to favor industries in which growth was very slow or even negative and in which the technology was stable. In addition, small LBOs were relatively immune from foreign competition.

The internal operating changes after the LBO did not include a shift in the decision-

---

[11] Ibid., 20; Gaffin, p. 20.

[12] Stewart C. Malone, ''Characteristics of Smaller Company Buyouts,'' *Journal of Business Venturing* (September 1989): 349–59.

Year	Present Value Factor for 24% Rate of Return
Today	1.000
1	0.806
2	0.650
3	0.524
4	0.423
5	0.341

All that is needed now is to prepare a table showing the net cash flows for the five-year period. You then multiply the present value factor (for a 24 percent return) by the net cash flow for each year.

Year	Net Cash Flow	Present Value Factor	Today's Value
1998	$ 0	0.806	$ 0
1999	40,000	0.650	26,000
2000	80,000	0.524	41,920
2001	110,000	0.423	46,530
2002	550,000[a]	0.341	187,550[a]
Totals	$780,000		$302,000

[a] Includes $150,000 net cash flow and $400,000 net worth of division at end of fifth year.

As computed, the total value of the projected net cash flow stream is $302,000 today—and this includes the projected $400,000 net worth at the end of year five.

In other words, if the division were purchased *today* for its net cash flow value of $302,000, and if the projected cash flows for the five years were generated (including the projected net worth value of $400,000), you would realize a 24 percent annual rate of return on your $302,000 investment over the five-year period.

SOURCE: Thomas J. Martin, *Valuation Reference Manual* (Hicksville, NY: Thomar Publications, 1987), 68.

making power to the lead investor. The most common operating changes seemed to focus on such revenue-generating efforts as increased sales and marketing as well as on more stringent capital-budgeting requirements.

Overall, the research found that the once-stable environments in which the firms had operated became far more exciting. In addition, these small companies were being operated by owner-managers experienced in both the company and the industry. The financial requirements of the high-debt levels and the resulting emphasis on cash flow rather than profitability made these firms extremely fierce competitors.[13]

It should be noted that the effects of government regulation, the economic slowdown in the 1990s, and changes in tax structures will all impact the use and popularity of LBOs.[14] Tax considerations may have the most dramatic impact on the continued use of LBOs for small firms.

[13] Ibid., 350.

[14] Alan Gart, "Leveraged Buyouts: A Reexamination," *SAM Advanced Management Journal* (summer 1990): 38–46.

ENTREPRENEURIAL

EDGE

"Acquisition Entrepreneurs"

The 1980s represented new start-ups, fast-growth companies, and creative entrepreneurs. In a ten-year period of solid economic growth, an astonishing number of new businesses developed. New incorporations were being established at a rate of 600,000 per year. However, the activity of the 1980s set the stage for a new entrepreneurial marketplace in the 1990s.

The 1990s are being characterized as one of business purchases and expansions rather than fresh start-ups. Numerous start-up companies from the 80s are available to purchase in the 90s. As an example, Steve McDonnell purchased Jugtown Mountain Smokehouse, a tiny specialty meats producer located in Flemington, New Jersey. The company had sales of approximately $300,000 in 1987. McDonnell invested in new processing equipment and a computer system. Introducing contemporary business methods in accounting, budgeting, and marketing paid off for McDonnell's company. In 1990, sales rose to $1.4 million. As for the future, McDonnell plans to merge or acquire a major competitor that would result in a tripling of his company's size.

As these new "acquisition entrepreneurs" avoid the agonies of start-up activities, they develop a new model of aggressive entrepreneurial growth: purchase/invest/grow. If the formula works, the 90s will show a constant increase in the purchase of existing firms.

SOURCE: John Case, "Buy Now—Avoid the Rush," *Inc.*, February 1991, 36–45.

LBO Tax Considerations

The ideas presented on the LBO provide a basic understanding for entrepreneurs. As with many situations for businesses being purchased, the tax and legal implications of a leveraged buyout are too complex to be analyzed completely in this section. Thus, the advice of an attorney and an accountant skilled in buyout transactions is always needed.

As an example of the tax complexities, consider how the Revenue Reconciliation Act of 1993 changed a number of business items:

- The top corporate tax rates are now lower than top individual tax rates.
- Capital gains were treated the same as ordinary income and taxed at the ordinary income tax rate until 1990. Then it became 28 percent for capital gains and as high as 39.6 percent for ordinary income.

These highlights of the new tax changes affect buyout situations in different ways. First, proprietorships, partnerships, and S corporations may become more popular due to higher individual tax rates. Second, conflicts over allocation of the purchase price over the assets previously had occurred. The buyer wanted it reflected in tax-deductible assets, and the seller sought to have it in the purchase price in order to take advantage of lower capital gains treatment. Now capital gains are given no special treatment, thus minimizing the conflict. Finally, corporations now must claim the capital gains they receive from a sale of a business and pay 34 percent on the realized gain. This may have an effect on the price of privately held businesses.

Many of the tax reform provisions took effect in different years from 1987 to 1993, depending on a variety of clauses in the tax codes. Therefore, it is imperative that a tax accountant work closely with an entrepreneur on the various tax implications. In most transactions, the tax considerations will have a significant impact on the structure of the buyout or on the final negotiations. Either way, an entrepreneur needs to have the most current and favorable tax information.

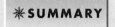

Many entrepreneurs start by purchasing a venture already in existence. Major steps were described that are critical to the purchase of any business. In addition, ten key questions were presented and described for evaluating a particular business that has been selected for purchase.

Entrepreneurs need to understand how to valuate a business for either purchase or sale. Many would like to know the value of their businesses. Sometimes this is strictly for informational purposes, and at other times it is for selling the operation. In either case, a number of ways of valuing an enterprise exist.

The first step is to analyze the business's overall operations, with a view to acquiring a comprehensive understanding of the firm's strong and weak points. Table 18.3 provides a checklist for this purpose. The second step is to establish a value for the firm. Table 18.4 sets forth ten methods for the valuation of a venture. Three of the most commonly used are (1) adjusted tangible assets, (2) price/earnings (multiple of earnings), and (3) discounted future earnings.

The adjusted tangible book value method computes the value of the business by revaluing the assets and then subtracting the liabilities. This is a fairly simple, straightforward process.

The price/earnings ratio method divides the market price of the common stock by the earnings per share and then multiplies by the number of shares issued. For example, a company with a price/earnings multiple of 10 and 100,000 shares of stock would be valued at $1 million.

The discounted earnings method takes the estimated cash flow for a predetermined number of years and discounts these sums back to the present using an appropriate discount rate. This is one of the most popular methods of valuing a business. Other factors to consider for valuing a business include start-up costs, accuracy of projections, and the control factor.

Finally, the concept of a leveraged buyout (LBO) was discussed as an alternative for entrepreneurs who lack the cash needed to purchase a business. Asset-based buyouts were described in comparison to cash-flow buyouts. A final section mentioned the importance of tax implications and the need to use a skilled tax accountant in buyout situations.

Key Terms and Concepts

Adjusted tangible book value	Emotional bias
Business assets	Entrepreneurial leveraged buyout (E-LBO)
Business environment	Leveraged buyout (LBO)
Business valuation	Price/earnings ratio
Cash-flow leveraged buyout (LBO)	Profit, sales, and operating ratios
Discounted earnings method	

Review and Discussion Questions

1. What are the four basic steps to follow when buying a business?
2. Identify five (out of ten) key questions to ask when buying an ongoing venture.
3. Identify and discuss the three underlying issues in the evaluation of a business.
4. Taxes will affect the purchase or sale of an enterprise. What does this statement mean? Include a discussion of Table 18.2 in your answer.
5. To analyze a business, what types of questions or concerns should the entrepreneur address in the following areas: history of the business, market and competition, sales and distribution, and manufacturing?
6. To analyze a business, what types of questions or concerns should the entrepreneur address in the following areas: employees, physical facilities, ownership, and trade and professional checks?
7. To analyze a business, what types of questions or concerns should the entrepreneur address in the following areas: financial, management?
8. One of the most popular methods of business valuation is the adjusted tangible book value. Describe how this method works.
9. Explain how the price/earnings ratio method of valuation works. Give an example.
10. What are the steps involved in using the discounted earnings method? Give an example.
11. How do the following methods of valuing a venture work: fixed price, multiple of earnings, return on investment, replacement value, liquidation value, excess earnings, and market value? In each case, give an example.
12. Explain why the following are important factors to consider when valuing a business: start-up costs, accuracy of projections, degree of control.

Experiential Exercise   *What Would You Recommend?*

Jane Winfield would like to buy Ted Garner's company. She has conducted a detailed financial analysis of Ted's firm and has determined the following:

1. Book value of the inventory: $250,000
2. Discount rate on future earnings: 24 percent
3. Book value of the plant and equipment: $150,000
4. Fair market value of the inventory: $400,000
5. Fair market value of other intangibles: $60,000
6. Number of shares of common stock: 100,000
7. Fair market value of the plant and equipment: $400,000
8. Price/earnings multiple: 9
9. Book market value of other intangibles: $30,000
10. Estimated earnings over the next five years:

Year 1	$200,000
Year 2	300,000
Year 3	400,000
Year 4	500,000
Year 5	600,000

Based on this information, how much should Jane valuate the business according to each of the following methods: adjusted tangible assets, price/earnings, and discounted future earnings? Based on your findings, recommend the valuation method she should use. Finally, given all of your calculations, estimate what the final price will be. Give reasons for this estimate. Enter your answers here.

a) Adjusted tangible assets valuation:_____

b) Price/earnings valuation:_____

c) Discounted future earnings valuation:_____

d) Final sales price:_____

VIDEO CASE **18.1**

Pier 1 Imports: Managing Worldwide Growth

More than thirty years after its Texas founders invited shoppers on an "affordable" adventure, Pier 1 Imports is enjoying the kind of growth and profitability other retailers can only dream about. "At Pier 1, we're fond of saying that our competitive advantage is there are no Pier 2s," says Katie McAbee, vice president of communication. "We like to think of it in terms of we have product, we have presentations, and we have people. Our product is fabulous merchandise that you can't find anywhere else. Our presentation is a shopping experience that's discovery-oriented. And we go out of our way to be friendly, helpful and offer our customers the best."

Not so long ago, Pier 1 was best known for groovy bean bag chairs, incense, batik-print linens, and wicker *everything*. But like the baby boomers who first discovered Pier 1, the retail chain has grown up and become more sophisticated. With nearly 650 retail stores in the United States, Puerto Rico, Canada, and Mexico, Pier 1 is now one of the leading retail specialty stores in North America. In 1995, Pier 1 sold $712 million in decorative home furnishings, dinnerware, casual clothing, and unique gift items imported from more than 42 countries around the world—earning the company a record net income. "Our attitude is one of the primary things that have guided us on a course of productivity and helped us be an outstanding retailer," reveals Steve Woodward, vice president of merchandise furniture. "This attitude permeates the company from the chairman to the president, all the way down through the associates on the sales floor. We're willing to take risks, we try things that other retailers might shy away from, but that's just a culturally accepted part of being with Pier 1."

Pier 1's can-do attitude has inspired the company to expand beyond domestic borders. "We realized that our product mix was a strong enough mix to sell worldwide," says Jim Prucha, vice president of merchandise shelf goods. "We've had people all over the globe approaching us and wanting to partner with us because our concept is so unique," adds McAbee. In the early 1990's, Pier 1 invested in an extensive strategic planning process for worldwide growth. "Our strategy for profitable worldwide growth truly grew out of a vision," reveals McAbee. "It came out of our chairman and CEO, Clark Johnson, and our president, Marvin Girouard. They sincerely believe that as we begin to mature as a company in this country, we need to seek outside our own geographic boundaries and begin to look for opportunities for Pier 1 to be known beyond the United States and Canada." Recently, Pier 1 has formed lucrative partnerships with Sears de Mexico and Sears de Puerto Rico. They have also teamed with an English company called The Pier in the United Kingdom and a Japanese partner to open Pier 1 stores in Japan.

In a corporate document entitled *A Strategy for Worldwide Growth,* Pier 1 clearly defines the major goals it plans to achieve by the year 2000. These goals include expanding the company's North American retail base to 900 stores doing $1.25 billion in sales and producing $475 million in net income by January 1, 2000. The company also plans to continue introducing Pier 1 stores internationally with direct investments in selected countries; expand its market presence in Southeast Asia, Mexico, and Central and South America through master franchise agreements and joint ventures; enter new specialty markets in North America; and establish a major procurement, logistics, and distribution presence in Singapore to reinforce the company's international sourcing capacity. "We are lucky to have a very strong, very united team of senior management who were all involved not only in the development of our strategy, but also how it would take shape, and what it would take to get us there," says McAbee.

"We have been very, very good at importing for years and years," says Prucha. "Now we have to become equally proficient at exporting. Exporting is a little different learning curve for us. But quite frankly, the only other obstacle we've encountered in international is we just can't keep up with the demand. We have people sending in letters and calling every day wanting to know if Pier 1's in their particular country. And we feel this is a very logical worldwide concept that can grow to who knows how large in the future."

 **CASE** **18.2**

Which Will It Be?

Georgia Isaacson and her son Rubin have been thinking about buying a business. After talking to seven entrepreneurs, all of whom have expressed an interest in selling their operations, the Isaacsons have decided to make an offer for a retail clothing store. The store is very well located, and its earnings over the past five years have been excellent. The current owner has told the Isaacsons he will sell for $500,000. The owner arrived at this value by projecting the earnings of the operation for the next seven years and then using a discount factor of 15 percent.

The Isaacsons are not sure the retail store is worth $500,000, but they do understand the method the owner used for arriving at this figure. Georgia feels that since the owner has been in business for only seven years, it is unrealistic to discount seven years of future earnings. A five-year estimate would be more realistic, in her opinion. Rubin feels that the discount factor is too low. He believes that 20–22 percent would be more realistic.

In addition to these concerns, the Isaacsons feel they would like to make an evaluation of the business using other methods. In particular, they would like to see what the value of the company would be when the adjusted tangible book value method is employed. They also would like to look at the replacement value and liquidation value methods.

"We know what the owner feels his business is worth," Georgia noted to her son. "However, we have to decide for ourselves what we think the operation is worth. From here on we can negotiate a final price. For the moment, I think we have to look at this valuation process from a number of different angles."

Questions

1. If the owner reduces the earnings estimates from seven to five years, what effect will this have on the final valuation? If the individual increases the discount factor from 15 percent to 20–22 percent, what effect will this have on the final valuation?
2. How do the replacement value and liquidation value methods work? Why would the Isaacsons want to examine these methods?
3. If the Isaacsons conclude that the business is worth $410,000, what will be the final selling price, assuming a sale is made? Defend your answer.

Chapter 19

MANAGEMENT SUCCESSION AND CONTINUITY: A FAMILY BUSINESS PERSPECTIVE

CHAPTER OBJECTIVES

1. To describe the importance of family businesses and their unique problems

2. To examine the key factors in management succession

3. To identify and describe some of the most important sources of succession

4. To discuss the potential impact of recent legislation on family business succession

5. To relate the ways to develop a succession strategy

6. To explain the steps involved in carrying out a succession plan

7. To present a "harvest strategy" for selling out as a final alternative

Contrary to popular opinion, America's family-owned and privately held corporations are not being destroyed by confiscatory taxation, ruthless competitors, unproductive labor, technological change, or insidious regulation. Family businesses fail because they allow themselves to be destroyed, slowly but surely, by the inaction of their owner/managers. The businesses fail because, more often than not, these people never make the decisions needed to ensure the vitality of their companies in an ever-changing, ever more complex world. Family business owners typically fail to recognize the needs of the future in managing their businesses.

Leon A. Danco,
Center for Family Business, Cleveland, Ohio

FAMILY-OWNED BUSINESS

Family businesses account for the largest percentage of our nation's businesses, according to expert estimates at the federal level. These family businesses also account for nearly 50 percent of the gross domestic product (GDP) and employ about half of the private sector workforce.[1] Over the past ten years, more than 600,000 new business start-ups occurred yearly in this country.[2] Many of these were family firms that will help increase GDP and employment. However, small business survival is becoming more difficult each year.

Family-owned companies can succeed and grow in spite of complex challenges. A variety of reasons help account for this. One is that these businesses have not been encumbered by demanding stockholders who want to dictate operating strategy. A second is that the family members are willing to sacrifice short-term profits for long-term gains. Research shows that family members are more productive than other employees.[3] A third is the companies' flexibility, a trait that has allowed family firms to respond to challenges and opportunities in an unrestricted manner. In addition, owners of family firms can convey an

---

[1] John L. Ward, "What Is a Family Business and How Can We Help?" *Small Business Forum* (winter 1991): 63–71; see also Melissa Carey Shanker and Joseph H. Astrachan, "Myths and Realities: Family Businesses' Contribution to the U.S. Economy," *Family Business Review* (summer 1996): 107–24.

[2] *The State of Small Business: A Report to the President* (Washington, DC: Government Printing Office, 1995), 38–40.

[3] Bruce A. Kirchhoff and Judith J. Kirchhoff, "Family Contributions to Productivity and Profitability in Small Businesses," *Journal of Small Business Management* (October 1987): 25–31.

image of stability—that the company is in business for the long haul and will provide continuity for customers and employees alike.[4]

Family values and influences can help the operation of a business. According to researcher Peter Davis, three advantages may be forthcoming after start-up:[5]

1. *Preserving the humanity of the workplace.* A family business can easily demonstrate higher levels of concern and caring for individuals than are found in the typical corporation.

2. *Focusing on the long run.* A family business can take the long-run view more easily than corporate managers who are judged on year-to-year results.

3. *Emphasizing quality.* Family businesses have long maintained a tradition of providing quality and value to the consumer.

Psychologist Manfred Kets de Vries examined the advantages and disadvantages associated with family businesses.[6] Table 19.1 provides an overview of his particular items. Some of the key advantages already have been touched on (greater flexibility of action, long-term orientation, stability, resilience, and less bureaucracy). The disadvantages include family disputes, paternalistic (or maternalistic) rule, confusing organization (no clear division of tasks), nepotism (promoting inept family members), and succession dramas. It is the succession challenge that Chapter 19 focuses on. We begin by examining the issues involved with managerial succession.

THE MANAGEMENT SUCCESSION ISSUE

Research shows that many family firms go out of existence after ten years; only three out of ten survive into a second generation. More significant, only 16 percent of all family enterprises make it to a third generation. One important study demonstrated these facts by examining the life expectancy of 200 successful manufacturing firms.[7] The average life expectancy for a family business is 24 years, which is also the average tenure for the founders of a business.[8]

One of the major problems most family businesses have is the lack of preparation for passing managerial control to the next generation. The cruel fact is that one generation succeeds the other with biological inevitability, yet most family businesses never formulate succession plans.

Management succession, which involves the transition of managerial decision making in a firm, is one of the greatest challenges confronting owners and entrepreneurs in family businesses. At first glance, succession would not seem to be a major problem. All an owner has to do is designate which heir will inherit the operation or, better yet, train one (or more) of them to take over the business during the founder's lifetime. Unfortunately, this is easier

[4] Leslie Brokaw, "Why Family Businesses Are Best," *Inc.,* March 1992, 20–22.

[5] Peter Davis, "Realizing the Potential of the Family Business," *Organizational Dynamics* (summer 1983): 53–54.

[6] Manfred F. R. Kets de Vries, "The Dynamics of Family-Controlled Firms: The Good News and the Bad News," *Organizational Dynamics* (winter 1993): 59–71.

[7] John L. Ward, *Keeping the Family Business Healthy* (San Francisco: Jossey-Bass, 1987), 1–2.

[8] Richard Beckhard and W. Gibb Dyer Jr., "Managing Continuity in the Family-Owned Business," *Organizational Dynamics* (summer 1983): 7–8.

TABLE 19.1   **ADVANTAGES AND DISADVANTAGES OF FAMILY-CONTROLLED FIRMS**

Advantages	Disadvantages
Long-term orientation	Less access to capital markets may curtail growth
Greater independence of action	Confusing organization
• Less (or no) pressure from stock market	• Messy structure
• Less (or no) takeover risk	• No clear division of tasks
Family culture as a source of pride	Nepotism
• Stability	• Tolerance of inept family members as managers
• Strong identification/commitment/ motivation	• Inequitable reward systems
• Continuity in leadership	• Greater difficulties in attracting professional management
Greater resilience in hard times	Spoiled-kid syndrome
• Willing to plow back profits	Internecine strife
Less bureaucratic and impersonal	• Family disputes overflow into business
• Greater flexibility	Paternalistic/autocratic rule
• Quicker decision making	• Resistance to change
	• Secrecy
Financial benefits	• Attraction of dependent personalities
• Possibility of great success	Financial strain
Knowing the business	• Family members milking the business
• Early training for family members	• Disequilibrium between contribution and compensation
	Succession dramas

SOURCE: Manfred F. R. Kets de Vries, "The Dynamics of Family-Controlled Firms: The Good News and the Bad News," *Organizational Dynamics* (winter 1993): 61.

said than done. A number of problems exist. One of the major ones is the owner. To a large degree, the owner *is* the business. The individual's personality and talents make the operation what it is. If this person were to be removed from the picture, the company might be unable to continue. Additionally, this individual may not want to be removed. So if the owner-manager begins to have health problems or is unable to manage effectively, he or she may still hang on. The owner often views any family attempt to get him or her to step aside as greedy efforts to plunder the operation for personal gain. What's more, the owner and family members may feel anxiety over death, since raising the topic of death conjures up a negative image in everyone's mind.

Other barriers to succession include sibling rivalry, family members' fear of losing status, or a complete aversion to death for fear of loss or abandonment.[9] Table 19.2 provides a list of barriers to succession attributed to the owner and to the family.

The basic rule for family-owned businesses is this: The owner should develop a succession plan. Since many people want to keep the business in the family, a decision has to be made regarding an heir. This is often psychologically difficult. Choosing an heir can be like buying a cemetery plot. It is an admission of one's mortality. Owners who refuse to face the succession issue, however, place an unnecessary burden on those whom they leave

[9] Kets de Vries, "The Dynamics of Family-Controlled Firms."

TABLE 19.2	BARRIERS TO SUCCESSION PLANNING IN FAMILY FIRMS

Founder/Owner	Family
Death anxiety	Death as taboo
Company as symbol	• Discussion is a hostile act
• Loss of identity	• Fear of loss/abandonment
• Concern about legacy	Fear of sibling rivalry
Dilemma of choice	Change of spouse's position
• Fiction of equality	
Generational envy	
• Loss of power	

SOURCE: Manfred F. R. Kets de Vries, "The Dynamics of Family-Controlled Firms: The Good News and the Bad News," *Organizational Dynamics* (winter 1993): 68.

behind. Family successor problems are not insurmountable. For our consideration of these problems, the best place to begin is with an identification of the key factors in succession.

KEY FACTORS IN SUCCESSION

It has been said that the concept of "smooth succession" in a family firm is a contradiction of terms. This contradiction is because succession is a highly charged emotional issue that requires not only structural changes but cultural changes as well.[10] Family succession includes the transfer of ethics, values, and traditions along with the actual business itself. The "family business" and the "business family" are two distinct components that must be dealt with and disentangled if progress toward succession is to be made.[11]

A number of considerations affect the succession issue.[12] One way to examine them is in terms of pressures and interests inside the firm and outside the firm. Another way is to examine forcing events. A third way is to examine the sources of succession. Finally we will discuss the legal restrictions that may affect succession decisions.

Pressures and Interests inside the Firm

Two types of succession pressures originate within the family firm (see Figure 19.1). One comes from the family members. The other comes from nonfamily employees.[13]

[10] Davis, "Realizing the Potential," 47.

[11] Phyllis G. Holland and William R. Boulton, "Balancing the 'Family' and the 'Business' in the Family Business," *Business Horizons* (March/April 1984): 19.

[12] See Donald F. Kuratko, "Understanding the Succession Challenge in Family Business," *Entrepreneurship, Innovation, and Change* (September 1995): 185–91.

[13] See Neil C. Churchill and Kenneth J. Hatten, "Non-Market-Based Transfers of Wealth and Power: A Research Framework for Family Business," *American Journal of Small Business* (fall 1987): 53–66.

FIGURE 19.1 **PRESSURES AND INTERESTS IN A FAMILY BUSINESS**

	Inside the Family	Outside the Family
Inside the Business	**The Family Managers** Hanging onto or Getting Hold of Company Control Selection of Family Members as Managers Continuity of Family Investment and Involvement Building a Dynasty Rivalry	**The Employees** Rewards for Loyalty Sharing of Equity, Growth, and Success Professionalism Bridging Family Transitions Stake in the Company
Outside the Business	**The Relatives** Income and Inheritance Family Conflicts and Alliances Degree of Involvement in the Business	**The Outsiders** Competition Market, Product, Supply, and Technology Influence Tax Laws Regulatory Agencies

SOURCE: Adapted and reprinted by permission of the *Harvard Business Review.* An exhibit from "Transferring Power in the Family Business," by Louis B. Barnes and Simon A. Hershon, July/August 1976, 106. Copyright © 1976 by the President and Fellows of Harvard College; all rights reserved.

FAMILY MEMBERS When members of the family are also employees, a number of succession-type problems can arise. One is that the family members may want to keep the business in existence so that they and their families will be able to manage it. Sometimes this results in the members wanting to get, or increase, control over operations. Another common development is pressure on the owner-manager to designate an heir. A third possible development is rivalry among the various branches of the family. For example, each of the owner's children may feel that the owner should put him or her (or one of his or her children) in charge of the operation. Given that only one of the family branches can win this fight, the rivalry can lead to the sale or bankruptcy of the business.

NONFAMILY EMPLOYEES   Nonfamily employees sometimes bring pressure on the owner-manager in an effort to protect their personal interests. For example, long-term employees often think the owner should give them an opportunity to buy a stake in the company, or they believe they should be given a percentage of the business in the owner's will. Such hopes and expectations are often conveyed to the owner and can result in pressure for some form of succession plan. Moreover, to the extent the nonfamily employees are critical to the enterprise's success, these demands cannot be ignored. The owner must reach some accommodation with these people if the business is to survive.

Pressures and Interests outside the Firm

Outside the firm, both family members and nonfamily elements exert pressure on and hold interest in the firm's succession.

FAMILY MEMBERS   Even when family members do not play an active role in the business, they can apply pressure. Quite often these individuals are interested in ensuring that they inherit part of the operation, and they will put pressure on the owner-manager toward achieving that end. In some cases they pressure for getting involved in the business. Some family members will pressure the owner-manager to hire them. Quite often these appeals are resisted on the grounds of the firm not needing additional personnel or needing someone with specific expertise (sales ability or technical skills), and thus the owner sidesteps the request.

NONFAMILY ELEMENTS   Another major source of pressure comes from external environmental factors. One of these is competitors who continually change strategy and force the owner-manager to adjust to new market considerations. Other factors include customers, technology, and new-product development. These forces continually change, and the entrepreneur must respond to them. Tax laws, regulatory agencies, and trends in management practices constitute still other elements with which the owner-manager must contend.[14]

Depending on the situation, any of these sources of pressure can prove troublesome.

Forcing Events

Forcing events are those happenings that cause the replacement of the owner-manager. These events require the entrepreneur to step aside and let someone else direct the operation. The following are typical examples:

[14] See Donald F. Kuratko, Helga B. Foss, and Lucinda L. VanAlst, "IRS Estate Freeze Rules: Implications for Family Business Succession Planning," *Family Business Review* (spring 1994): 61–72; and Joseph H. Astrachan and Roger Tutterow, "The Effect of Estate Taxes on Family Business: Survey Results," *Family Business Review* (fall 1996): 303–14.

ENTREPRENEURIAL
EDGE

Thinking Power

It's here. It's now. It's artificial intelligence. Everyone's been talking about it for years, wondering how it actually worked, what it would be capable of, and how expensive it would be; the list goes on and on. But no more wondering. It's here in law enforcement; it's here in the hospitals. And now it's in businesses of all shapes and sizes, including family-owned businesses.

Artificial intelligence, referred to as *neural networks* or *neural nets,* represents a whole new era of computer applications. They are designed to approach and solve problems the same way the human brain does: by trying to recognize the patterns that underlie a complex set of data. Neural nets can be "trained" just like people can be trained. Initially, the net begins with wild guesses. As time goes by, the net learns to refine its guesswork until it can pick out even the most subtle patterns. The true power that lies within the neural network is its ability to analyze nearly endless combinations of variables

more quickly and accurately than traditional statistical models.

Artificial intelligence applications are most commonly associated with law enforcement and hospitals. Some law enforcement agencies use neural nets to pinpoint possible drug dealers by identifying travel patterns. Some hospitals use neural nets to determine a patient's chance of contracting cancer or other diseases. Soon, neural nets also will be widely associated with business applications of all types. They are already making their way into marketing and other business arenas.

According to Bob Barrie of Global Management Technologies, a software-development company in Atlanta, neural nets work especially well when they are used to analyze down-to-the-minute trends. Although Barrie's clients include industry giants such as Walt Disney, an increasing number of considerably smaller businesses are becoming armed with neural

- Death, resulting in the heirs immediately having to find a successor to run the operation
- Illness or some other form of nonterminal physical incapacitation
- Mental or psychological breakdown, resulting in the individual having to withdraw from the business
- Abrupt departure, such as when an entrepreneur decides, with no advance warning, to retire immediately
- Legal problems, such as incarceration for violation of the law (If this period of confinement is for more than a few weeks, succession usually becomes necessary if in name only.)

nets to battle the abundance of available data and find victory in identifying precise customer traits and buying habits.

One such company is Plow & Hearth, a $30 million catalog company that sells yard and garden wares and is based in Madison, Virginia. John Popowski, the marketing manager until 1995, and Pete Rice, the circulation manager, decided after endless efforts that traditional marketing strategies weren't going to work for them. They needed a new approach for identifying valuable customers. They needed something cutting edge. Advanced Software Applications (ASA) had the solution. ModelMAX is a polished, ready-to-use marketing tool with a Windows interface. The application is simple. Users don't have to know how neural nets work; they only need to know how their company operates and to have access to its information on purchasing behavior. This is how it works. Each time Plow & Hearth is preparing to do a catalog mailing, the information about customers and their buying habits is gathered from previous mailings and purchases. All the key variables, such as time of year the customer made the first purchase, which products the customer buys most often, and where the customer lives, are entered into the ModelMAX program. ModelMAX then sorts through the information to determine which combinations of customer characteristics are most important in predicting customer value. For example, the company has learned that customers whose first purchase is clothing tend to stay customers. This finding was quite surprising since Plow & Hearth sells clothing only as a peripheral product.

Rice admits that learning how to organize and sort through the company's information so that the program would run efficiently was the hardest part. It took nearly a year before the program was used at its greatest capacity. Despite the extra effort required to learn the new application, Rice says, the information generated from ModelMAX has been extremely helpful in targeting which customers to pursue aggressively. Since the application inception three years ago, Plow & Hearth's per-catalog sales have gone up 32 percent, and its hit rates have risen by 19 percent.

SOURCE: Sarah Schafer, "Software That Thinks," *Inc. Technology,* 19 November 1996, 109–10.

- Severe business decline, resulting in the owner-manager deciding to leave the helm
- Financial difficulties, resulting in lenders demanding the removal of the owner-manager before lending the necessary funds to the enterprise

These types of events are often unforeseen, and the family seldom has a contingency plan for dealing with them. As a result, when they occur they often create a major problem for the business.

These considerations influence the environment within which the successor will operate. Unless that individual and the environment fit well, the successor will be less than maximally effective.

TABLE 19.3 COMPARISION OF ENTRY STRATEGIES FOR SUCCESSION IN FAMILY BUSINESS

	Advantages	Disadvantages
Early Entry Strategy	Intimate familiarity with the nature of the business and employees is acquired. Skills specifically required by the business are developed. Exposure to others in the business facilitates acceptance and the achievement of credibility. Strong relationships with constituents are readily established.	Conflict results when the owner has difficulty with teaching or relinquishing control to the successor. Normal mistakes tend to be viewed as incompetence in the successor. Knowledge of the environment is limited, and risks of inbreeding are incurred.
Delayed Entry Strategy	The successor's skills are judged with greater objectivity. The development of self-confidence and growth independent of familial influence are achieved. Outside success establishes credibility and serves as a basis for accepting the successor as a competent executive. Perspective of the business environment is broadened.	Specific expertise and understanding of the organization's key success factors and culture may be lacking. Set patterns of outside activity may conflict with those prevailing in the family firm. Resentment may result when successors are advanced ahead of long-term employees.

SOURCE: Jeffrey A. Barach, Joseph Ganitsky, James A. Carson, Benjamin A. Doochin, "Entry of the Next Generation: Strategic Challenge for Family Firms," *Journal of Small Business Management* (April 1988): 53.

Sources of Succession

An **entrepreneurial successor** is someone who is high in ingenuity, creativity, and drive. This person often provides the critical ideas for new-product development and future ventures. The **managerial successor** is someone who is interested in efficiency, internal control, and the effective use of resources. This individual often provides the stability and day-to-day direction needed to keep the enterprise going.

When looking for an inside successor, the entrepreneur usually focuses on a son or daughter or nephew or niece with the intent of gradually giving the person operational responsibilities followed by strategic power and ownership. An important factor in the venture's success is whether the founder and the heir can get along. The entrepreneur must be able to turn from being a leader to being a coach, from being a doer to being an adviser. The heir must respect the founder's attachment to the venture and be sensitive to this person's possessive feelings. At the same time the heir must be able to use his or her entrepreneurial flair to initiate necessary changes.[15]

When looking ahead toward choosing a successor from inside the organization, the founder often trains a team of executive managers consisting of both family and nonfamily members. This enables the individual to build an experienced management team capable

[15] For an interesting perspective, see Sue Birley, "Succession in the Family Firm: The Inheritor's View," *Journal of Small Business Management* (July 1986): 36–43; and T. Roger Peay and W. Gibb Dyer, "Power Orientations of Entrepreneurs and Succession Planning," *Journal of Small Business Management* (January 1989): 47–52.

of producing a successor. The founder assumes that, in time, a natural leader will emerge from the group.[16]

Two key strategies center around the entry of the inside younger generation and when the "power" actually changes hands. Table 19.3 illustrates the advantages and disadvantages of the **early entry strategy** versus the **delayed entry strategy.** The main question is the ability of the successor to gain credibility with the firm's employees. The actual transfer of power is a critical issue in the implementation of any succession plan.[17]

If the founder looks for a family member outside the firm, he or she usually prefers to have the heir first work for someone else. The hope is that the individual will make his or her initial mistakes early on, before assuming the family business reins.

Sometimes the founder will look for a nonfamily outsider to be the successor, perhaps only temporarily. The entrepreneur may not see an immediate successor inside the firm and may decide to hire a professional manager, at least on an interim basis, while waiting for an heir to mature and take over.

Another form of nonfamily outsider is the specialist who is experienced in getting ventures out of financial difficulty. The founder then usually gives the specialist total control, and this person later hands the rejuvenated venture to another leader.

Still another nonfamily approach is for the founder to find a person with the right talents and to bring this individual into the venture as an assistant, with the understanding that he or she will eventually become president and owner of the venture. No heirs may exist, or perhaps no eligible family member is interested.

Legal Restrictions

The first source for succession often is family and in-house personnel prospects. However, such traditions of succession practices in family businesses have been challenged in the Oakland Scavenger Company case.

This suit was brought in 1984 by a group of black and Hispanic workers in the California-based **Oakland Scavenger Company** (a garbage collection firm) who complained of employment discrimination because of their race. The U.S. District Court of Northern California dismissed the suit on the basis that it had no relation to antidiscrimination laws. However, the U.S. Court of Appeals for the Ninth Circuit reviewed the decision and held that "nepotistic concerns cannot supersede the nation's paramount goal of equal economic opportunity for all."[18]

According to Oakland Scavenger's legal brief, the question focused on the Fifth Amendment versus Title VII of the 1964 Civil Rights Act: If discrimination overrides the protection of life, liberty, and property from unreasonable interference from the state, then the rights of parents leaving their property and business to anyone can be abolished. This decision can have a major effect on the management succession plans of family businesses.

The case was appealed to the Supreme Court. However, before the Court could make a ruling, the Oakland Scavenger Company was purchased by the Waste Management Corporation, and an out-of-court settlement was reached. The company agreed to an $8 million settlement. The settlement allocated sums of at least $50,000 to 16 black and Hispanic

[16] See Kevin C. Seymour, "Intergenerational Relationships in the Family Firm: The Effect on Leadership Succession," *Family Business Review* (fall 1993): 263–82.

[17] Jeffrey A. Barach, Joseph Ganitsky, James A. Carson, Benjamin A. Doochin, "Entry of the Next Generation: Strategic Challenge for Family Firms," *Journal of Small Business Management* (April 1988): 49–56.

[18] "Nepotism on Trial," *Inc.,* July 1984, 29.

plaintiffs, depending on their length of service, and also provided for payments to a class of more than 400 black and Hispanic workers Oakland Scavenger employed after January 10, 1972.[19]

As K. Peter Stalland, legal representative for the National Family Business Council, has stated, "The effect this case can have on small business is tremendous. It means, conceivably, that almost any small business can be sued by an employee of a different ethnic origin than the owner, based upon not being accorded the same treatment as a son or daughter. The precedent is dangerous."[20]

The Oakland Scavenger case has started a movement that is sure to result in more guidelines and limitations for family employment, and family businesses will have to be aware of this challenge when preparing succession plans. (See the Contemporary Entrepreneurship box on legal concerns over **nepotism.**)

DEVELOPING A SUCCESSION STRATEGY

Developing a succession strategy involves several important steps: (1) understanding the contextual aspects, (2) identifying successor qualities, (3) understanding influencing forces, and (4) carrying out the succession plan.[21]

Understanding the Contextual Aspects

The five key aspects that must be considered for an effective succession follow.

TIME   The earlier the entrepreneur begins to plan for a successor, the better the chances of finding the right person. The biggest problem the owner faces is the prospect of events that force immediate action and result in inadequate time to find the best replacement.

TYPE OF VENTURE   Some entrepreneurs are easy to replace; some cannot be replaced. To a large degree, this is determined by the type of venture. An entrepreneur who is the idea person in a high-tech operation is going to be difficult to replace. The same is true for an entrepreneur whose personal business contacts throughout the industry are the key factors for the venture's success. On the other hand, a person running an operation that requires a minimum of knowledge or expertise usually can be replaced without much trouble.

CAPABILITIES OF MANAGERS   The skills, desires, and abilities of the replacement will dictate the future potential and direction of the enterprise. As the industry matures, the demands made on the entrepreneur also may change. Industries where high tech is the name of the game often go through a change in which marketing becomes increasingly important. A technologically skilled entrepreneur with an understanding of marketing, or with the ability to develop an orientation in this direction, will be more valuable to the enterprise than will a technologically skilled entrepreneur with no marketing interest or background.

---

[19] David Graulich, "You Can't Always Pay What You Want," *Family Business,* February 1990, 16–19.

[20] "Feuding Families," *Inc.,* January 1985, 38.

[21] Donald F. Kuratko and Richard M. Hodgetts, "Succession Strategies for Family Businesses," *Management Advisor* (spring 1989): 22–30.

CONTEMPORARY ENTREPRENEURSHIP

Legal Concerns over Nepotism

In certain cases, entrepreneurs may be in violation of the law if they employ too many family members. The law considers nepotism a neutral policy—that is, it's not discriminatory by itself. Such a policy is lawful unless it has an "adverse impact" on women or minority groups (as in the Oakland Scavenger Company case). In another case, the Supreme Court increased the burden of proving adverse impact to plaintiffs and, at the same time, made it easier for employers to defend such lawsuits. It is expected, however, that Congress will eventually enact a civil rights bill, with or without the president's signature, that will require employers to provide a strong business justification for a policy that results in racial or gender imbalance.

Nepotism is more vulnerable to attack for "disparate impact" by racial minorities than by women. As the U.S. Court of Appeals noted in *Platner* v. *Cash & Thomas*: "It is difficult to see how nepotism could mask systematic gender discrimination. While a person's relatives will usually be of the same race, men and women will presumably be equally represented both within and without the family."

The smallest companies—those with 15 or fewer employees—are specifically excluded from the provisions of the Civil Rights Law of 1964 dealing with employment discrimination. But many states have similar statutes with broader coverage. The following guidelines may help growing ventures avoid any charge of employment discrimination.

- Find out as much as you can about the racial and gender composition of the labor pool in your area, and try to bring your own shop in line with it.
- The argument that most hiring in your business is through industry connections or word of mouth is a weak defense, since these traditional sources often perpetuate an in-group.
- Avoid stereotyping in job assignments or communications. Jokes or epithets aimed at women or minority-group members will be taken in court as evidence of a "hostile environment" for these groups.
- When hiring or promoting a family member, explain the decision in job-related terms. If a disappointed applicant asks why he or she was passed over, emphasize the qualifications for the job, commitment to the long-term success of the company, and firsthand knowledge or skills—for whoever was selected.
- Never make or explain a hiring decision or promotion by reasoning that "our customers won't like it if we send them a black salesman or a woman." Customer preference is not a defense in a lawsuit based on a discrimination claim.

SOURCE: Howard Muson, "Dangerous Liaisons," *Family Business,* January/February 1991, 22–27.

ENTREPRENEUR'S VISION   Most entrepreneurs have expectations, hopes, and desires for their organization. A successor, it is hoped, will share this vision, except, of course, in cases where the entrepreneur's plans have gotten the organization in trouble and a new vision is needed. An example is Apple Computer, when one of the founders, Steven Jobs, was replaced by John Sculley because the board of directors felt that a more managerial, day-to-day entrepreneur was needed to replace the highly conceptual, analytical Jobs.

ENVIRONMENTAL FACTORS   Sometimes a successor is needed because the business environment changes and a parallel change is needed at the top. The Sculley/Jobs example is one case in point. Another is Edwin Land of Polaroid. Although his technological creativity had made the venture successful, Land eventually had to step aside for someone with more marketing skills. In some cases owners have had to allow financial types to assume control of the venture because internal efficiency was more critical to short-run survival than was market effectiveness.

Identifying Successor Qualities

Successors should possess many qualities or characteristics. Depending on the situation, some will be more important than others. In most cases, however, all will have some degree of importance. Some of the most common of these successor qualities are sufficient knowledge of the business or a good position (especially marketing or finance) from which to acquire this knowledge within an acceptable time; fundamental honesty and capability; good health; energy, alertness, and perception; enthusiasm about the enterprise; personality compatible with the business; high degree of perseverance; stability and maturity; reasonable amount of aggressiveness; thoroughness and a proper respect for detail; problem-solving ability; resourcefulness; ability to plan and organize; talent to develop people; personality of a starter and a finisher; and appropriate agreement with the owner's philosophy about the business.

Understanding Influencing Forces

Locating an individual with the desired traits can be difficult. If the ideal cannot be achieved, the entrepreneur should emphasize selecting a successor with the potential to develop the attributes mentioned previously within an appropriate time frame. This choice must take into account (1) family and business culture issues, (2) the owner's concerns, and (3) family member concerns. The specific aspects of each of these influencing forces follow:

Family and Business Culture Issues

- Business environment
- Stage of the firm's development
- Business's traditions and norms
- Family culture, strength, and influence
- Owner's personal motivations and values

Owner's Concerns

- Relinquishing power and leadership
- Keeping the family functioning as a unit
- Defining family members' future roles in the business

CONTEMPORARY ENTREPRENEURSHIP

Buy/Sell Agreements for Succession

Many entrepreneurs owe their continued success to the combined skills of two or more owners. And when one of those owners dies, becomes disabled, or retires, it is imperative the transfer of his or her ownership interest is carried out in a way that protects the future of the business, the ownership interests of remaining shareholders, and the financial security of the departing owner's family. A buy/sell agreement can provide just such protection. It ensures that interest in a closely held business is transferred in a manner advantageous to all involved parties. This type of agreement can be designed to make certain the following:

1. The remaining shareholder(s) has the first right to retain the ownership interest.
2. The departing owner (or beneficiaries) receives a fair market price for the ownership interest.
3. Lawsuits and disputes that could threaten the company's existence are avoided.
4. Funds are available to purchase the ownership interest.

Legal counsel is necessary to ensure that a buy–sell agreement addresses all of the unique circumstances of a particular company.

The two basic types of agreements are the "cross-purchase agreement," in which the shareholders are obligated to purchase the departing owner's stock, and the "redemption agreement" in which the company is obligated to purchase the departing owner's stock. Each case has certain advantages, disadvantages, and tax implications that need to be considered. Thus, both a lawyer and a tax accountant should be consulted.

SOURCE: Thomas Owens, "Buy-Sell Agreements," *Small Business Reports* (January 1991): 57–61.

- Assuring competent future leadership in the firm
- Educating family and nonfamily members about key roles
- Keeping nonfamily resources in the firm

Family Member Concerns

- Gaining and losing control of family assets
- Having control over decisions made by business leadership
- Protecting interest when ownership is dispersed among family members
- How to get money out of the business, if necessary
- Assurance that the business will continue[22]

These forces and concerns prepare the entrepreneur for developing a management continuity strategy and policy. A written policy can be established in one of the following strategies:

[22] Beckhard and Dyer Jr., "Managing Continuity"; see also Wendy C. Handler, "The Succession Experience of the Next Generation," *Family Business Review* (fall 1992): 283–308.

1. The owner controls the *management continuity strategy* entirely. This is very common, yet legal advice is still needed and recommended.

2. The owner consults with selected family members. Here the legal adviser helps to establish a *liaison* between family and owner in constructing the succession mechanism.

3. The owner works with professional advisers. This is an actual board of advisers from various professional disciplines and industries that works with the owner to establish the mechanism for succession (sometimes referred to as a "quasi board").

4. The owner works with family involvement. This alternative allows the core family (blood members and spouses) to actively participate in and influence the decisions regarding succession.

If the owner is still reasonably healthy and the firm is in a viable condition, the following additional actions should be considered:

5. The owner formulates **buy/sell agreements** at the very outset of the company, or soon thereafter, and whenever a major change occurs. This is also the time to consider an appropriate insurance policy on key individuals that would provide the cash needed to acquire the equity of the deceased.

6. The owner considers **employee stock ownership plans (ESOPs).** If the owner has no immediate successor in mind and respects the loyalty and competence of his or her employees, then an appropriate ESOP might be the best solution for passing control of the enterprise. After the owner's death, the employees could decide on the management hierarchy.

7. The owner sells or liquidates the business when losing enthusiasm for it but is still physically able to go on. This could provide the capital to launch another business. Whatever the owner's plans, the firm would be sold before it fails due to disinterest.

8. The owner sells or liquidates after discovering a terminal illness but still has time for the orderly transfer of management or ownership.[23]

For all of these strategies, legal advice is beneficial, but of greater benefit is having advisers (legal or otherwise) who understand the succession issues and are able to recommend a course of action.

Entrepreneurial founders of family firms often reject thoughts of succession. Yet neither ignorance nor denial will change the inevitable. It is therefore crucial for entrepreneurs to design a plan for succession very carefully. Such plans prevent today's flourishing family businesses from becoming a statistic of diminishing family dynasties.

---

[23] Adapted from Harold W. Fox, "Quasi-Boards: Useful Small Business Confidants," *Harvard Business Review* (January/February 1982): 64–72; Kenneth W. Olm and George G. Eddy, *Entrepreneurship and Venture Management* (Columbus, OH: Merrill, 1985), 282; "CEO Profile, The Case for Succession Planning," *Small Business Reports* (February 1985): 79–85; Glenn R. Ayres, "Rough Family Justice: Equity in Family Business Succession Planning," *Family Business Review* (spring 1990): 3–22; and Ronald E. Berenbeim, "How Business Families Manage the Transition from Owner to Professional Management," *Family Business Review* (spring 1990): 69–110.

Carrying Out the Succession Plan

History reveals that although succession can be a problem, effective ways of dealing with it exist.[24] The following are four important steps to remember.

IDENTIFY A SUCCESSOR   As difficult as it is, every owner-manager should identify a successor or at least the characteristics and experience needed of such an individual.[25] The basic question that must be answered is Who can do the best job keeping the firm going? Survival and growth should be the primary areas of concern. The greatest hurdle is getting the key manager(s) to select someone. If it is a public firm with one person running the show, the individual may never get around to it. Privately held firms require an additional consideration. If one relative is designated as the heir apparent, how will the other relatives take it? Some founders, not wishing to hurt anyone, never make a decision. If no successor is identified, the next two steps are also ignored.

GROOM AN HEIR   In some firms the entrepreneur will pick a successor and let it be known. However, many top managers waver when it comes to actually announcing a choice. One person may appear to have the inside track, or a small number of people may exist from whom the successor will be chosen, but no one knows for sure who will get the job. In order to keep the guessing game going, the entrepreneur does not provide formal grooming. Regardless of who eventually heads the firm, precious time is lost for the person to learn the job. In small firms, the problem can be more acute. Even if the heir is designated, the founder finds it difficult to relinquish (or at least share) the authority necessary for effective grooming. The ego factor proves to be a major stumbling block.

AGREE ON A PLAN   Effective succession requires a plan. In large enterprises this often is worked out through a series of meetings designed to ensure an orderly transfer of power and a smooth flow of operations. Smaller organizations usually need a detailed person-to-person discussion of how responsibilities will be transferred to the successor. Since large enterprises continually go through succession changes at all levels, the mechanics of power transfer need not be excessively time consuming. The basic procedures should be fairly routine. Small owner-manager firms, however, are not so accustomed to such changes; for them a detailed plan is in order. In both cases the future direction of the firm will be a major issue.

No owner wants to step aside for a person who will change things dramatically; no entrepreneur wants to see a lifetime of effort unraveled. If the person leaving the position has any power to influence future decision making, this is the time to use it, if only by spelling out a philosophy or general course of action. Of course, if operations have not been going well, the person stepping aside will have limited influence on the successor; and if a review of operations shows that changes should be made, promises are likely to be broken (or at least modified).

Especially in small firms, attention should be given to day-to-day operations. Such consideration helps eliminate (or at least reduce) feuding. A detailed discussion of duties, obligations, and operations is imperative for family businesses. At this point, it can be helpful to bring into the plan those who will be most affected by it. This participatory

[24] Ivan Lansberg, "Twelve Tasks in Succession," *Family Business,* summer 1993, 18–24.

[25] Steven D. Goldberg, "Research Note: Effective Successors in Family-Owned Businesses—Significant Elements," *Family Business Review* (summer 1996): 185–97.

TABLE 19.4   **A CHECKLIST FOR SUCCESSION: SOME IMPORTANT STEPS**

For the Owners of Family-Run Firms

_____ Learn to delegate authority and decentralize operations.

_____ Develop an organizational chart.

_____ Plan for more than one successor—increase the possibilities.

_____ Establish a personnel development program.

_____ Encourage the potential successor to gain experience outside of the business.

_____ Do not neglect daughters.

_____ Keep plans updated—continually review the progress of the business and possible successors.

_____ Strategically plan for the future—do not always focus on putting out daily fires.

_____ Establish family business meetings to air issues.

For the Children of Family-Run Firms

_____ Announce your interest in taking over the family firm.

_____ Take responsibility for your personal development.

_____ Get a mentor (someone "outside" that you respect).

_____ Gain experience outside the family business.

_____ Get some accountability training—hold positions that teach responsibility and offer opportunities for decision making.

_____ Learn to blend family traditions with future business goals.

_____ Avoid family feuds—work with the family, not against it.

_____ Eliminate "Dad's (or Mom's) ghost"—prepare a clear takeover plan that eventually phases out older family leaders and allows changes.

approach often will co-opt some critics and alleviate the fears of others. In any event, it is a useful management tactic for helping to create unity behind the new person.[26]

CONSIDER OUTSIDE HELP   Promotion from within is a morale-building philosophy. Sometimes, however, it is a mistake. When the top person does a poor job, does promoting the next individual in line solve the problem? The latter may be the owner-manager's clone. Or consider family-owned businesses that start to outgrow the managerial ability of the top person. Does anyone in the firm *really* have the requisite skills for managing the operation? The question that must be answered is How can the business be effectively run, and who has the ability to do it? Sometimes this calls for an outside person. Family businesses face the ever-present ego factor.[27] Does the owner-manager have the wisdom to step aside and the courage to let someone else make strategic decisions? Or is the desire for control so

[26] Leslie W. Rue and Nabil A. Ibrahim, "The Status of Planning in Smaller Family-Owned Businesses," *Family Business Review* (spring 1996): 29–44.

[27] Paul C. Rosenblatt, "Blood May Be Thicker, but in the Boardroom It Just Makes for Sticky Business," *Psychology Today,* July 1985, 55–56.

great that the owner prefers to run the risks associated with personally managing the operation? The lesson is clear to the dispassionate observer; unfortunately, it is one many owners have had to learn the hard way.[28]

The checklist presented in Table 19.4 recaps some of the material in this chapter and sets forth important steps that should be taken to address the family succession issue.

THE HARVEST STRATEGY: SELLING OUT

After considering the various succession ideas presented in this chapter, many family-business entrepreneurs choose a **harvest strategy,** which means the venture will be sold. If this becomes the proper choice for an entrepreneur (and keep in mind it may be the best decision for an entrepreneur who has no interested family members or key employees), then the owner needs to review some important considerations. The idea of "selling out" actually should be viewed in the positive sense of "harvesting the investment."

Entrepreneurs consider selling their venture for numerous reasons. Based on 1,000 business owners surveyed, some of the motivations are (1) boredom and burnout, (2) lack of operating and growth capital, (3) no heirs to leave the business to, (4) desire for liquidity, (5) aging and health problems, and (6) desire to pursue other interests.[29]

Whether due to a career shift, poor health, a desire to start another venture, or retirement, many entrepreneurs face the sellout option during their entrepreneurial lifetime. This harvesting strategy needs to be carefully prepared in order to obtain the adequate financial rewards.[30]

Steps for Selling a Business

Charles O'Conor, a corporate financial consultant, recommends eight steps for the proper preparation, development, and realization of the sale.[31]

STEP 1: PREPARE A FINANCIAL ANALYSIS The purpose of such an analysis is to define priorities and forecast the next few years of the business. These fundamental questions must be answered:

- What will executive and other workforce requirements be, and how will we pay for them?
- If the market potential is so limited that goals cannot be attained, should we plan an acquisition or develop new products to meet targets for sales and profits?
- Must we raise outside capital for continued growth? How much and when?[32]

---

[28] Johannes H. M. Welsch, "The Impact of Family Ownership and Involvement on the Process of Management Succession," *Family Business Review* (spring 1993): 31–54.

[29] Ellen Goldschmidt, "Selling Your Business Successfully," *Personal Finance,* December 1987, 62; see also James Fox and Steven Elek, "Selling Your Company," *Small Business Reports* (May 1992): 49–58.

[30] See Donald Reinardy and Catherine Stover, "I Want to Sell My Business. Where Do I Begin?" *Small Business Forum* (fall 1991): 1–24.

[31] From the *Harvard Business Review,* "Packaging Your Business for Sale," by Charles O'Conor, March/April 1985, 52–58. Copyright © 1985 by the President and Fellows of Harvard College; all rights reserved.

[32] Ibid., 52.

STEP 2: SEGREGATE ASSETS   Tax accountants and lawyers may suggest the following steps to reduce taxes:

- Place real estate in a separate corporation, owned individually or by members of the family.
- Establish a leasing subsidiary with title to machinery and rolling stock. You can then lease this property to the operating company.
- Give some or all of the owner's shares to heirs when values are low, but have the owner retain voting rights. Thus when a sale is made, part or all of the proceeds can go directly to another generation without double taxation.
- Hold management's salaries and fringe benefits at reasonable levels to maximize profits.[33]

STEP 3: VALUE THE BUSINESS   The various methods used to valuate a venture were discussed in Chapter 18. Obviously, establishing the valuation of a company constitutes a most important step in its sale.[34]

STEP 4: APPROPRIATE TIMING   Knowing when to offer a business for sale is a critical factor. Timing can be everything. A few suggestions follow:

- Sell when business profits show a strong upward trend.
- Sell when the management team is complete and experienced.
- Sell when the business cycle is on the upswing, with potential buyers in the right mood and holding excess capital or credit for acquisitions.
- Sell when you are convinced that your company's future will be bright.[35]

STEP 5: PUBLICIZE THE OFFER TO SELL   A short prospectus on the company that provides enough information to interest potential investors should be prepared. This prospectus should be circulated through the proper professional channels: bankers, accountants, lawyers, consultants, and business brokers.

STEP 6: FINALIZE THE PROSPECTIVE BUYERS   Inquiries need to be made in the trade concerning the prospective buyers. Characters and managerial reputation should be assessed in order to find the best buyer.

STEP 7: REMAIN INVOLVED THROUGH THE CLOSING   Meeting with the final potential buyers helps to eliminate areas of misunderstanding and to negotiate the major requirements more effectively. Also, the involvement of professionals such as attorneys and accountants usually precludes any major problems arising at the closing.

STEP 8: COMMUNICATION AFTER THE SALE   Problems between the new owner and the remaining management team need to be resolved in order to build a solid transition. Communication between the seller and the buyer and between the buyer and the current management personnel is a key step.

---

[33] Ibid., 56.

[34] See Stephen Nelson, "When to Sell Your Company," *Inc.*, March 1988, 131–32.

[35] O'Conor, "Packaging Your Business," 56.

In addition to these eight steps, an entrepreneur must be aware of the tax implications arising from the sale of a business. For professional advice, a tax accountant specializing in business valuations and sales should be consulted.

The eight steps outlined here combined with the information on valuation in Chapter 18 will help entrepreneurs harvest their venture. The steps provide a clear framework within which entrepreneurs can structure a fair negotiation leading to a sale. If the purpose of a valuation is to sell the business, then the entrepreneur must plan ahead and follow through with each step.

This chapter has focused on family business and family management succession, which is one of the greatest challenges for entrepreneurs. A number of considerations affect succession. Family and nonfamily members, both within and outside the firm, often bring pressure on the entrepreneur. Some want to be put in charge of the operation; others simply want a stake in the enterprise.

Two types of successors exist: An entrepreneurial successor provides innovative ideas for new-product development whereas a managerial successor provides stability for day-to-day operations. An entrepreneur may search inside or outside the family as well as inside or outside the business. The actual transfer of power is a critical issue, and the timing of entry for a successor can be strategic.

The Oakland Scavenger case revealed a new legal concern about the hiring of only family members. Thus, nepotism is now being challenged in the courts on the basis of discrimination.

Developing a succession plan involves understanding these important contextual aspects: time, type of venture, capabilities of managers, the entrepreneur's vision, and environmental factors. Also, forcing events may require the implementation of a succession plan regardless of whether or not the firm is ready to implement one. This is why it is so important to identify successor qualities and carry out the succession plan.

The chapter closed with a discussion of the entrepreneur's decision to sell out. The process was viewed as a method to "harvest" the investment, and eight specific steps were presented for entrepreneurs to follow.

Key Terms and Concepts

Buy/sell agreement	Harvest strategy
Delayed entry strategy	Management succession
Early entry strategy	Managerial successor
Employee stock ownership plans (ESOP)	Nepotism
Entrepreneurial successor	Oakland Scavenger Company
Forcing events	

Review and Discussion Questions

1. Describe the importance of family businesses to the U.S. economy.
2. What are some of the advantages and disadvantages of family firms?

3. A number of barriers to succession in family firms exist. Using Table 19.2, identify some of the key barriers.
4. What pressures do entrepreneurs sometimes face from inside the family? (Use Figure 19.1 in your answer.)
5. What pressures do entrepreneurs sometimes face from outside the family? (Use Figure 19.1 in your answer.)
6. An entrepreneur can make a number of choices regarding a successor. Using Table 19.3 as a guide, discuss each of these choices.
7. How might the Oakland Scavenger case affect succession decisions in small businesses?
8. What are three of the contextual aspects that must be considered in an effective succession plan?
9. In what way can forcing events cause the replacement of an owner-manager? Cite three examples.
10. What are five qualities or characteristics successors should possess?
11. What are four steps that should be taken in carrying out a succession plan? Describe each of these steps.
12. What eight steps should be followed to harvest a business? Discuss each of these steps.

Experiential Exercise *Passing It On*

Management succession and continuity are two of the critical concerns of most entrepreneurs. In your library, look through the past year of these magazines: *Business Week, Forbes, Inc., In-Business, Success, Working Woman,* and *Family Business.* Focus on articles related to the management succession and continuity of specific firms. Then choose the two you find to be most interesting and informative and answer the following questions:

Firm 1

1. What business is this company in?_____
2. What difficulties did the owner have formulating a strategy regarding his or her succession?_____
_____
_____
_____

3. What was the entrepreneur's final decision on how to handle the succession?_____
_____
_____
_____
_____

4. What lessons can be learned from this individual's experience?_____
_____
_____
_____
_____

Firm 2

1. What business is this company in?_____

2. What difficulties did the owner have formulating a strategy regarding his or her succession?_____

_____

_____

_____

3. What was the entrepreneur's final decision on how to handle the succession?_____

_____

_____

_____

_____

4. What lessons can be learned from this individual's experience?_____

_____

_____

_____

_____

In Conclusion

Based on what you have learned from these two cases, what recommendations would you give to an entrepreneur who is in the process of developing a succession plan? Be as helpful as possible._____

_____

_____

_____

_____

 **CASE 19.1**

Just as Good as Ever

When Pablo Rodriguez was found in the storage area, no one knew for sure how long he had been unconscious. Within 30 minutes he was in the emergency room of Mercy Hospital, and by early evening the doctors had determined that Pablo had suffered a mild heart attack.

During the first couple of days he was in the hospital, Pablo's family was more concerned with his health than anything else. However, as it became clear Pablo would be released within a week and would be allowed back at work within two weeks, family members talked about his stepping aside as president of the operation and allowing someone else to take over the reins.

Pablo is president of a successful auto parts supply house. Gross sales last year were $3.7 million. Working with him in the business are his son, daughter, and two nephews. Pablo started the business 22 years ago when he was 33. After working for one of the large oil firms for 10 years as a sales representative to auto parts supply houses, Pablo broke away and started his own company. At first, he hired outside help. Over the past 5 years, however, he has been slowly bringing his family on board. It was Pablo's hope that his son would one day take over the business, but he did not see this happening for at least another 10 to 15 years.

Pablo's wife, Rebecca, believes that although he should continue to work, he should begin to train his son to run the business. On the day before he left the hospital, she broached this idea with him and asked him to think about it. He replied: "What is there to think about? I'm too young to retire and José does not know the business well enough to take over. It will take at least 5 more years before he is ready to run the operation. Besides, all I have to do is slow down a bit. I don't have to retire. What's the hurry to run me out of the company? I'm as good as ever."

Rebecca and José believe that over the next couple of months they must continue working on Pablo to slow down and to start training José to take over the reins.

Questions

1. Why is Pablo reluctant to turn over the reins to José? Include a discussion of Figure 19.1 in your answer.
2. Cite and discuss two reasons Pablo should begin thinking about succession planning.
3. What would you recommend Rebecca and José do to convince Pablo they are right? Offer at least three operative recommendations.

 **CASE 19.2**

Needing Some Help on This One

In the past, most people who wanted to get their foreign sports cars fixed had to turn to the dealer from whom they had purchased the car. In recent years, however, auto repair shops that specialize in foreign sports cars have become popular in some areas of the country. When Jack Schultz started his company ten years ago, he was lucky if he had two cars a day to work on. Today, Jack has 15 people working for him, and he usually has a backlog of about five days' work. Some of this work is repairs caused by auto accidents; a lot of it is a result of improper maintenance by the owners.

Jack is 64 years old and feels he will work for about six more years before retiring. The business is very profitable, and Jack and his wife do not need to worry about retirement income. They have saved more than enough. However, Jack is concerned about what to do with the business. He has two children who work with him, Bob (31 years old) and Tim (29 years old). Jack has not asked either of them if they would want to take over the operation. He assumes they will. He also has a nephew, Richard (35 years old), working for him. All three of these relatives have been with Jack for nine years.

Jack believes that any one of the three could successfully head the venture. But he is concerned about in-fighting should he favor one over the others. On the other hand, if he turns the business over to all three of them collectively, will they be able to get along with one another? Jack has no reason to believe the three cannot work things out amicably, but he is unsure.

Jack has decided he cannot wait much longer to groom an heir. The major stumbling block is identifying who that person will be. Additionally, Jack really does not know anything about picking a successor. What characteristics should the individual possess? What types of training should the person be given? What other steps should be followed? Jack feels he needs to answer these questions as soon as possible. "I know how to plan business operations," he told his wife last week, "but I don't know how to go about planning for the succession of business operations. It's a whole different idea. I need some help on this one."

Questions

1. Identify and briefly describe four characteristics you would expect to find in a successful manager of this type of venture.
2. What steps does Jack need to follow to successfully identify and groom a successor? Be complete in your answer.
3. If you were going to advise Jack, what would you recommend he do first? How should he get started with his succession plan? What should he do next? Offer him some general guidance on how to handle this problem.

Chapter 20

Total Quality and the Human Factor: Continuous Challenges for Entrepreneurs

CHAPTER OBJECTIVES

1. To define the term *total quality management* (TQM)

2. To review the core values and concepts of TQM

3. To examine some of the most commonly used TQM tools and techniques entrepreneurial firms employ to increase the quality of goods and services

4. To present some ways TQM firms focus on meeting customer needs

5. To study some ways cutting-edge entrepreneurial firms use employee-focus and continuous-improvement concepts to remain highly competitive

The quality movement is the first industrial change that is based on the importance of people thinking, where brains are more critical than machines. . . .

Quality, remember, isn't just desirable, it's essential. The economy is real; it's not an abstraction. . . .

Quality drives productivity, productivity drives standard of living, and standard of living is the future.

Lloyd Dobyns and Clare Crawford-Mason,
Quality or Else

Entrepreneurial ability is important for running both small and large firms, and many companies spend a great deal of time trying to keep this "entrepreneurial fire" alive.[1] One helpful way is to introduce and maintain a total quality management philosophy throughout the enterprise, and this is true not just in the United States but internationally.[2] **Total quality management (TQM)** is a people-focused management system that aims at continuous increases in customer service at continuously lower real costs. At first glance, this may appear to be an impossible goal. In fact, entrepreneurially driven firms are able to accomplish this. They do it in three ways.

One way is to find out what customers really want and to design goods and services to meet these needs. A second way is to learn how to provide this output as efficiently as possible by eliminating both time and cost. A third is to continue to enhance the process by looking for improvements.

When companies implement total quality management, they follow what is called the primary rule of total quality: *do it right the first time.* Defective-free goods and services are provided, and the money spent correcting mistakes is then saved. This strategy rests heavily on managers understanding the nature of TQM and on their willingness to accept these ideas.[3]

THE NATURE OF TOTAL QUALITY MANAGEMENT

The nature of total quality management encompasses core TQM values, a formulation of vision, top management support, careful planning and organization of the TQM effort, and

[1] See, for example, "New Entrepreneurs Using Their Noodles with Pasta Factory," *Miami Herald,* 3 April 1994, 16A.

[2] Sang M. Lee, Fred Luthans, and Richard M. Hodgetts, "Total Quality Management Implications for Central and Eastern Europe," *Organizational Dynamics* (spring 1992): 42–55; and Louis Kraar, "Korea Goes for Quality," *Fortune,* 18 April 1994, 153–59.

[3] Sanjay L. Ahire and Damodar Y. Golhar, "Quality Management in Large versus Small Firms: An Empirical Investigation," *Journal of Small Business Management* (April 1996): 1–13.

619

ENTREPRENEURIAL

EDGE

Making ISO 9000 Work for You

Although an organization's motivation for adopting ISO 9000 might be to compete in the marketplace or to improve its internal quality system, the return on investment of time and money can be delayed one or two years while a gap assessment takes place, a documentation effort is launched to fill those gaps, internal operations are developed to adhere to the documentation, and the external audits are conducted. During this certification preparation period, however, companies can take advantage of productive opportunities. These opportunities include the following:

1. *Positive management.* When preparing for ISO 9000 certification, companies must systematically determine how their internal processes work and how their employees perform these processes. This gives management an eye-opening glimpse of how things actually happen in the organization, how groups and individuals relate, and what the organizational power structure is.

2. *Process improvement.* By improving its primary production process, a company is almost guaranteed to make a lot of money fast, thereby debunking the myth that it takes years for quality to pay off. Building on this success, a company can repeat this procedure with its other processes.

3. *Using the creative power of the workforce.* Seeking hands-on knowledge from task performers also changes the organization's culture and builds morale. It demonstrates to everyone

a well-thought-through system for implementing and controlling the process.[4] The following examines each of these.

Core Values and Concepts

Ten core values and concepts form the basis of TQM-driven firms:[5]

1. *Customer-driven quality.* All goods/services the organization provides are a result of feedback from customers who have told the company what they want. Drawing on this information, companies try to give customers more than what they desire and thus to create "customer delight."

---

[4] See Thomas A. Mahoney and John R. Deckop, "Y'Gotta Believe: Lessons from American- vs. Japanese-Run U.S. Factories," *Organizational Dynamics* (spring 1993): 27–38.

[5] For additional insights, see Warren H. Schmidt and Jerome P. Finnigan, *The Race without a Finish Line* (San Francisco: Jossey-Bass, 1992).

that management is really interested in quality, not quantity. People will get the message that quality pays, and recognition can be earned by making quality-enhancing, not quantity-enhancing, decisions.

4. *Direct management link to improvement efforts.* ISO 9000 requires top management to systematically review the company's quality system, the results of internal audits, and all corrective and preventive actions undertaken throughout the organization. The quality system is necessary to measure the effectiveness of those activities and their compliance to the ISO 9000 standards and to provide the resources and direction to maintain the standards. When top management takes this responsibility seriously and does not reassign it to employees, the organization will make money.

5. *Improved communication system.* ISO 9000 is as much a communication system as a quality tool. If implemented correctly in a company, ISO 9000 does the following:

- Builds interpersonal communication between managers and employees
- Helps resolve political conflicts, work procedure inconsistencies, and the conflict between formal and informal communication flows
- Trains management and employees in communication skills, such as interviewing, writing, and editing
- Creates a documentation system and a system for disseminating information company-wide and to all customers
- Provides the basis for a networked communication system
- Lays a foundation for using employees as sophisticated information gatherers and sorters

SOURCES: Adapted from Michael J. Scotto, "Seven Ways to Make Money from ISO 9000," *Quality Progress* (June 1996): 39–41; and Amy Zuckerman and Alan Hurwitz, "How Companies Miss the Boat on ISO 9000," *Quality Progress* (July 1996): 23–24.

2. *Leadership.* The firm's managers must understand what TQM is all about, be trained in the process, and be prepared both to implement these ideas and to encourage the rest of the personnel to do so.

3. *Continuous improvement.* No matter how well the enterprise does, it must make continual efforts to do even better. Thus, if a particular product cannot be built any better because it is error-free, the company can seek ways to produce it faster. TQM efforts have no end; every procedure, process, product, and service is continuously examined for ways to do things better than before.

4. *Full participation.* The company must develop a reward and recognition system that encourages full employee participation in the TQM effort. Examples include education and training programs that impart skills for improving work quality and solving job-related problems, as well as rewards that recognize and remunerate employees for a job well done.

5. *Rapid response.* The firm must continuously strive to reduce the amount of time needed to deliver goods and services. This means streamlining processes, eliminating

unnecessary tasks, and finding shortcuts that will get the output to the customer in the desired time (or earlier).

6. *Prevention, not detection.* Attention must be given to determining ways to prevent mistakes or problems, rather than identifying and correcting them after they have occurred. Management thus acts in a proactive rather than a reactive manner.

7. *Long-range outlook.* In addition to continuously identifying the goods and services customers desire, TQM firms seek to identify the output that will be needed in the future and begin planning today to reach that objective. For example, if a firm learns that the production of its microcomputer chips must be 99.9 percent perfect within 12 months and 99.999 percent perfect within 36 months, it will begin moving toward the latter goal immediately. In this way, the company anticipates customer needs and tries to stay ahead of them through effective long-range planning.

8. *Management by fact.* TQM companies document all of their efforts through data collection, analysis, and comparison. For example, if they are trying to reduce error rates, they will find out where they are today and then gather information on these rates over the next 12 months. In this way, they can use quantitative data to compare changes in error rates and can know exactly how much they have improved and how much further they have to go. This management by fact helps the firm ''prove'' its progress, rather than relying on hunches, opinions, or intuitive feelings regarding how well it is doing.

9. *Partnership development.* TQM firms get their suppliers, vendors, unions, and all other outside groups to help improve the delivery of goods and services. These outside groups, regarded as partners who can help improve quality, are brought into the planning process so that they can see their role and learn how they can help.

10. *Public responsibility.* TQM firms also are interested in good corporate citizenship. They accept the responsibility of providing their customers with safe, defect-free goods and services; work to produce less product waste; and are prepared to share their experiences to help other firms gain better corporate citizenship.

Vision Formulation

Although it is critical that firms accept and adhere to these ten TQM core values and concepts, the management of the company also must formulate a vision regarding its view of total quality.[6] How does TQM fit with the company's values? What is the firm's quality policy? Here are examples of corporate value statements from Zytec, a small entrepreneurially driven firm that manufactures power supplies and is regarded as one of the best in the world; Xerox, an internationally known company most famous for its photocopying products; and Motorola, the world's leading manufacturer of cellular phones and pagers:

> Zytec is a company that competes on value, is market-driven, provides superior quality and service, builds strong relationships with its customers, and provides technical excellence in its product.

> Xerox is a quality company. Quality is the basic business principle for Xerox. Quality means providing our external and internal customers with innovative products

---

[6] Leonard L. Berry and A. Parasuraman, ''Prescriptions for a Service Quality Revolution in America,'' *Organizational Dynamics* (spring 1992): 5–16.

and services that fully satisfy their requirements. Quality improvement is the job of every Xerox employee.

It is the objective of Motorola, Inc., to produce and provide products and services of the highest quality. In its activities, Motorola will pursue goals aimed at the achievement of quality excellence. These results will be derived from the dedicated efforts of each employee in conjunction with supportive participation from management at all levels of the corporation.[7]

Top Management Support

Every successful TQM-driven company has a top management that fully supports its effort.[8] This takes a number of forms. One of the most important is that all senior-level managers are trained in TQM tools and techniques so that they understand how the process works and how they can use these ideas in their own jobs.

In addition, this experience puts the managers in an ideal position to support the total quality management effort, because they understand what needs to be done and how it should be done. They also are insulated from criticism by lower-level personnel, who otherwise may feel that management gives lip service to total quality but is not part of the process itself.

Third, in some companies senior-level managers will help train others throughout the firm. Because they know what TMQ is all about, this puts them in an ideal position to share the information. This type of top involvement helps prepare companies for TQM excellence in three ways. First, it sets up senior managers as role models. Second, it ensures that these managers can actively help others become more total quality driven. Third, it helps the managers oversee the organizing and implementing stages of the process.

Planning and Organizing

The next step in setting up a total quality management program is to plan and organize the effort. At this stage companies set the quality objective they want to accomplish. For example, Motorola, one of the nation's foremost entrepreneurially driven organizations, decided in 1987 to increase its quality by 1992 so it would have fewer than four defects per million efforts. This objective is particularly important for understanding the relationship between cost and quality. Motorola found that as failure rates declined so did cost. Today the company produces goods that are so well manufactured that the error rate is measured in mistakes per billion. Motorola is not only the leader in manufacturing both cellular phones and pagers but also is regarded as one of the best-run high-technology firms in the world. (See the next Contemporary Entrepreneurship.)

In addition to setting objectives, TQM firms also must organize their efforts. This includes designating someone to head the total quality effort and to appoint a total quality management committee. Marlow Industries, a small firm that produces thermoelectric coolers, has created a Total Quality Management Council to oversee the quality process and to establish, review, and assess quality goals and implementation plans. This council— composed of six senior executives, who serve as permanent members, and seven other

---

[7] Richard M. Hodgetts, *Blueprints for Continuous Improvement: Lessons from the Baldrige Winners* (New York: American Management Association, 1993), 25.

[8] Kenneth R. Thompson, "A Conversation with Robert W. Galvin," *Organizational Dynamics* (spring 1992): 56–69.

CONTEMPORARY ENTREPRENEURSHIP

Staying the Best

Motorola is a giant firm that has never lost its entrepreneurial drive. In 1984 annual sales were just over $5 billion. By 1994 they were in the range of $20 billion, helping the company maintain its goal of doubling sales every five years. At the same time, Motorola's earnings surpassed the $1 billion mark, and the company was the second largest American firm in the electronics and electronic equipment industry. Only General Electric, another entrepreneurially driven firm, was larger and more profitable.

A number of developments help account for Motorola's success. One is its strong emphasis on total quality management, which helps the company produce goods virtually free from errors. Another is its emphasis on using these same ideas with white-collar workers, an effort the firm hopes will take $2 billion off its annual overhead. A third is the ability to transfer this efficiency into providing low-cost, high-quality products for world markets. Motorola controls 85 percent of the global market for pagers, easily besting Sony, Panasonic, and Casio. It also holds a major share of the cellular phone market, which is growing by 40 percent annually in the United States and even faster overseas. The company is also be-

coming a major force in the semiconductor market, where it is the third largest producer in the world. Motorola launched the PowerPC, which is an advanced microprocessor developed jointly with IBM and Apple and which promises to challenge Intel, the world's largest semiconductor company.

The rest of this decade will present even greater challenges to Motorola. One step the firm is implementing is that of making obsolete some current products in favor of better ones. The company's philosophy is that it should design and manufacture the very best products and that it is okay if these supplant some of its current offerings. Another challenge will be to keep the technical personnel motivated. As one manager recently put it, "We've met the challenge of the Japanese; our quality is high; demand for our product is strong. Our technical people are bordering on being cocky. That keeps me awake at night. I've got to figure out how to keep these people unhappy." This may prove to be the firm's biggest challenge.

SOURCE: Ronald Henkoff, "Keeping Motorola on a Roll," *Fortune,* 18 April 1994, 67–78.

employees, who rotate annually—is responsible for seeing that the TQM system is implemented throughout the company. In addition, the group works with the board of directors and senior management staff to tie total quality into the firm's strategic plan. The group also helps create action teams throughout the organization to manage specific total quality management projects. The result is a well-planned effort that ensures cooperation of all personnel.

Implementing and Controlling

The implementation and controlling steps are often determined when the firm formulates its total quality plan. In most cases the focus is on key results that can be measured and charted. For example, Federal Express uses 12 service quality indicators (SQI) that track how well service is being provided to customers. Examples include damaged packages, lost packages, and missed pickups. These three are so important to effective customer service that on a scale of one to ten, they have a weight of ten. Other indicators have a lesser weight, such as packages that have lost their identifying labels in shipment and packages delivered after the commitment date, both of which have a weight of five. IBM Rochester follows a similar approach, carefully implementing and then closely monitoring such areas as customer service, quality-related training, supplier-improvement activities, and employee cross-training.

TQM TOOLS AND TECHNIQUES

Although most employees want to see the quality of their output increase, many do not know how to go about measuring, evaluating, and correcting their mistakes. This is why all TQM firms provide training in specific tools and techniques. The following examines some of the most common.

Data Collection Sheets

Data collection sheets are used to gather information on performance so that problems can be identified and corrected. These sheets are designed so that the information can be easily recorded, tabulated, and analyzed. Figure 20.1 provides an example. Notice in the figure that the time period during which the information was collected has been clearly indicated, the name of the department has been written down, and both the types of errors and their number of occurrences have been indicated. A quick examination of the chart shows that typists in Department A most need to improve their punctuation and spelling. These two errors account for 59 percent of all their typing mistakes. Carefully designed data collection sheets are critical to total quality management efforts because they can help organizations quickly pinpoint problems. Quite often these sheets are used in conjunction with other TQM tools, such as the Pareto chart.

Pareto Charts

A **Pareto chart** is a vertical bar graph that helps identify which problems are to be solved and in what order. The basic concept behind this chart is explained by the **Pareto principle,** which holds that 80 percent of all outcomes can be attributed to 20 percent of all causes. Thus, entrepreneurs can increase the quality of their output by correcting a handful of problems.

The first step in constructing a Pareto chart is to gather information. Many firms use the format of a problem/error check sheet, such as the one shown in Figure 20.1, to obtain this information. Then the data are put into a table (see Table 20.1), where the number and rate of occurrence for each error are identified. Next the information is put into a bar chart, as seen in Figure 20.2, beginning with the most-common occurrence and continuing on to the least-common occurrence. Finally, a cumulative frequency line (each occurrence rate is added to the previous one) is constructed. This line in Figure 20.2 shows that after the third

FIGURE 20.1 ILLUSTRATION OF A PROBLEM/ERROR CHECK SHEET

Time Period: *August 16-20 1997*   Date: *9/6/97*

Purpose: *Determine typing mistakes in Department A*   Name: *L. Winslow*

Department: *A*

Problem/Error	August 15	August 16	August 17	August 18	August 19	Total	%
Bold Lettering	111	11	1111	11	111	14	5%
Centering	11	1	11	1	111	9	4%
Incorrect Page Numbers	1	11	1		1	6	2%
Missed Paragraphs	11	11	1	11	1	8	3%
Punctuation	LHT LHT 11	LHT LHT LHT LHT LHT	LHT LHT LHT 111	LHT LHT LHT LHT LHT	LHT LHT LHT 111	98	38%
Spacing	LHT	1111	LHT 1	LHT 11	111	25	10%
Spelling	LHT 1111	LHT LHT	LHT LHT LHT 11	LHT LHT	LHT 1111	55	21%
Tables	11	1		1	1	5	2%
Underlining	LHT LHT 11	LHT	LHT 111	LHT 11	LHT 11	40	15%
				Totals:		260	100%

major error (underlining), the percentage of errors begins to increase at a decreasing rate. Management would begin working with punctuation, spelling, and underlining errors, since these collectively account for 74 percent of all the mistakes.

Cause-and-Effect Diagrams

Cause-and-effect diagrams are often used as a follow-up to Pareto analysis. The Pareto chart identifies the problems; the **cause-and-effect diagram** helps explain the reasons and

TABLE 20.1   **AN ANALYSIS OF THE PROBLEM/ERROR CHECK SHEET**

Error	Number	Rate of Occurrence
Punctuation	98	38%
Spelling	55	21
Underlining	40	15
Spacing	25	10
Bold lettering	14	5
Centering	9	4
Missed paragraphs	8	3
Incorrect page numbers	6	2
Tables	5	2

FIGURE 20.2   **A PARETO ANALYSIS OF TYPING MISTAKES IN DEPARTMENT A**

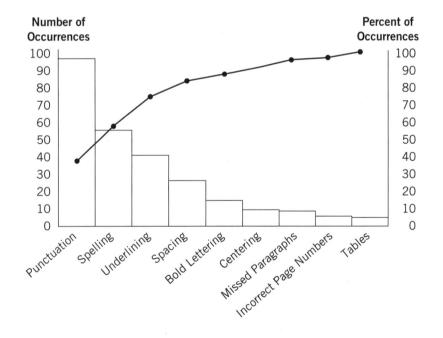

points the way toward solutions or improvements. This TQM tool typically begins with a brainstorming session designed to identify some of the causes of the problem. For example, consider a department that feels its meetings are unproductive. How can meetings be run so that more is done in a shorter period? The group begins by brainstorming possible reasons for the inefficient meetings, while someone writes down what members say. Then the reasons are put into categories such as (a) environment—it is too noisy in the meeting room, or the room temperature makes it uncomfortable; (b) resources/people—the participants are not prepared for the meeting, or they have poor problem-solving skills; or (c) procedures—no agenda exists, or the group does not stick to its agenda. These categories and reasons are put into the cause-and-effect diagram. An example is illustrated in Figure 20.3. Notice that the group classified its reasons into five major categories. In some cases, the diagram may have as few as two categories or as many as eight. However, it is usually best to keep the categories to a minimum number, since this helps reduce the difficulty of implementing the solutions.

Scatter Diagrams

Another widely used TQM tool is the **scatter diagram,** which illustrates the relationship between two variables. For example, suppose a company wants to know the value of conducting preventive maintenance on its machinery. The question to be investigated is What is the relationship between the amount of preventive maintenance on a machine and the amount of time the unit is down for repairs? After gathering information on these two variables, the company can construct a scatter diagram showing their relationship. Figure 20.4 provides an example.

Notice that machines that received 1 hour of preventive maintenance per month had downtimes of 11 hours or more. Conversely, machines that received 10 hours of maintenance a month had 3 or fewer hours of downtime. Based on these results, the company could decide the amount of maintenance to give to each machine and thus could minimize the cost of downtime. Similar investigations could be applied to other variables, such as the amount of training given to new salespeople and the dollar volume of sales for the first 90 days on the job. For example, a scatter diagram could help answer the question How effective is sales training for new salespeople? The same approach could be used to examine the effect of safety training on the number of accidents in the company's warehouse. By comparing training and accidents, the company could determine how valuable the training is and whether an ideal amount of training exists.

"Tool Box"

The first four examples are common TQM tools. Others include frequency histograms, statistical process controls, and control charts. It is important that entrepreneurs remember that depending on the problem, some tools and techniques will be of more value than others. The personnel must think of these tools as part of a "tool box," and, with the right tool or TQM technique, they can accurately investigate the problem and arrive at an action plan likely to resolve the problem. Typically, this analysis involves a five-step process that contains key questions that must be answered at each step. Here is one version of the process:

Step 1: Define the problem.
- What is happening?
- What results are being achieved?
- What seems to be going wrong?

FIGURE 20.3 **A CAUSE-AND-EFFECT DIAGRAM FOR DEALING WITH UNPRODUCTIVE MEETINGS**

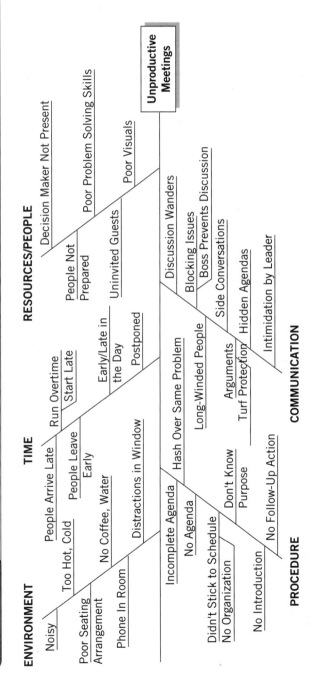

SOURCE: Richard M. Hodgetts, *Blueprints for Continuous Improvement: Lessons from the Baldrige Winners* (New York: American Management Association, 1993), 18.

FIGURE 20.4   **A SCATTER DIAGRAM SHOWING THE RELATIONSHIP BETWEEN PREVENTIVE MAINTENANCE AND DOWNTIME**

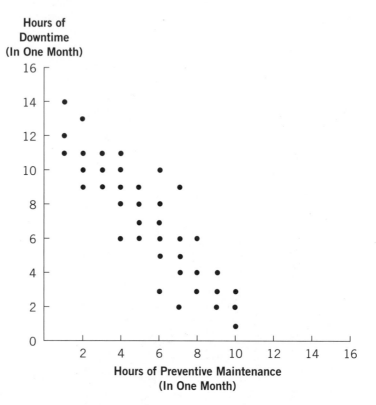

SOURCE: Richard M. Hodgetts, *Blueprints for Continuous Improvement: Lessons from the Baldrige Winners* (New York: American Management Association, 1993), 50.

Step 2: Formulate the hypothesis.
• What is causing the problem?
• What does an analysis of past data reveal?

Step 3: Test the hypothesis.
• What are the cause-and-effect relationships?
• What are the reasons for these relationships?

Step 4: Introduce the necessary changes.
• What needs to be done?
• In what order should these changes be carried out?
• How much time will be needed?

Step 5: Evaluate the results.
• Did things work as expected?
• What data support this evaluation?
• How can these results be used to continue "looping into" the process by going back to an earlier step and taking a fresh look at things?

| TABLE 20.2 | ZYTEC'S CUSTOMER STATEMENT |

CUSTOMERS are the most important people in our business, either in person, over the phone, or by mail.

CUSTOMERS are not dependent on us. We are dependent on them.

CUSTOMERS are not an interruption of our work—they are the purpose of it.

CUSTOMERS are not outsiders to our business. They are the most important part of it.

CUSTOMERS are not just names or numbers. They are people with feelings and emotions like our own.

CUSTOMERS are not people to argue with. No one wins in a business argument.

CUSTOMERS are people who bring us their needs. It is our job to satisfy them, and to do so profitably for them and for ourselves.

SOURCE: Zytec Corporation. Reprinted with permission.

Based on the questions that must be answered, participants are then taught to use the proper TQM tools. Here are examples of general questions applied to three of the tools discussed earlier:

In Answering This Question	Use This Tool
What are the major problems?	Pareto chart analysis
What are the causes of the major problems?	Cause-and-effect diagram
What are the cause/effect relationships?	Scatter diagram

CUSTOMER SERVICE FOCUS

The primary focus of all TQM efforts is the customer. For this reason, every total quality management strategy must be designed to find out what the customer wants, how well the firm is providing this output, and what the company needs to do to improve its performance to match, if not stay ahead of, customer expectations. This is typically done by placing attention on three areas: beliefs and values, gathering data, and data analysis.

Beliefs and Values

Total quality firms clearly think through their beliefs and values about customer service and then communicate these to the personnel. At AT&T Universal Card Service (UCS), for example, four factors are regarded as critical to effective customer service: (a) Personnel must be accessible to the customer; (b) employees must have a professional manner; (c) employees must evince a positive attitude toward the customer; and (d) all inquiries, requests, or problems must be handled efficiently. Motorola makes it clear that the customer is in the driver's seat and determines production and delivery schedules. When a customer contacts Motorola and wants to place an order, the employee finds out when the individual needs the product and uses this time to determine when the product will be built and shipped. Zytec reinforces its philosophy that the customer is number one by adhering to the customer statement in Table 20.2.

Gathering Data

Customer-related information can be gathered in a number of ways. One of the most common is customer surveys, which are used to gather information on a wide variety of topics, including product quality, delivery time, and employee helpfulness. Another is customer panel surveys, which provide face-to-face meetings between the company and those who buy its goods and services. For example, UCS interviews 200 customers every month and conducts panel surveys of customers biannually. Cadillac Motor, winner of the Malcolm Baldrige award for world-class quality, uses a combination of data-gathering techniques, including focus groups and product clinics, as well as more than 2.5 million customer interviews each year. Another common approach total quality management firms use is demographic surveys, which provide information on industry trends and developments, market segmentation practices, and newly developing markets. This is often supplemented by psychographic surveys, which identify product features and concepts that will be of value to customers in the future.

Data Analysis

After the data are gathered, the next step is to analyze the information and draw conclusions for action. One of the most direct ways to do this is to determine the frequency of responses to the various questions and then construct a Pareto chart. Sometimes this analysis reveals unexpected results. For example, a few years ago a Motorola task force evaluating the results of customer interviews found that customers wanted three things: high product quality, on-time delivery, and responsiveness to questions and concerns. Breaking the data down on the basis of customer account size, the company found that large customers were most interested in on-time delivery because their experience with Motorola convinced them that the firm always produced defect-free products. New customers, on the other hand, were more concerned with product quality because they had limited experience with the company. Zytec found that its customers were most interested in products that had state-of-the-art technology and could be produced quickly so that no shortage occurred. At the same time, these customers were not highly concerned with price; they were willing to pay more to ensure a high-quality product. As a result, the company is focusing its attention on these two areas.

CYCLE TIME FOCUS

Cycle time is the time needed to complete a task. This time is critical to quality improvement because of its effect on productivity. If more output can be achieved in the same amount of time, then productivity will increase because the cost per unit will decline. For example, if a person making $10 an hour turns out four units hourly, the labor cost per unit is $2.50. If the individual increases output to five per hour, the labor cost per unit is $2.00. Additionally, when the quality of a good or service reaches the point where it cannot be increased, such as a cellular phone that works perfectly, a firm has only one other way to increase quality—reduce the cycle time. This follows the quality-related maxim "If the work cannot be done any better, focus on doing it faster."

Paring Time

One of the most common approaches to improving cycle time is to examine how the work is currently done and then identify and eliminate extraneous steps. A good example is

Motorola's communications sector, which managed to cut four days from its order/delivery cycle time and generate an increase in billings of $100 million. The procedure involves a TQM tool known as **flow charting,** in which all the steps in a job or process are written out in the form of a flow diagram. The diagram is examined to identify steps that can be eliminated or combined.

A related approach is to eliminate nonvalue-added tasks and activities. All of the steps in a particular job are studied to determine which do not add any value to the good or service. For example, one small firm recently learned that its customers were just as happy with two-day delivery as with overnight delivery. As a result, the company stopped sending products overnight and cut its annual shipping costs by more than $100,000.

Another approach to paring time is to determine how to pass on the work to someone else. Wal-Mart, the giant retailer, has cut its inventory supply by passing this responsibility to suppliers. Procter & Gamble, one of its major suppliers, has the authority to determine when a resupply of goods is needed so that Wal-Mart stores can operate on a more hand-to-mouth basis. It is up to Procter & Gamble to determine the production and shipment of these goods, freeing Wal-Mart from time-consuming tasks and ensuring more frequent deliveries of smaller amounts of inventory. A similar approach is used by Zytec, which purchases inventory in small lots and keeps most of it on the shop floor, where it flows through the production process and out to the shipping dock. As a result, the firm has dramatically reduced the amount of money tied up in warehoused inventory.

Still another way to pare time is to break down walls between departments and get everyone to cooperate. For example, to bring its AS/400 minicomputer to market in record time, IBM created a design team that involved people from research and development, manufacturing, and marketing, as well as suppliers and customers. Working as a group, the team designed and built a computer that proved to be the most successful new product in the company's history.

Many firms find that they can reduce cycle time by creating a partnership with their suppliers. They bring in suppliers, show how they do things, teach their needs and practices, and then link their operations more closely together. This strategy is particularly useful for ensuring that products are delivered on time and built to proper specifications. It is also useful for helping both groups minimize their inventory, since suppliers can link their own production cycle more closely to the company's needs and thus ensure a hand-to-mouth delivery system.

EMPLOYEE FOCUS

Total quality management depends heavily on employee cooperation and contribution. For this reason, effective TQM firms always spend a great deal of attention on employee training, empowerment, involvement, and recognition.[9]

Training

Training is critical to total quality management efforts, because many times the personnel have to be taught how to do things somewhat differently from the way they did them in the past. One way to minimize this problem from the start is to develop an orientation program that focuses on total quality management and familiarizes all new employees with the

---

[9] For more on this, see Ronald Henkoff, "Keeping Motorola on a Roll," *Fortune,* 18 April 1994, 67–78.

company's philosophy and operating system. At the Ritz-Carlton hotels, for example, every new hire attends a specially designed orientation program that clearly spells out the firm's value system and operating methods. Employees learn that the customer is the focus of all attention. For example, when a guest asks an employee for directions to a particular place in the hotel, the employee stops whatever he or she is doing and personally escorts the individual there. Employees also are trained to remember the names of guests so that they can address them directly when they pass them in the hallway or are approached by them for assistance. In addition, employees are trained in teamwork and problem solving so that they can work together to identify ways to further improve customer services, such as reducing cycle time in the restaurant and at the front desk.

Although total quality firms offer a wide variety of training programs, the firms all have one thing in common: Every year they devote an increased amount of their budget for training. For example, at Solectron, a highly successful small manufacturer of complex circuit boards and subsystems, all employees received a minimum of 85 training hours in 1991; by 1995 this had risen to 160. Motorola has increased the number of training hours for its personnel to more than 40 hours annually.

Training typically involves both mandatory and optional courses, and, although inside personnel are used for most training, outside trainers often are used to supplement this process. At Zytec, for example, everyone is required to take a course called Zytec Involved People (ZIP), which teaches participants to become team players, to respond more effectively to customer needs, and to reward and reinforce one another for doing a good job.

Empowerment

Empowerment is the authority to take control and make decisions. This process typically involves two critical elements: delegation of authority and assignment of resources for completing the work. Employees are given the authority to make decisions that will increase the organization's quality of output, and they are given financial resources to ensure that this goal is attained. For example, at the Ritz-Carlton hotel chain, employees are authorized to spend up to $2,000 to handle a problem. If a guest is making a business presentation in a conference room and the overhead projector goes on the blink, the employee who is coordinating the equipment for the meeting can rent a machine at an office supply store without having to get permission. Zytec personnel have $1,000 each and are urged to spend these funds anytime it will help ensure improved customer service.

At AT&T's Universal Card System, employees are empowered to take whatever steps they need to reduce costs and improve customer service. One way the firm encourages this is to assign people to teams that plan strategies for eliminating problems on the company's "10 Most Wanted" list. As each problem is resolved, it is removed from the list and another item is put in its place. Thus the teams face a never-ending list of issues and problems, and members are encouraged to take responsibility for formulating solutions. At the same time, throughout the organization all employees are empowered to make decisions that will reduce costs and increase "customer delight." As a result, UCS is one of the best customer-driven firms in the country.

Involvement

TQM firms also maintain employee focus by keeping everyone informed about what is going on and getting all personnel involved in the quality-driven process.[10] For example,

[10] See Richard M. Hodgetts, "Quality Lessons from America's Baldrige Winners," *Business Horizons* (July/August 1994): 74–79.

Wild Oats, a natural foods and health care products company based in Colorado, puts a major emphasis on communicating with all associates and, in turn, gives each an opportunity to express his or her opinions, suggestions, or complaints. The company believes that this process is essential for making everyone feel he or she is a valuable member of the organization. This two-way flow of communication is promoted in a number of ways. One way is with monthly meetings between department managers and the staff and between the store managers and the department managers. A second way is with mandatory store meetings. Full attendance at these meetings helps ensure that everyone knows what is going on and that all questions are answered. Additionally, since the owners come to these meetings, those present can be assured that their concerns are being heard and will be acted on.[11]

Another form of feedback at Wild Oats is provided by staff surveys (see Table 20.3), which are conducted twice a year and at exit inverviews held with people leaving the company. The purpose of this feedback is to determine how well operations are going and to identify better ways to involve and manage the staff.

A common approach to gaining employee involvement is to encourage employees to submit quality-related ideas and then let them know the status of their suggestions. Henry Lee, a family-founded food distributor in Miami, Florida, has developed a system for employees to submit ideas for improvement. Associates who are interested in submitting a quality tip ("Q-Tip," for short) are asked to fill out a form on which they detail the problem they have identified, to describe their suggestion for improvement, and to note the value of implementing the suggestion. Each Q-Tip is then evaluated, and a decision is made regarding its usefulness. All new Q-Tips are then eligible for a prize, thus helping to encourage continuous involvement.

Another popular approach that promotes employee involvement is the use of newsletters to keep associates informed about what is going on and to praise individuals for outstanding performance. These in-house organs are particularly effective when operations are geographically dispersed and the employees do not see each other on a regular basis. The newsletter not only can keep everyone aware of activities but also can run pictures of individuals and work teams who have instituted new TQM practices or reached new productivity goals.

Recognition

Total quality management firms maintain their quality-driven momentum through the effective use of rewards. These rewards come in a variety of different forms. Table 20.4 provides some examples. Most companies use a combination of rewards in the table; the most common are financial rewards, Employee of the Month awards, and memos or letters praising people for a job well done.

At the Ritz-Carlton, an employee who feels that another worker has done an outstanding job can send the individual a "First Class" card—a three-by-five-inch card designed with the company logo—to express appreciation. The company also uses "Lightning Strikes," which are monetary rewards a member of the Executive Committee grants to any employee for outstanding service. In addition, employees who submit the best ideas for improvement are listed on a bulletin board and are given a buffet dinner for two, and those who generate the greatest number of useful ideas are honored at quarterly receptions.

---

[11] For additional ways companies get their employees actively involved, see "A Conversation with Steve Kerr," *Organizational Dynamics* (spring 1996): 68–79.

TABLE 20.3   **WILD OATS STAFF SURVEY**

This survey has been created so that you can anonymously relate your experiences as a staff member of Wild Oats. We will be using the numerical portion to come up with a store "Happiness Index," which will tell us if morale is giddy or suicidal. This feedback will help us create a better working environment for everyone. Please do your best to complete this survey in an honest and open manner and with as much detail and explanation as possible.

Please rate your responses by circling the number that most closely describes your experience. Feel free to use the back of these sheets for additional comments.

1. *How happy are you with your job overall?*
   Not happy at all .... Ecstatic

   | 1 | 2 | 3 | 4 | 5 | 6 | 7 | 8 | 9 | 10 |

   Any comments or suggestions?

2. *How do you feel about your benefits at Wild Oats?*
   Terrible .... Great

   | 1 | 2 | 3 | 4 | 5 | 6 | 7 | 8 | 9 | 10 |

   Any comments or suggestions?

3. *How do you feel about the pay levels at Wild Oats as compared to similar employees?*
   Worse than most .... Ecstatic

   | 1 | 2 | 3 | 4 | 5 | 6 | 7 | 8 | 9 | 10 |

   Any comments or suggestions?

4. *How do you feel about the employee review system at Wild Oats?*
   Hate it .... Love it

   | 1 | 2 | 3 | 4 | 5 | 6 | 7 | 8 | 9 | 10 |

   Any comments or suggestions?

5. *How is the overall morale in your store?*
   Awful .... Wonderful

   | 1 | 2 | 3 | 4 | 5 | 6 | 7 | 8 | 9 | 10 |

   Any comments or suggestions?

6. *How do you feel about the responsibilities of your job?*
   Too little .... Too much

   | 1 | 2 | 3 | 4 | 5 | 6 | 7 | 8 | 9 | 10 |

   Any comments or suggestions?

Marlow Industries maintains a hall of fame in which the pictures of outstanding performers are hung. The firm also gives service awards, perfect-attendance awards, good-housekeeping awards, team recognition awards, individual team bonuses, and profit sharing as recognition tools. Zytec uses a detailed **implemented improvement system (IIS),** which is a Japanese-style suggestion system that emphasizes employee involvement with the goal of generating ideas for increased productivity. The system works this way:

1. For each idea an employee submits, the individual receives a $1 token cash award plus a lottery ticket, which is presented at the person's workstation.

7. *How effectively is your store managed?*
Very poorly .... Very well

| 1 | 2 | 3 | 4 | 5 | 6 | 7 | 8 | 9 | 10 |

Any comments or suggestions?

8. *How effective is your department manager?*
Remarkably bad .... Terrific

| 1 | 2 | 3 | 4 | 5 | 6 | 7 | 8 | 9 | 10 |

Any comments or suggestions?

9. *Why do you come to work every day?*
Have to .... Want to

| 1 | 2 | 3 | 4 | 5 | 6 | 7 | 8 | 9 | 10 |

Any comments or suggestions?

10. *How does Wild Oats compare to your previous employers?*
Worse .... Same .... Much better

| 1 | 2 | 3 | 4 | 5 | 6 | 7 | 8 | 9 | 10 |

Any comments or suggestions?

11. What department do you work in? (optional) _____

12. How long have you worked for Wild Oats? _____

13. How do you feel about the training and orientation program you experienced when you started? Do you feel you understand the procedures, policies, and responsibilities that are part of your job? How would you change things?

14. What do you like *least* about your job and/or the company? Please explain.

15. What do you like *most* about your job and/or the company? Please explain.

16. What would you change if you were the owner?

SOURCE: Courtesy of Wild Oats.

2. The work group with the highest percentage of employee participation gets to display a trophy for a month.

3. Each month the names of all employees participating in the program are put in a hat, and one name is drawn for a day off with pay.

4. The winner of the day off with pay chooses a support or staff person to take over his or her job for one day.

5. Each month the program administrator asks for a volunteer from each work group to serve on the review board, which reviews all ideas submitted that month and chooses

TABLE 20.4   TYPICAL REWARDS TOTAL QUALITY MANAGEMENT COMPANIES USE

Plaques	Logo items	Special parking space
Trophies	• hats	Special luncheon
Certificates	• shirts	Dinner with spouse or friend
Letter from CEO	• pens	Trip (local or distant)
Honor roll	• mugs	Seminar attendance
Letter to personnel file	• coasters	Pick-your-own-gift certificate
Picture in company paper	• shorts	Day off
Use of limousine	• decals	Cash
Savings bond	• paper weights	Tickets to special events
Banner for office	• desk sets	

the top three. The employees who submit the top three ideas are given $100, $75, and $50, respectively.

6. Each month the program administrator takes pictures of the three winners and places them on the bulletin boards.

7. A copy of the review board's minutes is published in the company newsletter each month.[12]

The Wild Oats company gives a Moment of Truth Award, which honors staff members for performance beyond the call of duty. The award consists of a recommendation that remains in the individual's personnel file and a $10 gift certificate usable at Wild Oats Marts. Any staff member can recommend another person for this award, and the general manager gives final approval.

At the Henry Lee company rewards are given to everyone who submits a quality-related idea, regardless of whether it is implemented. In addition, the company carefully details eligibility levels for these awards, thus encouraging personnel to continue their TQM efforts and not stop after they have achieved a first-level award.[13] Table 20.5 describes how people earn points toward the various awards through the company's Shining Star Program. A close reading of the material in the table shows that some of these points are given for providing ideas and others are given for participation on quality teams. A person can earn high-tier awards in a number of ways. A Tier VI award earns the associate a $25 gift certificate at a local supermarket, a Tier VII award gives the individual a day off with pay, a Tier VIII award provides a $50 dinner certificate, and a Tier IX award entitles the individual to a one-night hotel stay worth a maximum of $150.

[12] Hodgetts, *Blueprints,* 96.

[13] Richard M. Hodgetts, *Implementing TQM in Small and Medium-Sized Organizations* (New York: AMACOM, 1996), 147–53.

These programs are all designed to keep the focus on employees and to get them involved in promoting the quality effort. They also help the organization maintain its continuous improvement effort.[14]

CONTINUOUS IMPROVEMENT

Continuous improvement is the process of increasing the quality of goods and services through incremental gains accompanied by occasional innovation.[15] Table 20.6 contrasts constant improvement with innovation. A close look at the table shows that although innovation can help bring about important changes, constant improvement is even more important because it requires a continuous emphasis on this process.[16]

Benefits and Characteristics

Entrepreneurially driven firms can achieve a number of benefits from continuous improvement. One is increased quality of output, because steady improvement in the way goods and services are delivered occurs.[17] A second is increased competitiveness, because the company is continuously getting better and thus keeping up with (or surpassing) the competition. A third is higher profitability, because increased quality brings about greater market demand and reduces costs caused by the need to correct mistakes. A fourth accompanying benefit is a lower operating break-even point, a result of lower cost per unit.

One of the ways total quality firms pursue these objectives is by "attacking themselves"—looking for ways to improve what they are doing.[18]

A good example is provided by Motorola, which reviews every quality problem in order to resolve the issue and to institutionalize the answer. Robert Galvin [the president] himself often participates in this process, taking one customer problem each day and asking his staff to trace it back to "first causes." This activity often involves multiple departments and creates what Galvin terms a *cycle of learning.* "What we learn from this experience will revise how we conduct our business, in general, with a lot of other customers," Galvin comments, "because this single problem could affect five other customers somewhere along the line."[19]

Guidelines and Principles

To achieve continuous improvement, organizations implement a number of steps. Examples include (a) keeping the workplace clean so that it is easy to find things and maintaining machinery and equipment; (b) developing procedures for getting things done quickly and correctly and following these procedures each time so that it takes less time to complete work assignments; and (c) communicating openly and honestly with other employees so that information is shared and ideas that will result in continuous improvement are known

---

[14] See Don L. Bohl et al., "Ideas That Will Shape the Future of Management Practice," *Organizational Dynamics* (summer 1996): 7–14.

[15] See Henkoff, "Keeping Motorola."

[16] See, for example, Alex Taylor III, "The New Golden Age of Autos," *Fortune,* 4 April 1994, 50–66.

[17] Louis S. Richman, "Reengineering under Fire," *Fortune,* 18 April 1994, 186.

[18] Henkoff, "Keeping Motorola."

[19] Hodgetts, *Blueprints,* 102.

TABLE 20.5 SHINING STAR PROGRAM AT THE HENRY LEE COMPANY

What is it?
A reward system for the associates of Henry Lee.

Why does Henry Lee need a reward system?
The *new* environment at Henry Lee is about positive change. Henry Lee associates that courageously embrace and contribute to the *new* environment shall be rewarded as well as associates that go above and beyond the call of duty from their everyday duties.

How does an associate participate?
There are numerous ways for an associate to participate. A list has been provided below:

Q-TIP, Q-TIP Third Place, Q-TIP Second Place, Q-TIP First Place, Q-TIP Suggestion of the Year, Leadership Training Course, *Q-TEAM, *85%+ Attendance, *Inner Q-TEAM, *Q-STAFF member, Q-STAFF member as a Facilitator, *Sub Team, Implemented Recommendations (teams only), Customer Calls or Writes about an Associate, Associate to Associate, Star of the Month, *Recording Secretary, Team Leader (Q-TEAM, Inner Q-TEAM, Sub Team), Implemented Q-TIP

*associated with TIER III

Q-TIPS

TIER I	1 lottery ticket (25 monthly) awarded along with **5 point(s)** for every complete nondupli-cated Q-TIP suggestion.
TIER II	**15 Point(s)** for implemented Q-TIPS awarded monthly along with the following cash prizes:

10 Points and $50.00 for Third Place
15 Points and $75.00 for Second Place
20 Points $125.00 and Associate of the Month parking spot for First Place
30 Points and a "Star burst" of cash for the "Suggestion of the Year"

Team Participation

TIER III	Q-Team, Inner Q-Team, and Sub team. **15 Points** to associates for 85%+ attendance and participation for every team a person contributes on. In addition, a Q-STAFF member as a facilitator. Minutes of all the meetings held by one team determine the 85%+ requirement. A copy of the completed minutes provided for the TQM Coordinator.

Implemented Recommendations

TIER IV	Certificates for all implemented recommendations presented by Q-Teams, Inner Q-Teams, and Sub teams. Certificates provided for all participants of Q-STAFF because they are the keepers of the Q-TREK system.

75 Points Q-STAFF	Certificate and "T" Shirt Annual luncheon with Ed Sternlieb
25 Points Q-Team	Certificate and "T" Shirt
15 Points Inner Q-Team	Certificate
10 Points Sub team	Certificate

to everyone. Another set of useful guidelines relates to asking the right questions so that work situations are properly analyzed and solutions can be quickly generated. These questions include the following:

Who? Who does this work? Who should be doing it? Who else can do it? Who else should do it? Who is responsible for putting together a checklist that details everything that needs to be done?

| TABLE 20.5 | SHINING STAR PROGRAM AT THE HENRY LEE COMPANY *(continued)* |

Star of the Month

TIER V   **25 Points** awarded for the associate chosen by a vote of the steering committee. Henry Lee managers nominate any one associate for star of the month based on the set criteria. The steering committee votes for one associate based on the nominations the third Wednesday of the month.

                   The Q-TREK board features the star of the month.

TIER VI   **150 Points** earns an associate a $25.00 gift certificate for Publix.

TIER VII   **200 Points** earns an associate 1 Day off per year with pay.

ELITE CLUB

TIER VIII   **300 Points** earned inducts the associate into the **ELITE CLUB.** Members receive a $50.00 certificate for dinner (no alcohol), star pin and their name listed on a certificate with the other **ELITE CLUB** members to hang on the *Shining Stars of the Henry Lee Galaxy* wall.

PRESIDENT'S CLUB

TIER IX   **400 Points** put the associate at the pinnacle of TQM. Members are treated to a coordinated 1 night Hotel stay worth a maximum $150.00 (no alcohol). Members are given a star pin and their name listed on a certificate with the other *PRESIDENT'S CLUB* members to hang on the *Shining Stars of the Henry Lee Galaxy* wall.

Q-TREK Boards

A Q-TREK board located at all Henry Lee News stations tracks the following: all Q-Teams, Inner Q-Teams, Q-Tips, and Sub teams for every department. *Finance—Operations—Sales—Merchandising—Tampa—Orlando*

The TQM Coordinator will update these boards and keep a database on all associates' points earned from program participation.

The *Shining Stars of the Henry Lee Galaxy* will be an annual program. All awards presented annually with the exception of the Star of the month and Associate of the month.

Associates can give stars to other associates for going above and beyond the call of duty. "Who's your Lucky Star?" forms are available for anything positive.

    Thank you for the hard work
    You're really appreciated around here
    That's a great idea
    Great teamwork
    Anything positive given to or received by anyone

These will be placed in the Q-TIP suggestion box or by leaving a message on the TQM's phonemail.

This program is at the sole discretion of the Henry Lee Company. The company reserves the right to change, modify or discontinue the program at any time with or without notification.

SOURCE: Courtesy of the Henry Lee Company.

What? What should be done? What is currently being done? What else should be done? What else can be done? What checklists have been created for doing all of this?

Where? Where is the work being done? Where should it be done? Where else can it be done? Where else should it be done?

When? When is the work being done? When should it be done? At what other times can it be done? At what other times should it be done? Does a time checklist exist?

TABLE 20.6   **A COMPARISON OF CONSTANT IMPROVEMENT AND INNOVATION**

	Constant Improvement	Innovation
Effect	Long term and long lasting but not dramatic	Short term and dramatic
Pace	Small steps	Large steps
Time frame	Continuous and incremental	Intermittent and nonincremental
Change	Gradual and constant	Abrupt and volatile
Involvement	Everyone in the firm	A select few "champions"
Approach	Group efforts	Rugged individuals
Mode	Maintain and improve	Scrap and rebuild
Spark	Conventional know-how	Technological state-of-the-art breakthroughs, new inventions, new theories
Practical requirements	Little investigation, great effort to maintain improvement	Large investigation, little effort to maintain improvement
Effort orientation	People	Technology
Evaluation criteria	Process and efforts for better results	Results for profit
Advantage	Works well in slow-growth economy	Works well in fast-growth economy

Why? Why does this work have to be done? Why is it being done by these employees and not others? Why it is being done here and not in a different place? Why is it being done at this time and not at another time? Why is it being done this way and not another way?

How? How is it being done? How should it be done? Can this method be used in other areas? Does any other way to do it exist? Have any checklists been developed to help answer these types of questions?

This type of questioning forces organizations to review current ways of operating and to examine other ways. In the process, companies often change the way they do things by making small, gradual improvements that result in higher-quality output.[20] (See the final Contemporary Entrepreneurship box.)

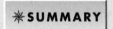 **SUMMARY**

Total quality management is a people-focused management system that aims at continuous increases in customer service at continuously lower real costs. This is typically done in three ways. One way is to find out what customers really want and then designing goods

[20] Fred Luthans, Richard M. Hodgetts, and Sang M. Lee, "New Paradigm Organizations: From Total Quality to Learning to World Class," *Organizational Dynamics* (winter 1994): 5–19.

CONTEMPORARY ENTREPRENEURSHIP

Good and Getting Better

When Betty Wagner purchased Cavalier Gage & Electronic, a small metal fabricator and printed circuit board manufacturer, she thought she had a good deal. Having worked for the company for 14 years, she knew the business and was certain that the firm would continue to prosper thanks to its long-standing relationship with IBM. For more than 40 years the giant computer maker had been Cavalier's biggest customer. Then in 1992, IBM, trying to straighten out its own business, suspended all orders to Cavalier. Most firms would have had to close their doors, but Wagner believed that the company could survive without IBM's business.

She called together the managers, opened up the company's books to show their status with IBM's business gone, and asked the managers to participate with her in developing a business plan that would save the company. The group analyzed overall operations and concluded that the firm's major strength was its production technology, including computerized machine tools and computer-aided design software. They believed they could build on this flexible manufacturing base and transform Cavalier into a contract manufacturer serving a diverse client base. They identified a fast-growing target market: small medical-equipment makers who had bright prospects but little knowledge of how to design and package parts for low-cost assembly. The employees also began to work together more closely, identifying ways to improve operations and deliver goods and services less expensively.

Thanks to these incremental refinements, the company began gaining new clients who in 1994 collectively accounted for $1 million in business. At the same time, IBM began giving the company more business, and the firm started to get back to where it was five years before. The company is continuing to develop or acquire new technologies that can help it garner additional sales. For example, Cavalier now has an energy-efficient lighting technology and is manufacturing a light-emitting-diode exit sign that it sells to commercial property owners. Slowly but surely, following a philosophy of continuous improvement, the firm is drawing back from the brink of disaster and, in the process, becoming a world-class, flexible manufacturer. It's all a matter of a company becoming increasingly better at what it does.

SOURCE: Louis S. Richman, "Reengineering under Fire," *Fortune,* 18 April 1994, 186.

and services to meet these needs. A second way is to learn how to provide this output as efficiently as possible by decreasing both time and cost. A third is to continue to enhance the process by looking for improvements.

Total quality management encompasses ten core values and concepts: (1) customer-driven quality; (2) leadership; (3) continuous improvement; (4) full participation; (5) rapid response; (6) prevention, not detection; (7) long-range outlook; (8) management by fact; (9) partnership development; and (10) public responsibility. Other steps that are critical to TQM include a formulation of the organization's vision of quality, top management support, planning and organizing the effort, and careful implementation and control of the process.

A number of widely used TQM tools and techniques exist. Some of the most useful include data collection sheets, Pareto charts, cause-and-effect diagrams, and scatter diagrams. The application of each is typically accomplished through the use of a "tool box" approach.

The primary focus of all TQM efforts is the customer. For this reason, every total quality management strategy is designed to find out what the customer wants, how well the firm is providing this output, and what the company needs to do to improve its performance and at least match, if not stay ahead, of customer expectations. Companies typically attend to three areas for this strategy: beliefs and values, data gathering, and data analysis. Other key areas of attention include *(a)* cycle time; *(b)* the training, empowering, involvement, and recognizing of employees; and *(c)* continuous improvement.

The overriding emphasis of all TQM efforts is to provide the customer with goods and services that meet (and oftentimes exceed) the customer's needs. To the extent that entrepreneurial firms accomplish this objective, they are able to maintain high profitability and survive in the face of increasing competition.

Key Terms and Concepts

Cause-and-effect diagram	Implemented improvement system (IIS)
Continuous improvement	Pareto chart
Cycle time	Pareto principle
Data collection sheets	Scatter diagram
Empowerment	Total quality management
Flow charting	

Review and Discussion Questions

1. What is meant by the term *total quality management?* How does the primary rule of total quality tie into this definition? Explain.
2. In what way do each of the ten core values and concepts of TQM help ensure that goods and services are provided in highly cost-effective ways?
3. Why is top management support critical to all TQM efforts?
4. How is a data collection sheet used in the TQM process?
5. How does a Pareto chart work, and of what value is it in the TQM process?
6. How does a cause-and-effect diagram work?
7. A company would like to know if any relationship exists between the amount of training being given to its salespeople and the effectiveness of these people out in the field. How could a scatter diagram be of any value in this investigation?
8. How does the concept of "tool box" help personnel apply TQM tools and techniques?
9. Why is a customer service focus so important to all TQM efforts?
10. How is cycle time related to quality? Why does a reduction in cycle time increase quality? Explain.
11. In what way do employee training, empowerment, involvement, and recognition help an organization maintain an employee focus during its TQM effort?
12. What is meant by continuous improvement? Why is this idea so important to every total quality management effort?

Experiential Exercise   *Knowing TQM Practices*

Entrepreneurs need to know how to apply TQM practices so that they can improve the quality of their goods and services and remain highly competitive. Below are 11 terms with which entrepreneurs should be familiar. Match each with its correct definition or description.

A. Cause-and-effect diagram
B. Continuous improvement
C. Cycle time
D. Data collection sheet
E. Empowerment
F. Flow charting
G. Implemented improvement system
H. Pareto chart
I. Pareto principle
J. Scatter diagram
K. Total quality management

_____ 1. A tool used in the TQM process to gather information on performance, so that problems can be identified and corrected.

_____ 2. A vertical bar graph often used in the TQM process to help identify which problems are to be solved and in what order.

_____ 3. A tool used in TQM to help explain the reasons for a particular problem and pinpoint some of the steps that can be taken to correct the problem.

_____ 4. A TQM tool used to illustrate and examine relationships between two variables.

_____ 5. The authority to take control and make decisions.

_____ 6. The process of increasing the quality of goods and services through small incremental gains accompanied by occasional innovation.

_____ 7. A people-focused management system that aims at continuous increases in customer service at continuously lower real costs.

_____ 8. A process in which all the steps in a job or procedure are identified and written out in the form of a flow diagram.

_____ 9. The period needed to complete a task.

_____ 10. A maxim that holds that 80 percent of all outcomes can be attributed to 20 percent of all causes.

_____ 11. A Japanese-style suggestion system that is often used by total quality management firms.

Answers

1. D	5. E	9. C
2. H	6. B	10. I
3. A	7. K	11. G
4. J	8. F	

JC Penney: Valuing Diversity

When an idealistic, young entrepreneur named James Cash Penney opened his first retail shop in Kemmerer, Wyoming, in 1902, he named his flagship store "The Golden Rule." Penney pledged that customers would find store shelves stocked with the best quality merchandise at the lowest possible prices. And just as important, customers always would be served with courtesy and respect. This precept also was extended to Penney's employees—or, as he chose to call them, associates. "If there is a secret to good management in the business of living, it lies in the partnerships we make," Penney told his employees in 1944. "Each of us needs the friendship, the companionship, the love, and the sympathy of our fellow man. In other words, we all need partners. I say partners because we believe all of our associates work together as partners and build into the principles of our business—honor, confidence, service, and cooperation."

Much has changed since Penney first conceived "The Penney Idea." Today, more than 1,200 JC Penney stores operate in the United States, Puerto Rico, and Santiago, Chile. Nearly 200,000 associates serve 98 million customers each year. But Penney's partnership philosophy is still at the cultural core of the nation's largest department store chain. Recently, it has inspired an aggressive company-wide initiative to nurture diversity. "The JC Penney company does place a tremendous value on diversity," Charles Brown, vice president and director of Penney's credit division, says. "We see it as having a direct link with our associates. There are more women in the workplace. There are more minorities in the workplace, more seniors. We see the consumer becoming more diverse. All those elements are part of our need to understand and value diversity."

The company has implemented several steps to promote employee understanding of diversity. Each associate is required to attend a one-and-a-half-day workshop—"Valuing Cultural Differences"—designed to create understanding and mutual respect among associates. In addition, JC Penney has formed two internal advisory boards: the Minority Advisory Team and the Women's Advisory Team. "We participated in the development of a diversity positioning statement, which for the first time established the company's position," Brown explains. "More important, we took that position statement and put it in the hands of every associate in the JC Penney company so they clearly understand that it's everyone's responsibility to embrace diversity within this company."

JC Penney introduces employees to the position statement with a video message by Chairman W. R. Howell. "Each of us is a one-of-a-kind combination of physical characteristics, personality, gender, race, religion, skills, and ethnic and cultural backgrounds," Howell says at the start. "This uniqueness of individuals is what we call diversity. Valuing diversity means respecting individual differences and appreciating the advantages our diversity offers."

Once the company's position was clearly on record, both advisory teams began to focus on specific ways JC Penney could be more responsive to its associate population. First, they established a mentor program to help promote women and minorities into senior management positions. "Sixty percent of the JC Penney company has almost always been women," Cathy Mills, vice president of corporate communication, explains. "It's just that they were at certain levels of the company, and the glass ceiling was very defined within our company. The goal of the advisory team is 46 percent [women] at all levels, all the way to the executive committee." The Minority Advisory Team also has launched an aggressive recruitment campaign. "As more and more minorities enter into our company, as they enter positions of decision making and achieve positions of senior management, it will have a positive, resounding impact on this company," Brown says.

Today, the early ideals of the late James Cash Penney still form the cultural core of his company. "The early partners who formulated the Penney Idea started us down this road when they said, 'We would improve constantly the human factor of our business,'" Howell told associates in his video address. "I think they knew, as we know today, that the common thread that binds our associates together is their desire to serve our customers—each person contributing his or her own special talents, so as a company we can be the best."

Questions

1. How is JC Penney exemplifying the human side of total quality management?
2. Compare the efforts of the Henry Lee Company with JC Penney's efforts.
3. Discuss continuous improvement as it applies to JC Penney.

 **CASE** **20.2**

It's All a Matter of Quality

The computer industry is very competitive, but Harry Brownell believes he has found a market niche where he can prosper. Harry's company offers troubleshooting and specialized services such as software packages specifically written to meet customer needs.

Harry has six employees besides himself: a bookkeeper who doubles as an accountant, a salesperson, three technicians, and a programmer. He hopes to add more as the firm grows, but, since he has been in operation for only four months, he does not have enough business to keep everyone busy full-time.

The company has had a number of clients. The primary ones are small businesses that have computer-related problems and need help backing up their systems. This is where the technicians play a key role, and collectively they have generated 85 percent of the firm's income. The other 15 percent comes from special programs the programmer writes. An example is a program designed to allow a client's salespeople to communicate information directly from their notebook computers to their company's minicomputer at the home office. This program has saved the client thousands of dollars and helped build Harry's firm's reputation for high-quality work.

Last week a local reporter came by to interview Harry about his fledgling enterprise. Here is part of what Harry had to say:

> The success of my business depends heavily on being client responsive. I'm just a little guy who has to compete on the basis of both price and quality. I can't ask the same price that large competitors can because I don't have a track record that shows what I can really do. So every job has to be carefully priced and then completed on time and done correctly so the customer is completely satisfied. Quality is critical in this business. It drives both price and repeat sales. If I can keep my focus on providing quality output, I believe I can grow this business by 30 percent annually for the indefinite future. It's all a matter of quality.

Questions

1. How can the ten core values and concepts of TQM be of value to Harry?
2. How can Harry ensure that he is providing the best service to his customers? Give two examples.
3. What type of TQM training should Harry provide to his people? Give two examples.

 **CASE   20.3**

Clara's Plan

Clara Weintaub owns a small restaurant chain consisting of three units located within five miles of one another. Clara's restaurants cater to family dining, and more than half the waiters and waitresses are over the age of 60. These individuals are particularly effective because most are grandparents who know how to interact well with young children and who help promote the desired family atmosphere.

In addition, Clara offers typical family dining and stays away from frills such as expensive French wines or elaborately prepared continental meals. Customers come to Clara's because of the friendly environment and the wholesome meals. She has a loyal following and is considering opening a new unit. Before doing so, however, she would like to evaluate her current operations and make any necessary changes. She would like to incorporate those ideas into her new unit.

Clara has designed a questionnaire and distributed it to her customers. In all, 290 have been returned. They show the following:

Complaint	Number of Responses
Poor quality of food	19
Small selection of food on menu	91
Slow service	122
Poor parking	27
Poor attitudes of waiters/waitresses	31

Clara intends to act on this information appropriately. In particular, she wants to use it as a basis for developing a total quality management program.

Questions

1. What steps should Clara take first if she wants to introduce a TQM approach in her organization? Identify and describe two.
2. Which two total quality management tools would you suggest she use in analyzing the data and deciding what to do? Explain how this process should be carried out.
3. What role should training play in Clara's TQM effort? Explain your reasoning.

PART 6

ENTREPRENEURIAL CASE ANALYSIS

Emge Packing Company, Inc.

In the late nineteenth century, Peter and Barbara Emge opened a small butcher shop in Fort Branch, a small southern Indiana rural community. The shop provided an adequate existence for Peter and Barbara, who had four children—Oscar, Ralph, Christina, and Alma. Oscar and his father dedicated their lives to the meat shop and built a reputation of providing high-quality meat at fair prices to the community.

In 1919, it was apparent that Emge could no longer serve the growing community with the small one-room shop. Oscar acquired a parcel of land in the town and began construction of a full slaughtering operation for beef and pork. The company was named Emge and Sons. Emge served southern Indiana through truck route distribution. A truck would be stocked early in the morning with a variety of fresh beef and pork as well as a few processed items (e.g., sausages) and would make several stops throughout the community during the day. The name *Emge* began to catch on in the southern part of the state, and the firm began to supply grocery stores and restaurant accounts. Oscar and his brother Ralph became very active in running the company as their father began to age. The company was built up slowly, always funding capital purchases with income from operations. Emge did not believe in doing business with borrowed money and therefore never incurred debt financing.

Over the next 20 years, the company continued to grow and expand its territory. The business became successful mainly from the "mom-and-pop" grocery store accounts that it had worked hard to gain the support of. In 1948, it was decided that the company could easily serve the entire state of Indiana if it had another plant in the northern part of the state. Oscar found a small operation in Anderson, Indiana, and acquired the business. It was at this time that the business became Emge Packing Company, Incorporated. Oscar became the president and CEO, while Ralph helped manage the operations. The rest of Peter and Barbara's descendants continued to work for the company in both the Fort Branch and Anderson operations. The company continued to grow which necessitated expansion and modernization of both plants. By 1960, *Emge* became a well-known name to grocers in Indiana, Illinois, Ohio, Michigan, and Kentucky. The Emge name continued to be associated with fresh, high-quality beef and pork at fair prices with good customer service. Emge's slogan, "Just Like a Family," was symbolic of the association of customers with their own family.

In 1978, Walter Emge, son of Oscar Emge, became president while his father remained CEO until 1980. Oscar Emge passed away in 1986.

Through the years, Emge continued to grow until today [1990] it employs 1,000 people at the two plants. Both plants are represented by the United Food and Commercial Workers Union. Annual sales are approximately $170 million.

Mission and Objectives

Emge's business mission is to become a major wholesale meatpacking/processing company serving the Midwest retail, hotel, and institutional market with fresh beef and pork as well as processed items such as hams, bacon, luncheon meats, sausage, and hot dogs. Emge attracts and maintains customers by offering fresh, high-quality products at low prices with excellent customer service.

SOURCE: This case was written by Michael E. Busing, College of Business, Clemson University, and is intended to be used as a basis for class discussion. All rights reserved to the author. Copyright © 1990 by Michael E. Busing. Reprinted with permission.

The objectives of the firm are as follows:

1. Protect Emge's market share in the Midwest by becoming a major force in the warehouse distribution system;
2. Begin to offer more value-added, higher-margin processed items;
3. Cut low-margin fresh pork production;
4. Purchase modern packaging equipment to increase efficiency, quality, and appearance of packaging;
5. Continue buying top quality raw materials (hogs and cattle) for operations. Pay for quality.

General Environment

Although meat and meat products shipments grew 1 percent in 1988, per capita consumption of *beef* declined 3.4 percent (*U.S. Industrial Outlook,* 1988). Poultry consumption rose due mainly to consumers' concerns about health and diet. Poultry is also cheaper per pound on average than red meat, which tends to weaken red meat sales (Standard & Poor's, 1989).

The industry itself consists of three major companies who slaughter more than 70 percent of grain-fed cattle used for steaks and roasts (*U.S. Industrial Outlook,* 1988).

More red meat producers are beginning to expand into poultry production and are closing inefficient plants.

Imports of red meat are increasing. Australia, New Zealand, Canada, and Denmark supply about 80 percent of all U.S. meat imports. Fifty-nine percent of U.S. meat imports are beef, while 31 percent are pork (*U.S. Industrial Outlook,* 1988).

At the same time, however, U.S. exports of red meat increased 23 percent in 1988. The main share of this is to Japan (Bjerklie, 1989).

Per capita poultry consumption rose from 53.2 pounds in 1977 to 82.5 pounds in 1988 (*U.S. Industrial Outlook,* 1988).

It is estimated that when adjusted for inflation, shipment of red meat grew less than 1 percent in 1989 (*U.S. Industrial Outlook,* 1989). Beef production will continue to decline, while pork production will reach a plateau. Poultry consumption per capita will be at an all-time high by the end of this year.

Long-term trends are calling for leaner meat. Research suggests that by redirecting substances in animal hormones, fat content could be decreased 50 percent (*U.S. Industrial Outlook,* 1988).

While the consumption of red meat continues to fall, it is suggested that continued profitability is achievable by introducing new products that are more value added, convenient, and nutritious (Duewer, 1989).

Industry Environment

KEY SUCCESS FACTORS IN INDUSTRY

In the meatpacking industry (beef, pork, and poultry), ultimate success of course depends on a firm's ability to offer high quality at competitive prices. However, it seems to go much beyond this.

Distribution is extremely important. Since meat is a perishable product, the customer expects products to be delivered when they need them in the store—not before, and not after. This requires a firm to establish a distribution system that is not only agreeable to each customer, but that is economical to the firm. For example, a firm in Illinois cannot profitably send a half-full truck to Ohio five days per week. However, there is a fine line of customer service and economies of scale in distribution.

Since meat products are perishable, it is impossible for firms to have extensive inventories. Therefore, it is difficult to stock up for peak periods such as Easter and Christmas (when ham demand is greatest). It is likely, then, that the firm would need somewhat greater capacity than utilized on average throughout the year for satisfying demand during these peak periods. Also, when part of the animal is being demanded at a high rate, the other, less desirable, parts must be able to be sold in the marketplace quickly (before they perish) at prices that still allow the producer to profit or at least break even. There are three or four big names such as Kahns, Eckrich, Swift, and Oscar Mayer whose marketing campaigns have gained them extensive amounts of brand loyalty. The smaller players rely on their track record for customer support. The name brand recognition is much more important in processed (packaged) items than in fresh beef and pork.

DRIVING FORCES CAUSING CHANGE IN MEAT PACKING INDUSTRY

Recently, there have been several changes occurring in the meatpacking industry that affect its structure and attractiveness. The health concerns of many

HOGS ARE GETTING LEANER

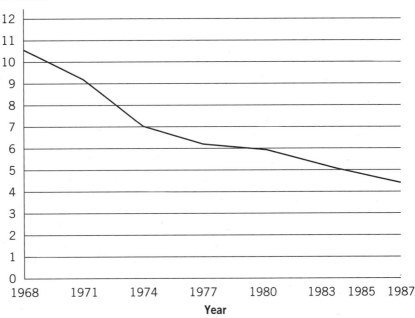

SOURCE: *Livestock Slaughter,* National Agriculture Statistics Services USDA Summary, 1988.

Americans are causing changes in the type of meat products being purchased (Duewer, 1989). The focus by many consumers has been on the amount of fat present in the various meat products. This is leading to closer trimming of beef and pork by the meat packaging plants, which, in turn, leads to fewer pounds of meat being shipped to the retailers. Hog producers are being forced to produce leaner animals (see Figure 1). Consumers are also demanding innovative ways in which the product can be prepared as well as preparations which take less time. This causes packing plants to become more consumer and product conscious.

Cost saving operations have recently been implemented in the meat industry. The major trend related to cost savings is the cutting of beef carcasses into smaller, more packagable pieces. This change to "boxed beef" has caused a shift in the way beef is leaving the packing plant (Duewer, 1989). Boxed beef refers to beef that is cut, vacuum packaged, and shipped in boxes. This trend in the industry is causing a movement away from the traditional hanging car-

casses (see Figure 2). Boxed beef reduces the overall system cost, yet increases the meat packer's costs many times as their plants are not geared toward boxed beef.

Boxed beef reduces overall cost in several ways. The labor rates are usually lower in the packing firm than in the retail stores. In addition, the equipment in the packaging plants allows faster and more efficient cutting. Because beef is boxed, transportation costs are decreased as heavy carcasses are no longer being transported because scrap and bones are removed prior to distribution. The main problem this presents to the meat packer is that margins are decreased as more actual labor is going into the product and more scrap is removed before sale (i.e., less weight actually purchased by the retailer). Therefore, meatpacking firms must find other innovative ways to command a high price for the product.

Retailers are also able to eliminate costs associated with selling all the cuts of the carcass. Because the cuts available are more customized, the retailers do not need to lower prices on the less popular items.

FIGURE 2   **TREND TOWARD BOXED BEEF**

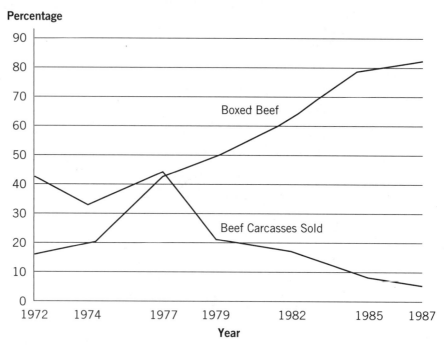

SOURCE: *National Food Review* 12 (1989).

This again presents a new challenge to the meat packer in that it must smooth demand for all the various cuts without accepting a loss due to lack of demand for certain cuts and excess demand for others.

Strong marketing innovation is very important in order to persuade retailers to carry a particular producer's brand. The trend for leaner meats which have simpler preparations must be responded to quickly by firms who wish to have their products on the shelves.

FINANCIAL CHARACTERISTICS OF PARTICIPATION IN INDUSTRY

The financial characteristics of participation in the meatpacking industry have remained fairly stable over the six years between 1983 and 1988 (see Table 1). The profit margin of meatpacking is lower than other industries in general. It is a business in which profits depend on volume.

Total industry sales have been steadily decreasing over the past five years ([1983–1987] see Figure 3). The 1988 dollar sales have increased substantially,

however. The main reason for the increase in sales dollars is due to a drought which weakened supply and bid prices up (Standard & Poor's, 1989).

Fixed assets and long-term debt have been steadily increasing over the six-year period. This would suggest that perhaps investment in newer, automated equipment is being made.

Intangibles are low relative to other industries. This indicates that a lack of research and development dollars are being invested, which is crucial for patents and trademarks.

The increase in long-term debt requires firms in the meatpacking industry to generate more revenues to meet these obligations. In an industry such as this with total sales stabilized, lowering operating cost is the best way to generate higher profit margin.

Current assets are 1.5 times current debt in the meatpacking industry. This is fairly consistent with other industry groups. Average collection time is low relative to other industries. Normally 30 days is considered good. However, this industry requires quick collection due to the narrow margins available on

TABLE 1		FINANCIAL CHARACTERISTICS OF MEATPACKING INDUSTRY				
	1983	**1984**	**1985**	**1986**	**1987**	**1988**
Assets (percentage of total assets)						
Cash and equiv.	7.9	7.3	6.0	6.8	5.5	7.3
Acct. recv.	30.6	30.3	32.0	29.9	30.9	28.2
Inventory	22.3	22.6	23.0	22.8	22.3	21.6
All other curr.	2.3	1.1	1.3	1.5	1.6	1.8
Total current	63.1	61.3	62.3	61.0	60.1	58.9
Fixed assets	29.1	29.9	29.0	31.0	31.5	32.1
Intangibles	1.0	0.6	0.7	0.7	0.8	0.7
Other n-curr.	6.7	8.2	8.0	7.3	7.6	8.3
Liabilities and Net Worth (percentage of total liabilities and net worth)						
Accounts pay.	14.3	14.1	13.5	13.5	14.1	12.9
Notes payable	14.4	14.4	17.4	14.7	14.7	15.3
Income tax pay.	0.0	0.9	0.7	0.9	0.6	0.6
All other curr.	12.7	11.8	10.3	11.1	11.3	10.6
Total current	41.4	41.2	41.9	40.2	40.7	39.4
Long-term debt	16.3	16.8	14.3	16.7	16.3	17.5
Deferred tax	0.0	0.9	0.8	1.1	0.8	0.9
Other n-curr.	1.9	1.8	3.7	2.2	3.2	1.1
Net worth	40.4	39.4	39.3	39.8	39.1	41.1
Ratios						
Profitability						
Net prof. marg.	0.7	0.7	0.9	0.7	1.0	0.9
Return on assets	5.7	5.4	6.0	6.1	7.5	5.3
Ret. on stockholder eqy.	8.8	8.4	9.3	9.5	11.6	8.2
Liquidity						
Curr. ratio	1.7	1.6	1.5	1.5	1.4	1.5
Quick ratio	0.9	0.9	0.9	0.9	0.9	0.8
Leverage						
Debt/equity	1.5	1.6	1.5	1.7	1.9	1.7
Activity						
Inv. turnover (no. of times)	35.0	29.6	32.0	31.1	40.2	33.9
Fixed assets turnover (no. of times)	23.9	20.8	26.2	22.2	24.9	18.8
Total assets turnover (no. of times)	6.8	6.2	6.9	6.6	7.2	5.6
Avg. coll. period (days)	14.5	13.9	14.2	15.1	14.5	13.7

SOURCE: *Industry Norms and Key Business Ratios,* 1988, 1989; and *RMA Annual Statement Studies,* 1989.

sales and obligations of the sellers to their suppliers and employees.

Fixed assets turnover has been decreasing over the past six years [1983–1988]. Between 1987 and 1988, the ratio decreased substantially. With higher sales dollars in 1988, it seems logical to believe that this is a result of higher increases in automation relative to sales.

FIGURE 3   **TOTAL SALES**

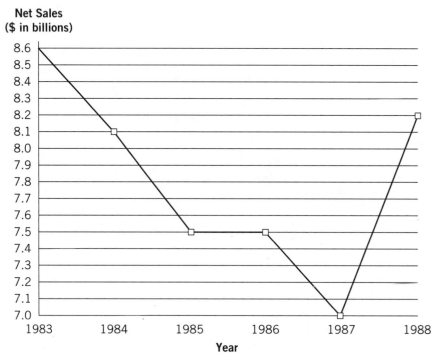

Net Sales
($ in billions)

SOURCE: *RMA Annual Statement Studies*, 1989.

Overall, no great changes are observed in the financial characteristics of the industry for the past six years. This is generally a low profit margin business with high capital requirements and a need for close control over collection of accounts receivable and manufacturing cost. Profitability is generally a function of volume.

STRATEGIC GROUP STRUCTURE OF INDUSTRY COMPETITORS

The main way in which rival firms in the meatpacking industry compete is through product line breadth and geographical market coverage (see Figure 4).

There are competitive advantages associated with being a small independent wholesaler with local market coverage as well as from being a large multinational full-line producer. Smaller, local companies have the advantage of being able to respond quickly to customer needs (Thompson, 1989). By being small and local, they are able to customize products for individual customer needs. Also, since firms covering

a national or global market are unable to provide this level of customer service, the local competitor can demand a higher price for its product.

Larger companies who compete in a broader geographic area, while having fewer customer service capabilities, enjoy the economies of scale associated with raw material quantity discounts and efficient utilization of plant and production equipment, distribution systems, and marketing efforts from which smaller firms do not benefit (Thompson, 1989).

Competitive advantages are also associated with product-line scope. Firms with broad product lines are able to divide risk of uncertain conditions adversely affecting each product over a much broader range than firms specializing in one or two products. Narrow-scope firms are able to concentrate on quality and product/process innovations for their specialized products. This allows them to respond better to specific customer needs than firms producing a wide array of products.

FIGURE 4   **STRATEGIC GROUP MAP**

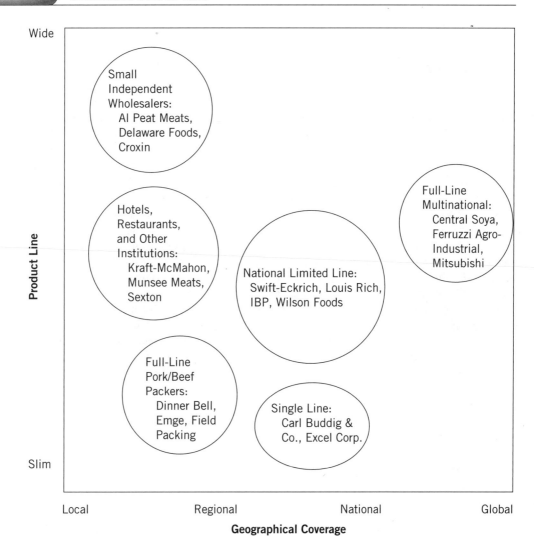

DESCRIPTION OF MAJOR COMPETITORS

The major competitors can be classified into six basic groups. These are small independent wholesalers, hotel/restaurant/institutional suppliers, regional full-line producers, national limited-line producers, single-line producers, and full-line multinationals.

Small Independent Wholesalers   Al Pete Meats, Delaware Foods, and Croxin Wholesale Meats are firms which can only serve a limited geographic market. These firms serve mainly "mom-and-pop" grocery store accounts. The main reason for success here

is their high level of customer service and high-quality, specialty product approach. "Mom-and-pop" stores are generally not able to buy in volume and therefore rely on these producers for a limited volume distribution to their business. These competitors normally do not have extensive distribution systems; therefore, customers oftentimes must actually go to the plant to receive the product.

Hotel/Restaurant/Institutional Suppliers   Kraft-McMahon, Munsee Meats, and Sexton are key firms that service restaurant accounts with portion-controlled products. These are ready-to-prepare steaks, hamburger patties, pork chops, and, oftentimes, entrees that only need to be heated before serving. The distribution system is more extensive here than with the small independents. Since portion control requires more extensive labor input, a premium price is commanded.

Full-Line Pork/Beef Producers (Regional) Dinner Bell Foods, Emge, and Field Packing are the main full-line pork/beef producers competing in the Midwest. They all provide basically the same line of products (fresh beef and pork as well as bacon, sausage, luncheon meats, and hot dogs) and compete on the basis of price and brand name recognition. Dinner Bell has a good reputation in the Ohio area for its ham and ham-related products. Emge is well known in a tristate area (Indiana, Kentucky, and Ohio), but also serves Illinois and Tennessee for fresh pork, hams, and bacon products. Field Packing is based in Kentucky, but competes with Emge and Dinner Bell in their home states.

These three firms have typically relied on grocery chains and warehouse distributors as their main customers. Emge and Dinner Bell jointly supply a majority of the meat to Scot Lad foods, a warehouse distributor in Defiance, Ohio. Marsh Supermarkets based in Yorktown, Indiana, with over 100 stores purchases more than 25 percent of their fresh beef and pork from Emge.

Limited-Line National Firms Swift-Eckrich, Louis Rich (Oscar Mayer), Iowa Beef Producers, and Wilson Foods are the name brand nationals who have broad geographic coverage throughout the United States. They are currently the innovators in product offerings. For example, Wilson Foods has recently developed a deli-type ham that is 95 percent fat-free. This boosts its brand name recognition as an innovative, high-quality producer. These firms traditionally set the industry pace.

Single-Line Nationals Carl Buddig and Excel Corporation are national firms who provide one single product line. For example, Buddig is the leader in slender-sliced luncheon meats. Excel, on the other hand, sells only fresh boxed beef and is quickly becoming a major competitor in boxed beef with its "brand name" beef (Kay, 1989).

Full-Line Multinational Mitsubishi, a Japanese firm, and Central Soya, a U.S.-based manufacturer, process hogs into a full line of consumer-ready products such as boneless pork, ham, bacon, and sausage, as well as by-products such as pharmaceutical commodities and feed ingredients. They provide top-quality products and focus on buying lean, high-quality animals. They are known to buy value and pay accordingly (Central Soya, 1989).

COMPETITIVE FORCES (PORTER)

Rivalry Rivalry in the meat packing industry is intense. Although three very large competitors hold 70 percent of the market (*U.S. Industrial Outlook,* 1989), there are many firms of approximately equal size competing for the other 30 percent. While demand is expected to increase [over the next ten years] for meat in general (Thompson, 1989), there are plenty of competitors who are competing for the business.

Demand for the product is growing very slowly. Many firms have merged in the past few years, which makes the overall group of firms smaller but stronger. The existence of the conglomerate interest in the meatpacking industry has meant lower costs for these firms and decreasing market share for the independents.

The structure of the industry as low volume-based combined with the product being perishable means that rival firms oftentimes resort to price concessions in order to gain sales. This is evidenced by Excel Corporation's supplying its products in two Midwest Kmart Stores in order to give its beef program a much-needed boost (Kay, 1989).

Customers do not have a high switching cost between suppliers because the products are not highly differentiated—pork is basically pork. Also, the processed items on the market are all basically the same. Every company in the processed luncheon meat business, for example, offers bologna, salami, and summer sausage. For all practical purposes, these products are not highly differentiated. Therefore, an incentive on the part of rival firms to induce customers to switch from one brand to another exists.

In the past, payoffs for successful strategic moves were not great in the meatpacking industry. However, there has been a recent move toward fat content reduction in raw materials that packing firms have invested a lot of money in. At the same time, automation can help reduce production costs greatly. These two moves are not easily copied. First, the genetic engineering involved in raising livestock can take years, and automation requires serious consideration because of high capital requirements.

Threat of Entry   The threat of entry is weak because of the requirement of new firms to enter on a large scale basis with state-of-the-art equipment. Combine this with a shortage of raw materials because of a small number of raw material suppliers, and a new entrant suddenly realizes a lack of capacity utilization.

Brand preference and consumer loyalty are mostly present in the packaged or branded products such as lunch meats, hot dogs, and the newly branded beef that Excel Corporation pioneered. This causes new, unknown firms to have difficulty in gaining business required for survival. The only areas in which they could be successful in gaining share quickly are in fresh, unbranded beef and pork.

The requirement of firms to enter with state-of-the-art equipment means a high capital dollar investment. In order to establish a clientele, a new firm must usually meet or beat the prices at which existing firms are offering identical products. This may involve taking a loss for a period of time until a reputation for the product itself can be built.

The main advantage available to existing firms, independent of size, is the fact that their plants and equipment are generally very old and thus were purchased at preinflation prices. Potential entrants could possibly acquire equipment of existing firms who are liquidating or modernizing their plants. However, timing is a key factor and automation is the road to a successful future.

Governmental actions actually encourage entry into the meatpacking industry. The Indiana Department of Commerce recently offered a $2.5 million grant from state taxpayers to Mitsubishi and Central Soya Corporation to place a new highly automated packing plant in Delphi, Indiana. The plant would be a major force in the United States in that it would process 3,000 hogs per day (Juday, 1989).

Substitute Products   Substitutes for meat are fish, seafood, soybean products, and certain vegetables. While seafood consumption per capita is growing, it does not represent a significant threat to the meatpacking industry.

Economic Power of Suppliers   The input, live animals, is definitely a vital part of the production process. There are other input suppliers in the meatpacking industry as well—labor, packaging suppliers, and equipment suppliers being the main players.

The live animal production is beginning to be dominated by a few large producers who are forming exclusive contracts with meat packers who are willing to invest money in genetic engineering of their feedlots. There is beginning to be more and more differentiation across supplying firms with respect to animal fat contents as well. This results in suppliers having more power over the customers.

The buying firms do represent important customers to farmers, but currently there is much more production capacity than raw material availability (Thompson, 1989). This allows suppliers the ability to command a premium price for their quality products.

The future may see a backward integration on the part of meat packers into livestock development. The big producers are investing large amounts of capital into research and development for lean animal development. The next step is to see large firms begin feedlots of their own. This is the only way to lessen the power of the suppliers.

Economic Power of Buyers   Customers in this industry are mainly grocery stores, restaurants, and other smaller restaurant/hotel/institutional suppliers. As there is a move toward central warehousing, customers become larger in size, smaller in number, and generally more powerful.

With the standardized product, brand switching is easy. However, there is a resistance to do so because of high brand loyalty on the part of the ultimate buyer, the consumer. The threat of switching can give the retail buyer a certain amount of power. Also, buyers are not locked in to just one brand at a time. It is not feasible for buyers to rely on just one producer. Competing brands can be carried simultaneously, which allows a buyer to pick and choose among the various brands, carrying only products that allow the best margin from each producer.

Sellers have been known to forward integrate, as Bob Evans did with its restaurant chain. However, this does not really affect the economic power of most buyers, because of its small scale.

In conclusion, rivalry among competing firms in the meatpacking industry is high. There is a limited amount of market share available and growth is slow. Thus, firms must work to gain share at the expense of competitors.

Entry barriers are relatively high. In order to enter, a firm must invest a great amount in plant, equipment, and promotion efforts. This often involves taking a loss until the product gains brand recognition and is able to compete at prices comparable to other brands.

Substitutes exist but are not a significant threat to meat packers.

Supplier power is increasing. This is mainly because the capacity of plants is greater than supply of hogs and cattle. This gives the supplying firm economic power to demand a higher price for its product.

Buyer power is high because buyers are generally becoming smaller in number and larger in size. Also, there are plenty of producers available to choose from and switching cost is low.

The industry is not particularly attractive because of the extent to which environmental factors affect meatpacking firms.

Conclusions about Major Problems Emge Faces from Environment   The major environmental problems that Emge faces are:

1. Trend toward chicken (poultry) consumption;
2. Warehousing distribution and buyer power;
3. Automation of major competitor firms;
4. More competitors having backing of larger conglomerate;
5. Buyouts/mergers;
6. Competitors from foreign shores.

Emge is solely in the business of providing beef and pork products. It does not have the facilities to process poultry. It would be difficult, if not impossible, for it to become well established in poultry, since there are many existing well-known brands. If the trend toward poultry continues, Emge could face serious problems in future sales.

Emge was built on its ability to serve the "mom-and-pop" grocery store and restaurant accounts. With the trend toward centralized warehousing, Emge must be able to remain competitive on the basis of price in order to compete with larger firms who have

the advantage of lower costs as a result of automation and lower labor costs.

Larger firms have been employing automation in order to gain competitive advantage through lower cost, more consistent quality of products, and increased daily production. With automation of other firms, Emge is in a position to lose its competitive edge.

The existence of a market niche which Emge may be able to serve is seriously affected by firms equal in size who have backing of a large conglomerate. The deep pockets of parent firms combined with their marketing experience pose a threat to Emge's competitive position.

Diversified food giants are taking over meatpacking firms and driving smaller companies out of business through their knowledge of marketing and preestablished distribution channels.

Japanese firms such as Mitsubishi are entering the Midwest region and competing head-to-head with smaller firms like Emge through new high technology plants that allow them lower costs and higher consistency of quality.

Emge Organization Analysis

CURRENT STRATEGY

Emge's business level strategy focuses on maintaining its current market share. It has continued to focus on the Midwest market with little effort to expand its geographic coverage. Its main competitive approach is low-cost/low-price. This is how it is able to compete with well-known national brands. Product differentiation is based mainly on customer service. Since Emge is physically closer to customers than its national brand competitors, it can respond to customer needs in a more timely manner.

Emge does not have any specific strategic plans in response to changing industry conditions and other emerging developments in the external environment, even though the management does realize the importance of the environment.

FUNCTIONAL AREA STRATEGY

Human Resources/Labor Relations   Emge realizes that automation is the key to future success. Along with the automation comes a reduction in labor force. The company is not expanding its labor base and is actually allowing it to decrease by means of attrition. This supports its overall strategy of being a low-cost producer while not causing union retaliation.

Marketing, Promotion, and Distribution Emge's strategy of serving its customer base is supported by marketing, promotion, and distribution. It is not uncommon for the firm to do custom packaging for various large accounts. For example, Emge vacuum packages hot dogs with the Marsh Supermarket "Val-U" logo.

Distribution is efficient in delivering products to the customers, mainly because the firm insists on serving only the Midwest market.

Manufacturing and Operations Emge does not invest extensively in its operations. Equipment is normally replaced when it is fully depreciated and obsolete to the point that it cannot be repaired any longer. The firm concentrates on a simple, low-cost package with a quality product inside. This has traditionally kept manufacturing costs low.

Finance Capital investment has always been financed through retained earnings from operations. Emge's financial strategy has been to build capital reserves while incurring no debt and keeping operating costs low.

Like many corporations, Emge's functional areas do not support one another. Finance and production, having a conservative approach, do not make it feasible for marketing and production to serve changing customer needs in the long run.

QUALITATIVE RESOURCES

Personnel Emge's top-level managers have a willingness for the corporation to prosper mainly because they have a personal financial interest in the company. The CEO is aging, however, and no plan for succession has been made. In fact, there is a power struggle for his position. The older generation of managers are all near retirement age and it is questionable whether or not the younger family members will be able to meet the challenges that the competitive environment of the future is expected to present. Few middle-level managers exist. This is a lean organization.

Production workers have strong union support. The union presents a barrier between the company and its employees in that management feels the union places many unnecessary restrictions on management's reign of the company.

The sales force is dedicated to the success of the company. It is apparent that they take pride in the company name and the products it produces.

Image Emge has a good image among suppliers as well as with its customers. Suppliers are always paid for raw materials on time, and Emge is willing to pay the extra price for quality products. Customers feel that they receive quality products at reasonable prices. If problems with quality arise, the company is always willing to compensate the customer.

Facilities The facilities are becoming older and there is a need for newer, more advanced technological equipment to remain competitive with other producers. Capacity utilization is nearing 100 percent for much of the plants' equipment. This could cause the company problems in serving customers' future demands.

Willingness to Compete The company's objective has been to remain conservative and not compete in areas in which it does not have a sure competitive advantage. This may have resulted in lost opportunity for gaining competitive edge many times.

As far as challenges in the future, management succession and aging plant and equipment are most prevalent.

FINANCIAL RESOURCES AND PERFORMANCE
Emge's 1988 financial performance at first glance appears to be satisfactory compared to the industry averages (see Tables 2, 3, and 4).

Assets Emge's high liquidity ratios exemplify its ability to meet its obligations to short-term creditors. Cash is a high percentage of total assets compared to the industry, which allows Emge to easily meet short-term obligations. Accounts receivable, inventory, and fixed assets are all low as a percentage of total assets. The large portion of cash assets is good in that it gives Emge protection against environmental uncertainties. High levels of cash and marketable securities can represent a lost opportunity if these could be better utilized for operations. The firm has no intangible assets.

TABLE 2	FINANCIAL CHARACTERISTICS: EMGE VERSUS INDUSTRY		

	1988	
	Industry	**Emge**
Assets (percentage of total assets)		
Cash and equiv.	7.3	14.9
Acct. Recv.	28.2	15.8
Inventory	21.6	12.2
All other curr.	1.8	36.6
Total current	58.9	79.5
Fixed assets	32.1	8.2
Intangibles	0.7	0
Other n-curr.	8.3	12.3
Liabilities and net worth **(percentage of total liabilities and net worth)**		
Accounts pay.	12.9	2.0
Notes payable	15.3	0
Income tax pay.	0.6	0.4
All other curr.	10.6	3.8
Total current	39.4	6.2
Long-term debt	17.5	0
Deferred tax	0.9	1.5
Other n-curr.	1.1	0
Net worth	41.1	92.2
Ratios		
Profitability		
Net prof. marg.	0.9	2.7
Return on assets	5.3	10.1
Ret. on s.h. eqy.	8.2	10.9
Liquidity		
Curr. ratio	1.5	12.8
Quick ratio	0.8	10.8
Leverage		
Debt/equity	1.7	0
Activity		
Inv. turnover (no. of times)	33.9	77.8
Fixed assets turnover (no. of times)	18.8	45.1
Total assets turnover (no. of times)	5.6	3.67
Avg. coll. period (days)	13.7	15.7

SOURCE: *Industry Norms and Key Business Ratios, 1988, 1989; RMA Annual Statement Studies, 1989;* and Geo. S. Olive Audited Financial Statement of Emge as of Dec. 31, 1988.

TABLE 3	EMGE PACKING COMPANY, INC.: STATEMENT OF INCOME

(YEAR ENDED DECEMBER 31, 1988)

Net sales		$175,954,700
Cost of sales		161,327,381
Gross profits		$ 14,627,319
Selling and administrative expenses		8,999,393
Operating income		$ 5,627,926
Other income		
Sale of scrap	$ 30,625	
Rental income	7,571	
Interest income	1,938,023	
Gain on sale of assets	7,707	
Increase in cash surrender value and proceeds received, net of premiums paid	49,781	
Other miscellaneous income	80	
		$ 2,033,787
Income before income taxes		$ 7,661,713
Income taxes		2,848,705
Net income		$ 4,813,008

Liabilities   Emge has no long-term liabilities. Greater than 92 percent of the liabilities and net worth are stockholders' equity. Stockholders in this corporation have great control. They are small in number (less than 100), and all of the senior-level managers are major stockholders. This forces management to have a strong commitment to the company.

Profitability   Emge's profitability level has outperformed the industry average. Its net profit margin is three times the industry average for 1988, mainly because Emge's revenues contain a large percentage of nonoperational interest income (see Table 3). Its high return on assets demonstrates that Emge is gaining more return on its investments relative to the industry. This is again due to the high amount of cash, which

earns interest at a higher rate than the industry profit margin from operations (see Table 4).

Activity   Emge has more inventory turns than does the industry. This suggests that they may not keep enough inventory on hand to adequately serve their customer base. This may result in a loss of accounts over time.

Fixed assets turnover is higher than the industry average. This shows that Emge is utilizing its plants and equipment efficiently relative to the industry as a whole. Total assets turnover, however, is low relative to the industry, because of the large percentage of total assets in cash and equivalents.

In summary, Emge has very high amounts of cash and equivalents and low investment in plant and

TABLE 4   **EMGE PACKING COMPANY, INC.: BALANCE SHEET AT DECEMBER 31, 1988**

Assets

Current assets

Cash and cash equivalents	$ 7,118,754	
Investments at cost (approximates market)	16,846,843	
Accounts receivable	7,572,636	
Inventory	5,822,309	
Deferred income tax benefit	356,964	
Prepaid expenses	327,029	
Total current assets		$38,044,535

Property and equipment

Land	$ 555,323	
Buildings	3,686,186	
Machinery and equipment	5,116,665	
	9,358,174	
Less accumulated depreciation	5,456,343	$ 3,901,831

Other assets

Cash surrender value of life insurance	$ 893,777	
Trust account	1,254,913	
Investments at cost	1,946,312	
Prepaid pension	1,811,332	
		$ 5,906,334
		$47,852,700

Liabilities and Stockholders' Equity

Current liabilities

Accounts payable	$ 970,678	
Salaries and wages	1,086,001	
Accrued expenses	687,879	
Federal and state income taxes	185,815	
Deferred farm income	50,000	
Total current liabilities		$ 2,980,373
Deferred income taxes		$ 734,876

Stockholders' equity

Common stock: no par value

Authorized: 50,000 shares

Issues and outstanding: 10,003 shares	$ 1,914,200	
Additional paid-in capital	44,353	
Retained earnings	42,178,898	
		$44,137,451
		$47,852,700

equipment. The cash surplus of the firm could probably be better utilized.

COMPETITIVE POSITION

Emge's short-term competitive position seems strong in the Midwest as it is the only full-line meat packer in the state of Indiana and competes very well in this market on the basis of price and customer service.

The long-term competitive position may be hindered by such environmental changes as the decreasing per capita consumption of beef and pork. Rival firm conglomerate financial backing as well as the internal challenges the firm is confronted with in areas of strategic direction, managerial succession, and facilities present problems. Emge's financial resources may assist its future competitive efforts only if management is willing to make the commitment.

Problems as a Result of Resources and Past Strategy

Emge's main problems are a result of not using resources to prepare for future competitiveness and a strategy which doesn't develop the company for long-term survival. The strategy combined with Emge's limited resources has posed the following problems:

1. Plant and equipment are not consistent with industry norms. The conservative strategy of management has neglected to implement new technology necessary for competing with a new industry of high automation. For example, Emge's plants are more compatible with hanging beef, which has been replaced by boxed beef.
2. Emge has not invested R&D dollars into consumer health concerns which are changing demand patterns for meat. For example, many beef and pork producers are investing in poultry plants. Emge has made the same products for years. It has not moved forward with lowering fat contents of processed items in order to address health concerns.
3. Managerial succession problems are inevitable. Emge has not planned for replacement of the current chief executive. The power struggle suggests that any family member who takes over this position will be challenged in gaining

control and following of other managers. This will affect the direction of the firm and its ability to move forward or even hold its own in the market. Internal problems will surely cause Emge to lose sight of the environment.
4. Emge is sure to find its competitive future challenging with the decrease of independent firms and the increase of large conglomerate and international parent company financial backing. This will no doubt give competitors cost as well as distribution advantages which Emge does not have.
5. With respect to the strategic structure of the industry (Figure 4), Emge is more or less caught in the middle. It is not able to concentrate as well on customer service as are small firms, but also doesn't enjoy the economies of scale which larger national and multinational firms experience.

Date: Saturday, March 31, 1990
Time: 9:00 A.M. (C.S.T.)
Event: 44th Annual Meeting of Stockholders

The directors of the corporation of Emge Packing Company gathered at the Fort Branch, Indiana, office for what was planned to be an average, unexciting annual meeting. This was unfortunately not the case. This year, many more non-management shareholders were present for the meeting and were ready with questions for the board of directors.

Specifically, they were very concerned that the net income after taxes fell from nearly $5.5 million in 1988 to just over $2 million in 1989. Also, of concern was that for the first time in many years, the operating portion of income was negative. This sent a red flag to many stockholders that their investment was at great risk.

Walter Emge, the CEO, seemed to be the target of much criticism. One of the founder's grandchildren was very much against Mr. Emge and let it be known that she does not believe he has any notion of a long- or short-term strategic plan for Emge. A very hectic, out of control meeting with many personal insults followed. The stockholders were concerned that their investments would be lost if the firm continued in the direction it was headed. They additionally felt that Mr. Emge did not have confidence in the Emge family managers. It was pointed out that the industry is becoming increasingly more difficult to compete in as more months go by.

Many stockholders are becoming money hungry and have a great desire to liquidate the stock of the company—either by sale of the company to an outside investor or by a discontinuation of operations. They feel strongly that Emge's current dividend policy is much too conservative. Mr. Emge as well as other board members do not wish to see this happen on the basis that they feel an obligation to the employees of the company for as long as the firm can turn a profit. Walter also feels an obligation on behalf of his deceased father to carry on the family business.

Walter, now 67 years old, sat in his chair at the head table looking very grim and fatigued. It was obvious that he knew something had to be done— but what?

EMGE'S PROBLEM

Properly determining the root cause of business problems is the key to the success of proper strategy formulation and implementation (McNichols, 1983).

Emge has one main problem caused by two factors. One is industry environment changes and the other is Emge resources and past strategy.

ENVIRONMENT

Automation of Major Competitor Firms In this relatively mature industry there are many firms leaving the business of meatpacking/processing. The firms who choose to remain and compete have found it necessary to emphasize automation on the production floor—as well as in procurement of live animal raw material.

More Competitors Receiving Backing from Large Conglomerate Firms The expense of automation has caused most remaining firms to seek financial backing as well as distribution channels from the deep pocketed conglomerate companies.

Foreign Competition Foreign companies, especially the Japanese, have found the U.S. market attractive and have decided to enter the meat packing industry. The foreign firms generally have substantial financial resources as well as technological know-how. This has provided them lower costs as well as a higher consistency of quality. In short, foreign competition is presenting firms such as Emge with competitive pressures.

Poultry Consumption Trend The consumer trend toward leaner meats—especially poultry—could cause Emge serious problems, since it currently focuses on beef and pork exclusively and current production facilities cannot be easily adapted for poultry processing. Also, the problem of government inspection arises as it may be difficult, if not impossible, to persuade the U.S.D.A. to grant inspection for poultry as well as for beef and pork in the same facility.

PROBLEMS AS A RESULT OF EMGE RESOURCES AND PAST STRATEGY

Outdated Plant and Equipment The plant and equipment at both the Fort Branch and Anderson plants are not consistent with industry norms. The conservative strategy of current management has neglected to allow for implementation of new technology necessary for competing in an industry of highly automated production.

R&D Investment Emge has not directed R&D dollars toward consumer health concerns, which are changing demand patterns for meat. For example, many beef and pork producers are investing in poultry plants. Emge has been producing the same line of products for years. They have not moved forward by investing in procurement of leaner animals and thereby lowering fat contents of processed items. Actions such as this will address consumers' health concerns.

Managerial Succession Managerial succession problems are inevitable. Emge has not planned for replacement of the chief executive. The power struggle that exists would suggest that any family member taking over will be challenged in gaining control and following of other managers.

MAIN PROBLEM RESULTING FOR EMGE

Emge's main problem is that they are simply not able to compete effectively in today's market. This is a result of management's conservative nature and lack of response to the environment in a timely manner. A factor out of Emge's direct control is the conglomerate backing and foreign competitor entry. Emge is a small force in a relatively overcrowded, mature industry.

The future does not look bright for Emge. Many of its problems are not a result of the environment, but rather internal in origin. Nonmanagement stockholders want larger dividends—perhaps even liquidation of the cash surplus. Management, on the other hand, is divided as to what should be the fate of the company and the strategic plan necessary to carry the corporation to this goal.

STRATEGIC ALTERNATIVES

Emge can take one of two routes in making a strategy decision.

1. Exit: Hofer (1978) addresses appropriate strategies for firms with weak competitive position in mature or saturated markets. It is pointed out that even when bankruptcy is not imminent, exiting may be a viable alternative.

    Emge would discontinue operations in the meatpacking business. This can be carried out in one of two ways.

    a) Liquidation of cash and other assets after locating an existing packing firm to purchase plants, equipment, Emge trademark, etc.

    b) Liquidate completely; discontinue operations. This involves selling the plants and equipment in a piecemeal fashion as quickly as possible, as they would become a liability under this plan.

2. Option to Stay in Business: One common approach to formulating strategy is to seek competitive advantage in the form of cost leadership or differentiation (Stringer, 1986). If Emge is to stay in business, an appropriate strategy would need to facilitate achievement of these advantages. The extent to which Emge would be able to gain a competitive advantage is directly related to its financial constraints (Hamermesh, 1986).

    Emge could restructure and continue operations in the meatpacking industry. They could follow one of two alternate plans.

    a) Modernize current operations with highly automated computer-integrated equipment.

    Recently, Hatfield, a regional meat processor, invested $19 million in modernization of its plant (Murphy, 1989). Emge could duplicate this automation effort for approximately the same cost. Cash surplus from past operations can be used to fund this project. This may include any combination of the following:

    (1) Build highly automated plant at a location found to be strategically advantageous with respect to raw materials procurement, distribution, labor rates, tax rates, etc.

    (2) Close Fort Branch plant, Anderson plant, or both.

    (3) Refurbish Fort Branch plant, Anderson plant, or both, adding state-of-the-art computer-integrated equipment.

    b) Pay out as dividend to shareholders cash and other assets not needed for day-to-day operations (approximately $19 million). If current/future management can operate successfully without interest income from these nonoperating assets, then continue operations.

    The option to stay in business would require restructuring in order to combat problems of managerial succession and to reduce fixed overhead expenses resulting from the current high degree of labor intensity.

Bibliography

Bjerklie, Steve, "Technology: Solutions from Problems," *Meat & Poultry* 35 (September 1989), 19.

Central Soya, "Central Soya Selects Delphi, Indiana, for Pork Processing Plant," News Release, September 20, 1989.

Duewer, Lawrence A., "Changes in the Beef and Pork Industries," *National Food Review* 12 (1989), 5–9.

Emge Packing Company, Inc., Audited Financial Statements, December 31, 1988.

Galbraith, Jay R., and Daniel Nathanson, *Strategy Implementation: The Role of Structure and Process,* West: St. Paul (1978), 19–25.

Hamermesh, Richard G., *Making Strategy Work,* Wiley: New York (1986), 57–63.

Hofer, Charles W., and Dan Schendel, *Strategy Formulation: Analytical Concepts,* West: St. Paul (1978), 104–106.

Industry Norms and Key Business Ratios, New York: Dun & Bradstreet (1989), 36.

Juday, Paul, "Really Necessary?" *Anderson Herald Bulletin,* 121, November 22, 1989, Editorial.

Kay, Steve, "Big 3 Plans," *Meat & Poultry* 35 (September 1989), 16.

Livestock Slaughter, National Agriculture Statistics Services, U.S.D.A. Annual Summary, 1988.

McNichols, Thomas J., *Executive Policy and Strategic Planning,* McGraw-Hill: New York (1977), 74–78.

———, *Executive Policy and Strategic Planning,* McGraw-Hill: New York (1983), 90–95.

Murphy, Dan, "Phenomenal Family, Futuristic Facility," *Meat Processing* 28 (June 1989), 28–34.

Pearce, John A., and Richard B. Robinson, *Strategic Management,* Irwin: Homewood (1982), 240–253.

RMA Annual Statement Studies, Philadelphia: Robert Morris Associates (1989), 76.

Standard & Poor's *Industry Surveys,* New York: Standard & Poor's Corp., February 2, 1989, 15–21.

Stringer, Robert A., *Strategy Traps,* Lexington Books: Lexington (1986), 25–28.

Thompson, Kevin, "Business: It Could Be a Joy Ride," *Meat & Poultry* 35 (September 1989), 14–16.

U.S. Industrial Outlook, Washington, DC: U.S. Department of Commerce (1988), 39: 1–5.

U.S. Industrial Outlook, Washington, DC: U.S. Department of Commerce (1989), 40: 1–5.

PART 6

EXERCISE

Surveying Family Business Values

Using the following questionnaire, interview the owner of a family business to determine some of the owner's key values. The questions are designed to gather information quickly on two distinct subjects— the goals of the business and factors for business success. However, you are encouraged to gather additional interesting information about the family business.

I. Goals for the Business
    A. Rank and compare your preference for business performance measures (1 = highest, 8 = lowest).
        _____ Market share
        _____ Sales growth rate
        _____ Return on sales now
        _____ Return on assets now
        _____ Return on sales in 5 years
        _____ Return on assets in 5 years
        _____ Profit stability/consistency
        _____ Reputation for excellence in your industry
    B. What do you believe to be appropriate goals for your company? (Mention the goals of the family as well as the goals of the business.)

II. Factors for Business Success
    A. Which is the greater strategic threat to a healthy, successful business?
        _____ Deviation from what made it successful in the past
        _____ Inability to adapt to new opportunities as they occur
    B. Which of the following do you consider to be the critical threat or threats to the future of your business? (Check no more than three.)
        _____ New competition
        _____ Aggressiveness of current competition
        _____ Declining market(s)
        _____ Labor demands

_____ Changing end-user desires (final customers)
_____ Changing immediate customer desires (immediate customers)
_____ Aging assets
_____ Inadequate cash flow
_____ Declining product/service quality

    C. Rank the following management tools according to their importance to your business (1 = most, 10 = least).
        _____ Forecasting
        _____ Market research
        _____ Variable budgets
        _____ Standardized costs
        _____ Computer simulation
        _____ Financial analysis
        _____ Discounted cash flows
        _____ Materials requirement plan
        _____ Inventory order models
        _____ Capital budgeting
    D. Rank the following key areas according to their importance for success in your business (1 = most, 8 = least).
        _____ Production
        _____ Purchasing
        _____ Marketing
        _____ Distribution
        _____ Research and development
        _____ Engineering
        _____ Organization
        _____ Finance
    E. Rank the following according to their importance for business success (1 = most, 6 = least).
        _____ Attention to detail
        _____ Consistent execution
        _____ Creative thinking
        _____ Aggressive decision making
        _____ Experimentation
        _____ Happy employees

F. Score the following statements as to how much you agree or disagree with them (10 = agree completely, 1 = disagree completely).

_____ Growth in sales would solve most of our profit goals.

_____ Our costs are mostly fixed costs.

_____ Marginal pricing (by variable cost) is necessary.

_____ Prices should be based on competition.

_____ Prices should be based on desired profit margin.

_____ Our market is not very price sensitive.

_____ We should spend more money on competitive and market research.

_____ Our hourly workers are satisfied with their jobs.

_____ We have plenty of plant capacity for growth.

_____ Our people are productive.

_____ Our competition will react quickly to any changes we make.

_____ We should spend more money and time learning our true product and/or process costs.

_____ The physical appearance of our administrative offices is very important.

_____ Our people want employment and personal security more than take-home pay.

_____ Increasing our product line increases our average costs significantly.

_____ Salespeople are mostly motivated by money.

GLOSSARY

The following are key terms and concepts that have been used in this book. In some cases, the description or definition has been expanded to provide information in addition to that presented in the text.

Abandonment Nonuse of a trademark for two consecutive years without justification or a statement regarding abandonment of the trademark.

Accounts receivable financing Short-term financing that involves either the pledge of receivables as collateral for a loan or the outright sale of receivables. (Also see **Factoring.**)

Accredited purchaser A category used in Regulation D that includes institutional investors; any person who buys at least $150,000 of the offered security and whose net worth is in excess of $1 million; a person whose individual income was greater than $200,000 in each of the last two years; directors, partners, or executive officers selling securities; and certain tax-exempt organizations with more than $500,000 in assets.

Active partner A person who is active in the business. This person may also be an ostensible partner. (Also see **Ostensible partner.**)

Adaptive firm A venture that remains adaptive and innovative both through and beyond the growth stage.

Adjusted tangible book value A common method of valuing a business by computing its net worth as the difference between total assets and total liabilities.

Adjustment of debts Under Chapter 13 of the Bankruptcy Act, individuals are allowed to avoid a declaration of bankruptcy, have the opportunity to pay their debts in installments, and are protected by the federal court. (Also see **Bankruptcy Act.**)

Administrative culture A culture typified by the presence of such characteristics as a hierarchical management structure, ownership of enterprise resources, a competitive commitment of resources, and a long-run time perspective. (Also see **Entrepreneurial culture.**)

Advisory board A board of professionals established to enhance a venture's growth.

Amoral management Management is neither moral nor immoral, but decisions lie outside the sphere to which moral judgments apply.

Angel financing Investments in new ventures that come from wealthy individuals referred to as "business angels."

Appositional relationship A relationship among things and people existing in the world in relation to other things and other people.

Background or knowledge accumulation The first step in the creative thinking process, which involves investigation and information gathering related to the matter under analysis.

Balance sheet A financial statement that reports the assets, liabilities, and owners' equity in the venture at a particular point in time.

Balance sheet equation A basic accounting equation that states that assets equal liabilities plus owners' equity.

Bankruptcy Act Federal law that provides for specific procedures in handling insolvent debtors.

Barriers to entry Elements restricting an emerging industry, such as proprietary technology, access to distribution channels, access to raw materials and other inputs, cost disadvantages due to lack of experience, and risk.

Better widget strategy Innovation that encompasses new or existing markets.

Book value The value of a business determined by subtracting total liabilities (adjusted for intangible assets) from total assets.

Bootlegging Secretly working on new ideas on company time as well as on personal time.

Break-even analysis A technique commonly used to assess expected product profitability, which helps to determine how many units must be sold in order to break even at a particular selling price.

Break-even point The point at which the company neither makes nor loses money on a particular project. The formula for computing this point (in units) is Fixed Cost/Selling Price per Unit − Variable Cost per Unit.

Budget A statement of estimated income and expenses over a specified period of time.

Business assets The tangible (physical) and intangible (e.g., reputed) assets of the business.

Business description segment That segment of a business plan that provides a general description of the venture, industry background, company history or background, goals, potential of the venture, and uniqueness of the product or service.

Business environment The local environment for business that should be analyzed to establish the potential of the venture in its present location.

Business incubator A facility with adaptable space that small businesses can lease on flexible terms and at reduced rent.

Business plan The written document that details a proposed venture. It must illustrate current status, expected needs, and projected results of the new business.

Business valuation The calculated value of the business, used to track its increases or decreases.

Buy/sell agreement An agreement designed to handle situations in which one or more of the entrepreneurs wants to sell their interest in the venture.

Calculated risk taking Occurs when successful entrepreneurs carefully think out a venture and do everything possible to get the odds in their favor.

Cancellation proceedings A third party's challenge to the trademark's distinctiveness within five years of its issuance.

Capital budgeting A budgeting process used to determine investment decisions. It relies heavily on an evaluation of cash inflows.

Career risk Whether or not an entrepreneur will be able to find a job or go back to an old job if his or her venture fails.

Cash-flow budget A budget that provides an overview of inflows and outflows of cash during a specified period of time.

Cash-flow leveraged buyout (LBO) Type of buyout that relies heavily on the target company's cash receipts with indicators of that positive cash flow continuing.

Cash-flow statement A financial statement that sets forth the amount and timing of actual and/or expected cash inflows and outflows.

Cause-and-effect diagram A tool used in total quality management to help explain the reasons for a particular problem and pinpoint some of the steps that can be taken to correct the problem.

Champion A person with a vision and the ability to share it.

Claims A series of short paragraphs, each of which identifies a particular feature or combination of features, protected by a patent.

Cleaning-out procedure The failure of a trademark owner to file an affidavit stating that it is in use or justifying its lack of use within six years of registration.

Close corporation A corporation in which all shares of stock are held by one person or a small group of persons and in which purchase of the stock is not available to the general public.

Code of conduct A statement of ethical practices or guidelines to which an enterprise adheres.

Collective entrepreneurship Individual skills integrated into a group wherein the collective capacity to innovate becomes something greater than the sum of its parts.

Common stock The most basic form of ownership, usually carrying the right to vote for the board of directors.

Community demographics Determines the composition or makeup of consumers who live within a community.

Competitive analysis The quality and quantity of the competition, which needs to be carefully scrutinized by the entrepreneur.

Comprehensive feasibility approach A systematic analysis incorporating external factors.

Consumer-driven philosophy A marketing philosophy that relies on research to discover consumer preferences, desires, and needs before production actually begins. (See also **Product-driven philosophy** and **Sales-driven philosophy.**)

Continuous improvement The process of increasing the quality of goods and services through small incremental gains accompanied by occasional innovation.

Contribution margin approach A common approach to break-even analysis, determined by calculating the difference between the selling price and the variable cost per unit.

Convenience goods Goods that consumers want but are not willing to spend time shopping for.

Convertible debentures Unsecured loans that can be converted into stock.

Copyright A legal protection that provides exclusive rights to creative individuals for the protection of their literary or artistic productions.

Corporate entrepreneurship A new "corporate revolution" taking place due to the infusion of entrepreneurial thinking into bureaucratic structures.

Corporation An entity legally separate from the individuals who own it, created by the authority of state laws and usually formed when a transfer of money or property by prospective shareholders takes place in exchange for capital stock in the corporation.

Corridor principle States that with every venture launched, new and unintended opportunities arise.

Creative process The four phases of creative development: background or knowledge accumulation, incubation process, idea experience, and evaluation or implementation.

Creativity The generation of ideas that results in an improvement in the efficiency or effectiveness of a system.

Critical factors Important new-venture assessments.

Critical risks segment The segment of the business plan that discusses potential problems, obstacles and risks, and alternative courses of action.

Customer availability Having customers available before the venture starts.

Cycle time The time needed to complete a task.

Dark side of entrepreneurship A destructive side existing within the energetic drive of successful entrepreneurs.

Data collection sheets Sheets used in the TQM process to gather information on performance so that problems can be identified and corrected.

Debt financing Borrowing money for short- or long-term periods for working capital or for purchasing property and equipment.

Debtor-in-possession When a debtor involved in a Chapter 11 proceeding continues to operate the business.

Decision support system (DSS) An information system used to provide management with data critical to decision making.

Decline The fifth stage of a new venture's life cycle, typified by a dramatic drop-off in revenues and an eventual termination of operations. It can be avoided if the entrepreneur is able to innovate and keep sales growing. (See also **Innovation.**)

Delayed entry strategy Entering the workforce at a later date.

Delegating Having trained people complete tasks for entrepreneurs to help them save time.

Deservedness The strength of the relationship between the perceived deservedness and the community's identification with the new venture.

Design patent Gives the owner exclusive rights to hold, transfer, and/or license the production and sale of the product or process for 14 years.

Direct foreign investment A domestically controlled foreign production facility.

Discounted earnings method A method that determines the true value of the firm with a pricing formula that includes earning power as well as adjusted tangible book value.

Displacement school of thought A school of entrepreneurial thought that focuses on group phenomena such as the political, cultural, and economic environments.

Diversified marketing A marketing stage during which the organization focuses on decentralizing operations by examining individual product life cycles and developing portfolio management approaches to product lines.

Domestic corporation A corporation doing business in the state in which it has been incorporated.

Domestic international sales corporation (DISC) A legal entity that provides special tax benefits for firms engaged in exporting, created by Congress to combat an increasingly unfavorable trade balance.

Dormant partner A person who is inactive in the firm and is not known or held out to be a partner.

Drive to achieve A strong desire to compete, to excel against self-imposed standards, and to pursue and attain challenging goals.

Duplication A basic type of innovation involving the replication of an already existing product, service, or process.

Early entry strategy The younger generation entering the workforce.

Economic base The base that includes the nature of employment (which influences the size and distribution of income) and the purchasing trends of consumers in the area.

Effective delegation Assignment of specific duties, granting authority to carry out these duties, and creating the obligation of responsibility for necessary action.

Emotional bias The tendency to believe an enterprise is worth a great deal more than outsiders believe it is worth.

Employee stock ownership plan (ESOP) Passing control of the enterprise to the employees if the owner has no immediate successor in mind.

Empowerment The authority to take control and make decisions.

Entrepreneur An innovator or developer who recognizes and seizes opportunities; converts these opportunities into workable/marketable ideas; adds value through time, effort, money, or skills; assumes the risks of the competitive marketplace to implement these ideas; and realizes the rewards from these efforts.

Entrepreneurial behavior An entrepreneur's decision to initiate the new-venture formation process.

Entrepreneurial culture A culture typified by the presence of characteristics such as a flat management structure with multiple informal networks, episodic use or rent of required resources, a long-run time perspective, and a strategic orientation driven by perception of opportunity. (Also see **Administrative culture.**)

Entrepreneurial economy A new emphasis on entrepreneurial thinking that developed in the 1980s.

Entrepreneurial events approach The process of entrepreneurial activity including such factors as initiative, organization, administration, relative autonomy, risk taking, and environment.

Entrepreneurial leveraged buyout (E-LBO) Having at least two-thirds of the purchase price generated from borrowed funds; more than 50 percent of the stock after acquisition owned by a single individual or his or her family; and the majority investor devoted to the active management of the company after acquisition.

Entrepreneurial management The theme or discipline that suggests entrepreneurship is based on the same principles, whether the entrepreneur is an exist-

ing large institution or an individual starting his or her new venture single-handedly.

Entrepreneurial marketing A marketing stage in which the enterprise attempts to develop credibility in the marketplace by establishing a market niche.

Entrepreneurial motivation The willingness of an entrepreneur to sustain his or her entrepreneurial behavior.

Entrepreneurial perspective All the characteristics and elements that comprise the entrepreneurial potential in every individual.

Entrepreneurial stress A function of discrepancies between one's expectations and one's ability to meet those demands.

Entrepreneurial successor A successor to a venture who is highly gifted with ingenuity, creativity, and drive.

Entrepreneurial trait school of thought A school of entrepreneurial thought that focuses on identifying traits that appear common to successful entrepreneurs.

Entrepreneurial ways A strategy that allows new ideas to flourish in an innovative environment.

Entrepreneurship The process of organizing, managing, and assuming the risks of a business.

Environmental assessment Entails evaluating the general economic environment, the government-regulating environment, and the industry.

Environmental awareness A reawakening of the need to preserve and protect our natural resources.

Environmental school of thought A school of entrepreneurial thought that focuses on the external factors and forces—values, mores, and institutions—that surround a potential entrepreneur's lifestyle.

Equal Access to Justice Act Federal law that provides greater equity between small business and regulatory bodies. It states, among other things, that if a small business challenges a regulatory agency and wins, then the agency must pay the legal costs of the small business.

Equity financing The sale of some ownership in a venture in order to gain capital for start-up.

Ethics A set of principles prescribing a behavioral code that explains what is good and right or bad and wrong.

European Union (EU) A dramatic international development intended to create a single market in Europe by removing barriers to the free movement of goods, people, and capital.

Evaluation and implementation The fourth step in the creative thinking process, during which the individual makes adjustments in the approach so that it more closely approximates the necessary solution.

Excess earnings A method of determining a firm's intangible assets. It is a method of last resort that does not include intangibles with estimated useful lives such as patents and copyrights.

Experimentation A form of research that concentrates on investigating cause-and-effect relationships.

Export/Import Bank (Eximbank) Governmental agency that offers direct loans for large-project and equipment sales that require long-term financing. It also offers credit guarantees to commercial banks that finance export sales.

Export management company A firm that serves as an export department for a manufacturer by soliciting business and exporting the product(s) for the client in return for a commission, salary, or retainer plus commission.

Exporting Participating actively in the international arena as a seller rather than a buyer.

Extension A basic type of innovation that involves extending the life of a product, service, or process already in existence.

External locus of control A point of view in which external processes are sometimes beyond the control of the individual entrepreneur.

External optimism Ceaseless optimism emanating from entrepreneurs as a key factor in the drive toward success.

External resources Resources outside the venture.

Factoring The sale of accounts receivable.

Fair-use doctrine An exception to copyright protection that allows limited use of copyrighted materials.

Feasibility criteria approach A criteria selection list from which entrepreneurs can gain insights into the viability of their venture.

Finance company Asset-based lender that lends money against assets such as receivables, inventory, and equipment.

Financial/capital school of thought A school of entrepreneurial thought that focuses on the ways entrepreneurs seek seed capital and growth funds.

Financial risk The money or resources at stake for a new venture.

Financial segment The segment of the business plan that discusses the financial forecast, the sources and uses of funds, budgeting plans, and stages of financing.

Five-minute reading A six-step process venture capitalists use when they are reviewing a business plan for potential investment.

Fixed cost One that does not change in response to changes in activity for a given period of time.

Flow charting A process in which all the steps in a job or process are identified and written out in the form of a flow diagram.

Forcing events Happenings that cause the replacement of the owner-manager.

Foreign corporation A corporation doing business in a state other than the one in which it is incorporated.

Foreign economic trends Publications that provide information on current business conditions in foreign countries: current and near-term prospects, gross national product, foreign trade, wage and price indexes, unemployment rates, and construction starts.

Foreign sales corporation (FSC) An entity, created by the domestic international sales corporation legislation to encourage exports, that receives tax-exempt treatment on a portion of its export income.

Franchise Any arrangement in which the owner of a trademark, tradename, or copyright has licensed others to use it to sell goods or services.

Free Trade Agreement (FTA) Global economic development that has provided new potential environments within which entrepreneurs could prosper.

Freight forwarder An independent business that handles export shipments in return for compensation.

Functional perspective Viewing things and people in terms of how they can be used to satisfy one's needs and to help complete a project.

Funding gap A barrier women entrepreneurs experience when beginning a venture and are frustrated in an attempt to secure initial financing.

General Agreement on Tariffs and Trade (GATT) A major trade liberalization organization whose objectives are to create a basic set of rules under which trade negotiations take place.

General partner A person who is active in the business, is known to be a partner, and has unlimited liability.

Generic meaning Allowance of a trademark to represent a general grouping of products or services (i.e., Kleenex has come to represent tissue).

Growth stage The third stage of a new-venture life cycle, typically involving activities related to reformulating strategy in the light of competition.

Growth wall A psychological wall against changes that prevents entrepreneurs from developing a managerial ability to deal with venture growth.

Harvest strategy Family-business entrepreneurs' decision to sell the venture.

High-growth venture When sales and profit growth are expected to be significant enough to attract venture capital money and/or funds raised through public or private placements.

Idea experience The third step in the creative thinking process, during which the individual discovers the answers he or she has been pursuing.

Immersion in business When the successful entrepreneur devotes all of his or her time to the business rather than taking some time for leisure activities.

Immoral management Management decisions imply a positive and active opposition to what is ethical.

Implemented improvement system (IIS) A Japanese-style suggestion system that is often used by total quality management firms.

Importing Buying and shipping foreign-produced goods for domestic consumption.

Income statement A financial document that reports the sales, expenses, and profits of the enterprise over a specified period, usually one year.

Incongruities Whenever a gap or difference exists between expectations and reality.

Incremental innovation The systematic evolution of a product or service into newer or larger markets.

Incubation process The second step in the creative thinking process during which one's subconscious is allowed to mull over the information gathered during the preparation phase.

Informal risk capitalists Wealthy people who invest capital in public and private placements but are considered professional venture capitalists.

Initial public offering (IPO) A corporation's raising capital through the sale of securities on the public markets.

Innovation The process by which entrepreneurs convert opportunities into marketable ideas.

Interactive learning Learning ideas within an innovative environment that cuts across traditional, functional lines in the organization.

Internal locus of control The viewpoint in which the potential entrepreneur has the ability or control to direct or adjust the outcome of each major influence.

Internal rate of return A capital-budgeting technique that involves discounting future cash flows to the present at a rate that makes the net present value of the project equal to zero.

Interrole conflict A work/home role conflict arising from the incompatibility of pressures from the entrepreneurial role and the homemaker role.

Intracapital Special capital set aside for the corporate entrepreneur to use whenever investment money is needed for further research ideas.

Intrapreneurship Entrepreneurial activities that receive organizational sanction and resource commitments for the purpose of innovative results.

Invention A basic type of innovation that involves the creation of a new product, service, or process that is often novel or untried.

Joint venture An organization owned by more than one company—a popular approach to doing business overseas.

Lack of expertise/skills When small-business managers lack the specialized expertise/skills necessary for the planning process.

Lack of knowledge Small-firm owners/managers' uncertainty about the components of the planning process and their sequence due to minimal exposure to, and knowledge of, the process itself.

Lack of trust and openness When small-firm owners/managers are highly sensitive and guarded about their businesses and the decisions that affect them.

Learning curve concept The time needed for new methods or procedures to be learned and mastered.

Left brain The part of the brain that helps an individual analyze, verbalize, and use rational approaches to problem solving. (See also **Right brain.**)

Leveraged buyout (LBO) Allowing the entrepreneur to finance the transaction by borrowing on the target company's assets.

Licensing A business arrangement in which the manufacturer of a product (or a firm with proprietary rights over technology or trademarks) grants permission to a group or an individual to manufacture that product in return for specified royalties or other payments.

Life-cycle stages The typical life cycle through which a venture progresses, including venture development, start-up, growth, stabilization, and innovation or decline.

Life-style venture A small venture where the primary driving forces include independence, autonomy, and control.

Limited liability A restriction on the amount of financial responsibility assumed by a partner or stockholder. (See also **Unlimited liability.**)

Limited partnership Organizational arrangement that allows investors to put money into a partnership without assuming liability for any losses beyond this initial investment.

Liquidation See **Straight bankruptcy.**

Liquidation value A method of valuing a business in which the value of all assets is determined on the basis of their current sale value.

Loan with warrants A loan that provides the investor (lender) with the right to buy stock at a fixed price at some future date.

Loneliness Isolation from persons with whom entrepreneurs can confide because of their long hours at work.

Macroview of entrepreneurship A broad array of factors that relate to success or failure in contemporary entrepreneurial ventures.

Management by walking around (MBWA) A management approach to communicating with personnel and getting feedback from them. It consists of the entrepreneur walking around the company, talking to personnel, asking questions, and learning about operations on a firsthand basis.

Management segment The segment of a business plan that discusses the management team, legal structure, board of directors, advisers, and consultants.

Management succession The transition of managerial decision making in a firm, one of the greatest challenges confronting owners and entrepreneurs in family businesses.

Managerial successor A successor to a venture who is interested in efficiency, internal control, and the effective use of resources.

Manufacturing segment The segment of a business plan that discusses location analysis, production needs, suppliers, transportation, labor supply, and manufacturing cost data.

Market A group of consumers (potential customers) who have purchasing power and unsatisfied needs. (Also see **Market niche** or **Niche.**)

Market niche A homogeneous group of consumers with common characteristics.

Market planning The process of determining a clear, comprehensive approach to the creation of a consumer.

Market segmentation The process of identifying a specific set of characteristics that differentiate one group of consumers from the rest.

Market strategy A general marketing philosophy and strategy of the company developed from market research and evaluation data.

Market value A method of valuing a business that involves an estimation based on prices recently paid for similar enterprises as well as on the methods of sale.

Marketability Assembling and analyzing relevant information about a new venture to judge its potential success.

Marketing information system A system that compiles and organizes data relating to cost, revenues, and profit from the customer base.

Marketing research A gathering of information about a particular market, followed by an analysis of that information.

Marketing segment The segment of a business plan that describes aspects of the market such as the target market, the market size and trends, the competition, estimated market share, market strategy, pricing, and advertising and promotion.

Microenvironmental assessment Analysis directed toward the community within which the new venture is to be launched.

Microview of entrepreneurship   Examines the factors specific to entrepreneurship and part of the internal locus of control.

Milestone planning approach   A planning approach based on the use of incremental goal attainment that takes a new venture from start-up through strategy reformulation.

Milestone schedule segment   The section of a business plan that provides investors with timetables for the accomplishment of various activities such as completion of prototypes, hiring of sales representatives, receipt of first orders, initial deliveries, and receipt of first accounts receivable payments.

Minority-owned business   Business owned and operated by a minority, which may include blacks, Asians, Native Americans, and Hispanics.

Moral management   Management activity that conforms to a standard of ethical behavior.

Mountain gap strategies   Identifying major market segments as well as interstice (in-between) markets that arise from larger markets.

Muddling mindsets   When creative thinking is blocked or impeded.

Multidimensional approach   Viewing entrepreneurship as a complex, multidimensional framework that emphasizes the individual, the environment, the organization, and the venture process.

Multiple of earnings   A method of valuing a venture that consists of multiplying earnings by a predetermined multiple to arrive at a final value.

Multistage contingency approach   Strategic analysis that includes the individual, the venture, and the environment in relation to a venture's stages as well as to the entrepreneur's career perspective.

Need for control   The strong desire entrepreneurs have to control both their venture and their destiny.

Nepotism   The hiring of relatives in preference to other, more qualified candidates.

Net present value   A capital-budgeting technique used to evaluate an investment that involves a determination of future cash flows and a discounting of these flows to arrive at a present value of these future dollars.

Networking   Sharing experiences with other business owners as a way to relieve loneliness.

New products   Products that are unknown due to a lack of advertising or that take time to be understood.

New-venture development   The first stage of a venture's life cycle that involves activities such as creativity and venture assessment.

Niche   A homogeneous group with common characteristics, such as people who all have a need for a newly proposed good or service.

Nominal partner   A person who holds himself or herself out as a partner or who permits others to make such representation by use of his or her name or by other means.

Nonprofit corporation   A corporation whose main objective is not profit, such as a religious, charitable, or educational institution.

Nonprofit-sponsored incubator   An incubator organized and managed through industrial development associations of private industry, chambers of commerce, or community-based organizations and whose primary objective is area development.

Nonrole   Refers to unethical instances where the person is acting outside of his or her role as manager yet committing acts against the firm.

North American Free Trade Agreement (NAFTA)   An international agreement between Canada, Mexico, and the United States whereby eventually no trade barriers will exist among the three nations.

Oakland Scavenger Company   A garbage collection firm based in California that was involved in a legal dispute over nepotism in a family business.

Observational methods   Methods of collecting primary data that do not involve any direct contact with the respondents. (See also **Questioning methods.**)

Ongoing operations   A perceived problem area among entrepreneurs involving lack of experience in financial planning, poor cash flow, and difficulty in attracting business.

Operating budget   A budget that sets forth the projected sales forecast and expenses for an upcoming period.

Operational planning   Short-range or functional planning consisting of specific practices established to carry out the objective set forth in the strategic plan.

Opportunistic marketing   A marketing stage in a growing venture in which the organization attempts to develop high sales volume through market penetration.

Opportunity management approach A planning approach based heavily on environmental analysis that involves an evaluation of internal resources, a forecast of external market conditions, an evaluation of company strengths and weaknesses, and a formulation of business objectives.

Opportunity orientation A pattern among successful, growth-minded entrepreneurs to focus on opportunity rather than on resources, structure, or strategy.

Ostensible partner A partner who is active in the business and is known to be a partner. This individual is also known as a general partner. (See also **General partner.**)

Overseas business reports (OBR) Publications that evaluate various foreign markets by discussing pertinent marketing factors, presenting economic and commercial profiles, issuing semiannual outlooks for U.S. firms in the respective countries, and publishing selected statistical reports on the direction, volume, and nature of U.S. foreign trade.

Overseas Private Investment Corporation (OPIC) A governmental agency that provides special insurance for overseas investments, including protection against losses suffered by inconvertibility of funds, expropriation, and political violence.

Pareto chart A special form of vertical bar graph often used in the total quality management process to help identify which problems are to be solved and in what order.

Pareto principle A principle that holds that 80 percent of all outcomes can be attributed to 20 percent of all causes.

Partnership An association of two or more persons acting as co-owners of a business for profit.

Patent An intellectual property right granted to an inventor giving him or her the exclusive right to make, use, or sell an invention for a limited time period (usually 17 years).

Payback method A capital-budgeting technique used to determine the length of time required to pay back an original investment.

Perception of high cost When small-business owners perceive the cost associated with planning to be very high.

Planning The process of transforming entrepreneurial vision and ideas into action, involving three steps: (1) commitment to an open planning process, (2) accountability to a corporate conscience, and (3) establishment of a pattern of subordinate participation in the development of the strategic plan.

Policies Fundamental guides for the venture as a whole.

Preferred stock Equity that gives investors a preferred place among the creditors in case the venture is dissolved.

Previous work experience An influence on the decision to create an entrepreneurial venture, such as losing one's job, dissatisfaction with one's current job, etc.

Price/earnings ratio A method of valuing a business that divides the price of the common stock in the market by the earnings per share and multiplies the result by the number of shares of stock issued.

Primary data New data that are often collected by using observational or questioning methods.

Private corporation A corporation created either wholly or in part for private benefits; another name for a *close corporation* or *family corporation,* where the rights of shareholders are restricted regarding transfer of shares.

Private offering The raising of capital through the private placement of securities to groups such as friends, employees, customers, relatives, and local professionals. (Also see **Public offerings.**)

Private placements A method of raising capital through securities; often used by small ventures.

Privately sponsored incubators An incubator organized and managed by a private corporation for the purpose of making a profit for that corporation.

Pro forma financial statement A financial statement that projects the results of future business operations, such as a pro forma balance sheet, an income statement, or a cash-flow statement.

Probability thinking Relying on probability to make decisions in the struggle to achieve security.

Procedures Policies that have been standardized as a continuing method.

Product availability The availability of a salable good or service at the time the venture opens its doors.

Product-driven philosophy A market philosophy based on the principle of producing efficiently and letting sales take care of themselves. (See also **Consumer-driven philosophy** and **Sales-driven philosophy.**)

Professional corporation A corporation made up of practicing professionals such as lawyers, accountants, or doctors.

Profits, sales, and operating ratios Used to estimate a business's potential earning power, which is a key factor in evaluating the attractiveness of the venture and in later determining a reasonable buying price.

Prompt Payments Act A federal law requiring that small businesses doing work for the federal government be paid within 30 days with an additional 15-day grace period; otherwise, interest penalty charges become retroactive from the 30-day point.

Psychic risk The great psychological impact on and the well-being of the entrepreneur creating a new venture.

Public corporation A corporation the government forms to meet a political or governmental purpose.

Public offerings The raising of capital through the sale of securities on public markets. (See also **Private offerings.**)

Publicly sponsored incubators An incubator set up by a public entity such as a municipal economic development department, urban renewal authority, or a regional planning and development department with the main objective of job creation.

Questioning methods Methods of collecting primary data directly from the respondents, such as surveys and telephone interviews. (Also see **Observational methods.**)

R&D limited partnership A popular tool for funding research and development expenses in entrepreneurial ventures; it is a limited partnership in many ways.

Radical innovation The inaugural breakthroughs launched from experimentation and determined vision that are not necessarily managed but must be recognized and nurtured.

Ratio analysis Financial analysis designed to show relationships among financial statement accounts.

Rationalizations What managers use to justify questionable conduct.

Regulation D Regulation and exemption for reports and statements required for selling stock to private parties based on the amount of money being raised.

Regulatory Flexibility Act A federal law that puts the burden on government to ensure that legislation does not unfairly impact small business.

Reliance The strength of the community's need for the entrepreneur's venture and the entrepreneur's willingness to make a commitment to the community.

Reorganization A common form of bankruptcy in which the debtor attempts to formulate a plan to pay a portion of the debts, have the remaining sum discharged, and continue to stay in operation.

Replacement value A method of valuing a business in which the cost of replacing each asset is determined at current cost.

Research, design, and development segment The part of a business plan that discusses the development and design plan, technical research results, research assistance needs, and cost structure.

Responsibility charting Uses the three components of decisions, roles, and types of participation to form a matrix so that a respondent can assign a type of participation to each of the roles (at the top) for a specific decision (on the left).

Responsive marketing A marketing stage during which the organization attempts to develop high customer satisfaction through product market development.

Return on investment Net profit divided by investment.

Right brain The part of the brain that helps an individual understand analogies, imagine things, and synthesize information. (See also **Left brain.**)

Role assertion Unethical acts committed on the basis of "for the firm" involving managers/entrepreneurs who represent the firm and who rationalize that the firm's long-run interests are foremost.

Role distortion Unethical acts committed on the basis of "for the firm" involving managers/entrepreneurs who commit individual acts and who rationalize that they are in the firm's long-run interests.

Role failure Unethical acts against the firm involving a person failing to perform his or her managerial role, including superficial performance appraisals (not being totally honest) and not confronting someone who is cheating on expense accounts.

S corporation   A corporation that retains some of the benefits of the corporate form while being taxed similarly to a partnership.

Sales-driven philosophy   A marketing philosophy that focuses on personal selling and advertising to persuade customers to buy the company's output. (See also **Consumer-driven philosophy** and **Product-driven philosophy.**)

Sales/forecasting   The process of projecting future sales by applying statistical techniques to historical sales figures.

Scatter diagram   A total quality management tool used to illustrate and examine relationships between two variables.

Secondary data   Data that have already been compiled. Examples are periodicals, articles, trade association information, governmental publications, and company records.

Secret partner   A person who is active in the business but is not known or held out to be a partner.

Self-management concept   A technique designed to identify management behaviors requiring change and to help the entrepreneur make those changes.

Shopping goods   Goods that consumers will take time to examine carefully and compare for quality and price.

Silent partner   A person who is inactive in the business operation but may be known to be a partner.

Simple linear regression   A technique in which a linear equation states the relationship among three variables used to estimate the sales forecast.

Skunkworks   A highly innovative enterprise that uses groups functioning outside traditional lines of authority.

Small Business Administration   A governmental agency that aids small business by providing financial, consulting, and managerial assistance.

Small, profitable venture   A venture in which the entrepreneur does not want venture sales to become so large that he or she must relinquish equity or ownership position and thus give up control over cash flows and profits, which it is hoped will be substantial.

Social obligation   Reacting to social issues through obedience to the laws.

Social responsibility   Reacting to social issues by accepting responsibility for various programs.

Social responsiveness   Proactive to social issues by being associated with various activities for the social good.

Sole proprietorship   A business owned and operated by one person.

Specialty goods   Products or services that consumers make a special effort to find and purchase.

Specification   The text of a patent; it may include any accompanying illustrations.

Stabilization stage   The fourth stage of a new-venture life cycle, typified by increased competition, consumer indifference to the entrepreneur's good(s) or service(s), and saturation of the market with a host of "me too" look-alikes. During this stage the entrepreneur begins planning the venture's direction over 'the next three to five years.

Start-up activities   The second stage of a new-venture life cycle, encompassing the foundation work needed for creating a formal business plan, searching for capital, carrying out marketing activities, and developing an effective entrepreneurial team.

Start-up problems   A perceived problem area in the start-up phase of a new venture, such as lack of business training, difficulty obtaining lines of credit, and inexperience in financial planning.

Stereotyping   Refers to averages that people fabricate and then, ironically, base decisions on as if they were data entities existing in the real world.

Straight bankruptcy   A bankruptcy arrangement in which the debtor is required to surrender all property to a court-appointed trustee who sells the assets and turns the proceeds over to the creditors; sometimes known as *liquidation.*

Strategic model approach   A normative approach to strategic planning that begins with a formulation of the basic idea for the new venture, continues on to raising capital, conducting a pilot operation, market testing, and starting up operations and ends with selling, evaluating the competition's reaction, and redesigning or redirecting the strategy.

Strategic planning   The primary step in determining the future direction of a business influenced by the abilities of the entrepreneur, the complexity of the venture, and the nature of the industry.

Strategy formulation school of thought A school of entrepreneurial thought that focuses on the planning process used in successful venture formulation.

Subpartner A person who is not a member of a partnership but who contracts with one of the partners to participate in the interest of that partner in the firm's operation.

Surveys A method of collecting primary data, such as a mail, telephone, or personal interview.

SWOT analysis A strategic analysis that refers to Strengths, Weaknesses, Opportunities, and Threats.

Synthesis A basic type of innovation that involves combining existing concepts and factors into a new formulation.

Technical feasibility Producing a product or service that will satisfy the expectations of potential customers.

Telemarketing The use of telephone communications to directly contact and sell merchandise to consumers.

Time scarcity Lack of time and the difficulty of allocating time for planning in the face of continual day-to-day operating problems.

Tolerance for ambiguity Uncertainty compounded by constant changes introducing ambiguity and stress into every aspect of the enterprise.

Tolerance for failure The iterative, trial-and-error nature of a successful entrepreneur due to serious setbacks and disappointments that are an integral part of the entrepreneur's learning experience.

Top management support When upper-level managers in a corporation can concentrate on helping individuals within the system develop more entrepreneurial behavior.

Total quality management (TQM) A people-focused management system that aims at continuous increases in customer service at continuously lower real costs.

Trade credit Credit given by a supplier who sells goods on account. A common arrangement calls for the bill to be settled within 30 to 90 days.

Trademark A distinctive name, mark, symbol, or motto identified with a company's product(s).

Uniform Franchise Offering Circular (UFOC) A disclosure form the Federal Trade Commission requires of all potential franchisors.

Uniform Partnership Act Generally followed by most states as the guide for legal requirements of forming a partnership.

Uniqueness Special characteristics and/or design concepts that draw the customer to the venture and should provide performance or service superior to competitive offerings.

University-related incubators An incubator that is a spin-off of an academic research project with the major goal to transfer the findings of basic research and development into a new product or technology.

Unlimited liability A condition existing in sole proprietorships and partnerships wherein someone is responsible for all the enterprise's debts. (See also **Limited liability.**)

Unsought goods Goods that consumers neither currently need nor seek, such as encyclopedias and cemetery plots.

Value added A basic form of contribution analysis in which sales minus raw material costs equals the value added.

Variable cost A cost that changes in the same direction as, and in direct proportion to, changes in operating activity.

Venture capitalist An individual who provides a full range of financial services for new or growing ventures, such as capital for start-ups and expansions, marketing research, management consulting, assistance with negotiating technical agreements, and assistance with employee recruitment and development of employee agreements.

Venture opportunity school of thought A school of entrepreneurial thought that focuses on the search for idea sources, on concept development, and on implementation of venture opportunities.

Venture teams A small group of people who operate as a semiautonomous unit to create and develop a new idea.

Vision A concept of what the entrepreneur's idea can become.

Water well strategies The ability to gather or harness special resources (land, labor, capital, raw materials) over the long term.

Women entrepreneurs Women who own their own businesses.

Women-owned businesses Businesses women own, the fastest growing segment of small business in the nation.

Women's Business Ownership Act A law to establish programs and initiate efforts to help develop women-owned businesses.

World Trade Organization (WTO) A newly created international organization which replaced GATT (General Agreement on Tariffs and Trade). It is responsible for enforcing rulings on trade disputes as well as creating systems to monitor trade policies among nations.

Name Index

Subject Index

A

ABA. *See* American Bar Association (ABA)

Abandonment, 417

Accounts payable turnover, 282

Accounts receivable financing, 432

Accounts receivable turnover, 281

Accredited purchaser, 438–439

Accrual system of accounting, 258

Achievement needs, 110, 116–118

Acordia, Inc., 54, 552–562

Acquisition entrepreneurs, 588

Activity ratios, 419

Adaptive firms, 496–498

Adjusted tangible book value, 574–575, 580

Administrative culture versus entrepreneurial culture, 500–502

Advanced Software Applications (ASA), 601

Advertising plan, 301–302

Advisory boards, 384–385

African American women in labor force, 15

African American owned businesses, 20–22

Alaskan Native Americans. *See* North American Indians

American Bar Association (ABA), 434

American Indians. *See* North American Indians

American Optical Company, 84

American Research & Development (AR&D), 311

Amoral management, 156, 157

Amy's Ice Creams, 482

"Angel" financing, 21, 450–452

Appendix of business plans, 306

Apple Computer, 103–104, 128

Appositional relationship, 129–130

Argentina, 539

Arthur Andersen Center for Family Business, 508

Artificial intelligence, 600–601

ASA. *See* Advanced Software Applications (ASA)

Asia, 525

B

Asian American women in labor force, 15

Asian Americans and Pacific Islanders, 20, 21

Assessment. *See* Environmental assessment; Evaluation

Asset turnover, 279

Assets, 258, 568

Associated Group, 552–562

AT&T, 54, 634

Atlanta, Georgia, 201–202

Automatic Door Specialists, 572

Average age of payables, 279

Average collection period, 279, 281, 419

Average payment period, 282

Avon Products, Inc., 163

Avon Worldwide Fund for Women's Health, 163

Background or knowledge accumulation phase of creativity, 125, 127

Balance sheet, 256, 258, 345–349

Bank of America, 153

Bankruptcy. *See also* Failures

Bankruptcy Act, 421–422

Chapter 7 bankruptcy, 421, 422

Chapter 11 bankruptcy, 415, 421, 422

Chapter 12 bankruptcy, 421

Chapter 13 bankruptcy, 421, 422–423

liquidation, 421, 422

ratio analysis for detection of, 419

reorganization, 421, 422

statistics on business failures, 419–420

warning signs of, 418–419

Bankruptcy Act, 421–422

Banks, 430–431, 432, 543, 546

Barriers to entry, 205

Bell Atlantic, 54, 62–63

BEMs. *See* "Big Emerging Markets" (BEMs)

Ben & Jerry's Ice Cream, 508

Best Cities list, 200–202

Better widget strategies, 42

Bibliography in business plans, 306

"Big Emerging Markets" (BEMs), 538–539

Black Diamond Equipment, 483

Blacks. *See* headings beginning with African American

BMW, 145

Book value, 574–575, 580

Bootlegging, 61

Brain hemispheres, 131–132, 133

Brazil, 538

Break-even analysis, 272–277

Break-even point computation, 272–277

Breast Cancer Awareness Crusade, 163

Budgets

capital budgeting, 257, 266–272

cash budget, 257

cash-flow budget, 262–265

definition of, 257

infringement budget, 408

operating budget, 257, 259–262, 263

as planning documents, 485

Bureau of Labor Statistics, 22

Bureaucratization versus decentralization, 505

Business angels, 21, 450–452

Business assets, 568

Business climate, 209

Business decisions, ethics of, 160–161

Business description, in business plans, 298, 307, 321–326

Business environment, 568

Business failures. *See also* Bankruptcy

examples of, 359

failure prediction model, 366–369

failure rates for entrepreneurs, 35

of new ventures, 359, 364–369

statistics on, 419–420

Business forums, 300

Business incubators, 211–215, 220

TQM. *See* Total quality management (TQM)
Trade credit, 431–432
Trade Opportunities Program (TOP), 542
Trade secrets, 417–418
Trademark Revision Act, 414–415
Trademarks, 413–418, 457–461, 537
Training of employees, 633–634
Type A personality, 108–109

U
U-7, 434
UFOC. *See* Uniform Franchise Offering Circular (UFOC)
ULOR (Uniform Limited Offering Registration), 434
ULPA. *See* Uniform Limited Partnership Act (ULPA)
Unethical behavior. *See* Ethics
Uniform Franchise Offering Circular (UFOC), 400
Uniform Limited Offering Registration (ULOR), 434
Uniform Limited Partnership Act (ULPA), 389
Uniform Partnership Act, 384
Uniqueness of new ventures, 358
United Artists, 359
University programs for entrepreneurs, 12–13
Unlimited liability, 382
Unsought goods, 234, 236
Unstructured planning (UP), 474–475
UP. *See* Unstructured planning (UP)
Upjohn, 250–251
US West, 39

V
Valuation
  accuracy of projections, 584
  adjusted tangible book value, 574–575, 580
  analyzing the business, 573–574, 576–579
  buying a business venture, 567–569, 570

case studies on, 572, 586–587, 591–592
control factor and, 585
discounted earnings method, 580–581, 582–584
due-diligence inspection, 572
emotional bias and, 571
establishing firm's value, 574–575, 580–584
and goals of buyer and seller, 570–571
importance of, 569–570
leveraged buyout and, 585–589
methods for, 574–575, 580–584
price/earnings ratio method, 575, 580, 582
pricing formula, 583
questions on buying a business, 568–569
reasons for acquisition, 571–573
start-up costs and, 584
underlying issues in, 570–573
Value added, 208
Variable costs, 258, 262
Venture capital market
  criteria for evaluating new-venture proposals, 445–447, 448, 449
  definition of venture capitalists, 439
  environment of, 140–142
  and evaluation of product/service and management, 444
  evaluation of venture capitalists, 447–450, 451
  financial services provided by venture capitalists, 439
  myths of, 441–442
  objectives of venture capitalists, 442, 444–445
  recent development in, 439–441
  research on, 10
  responses of venture capitalists to business plans, 310–311

returns on investment sought by venture capitalists, 445
sources of venture capital, 440
statistics on, 439–440
venture capital disbursements by stage of new ventures, 441
venture club networks, 443
Venture club networks, 443
Venture opportunity school of thought, 41
Venture teams, 71–73
Vertical analysis, 279
VMG, 410–411
V-Teams, 71–73

W
Wal-Mart, 633
Walt Disney Company, 128, 145, 483
Wang Associates Health Communications, 384
Water well strategies, 42
Weatherly Private Capital Co., 410–411
White House Conferences on Small Business, 202
Wild Oats company, 635, 636–637, 638
Women-owned businesses, 14–20, 26–28
Women's Business Ownership Act, 14
Women's employment, 14–15
Working capital, 258, 279
World Eye Bookstore, 163
World Trade Organization (WTO), 522
WTO. *See* World Trade Organization (WTO)

X
Xerox, 622–623

Y
Young Entrepreneurs Network, 104

Z
Zytec, 622, 631, 632, 634

DRYDEN

soon to become

Harcourt
College Publishers

A Harcourt Higher Learning Company

Soon you will find The Dryden Press'
distinguished innovation, leadership, and
support under a different name . . . a new
brand that continues our unsurpassed
quality, service, and commitment to
education.

We are combining the strengths of our
college imprints into one worldwide
brand: Harcourt Our mission is to make
learning accessible to anyone, anywhere,
anytime—reinforcing our commitment to
lifelong learning.

We'll soon be Harcourt College Publishers.
Ask for us by name.

One Company
"Where Learning
Comes to Life."